Neuropsychological Conditions across the Lifespan

This unique analysis of neuropsychological conditions provides readers with a review of both pediatric and adult presentations in one convenient place. Covering the most common disorders encountered in clinical practice, including those specific to the extremes of the age spectrum, this book provides dedicated chapters on:

- Preterm and Low-Birth-Weight Birth
- Spina Bifida Myelomeningocele
- Autism Spectrum Disorder
- Intellectual Disability Syndromes
- Fetal Alcohol Spectrum Disorders
- Attention-Deficit/Hyperactivity Disorder
- Learning Disabilities
- Traumatic Brain Injury
- Cancer
- Epilepsy
- Human Immunodeficiency Virus
- Multiple Sclerosis
- Stroke
- Dementia

Each chapter provides evidence-based guidelines that can be readily applied to daily practice.

Jacobus Donders is Chief Psychologist at Mary Free Bed Rehabilitation Hospital in Grand Rapids, Michigan. He is board certified in clinical neuropsychology, pediatric clinical neuropsychology, and rehabilitation psychology.

Scott J. Hunter is Professor of Psychiatry and Behavioral Neuroscience, and Pediatrics at the University of Chicago and Director of Neuropsychology for the University of Chicago Medicine and Comer Children's Hospital, Chicago, Illinois.

Neuropsychological Conditions across the Lifespan

Edited by

Jacobus Donders
Mary Free Bed Rehabilitation Hospital, Grand Rapids, Michigan

Scott J. Hunter
University of Chicago, Chicago, Illinois

CAMBRIDGE
UNIVERSITY PRESS

CAMBRIDGE
UNIVERSITY PRESS

University Printing House, Cambridge CB2 8BS, United Kingdom

One Liberty Plaza, 20th Floor, New York, NY 10006, USA

477 Williamstown Road, Port Melbourne, VIC 3207, Australia

314–321, 3rd Floor, Plot 3, Splendor Forum, Jasola District Centre, New Delhi – 110025, India

79 Anson Road, #06–04/06, Singapore 079906

Cambridge University Press is part of the University of Cambridge.

It furthers the University's mission by disseminating knowledge in the pursuit of
education, learning, and research at the highest international levels of excellence.

www.cambridge.org
Information on this title: www.cambridge.org/9781107190016
DOI: 10.1017/9781316996751

First published 2018

Printed and bound in Great Britain by Clays Ltd, Elcograf S.p.A.

A catalogue record for this publication is available from the British Library.

Library of Congress Cataloging-in-Publication Data
Names: Donders, Jacobus, editor. | Hunter, Scott J., editor.
Title: Neuropsychological conditions across the lifespan / edited by Jacobus Donders, Scott J. Hunter.
Description: New York, NY : Cambridge University Press, [2018] | Includes bibliographical references.
Identifiers: LCCN 2018006516 | ISBN 9781107190016 (hardback)
Subjects: | MESH: Neurobehavioral Manifestations | Neurodevelopmental Disorders – psychology | Brain Diseases
– psychology | Central Nervous System – injuries | Child | Adult
Classification: LCC RC360 | NLM WL 340 | DDC 616.8/4–dc23
LC record available at https://lccn.loc.gov/2018006516

ISBN 978-1-107-19001-6 Hardback

....

Contents

List of Contributors   vi

Introduction   1

1   **Preterm and Low-Birth-Weight Birth**   2
Julia Jaekel and Megan Scott

2   **Spina Bifida Myelomeningocele**   24
Colleen F. Bechtel Driscoll, Diana Ohanian,
Jaclyn Lennon Papadakis, Alexa Stern,
T. Andrew Zabel, Kathy Zebracki, and
Grayson N. Holmbeck

3   **Autism Spectrum Disorder**   45
Julie M. Wolf, Marianne Barton, and
Roger Jou

4   **Intellectual Disability Syndromes**   61
Kelly Janke and Lisa Jacola

5   **Fetal Alcohol Spectrum Disorders**   79
Israel M. Gross and Doug Bodin

6   **Attention-Deficit/Hyperactivity Disorder**   93
Jodene G. Fine, David J. Marks, Danielle
Wexler, Victoria M. Dahl, and Elizabeth
P. Horn

7   **Learning Disabilities**   116
Richard Boada, Robin L. Peterson, and
Robert L. Mapou

8   **Traumatic Brain Injury**   139
Tresa Roebuck-Spencer, Naddley Désiré,
and Miriam Beauchamp

9   **Cancer**   162
Iris Paltin, Darcy E. Burgers, Marsha
Gragert, and Chad Noggle

10   **Epilepsy**   186
Julie Janecek, Klajdi Puka, Evan Schulze,
and Mary Lou Smith

11   **Human Immunodeficiency Virus**   210
Steven Paul Woods, Kelli L. Sullivan,
Sharon Nichols, and Scott J. Hunter

12   **Multiple Sclerosis**   228
Lana Harder, Julie A. Bobholz, and William
S. MacAllister

13   **Stroke**   244
Robyn Westmacott, Angela Deotto, and
David Nyenhuis

14   **Dementia**   268
Laura Lacritz, Heidi Rossetti, and Christian
LoBue

Index   286

Contributors

Marianne Barton, PhD
University of Connecticut

Miriam Beauchamp, PhD
University of Montreal

Colleen F. Bechtel Driscoll, MA, MS
Loyola University Chicago

Richard Boada, PhD, ABPP
Children's Hospital Colorado

Julie A. Bobholz, PhD, ABPP
Medical College of Wisconsin

Douglas Bodin, PhD, ABPP
Nationwide Children's Hospital

Darcy E. Burgers, PhD
Temple University

Victoria M. Dahl
New York University

Angela Deotto
York University, Canada

Naddley Désiré, PhD
CHU Sainte-Justine Research Center
Alberta Children's Hospital

Jodene G. Fine, PhD
Michigan State University

Marsha Gragert, PhD, ABPP
Texas Children's Hospital

Israel M. Gross, PhD
Stroger Hospital of Cook County

Lana Harder, PhD, ABPP
UT Southwestern Medical
Center

Grayson N. Holmbeck, PhD
Loyola University Chicago

Elizabeth P. Horn
New York University

Scott J. Hunter, PhD
University of Chicago

Lisa Jacola, PhD
St. Jude Children's Research Hospital

Julia Jaekel, PhD
The University of Tennessee Knoxville

Julie Janecek, PhD, ABPP
ProHealth Waukesha Memorial
Hospital

Kelly Janke, PhD, ABPP
Columbia University Medical Center

Roger Jou, MD, PhD, MPH
Yale Child Study Center

Laura Lacritz, PhD, ABPP
UT Southwestern Medical Center

Jaclyn Lennon Papadakis, MA
Loyola University Chicago

Christian LoBue, PhD
UT Southwestern Medical Center

William S. MacAllister, PhD, ABPP
New York University Langone Health
Alberta Children's Hospital

Robert L. Mapou, PhD, ABPP
Oceanside Neuropsychology

David J. Marks, PhD
New York University Langone Health

Sharon Nichols, PhD
University of California, San Diego

Chad Noggle, PhD
Southern Illinois University School of Medicine
Neuroscience Institute

David Nyenhuis, PhD, ABPP
Mercy Health Hauenstein Neurosciences

Diana Ohanian, MA
Loyola University Chicago

Iris Paltin, PhD
Children's Hospital of Philadelphia

Robin L. Peterson, PhD, ABPP
Children's Hospital Colorado

Klajdi Puka, BSc
University of Western Ontario

Tresa Roebuck-Spencer, PhD, ABPP
Jefferson Neurobehavioral Group

Heidi Rossetti, PhD
UT Southwestern Medical Center

Evan Schulze, PhD
University of Illinois at Chicago Medical Center

Megan Scott, PhD
University of Chicago

Mary Lou Smith, PhD
University of Toronto Mississauga

Alexa Stern, MA
Loyola University Chicago

Kelli L. Sullivan, PhD
University of Houston

Robyn Westmacott, PhD, ABPP
The Hospital for Sick Children

Danielle Wexler
Michigan State University

Julie M. Wolf, PhD
Yale Child Study Center

Steven Paul Woods, PsyD
University of Houston

T. Andrew Zabel, PhD
Kennedy Krieger Institute

Kathy Zebracki, PhD
Northwestern University Feinberg
School of Medicine

Introduction

Jacobus Donders and Scott J. Hunter

Our understanding and management of brain-behavior relationships over the lifespan has advanced significantly since we published our first book on this topic in 2007 (Donders & Hunter, 2007) and a similar text that was published by others six years later (Baron & Rey-Casserly, 2013). In this volume, we wanted to provide an updated account of the most common neuropsychological conditions that most clinicians may encounter in their practice. Whenever possible, we aspired to include within the same chapter descriptions of the different manifestations across the lifespan, although understandably some conditions (e.g., low birth weight, dementia) are unique to the extremes of the age spectrum.

It was our goal that each chapter in this volume provide a concise but sufficiently in-depth review of the clinical manifestations of the condition at hand, with particular attention paid to the role of neuropsychological assessment and intervention,

culminating in pragmatic suggestions for clinical practice as well as future research. Each chapter was written by contributors who have considerable clinical as well as empirical expertise with the condition being discussed. We hope that this book serves as an updated reference point for our current understanding of a wide range of commonly encountered neuropsychological conditions across the lifespan. We anticipate that it will be of interest to not only neuropsychologists but also to professionals in rehabilitation, neurology, and a variety of related health professions.

References

Baron, I. S., & Rey-Casserly, C. (Eds.) (2013). *Pediatric neuropsychology: Medical advances and lifespan outcomes.* New York: Oxford University Press.

Donders, J., & Hunter, S. J. (Eds.) (2007). *Principles and practice of lifespan developmental neuropsychology.* Cambridge: Cambridge University Press.

Preterm and Low-Birth-Weight Birth

Julia Jaekel and Megan Scott

Introduction

Two of the most significant risk factors for long-term developmental outcomes are preterm birth (<37 weeks gestational age [GA]) and low birth weight (<2,500 g). Prematurity is the leading cause of infant mortality and long-term morbidity (March of Dimes, PMNCH, Save the Children, & WHO, 2012). According to the World Health Organization (WHO), about 15 million babies worldwide (>10% of all births) are born preterm every year, and nearly 22 million infants (16%) have low birth weight (Blanc & Wardlaw, 2005). In addition, prematurity is associated with intrauterine growth restriction and small for gestational age (SGA) birth, commonly defined as birth weight below the 10th percentile for GA according to national sex-specific norms. Based on recent findings on a progressive impact of prematurity on long-term outcomes with increased prematurity (Lipkind, Slopen, Pfeiffer, & McVeigh, 2012; MacKay, Smith, Dobbie, & Pell, 2010; Poulsen et al., 2013; Quigley et al., 2012), fine-grained definitions for groups of preterm and low-birth-weight children have been established (see Table 1.1 and abbreviations therein). Accordingly, in this chapter we refer to the highest risk groups of premature infants as VP/VLBW and EP/ELBW.

Clinical Manifestation

Epidemiology and Pathophysiology

The etiology of preterm birth can be differentiated into spontaneous and medically indicated, often as a result of intrauterine growth restriction and maternal conditions such as preeclampsia. A number of diverse risk factors for preterm birth have been identified (e.g., infection/inflammation, social adversity, Black ethnicity, maternal stress, and preconception and prenatal smoking); however, the precise mechanisms and majority of variance remain unexplained (Goldenberg, Culhane, Iams, & Romero, 2008; Raisanen, Gissler, Saari, Kramer, & Heinonen, 2013). The preterm birth rate in the United States is now 9.6% (March of Dimes, 2016). The preterm birth rate has increased in most countries in the last two decades due to changing demographics (e.g., older mothers), increased fertility treatment leading to increased multiple births, which are often preterm, and the increased use of elective cesarean sections, which often occur early in the term (Cheong & Doyle, 2012; Goldenberg et al., 2008). However, the preterm live birth weight peaked in 2006 and has declined or remained relatively stable from year to year since then (March of Dimes, 2016). This decline has been attributed to improved medical

Table 1.1 Classification of Premature Children According to Birth Weight and Gestational Age Groups and Their Overall Percentage Among All Live Births in the United States (CDC, 2016)

Birth Weight (BW) Groups (%)	BW (g)	Preterm Birth in GA Groups (%)	GA (weeks)
Extremely low BW (ELBW), 0.7	<1,000	Extremely preterm (EP), 0.7	<28
Very low BW (VLBW), 0.7	1,000–1,499	Very preterm (VP), 0.9	28–31
		Moderately preterm, 1.5	32–33
Low BW (LBW), 6.6	1,500–2,499	Late preterm (LP), 6.8	34–36
		Early term, 24.8	37–38
Normal BW (NBW), 92	>2,499	Full term, 58.7	>38

interventions as well as changes in clinical practice around LP birth. With increasing recognition of risks associated with LP birth, delivery before 39 weeks' gestation is now discouraged unless there is a clear medical rationale (ACOG Committee, 2008; Ashton, 2010).

Due to continuous advances in neonatal care (i.e., early surfactant administration and less-invasive treatment), more EP/ELBW infants are surviving (Gopel et al., 2011; Halliday, 2008). Although medical advances have improved the survival rate and decreased the rates of severe medical and neurodevelopmental complications, the prevalence of cognitive problems in preterm populations has not changed with these improvements in viability (Moore et al., 2012). In addition, although significant deficits have been clearly documented in individuals with a history of EP/ELBW, specific patterns of neurocognitive weakness have been identified in LP groups as well (Baron, Litman, Ahronovich, & Baker, 2012).

Neurodevelopmental and Medical Complications

In addition to cognitive outcomes discussed in greater detail in the section on Cognition, there are a number of significant medical and neurodevelopmental challenges with EP/ELBW and VP/VLBW infants. EP/ELBW birth means that these infants are born with immature organs, including their lungs and brains, and they often experience organ complications (e.g., bleeding into the brain). Severe neurological injuries such as periventricular leukomalacia (PVL) have become rare today, but diffuse white matter injuries remain common and can be used to predict neurodevelopmental outcomes (Woodward, Anderson, Austin, Howard, & Inder, 2006; Woodward, Clark, Bora, & Inder, 2012). A number of factors have been identified that are associated with PVL and intraventricular and cerebellar hemorrhage in VP/VLBW infants, including low Apgar scores, necrotizing enterocolitis, inotropic support, and patent ductus arteriosus (Kidokoro et al., 2014). Moreover, PVL is often associated with neuronal/axonal disease in a destructive amalgam termed encephalopathy of prematurity, affecting cerebral white matter and cortex, the thalamus, basal ganglia, the brain stem, and the cerebellum (Volpe, 2009). Research has also documented that an important cellular mechanism for explaining changes to the preterm brain is the developing oligodendrocyte (Volpe, Kinney, Jensen, & Rosenberg, 2011) and the timing of its exposure to oxygen (Felderhoff-Müser et al., 2004; Prager et al., 2013).

In terms of broader neurodevelopmental outcomes, rates of cerebral palsy (CP) in preterm children are variable in the literature. A 2008 meta-analysis of 26 studies indicated that the prevalence of CP increases with lower GA; <1% of children born between 32 and 36 weeks GA have CP, and the numbers increase to 6% at 28–31 weeks GA and to 14% at 22–27 weeks GA (Himpens, Van den Broeck, Oostra, Calders, & Vanhaesebrouck, 2008). Moreover, developmental coordination disorder is common in VP/VLBW children, with highly variable rates in the literature that range from 9.5% to 51% when compared with a 6% rate of occurrence in the general population (Arpino et al., 2010). Children born preterm also have higher rates of vision impairments, including retinopathy of prematurity (occurring in up to 56% of EP/ELBW), strabismus, and low visual acuity, and of hearing deficits (occurring in up to 3% of EP/ELBW) (Arpino et al., 2010). It is notable that despite these frequent problems, parents and teachers of preterm children often expect developmental catch-up before school entry; however, patterns of developmental difficulties are relatively stable from age 2 years onward (Breeman, Jaekel, Baumann, Bartmann, & Wolke, 2015). In fact, specific developmental problems often become more apparent during primary school because of the larger demands on differential abilities such as mathematics.

Prevention

As described in the section on Epidemiology and Pathophysiology, up to 78% of the variation in preterm birth remains unexplained. This is found even when looking at data from large whole-population studies (Goldenberg et al., 2008; Raisanen et al., 2013). Thus, although there are techniques to delay birth under some conditions, with variable success, it is currently not possible to identify women who are at risk for preterm birth and to prevent preterm birth (Rubens et al., 2014). In addition, research in this area is complicated by a lack of standardization and consistency in primary outcomes used to measure prevention of preterm birth in randomized controlled studies and systematic reviews (Meher & Alfirevic, 2014).

Long-Term Neuropsychological Outcomes

When reviewing literature on outcomes of VP/VLBW and EP/ELBW children, it is important to be careful about generalizing results of outcome research from older birth cohorts to more recent cohorts born after 2000. Although the outcome data regarding neuropsychological impairment are fairly consistent across studies, Table 1.2 indicates a large range of effects when compared across the available literature. Given the significant advances in neonatal care implemented since 1980, there have been substantial changes in the mortality and disability rates in these populations, a fact that has likely contributed to significant differences in cohorts across time. In addition, significant research methodology changes in the 1990s, including a shift toward longitudinal analyses and the use of neuropsychological measures to examine neurodevelopmental profiles beyond broad cognitive outcomes, led to vast differences in the information available for these different cohorts (Baron & Rey-Casserly, 2010). Beyond these methodological and cohort differences, researchers have often interpreted findings about temporal change or stability in developmental outcomes differently, contributing to continued variability in rates and profiles of impact.

Table 1.2 Overall Rates of Neuropsychological and Related Problems After VP/VLBW Birth

Outcome Area Affected by VP/VLBW Birth	Range of Problems Reported in the Literature (%)
General cognitive impairment	20–30
Attention problems, attention-deficit/hyperactivity disorder	10–25
Executive function deficits	10–70
Visual-motor skills	30–60
Mathematics deficiencies	10–25
Reading/language deficiencies	24–34
Special educational needs	20–45
Below average attainment	40–48
Emotional problems	10–40
Social relationship difficulties	10–30
Autism spectrum disorder	3–8

Research on brain development in VP/VLBW children suggests that their brains grow more slowly and differently than the brains of children born at full term (Ball et al., 2012; Kapellou et al., 2006; Woodward et al., 2012). As a result, VP/VLBW children are at highly increased risk for a range of neurodevelopmental, cognitive, attention, mental health, and social relationship difficulties (Farooqi, Hagglof, Sedin, Gothefors, & Serenius, 2007). VP/VLBW children more often struggle in school and have persistent difficulties throughout adolescence (Johnson & Wolke, 2013). In adulthood, preterm individuals, across periods of prematurity, have lower academic attainment and income, increased reliance on social benefits, and increased risk of psychiatric problems, and these individuals report poorer interpersonal relationships and less satisfaction with their lives (Darlow, Horwood, Pere-Bracken, & Woodward, 2013a; D'Onofrio et al., 2013; Hack, 2009, 2013; Heinonen et al., 2013; Johnson & Marlow, 2014; Moster, Lie, & Markestad, 2008).

Cognition

Recent studies suggest that delivery at any gestation other than full term may confer an insult to brain development, rendering survivors at risk for adverse neurocognitive outcomes (MacKay et al., 2010; Quigley et al., 2012). Depending on the timing and severity of gestational insults, reorganization of cortical structures is still detectable throughout childhood and adolescence in multiple regions (Nosarti, Murray, & Hack, 2010; Peterson, 2003). As neuroimaging techniques have advanced, widespread brain changes in preterm infants, adolescents, and adults have been demonstrated (Ball et al., 2012; Kapellou et al., 2006; Nosarti, 2013; Nosarti et al., 2010; Peterson, 2003). For example, effects of preterm birth on the brain's large-scale intrinsic networks with related changes of intrinsic connectivity and gray matter structure in the ventral brain of preterm adults have been documented at 26 years of age (Bäuml et al., 2014). Across development, cortical changes are prospectively related to academic achievement because they functionally manifest in poor attention (Woodward et al., 2012) and slower processing speed (Mulder, Pitchford, & Marlow, 2010). Attention, for example, is an important prerequisite for learning in the classroom but preterm children's attention problems make it hard for them to profit from teaching input in school.

General Cognitive Ability. A number of meta-analyses and systematic reviews have examined general cognitive ability (otherwise discussed as IQ) in preterm children, beginning with the earliest cohorts studied systematically. One seminal meta-analysis of children born between 1975 and 1988 found a weighted mean difference of 10.9 IQ points in favor of term controls (Bhutta, Cleves, Casey, Cradock, & Anand, 2002). In a more recent meta-analysis of studies examining cognitive outcomes in preterm children born between 1975 and 2000, the mean IQ score difference was 11.9 points in favor of term controls (Kerr-Wilson, Mackay, Smith, & Pell, 2012). In both studies, IQ was associated with GA, and there was an increasing difference in IQ scores between preterm and term-matched controls with lower GA, indicating a nonlinear quadratic trend (Jaekel, Baumann, & Wolke, 2013).

Both meta-analyses included studies of preterm birth cohorts from different eras of neonatal care, which limits the generalizability of these findings to more recent birth cohorts. Nevertheless, results of cognitive deficits seem to remain consistent. In a large cohort of children born in Australia in the 1990s, ELBW children also performed significantly below NBW controls with a mean Full Scale IQ difference on the Wechsler Intelligence Scale for Children-III of 9.4 points (Anderson, Doyle, & Victorian Infant Collaborative Study Group, 2003). Although significant mean differences were identified across test indices, the most significant group differences were found for the following IQ indices: perceptual organization (9.9 points) and freedom from distractibility (8.1 points), whereas the verbal comprehension (6.8 points) and processing speed (6.7 points) indices indicated a less significant discrepancy in the favor of NBW controls. Similarly, in a 2001–2003 birth cohort, cognitive deficits were three to six times higher at 6 years of age in an EP/ELBW cohort as compared with term controls (Orchinik et al., 2011). In a recent large multisite study of EP children's neurocognitive outcomes at age 10 years, the distribution of test scores was significantly shifted, situated below normative expectations on the Differential Ability Scale, 2nd ed. In this US cohort, 17% of the EP group demonstrated Verbal Cluster scores that were more than 2 SD below the population mean and 19% fell between 1 and 2 SD below the mean (Joseph et al., 2016). On the Nonverbal Cluster of the same scale, 15% of the EP group demonstrated scores that were more than 2 SD

below the population mean and 24% fell between 1 and 2 SD below the mean (Joseph et al., 2016). Although there was no term control group available, these rates of cognitive impairment are significantly greater than expected based on normative data.

Attention and Executive Functioning. Attention regulation is often compromised in VP/VLBW individuals (please see the section on attention-deficit/hyperactivity disorder [ADHD] for more details on this condition). Research has investigated the underlying mechanisms that may explain the association between different markers of prematurity (i.e., low GA, low BW, SGA birth) and attention problems (Hall, Jaekel, & Wolke, 2012) and found specific developmental pathways; for example, SGA affected attention problems at age 6 years in response to reduced brain volume, and preterm birth impacted attention problems in response to altered brain function (Hall et al., 2012). Moreover, although boys in general are more often found to have attention problems, attention problems after preterm birth are more apparent in girls. This finding has important implications for clinical practice, such that regular childhood follow-up assessments of preterm children are more sensitive to potential gender differences in potential challenges.

With regard to the neural mechanisms underlying attention in VP/VLBW, it is not clear which specific attentional submechanisms are affected and how they relate to broader unfolding brain circuitry. There is recent evidence for selectively changed attention mechanisms in relation to preterm adults' altered intrinsic brain networks (Finke et al., 2015). Intrinsic functional connectivity is organized by brain networks that are defined by synchronous ongoing activity (i.e., circuits). One such brain circuit is the attentional network that is involved in alerting, orienting, and executive control. Anatomically, this includes the anterior cingulate and anterior insula as well as areas of the prefrontal cortex (for inhibition of dominant responses) (Petersen & Posner, 2012). The computational theory of visual attention further separates components for the assessment of specific attention submechanisms including visual perceptual processing speed, visual short-term memory storage capacity, efficiency of top-down control, and spatial laterality of attention. When comparing preterm and term-born adults, Finke and colleagues (2015) found specific impairments in visual short-term memory storage capacity that was predicted by the degree of neonatal medical complications. Most importantly, patterns of changed connectivity in preterm versus full term adults were systematically associated with short-term storage capacity (i.e., the more connectivity differences the better preterm adults' storage capacity) (Finke et al., 2015). This suggests that changes in intrinsic functional connectivity patterns may have the potential to compensate adverse developmental consequences of prematurity on visual short-term memory capacity.

In a meta-analysis of attention and executive functioning (EF) outcomes in EP/ELBW, deficits in a number of specific domains of attention were identified, i.e., selective attention, sustained attention, response inhibition, working memory, verbal fluency, planning and shifting (Mulder, Pitchford, Hagger, & Marlow, 2009). Results across individual studies of selective attention have gleaned variable results in the EP literature. In the preterm population, development of selective attention is impacted by sex, socioeconomic status, chronological age, and gestational age. In the EP group, studies demonstrated a moderate effect of prematurity on selective attention (0.58), which was relatively stable over time. In preterm children born later than 26 weeks GA a large effect size was identified in the preschool years, but this appeared to decline over time with preterm children catching up to term controls in their later school-age years (Mulder et al., 2009).

Across studies of sustained attention, there was variability in findings. As part of the meta-analysis, studies were split based on GA. For studies that examined sustained attention in an EP cohort, a moderate to large effect size (0.67) was identified with a significant relationship between the effect size and GA (Mulder et al., 2009). Across analyses of EF, Mulder and colleagues also demonstrated a number of areas of impact in preterm children compared with term controls. Given the interaction between GA and task performance, studies were again split by GA, revealing a moderate effect size for studies of children born before 26 weeks GA. There were not enough studies with similar assessments to measure working memory, although results indicated that spatial working memory was impacted in preterm children when compared with term controls, whereas performances on nonspatial working memory tasks were not different. On verbal fluency tasks, both semantic and phonemic verbal fluency

skills were affected in preterm children with small to moderate effect size. On studies of planning on a tower test, the mean effect size was moderated by GA. When examining studies of children born less than 26 weeks GA the mean effect size was moderate to large, but the effect size became nonsignificant when focusing on studies of preterm children born more than 26 weeks GA. Finally, studies assessing shifting abilities (Trail Making Test part B) revealed a moderate mean effect size. Overall, results support a pattern of less effective attention and EF skills in preterm children compared with term controls (Mulder et al., 2009).

In a large Australian EP/ELBW cohort, specific aspects of attention and EF were examined compared with term controls at 8 years of age (Anderson et al., 2011). The EP/ELBW performed significantly below the term control group across assessments of selective attention, sustained attention, attention encoding, shifting, and divided attention. In addition, the EP/ELBW group demonstrated significantly higher ADHD symptoms. In contrast to many of the findings from the meta-analysis by Mulder et al. (2009), the authors did not find a significant interaction with GA.

A number of studies have identified EF deficits across the lifespan in preterm populations. Significantly higher rates of deficits across measures of response inhibition, cognitive set-shifting, and working memory were identified in a geographical cohort of kindergarten-age EP/ELBW children compared with term controls (Orchinik et al., 2011). These differences remained significant even when controlling for verbal knowledge (Orchinik et al., 2011). Parent and teacher reports of ADHD symptoms and impaired self-regulation were associated with deficits on tests of EF in this EP/ELBW cohort (Scott et al., 2012). These results indicate that differences in the development of EF skills are present early in life in preterm children and impact functioning in daily life. When examining early EF skills in ELBW, late-preterm, and term-born preschoolers, ELBW children performed significantly poorer than term-born controls on assessments of working memory and inhibition as well as sustained attention (Baron, Kerns, Muller, Abronovich, & Litman, 2012). Importantly, LP preschoolers performed significantly poorer than term controls on assessments of working memory, indicating subtle neurocognitive weaknesses in this group often considered to be at low risk for negative neurocognitive outcomes.

EF deficits appear to remain throughout adolescence and young adulthood. In a meta-analysis of neurobehavioral outcomes in VP/VLBW children, Aarnoudse-Moens, Weisglas-Kuperus, van Goudoever, and Oosterlaan (2009) examined EF outcomes in 12 studies of VP/VLBW outcomes with mean participants ages ranging from 7.5 to 23.2 years. Results of this meta-analysis indicated that VP/VLBW children performed significantly poorer than controls across assessments of verbal fluency, working memory, and cognitive flexibility, with small to medium effect sizes ranging from −0.36 to −0.57 across these domains of EF (Aarnoudse-Moens et al., 2009). Adolescents born very prematurely demonstrated deficits in numerous domains of EF including verbal fluency, inhibition, cognitive flexibility, planning/organization, and working memory when compared with term controls (Luu, Ment, Allan, Schneider, & Vohr, 2011). These results remained significant when controlling for intellectual impairment. Consistent with performance on neuropsychological assessments, VP adolescents were rated by their parents as exhibiting more difficulties with EF in daily life, with elevated scores on the Metacognition Index and Global Executive Composite of the Behavior Rating Inventory of Executive Function. Finally, in addition to EF, VP subjects demonstrated more difficulty with verbal and visuospatial memory. These results suggest that deficits in EF may impact academic functioning including learning and memory.

Several studies have identified potential neuroanatomical correlates of EF deficits. White matter abnormalities on neonatal magnetic resonance imaging have been identified as a predictors of poorer outcomes at 4 and 6 years of age on assessments of general intelligence, language, and executive function, with more severe white matter abnormalities associated with poorer cognitive outcomes (Woodward, Clark, Pritchard, Anderson, & Inder, 2011; Woodward et al., 2012). When examining the associations between brain abnormalities and neurocognitive outcomes in VLBW adolescents, Taylor and colleagues (2011) identified smaller brain volumes, larger lateral ventricles, and smaller surface area of the corpus callosum in the VLBW group compared with NBW controls. Additional findings included white matter abnormalities as well as differences in subcortical gray matter and the cerebellum. Reduced performance on one or more measures of cognitive functioning (e.g., IQ, language, memory, perceptual-motor organization, EF) was associated with greater reductions in whole brain volume, cerebral white matter, subcortical gray matter nuclei, cerebellar white and gray matter, brain stem, and corpus callosum (Taylor et al., 2011).

Visual Motor Skills. Previous studies of extremely premature samples have identified significant deficits in visuomotor integration that are present beyond the generalized cognitive weaknesses seen in this population. Visual motor skills are influenced by different cognitive processes, such as fine motor, visual, proprioceptive, and tactile skills as well as working memory. Studies report lower proprioceptive and tactile skills in preterm compared with full-term children, but their validity may be limited due to a lack of internationally standardized assessments. A recent meta-analysis of 32 case-control studies of VP children with standardized assessments of visual perception and visual-motor integration published from 1985 to 2010 demonstrated lower performance of preterm compared with full-term children (Geldof, van Wassenaer, de Kieviet, Kok, & Oosterlaan, 2012). In a review of 12 studies of fine motor skills in preterm infants published between 1997 and 2012, the prevalence of deficits ranged from 40% to 60% (Bos et al., 2013).

Academic Outcomes and Learning Disabilities. Research has consistently identified poorer educational outcomes in preterm children. As in many other domains, a GA or BW gradient is observed in educational outcomes, with the EP/ELBW infants at the greatest risk for academic underachievement when compared with full-term and normal-birth-weight peers. In a meta-analysis of neurobehavioral outcomes in VP/VLBW children, 14 studies assessing academic outcomes were included to examine outcomes from school age to adulthood with the mean age ranging from 8.0 to 20.0 across these studies (Aarnoudse-Moens et al., 2009). Results indicated that VP/VLBW children performed significantly more poorly across assessments of reading, spelling, and mathematics in comparison with term control groups. Combined effect sizes were medium to large with effect sizes of −0.48 for reading, −0.60 for mathematics, and −0.76 for spelling.

Difficulties in educational progress have been identified in EP children at the time of school entry (Taylor et al., 2011). EP children had significantly lower mean scores on standardized assessments of mathematics and spelling achievement compared with term controls and higher rates of teacher report of poor academic progress in written language and mathematics in kindergarten. These group differences remained when controlling for neurosensory impairment and low cognitive functioning (Taylor et al., 2011). Deficits persist into the school-age years. In a large geographic cohort of EP/ELBW children, assessments of academic achievement revealed that 8-year-old EP/ELBW participants performed significantly lower than the control group on standardized assessments of reading, spelling, and math with the group differences falling between 0.5 SD for reading and spelling and 0.6 SD for mathematics (Hutchinson, De Luca, Doyle, Roberts, & Anderson, 2013). In the EPICure cohort of EP children, Johnson and colleagues (Johnson, Hennessy, et al., 2009) found that at 11 years of age, EP children had significantly lower scores on assessments of reading (−18 points) and mathematics (−27 points) than term peers. These differences remained significant when controlling for cognitive ability. In addition, teachers rated half of the EP population as having poor educational attainment as compared with 5% of their term peers (Johnson, Hennessy, et al., 2009).

As has been found in a number of other studies, EP/ELBW children also require higher utilization of special education services (Aarnoudse-Moens et al., 2011; Anderson et al., 2003; Buck, Msall, Shisterman, Lyon, & Rogers, 2000). ELBW adolescents had significantly lower academic achievement than normal-birth-weight peers on assessments of academic achievement in reading and mathematics (Litt et al., 2012). Higher rates of mathematics learning disabilities, as defined by a low achievement scores in cognitively average teens, were found in the EP group, with 50% of EP adolescents versus 28% of term controls meeting criteria. Rates of special education involvement at age 14 were also significantly higher in the EP group (OR = 11.78) (Litt et al., 2012).

Studies consistently show that EP/ELBW individuals are at high risk for learning disabilities, and these are often comorbid with intellectual impairments (Johnson et al., 2016). In addition to general cognitive and attention problems, neurodevelopmental deficits of VP/VLBW individuals profoundly affect their ability to perceive, integrate, and process stimuli simultaneously; thus their mathematical performance appears particularly compromised (Taylor, Espy, &

Anderson, 2009). Some have suggested that VP/VLBW children's mathematic deficits are specific and not explained by global cognitive function (Johnson, Wolke, Hennessy, & Marlow, 2011; Litt et al., 2012; Simms, Cragg, Gilmore, Marlow, & Johnson, 2013). However, comparing different diagnosis alternatives (fixed cutoff scores vs. discrepancy-based residual scores), others have shown that although the risk for general cognitive and mathematic impairments increases with lower GA, preterm children have no increased risk of dyscalculia after statistically adjusting for gender, family socioeconomic status, and SGA birth (Jaekel & Wolke, 2014).

To tailor specific educational support and develop effective interventions we need to understand the underlying mechanisms that explain preterm children's long-term problems. One such example is a cognitive workload model that may help explain the association between cognitive task complexity and incremental performance deficits: cognitive performance of preterm children decreases as the cognitive workload of tasks increases (Jaekel, Baumann, et al., 2013). Current studies point to a possibly universal effect of GA on later mathematics attainment (Johnson, Hennessy, et al., 2009; Lipkind et al., 2012; Quigley et al., 2012; Saigal et al., 2003), but there is uncertainty about the specific shape and magnitude of this effect. Study populations are heterogeneous and may be affected by a number of confounding factors such as socioeconomic, cultural, and health-care standards, as well as opportunities available within education systems. One study has investigated whether the effects of GA on IQ and mathematic abilities that were found in the Bavarian Longitudinal Study (Jaekel, Baumann, et al., 2013; Jaekel & Wolke, 2014) are universal (e.g., whether similar associations are found across cohorts assessed in different countries and during different eras of neonatal care). Prematurity had significant adverse effects on IQ and basic mathematic processing following birth at all gestations <36 weeks and on IQ <34 weeks GA (Wolke, Strauss, et al., 2015). These prediction functions then accurately predicted IQ and mathematic processing in the EPICure Study of 171 children born <26 weeks GA in the United Kingdom in 1995. Thus, despite significant improvements in neonatal intensive care, there is considerable temporal and cross-national consistency in long-term cognitive abilities as evidenced in IQ and basic numerical processing (Wolke, Strauss, et al., 2015). The ability to predict long-term outcomes from one cohort to another suggests that neurodevelopmental rather than environmental factors explain the long-term effects of gestation at birth.

Behavior

Premature birth is associated with a specific cluster of behavioral problems including attention, emotional, and sociocommunication difficulties (Farooqi et al., 2007; Hille et al., 2001). This preterm behavioral phenotype manifests in a high prevalence of internalizing disorders, autism, and ADHD (D'Onofrio et al., 2013; Johnson & Marlow, 2011; Johnson & Wolke, 2013) and is evident in studies using behavioral screening measures as well as diagnostic psychiatric interviews. Recently, generally increased risks for non–substance use disorders (Van Lieshout, Boyle, Saigal, Morrison, & Schmidt, 2015), low self-esteem, and the need for social assistance have been reported for ELBW adults (Saigal et al., 2016). However, most studies report that differences between groups disappear when individuals with neurosensory or neurodevelopmental impairments (percentages range from 5% to 40% depending on the degree of neonatal risk and sampling criteria in different populations) are excluded from analyses.

ADHD. This condition is one of the psychiatric disorders most consistently associated with the preterm behavioral phenotype (Aarnoudse-Moens et al., 2009; Bhutta et al., 2002; Hack et al., 2009; Hille et al., 2001). Prevalence rates of up to 25% have been reported for preterm children and adolescents (Johnson & Marlow, 2011; Johnson & Wolke, 2013), and a meta-analysis of VP/VLBW compared with full-term children found a pooled relative ADHD risk of 2.6 (Bhutta et al., 2002). In a study examining behavior outcomes at school entry in ELBW compared with classroom-matched NBW control children, rates of ADHD combined subtype assessed with psychiatric interviews were about twice as high for the ELBW group. The ELBW group also had much higher rates of teacher-identified deficits in attention, self-regulation (Behavior Rating Inventory of Executive Function), and social functioning. ADHD and impaired behavioral self-regulation were associated with deficits on tests of EF but not with global cognitive impairment (Scott et al., 2012).

Recent studies have shown that the increased risk for ADHD may be specific to attention problems without hyperactivity/impulsivity and stable across childhood and adulthood in preterm individuals (i.e., ADHD inattentive subtype) (Breeman, Jaekel, Baumann, Bartmann, & Wolke, 2016; Jaekel, Wolke, & Bartmann, 2013). Moreover, in the general population ADHD is often comorbid with conduct disorder/oppositional defiant disorder (Biederman et al., 2008), whereas ADHD in preterm children is not accompanied by comorbid conduct problems (Hack et al., 2009; Samara, Marlow, & Wolke, 2008). Together, these findings suggest a predominantly neurodevelopmental etiology for ADHD in preterm populations.

Social Difficulties and Autism Spectrum Disorder. There is increasing evidence that VP/VLBW individuals are at an increased risk of autism spectrum disorders (ASD) than term-born peers, with a prevalence of up to 8% compared with a median prevalence of 0.6% in the general population (Elsabbagh et al., 2012). In a recent study of EP children, prevalence rates of ASD were assessed using gold standard assessment measures, the Autism Diagnostic Interview-Revised (Rutter, LeCouteur, & Lord, 2003, 2008) and Autism Diagnostic Observation Schedule, 2nd Edition (Lord et al., 2012). In a large, national EP cohort assessed at 10 years of age, 7.1% of the cohort met criteria for ASD (Joseph et al., 2017). However, general problems with social interaction and cognitive impairment may explain VP/VLBW children's elevated risk for an ASD diagnosis (Johnson et al., 2010a, 2010b; Pinto-Martin et al., 2011). VP/VLBW children more often experience peer relationship difficulties and tend to be socially isolated (Bora, Pritchard, Moor, Austin, & Woodward, 2011; Hutchinson et al., 2013; Jones, Champion, & Woodward, 2013; Larroque et al., 2011; Ritchie, Bora, & Woodward, 2015). It has been postulated that these social difficulties may be due to VP/VLBW children's cognitive and neurosensory deficits (Delobel-Ayoub et al., 2009), potentially resulting in difficulties processing complex social stimuli (Jaekel, Baumann, et al., 2013; Johnson & Wolke, 2013); however, differences in social adjustment usually remain significant even after statistically adjusting for neurodevelopmental impairment (Eryigit-Madzwamuse, Strauss, Baumann, Bartmann, & Wolke, 2015; Samara et al., 2008; Scott et al., 2012). Growing evidence also suggests that VP/VLBW children are more often targets of bullying and victimization than their full-term peers (Day et al., 2015; Wolke, Baumann, Strauss, Johnson, & Marlow, 2015). With survivors of some of the best-documented VP/VLBW cohorts entering adulthood, more research has emerged on self-reports of young adults' social relationships and friendships, with all studies consistently reporting very limited social support from friends and romantic partners (Darlow, Horwood, Pere-Bracken, & Woodward, 2013b; Lund et al., 2012; Mannisto et al., 2015; Wolke, Chernova, et al., 2013).

Emotional Problems. Studies have shown mixed results in relation to the risk for internalizing symptoms (i.e., anxiety and depression) in preterm cohorts (Bhutta et al., 2002; Hille et al., 2001; Samara et al., 2008), but meta-analyses have consistently shown that preterm adolescents are at a 2- to 3-fold increased risk for emotional disorders (Burnett et al., 2011; Somhovd, Hansen, Brok, Esbjorn, & Greisen, 2012). In general, VP/VLBW individuals present a higher rate of anxiety problems and are more often diagnosed with anxiety disorders in childhood, adolescence, and adulthood (Johnson & Wolke, 2013; Lund, Vik, Skranes, Brubakk, & Indredavik, 2011). Evidence for depression has been mixed, depending on the age at assessment, number of participants, inclusion criteria for preterm and term comparison groups, type of assessment instrument (e.g., dimensional measures vs. psychiatric diagnoses), and sources of information (e.g., self-report vs. parent rating) (Jaekel, Baumann, Bartmann, & Wolke, 2018; Johnson & Marlow, 2011; Johnson & Wolke, 2013; Nosarti et al., 2012; Westrupp, Northam, Doyle, Callanan, & Anderson, 2011). Inconsistencies between studies may also partly be explained by the fact that mood disorders, in general, show a rise in onset in adolescence and early adulthood but most studies of those born VP/VLBW were limited to cross-sectional childhood data. Overall, the clinical risk after VP/VLBW birth seems to be higher for anxiety rather than depression (Johnson et al., 2010b; Treyvaud et al., 2013). It has also been suggested that emotional problems may be more stable over time in VP/VLBW compared with full-term children and adolescents (Hall & Wolke, 2012), resulting in a greater relative risk for morbidity in adulthood among preterm individuals (Van Lieshout et al., 2015).

Personality. Recent studies have shown that the described VP/VLBW behavioral phenotype in adults may not be limited to certain behaviors such as shyness and low risk-taking but may include a more general socially withdrawn personality tendency. This VP/VLBW personality has been described as being easily worried, rigid in communication, minimally socially engaged, and not interested in physical or social risks that underlie novel, complex, or sensation-seeking experiences (Eryigit-Madzwamuse, Strauss, et al., 2015; Waxman, Van Lieshout, Saigal, Boyle, & Schmidt, 2013). Overall, VP/VLBW birth increases the risk for behavioral and socioemotional difficulties that may adversely affect long-term developmental outcomes, including life satisfaction, social support, wealth, and health. Not surprisingly, VP/VLBW adults consistently report lower quality of life than their term-born peers (Wolke, 2016). Early identification and treatment of behavioral, social, and emotional problems may not only help reduce the individual lifelong burden of the sequelae of preterm birth but also increase overall life satisfaction and happiness.

Neuropsychological Assessment

There are a number of considerations to address when using normative data with preterm and LBW populations. In research studies, use of test norms is believed to lead to underestimations of impairment when compared with using a local term control group. In clinical practice, care should be taken to consider the sociodemographic characteristics of the standardization sample and how they may differ from the characteristics of a VP/VLBW or EP/ELBW sample. Given the rates of neurosensory impairment, specifically visual perceptual abnormalities, careful test selection should consider the potential impact of deficits in visual acuity and tracking on test performance beyond the domain of visual perception. Finally, given high rates of CP and developmental coordination disorder, providers and researchers should consider the negative impact of motor deficits on assessments of domains outside the strictly motor, including measures of attention, processing speed, visual memory, and academic achievement, which may negatively impact test performance and lead to an underestimate of functioning.

During early developmental evaluations, "corrected age" (chronological age minus the numbers of weeks born before full term, or 40 weeks' gestation) is often used for preterm infants to account or control for delays in neurological maturation related to preterm birth. Standard practice has often been to use age-corrected norms until 24–30 months of age (Baron & Rey-Casserly, 2010), although some researchers have advocated for extending the use of age-corrected norms, given that more infants are surviving in the EP/ELBW group, with a protracted course of immature neurological development (Raz, Debastos, Newman, & Batton, 2010). Although these questions have been raised in research, no clear guidelines are available to provide a rationale for when it is appropriate to stop using "corrected age" normative data in research or clinical settings. Given the importance of early identification of preterm children who are at risk for negative neurodevelopmental outcomes, further research in this area is believed imperative to inform practice guidelines in this area.

With regard to attention problems and ADHD, it has been suggested that observational, continuously scored ratings of attention may be more reliable and useful to detect ADHD-related symptoms in clinical and educational practice as opposed to categorical clinical diagnoses (Jaekel, Wolke, et al., 2013). Observational measures of attention during standard testing provide an added advantage of detecting subclinical levels in children that are relevant for learning. Thus, it may be recommended to implement standardized behavior ratings in clinical and educational settings as sensible practice tools to identify children with subtle attention problems who may benefit from early intervention.

With regard to developmental disorders, children are usually diagnosed when there is a clear discrepancy between their respective test scores (i.e., reading, mathematics) and expected performances based on general intelligence (IQ) and age (APA, 2013). However, preterm children often have lower than typical IQ scores (Johnson, Fawke, et al., 2009; Wolke & Meyer, 1999), thus fixed definitions of developmental disorders may miss many children who have low IQ combined with low test performance. Some have used residuals from a regression analysis, for example, when predicting math by general IQ, to obtain specific math scores that are independent of IQ (Jaekel & Wolke, 2014). The goal for future research as well as for clinical and educational practice is to establish transdisciplinary and internationally consistent terms, definitions, and diagnosis standards for developmental deficiencies and learning disorders.

Intervention

Preterm children have an adverse start into life, but devising successful intervention strategies may help them unfold their full potential and have effective, productive lives (Saigal, 2014). The costs of educational remediation for preterm survivors typically outstrips the costs for post-discharge medical care; a reduction in academic problems would lead to both substantial public cost savings (Heckman, 2006), and a likely better quality of life for those individuals affected by preterm birth. In general, VP/VLBW individuals' developmental outcomes may be impeded by neurodevelopmental adversity, whereas environmental factors may promote adaptation or compensation. For instance, providing skin-to-skin contact ("kangaroo care") to preterm neonates can improve parental sensitivity across childhood (Feldman, Rosenthal, & Eidelman, 2014; Tessier et al., 2009), and sensitive parenting predicts more optimal functioning in preterm children and adolescents (Feldman et al., 2014; Jaekel, Pluess, Belsky, & Wolke, 2015; Wolke, Jaekel, Hall, & Baumann, 2013).

Several researchers have examined the impact that early intervention programs have on motor and cognitive development in early childhood in VP/VLBW children. A meta-analysis examined the effectiveness of early interventions with preterm children on neurodevelopmental outcomes at 12 months of age (Vanderveen, Bassler, Robertson, & Kirpalani, 2009). Researchers identified 25 randomized controlled trials (RCTs) including a range of early interventions (e.g., parent education, home visits, developmental intervention). Pooled results revealed significantly higher scores in the intervention group on cognitive/mental and physical assessments at 12 months. The higher cognitive scores in the intervention group were sustained at 24 months, but not by 36 months. Intervention effects on physical development were no longer significant by 24 months (Vanderveen et al., 2009).

Several studies have assessed early interventions that focus on improving the parent–infant interaction. Koldewijn and colleagues (2009) examined the impact of the Infant Behavior Assessment and Intervention Program (Hedlund, 1998; Hedlund & Tatarka, 1988) implemented between birth and 8 months of age, on early cognitive development and behavior in VLBW infants at 24 months of age. In this RCT, interventions were received until 6 months of age. At 24 months, significant intervention effects were only found for motor development on the Bayley Scales of Infant Development, Second Edition (Bayley-II) (Bayley, 1993) when controlling for perinatal and background variables (e.g., gestation age, gender, abnormal ultrasound, receipt of oxygen therapy, and low maternal education). No intervention effects were found for the cognitive scores (Koldewijn et al., 2009). Nordhov and colleagues (2010) examined the impact of another early intervention program implemented after delivery on cognitive and motor outcomes in preterm children at ages 3 and 5 years (Nordhov et al., 2010). This study used a modified version of the Mother-Infant Transaction Program (Rauh, Nurcombe, Achenbach, & Howell, 1990) for their early intervention approach, which also focused on both the infant and the parent–infant interaction. In this RCT, when controlling for maternal education, significant group differences were found in Full Scale IQ scores on the Wechsler Preschool and Primary Scale of Intelligence, Revised (Wechsler, 1989) at 5 years of age, with the intervention group showing higher IQ scores (Nordhov et al., 2010). Interestingly, group differences on the Bayley-II Mental Development Index were not significant at age 3 when controlling for maternal education (Nordhov et al., 2010). These studies highlight the potential for early interventions that focus on the parent–infant interaction to improve long-term outcomes, although results are inconsistent.

As described in the two paragraphs above, most interventions for improving preterm children's cognitive development have been applied in infancy and focus on increasing maternal sensitivity and stimulation. However, these interventions may not benefit preterm children into school age (Orton, Spittle, Doyle, Anderson, & Boyd, 2009). Why could this be? In infancy, consistent differences between full-term and preterm mother–infant dyads have been reported, with preterm infants being described as more compliant and less active (Forcada-Guex, Pierrehumbert, Borghini, Moessinger, & Muller-Nix, 2006) and their mothers as less sensitive and more controlling (Feldman & Eidelman, 2007; Muller-Nix et al., 2004). These differences have been attributed to stress (Muller-Nix et al., 2004) and increased social disadvantage (Saigal & Doyle, 2008) associated with preterm birth. Studies have shown, however, that this assumption needs to be revised: indeed, the quality of interaction crucially depends on the child's cognitive level of functioning, especially in situations that are challenging for the child (Jaekel, Wolke, & Chernova, 2012). Most importantly, a recent meta-analysis showed that there is no difference in sensitivity between preterm and full-term children's mothers (Bilgin & Wolke, 2015). Although systematic reviews of parenting interventions in infancy to increase sensitivity found only

limited impact on preterm children's long-term performance (Benzies, Magill-Evans, Hayden, & Ballantyne, 2013; Spittle, Orton, Anderson, Boyd, & Doyle, 2012), this may be explained by the hypothesis that the brains of preterm infants are organized differently than those of healthy full-term children and are less able to process complex inputs such as social stimulation (Als, 2009; De Schuymer, De Groote, Desoete, & Roeyers, 2012; Treyvaud et al., 2009). Brain imaging research suggests that interventions at later ages (pre- and primary school) may be more effective, when preterm children's brains are more developed and capable of profiting from learning opportunities and a positive environment (Grunewaldt, Lohaugen, Austeng, Brubakk, & Skranes, 2013; van der Kooy-Hofland, van der Kooy, Bus, van Ijzendoorn, & Bonsel, 2012). Sensitive parenting at age 6 years is a protective factor that may compensate for preterm children's academic underachievement (Wolke, Jaekel, et al., 2013). Importantly sensitive parenting around school-entry and elementary school age (e.g., 6 years) may look different than sensitive parenting in infancy. For example, parents may provide gentle feedback, adapt tasks to the children's ability to deal with increasing workload, and suggest potential solutions rather than taking over and solving tasks for the child, thereby allowing VP/VLBW children to attain the same school performance as full-term children in adolescence, based on secondary school track, grade retention, and teacher ratings of performance in the main subjects. Accordingly, Differential Susceptibility Theory suggests that some children who would, within a traditional diathesis-stress framework, be considered more vulnerable (Zuckerman, 1999), are more susceptible to environmental factors such as parenting (Belsky, Bakermans-Kranenburg, & van Ijzendoorn, 2007; Belsky & Pluess, 2009; Roisman et al., 2012). We have investigated this hypothesis and documented that LBW and VLBW children are more vulnerable than NBW children to the adverse effects of low-sensitive parenting (Jaekel et al., 2015), i.e., LBW and VLBW children who experienced highly sensitive parenting showed academic catch-up with their NBW peers, whereas those who experienced less sensitive parenting showed much poorer functioning. Altogether these findings suggest that LBW and VLBW children may be more susceptible to their environments but neurodevelopmental deficits may limit their potential for functional adaptation in performance. The conceptualization of two competing forces of increased susceptibility (i.e., developmental plasticity) versus limited neurobiological resources (e.g., low potential for functional adaptation) in VP/VLBW children may help explain the knowledge we already have acquired. More specifically, VP/VLBW children may be highly susceptible to the environment, but may not have sufficient neurobiological resources to profit from stimulation. Under optimal conditions, they may be able to compensate or catch up with healthy full-term children, but it is unlikely that they will outperform them. The theoretical and practical implications of this assumption are innovative and far-reaching, as this would provide the basis for designing targeted interventions. For example, children could be identified for participation in novel interventions based on their predicted environmental susceptibility and learning potential, i.e., VP/VLBW children without severe neurodevelopmental impairments may be expected to benefit most from investments in intervention according to the Differential Susceptibility Theory framework. In addition, such future interventions may target parents of preterm children beyond infancy in late preschool or early school age (Jaekel, 2016), and aim to increase their sensitivity, for example via video-feedback training.

Tentative evidence has emerged that an adaptive computerized training program may improve the working memory capacity of ELBW preschool children (Grunewaldt et al., 2013) and adolescents (Lohaugen et al., 2011). Accordingly, training-induced changes in structural brain connectivity (Takeuchi et al., 2010; Zatorre, Fields, & Johansen-Berg, 2012) and activity (Olesen, Westerberg, & Klingberg, 2004; Westerberg & Klingberg, 2007) were identified and were attributed to increased working memory capacity (Klingberg, 2010). However, although working memory is, in general, associated with academic achievement, transfer effects of cognitive training on long-term academic achievement were not empirically evaluated with this study. Very recently, new findings from a large population-based Australian RCT showed that academic outcomes of children with low working memory were not improved by working memory training (Roberts, Quach, Spencer-Smith, & et al., 2016); more directly, their math performance was even lower after the intervention (please note: not all children in this sample were born preterm, whereas VP/VLBW children have an increased risk for working memory problems). These results are further substantiated by two recent meta-analytic reviews that dispute previously reported transfer effects of working memory training onto other cognitive and academic domains of functioning (Melby-Lervåg, Redick, & Hulme, 2016; Soveri, Antfolk, Karlsson, Salo, & Laine, 2017).

To date, it is not clear to what extent it may be possible to positively influence children's developmental trajectories with training (Jolles & Crone, 2012; Pascoe et al., 2013). In addition to the classic approaches to intervention described in earlier sections, such as targeting parenting behavior or computerized training, we still need to investigate how preterm children can be better supported in school. Despite their frequent developmental problems, most preterm children attend mainstream schools, thus teachers are responsible for identifying and providing special support for an increasing number of children with complex learning difficulties. However, teachers lack knowledge and formal training about preterm children's characteristic problem areas (i.e., attention, cognition, and mathematics) (Johnson, Gilmore, Gallimore, Jaekel, & Wolke, 2015), how they affect their ability to adapt in class (Jaekel, Baumann, et al., 2013), and how to appropriately facilitate their learning progress. Teachers need to understand who are the high-risk groups for specific learning problems because early identification and individually tailored support may help all preterm children live up to their full academic potential.

Table 1.3 Primary Recommendations for Clinical Practice for VP/VLBW Patients

- Begin developmental evaluations around age 2 years
- Use "corrected age" normative data until between 24 and 30 months of age
- Complete serial neuropsychological evaluations to monitor progress and provide appropriate accommodations
- Include the following elements in all evaluations:
  - Review of medical, developmental, academic records
  - Interview with caregivers and seeking information from other informants
  - Evaluation of domains of neuropsychological functioning (e.g., general intellectual functioning; attention and EF; and language, visual-spatial, visual-motor, and memory skills) and academic achievement
  - Appropriate diagnoses and recommendations for accommodations and interventions based on evaluation results

Implications for Clinical Practice

Given the presence of early developmental differences between VP/VLBW and healthy full-term children, regular follow-up assessments are recommended to guide intervention service decisions. Early developmental evaluations are generally recommended by 20 months of corrected age at the latest, to guide early intervention (e.g., speech/language, occupational, physical, and developmental therapy) as well as inclusion in therapeutic or early childhood preschool programs where appropriate. There are no clear guidelines available to provide a rationale for when it is appropriate to stop using "corrected age" normative data in clinical developmental evaluation. Standard of practice is to use "corrected age" until 24–30 months of age (Baron & Rey-Casserly, 2010), although some researchers have advocated for extending the use of age-corrected norms beyond the toddler period (Raz et al., 2010). Clinical judgment should guide decisions around the use of "corrected age" norms in these early evaluations.

Deficits in cognitive abilities, attention, EF, and early academic achievement have been found at or before the time of school entry (Orchinik et al., 2011; Scott et al., 2012; Taylor et al., 2011), thus thorough evaluations are recommended within 6–12 months before school entry to identify VP/VLBW children who are at risk for underachievement. For those children identified as demonstrating areas of neurocognitive impairment, regular follow-up evaluations are recommended throughout the school years to guide intervention and educational accommodations. Moreover, strategies for sharing information between families, health professionals, and teachers need to be developed and established.

Neuropsychological evaluations of VP/VLBW and EP/ELBW children should meet the standards for a typical comprehensive neuropsychological evaluation (Taylor, 2016). Specifically, the evaluation should include the following elements:

(1) An interview with the child's caregiver regarding medical, developmental, family, educational, and psychosocial history and a review of available medical records.

(2) A neurobehavioral status examination and interview with the child.

(3) A thorough assessment of neurocognitive functioning and academic skills, including an evaluation of multiple cognitive domains (i.e., general intellectual abilities; attention and EF; and language, visual-motor, visual-spatial, and memory skills).

(4) Input from additional informants such as teachers regarding social-emotional and behavioral functioning in the school setting as well as a review of records of prior educational interventions and accommodations (e.g., 504 Plan, individualized education program) and results of prior testing.

Evaluations should include both broad-band evaluations as well as in-depth assessments of areas of concern that are identified through caregiver interview, information from other sources, and review of records. Care should be taken when choosing assessment tools to ensure that normative sample data is appropriate given the socioeconomic, cultural, racial, and language background of the child. Test results and behavioral observations should be interpreted within the context of non-neurocognitive factors such as the child's behavior, cooperation, and motivation, socioemotional and behavioral presentation, social and family stressors, educational history and socioeconomic background, as well as educational system and intervention history.

Based on these complex factors (i.e., history, behavioral observations, and evaluation results), diagnostic impressions should be provided to the family as appropriate, as well as a discussion of neurocognitive strengths and weaknesses and recommendations for interventions and accommodations. Serial assessments throughout the school years can evaluate change over time and guide updated recommendations for interventions and accommodations as demands change across settings throughout the lifespan. Although there is no specific special education category for children with a history of prematurity or LBW, consideration should be given to eligibility for special education services under the label of "other health impairment" when the profile of neuropsychological deficits is consistent with expectations for children with a history of VP/VLBW or EP/ELBW. Given that there are higher rates of broader cognitive impairment and academic underachievement in the VP/VLBW population, consideration should be given to other educational labels such as "cognitive disorder" or "specific learning disability." In addition to the development of an individualized education program or a 504 Plan, it is important for mental and physical health providers to educate parents, teachers, and interventionists about the frequent consequences of VP/VLBW birth to facilitate an understanding of the child's challenges (Johnson et al., 2015). In addition, facilitating communication among families, teachers, interventionists, and medical providers will be important in coordinating care and advocacy for children affected by VP/VLBW.

Future Directions

Delivery at any gestation other than full term confers potential alterations to brain development and increases the risk for academic underachievement. Research has shown that there are specific problem areas that are characteristically affected in the preterm phenotype (Johnson & Marlow, 2011; Wolke, 2011) such as attention deficits and social difficulties, whereas many functional problems may be explained by general cognitive impairments of preterm children. Indeed, VP/VLBW adult studies suggest that lifespan consequences of preterm birth may predominantly involve general cognitive and multiple problems instead of specific deficits (Eryigit Madzwamuse, Baumann, Jaekel, Bartmann, & Wolke, 2015). If this finding is replicated by other studies of preterm populations, it may imply that alleviating long-term problems after VP/VLBW birth may be even harder than currently believed. There is no doubt that medical and neonatal care has fundamentally changed since those preterm infants who are now adults were born, and these changes (e.g., introduction of corticosteroid and surfactant therapies) have resulted in increased survival of ever lower gestation infants. However, rates of cognitive problems have remained at similar levels (Moore et al., 2012), and although severe neural abnormalities such as cystic PVL are now relatively rare, focal noncystic white matter injuries remain common (Woodward et al., 2006, 2012). Although this shift may be partly explained by shorter periods of neonatal ventilation (Miller & Ferriero, 2009), focal white matter injuries have been related to cognitive and neuromotor disabilities as severe as those following PVL (Bora, Pritchard, Chen, Inder, & Woodward, 2014; Spittle et al., 2011; Woodward et al., 2006), suggesting that the underlying neurodevelopmental mechanisms may not have changed.

Over the last decade, we have learned that every lost week of gestation confers an insult to brain development and that there is a dose–response effect of low GA on developmental risk, even for LP and early-term children. Considering the large number of children

born moderately preterm to LP and early term (see Table 1.1), even small increases in cognitive impairments may have large effects on a population level. Thus, as the total number of children born preterm increases, there will be parallel increases in the prevalence of learning problems and special education needs, placing new demands on the education system. This increased demand will have profound financial implications because preterm children incur high public sector costs over the first 18 years of life, with education costs representing the highest contributor (Petrou, Johnson, Wolke, & Marlow, 2013; Petrou & Khan, 2012).

Although preterm birth is on the rise worldwide, most studies have involved only White, nonimmigrant families, but Black infants have the highest risk of being born preterm (March of Dimes, 2007). In September 2014, *The Lancet* published a new series on child deaths in high-income countries (Editorial, 2014), arguing for prioritizing context-specific studies and preventive strategies for the most vulnerable communities. The main obstacles when studying social determinants of health in deprived populations are difficulties in gaining access to certain high-risk groups and the lack of standardized data collection. Nevertheless, there is an urgent need for targeting the most vulnerable populations to learn more about effects of preterm birth in socioeconomically deprived regions and racial minority groups.

In general, regular developmental follow-up assessments during the preschool years can help early identification of preterm children who may profit from special support to develop their full academic potential (Doyle et al., 2014). However, we still lack information about the mechanisms influencing preterm children's neuropsychological development and, in particular, potential avenues to successful intervention. With regard to prevention and intervention, one of the most important factors to consider is their cost–benefit ratio and if there are certain target groups who would profit more from support than others. For example, cognitive problems of moderately preterm and LP children are subtle and they have been neglected in follow-up services. However, considering the large number of children born moderately preterm and LP, even small increases in cognitive abilities may have large effects on academic performance on a population level (MacKay et al., 2010; Shapiro-Mendoza & Lackritz, 2012). Thus it is timely to not only document preterm children's gradual impairments (Boyle, 2012; Boyle et al., 2012; Poulsen et al., 2013; Quigley et al., 2012), but also to investigate their learning ability (i.e., developmental plasticity, potential for functional adaptation) to identify those who may benefit most from intervention (McCormick et al., 2006). We need more RCTs to develop long-term effective interventions for preterm individuals across the full spectrum of GA and to identify the right target groups within this population. Increasingly inter- and transdisciplinary research collaborations will be needed to accomplish this goal. Preterm children had an adverse start into life, but by trying to understand the mechanisms underlying their long-term development we may progressively be able to meet their specific needs to promote lifelong personal success and a good quality of life.

References

Aarnoudse-Moens, C. S. H., Weisglas-Kuperus, N., van Goudoever, J., & Oosterlaan, J. (2009). Meta-analysis of neurobehavioral outcomes in very preterm and/or very low birthweight children. *Pediatrics, 124*(2), 717–728.

Aarnoudse-Moens, C. S., Oosterlaan, J., Duivenvoorden, H. J., van Goudoever, J. B., & Weisglas-Kuperus, N. (2011). Development of preschool and academic skills in children born very preterm. *Journal of Pediatrics, 158*(1), 51–56.

Als, H. (2009). NIDCAP: Testing the effectiveness of a relationship-based comprehensive intervention. *Pediatrics, 124*(4), 1208–1210.

American College of Obstetrics and Gynecology. (2008). ACOG Committee Opinion No. 404 April 2008. Late-preterm infants. *Obstetrics & Gynecology, 111*(4), 1029–1032. doi:10.1097/AOG.0b013e31817327d0

American Psychiatric Association. (2013). *Diagnostic and statistical manual of mental disorders* (5th ed.). Arlington, VA: American Psychiatric Publishing.

Anderson, P. J., De Luca, C. R., Hutchinson, E., Spencer-Smith, M. M., Roberts, G., Doyle, L. W., & Victorian Infant Collaborative Study Group. (2011). Attention problems in a representative sample of extremely preterm/extremely low birth weight children. *Developmental Neuropsychology, 36*(1), 57–73. doi:10.1080/87565641.2011.540538

Anderson, P., Doyle, L. W., & the Victorian Infant Collaborative Study Group. (2003). Neurobehavioral outcomes of school-age children born extremely low birth weight or very preterm in the 1990s. *Journal of the American Medical Association, 289*(24), 3264–3272.

Arpino, C., Compagnone, E., Montanaro, M. L., Cacciatore, D., De Luca, A., Cerulli, A., Di Girolamo, S., & Curatolo, P. (2010). Preterm birth and neurodevelopmental outcome: A review. *Childs Nervous System, 26*(9), 1139–1149. doi:10.1007/s00381-010-1125-y

Ashton, D. D. (2010). Elective delivery at less than 39 weeks. *Current Opinion in Obstetrics and Gynecology, 22*, 506–510.

Ball, G., Boardman, J. P., Rueckert, D., Aljabar, P., Arichi, T., Merchant, N., ... Counsell, S. J. (2012). The effect of preterm birth on thalamic and cortical development. *Cerebral Cortex, 22*, 1016–1024.

Baron, I. S., Kerns, K. A., Muller, U., Ahronovich, M. D., & Litman, F. R. (2012). Executive functions in extremely low birth weight and late-preterm preschoolers: Effects on working memory and response inhibition. *Child Neuropsychology, 18*(6), 586–599. doi:10.1080/09297049.2011.631906

Baron, I. S., Litman, L., Ahronovich, M. D., & Baker, R. (2012). Late preterm birth: A review of medical and neuropsychological childhood outcomes. *Neuropsychological Review, 22*, 438–450.

Baron, I. S., & Rey-Casserly, C. (2010). Extremely preterm birth outcome: A review of four decades of cognitive research. *Neuropsychology Review, 20*(4), 430–452. doi:10.1007/s11065-010-9132-z

Bäuml, J. G., Daamen, M., Meng, C., Neitzel, J., Scheef, L., Jaekel J., ... Sorg, C. (2015). Correspondence between aberrant intrinsic network connectivity and gray matter volume in the ventral brain of preterm born adults. *Cerebral Cortex. 25*(11), 4135–4145. doi:10.1093/cercor/bhu133

Bayley, N. (1993). *Bayley scales of infant development* (2nd ed.). San Antonio, TX: The Psychological Corporation.

Belsky, J., Bakermans-Kranenburg, M. J., & van Ijzendoorn, M. H. (2007). For better and for worse: Differential susceptibility to environmental influences. *Current Directions in Psychological Science, 16*(6), 300–304. doi:10.1111/j.1467-8721.2007.00525.x

Belsky, J., & Pluess, M. (2009). Beyond diathesis-stress: Differential susceptibility to environmental influences. *Psychological Bulletin, 135*(6), 885–908.

Benzies, K., Magill-Evans, J., Hayden, K., & Ballantyne, M. (2013). Key components of early intervention programs for preterm infants and their parents: A systematic review and meta-analysis. *BMC Pregnancy and Childbirth, 13*(Suppl 1), S10.

Bhutta, A. T., Cleves, M. A., Casey, P. H., Cradock, M. M., & Anand, K. J. S. (2002). Cognitive and behavioral outcomes of school-aged children who were born preterm. A meta-analysis. *Journal of the American Medical Association, 288*(6), 728–737.

Biederman, J., Petty, C. R., Dolan, C., Hughes, S., Mick, E., Monuteaux, M. C., & Faraone, S. V. (2008). The long-term longitudinal course of oppositional defiant disorder and conduct disorder in ADHD boys: Findings from a controlled 10-year prospective longitudinal follow-up study. *Psychological Medicine, 38*(7), 1027–1036.

Bilgin, A., & Wolke, D. (2015). Maternal sensitivity in parenting preterm children: A meta-analysis. *Pediatrics*, *136* (1), 2014–3570.

Blanc, A. K., & Wardlaw, T. (2005). Monitoring low birth weight: An evaluation of international estimates and updated estimation procedure. *Bulletin of the World Health Organization*, *83*, 161–240.

Bora, S., Pritchard, V. E., Chen, Z., Inder, T. E., & Woodward, L. J. (2014). Neonatal cerebral morphometry and later risk of persistent inattention/hyperactivity in children born very preterm. *Journal of Child Psychology and Psychiatry*, *55*(7), 828–838. doi:10.1111/jcpp.12200

Bora, S., Pritchard, V. E., Moor, S., Austin, N. C., & Woodward, L. J. (2011). Emotional and behavioural adjustment of children born very preterm at early school age. *Journal of Paediatrics and Child Health*, *47*(12), 863–869. doi:10.1111/j.1440-1754.2011.02105.x

Bos, A. F., Van Braeckel, Koenraad N. J. A, Hitzert, M. M., Tanis, J. C., & Roze, E. (2013). Development of fine motor skills in preterm infants. *Development Medicine & Child Neurology*, *55*(Suppl 4), 1–4.

Boyle, E. M. (2012). The late and moderate preterm baby. *Seminars in Fetal and Neonatal Medicine*, *17*(3), 119. doi: http://dx.doi.org/10.1016/j.siny.2012.02.005

Boyle, E. M., Poulsen, G., Field, D. J., Kurinczuk, J. J., Wolke, D., Alfirevic, Z., & Quigley, M. A. (2012). Effects of gestational age at birth on health outcomes at 3 and 5 years of age: Population based cohort study. *British Medical Journal*, *344*. doi:10.1136/bmj.e896

Breeman, L. D., Jaekel, J., Baumann, N., Bartmann, P., & Wolke, D. (2015). Preterm cognitive function into adulthood. *Pediatrics*, *136*(3), 415–423. doi:10.1542/peds.2015-0608

Breeman, L. D., Jaekel, J., Baumann, N., Bartmann, P., & Wolke, D. (2016). Attention problems in very preterm children from childhood to adulthood: The Bavarian Longitudinal Study. *Journal of Child Psychology and Psychiatry*, *57*(2), 132–140. doi:10.1111/jcpp.12456

Burnett, A. C., Anderson, P. J., Cheong, J., Doyle, L. W., Davey, C. G., & Wood, S. J. (2011). Prevalence of psychiatric diagnoses in preterm and full-term children, adolescents and young adults: A meta-analysis. *Psychological Medicine*, *41*(12), 2463–2474. doi:10.1017/s003329171100081x

Centers for Disease Control and Prevention. (2016). CDC report of live births from 2014. Retrieved from www.cdc.gov/reproductivehealth/data_stats/state-profiles.htm:

Cheong, J. L. Y., & Doyle, L. W. (2012). Increasing rates of prematurity and epidemiology of late preterm birth. *Journal of Paediatrics and Child Health*, *48*(9), 784–788. doi:10.1111/j.1440-1754.2012.02536.x

Darlow, B. A., Horwood, L. J., Pere-Bracken, H. M., & Woodward, L. J. (2013a). Psychosocial outcomes of young adults born very low birth weight. *Pediatrics*, *132*(6), E1521–E1528. doi:10.1542/peds.2013-2024

Day, K. L., Van Lieshout, R. J., Vaillancourt, T., Saigal, S., Boyle, M. H., & Schmidt, L. A. (2015). Peer victimization in extremely low birth weight survivors. *Clinical Pediatrics*, *54* (14), 1339–1345. doi:10.1177/0009922815580770

Delobel-Ayoub, M., Arnaud, C., White-Koning, M., Casper, C., Pierrat, V., Garel, M., ... Larroque, B. (2009). Behavioral problems and cognitive performance at 5 years of age after very preterm birth: The EPIPAGE study. *Pediatrics*, *123*(6), 1485–1492. doi:10.1542/peds.2008-1216

De Schuymer, L., De Groote, I., Desoete, A., & Roeyers, H. (2012). Gaze aversion during social interaction in preterm infants: A function of attention skills? *Infant Behavior and Development*, *35*(1), 129–139.

D'Onofrio, B. M., Class, Q. A., Rickert, M. E., Larsson, H., Langstrom, N., & Lichtenstein, P. (2013). Preterm birth and mortality and morbidity: A population-based quasi-experimental study. *JAMA Psychiatry (Chicago, Ill.)*, *70*(11), 1231–1240. doi:10.1001/jamapsychiatry.2013.2107

Doyle, L. W., Anderson, P. J., Battin, M., Bowen, J. R., Brown, N., Callanan, C., ... Woodward, L. J. (2014). Long term follow up of high risk children: Who, why and how? *BMC Pediatrics*, *14*(1), 279. doi:10.1186/1471-2431-14-279

Editorial. (2014). Child deaths in high-income countries [Editorial]. *Lancet*, *384*(9946), 830.

Elsabbagh, M., Divan, G., Koh, Y.-J., Kim, Y. S., Kauchali, S., Marcín, C., ... Fombonne, E. (2012). Global prevalence of autism and other pervasive developmental disorders. *Autism Research*, *5*(3), 160–179. doi:10.1002/aur.239

Eryigit Madzwamuse, S., Baumann, N., Jaekel, J., Bartmann, P., & Wolke, D. (2015). Neuro-cognitive performance of very preterm or very low birth weight adults at 26 years. *Journal of Child Psychology and Psychiatry*, *56* (8), 857–864. doi:10.1111/jcpp.12358

Eryigit-Madzwamuse, S., Strauss, V. Y.-C., Baumann, N., Bartmann, P., & Wolke, D. (2015). Personality of adults who were born very preterm. *Archives of Disease in Childhood – Fetal and Neonatal Edition*. doi:10.1136/archdischild-2014-308007

Farooqi, A., Hagglof, B., Sedin, G., Gothefors, L., & Serenius, F. (2007). Mental health and social competencies of 10- to 12-year-old children born at 23 to 25 weeks of gestation in the 1990s: A Swedish national prospective follow-up study. *Pediatrics*, *120*(1), 118–133. doi:10.1542/peds.2006-2988

Felderhoff-Müser, U., Bittigau, P., Sifringer, M., Jarosz, B., Korobowicz, E., Mahler, L., ... Ikonomidou, C. (2004). Oxygen causes cell death in the developing brain. *Neurobiological Disorders*, *17*(2), 273–282.

Feldman, R., & Eidelman, A. I. (2007). Maternal postpartum behavior and the emergence of infant-mother and infant-father synchrony in preterm and full-term infants: The role of neonatal vagal tone. *Developmental Psychobiology*, *49*(3), 290–302.

Feldman, R., Rosenthal, Z., & Eidelman, A. I. (2014). Maternal-preterm skin-to-skin contact enhances child physiologic organization and cognitive control across the first 10 years of life. *Biological Psychiatry*, *75*, 56–64.

Finke, K., Neitzel, J., Bäuml, J. G., Redel, P., Müller, H. J., Meng, C., … Sorg, C. (2015). Visual attention in preterm born adults: Specifically impaired attentional sub-mechanisms that link with altered intrinsic brain networks in a compensation-like mode. *NeuroImage*, *107*, 95–106. doi:http://dx.doi.org/10.1016/j.neuroimage.2014.11.062

Forcada-Guex, M., Pierrehumbert, B., Borghini, A., Moessinger, A., & Muller-Nix, C. (2006). Early dyadic patterns of mother-infant interactions and outcomes of prematurity at 18 months. *Pediatrics*, *118*(1), e107–e114.

Geldof, C. J. A., van Wassenaer, A. G., de Kieviet, J. F., Kok, J. H., & Oosterlaan, J. (2012). Visual perception and visual-motor integration in very preterm and/or very low birth weight children: A meta-analysis. *Research in Developmental Disabilities*, *33*(2), 726–736.

Goldenberg, R. L., Culhane, J. F., Iams, J. D., & Romero, R. (2008). Epidemiology and causes of preterm birth. *The Lancet*, *371*(9606), 75–84.

Gopel, W., Kribs, A., Ziegler, A., Laux, R., Hoehn, T., Wieg, C., … on behalf of the German Neonatal Network (2011). Avoidance of mechanical ventilation by surfactant treatment of spontaneously breathing preterm infants (AMV): An open-label, randomised, controlled trial. *The Lancet*, *378*(9803), 1627–1634. doi:10.1016/s0140-6736(11)60986-0

Grunewaldt, K. H., Lohaugen, G. C., Austeng, D., Brubakk, A. M., & Skranes, J. (2013). Working memory training improves cognitive function in VLBW preschoolers. *Pediatrics*, *131*(3), e747–754. doi:10.1542/peds.2012-1965.

Hack, M. (2009). Adult outcomes of preterm children. *Journal of Developmental & Behavioral Pediatrics*, *30*(5), 460–470.

Hack, M. (2013). Psychosocial development of adolescent preterm children. *Early Human Development*, *89*(4), 197–198. doi:10.1016/j.earlhumdev.2013.01.011

Hack, M., Hudson, G. T., Schluchter, M., Andreias, L., Drotar, D., & Klein, N. (2009). Behavioral outcomes of extremely low birth weight children at age 8 years. *Journal of Developmental & Behavioral Pediatrics*, *30*, 122–130.

Hall, J., Jaekel, J., & Wolke, D. (2012). Gender distinctive impacts of prematurity and small for gestational age on age 6 attention problems. *Child and Adolescent Mental Health*, *17*(4), 238–245. doi:10.1111/j.1475-3588.2012.00649.x.

Hall, J., & Wolke, D. (2012). A comparison of prematurity and small for gestational age as risk factors for age 6–13 year emotional problems. *Early Human Development* *88*(10), 797–804. doi:10.1016/j.earlhumdev.2012.05.005

Halliday, H. L. (2008). Surfactants: Past, present and future. *Journal of Perinatology*, *28*(S1), S47–S56. doi:10.1038/jp.2008.50

Heckman, J. J. (2006). Skill formation and the economics of investing in disadvantaged children. *Science*, *312*(5782), 1900–1902. doi:10.1126/science.1128898

Hedlund, R. (1998). The Neurobehavioral Curriculum for Early Intervention. Retrieved 04/06/2017, from Washington Research Institute http://www.ibaip.org

Hedlund, R., & Tatarka, M. (1988). *The infant behavioral assessment*. Seattle: The Washington Research Institute.

Heinonen, K., Eriksson, J. G., Kajantie, E., Pesonen, A.-K., Barker, D. J., Osmond, C., & Raikkonen, K. (2013). Late-preterm birth and lifetime socioeconomic attainments: The Helsinki birth cohort study. *Pediatrics*, *132*(4), 647–655. doi:10.1542/peds.2013-0951

Hille, E. T. M., den Ouden, A. L., Saigal, S., Wolke, D., Lambert, M., Whitaker, A., … Paneth, N. (2001). Behavioural problems in children who weigh 1000 g or less at birth in four countries. *The Lancet*, *357*(9269), 1641–1643.

Himpens, E., Van den Broeck, C., Oostra, A., Calders, P., & Vanhaesebrouck, P. (2008). Prevalence, type, distribution, and severity of cerebral palsy in relation to gestational age: A meta-analytic review. *Developmental Medicine & Child Neurology*, *50*(5), 334–340. doi:10.1111/j.1469-8749.2008.02047.x

Hutchinson, E. A., De Luca, C. R., Doyle, L. W., Roberts, G., & Anderson, P. J. (2013). School-age outcomes of extremely preterm or extremely low birth weight children. *Pediatrics*, *131*(4), e1053–e1061. doi:10.1542/peds.2012-2311

Jaekel, J. (2016). Commentary: Supporting preterm children's parents matters–A reflection on Treyvaud et al. (2016). *Journal of Child Psychology and Psychiatry*, *57*(7), 822–823.

Jaekel, J., Baumann, N., & Wolke, D. (2013). Effects of gestational age at birth on cognitive performance: A function of cognitive workload demands. *PLoS One*, *8*(5), e65219.

Jaekel, J., Pluess, M., Belsky, J., & Wolke, D. (2015). Effects of maternal sensitivity on low birth weight children's academic achievement: A test of differential susceptibility versus diathesis stress. *Journal of Child Psychology and Psychiatry*, *56*(6), 693–701. doi:10.1111/jcpp.12331

Jaekel, J., & Wolke, D. (2014). Preterm birth and dyscalculia. *The Journal of Pediatrics*, *164*(6), 1327–1332. doi:10.1016/j.jpeds.2014.01.069

Jaekel, J., Wolke, D., & Bartmann, P. (2013). Poor attention rather than hyperactivity/impulsivity predicts academic achievement in very preterm and fulderm adolescents. *Psychological Medicine*, *43*, 183–196. doi:10.1017/S0033291712001031.

Jaekel, J., Wolke, D., & Chernova, J. (2012). Mother and child behaviour in very preterm and term dyads at 6 and 8 years. *Developmental Medicine & Child Neurology, 54* (8), 716–723.

Johnson, S., Fawke, J., Hennessy, E. M., Rowell, V., Thomas, S., Wolke, D., & Marlow, N. (2009). Neurodevelopmental disability through 11 years of age in children born before 26 weeks of gestation. *Pediatrics, 124* (2), e249–e257.

Johnson, S., Gilmore, C., Gallimore, I., Jaekel, J., & Wolke, D. (2015). The long-term consequences of preterm birth: What do teachers know? *Developmental Medicine & Child Neurology, 57*(6), 571–577. doi:10.1111/dmcn.12683

Johnson, S., Hennessy, E., Smith, R., Trikic, R., Wolke, D., & Marlow, N. (2009). Academic attainment and special educational needs in extremely preterm children at 11 years of age: The EPICure study. *Archives of Disease in Childhood - Fetal and Neonatal Edition, 94*(4), F283–F289. doi:10.1136/adc.2008.152793

Johnson, S., Hollis, C., Kochhar, P., Hennessy, E., Wolke, D., & Marlow, N. (2010a). Autism spectrum disorders in extremely preterm children. *Journal of Pediatrics, 156*(4), 525–U527. doi:10.1016/j.jpeds.2009.10.041

Johnson, S., Hollis, C., Kochhar, P., Hennessy, E., Wolke, D., & Marlow, N. (2010b). Psychiatric disorders in extremely preterm children: Longitudinal finding at age 11 years in the EPICure study. *Journal of the American Academy of Child and Adolescent Psychiatry, 49*(5), 453–463. doi:10.1016/j.jaac.2010.02.002

Johnson, S., & Marlow, N. (2011). Preterm birth and childhood psychiatric disorders. *Pediatric Research, 69*(5), 11R–18R. doi:10.1203/PDR.0b013e318212faa0

Johnson, S., & Marlow, N. (2014). Growing up after extremely preterm birth: Lifespan mental health outcomes. *Seminars in Fetal & Neonatal Medicine, 19*(2), 97–104. doi:10.1016/j.siny.2013.11.004

Johnson, S., Strauss, V., Gilmore, C., Jaekel, J., Marlow, N., & Wolke, D. (2016). Learning disabilities among extremely preterm children without neurosensory impairment: Comorbidity, neuropsychological profiles and scholastic outcomes. *Early Human Development, 103*, 69–75. doi:10.1016/j.earlhumdev.2016.07.009

Johnson, S., & Wolke, D. (2013). Behavioural outcomes and psychopathology during adolescence. *Early Human Development, 89*(4), 199–207.

Johnson, S., Wolke, D., Hennessy, E., & Marlow, N. (2011). Educational outcomes in extremely preterm children: Neuropsychological correlates and predictors of attainment. *Developmental Neuropsychology, 36*(1), 74–95.

Jolles, D., & Crone, E. A. (2012). Training the developing brain: A neurocognitive perspective. *Frontiers in Human Neuroscience, 6*. doi:10.3389/fnhum.2012.00076

Jones, K. M., Champion, P. R., & Woodward, L. J. (2013). Social competence of preschool children born very preterm. *Early Human Development, 89*(10), 795–802. doi:10.1016/j.earlhumdev.2013.06.008

Joseph, R. M., O'Shea, T. M., Allred, E. N., Heeren, T., Hirtz, D., Jara, H., ... Kuban, K. C. K. (2016). Neurocognitive and academic outcomes at age 10 years of extremely preterm newborns. *Pediatrics, 137*(4), 1–9. doi:10.1542/peds.2015-4343

Joseph, R. M., O'Shea, T. M., Allred, E. N., Heeren, T., Hirtz, D., Paneth, N., ... Kuban, K. C. (2017). Prevalence and associated features of autism spectrum disorder in extremely low gestational age newborns at age 10 years. *Autism Research, 10*(2), 224–232. doi:10.1002/aur.1644

Kapellou, O., Counsell, S. J., Kennea, N., Dyet, L., Saeed, N., Stark, J., ... Edwards, A. D. (2006). Abnormal cortical development after premature birth shown by altered allometric scaling of brain growth. *PLoS Med, 3*(8), e265.

Kerr-Wilson, C. O., Mackay, D. F., Smith, G. C., & Pell, J. P. (2012). Meta-analysis of the association between preterm delivery and intelligence. *Journal of Public Health (Oxford), 34*(2), 209–216. doi:10.1093/pubmed/fdr024

Kidokoro, H., Anderson, P. J., Doyle, L. W., Woodward, L. J., Neil, J. J., & Inder, T. E. (2014). Brain injury and altered brain growth in preterm infants: Predictors and prognosis. *Pediatrics, 134*(2), e444–453. doi:10.1542/peds.2013-2336

Klingberg, T. (2010). Training and plasticity of working memory. *Trends in Cognitive Science, 14*(7), 317–324.

Koldewijn, K., van Wassenaer, A., Wolf, M.-J., Meijssen, D., Houtzager, B., Beelen, A., ... Nollet, F. (2009). A neurobehavioral intervention and assessment program in very low birth weight infants: outcome at 24 months. *Journal of Pediatrics, 156*(3), 359–365. doi:10.1016/j.jpeds.2009.09.009

Larroque, B., Ancel, P. Y., Marchand-Martin, L., Cambonie, G., Fresson, J., Pierrat, V., ... Marret, S. (2011). Special care and school difficulties in 8-year-old very preterm children: The Epipage cohort study. *PLoS One, 6* (7), e21361. doi:10.1371/journal.pone.0021361

Lipkind, H. S., Slopen, M. E., Pfeiffer, M. R., & McVeigh, K. H. (2012). School-age outcomes of late preterm infants in New York City. *American Journal of Obstetrics and Gynecology, 206*(3), 222.e221–222.e226.

Litt, J. S., Gerry Taylor, H., Margevicius, S., Schluchter, M., Andreias, L., & Hack, M. (2012). Academic achievement of adolescents born with extremely low birth weight. *Acta Paediatrica, 101*(12), 1240–1245.

Lohaugen, G. C. C., Antonsen, I., Haberg, A., Gramstad, A., Vik, T., Brubakk, A. M., & Skranes, J. (2011). Computerized working memory training improves function in adolescents born at extremely low birth weight. *Journal of Pediatrics, 158*(4), 555–U556. doi:10.1016/j.jpeds.2010.09.060

Lord, C., Rutter, M., DiLavore, P. C., Risi, S., Gotham, K., & Bishop, S. (2012). *Autism diagnostic observation schedule*, 2nd ed. Torrance, CA: Western Psychological Services.

Lund, L. K., Vik, T., Lydersen, S., Lohaugen, G. C., Skranes, J., Brubakk, A. M., & Indredavik, M. S. (2012). Mental health, quality of life and social relations in young adults born with low birth weight. *Health and Quality of Life Outcomes, 10*, 146. doi:10.1186/1477-7525-10-146

Lund, L. K., Vik, T., Skranes, J., Brubakk, A.-M., & Indredavik, M. S. (2011). Psychiatric morbidity in two low birth weight groups assessed by diagnostic interview in young adulthood. *Acta Paediatrica, 100*(4), 598–604. doi:10.1111/j.1651-2227.2010.02111.x

Luu, T. M., Ment, L., Allan, W., Schneider, K., & Vohr, B. R. (2011). Executive and memory function in adolescents born very preterm. *Pediatrics, 127*(3), e639–e646. doi:10.1542/peds.2010-1421

MacKay, D. F., Smith, G. C. S., Dobbie, R., & Pell, J. P. (2010). Gestational age at delivery and special educational need: Retrospective cohort study of 407,503 schoolchildren. *PLoS Med, 7*(6), e1000289.

Mannisto, T., Vaarasmaki, M., Sipola-Leppanen, M., Tikanmaki, M., Matinolli, H.-M., Pesonen, A.-K., … Kajantie, E. (2015). Independent living and romantic relations among young adults born preterm. *Pediatrics, 135*(2), 290–297. doi:10.1542/peds.2014-1345

March of Dimes. (2016). 2015 premature birth report card. Retrieved 8/30/2016. http://www.marchofdimes.org/materi als/premature-birth-report-card-united-states.pdf

March of Dimes, PMNCH, Save the Children, & WHO. (2012). *Born too soon: The global action report on preterm birth*. Geneva: World Health Organization.

March of Dimes. (2007). *Born Too Soon: Premature Birth in the U.S. Black Population*. White Plains, NY: Author.

McCormick, M. C., Brooks-Gunn, J., Buka, S. L., Goldman, J., Yu, J., Salganik, M., … Casey, P. H. (2006). Early intervention in low birth weight premature infants: Results at 18 years of age for the Infant Health and Development Program. *Pediatrics, 117*(3), 771–780.

Meher, S., & Alfirevic, Z. (2014). Choice of primary outcomes in randomised trials and systematic reviews evaluating interventions for preterm birth prevention: A systematic review. *BJOG: An International Journal of Obstetrics & Gynaecology, 121*(10), 1188–1194.

Melby-Lervåg, M., Redick, T. S., & Hulme, C. (2016). Working memory training does not improve performance on measures of intelligence or other measures of "far transfer." *Perspectives on Psychological Science, 11*(4), 512–534. doi:doi:10.1177/1745691616635612

Miller, S. P., & Ferriero, D. M. (2009). From selective vulnerability to connectivity: Insights from newborn brain imaging. *Trends in Neurosciences, 32*(9), 496–505. doi:http://dx.doi.org/10.1016/j.tins.2009.05.010

Moore, T., Hennessy, E. M., Myles, J., Johnson, S., Draper, E. S., Costeloe, K. L., & Marlow, N. (2012). Neurological and developmental outcome in extremely preterm children born in England in 1995 and 2006: The EPICure studies. *BMJ, 345*. doi:10.1136/bmj.e7961

Moster, D., Lie, R. T., & Markestad, T. (2008). Long-term medical and social consequences of preterm birth. *New England Journal of Medicine, 359*(3), 262–273. doi:10.1056/NEJMoa0706475

Mulder, H., Pitchford, N. J., Hagger, M. S., & Marlow, N. (2009). Development of executive function and attention in preterm children: A systematic review. *Developmental Neuropsychology, 34*(4), 393–421. doi:10.1080/87565640902964524

Mulder, H., Pitchford, N. J., & Marlow, N. (2010). Processing speed and working memory underlie academic attainment in very preterm children. *Archives of Disease in Childhood - Fetal and Neonatal Edition, 95*(4), F267–F272. doi:10.1136/adc.2009.167965

Muller-Nix, C., Forcada-Guex, M., Pierrehumbert, B., Jaunin, L., Borghini, A., & Ansermet, F. (2004). Prematurity, maternal stress, and mother-child interactions. *Early Human Development, 79*, 145–158.

Nordhov, S. M., Rønning, J. A., Dahl, L. B., Ulvund, S. E., Tunby, J., & Kaaresen, P. I. (2010). Early intervention improves cognitive outcomes for preterm infants: Randomized controlled trial. *Pediatrics, 126*(5), e1088–e1094. doi:10.1542/peds.2010-0778

Nosarti, C. (2013). Structural and functional brain correlates of behavioral outcomes during adolescence. *Early Hum Dev, 89*(4), 221–227. doi:10.1016/j.earlhumdev.2013.02.002

Nosarti, C., Murray, R. M., & Hack, M. E. (2010). *Neurodevelopmental outcomes of preterm birth*. Cambridge: Cambridge University Press.

Nosarti, C., Reichenberg, A., Murray, R. M., Cnattingius, S., Lambe, M. P., Yin, L., … Hultman, C. M.(2012). Preterm birth and psychiatric disorders in young adult life. *Archives of General Psychiatry, 69*(6), 610–617. doi:10.1001/archgenpsychiatry.2011.1374

Olesen, P. J., Westerberg, H., & Klingberg, T. (2004). Increased prefrontal and parietal activity after training of working memory. *Nature Neuroscience, 7*(1), 75–79. doi:10.1038/nn1165

Orchinik, L. J., Taylor, H. G., Espy, K. A., Minich, N., Klein, N., Sheffield, T., & Hack, M. (2011). Cognitive outcomes for extremely preterm/extremely low birth weight children in kindergarten. *Journal of the International Neuropsychological Society, 17*(6), 1067–1079. doi:10.1017/s135561771100107x

Orton, J., Spittle, A., Doyle, L., Anderson, P. J., & Boyd, R. (2009). Do early intervention programmes improve cognitive and motor outcomes for preterm infants after discharge? A systematic review. *Developmental Medicine & Child Neurology, 51*(11), 851–859.

Pascoe, L., Roberts, G., Doyle, L. W., Lee, K. J., Thompson, D. K., Seal, M. L., ... Anderson, P. J. (2013). Preventing academic difficulties in preterm children: A randomised controlled trial of an adaptive working memory training intervention – IMPRINT study. *BMC Pediatrics, 13*:144.

Petersen, S. E., & Posner, M. I. (2012). The attention system of the human brain: 20 years after. *Annual Review of Neuroscience, 35*, 73–89. doi:10.1146/annurev-neuro-062111-150525

Peterson, B. S. (2003). Brain imaging studies of the anatomical and functional consequences of preterm birth for human brain development. *Annals of the New York Academy of Sciences, 1008*(1), 219–237. doi:10.1196/annals.1301.023

Petrou, S., Johnson, S., Wolke, D., & Marlow, N. (2013). The association between neurodevelopmental disability and economic outcomes during mid-childhood. *Child Care Health and Development, 39*(3), 345–357. doi:10.1111/j.1365-2214.2012.01368.x

Petrou, S., & Khan, K. (2012). Economic costs associated with moderate and late preterm birth: Primary and secondary evidence. *Seminars in Fetal and Neonatal Medicine, 17*(3), 170–178. doi:http://dx.doi.org/10.1016/j.siny.2012.02.001

Pinto-Martin, J. A., Levy, S. E., Feldman, J. F., Lorenz, J. M., Paneth, N., & Whitaker, A. H. (2011). Prevalence of autism spectrum disorder in adolescents born weighing < 2000 grams. *Pediatrics, 128*(5), 883–891. doi:10.1542/peds.2010-2846

Poulsen, G., Wolke, D., Kurinczuk, J. J., Boyle, E. M., Field, D., Alfirevic, Z., & Quigley, M. A. (2013). Gestational age and cognitive ability in early childhood: A population-based cohort study. *Paediatric and Perinatal Epidemiology, 27*(4), 371–379. doi:10.1111/ppe.12058

Prager, S., Singer, B. B., Bendix, I., Schlager, G. W., Bertling, F., Ceylan, B., ... Ergün, S. (2013). CEACAM1 expression in oligodendrocytes of the developing rat brain shows a spatiotemporal relation to myelination and is altered in a model of encephalopathy of prematurity. *Development Neuroscience, 35*(2–3), 226–240.

Quigley, M., Poulsen, G., Boyle, E. M., Wolke, D., Field, D., Alfirevic, Z., & Kurinczuk, J. J. (2012). Early term and late preterm birth is associated with poorer school performance at age 5 years: A cohort study. *Archives of Disease in Childhood – Fetal and Neonatal Edition.* doi:10.1136/archdischild-2011-300888

Raisanen, S., Gissler, M., Saari, J., Kramer, M., & Heinonen, S. (2013). Contribution of risk factors to extremely, very and moderately preterm births – register-based analysis of 1,390,742 singleton births. *PLoS One, 8*(4). doi:e6066010.1371/journal.pone.0060660

Rauh, V. A., Nurcombe, B., Achenbach, T., & Howell, C. (1990). The Mother-Infant Transaction Program. The content and implications of an intervention for the mothers of low-birthweight infants. *Clinics in Perinatology, 17*(1), 31–45.

Raz, S., Debastos, A. K., Newman, J. B., & Batton, D. (2010). Extreme prematurity and neuropsychological outcome in the preschool years. *Journal of the International Neuropsychological Society, 16*(1), 169–179. doi:10.1017/S1355617709991147

Ritchie, K., Bora, S., & Woodward, L. J. (2015). Social development of children born very preterm: A systematic review. *Developmental Medicine & Child Neurology, 57*(10), 899–918. doi:10.1111/dmcn.12783

Roberts, G., Quach, J., Spencer-Smith, M., Anderson, P. J., Gathercole, S., Gold, L., ... Wake M. (2016). Academic outcomes 2 years after working memory training for children with low working memory: A randomized clinical trial. *JAMA Pediatrics, 170*(5), e154568. doi:10.1001/jamapediatrics.2015.4568

Roisman, G. I., Newman, D. A., Fraley, R. C., Haltigan, J. D., Groh, A. M., & Haydon, K. C. (2012). Distinguishing differential susceptibility from diathesis–stress: Recommendations for evaluating interaction effects. *Development and Psychopathology, 24*(02), 389–409. doi:10.1017/S0954579412000065

Rubens, C. E., Sadovsky, Y., Muglia, L., Gravett, M. G., Lackritz, E., & Gravett, C. (2014). Prevention of preterm birth: Harnessing science to address the global epidemic. *Science Translational Medicine, 6*(262), 262sr265-262sr265.

Rutter, M., LeCouteur, A., & Lord, C. (2003, 2008). *Autism diagnostic interview, revised (ADI®-R).* Los Angeles, CA: Western Psychological Services.

Saigal, S. (2014). *Preemie voices.* Victoria, British Colombia: FriesenPress.

Saigal, S., Day, K. L., Van Lieshout, R. J., Schmidt, L. A., Morrison, K. M., & Boyle, M. H. (2016). Health, wealth, social integration, and sexuality of extremely low-birth-weight prematurely born adults in the fourth decade of life. *JAMA Pediatrics, 170*(7), 678–686. doi:10.1001/jamapediatrics.2016.0289

Saigal, S., & Doyle, L. W. (2008). An overview of mortality and sequelae of preterm birth from infancy to adulthood. *Lancet, 371*, 261–269.

Saigal, S., van Ouden, L., Wolke, D., Hoult, L., Paneth, N., Streiner, D. L., ... Pinto-Martin, J. (2003). School-age outcomes in children who were extremely low birth weight from four international population-based cohorts. *Pediatrics, 112*(4), 943–950.

Samara, M., Marlow, N., & Wolke, D. (2008). Pervasive behavior problems at 6 years of age in a total-population sample of children born at <=25 weeks of gestation. *Pediatrics, 122*(3), 562–573. doi:10.1542/peds.2007-3231

Scott, M. N., Taylor, H. G., Fristad, M. A., Klein, N., Espy, K. A., Minich, N., & Hack, M. (2012). Behavior disorders in extremely preterm/extremely low birth weight children in kindergarten. *Journal of Developmental and Behavioral Pediatrics, 33*(3), 202–213. doi:10.1097/DBP.0b013e3182475287

Shapiro-Mendoza, C. K., & Lackritz, E. M. (2012). Epidemiology of late and moderate preterm birth. *Seminars in Fetal and Neonatal Medicine, 17*(3), 120–125. doi:http://dx.doi.org/10.1016/j.siny.2012.01.007

Simms, V., Cragg, L., Gilmore, C., Marlow, N., & Johnson, S. (2013). Mathematics difficulties in children born very preterm: Current research and future directions. *Archives of Disease in Childhood - Fetal and Neonatal Edition, 98*(5), F457–F463. doi:10.1136/archdischild-2013-303777

Somhovd, M. J., Hansen, B. M., Brok, J., Esbjorn, B. H., & Greisen, G. (2012). Anxiety in adolescents born preterm or with very low birthweight: A meta-analysis of case-control studies. *Dev Med Child Neurol, 54*(11), 988–994. doi:10.1111/j.1469-8749.2012.04407.x

Soveri, A., Antfolk, J., Karlsson, L., Salo, B., & Laine, M. (2017). Working memory training revisited: A multi-level meta-analysis of n-back training studies. *Psychonomic Bulletin & Review, 24*(4):1077–1096. doi:10.3758/s13423-016-1217-0

Spittle, A., Orton, J., Anderson, P., Boyd, R., & Doyle, L. (2012). Early developmental intervention programmes post-hospital discharge to prevent motor and cognitive impairments in preterm infants. *Cochrane Database System Review, 12*, Cd005495. doi:10.1002/14651858.CD005495.pub3

Spittle, A. J., Cheong, J., Doyle, L. W., Roberts, G., Lee, K. J., Lim, J., … Anderson, P. J. (2011). Neonatal white matter abnormality predicts childhood motor impairment in very preterm children. *Developmental Medicine & Child Neurology, 53*(11), 1000–1006. doi:10.1111/j.1469-8749.2011.04095.x

Takeuchi, H., Sekiguchi, A., Taki, Y., Yokoyama, S., Yomogida, Y., Komuro, N., … Kawashima, R. (2010). Training of working memory impacts structural connectivity. *Journal of Neuroscience, 30*(9), 3297–3303. doi:10.1523/jneurosci.4611-09.2010

Taylor, H. G. (2016). Low birth weight. In J. E. Morgan & J. H. Ricker (Eds.), *Textbook of clinical neuropsychology* (pp. 308–332). New York, NY: Taylor & Francis.

Taylor, H. G., Espy, K. A., & Anderson, P. J. (2009). Mathematics deficiencies in children with very low birth weight or very preterm birth. *Developmental Disabilities Research Reviews, 15*(1), 52–59. doi:10.1002/ddrr.51

Taylor, H. G., Filipek, P. A., Juranek, J., Bangert, B., Minich, N., & Hack, M. (2011). Brain volumes in adolescents with very low birth weight: Effects on brain structure and associations with neuropsychological outcomes. *Developmental Neuropsychology, 36*(1), 96–117. doi:10.1080/87565641.2011.540544

Tessier, R., Charpak, N., Giron, M., Cristo, M., de Calume, Z. F., & Ruiz-Pelaez, J. G. (2009). Kangaroo Mother Care, home environment and father involvement in the first year of life: A randomized controlled study. *Acta Paediatrica, 98*(9), 1444–1450. doi:10.1111/j.1651-2227.2009.01370.x

Treyvaud, K., Anderson, V. A., Howard, K., Bear, M., Hunt, R. W., Doyle, L. W., … Anderson, P. J. (2009). Parenting behavior is associated with the early neurobehavioral development of very preterm children. *Pediatrics, 123*(2), 555–561. doi:10.1542/peds.2008-0477

Treyvaud, K., Ure, A., Doyle, L. W., Lee, K. J., Rogers, C. E., Kidokoro, H., … Anderson, P. J. (2013). Psychiatric outcomes at age seven for very preterm children: Rates and predictors. *Journal of Child Psychology and Psychiatry, 54*(7), 772–779. doi:10.1111/jcpp.12040

van der Kooy-Hofland, V. A. C., van der Kooy, J., Bus, A. G., van Ijzendoorn, M. H., & Bonsel, G. J. (2012). Differential susceptibility to early literacy intervention in children with mild perinatal adversities: Short- and long-term effects of a randomized control trial. *Journal of Educational Psychology, 104*(2), 337–349. doi:10.1037/a0026984

Vanderveen, J. A., Bassler, D., Robertson, C. M., & Kirpalani, H. (2009). Early interventions involving parents to improve neurodevelopmental outcomes of premature infants: A meta-analysis. *Journal of Perinatology, 29*(5), 343–351. doi:10.1038/jp.2008.229

Van Lieshout, R. J., Boyle, M. H., Saigal, S., Morrison, K., & Schmidt, L. A. (2015). Mental health of extremely low birth weight survivors in their 30s. *Pediatrics, 135*(3), 452–459. doi:10.1542/peds.2014-3143

Volpe, J. J. (2009). Brain injury in premature infants: A complex amalgam of destructive and developmental disturbances. *The Lancet Neurology, 8*(1), 110–124.

Volpe, J. J., Kinney, H. C., Jensen, F. E., & Rosenberg, P. A. (2011). The developing oligodendrocyte: Key cellular target in brain injury in the premature infant. *International Journal of Developmental Neuroscience, 29*(4), 423–440. doi:10.1016/j.ijdevneu.2011.02.012

Waxman, J., Van Lieshout, R. J., Saigal, S., Boyle, M. H., & Schmidt, L. A. (2013). Still cautious: Personality characteristics of extremely low birth weight adults in their early 30s. *Personality and Individual Differences, 55*(8), 967–971. doi:http://dx.doi.org/10.1016/j.paid.2013.08.003

Wechsler, D. (1989). *Wechsler preschool and primary scale of intelligence - revised.* San Antonio, TX: The Psychological Corporation.

Westerberg, H., & Klingberg, T. (2007). Changes in cortical activity after training of working memory – A single-subject analysis. *Physiology & Behavior*, *92*(1–2), 186–192. doi:10.1016/j.physbeh.2007.05.041

Westrupp, E. M., Northam, E., Doyle, L. W., Callanan, C., & Anderson, P. J. (2011). Adult psychiatric outcomes of very low birth weight survivors. *Australian and New Zealand Journal of Psychiatry*, *45*(12), 1069–1077.

Wolke, D. (2011). Preterm and low birth weight children. In P. Howlin, T. Charman, & M. Ghaziuddin (Eds.), *The SAGE handbook of developmental disorders* (pp. 497–527). London: Sage Publications.

Wolke, D. (2016). Born extremely low birth weight and health related quality of life into adulthood. *Journal of Pediatrics*, *179*, 11–12.e11. doi:10.1016/j.jpeds.2016.09.012

Wolke, D., Baumann, N., Strauss, V., Johnson, S., & Marlow, N. (2015). Bullying of preterm children and emotional problems at school age: Cross-culturally invariant effects. *Journal of Pediatrics*, *166*(6), 1417–1422. doi:10.1016/j.jpeds.2015.02.055

Wolke, D., Chernova, J., Eryigit-Madzwamuse, S., Samara, M., Zwierzynska, K., & Petrou, S. (2013). Self and parent perspectives on health-related quality of life of adolescents born very preterm. *Journal of Pediatrics*, *163*(4), 1020–1026.e1022. doi:10.1016/j.jpeds.2013.04.030

Wolke, D., Jaekel, J., Hall, J., & Baumann, N. (2013). Effects of sensitive parenting on the academic resilience of very preterm and very low birth weight adolescents. *Journal of Adolescent Health*, *53*(5), 642–647.

Wolke, D., & Meyer, R. (1999). Cognitive status, language attainment, and prereading skills of 6-year-old very preterm children and their peers: The Bavarian Longitudinal Study. *Developmental Medicine & Child Neurology*, *41*, 94–109.

Wolke, D., Strauss, V. Y.-C., Johnson, S., Gilmore, C., Marlow, N., & Jaekel, J. (2015). Universal gestational age effects on cognitive and basic mathematic processing: 2 cohorts in 2 countries. *Journal of Pediatrics*, *166*(6), 1410–1416.e2. doi:10.1016/j.jpeds.2015.02.065

Woodward, L. J., Anderson, P. J., Austin, N. C., Howard, K., & Inder, T. E. (2006). Neonatal MRI to predict neurodevelopmental outcomes in preterm infants. *New England Journal of Medicine*, *355*(7), 685–694.

Woodward, L. J., Clark, C. A. C., Bora, S., & Inder, T. E. (2012). Neonatal white matter abnormalities an important predictor of neurocognitive outcome for very preterm children. *PLoS One*, *7*(12), e51879. doi:10.1371/journal.pone.0051879

Woodward, L. J., Clark, C. A., Pritchard, V. E., Anderson, P. J., & Inder, T. E. (2011). Neonatal white matter abnormalities predict global executive function impairment in children born very preterm. *Developmental Neuropsychology*, *36*(1), 22–41. doi:10.1080/87565641.2011.540530

Zatorre, R. J., Fields, R. D., & Johansen-Berg, H. (2012). Plasticity in gray and white: Neuroimaging changes in brain structure during learning. *Nature Neuroscience*, *15*(4), 528–536. doi:10.1038/nn.3045

Zuckerman, M. (1999). *Vulnerability to psychopathology: A biosocial model*. Washington, DC: American Psychological Association.

Chapter 2

Spina Bifida Myelomeningocele

Colleen F. Bechtel Driscoll, Diana Ohanian, Jaclyn Lennon Papadakis, Alexa Stern, T. Andrew Zabel, Kathy Zebracki, and Grayson N. Holmbeck

Introduction

Spina bifida is a congenital birth defect that occurs during the first month of pregnancy when the embryonic neural tube fails to close completely (Copp et al., 2015). Spina bifida myelomeningocele (SBM), the most common form of spina bifida, is associated with the most severe complications and is the focus of this chapter. In individuals with SBM, the spinal cord and meningeal membranes protrude through the unfused portion of the spinal column enclosed by a sac. Individuals with SBM who survive to birth have these lesions closed surgically, either pre- or postnatally. They experience a wide range of difficulties, however, including motor, orthopedic, sensory, and cognitive impairments (summarized in Table 2.1). SBM is associated with complications with bladder and bowel functioning, varying degrees of lower-body paralysis, hydrocephalus, risk of meningitis, and increased risk of neurocognitive issues and/or learning disabilities (Kelly, Zebracki, Holmbeck, & Gershenson, 2008). These medical issues often have significant complications that require lifelong, ongoing care from a multidisciplinary team.

Clinical Manifestation

Epidemiology and Pathophysiology

SBM occurs in roughly 3 out of every 10,000 live births in the United States (Centers for Disease Control and Prevention, 2011). SBM is the most common congenital birth defect that involves the central nervous system, but its incidence varies by geographic location and ethnicity. Globally, incidence rates of SBM are higher in Mexico, northern China, and South America (Botto & Mulinare, 1999), with Hispanics and Caucasians at a generally higher risk than Blacks and Asians. In the United States, the prevalence of SBM has been found to be higher in

Table 2.1 Features of Spina Bifida Myelomeningocele

Primary Neurological Features
Myelodysplasia (spinal cord malformation)
Hydrocephalus
Chiari II malformation
Hypoplastic (thinned) corpus callosum
Neurogenic bladder and bowel

Secondary Features/Complications
Shunt malfunction
Epilepsy
Scoliosis
Orthopedic impairment
Urologic difficulties (e.g., urinary tract infections)
Spinal cord tethering
Sensorimotor impairment
Skin breakdown (e.g., pressure sores)
Reduced mobility
Obesity
Allergies (e.g., latex)

Hispanics and lower in Blacks than in non-Hispanic Whites (Copp et al., 2015).

The primary disorder in SBM is the failed closure of the neural tube in the embryonic spine (Copp et al., 2015). This condition exposures the spinal cord to amniotic fluid in utero, which ultimately leads to neurodegeneration. SBM is often associated with major orthopedic and urologic impairments, including paraplegia of the lower limbs and neurogenic bladder and bowel functioning (Copp et al., 2015). These medical issues have significant lifelong implications, such as use of assistive devices for mobility and adherence to medical regimens such as bowel and bladder programs.

Two neurological conditions frequently occur in the context of SBM: Chiari II malformation and hydrocephalus. Chiari II malformation is a deformity of the hindbrain and cerebellum that can obstruct the flow of cerebrospinal fluid within the brain. The Chiari II malformation frequently produces hydrocephalus, which typically requires shunting in most children with SBM (Yeates, Fletcher, & Dennis, 2008). Hydrocephalus can have significant effects on the corpus callosum, which often becomes hypoplastic, or thinned. Hydrocephalus in individuals with SBM is typically managed through the placement of a shunt, which permits excess cerebrospinal fluid to drain from the brain (Copp et al., 2015). Although shunting has positive effects (specifically, the resolution of hydrocephalus), the presence of a shunt carries its own risks. Shunts can require surgical revision due to malfunction, obstruction, or infection (Yeates, Fletcher, & Dennis, 2008). Shunt malfunctions and subsequent surgical shunt revisions can affect cognitive functioning in youth with SBM. Additionally, individuals with SBM are at increased risk for seizures, with an incidence of 5–15% in affected individuals (Noetzel & Blake, 1991). Recurrent seizures can have a profound impact on the cognitive, behavioral, and psychosocial functioning of these individuals.

This chapter will focus on the cognitive, psychosocial, and behavioral impairments associated with SBM across the lifespan. These impairments can range from minor to severe; the degree of severity is related to the level of the initial spinal lesion as well as secondary central nervous system insults (e.g., hydrocephalus; Copp et al., 2015).

Prevention

Although the etiology of SBM remains unclear, both genetic and nongenetic factors likely play a role in its development. Studies in twins have provided substantial evidence that genetic variations are a factor in the development of SBM (Yeates et al., 2008). Within families, the risk of recurrence increases substantially as the number of affected family members increases (Yeates et al., 2008). However, genetics alone do not explain the occurrence of SBM.

A nongenetic factor that significantly impacts the development of SBM and is a target of both medical and public health interventions is maternal folate deficits. Administration of prenatal multivitamins that contain folic acid supplements have been found to reduce the risk of neural tube defect by approximately 50–70% (Volcik et al., 2000). In addition to voluntary folic acid supplementation, policy decisions in many countries have led to the fortification of staple foods, such as cereal, with folic acid. This fortification has reportedly led to a 20% decrease in the incidence of SBM and anencephaly (Yeates et al., 2008).

The mortality rate among young people with SBM is ~1% per year between the ages of 5 and 30 years (Oakeshott, Hunt, Poulton, & Reid, 2010). Many individuals with SBM live well into adulthood. Therefore, it is imperative to identify ways to prevent or limit SBM-associated deficits and to promote independence and community participation in these individuals.

Early intervention services may help children with SBM achieve or maintain functioning in their first 3 years. Throughout childhood, youth may benefit from special education and therapeutic services, including physical therapy, occupational therapy, and speech therapy. The utilization of these services may allow individuals with SBM to reach the same milestones as their typically developing peers in childhood. Continuing support throughout adolescence and early adulthood may help prevent negative psychosocial outcomes and promote functional independence in individuals with SBM. Still, many individuals with SBM face significant challenges due to the physical, cognitive, behavioral, and social limitations of this condition.

Clinical Manifestation

SBM is a lifelong illness, and the difficulties faced by individuals with SBM change across the lifespan. Although SBM is often viewed as a physical or orthopedic disability, this condition affects the development of the brain and contributes to a number of unique neuropsychological strengths and weaknesses (Dennis & Barnes, 2010). This section aims to describe the most salient cognitive, behavioral, and psychosocial issues associated with this condition from infancy through adulthood (summarized in Table 2.2).

Attention. Individuals with SBM tend to exhibit subtle, but unique attentional deficits (Rose & Holmbeck, 2007). Children and adolescents with SBM exhibit clinically significant deficits in focused attention, which reflects the ability to select specific

Table 2.2 Primary Neuropsychological Domains Affected by Spina Bifida Myelomeningocele

Attention

Executive functioning

Language

Memory

Visual-spatial abilities

Motor functioning

Academic achievement

Psychological functioning

Social functioning

Family functioning

Functional adaptation

stimuli from a broad array (Rose & Holmbeck, 2007; Vinck, Mullaart, Rotteveel, & Maassen, 2009), as well as shifting, the ability to redirect one's focus of attention away from one fixation and toward a different focus of attention (Vinck, Mullaart, Rotteveel, & Maassen, 2009). These difficulties with orienting toward and disengaging from stimuli reflect impairment in the posterior (as opposed to the anterior) attention system, the "bottom-up" attention network that is responsible for prioritizing sensory input (Ramsundhar & Donald, 2014). Indeed, functional magnetic resonance imaging (fMRI) reveals decreased posterior activation during tests of selective attention and response inhibition (Ou, Snow, Byerley, Hall, & Glasier, 2013). In contrast, "top-down" attentional abilities (e.g., the ability to sustain concentration) that are driven by the anterior attention system, and are often problematic in youth <18 years with such disorders as attention-deficit/hyperactivity disorder (ADHD), may be relatively preserved in SBM (Rose & Holmbeck, 2007; Swartwout et al., 2008). Malformations in the midbrain and hindbrain that are unique to brain dysmorphology in SBM, such as "tectal beaking," may account for poor posterior attention function (Swartwout et al., 2008; Williams, Juranek, Stuebing, Cirino, Dennis, & Fletcher, 2013). The Chiari II malformation causes midbrain anomalies that have been found to be related to difficulties with attention orienting (Kulesz et al., 2015). Hydrocephalus and subsequent shunt-related surgery may further impact attention (Rose & Holmbeck, 2007); however, hydrocephalus does not solely account for the impaired attentional abilities in SBM (Swartwout et al., 2008; Kulesz et al., 2015).

Additionally, studies have demonstrated that the incidence of clinical ADHD symptoms, such as problems paying attention and difficulty with behavioral inhibition and broader regulation, is three times higher in children and adolescents with SBM (28%) than in typically developing peers (8%; Spellicy et al., 2012; Swartwout et al., 2008). Most children with both SBM and ADHD are diagnosed with the inattentive (as opposed to the hyperactive or combined) subtype, suggesting that individuals with SBM who also have ADHD display a different pathophysiology than children with solely ADHD, who tend to have more severe problems with sustained attention (Ramsundhar & Donald, 2014). The exact etiology of ADHD in SBM has yet to be determined, but preliminary research shows that the increased prevalence of ADHD may be linked to a specific variation in the gene that metabolizes folate, the vitamin widely implicated in neural tube defects (Spellicy et al., 2012). However, the attention problems seen widely in individuals with SBM appear to be different and separate from those seen in ADHD.

Executive Functioning. Individuals with SBM demonstrate deficits in several areas of executive functioning that persist even after accounting for the potential influence of intellectual ability. Particular areas of weakness include planning ability, problem-solving abilities, working memory, and initiation of goal-directed behavior (Rose & Holmbeck, 2007). Metacognition (e.g., goal-setting) appears to be a more prominent deficit in individuals with SBM than other components of executive functioning, such as behavior regulation (e.g., inhibition; Brown et al., 2008). Brain anomalies implicated in SBM-specific attentional deficits may also be associated with executive function deficits, because the posterior attention network undergirds both cognitive processes (Tuminello, Holmbeck, & Olson, 2012). SBM is also associated with increased frontal cortical thickness, decreased overall surface area (especially in the occipital lobe), and a reduction in cerebral white matter (Juranek et al., 2008). This pattern of disrupted brain development likely contributes significantly to executive functioning deficits in this population.

Neuroimaging research has shown that aberrances in the neural circuitry connecting the prefrontal cortex, basal ganglia, and thalamus are associated with some of the executive functioning difficulties found in SBM (Ware et al., 2016). Reduced superior parietal volume (that is potentially secondary to hydrocephalus) has also been associated with problems with executive control (Kulesz et al., 2015). Additionally, certain medical factors, including shunt-related surgeries and history of seizures, place children and adolescents with SBM at risk for poor metacognition (Brown et al., 2008). Executive functioning weaknesses in adolescents with SBM are associated with greater dependence on parents and lower levels of intrinsic motivation in the classroom over time (Tuminello, Holmbeck, & Olson, 2012). Metacognitive problems may explain the difficulties experienced by individuals <18 years with SBM, such as poor social competence, poor adaptive skills, and greater internalizing symptoms, across several areas of psychological functioning (Kelly et al., 2012). These impairments in executive functioning often stabilize but continue into adulthood, and can negatively impact educational, vocational, and self-help skills (Zabel et al., 2011).

Language. Individuals with SBM demonstrate a complex language profile. From infancy to early childhood, youth with SBM show slower rates of language growth when compared to typically developing children (Lomax-Bream, Barnes, Copeland, Taylor, & Landry, 2007). Demographic factors, such as lower socioeconomic background, can further slow the rate of language growth. Language deficits become increasingly apparent with age; deficits present at preschool age have been found to have a significant impact on later development of language comprehension (Pike, Swank, Taylor, Landry, & Barnes, 2013.) Nevertheless, these children typically show strong development of vocabulary and syntax. Still, they have been found to be less efficient and concise with their use of language than typically developing peers. They produce fewer clauses and require more time to reproduce a story than typically developing children. Moreover, children with SBM have difficulty conveying the meaning of a story (Taylor, Landry, English, & Barnes, 2010). In other words, although these youth are able to master the mechanics of language, they struggle with meaning and comprehension.

In social contexts, children with SBM struggle with the nuances of language, and these difficulties become increasingly apparent in adolescence and young adulthood. Conversations, which require the ability to use language flexibly, are difficult for individuals with SBM because they tend to favor language that is semantically retrieved rather than dynamically constructed (Holbein, Zebracki, & Holmbeck, 2014;

Dennis & Barnes, 2010). Moreover, they have been found to be tangential in conversation and demonstrate hyperverbosity (Holbein et al., 2014). These individuals also demonstrate poor inferential skills, a core component of conversation. Although their communication can be unclear, the interpersonal rhetoric remains intact. Specifically, they can initiate appropriate conversation and be friendly, polite, sociable, and cooperative in conversation (Dennis & Barnes, 2010).

Memory. Memory is a key cognitive resource that impacts multiple areas of functioning, and research has suggested that individuals with SBM have some memory dysfunction. Children with SBM demonstrate profound recency effects and perform poorly on long delay free recall exercises. They demonstrate deficits in immediate and delayed episodic memory or the recall and recognition of context-specific events (Dennis et al., 2007). These children also perform poorly on tasks requiring high information maintenance, largely due to impaired working memory. Additionally, Treble-Barna and colleagues (2015) found lower prospective memory to be associated with lower hippocampal volume in a sample of adults with SBM. Prospective memory also involves the frontal lobe system, and individuals with SBM have atypically large frontal lobe volume (Hasan et al., 2008), which impacts both their academic success and their ability to be self-sufficient. Furthermore, Dennis and colleagues (2007) found that retrospective memory problems were negatively correlated with communication, independence, and components of quality of life. These memory deficits are believed to increase with number of shunt revisions (Zebracki, Zaccariello, Zelko, & Holmbeck, 2010). Research has also recently shown that individuals with SBM may have more impairments in memory as they age, further reducing their ability to assert and maintain independence (Dennis et al., 2007). However, implicit memory and motor learning appear to be preserved in this population.

Visual-Spatial Abilities. Research indicates that individuals with SBM have unique difficulties with visual-spatial perception. Visual-spatial perception involves two processing systems: the dorsal (action-based) system and the ventral (object-based) system. The current literature does not support global visual-perceptual deficits in these individuals. Rather, they have specific difficulties with tasks requiring integration of a visual gestalt or detection of multiple dimensions (e.g., tasks that require synthesis of dorsal input; Fletcher et al., 1996). For example, they are able to identify faces but have difficulty with visual relations and visually guided goal-directed action, such as picking up an object. These perceptual difficulties have been related to posterior cortex thinning (Fletcher et al., 1996). The hypoplasia of the corpus callosum that is frequently found in SBM also impacts visual-motor integration (Fletcher et al., 1996). In fact, children with SBM and hydrocephalus were found to have consistently impaired performances on tasks of action-based visual perception tasks when compared with object-based visual perception tasks (Dennis, Fletcher, Rogers, Hetherington, & Francis, 2002). Generally, these visual-spatial abilities and difficulties are exhibited in childhood and are maintained through adolescence and adulthood.

Motor Functioning. Individuals with SBM have impaired upper and lower limb control and eye movement. In general, the higher the level of the initial lesion, the greater the impact on gross motor functioning (e.g., ambulation; Fletcher et al., 2004). During early development, infants show limb motor deficits, such as motor weakness, low motor speed, poor motor planning, and reduced coordination (Fletcher et al., 2004). Other motor deficits exhibited include decreased strength, balance, dexterity, and oculomotor and oral-motor skills. Many of these motor difficulties have been attributed to abnormalities of the cerebellum (Fletcher et al., 2004). Although motor abilities improve with age and practice, individuals with SBM demonstrate motor difficulties into adulthood. Difficulties with gross and fine motor abilities can be related to a lower level of functional ability and can necessitate the need for supports (e.g., occupational therapy, physical therapy) and accommodations.

In addition to gross motor problems, fine motor skills are often poor in youth with SBM. Difficulty with controlled motor performance tasks, especially tasks that require coordinating motor activities with visual input, such as writing and drawing (Fletcher, Ostermaier, Cirino, & Dennis, 2008), is frequently seen. One study using MRI analysis of youth ages 8–18 years with SBM found that fine motor dexterity decreased with increasing cortical thickness in the putamen as well as the dorsolateral prefrontal cortex (Ware et al., 2016). These individuals often struggle with precise motor movements and demonstrate difficulties with time and rhythm impairments, which

may be exacerbated by impairments in attention, memory, executive functioning, and visual-spatial abilities (Vinck et al., 2009).

Academic Achievement. Academic achievement is an area of difficulty for children and young adults with SBM. Sight-word reading is often a relative strength, but children, adolescents, and young adults with SBM frequently have difficulty with reading comprehension (Barnes, Dennis, & Hetherington, 2004) and drawing inferences from text (Pike et al., 2013). Although math fact retrieval is often intact, procedural math skills such as subtraction with regrouping can be an area of difficulty (Barnes et al., 2004). Cognitive difficulties early in development (i.e., preschool years), including deficits in visual-spatial working memory and phonological awareness, have been shown to contribute to school-age difficulties in math achievement (Barnes et al., 2014).

Although many children with SBM begin in regular education classrooms, a greater percentage of those with hydrocephalus begin receiving special education services as schooling progresses. In general, children with SBM who have below-average IQ, depend on wheelchair for mobility due to high lesion level, and have a history of multiple surgeries are more likely to receive special education (Dicianno et al., 2008). Demographic and other illness-specific factors have also been found to impact academic achievement. For example, Hispanic ethnicity, lower socioeconomic status (SES), presence of hydrocephalus, and shunt placement are predictors of worse performance on academic achievement measures (Swartwout, Garnaat, Myszka, Fletcher, & Dennis, 2010). Most adolescents with SBM successfully graduate high school (85%), but have lower rates of college attendance (14.6%) than healthy peers (Dicianno et al., 2008). Lack of education may lead to limited career and vocational options, decreased financial independence, and, therefore, greater reliance on family or other caregivers as these individuals enter young adulthood.

Psychological Functioning. Compared with their typically developing peers, children age 8–18 years with SBM are at risk for higher levels of internalizing symptoms, particularly depressive symptoms, as well as lower levels of self-concept compared with their typically developing peers (Kabra, Feustal, & Kogan, 2015; Shields, Taylor, & Dodd, 2008; Holmbeck et al., 2003, 2010; Kelly et al., 2012). They may also be at risk for externalizing symptoms, although the existing evidence is mixed. One meta-analytic review revealed that these individuals <18 years were at increased risk for externalizing symptoms (Pinquart & Shen, 2011), but another study found no difference in externalizing symptoms between 8- and 9-year-olds with SBM and their same-aged peers (Holmbeck et al., 2003). Emerging adults with SBM are at risk for depressive symptoms and anxiety (Bellin et al., 2010), but are less likely than their typically developing age-mates to engage in risky behaviors (e.g., alcohol use, multiple sexual partners; Murray et al., 2014). Youth <18 years with SBM are also at risk for reduced health-related quality of life (HRQOL) (Sawin & Bellin, 2010). Past studies have found they have lower HRQOL when compared with typically developing populations and youth with other chronic health conditions (Murray et al., 2015); such differences tend to be stable across age groups, gender, geographical location, and time (Murray et al., 2015; Sawin & Bellin, 2010). Research has found that a variety of factors predict psychological outcomes in this population, including parenting, parent functioning, pain, severity of SBM, neuropsychological functioning, attitudes toward SBM, healthcare services, and socioeconomic status (Bellin et al., 2010, 2013; Friedman, Holmbeck, Jandasek, Zukerman, & Abad, 2004; Holmbeck et al., 2003; Kelly et al., 2012; Lennon, Klages, Amaro, Murray, & Holmbeck, 2015; Oddson, Clancy, & McGrath, 2006).

Social Functioning. Individuals with SBM are also at risk for experiencing social difficulties, which appear during childhood and persist throughout adolescence (Holmbeck et al., 2010). Specifically, these children and adolescents are less socially competent compared with their typically developing peers, such that they tend to be more socially immature and passive, and demonstrate less-adaptive social behaviors when interacting with peers (Holbein et al., 2015; Holmbeck et al., 2003; Shields et al., 2008). They also report that they are less socially accepted, have smaller peer networks, spend less time with friends, participate in fewer organized social activities, and have friendships that are less likely to be reciprocated and are of poorer quality (Buran, Sawin, Brie, & Fastenau, 2004; Cunningham, Thomas, & Warschausky, 2007; Devine, Holmbeck, Gayes, & Purnell, 2012; Holmbeck et al., 2010). Young adults with SBM are less likely to have a romantic relationship compared with their typically developing peers (Zukerman, Devine, & Holmbeck, 2011), and parents are less likely to discuss

issues of sexuality with their children with SBM (Sawin, Brei, Buran, & Fastenau, 2002). With respect to community participation and social integration, participation in leisure and recreational activities tends to be low: more than 50% participate in no such activities (Boudos & Mukherjee, 2008).

Studies reveal a variety of sociodemographic factors that impact social functioning among these individuals. A camp-based intervention targeting independence for individuals with SBM found that campers in the lower income group showed greater improvement in their social skills over the course of the camp experience (Holbein et al., 2013). As discussed in the preceding paragraph, participation in community activities for these individuals is limited, and this limitation is even more pronounced for youth from families reporting lower income, lower parent education, and single-parent status (Law et al., 2006). Further, those of Hispanic ethnicity or those from homes where English is not the primary spoken language are less likely to participate in social and work activities (Liptak, Kennedy, & Dosa, 2010). Social skill development may be impacted by race or ethnicity or both: one study that examined social functioning during a structured interaction task with a close friend found that dyads of White youth with SBM were observed to exhibit greater maturity, collaboration, and social dominance as compared with mixed-race dyads (Holbein et al., 2015). Further, studies have found that SBM and SES status may have cumulative impacts on social adjustment outcomes. For example, studies have found that children with SBM from low-SES homes had the fewest social contacts outside of school and were reported to have more social problems (Holmbeck et al., 2003), and that lower SES was associated with having fewer friends in youth with SBM but not for a typically developing comparison sample (Zukerman et al., 2011).

Family Functioning. As many individuals with SBM continue to live with their immediate family throughout adulthood, the impact of family functioning extends across the lifespan. Research on families of youth <18 years with SBM supports a resilience–disruption view of family functioning, whereby the presence of a child with SBM disrupts normative family functioning. Nonetheless, many families exhibit considerable resilience (Lennon, Murray, Bechtel, & Holmbeck, 2015). Compared with families of typically developing youth, families of these children tend to display lower levels of cohesion during preadolescence, with families from lower SES backgrounds being particularly at risk (Holmbeck, Coakley, Hommeyer, Shapera, & Westhoven, 2002). However, families do not demonstrate increases in family conflict as a function of pubertal development as is seen in families of typically developing youth (Coakley, Holmbeck, Friedman, Greenly, & Thill, 2002), and some studies have found that overall levels of family stress were similar between groups (Holmbeck et al., 2002; Jandasek, Holmbeck, DeLucia, Zebracki, & Friedman, 2009).

In terms of parenting behaviors, parents of children with SBM exhibit higher levels of intrusiveness, psychological control, and authoritarian parenting (Holmbeck et al., 2002; Sawin et al., 2003), and these behaviors are linked with less desirable child outcomes. In terms of parent functioning, compared with parents of typically developing youth, parents of children with SBM experience more stress in their roles as parents, feel less satisfied and competent as parents, feel more isolated, are less adaptable to change, and hold less optimistic views about the future than comparison parents (Holmbeck & Devine, 2010). Parents who are single, socially isolated, older, or from a low SES background are particularly at risk for such outcomes (Holmbeck & Devine, 2010). In addition, compared with non-Hispanic White parents of youth age 8–17 years with SBM, Hispanic mothers and fathers reported lower levels of parenting satisfaction, competence as a parent, social support, and higher perceptions of child vulnerability, although these effect sizes were reduced when SES was included as a covariate (Devine, Holbein, Psihogios, Amaro, & Holmbeck, 2012).

Functional Adaptation. Functional adaptation is commonly defined as the attainment of major developmental milestones as expected for a given age and gender in a given culture (Heffelfinger et al., 2008). Risk factors for poor functional adaptation for an individual with SBM include the following condition variables: higher spinal lesion level, shunted hydrocephalus, shunt infections, shunt revisions, and presence of epilepsy (Zebracki et al., 2010). Functional adaptation specific to individuals with SBM includes health management, employment preparation, transportation independence, and other basic independence skills such as cooking and cleaning.

For all individuals, not just those with SBM, successful adaptation in adolescence usually predicts greater independence in adulthood, as adolescence is a developmental period that involves changing social roles and increasing responsibility, accountability, and status in interpersonal relationships. In general, individuals with SBM frequently do not navigate milestones as successfully as their typically developing peers. For example, they often have significant motor difficulties that impede them from getting a driver's license (Zebracki et al., 2010); only 45% of adults with SBM have a driver's license in the United States (Leger, 2005). Moreover, learning basic life skills such as cooking and cleaning is delayed or absent for young adults with SBM (Bellin, Sawin, Roux, Buran, & Brei, 2007). Other important elements of independent functioning include employment, independent living, and community participation. Rates of independent living and community participation for individuals with SBM are low (Mukherjee, 2007). In a qualitative study done by Bellin and colleagues (2007), adolescent women with SBM reported that they had goals of going to college and having a career. However, rates of employment are not very high in this population. In the United States, Mahmood and colleagues (2011) found that only 52.6% of young adults with SBM were employed, and only 10.5% were employed full time. Similarly, in a British study, only 33% of adults with SBM were employed (Oakeshott et al., 2010). Besides having to manage many of the same milestones required of typically developing individuals, individuals with SBM must also navigate the transfer of medical responsibility from parents to adolescents and young adults. If medical responsibilities are transferred prematurely, poor medical adherence may result; yet if these responsibilities are transferred too late, it may foster a sense of dependency and low self-efficacy (Zebracki et al., 2010).

Neuropsychological Assessment

Given the heterogeneity of this condition, comprehensive neuropsychological evaluations can highlight the specific strengths and weaknesses of individuals with SBM. Initial neuropsychological assessment in childhood can help to establish a baseline of functioning, as marked changes in cognitive functioning could be indicative of an underlying medical issue such as a shunt malfunction (Matson, Mahone, & Zabel, 2005). Reevaluations at times of transition (e.g., educational transitions, transitioning from adolescence to adulthood) can help with planning for significant life changes. Assessment is also important because neuropsychological functioning predicts other outcomes of interest (e.g., general cognitive and executive functioning predicting internalizing symptoms; Lennon, Klages, et al., 2015). The brain in SBM undergoes a complex reorganization compared with the typically developing brain, and it remains unclear how this reorganization impacts the normal effects of aging on cognitive functioning (Dennis, Nelson, Jewell, & Fletcher, 2010). Therefore, future research is necessary to identify time points in adulthood at which assessment would be beneficial for these individuals. This section aims to outline strategies to assess the most salient neuropsychological issues associated with SBM, which were described in detail in the previous section.

Assessment Strategies by Domain

Attention. Attentional deficits in SBM have been reported across a range of assessment contexts. Standardized neuropsychological test batteries, including the Cognitive Assessment System (Naglieri & Das, 1997), the Wechsler Intelligence Scale for Children (Wechsler, 2014), and the Stroop color-word test (Golden, 2004), have revealed poorer focused attention and distractibility skills in adolescents with SBM compared to both typically developing children and those with SBM without hydrocephalus (Rose & Holmbeck, 2007; Vinck, Mullaart, Rotteveel, & Maassen, 2009). Children with SBM display relatively intact levels of sustained attention, but they make more omission errors and respond more slowly than their peers on the Gordon Diagnostic System (Swartwout et al., 2008). Concurrently, parents rate their children with SBM as displaying more inattentive behaviors than impulsive or hyperactive behaviors on the Swanson, Nolan, and Pelham Teacher and Parent Rating Scale, a measure of ADHD symptoms in children (Swartwout et al., 2008).

Proper assessment of attention in individuals with SBM is difficult because traditional tests of attention may not be sensitive to the subtle, individual deficits exhibited. Indeed, studies have shown that parent ratings of attention behaviors in children with SBM do not share a significant amount of variance with attention-task performance measures. This result may highlight that different assessment methods better index different components of attention (Swartwout et al., 2008). Moreover, test results may be confounded by coexisting cognitive and visual-motor

impairments. Traditional neuropsychological tests usually require rapid visual-motor processing skills, fine motor manipulation, and hand-eye coordination (Vinck, Mullaart, Rotteveel, & Maassen, 2009). To circumvent this issue, researchers have begun using computerized or simplified tests that do not rely on complex motor demands, such as the Dual Attention to Response Task (Dockree et al., 2006), and tasks based on the Theory of Visual Attention (Bundesen, 1990). Findings have shown reduced performance differences between youth with SBM and typically developing youth for focused attention, visual distractibility, and sustained attention when using these alternative tests (Vinck et al., 2009).

Executive Functioning. Neuropsychological assessment can help identify specific executive functioning deficits in individuals with SBM. To obtain a comprehensive understanding of executive functioning in this population, it is important to include both subjective ratings (e.g., parent report) and objective measures (e.g., performance tasks) of executive functioning skills. Reports of executive functioning behaviors and performance on executive functioning tasks often do not correlate with each other, indicating that they may capture different aspects of functioning (Brown et al., 2008). Performance-based measures tap into the efficiency of the mental processes related to executive functioning, whereas behavioral ratings offer information about how individuals use these skills in everyday life (Brown et al., 2008). Incorporating multiple raters of executive functioning is important as well. Research has found that adolescents with SBM and their parents produce discrepant ratings of adolescent executive dysfunction, with parents rating their children as having clinically worse executive functioning skills than the children report themselves (Zabel et al., 2011). Such evidence suggests that children with SBM may have limited insight into their executive dysfunction, and may underestimate their deficits (Zabel et al., 2011).

Language. Detailed assessment of language skills in this population is important because many individuals with SBM present with language development that appears intact but is actually impaired (Fletcher et al., 2002). Tasks assessing both simple and complex receptive language skills are necessary because these individuals tend to perform relatively well on simple tasks. Still, one study found that preadolescents with SBM performed significantly lower on the Peabody Picture

Vocabulary Test – Revised (Dunn & Dunn, 1981) than a matched group of able-bodied peers (Holmbeck et al., 2003). The performance of the SBM group was in the low average range on this relatively simple assessment task. Performance on more complex tasks may be poorer for these individuals because they may lack complex comprehension skills (Fletcher, Barnes, & Dennis, 2002), so it is helpful to include a range of receptive language assessments.

Informally, examiners may notice that individuals with SBM tend to display the "cocktail party syndrome," that is, using articulate and coherent expressive language that is irrelevant, aimless, or inappropriate in the conversational context (Fletcher et al., 2002). This is an important behavioral observation to note because the use of empty language affects these individuals in educational, professional, and social settings. Additionally, formal assessments of semantic-pragmatic language, such as the Comprehensive Assessment of Spoken Language (Carrow-Woolfolk, 1999) can identify these discourse-level language difficulties (Fletcher et al., 2002).

Memory. There are a number of general assessment techniques for measuring memory functioning for children, adolescents, and adults with SBM. It is important to consider the motor component of potential memory tasks, as deficits in motor functioning in individuals with SBM could lower their scores on a memory task. For children <3 years old, assessments like the "six boxes task" are appropriate (Pike et al., 2013). This adapted, self-ordered pointing task requires a child to keep track of his or her search history, which involves working memory and inhibitory control. Significant impairments in prospective and episodic memory have been found in adults with SBM (Treble-Barna et al., 2015). These adults performed more poorly than typically developing same-age peers on multiple subtests of the Rivermead Behavioural Memory Test – Extended Version (Wilson, Cockburn, & Baddeley, 2003). Given concerns with practical memory skills, another appropriate test for adults with SBM is the Cambridge Prospective Memory Test (Wilson et al., 2005). This paper-and-pencil measure assesses a participant's goal-oriented memory.

Visual-Spatial Abilities. A number of tasks can be completed to assess visual-spatial abilities in individuals with SBM. First and foremost, it is imperative

that these individuals have up-to-date eye exams with an optometrist, and, when appropriate, wear eyeglasses or corrective lenses. Given the comorbid deficits in motor functioning experienced by these individuals, nonmotor assessments of visual perception such as the Motor-Free Visual Perception Test – 3rd ed. (Calarusso & Hammill, 2003) should be used when possible. Visual-spatial abilities are also frequently assessed using subtests from age-appropriate measures of general intellectual abilities (e.g., visual puzzles on the Wechsler Intelligence Scale for Children – 5th ed. and Wechsler Adult Intelligence Scale – 4th ed.). Visual-perceptual abilities can also be assessed separately from motor abilities, such as with the Visual Perception subtest of the Beery-Buktenica Developmental Test of Visual-Motor Integration (Beery & Beery, 2004).

Motor Functioning. At birth, doctors assess the potential motor abilities of infants with SBM based on lesion level and neuronal functioning (Copp et al., 2015). Gross motor functioning in individuals with SBM can be assessed regularly through orthopedic exams. The more nuanced fine motor deficits of individuals with SBM can be assessed through a variety of neuropsychological measures. Fine motor coordination, dexterity, and speed can be assessed using tasks such as the Grooved Pegboard (Trites, 1975). Graphomotor coordination and visual integration skills can be assessed through the Beery-Buktenica Developmental Test of Visual-Motor Integration (Beery & Beery, 2004) or the Rey-Osterrieth Complex Figure Test (Meyers & Meyers, 1995). Given the impact that other abilities (attention, executive functioning, memory, visual-spatial abilities) may have on performance on these measures, it is important to carefully observe the individual's behavioral strategies and specific fine motor difficulties.

Academic Achievement. A comprehensive assessment of the specific academic-related strengths and weaknesses in youth with SBM is necessary to effectively evaluate academic achievement. Scholastic achievement has been assessed in this population with standardized measures such as the Woodcock-Johnson IV Tests of Achievement (Schrank, Mather, & McGrew, 2014) and the Kaufman Test of Educational Achievement – 3rd Edition (Kaufman & Kaufman, 2014). It is important to take into account general intellectual, visual-motor, executive functioning, and attention abilities because deficits in these areas can undermine academic performance (Ramsundhar & Donald, 2014). Administration of a neuropsychological test battery in childhood can help identify potential problem areas early on, allowing time for the necessary supports to be put in place to address delays in achievement (Ramsundhar & Donald, 2014). Early indicators of math disability can be detected during preschool and kindergarten (Barnes, Smith-Chant, & Landry, 2005), and assessment of numeracy skills and early number sense (Mazzocco & Thompson, 2005) using instruments such as the Test of Early Mathematics Ability – 3rd Edition (Ginsburg & Baroody, 2003) can facilitate the early identification of those at higher risk for these problems. Because reading comprehension difficulties often persist despite adequate word-reading skills (Barnes et al., 2004), it is recommended that student screening not be limited to screening sight-word reading and decoding but that it also include reading comprehension tasks.

Psychological, Social, and Family Functioning. Impairments in psychological, social, and family functioning can impact the well-being of individuals with SBM, and, thus, are an important emphasis in a comprehensive evaluation. Assessment of functioning across these domains can occur through regular screenings by medical providers, through either interview or paper-and-pencil measures. In terms of psychological functioning, well-validated broad-band or symptom-specific measures can be completed by multiple reporters. Assessment of social functioning can occur through self-, parent, and teacher report on broad-based measures or measures specific to social functioning. Holbein and colleagues (2014) provided validation data for an adapted observational coding system designed to measure social competence during observed peer interactions. The observational coding system used to assess social functioning was originally adapted as a system to code observed family interactions, and it has been validated for families of youth with SBM (Kaugars et al., 2011). Otherwise, parent and self-report questionnaire measures assessing family functioning (such as the Family Environment Scale; Moos & Moos, 2002) can give providers an indication of family members' perception of the family environment.

Functional Adaptation. Assessing functional adaptation skills as early as possible can guide families and

individuals with SBM in holding realistic expectations and developing plans for the future. Broad-based adaptive skill inventories can be used to compare youth with SBM with typically developing children and help identify areas of disability and targets for intervention (e.g., the California Healthy and Ready to Work Transition Assessment Tool [Betz, Redcay & Tan, 2003], or the Adaptive Behavior Assessment System for Children-Third Edition [Harrison & Oakland, 2015]). Evaluation of adaptive skills using an SBM-specific measure of independence, to further document intervention need and/or adaptive capabilities, is also advised. The Adolescent Self-Management and Independence Scale-II (Buran, Brei, Sawin, Stevens & Neufeld, 2006) assesses the amount of assistance an adolescent with SBM needs when carrying out medical self-management activities. Another measure specific to this population is the Kennedy Krieger Independence Scales–Spina Bifida Version (Zabel, Jacobson, Tarazi, & Mahone, 2012). This parent report inventory addresses specific knowledge and skills fundamental to self-management. Finally, the Spina Bifida Needs Questionnaire (Kennedy et al., 1998) measures individuals' and families' needs for SBM-specific services.

Intervention

Given the wide range of challenges associated with SBM, affected individuals may benefit from a variety of interventions across the lifespan. To date, most research in SBM focuses on children, adolescents, and young adults. There is limited research with older adults, especially regarding intervention. Still, research on SBM-specific interventions across the lifespan for each domain described previously is presented in this section. However, it is important to note that more rigorously designed research studies are required before these intervention strategies can be supported as practice standards or guidelines.

Intervention Strategies by Domain

Attention. Due to the increased risk of attention deficits, routine screening assessments should become standard practice for clinicians to identify cognitive problems early in development. Documenting the presence of attention difficulties can help identify children and adolescents who require specific supports in school, as attention problems interfere with academic functioning (Dennis & Barnes, 2010).

Children with SBM are more likely to be treated with stimulant medication therapy than their peers with ADHD (Wasserman, Stoner, Stern, &Holmbeck, 2016). Stimulant medication as a sole therapy may not be sufficient to resolve attentional difficulties in this population because their pattern of attentional deficits differs from the deficits typically associated with ADHD (Rose & Holmbeck, 2007). Children with SBM, whether treated with stimulant medications or not, benefit from behavioral supports and school accommodations, such as preferential seating, frequent breaks, testing in an individual or small group setting to minimize distractions, repetition of information, and behavior reinforcement systems (Ramsundhar & Donald, 2014). Such accommodations can be provided informally at home and school or through an individualized education program.

Executive Functioning. Parent ratings of behavior collected during adolescence and young adulthood suggest that individuals with SBM can show improvement in executive functioning over time (Zabel et al., 2011). A randomized controlled trial (RCT) evaluated the effectiveness of a goal-management training program for adults with spina bifida who had clinically elevated executive dysfunction (Stubberud, Langenbahn, Levine, Stanghelle, & Schanke, 2013). Led by a neuropsychologist and a nurse/social worker, the intervention taught participants strategies for improving their attentional and problem-solving abilities, and found that participants' performance executive functioning skills improved over time, and that the improvements in these performance-based test scores generalized to models of "real-life" multitasking situations. It is promising that targeted interventions can ameliorate some of the executive functioning difficulties found in individuals with SBM. More RCTs are needed to evaluate the effectiveness of executive functioning interventions for youth with SBM, because early identification and treatment of these problems may lead to better adaptive outcomes. Additionally, assistive technologies, such as smart phones, can enhance complex planning and memory-related functions (Dicianno et al., 2008).

Language. Suggested interventions for language development for children with SBM primarily center on parental involvement. Many studies have found that responsive parenting has a positive impact on language skills for these children (Vacha & Adams, 2009; Lomax-Bream et al., 2007). For instance,

parental support, encouragement, and scaffolding can bolster children's confidence in speaking and ability to stay on topic in a conversation (Taylor et al., 2010; Holbein et al., 2015). Existing social skills interventions can be adapted to promote conversational language skills, such as making inferences, pragmatic judgments, understanding sarcasm, and nonliteral language (Holbein et al., 2015). Lastly, an association has been found between placing high value on participation in recreation activities and increased language development for youth age 7–16 years with SBM (Vacha & Adams, 2009). Therefore, interventions for language development might include encouraging more active participation in recreational activities, which can increase exposure to pragmatic language in multiple settings. Moreover, a positive relationship has been found between family engagement in intellectual and cultural activities and the development of multiple language systems (e.g., bilingualism) in youth age 7–16 years with SBM (Vacha & Adams, 2009). However, this study also found that when a child is pushed too far past his or her developed skill level, language learning may actually be slowed.

Memory. There is a lack of research on interventions for memory deficits in individuals with SBM. The research to date has focused on strategies to be used in the school setting, given that this is the setting in which memory and learning deficits are most noticeable for youth. It has been proposed that teachers underscore important material, to address what may not have been stored immediately due to reduced working memory capacity and attention difficulties in children with SBM (Vacha & Adams, 2005). Subsequent studies have echoed this suggestion, explaining that targeted academic supports may aid children with memory dysfunction (e.g., Dennis et al., 2007). Memory impacts individuals with SBM beyond the school setting because they must follow a medical regimen that requires adherence to a schedule (e.g., catheterization, bowel programs, and medications). For both children and adults, assistive technology (e.g., cell phone reminders) or the use of charts to remind an individual to complete certain tasks (e.g., catheterization) could help foster more self-efficacy and independence despite memory deficits (Dicianno et al., 2008; Zebracki et al., 2010). Despite evidence of progressive memory deficits in adulthood (Treble-Barna et al., 2015), interventions aimed at addressing these deficits with this population have yet to be developed.

Visual-Spatial Abilities. Although interventions addressing visual-spatial difficulties in individuals with SBM have not been studied empirically, generic interventions that target these abilities are applicable. There is evidence that early movement (e.g., crawling) influences the development of spatial cognition and problem-solving strategies (Fletcher et al., 1996). Therefore, although gross motor functioning is impaired in infants with SBM, it is necessary that affected infants be provided opportunities for movement and exploration of their environment to optimize development of visual-spatial abilities (Dennis et al., 2002). For older children, visual-perceptual deficits may cause difficulties at home (e.g., problems with dressing) and in the classroom (e.g., impairments in handwriting, difficulty identifying letters and words, issues with math computations that include more than one digit; Fletcher et al., 1996). These children may benefit from occupational therapy to help with daily tasks (e.g., writing) as well as accommodations in the classroom, such as minimizing distractions, using graph paper, and adaptive technology to ensure optimal performance (Fletcher et al., 1996). These types of accommodations can be adapted as individuals advance from elementary to high school.

Motor Functioning. Ongoing management of mobility is necessary in individuals with SBM. Regular orthopedic assessments, bracing and orthotics, and orthopedic surgeries (such as spinal fusion or hip, pelvic, or foot or ankle procedures) are often necessary (Copp et al., 2015). Additionally, weight management strategies are important for individuals with SBM because excessive weight gain can further limit mobility and increase the risk for pressure ulcers (Ottolini, Harris, Amling, Kennelly, & Phillips, 2013). It is critical to provide opportunities for infants and preschoolers with SBM to explore their environment, for the development of motor functioning as well as other cognitive abilities (Fletcher et al., 1996). Physical and occupational therapists can identify interventions addressing gross and fine motor limitations. These therapies may help improve functioning and independence in activities of daily living. For example, physical therapy can focus on improving efficiency of mobility, decreasing contractures, and increasing overall strength and balance. Additionally, occupational therapy interventions can help adolescents and adults with SBM achieve independence in medical tasks (such as catheterization) as well as dressing (e.g., manipulating buttons and tying shoes; Zebracki et al., 2010).

Academic Achievement. Children and adolescents with SBM can receive a variety of services to enhance their academic success. For children who qualify for special education, families can collaborate with their school administrators to create an Individualized Education Program, a formal plan that delineates what accommodations are needed to help their child succeed academically. Through special education programs, children with cognitive impairments can remain in an extended secondary education and participate in vocational programs until the age of 22 years (Spina Bifida Association, 2015). Although few disease-specific academic interventions have been designed for youth with SBM, a specialized intervention in cognitive strategy training for adolescents with spina bifida was found to lead to improvements in confidence in math skills and math performance (Coughlin & Montague, 2011). Additionally, increased instruction time in class or extra tutoring may improve arithmetic achievement in youth with SBM (Coughlin & Montague, 2011). Social difficulties can contribute to poor academic achievement in these youth (Brislin, 2008), and working with school counselors or social workers, as well as participation in social skills groups, may help address these issues (e.g., negative self-perceptions of inferiority, poor self-efficacy, and low intrinsic motivation). School counselors and social workers can also refer youth to available intervention programs and educational resources (Brislin, 2008).

Psychological, Social, and Family Functioning. There is a lack of clinical interventions specifically designed to improve psychological functioning among people with SBM. One exception is the RCT discussed previously, which aimed to address executive functioning impairments through goal-management training (Stubberud et al., 2013). The intervention was found to produce significant improvements in executive functioning, self-reported depressive and anxiety symptoms, HRQOL, and coping skills (Stubberud, Langenbahn, Levine, Stanghelle, & Schanke, 2015).

There are also few clinical interventions that focus on improving social and family functioning in individuals with SBM. In fact, to date, no clinical interventions designed to improve family functioning have been validated (Holmbeck, Greenley, Coakley, Greco, & Hagstrom, 2006). In terms of social functioning, a manualized summer camp-based intervention was developed to target independence and social skills among children, adolescents, and young adults with SBM, and it led to improvements in campers' social goal attainment (e.g., using appropriate eye contact, asking appropriate follow-up questions in conversation) and social independence. Although benefits were found for most campers, cognitive functioning and family income moderated some outcomes (Holbein et al., 2013; O'Mahar, Holmbeck, Jandasek, & Zukerman, 2010).

Functional Adaptation. Studies have shown that giving youth with SBM small tasks such as household chores is associated with better adaptation later in life, regardless of illness severity (Heffelfinger et al., 2008). Conversely, restrictive parenting is associated with less practical knowledge, less well developed independence skills, and poorer adaptation in adulthood (Bellin et al., 2007). Therefore, parents might consider gradually shifting responsibility to their children in a manner that is congruent with their child's maturity level. Responsibility transition topics might include lessons about shopping and money handling, and discussing employment interests and educational goals (Zebracki et al., 2010). Adolescents and young adults with SBM may also benefit from vocational training, within or outside of the context of school, to support the pursuit of higher education and employment. Indeed, individuals with a chronic health condition are more likely to be employed if they have received vocational training (Shandra & Hogan, 2008). Vocational training may also focus on general life skills, including navigating public transportation systems and managing finances. Furthermore, given the known difficulties with memory, assistive technology for reminding an individual to perform certain self-management tasks (e.g., catheterization) could aid in establishing and maintaining independence. Finally, psychotherapy can assist youth in managing and discussing the transition to adult health care (Zebracki et al., 2010).

Table 2.3 Important Components of Clinical Practice for Psychologists Working with an Individual with Spina Bifida Myelomeningocele

- Working within an interprofessional team
- Partnering in patient- and family-centered care
- Providing anticipatory guidance
- Providing psychoeducation regarding secondary health complications
- Monitoring meeting developmental milestones
- Considering the impact of SBM on academic performance and executive functions
- Providing information regarding vocational rehabilitation services and resources
- Monitoring mood and assessing for internalizing symptoms
- Providing support for the transition from pediatric to adult health care

Implications for Clinical Practice

This section highlights general and SBM-specific strategies for use in clinical practice. Effective and open communication (within the team and between the team and the patient and his or her caregivers) is a critical component within all of the following areas (summarized in Table 2.3).

Interprofessional Team Partnering with Families

An interprofessional team and the consideration of several domains of functioning within a developmental context is vital to facilitate optimal medical and psychosocial outcomes for individual with SBM. The team collaborates to develop a dynamic and evolving treatment plan that addresses deficits and promotes independence and participation specific to the individual's developmental stage and environmental context. Moreover, the team partners with the youth and family in treatment planning, implementation, and evaluation of care. Providing patient- and family-centered care has been shown to improve patient and family outcomes, promote a positive health-care experience, increase patient and family satisfaction, and promote more effective use of health-care resources (Committee on Hospital Care and Institute for Patient- and Family-Centered Care, 2012). Moreover, such partnering with patients and families can enhance the confidence, knowledge, and skills of youth and families and prepare youth to take responsibility for their own health care as they transition to the adult health-care system.

Anticipatory Guidance

The interprofessional team provides individuals and families with accurate and timely information on issues related to the various domains of functioning (e.g., physiological, developmental, academic, and psychosocial) that are likely to occur as the youth grows and matures. Anticipatory guidance describes natural trajectories of SBM and development, emphasizes strategies to minimize secondary health conditions and other negative outcomes, supports collaboration of treatment, and provides opportunities for active discussion of expectations of the youth. For example, the expectation that youth engage in and achieve developmental milestones, such as dating and employment, should be promoted, as applicable (Holbein et al., 2016).

Medical Care

Along with the medical provider, psychologists often provide psychoeducation on SBM and secondary health complications. Targeted education may help promote adherence to the provider's recommendations by increasing the youth's knowledge regarding the importance of engaging in these behaviors and learning the consequences of nonadherence. Psychological interventions may be utilized to promote behavioral strategies to increase adherence and cognitive strategies to promote problem-solving skills in managing care.

Developmental Issues

Individuals with SBM experience the typical challenges of development as well as unique challenges owing to their medical condition. A psychologist's role includes assessing attainment of developmental milestones, implementing interventions to promote development, and providing education on the interplay between normative development and SBM. For example, during middle childhood, as precocious puberty is common in girls with SBM (Fletcher et al., 2004), it is important to provide information about sexual development, including fertility and sexuality – including engaging in romantic relationships, to both the youth and families. Moreover, adolescents with SBM may have physical limitations that make it more challenging to participate in social activities and to establish autonomy. Psychological treatment may focus on promoting socialization with peers and addressing isolation. During emerging adulthood, counseling youth and families about employment, independent living, and other developmental issues is critical in promoting adaptive functioning and positive outcomes.

Academic Performance and Executive Function

Individuals with SBM may experience a range of deficits in academic performance and executive functions that would benefit from targeted psychological intervention. These neurological deficits also impact SBM management and adherence to treatment. For example, patients with executive dysfunction may have difficulty remembering and adhering to multistep treatment procedures. In such cases, strategies such as visual cues and simple step-by-step guidelines may be beneficial.

Vocational Training

Individuals with SBM may benefit from vocational training in determining an appropriate job or pursuing higher education. Individuals with SBM are less likely to go to college and be employed: 41–56% attend college compared with 66% of typically developing youth (Bowman, McLone, Grant, Tomita, & Ito, 2001; Holbein et al., 2016; Zukerman et al., 2011). Vocational training may also focus on general life skills, including navigating public transportation systems and financial management. In some cases, the interprofessional team may counsel the family to seek legal services in establishing a special-needs trust or guardianship or both.

Psychological Function

Across the lifespan, individuals with SBM are at risk for internalizing symptoms, including depression and anxiety, poor self-concept and self-image, social difficulties, and reduced HRQOL (Dicciano et al., 2008; Holbein et al., 2015; Murray et al., 2014). However, they are also less likely to engage in risk behaviors, including alcohol use and having multiple sexual partners (Murray et al., 2014), which may be due in part to greater social isolation and parent monitoring. Youth with disabilities, however, are at an increased risk of physical and sexual abuse for multiple reasons (e.g., because of dependence on others for intimate care, increased exposure to many caregivers and settings), making it imperative for the interprofessional team and caregivers to provide information to the youth with SBM on how to identify, avoid, and report abuse (Murphy & Elias, 2006).

Psychological treatment for youth <18 years with SBM and for the family, as well as individual therapy for the caregivers, is recommended when signs and symptoms of maladjustment and nonadherence are present. Effective interventions may include cognitive-behavioral therapy, coping effectiveness training, and motivational interviewing. Moreover, addressing parenting factors as well as family conflict can affect the well-being of the youth as well as adherence and self-management. Although routine monitoring and treatment for psychological maladjustment is critical, many youth with SBM and families demonstrate resilience and positive psychological adjustment (Lennon, Murray, et al., 2015).

Transition to Adult Care

Transition from pediatric care to adult care begins at birth. Each developmental stage provides the foundation for the next stage. Moreover, early involvement will help children develop the skills and expectations to independently manage or direct their care when developmentally appropriate and ready. Starting between the ages of 12 and 14 years, the interprofessional team should begin the process of transition to adult-care services. This may include directing medical questions to the child directly, meeting with the adolescent alone in addition to with the caregiver, encouraging adolescents to make appointments and initiate calls to providers with questions in between appointments, and providing education on how to navigate the health-care system, including insurance coverage and finding providers.

Future Directions

The treatment and care of individuals with SBM has changed significantly over the past decade, and innovative treatment options and approaches have made SBM a lifespan condition that is survivable well into adulthood. Prevention efforts have helped reduce the incidence of SBM, but there is little indication that the incidence will be dramatically reduced or eliminated in the foreseeable future. Rather, current innovations and treatments are, to a great extent, focused on reducing the severity of SBM and the related burden

of the condition on patients and their families. As these innovations are implemented on a larger scale, there will be new questions for neuropsychological research and clinical inquiry, particularly with regard to the preservation and improvement of cognitive outcomes.

Although most infants currently born with a myelomeningocele undergo surgical correction during the first several days following birth, there is compelling evidence that neurological outcomes may be improved if the myelomeningocele is surgically corrected *in utero*. The investigators of the Management of Myelomeningocele Study (Adzick et al., 2011) reported a reduction in hindbrain herniation and a reduced relative risk of postnatal shunting in their sample of patients undergoing prenatal (before 26 weeks' gestation) correction of myelomeningocele. Both the primary (brainstem malformation) and secondary (hydrocephalus) injuries associated with SBM (Dennis & Barnes, 2010) could be reduced or avoided using this surgical strategy, and there is preliminary evidence of positive outcomes concerning adaptive and executive functioning in the Management of Myelomeningocele Study cohort at age 10 (Danzer et al., 2016). As the use of prenatal surgical management of myelomeningocele likely expands, there will be a need to reconceptualize the neuropsychological sequelae of SBM and identify residual patterns of strengths and weaknesses of continued relevance to educational and vocational planning.

Innovations and new practices in the management of hydrocephalus have also raised new research questions for individuals with SBM. To avoid ongoing shunt dependence, endoscopic third ventriculostomy with choroid plexus cauterization has been utilized as a minimally invasive surgical technique for the management of hydrocephalus, including in individuals with SBM (Warf & Campbell, 2008). Studies examining potential differences in cognitive outcomes comparing children treated with endoscopic third ventriculostomy with choroid plexus cauterization versus shunts have been limited (e.g., Warf et al., 2009), and additional inquiry is needed to determine whether minimally invasive surgical measures can be utilized with a greater or at least comparable level of cognitive preservation relative to shunting. Similarly, with the introduction of "wait-and-see" methods of hydrocephalus management that delay or forego shunting of infants with mild to moderate ventricular dilatation (Sankhla & Khan, 2009), neuropsychological research is needed to determine whether these conservative approaches result in better or at least comparable outcomes relative to more aggressive shunting decisions. Finally, the neuropsychological benefit of "smart shunts" (e.g., a combination of sensors, fluid control mechanism, data communication, and implanted power source; Lutz, Venkataraman, & Browd, 2013) should be investigated, if such devices become viable and available.

At the other end of the age spectrum, there is extensive need for clinical investigation of the adaptive and cognitive functioning of adults with SBM. Because of technological innovation, individuals with SBM are now frequently living well into adulthood. This new research and treatment frontier involves the functioning of older adults with SBM and the interaction of their health needs with their cognitive abilities. To preserve or improve health outcomes in this population, there is an ongoing need for programs and approaches to support medical self-management and help avoid preventable conditions such as skin wounds (Parmanto, Pramana, Yu, Fairman, & Dicianno, 2015). The preservation of independence and medical self-management, however, is challenged by both cognitive issues associated with SBM and emerging evidence that suggests premature aging processes that may result in further functional declines (Treble-Barna et al., 2015). Integrated research using a model of older adult and geriatric care is needed to support functioning and calibrate care accordingly to this aging population.

This chapter has reviewed the core deficits and strengths across the lifespan for individuals with SBM and has highlighted implications for clinical practice with these individuals. Advances in medical care and procedures and changing technology necessitate continued monitoring of the functioning of these individuals, especially as they transition from childhood to adolescence and on to adulthood. Given the heterogeneous nature of SBM, it is important to continue to strive to understand the diverse individual and environmental factors that contribute to positive neuropsychological, social, and functional outcomes.

Notes

Completion of this chapter was supported in part by research grants from the National Institute of Child Health and Human Development (No. R01 HD048629), the March of Dimes Birth Defects Foundation (No. 12-FY13-271), the National Institute of Nursing Research and the Office of Behavioral and Social Sciences Research (No. R01 NR016235), and the Kiwanis Neuroscience Research Foundation. All correspondence should be sent to Grayson N. Holmbeck, PhD, Loyola University Chicago, Department of Psychology, 1032 W. Sheridan Road, Chicago, IL 60660 (gholmbe@luc.edu).

References

Adzick, N. S., Thom, E. A., Spong, C. Y., Brock, J. W. 3rd, Burrows, P. K., Johnson, M. P., … MOMS Investigators (2011). A randomized trial of prenatal versus postnatal repair of myelomeningocele. *New England Journal of Medicine, 364*(11), 993–1004.

Barnes, M., Dennis, M., & Hetherington, R. (2004). Reading and writing skills in young adults with spina bifida and hydrocephalus. *Journal of the International Neuropsychological Society, 10*(5), 655–663.

Barnes, M., Raghubar, K., English, L., Williams, J., Taylor, H., & Landry, S. (2014). Longitudinal mediators of achievement in mathematics and reading in typical and atypical development. *Journal of Experimental Child Psychology, 119*, 1–16.

Barnes, M. A., Smith-Chant, B., & Landry, S. (2005). Number processing in neurodevelopmental disorders: Spina bifida myelomeningocele. In: J. Campbell (Ed.) *Handbook of mathematical cognition* (pp. 299–314). New York: Psychology Press.

Beery, K. E., & Beery, N. A. (2004). *The Beery-Buktenica developmental test of visual motor integration: Administration, scoring, and teaching manual* (5th ed.) Minneapolis, MN: NCS Pearson.

Bellin, M. H, Dosa, N., Zabel, T. A., Aparicio, E., Dicianno, B. E., & Osteen, P. (2013). Self-management, satisfaction with family functioning, and the course of psychological symptoms in emerging adults with spina bifida. *Journal of Pediatric Psychology, 38*(1), 50–62. doi: 10.1093/jpepsy/jss095.

Bellin, M. H., Sawin, K. J., Roux, G., Buran, C. F., & Brei, T. J. (2007). The experience of adolescent women living with spina bifida part I: Self-concept and family relationships. *Rehabilitation Nursing, 32*(2), 57–67. https://doi.org/10.1002/j.2048-7940.2007.tb00153.x

Bellin, M. H., Zabel, T. A., Dicianno, B. E., Levey, E., Garver, K., Linroth, R., & Braun, P. (2010). Correlates of depressive and anxiety symptoms in young adults with spina bifida. *Journal of Pediatric Psychology, 35*(7), 778–789. doi: 10.1093/jpepsy/jsp094

Betz, C. L., Redcay, G., & Tan, S. (2003). Self-reported health care self-care needs of transition-aged youth: A pilot study. *Issues in Comprehensive Pediatric Nursing, 26*(3), 159–181.

Botto, L. D., & Mulinare, J. (1999). Maternal vitamin use, genetic variation of infant methylenetetrahydrofate reductase, and risk for spina bifida. *American Journal of Epidemiology, 150*(3), 323–324.

Boudos, R. M., & Mukherjee, S. (2008). Barriers to community participation: Teens and young adults with spina bifida. *Journal of Pediatric Rehabilitation Medicine, 1*(4), 303–310.

Bowman, R., McLone, D., Grant, J., Tomita, T., & Ito, J. (2001). Spina bifida outcome: A 25-year prospective. *Pediatric Neurosurgery, 134*, 114–120.

Brislin, D. (2008). Reaching for independence: Counseling implications for youth with spina bifida. *Journal of Counseling & Development, 86*(1), 34–38.

Brown, T., Ris, M., Beebe, D., Ammerman, R., Oppenheimer, S., Yeates, K., & Enrile, B. (2008). Factors of biological risk and reserve associated with executive behaviors in children and adolescents with spina bifida myelomeningocele. *Child Neuropsychology, 14*(2), 118–134.

Bundesen, C. (1990). A theory of visual attention. *Psychological Review, 97*, 523–547.

Buran, C. F., Sawin, K. J., Brei, T. J., & Fastenau, P. S. (2004). Adolescents with myelomeningocele: Activities, beliefs, expectations, and perceptions. *Developmental Medicine & Child Neurology, 46*(4), 244–252. doi: 10.1017/S0012162204000404

Buran, C. F., Brei, T. J., Sawin, K. J., Stevens, S., & Neufeld, J. (2006). Further development of the adolescent self management and independence scale: AMIS II. *Cerebrospinal Fluid Research, 3*(Suppl 1), S37.

Calarusso, R. P., & Hammill, D. D. (2003). *Motor-Free Visual Perception Test* (3rd ed.). Novata: CA: Academic Therapy Publications.

Carrow-Woolfolk, E. (1999). *Comprehensive assessment of spoken language*. Bloomington, MN: Pearson Clinical.

Centers for Disease Control and Prevention. (2011). Neural tube defect ascertainment project. Retrieved from http://www.nbdpn.org.

Coakley, R. M., Holmbeck, G. N., Friedman, D., Greenly, R. N., & Thill, A. W. (2002). A longitudinal study of pubertal timing, parent-child conflict, and cohesion in families of young adolescents with spina bifida. *Journal of Pediatric Psychology, 27*(5), 461–473. doi: 10.1093/jpepsy/27.5.461.

Committee on Hospital Care and Institute for Patient- and Family-Centered Care (2012). Patient- and family-centered care and the pediatrician's role. *Pediatrics, 129*(2), 394–404. doi:10.1542/peds.2011-3084.

Copp, A. J., Adzick, N. S., Chitty, L. S., Fletcher, J. M., Holmbeck, G. N., & Shaw, G. M. (2015). Spina bifida. *Nature Reviews Disease Primers, 1*, 1–18. doi: 10.1038/nrdp.2015.7

Coughlin, J., & Montague, M. (2011). The effects of cognitive strategy instruction on the mathematical problem solving of adolescents with spina bifida. *The Journal of Special Education, 45*(3), 171–183.

Cunningham, S., Thomas, P., & Warschausky, S. (2007). Gender differences in peer relations of children with neurodevelopmental conditions. *Rehabilitation Psychology, 52*(3), 331–337. doi: 10.1037/0090-5550.52.3.331

Danzer, E., Thomas, N. H., Thomas, A., Friedman, K. B., Gerdes, M., Koh, J., ... Johnson, M. P. (2016). Long-term neurofunctional outcome, executive functioning, and behavioral adaptive skills following fetal myelomeningocele surgery. *American Journal of Obstetrics and Gynecology, 214*(2), 269, e1–e8.

Dennis, M., & Barnes, M. A. (2010). The cognitive phenotype of spina bifida meningomyelocele. *Developmental Disabilities Research Reviews, 16*(1), 31–39.

Dennis, M., Fletcher, J. M., Rogers, T., Hetherington, R., & Francis, D. J. (2002). Object-based and action-based visual perception in children with spina bifida and hydrocephalus. *Journal of the International Neuropsychological Society, 8*(1), 95–106.

Dennis, M., Jewell, D., Drake, J., Misakyan, T., Spiegler, B., Hetherington, R., ... Barnes, M. (2007). Prospective, declarative, and nondeclarative memory in young adults with spina bifida. *Journal of the International Neuropsychological Society, 13*(2), 312–323.

Dennis M., Nelson, R., Jewell, D., & Fletcher, M. (2010). Prospective memory in adults with spina bifida. *Child's Nervous System, 26*(12), 1749–1755. doi:10.1007/s00381-010-1140

Devine, K. A., Holbein, C. E., Psihogios, A. M., Amaro, C. M., & Holmbeck, G. N. (2012). Individual adjustment, parental functioning, and perceived social support in Hispanic and non-Hispanic white mothers and fathers of children with spina bifida. *Journal of Pediatric Psychology, 37*(7), 769–778. doi:10.1093/jpepsy/jsr083

Devine, K. A., Holmbeck, G. N., Gayes, L., & Purnell, J. Q. (2012). Friendships of children and adolescents with spina bifida: Social adjustment, social performance, and social skills. *Journal of Pediatric Psychology, 37*(2), 220–231. doi: 10.1093/jpepsy/jsr075

Dicianno, B., Kurowski, B., Yang, J., Chancellor, M., Bejjani, G., Fairman, A., ... Sotirake, J. (2008). Rehabilitation and medical management of the adult with spina bifida. *American Journal of Physical Medicine & Rehabilitation, 87*(12), 1027–50.

Dockree, P. M., Bellgrove, M. A., O'Keeffe, F. M., Moloney, P., Aimola, L., Carton, S., & Robertson, I. H. (2006). Sustained attention in traumatic brain injury (TBI) and healthy controls: Enhanced sensitivity with dual task load. *Experimental Brain Research, 168*, 218–229.

Dunn, L. M. & Dunn, L. M. (1981). *Peabody Picture Vocabulary Test – Revised (PPVT)*. Circle Pines, MN: American Guidance Service.

Fletcher, J. M., Barnes, M., & Dennis, M. (2002). Language development in children with spina bifida. *Seminars in Pediatric Neurology, 9*(3), 201–208.

Fletcher, J. M., Bohan, T. P., Brandt, M. E., Kramer, L. A., Brookshire, B. L., Thorstad, K., … Baumgartner, J. E. (1996). Morphometric evaluation of the hydrocephalic brain: Relationships with cognitive development. *Children's Nervous System, 12*(4), 192–199.

Fletcher, J. M., Dennis, M., Northrup, H., & Francis, D. J. (2004). Spina bifida: Genes, brain, and development. *International Review of Research in Mental Retardation, 29*, 63–117.

Fletcher, J. M., Ostermaier, K. K., Cirino, P. T., & Dennis, M. (2008). Neurobehavioral outcomes in spina bifida: Processes versus outcomes. *Journal of Pediatric Rehabilitation Medicine, 1*(4), 311–324.

Friedman D., Holmbeck, G. N., Jandasek, B., Zukerman, J., & Abad, M. (2004). Parent functioning in families of preadolescents with spina bifida: Longitudinal implications for child adjustment. *Journal of Family Psychology, 18*(4), 609–619. doi: 10.1037/0893-3200.18.4.609

Ginsburg, H. P., & Baroody, A. J. (2003). *Test of early mathematics ability* (3rd ed.). Boston, MA: Houghton Mifflin Harcourt.

Golden, C. (2004). *Stroop Color and Word Test*. North Tonawanda, NY: Multi-Health Systems.

Hasan, K. M., Eluvathingal, T. J., Kramer, L. A., Ewing-Cobbs, L., Dennis, M., & Fletcher, J. M. (2008). White matter microstructural abnormalities in children with spina bifida myelomeningocele and hydrocephalus: A diffusion tensor tractography study of the association pathways. *Journal of Magnetic Resonance Imaging: JMRI, 27*(4), 700–709. https://doi.org/10.1002/jmri.21297

Harrison, P., & Oakland, T. (2015). *Adaptive behavior assessment system* (3rd ed.). Torrance, CA: WPS.

Heffelfinger, A. K., Koop, J. I., Fastenau, P. S., Brei, T. J., Conant, L., Katzenstein, J., … Sawin, K. J. (2008). The relationship of neuropsychological functioning to adaptaion outcome in adolescents with spina bifida. *Journal of the International Neuropsychological Society, 14*, 793–804.

Holbein, C. E., Lennon, J. M., Kolbuck, V. D., Zebracki, K., Roache, C., & Holmbeck, G. N. (2015). Observed differences in social behaviors exhibited in peer interactions between youth with spina bifida and their peers: Neuropsychological correlates. *Journal of Pediatric Psychology, 40*(3), 320–335. doi: 10.1093/jpepsy/jsu101

Holbein, C. E., Murray, C. B., Psihogios, A. M., Wasserman, R. M., Essner, B., & Holmbeck, G. N. (2013). A camp-based psychosocial intervention to promote independence and social function in individuals with spina bifida: Moderators of treatment effectiveness. *Journal of Pediatric Psychology 38*(4), 412–424. doi:10.1093/jpepsy/jst003

Holbein, C. E., Zebracki, K., Bechtel, C. F., Lennon Papadakis, J., Franks Bruno, E., & Holmbeck, G. N. (2016). Milestone achievement in emerging adulthood in spina bifida: A longitudinal investigation of parental expectations. *Developmental Medicine and Child Neurology*, epub ahead of print, doi: 10.1111/dmcn.13279.

Holbein, C. E., Zebracki, K., & Holmbeck. G. N. (2014). Development and validation of the peer interaction macro-coding system scales (PIMS): A new tool for observational measurement of social competence in youth with spina bifida. *Psychological Assessment, 26*(4), 1235–1246. doi: 10.1037/a0037062

Holmbeck, G. N., Coakley, R. M., Hommeyer, J., Shapera, W. E., & Westhoven, V. (2002). Observed and perceived dyadic and systemic functioning in families of preadolescents with spina bifida. *Journal of Pediatric Psychology, 27*(2), 177–189. doi: 10.1093/jpepsy/27.2.177

Holmbeck, G. N., DeLucia, C., Essner, B., Kelly, L., Zebracki, K., Friedman, D., & Jandasek, B. (2010). Trajectories of psychosocial adjustment in adolescents with spina bifida: A 6-year, four-wave longitudinal follow-up. *Journal of Consulting and Clinical Psychology, 78*(4), 511–525. doi: 10.1037/a0019599

Holmbeck, G. N., & Devine, K. A. (2010). Psychological and family functioning in spina bifida. *Developmental Disabilities, 16*(1), 40–46. doi: 10.1002/ddrr.90

Holmbeck, G. N., Greenley, R. N., Coakley, R. M., Greco, J., & Hagstrom, J. (2006). Family functioning in children and adolescents with spina bifida: An evidence-based review of research and interventions. *Journal of Developmental and Behavioral Pediatrics, 27*(3), 249–277.

Holmbeck, G. N., Westhoven, V. C., Phillips, W. S., Bowers, R., Gruse, C., Nikolopoulos, T., Tortura, C. M., & Davison, K. (2003). A multimethod, multi-informant, and multidimensional perspective on psychosocial adjustment in preadolescents with spina bifida. *Journal of Consulting and Clinical Psychology, 71*(4), 782–796. doi: 10.1037/0022-006X.71.4.782

Jandasek, B., Holmbeck, G. N., DeLucia, C., Zebracki, K., & Friedman, D. (2009). Trajectories of family processes across the adolescent transition in youth with spina bifida. *Journal of Family Psychology, 23*, 726–738. doi: 10.1037/a0016116

Juranek, J., Fletcher, J. M., Hasan, K. M., Breir, J. I., Cirino, P. T., Pazo-Alvarez, P., … Papanicolaou, A. C. (2008). Neocortical reorganization in spina bifida. *Neuroimage, 40*(4), 1516–1522. doi: 10.1016/j.neuroimage.2008.01.043.

Kabra, A. T., Feustal, P. J., & Kogan, B. A. (2015) Screening for depression and anxiety in childhood neurogenic bladder dysfunction. *Journal of Pediatric Urology*, *11*, 75.e1–75.e7. doi: 10.1016/j.jpurol.2014.11.017

Kaufman, A. S., & Kaufman, N. L. (2014). *Kaufman test of educational achievement* (3rd ed.). San Antonio, TX: Pearson.

Kaugars, A. S., Zebracki, K., Kichler, J. C., Fitzgerald, C. J., Greenley, R. N., Alemzadeh, R., & Holmbeck, G. N. (2011). Use of the Family Interaction Macro-coding System with families of adolescents: Psychometric properties among pediatric and healthy populations. *Journal of Pediatric Psychology*, *36*(5), 539–551. doi: 10.1093/jpepsy/jsq106

Kelly, N. C., Ammerman, R. T., Rausch, J. R., Ris, M. D., Yeates, K. O., Oppenheimer, S.G., & Enrile, B. G. (2012). Executive functioning and psychological adjustment in children and youth with spina bifida. *Child Neuropsychology*, *18*(5), 417–431. doi:10.1080/09297049.2011.613814

Kelly, L. M., Zebracki, K., Holmbeck, G. N., & Gershenson, L. (2008). Adolescent development and family functioning in youth with spina bifida. *Journal of Pediatric Rehabilitation Medicine*, *1*(4), 291–302.

Kennedy, S. E., Martin, S. G., Kelley, J. M., Walton, B., Vlcek, C. K., Hassanein, R. S., & Holmes, G. E. (1998). Identification of medical and nonmedical needs of adolescents and young adults with spina bifida and their families: A preliminary study. *Children's Health Care*, *27*(1), 47–61.

Kulesz, P. A., Treble-Barna, A., Williams, V. J., Juranek, J., Cirino, P. T., Dennis, M., & Fletcher, J. M. (2015). Attention in spina bifida myelomeningocele: Relations with brain volume and integrity. *NeuroImage Clinical*, *8*, 72–78.

Law, M., King, G., King, S., Kertoy, M., Hurley, P., Rosenbaum, P., … Hanna, S. (2006). Patterns of participation in recreational and leisure activities among children with complex physical disabilities. *Developmental Medicine & Child Neurology*, *48*, 337–342.

Leger, R. R. (2005). Severity of illness, functional status, and HRQOL in youth with spina bifida. *Rehabilitation Nursing*, *30*(5), 180–187.

Lennon, J. M., Klages, K. L., Amaro, C. M., Murray, C. B., & Holmbeck, G. N. (2015). Longitudinal study of neuropsychological functioning and internalizing symptoms in youth with spina bifida: Social competence as a mediator. *Journal of Pediatric Psychology*, *40*(3), 336–348. doi: 10.1093/jpepsy/jsu075.

Lennon, J. M., Murray, C. B., Bechtel, C. F., & Holmbeck, G. N. (2015). Resilience and disruption in observed family interactions in youth with and without spina bifida: An eight-year, five-wave longitudinal study. *Journal of Pediatric Psychology*, *40*(9), 943–955. doi: 10.1093/jpepsy/jsv033

Liptak, G. S., Kennedy, J. A., & Dosa, N. P. (2010). Youth with spina bifida and transitions: Health and social

participation in a nationally represented sample. *The Journal of Pediatrics*, *157*(4), 584–588. doi: 10.1016/j.jpeds.2010.04.004

Lomax-Bream, L. E., Barnes, M., Copeland, K., Taylor, H. B., & Landry, S. H. (2007). The impact of spina bifida on development across the first 3 years. *Developmental Neuropsychology*, *31*(1), 1–20. https://doi.org/10.1080/87565640709336884

Lutz, B. R., Venkataraman, P., & Browd, S. R. (2013). New and improved ways to treat hydrocephalus: Pursuit of a smart shunt. *Surgical Neurology International*, *4* (Suppl 1), S38–S50.

Mahmood, D., Dicianno, B., & Bellin, M. (2011). Self-management, preventable conditions and assessment of care among young adults with myelomeningocele. *Child: Care, Health and Development*, *37*(6), 861–865. https://doi.org/10.1111/j.1365-2214.2011.01299.x

Matson, M., Mahone, E. M., & Zabel, T. A. (2005). Serial neuropsychological assessment and evidence of shunt malfunction in spina bifida: A longitudinal case study. *Child Neuropsychology*, *11*(4), 315–332.

Mazzacco, M. M. M., & Thompson, R. E. (2005). Kindergarten predictors of math learning disability. *Learning Disabilities: Research and Practice*, *20*(3), 142–155.

Meyers, J. E., & Meyers, K. R. (1995). Rey complex figure test under four different administration procedures. *The Clinical Neuropsychologist*, *9*(1), 63–67.

Moos, R. H., & Moos, B. S. (2002). *Family environment scale manual: Development, applications, research*. Palo Alto, CA: Mind Garden, Inc.

Mukerhjee, S. (2007). Transition to adulthood in spina bifida: Changing roles and expectations. *The Scientific World Journal*, *7*, 1890–1895. doi: 10.1100/tsw.2007.179.

Murphy, N., & Elias, E. (2006). Sexuality of children and adolescents with developmental disabilities. *Journal of Pediatrics*, *118*(1), 398–403.

Murray, C. B., Holmbeck, G. N. Ros, A. M., Flores, D. M., Mir, S. A., & Varni, J. W. (2015). A longitudinal examination of health-related quality of life in children and adolescents with spina bifida. *Journal of Pediatric Psychology*, *40*(4), 419–430. doi: 10.1093/jpepsy/jsu098.

Murray, C. B., Lennon, J. M., Devine, K. A., Holmbeck, G. N., Klages, K., & Potthoff, L. M. (2014). The influence of social adjustment on normative and risky health behaviors in emerging adults with spina bifida. *Health Psychology*, *33*(10), 1153–1163. doi: 10.1037/hea0000050

Mukherjee, S. (2007). Transition to adulthood in spina bifida: Changing roles and expectations. *The Scientific World Journal*, *7*, 1890–1895. https://doi.org/10.1100/tsw.2007.179

Naglieri, J. A., & Das, J. P. (1997). *Cognitive assessment system*. Itasca, IL: Riverside Publishing Company.

Noetzel, M. J., & Blake, J. N. (1991). Prognosis for seizure control and remission in children with myelomeningocele. *Developmental Medicine and Child Neurology*, *33*(9), 803–810.

Oakeshott, P., Hunt, G. M., Poulton, A., & Reid, F. (2010). Expectation of life and unexpected death in open spina bifida: A 40-year complete, non-selective, longitudinal cohort study. *Developmental Medicine & Child Neurology*, *52*(8), 749–753. doi: 10.1111/j.1469-8749.2009.03543.x

Oddson, B. E., Clancy, C. A., & McGrath, P. J. (2006). The role of pain in reduced quality of life and depressive symptomology in children with spina bifida. *Clinical Journal of Pain*, *22*(9), 784–789. doi: 10.1097/01. ajp.0000210929.43192.5d

O'Mahar, K., Holmbeck, G. N., Jandasek, B., & Zukerman, J. (2010). A camp-based intervention targeting independence among individuals with spina bifida. *Journal of Pediatric Psychology*, *35*(8), 848–856. doi: 10.1093/jpepsy/jsp125

Ottolini, K., Harris, A. B., Amling, J. K., Kennelly, A. M., & Phillips, L. A. (2013). Wound care challenges in children and adults with spina bifida: An open-cohort study. *Journal of Pediatric Rehabilitation Medicine*, *6*(2013), 1–10.

Ou, X., Snow, J., Byerley, A., Hall, J., & Glasier, C. (2013). Decreased activation and increased lateralization in brain functioning for selective attention and response inhibition in adolescents with spina bifida. *Child Neuropsychology*, *19*(1), 23–36.

Parmanto, B., Pramana, G., Yu, D. X., Fairman, A. D., & Dicianno, B. E. (2015). Development of mHealth system for supporting self-management and remote consultation of skincare. *BMC Medical Informatics and Decision Making*, *15*, 114.

Pike, M., Swank, P., Taylor, H., Landry, S., & Barnes, M. A. (2013). Effect of preschool working memory, language, and narrative abilities on inferential comprehension at school-age in children with spina bifida myelomeningocele and typically developing children. *Journal of the International Neuropsychological Society*, *19*(4), 390–399. https://doi.org/10.1017/S1355617712001579

Pinquart, M., & Shen, Y. (2011). Behavior problems in children and adolescents with chronic physical illness: A meta-analysis. *Journal of Pediatric Psychology*, *36*(9), 1003–1216. doi:10.1093/jpepsy/jsr042

Ramsundhar, N., & Donald, K. (2014). An approach to the developmental and cognitive profile of the child with spina bifida. *South African Medical Journal*, *104*(3), 221. doi:10.7196/SAMJ.8048

Rose, B., & Holmbeck, G. (2007). Attention and executive functions in adolescents with spina bifida. *Journal of Pediatric Psychology*, *32*(8), 983–94.

Sankhla, S., & Khan, G. M. (2009). Reducing CSF shunt placement in patients with spinal myelomeningocele. *Journal of Pediatric Neurosciences*, *4*(1), 2–9.

Sawin, K. J., & Bellin, M. H. (2010). Quality of life in individuals with spina bifida: A research update. *Developmental Disabilities Research Reviews*, *16*, 47–59.

Sawin, K. J., Bellin, M. H., Roux, G., Buran, C. F., Brei, T. J., & Fastenau, P. S. (2003). The experience of parenting an adolescent with spina bifida. *Rehabilitation Nursing*, *28*(6), 173–185. doi: 10.1002/j.2048-7940.2003.tb02057.x

Sawin, K. J., Brei, T. J., Buran, C. F., & Fastenau, P. S. (2002). Factors associated with quality of life in adolescents with spina bifida. *Journal of Holistic Nursing*, *20*(3), 279–304. doi: 10.1177/089801010202000307

Schrank, F. A., Mather, N., & McGrew, K. S. (2014). *Woodcock-Johnson IV tests of achievement*. Boston, MA: Houghton Mifflin Harcourt.

Shandra, C. L., & Hogan, D. P. (2008). School-to-work program participation and the post-high school employment of young adults with disabilities. *Journal of Vocational Rehabilitation*, *29*(2), 117–130.

Shields, N., Taylor, N. F., & Dodd, K. J. (2008). Self-concept in children with spina bifida compared with typically developing children. *Developmental Medicine & Child Neurology*, *50*(10), 733–743. doi: 10.1111/j.1469-8749.2008.03096.x

Spellicy, C., Northrup, H., Fletcher, J., Cirino, P., Dennis, M., Morrison, A., … Yao, Y. (2012). Folate metabolism gene 5,10-methylenetetrahydrofolate reductase (MTHFR) is associated with ADHD in myelomeningocele patients (association of MTHFR to ADHD with myelomeningocele). *PLoS One*, *7*(12), E51330.

Spina Bifida Association. (2015). Learning & education. Retrieved December 09, 2016, from http://spinabifidaassociation.org/resource-directory/learning-education/

Stubberud, J., Langenbahn, D., Levine, B., Stanghelle, J., & Schanke, A. (2013). Goal management training of executive functions in patients with spina bifida: A randomized controlled trial. *Journal of the International Neuropsychological Society: JINS*, *19*(6), 672–85.

Stubberud, J., Langenbahn, D., Levine, B., Stanghelle, J., & Schanke, A. K. (2015). Emotional health and coping in spina bifida after goal management training: a randomized controlled trial. *Rehabilitation Psychology*, *60*(1), 1–16. doi: 10.1037/rep0000018.

Swartwout, M., Cirino, P., Hampson, A., Fletcher, J., Brandt, M., Dennis, M., & Rao, Stephen M. (2008). Sustained attention in children with two etiologies of early hydrocephalus.*Neuropsychology*, *22*(6), 765–775.

Swartwout, M., Garnaat, S., Myszka, K., Fletcher, J., & Dennis, M. (2010). Associations of ethnicity and SES with IQ and achievement in spina bifida meningomyelocele. *Journal of Pediatric Psychology*, *35*(9), 927–36.

Taylor, H., Landry, S., English, L. & Barnes, M. (2010). Infants and children with spina bifida. In Donders, J., & Hunter, S. J. (Eds.), *Principles and practice of lifespan developmental neuropsychology*. Cambridge, MA: Cambridge University Press.

Treble-Barna, A., Juranek, J., Stuebing, K. K., Cirino, P. T., Dennis, M., & Fletcher, J. M. (2015). Prospective and episodic memory in relation to hippocampal volume in adults with spina bifida myelomeningocele. *Neuropsychology, 29*(1), 92–101.

Trites, R. (1975). *Grooved Pegboard Test user instructions*. Lafayette, IN: Lafayette Instrument.

Tuminello, E., Holmbeck, G., & Olson, R. (2012). Executive functions in adolescents with spina bifida: Relations with autonomy development and parental intrusiveness. *Child Neuropsychology, 18*(2), 105–124.

Vachha, B., & Adams, R. C. (2005). Memory and selective learning in children with spina bifida-myelomeningocele and shunted hydrocephalus: A preliminary study. *Cerebrospinal Fluid Research, 2*, 10. https://doi.org/10.1186/1743–8454–2–10

Vachha, B., & Adams, R. (2009). Implications of family environment and language development: comparing typically developing children to those with spina bifida. *Child: Care, Health and Development, 35*(5), 709–716. https://doi.org/10.1111/j.1365–2214.2009.00966.x

Vinck, A, Mullaart, R., Rotteveel, J., & Maassen, B. (2009). Neuropsychological assessment of attention in children with spina bifida. *Fluids and Barriers of the CNS, 6*(1), 6.

Volcik, K. A., Blanton, S. H., Tyerman, G. H., Jong, S. T., Rott, E. J., Page, T. Z., ... Northrup, H. (2000). Methylenetetrahydrofolate reductase and spina bifida: Evaluation of level of defect and maternal genotypic risk in Hispanics. *American Journal of Medical Genetics, 95*(1), 21–27.

Ware, A., Kulesz, P., Williams, V., Juranek, J., Cirino, P., & Fletcher, J. (2016). Gray matter integrity within regions of the dorsolateral prefrontal cortical-subcortical network predicts executive function and fine motor dexterity in spina bifida. *Neuropsychology*, 2016.

Warf, B. C., & Campbell, J. W. (2008). Combined endoscopic third ventriculostomy and choroid plexus cauterization as primary treatment of hydrocephalus for infants with myelomeningocele: Long-term results of a prospective intent-to-treat study in 115 East African infants. *Journal of Neurosurgery: Pediatrics, 2*(5), 310–316.

Warf, B., Ondoma, S., Kulkami, A., Donnelly, R., Ampiere, M., Akona, J., ... Nsubuga, B. K. (2009). Neurocognitive outcome and ventricular volume in children with myelomeningocele treated for hydrocephalus in Uganda. *Journal of Neurosurgery: Pediatrics, 4*(6), 564–570.

Wasserman, R. M., Stoner, A. M., Stern, A. & Holmbeck, G. N. (2016). ADHD and attention problems in children with and without spina bifida. *Topics in Spinal Cord Injury Rehabilitation, 22*(4): 253–259. doi: 10.1310/sci2204-253

Wechsler, D. (2014). *Wechsler Intelligence Scale for Children* (5th ed.). Bloomington, MN: Pearson Clinical.

Williams, V. J., Juranek, J., Stuebing, K., Cirino, P. T., Dennis, M., & Fletcher, J. M. (2013). Examination of frontal and parietal tectocortical attention pathways in spina bifida meningomyelocele using probabilistic diffusion tractography. *Brain Connectivity, 3*(5), 512–522.

Wilson, B. A., Cockburn, J., & Baddeley, A. D. (2003). *The Rivermead Behavioural Memory Test* (2nd ed.). London: Pearson Assessment.

Wilson, B. A., Emslie, H., Foley, J., Shiel, A., Watson, P., Hawkins, K., ... Evans, J. J. (2005). *The Cambridge Prospective Memory Test (CAMPROMPT)*. London: Harcourt Assessment.

Yeates, K. O., Fletcher, J. M., & Dennis, M. (2008). Spina bifida and hydrocephalus. In J. E. Morgan & J. H. Ricker (Eds.), *Textbook of clinical neuropsychology* (pp. 128–148). New York, NY: Psychology Press.

Zabel, T. A., Jacobson, L. A., Tarazi, R., & Mahone, E. M. (2012). *The Kennedy Krieger independence scale–Spina bifida version (KKIS-SB)*. Baltimore, MD: The Kennedy Krieger Institute.

Zabel, T. A., Jacobson, L., Zachik, C., Levey, E., Kinsman, S., & Mahone, E. (2011). Parent and self-ratings of executive functions in adolescents and young adults with spina bifida. *The Clinical Neuropsychologist, 25*(6), 926–941.

Zebracki, K., Zaccariello, M., Zelko, F., Holmbeck, G. (2010). Adolescence and emerging adulthood in individuals with spina bifida: a developmental neuropsychological perspective. In Donders, J., & Hunter, S. J. (Eds.), *Principles and practice of lifespan developmental neuropsychology*. Cambridge, MA: Cambridge University Press.

Zukerman, J. M., Devine, K. A., & Holmbeck, G. N. (2011). Adolescent predictors of emerging adulthood milestones in youth with spina bifida. *Journal of Pediatric Psychology, 36*(3), 265–276. doi: 10.1093/jpepsy/jsq075

Chapter 3

Autism Spectrum Disorder

Julie M. Wolf, Marianne Barton, and Roger Jou

Introduction

Autism spectrum disorder (ASD) is a neurodevelopmental disorder characterized by impairments in social communication and restricted or repetitive patterns of interest or behavior. The disorder is present from early in development and is typically identifiable in the second year of life. Developmental delays, particularly with regard to language and social milestones, are common, as is regression or loss of previously acquired skills, typically between 12 and 24 months of age (e.g., a toddler may begin to use words, but then lose those words and no longer continue to progress in language development). ASD is pervasive and lifelong; although most individuals with ASD do continue to learn and make developmental gains throughout their lives, significant impairments most often persist into and throughout adulthood, with only a minority of adults with ASD living and working independently and most requiring supports throughout their lives.

The *Diagnostic and Statistical Manual of Mental Disorders*, 5th ed. (DSM-5; American Psychiatric Association, 2013) identifies three areas of social communication impairment, all of which must be present in an individual to meet diagnostic criteria. Specifically, the individual must present with (a) deficits in social reciprocity, which may include difficulties with reciprocal conversation, decreased sharing of enjoyment or interests with others, or impairments in social initiation or responsiveness; (b) impairments in nonverbal communication, which may include reduced or poorly integrated use of nonverbal forms of communication such as eye contact, gestures, facial expressions, and body language; and (c) deficits in "developing, maintaining, and understanding relationships," which may include a failure to develop appropriate peer relationships or lack of interest in peers, failure to appropriately adjust behavior to the social context, or difficulties sharing in imaginative play with others.

In the domain of restricted and repetitive patterns of behavior, interests or activities, the DSM-5 outlines four specific areas, at least two of which must be present in an individual to meet diagnostic criteria. These include (a) repetitive motor movements (e.g., motor stereotypies such as hand flapping), repetitive speech (e.g., echolalia or idiosyncratic language), or repetitive use of objects (e.g., lining up toys, repetitive banging, spinning, dropping, or flipping objects); (b) inflexible adherence to routines and need for sameness (e.g., distress at small changes in routine or environment, difficulty with transitions), or ritualized patterns of behavior (e.g., rigid thinking patterns, needing to do things in a prescribed way); (c) restricted areas of interest or intense fixations, such as a strong attachment to an unusual object or intense interest in an unusual topic; and (d) sensory abnormalities, including hyper- or hyporeactivity to sensory input (e.g., indifference to pain, hypersensitivity to sounds or light) or sensory-seeking behaviors (e.g., smelling, rubbing, or visually inspecting objects).

A number of other features commonly associated with ASD are not part of the diagnostic criteria. These include intellectual impairment, language impairment (many children with ASD have language delays or may not develop spoken language at all), impairment in adaptive functioning, motor impairment, disruptive behavior, and self-injurious behavior (such as head banging). Comorbid diagnoses of epilepsy, attention-deficit/hyperactivity disorder, anxiety disorder, or mood disorder are also common. The diagnostic criteria for ASD contain specifiers to indicate whether the individual presents with co-occurring intellectual impairment, language impairment, or catatonia, or whether the presentation is associated with another known disorder, such as medical or genetic condition (e.g., Rett's syndrome, fragile X syndrome) or neurodevelopmental factor (e.g., fetal alcohol syndrome, very low birth weight). Additionally, severity levels can be indicated for each of the two broad domains (social communication, and restricted/repetitive patterns of behavior) to indicate the degree of support that the individual requires in that domain.

Of note, some individuals who met diagnostic criteria under DSM-IV-TR (DSM 4th ed., Text Revision; American Psychiatric Association, 2000) may no longer meet the DSM-5 criteria outlined previously, perhaps because they exhibit some but not all of the social communication deficits, or because they have social communication impairments but do not demonstrate restricted areas of interest or repetitive behaviors. Many of these individuals held a diagnosis of pervasive developmental disorder, not otherwise specified under DSM-IV-TR. The DSM-5 criteria include a clause that those with a well-established DSM-IV-TR autism spectrum diagnosis may still receive a diagnosis of ASD under DSM-5. Additionally, the DSM-5 introduced a new diagnosis of social (pragmatic) communication disorder to address those individuals who display deficits in social communication but lack restricted or repetitive interests and behaviors.

Clinical Manifestation

Epidemiology and Pathophysiology

Estimates of the prevalence of autism have changed substantially since its original description in 1943 (Centers for Disease Control and Prevention [CDC], 2018). In the 1980s, estimates of 1 per 1,000 were commonly cited. Before that, prevalence of 0.5 per 1,000 or less were estimated. More recently, the CDC has been providing statistics on the condition through its Autism and Developmental Disabilities Monitoring Network. In the year 2000, estimates were 1 in 150. In 2004, the estimates changed to 1 in 125, which changed again to 1 in 88 in 2008, and then again to 1 in 68 in 2010. The current estimate is 1 in 59. Although the estimated prevalence has been increasing over time, creating concern for an "autism epidemic," the reasons for this increase remain a topic of debate and ongoing research. It is argued that the increasing changes reflect a combination of factors, including, without limitation, improved public awareness and ability to diagnose the condition and changes in diagnostic criteria (Lundström, Reichenberg, Anckarsäter, Lichtenstein, & Gillberg., 2015). Autism is reported in all racial, ethnic, and socioeconomic groups; however, group differences are

less clear with the exception of gender. Autism is 4 times more common in males, with an estimated prevalence of 1 in 37. In contrast, estimated prevalence in girls is 1 in 151. The reasons for this prominent gender difference are unclear, and this difference remains an active area of research. One theory asserts a "female protective model" with clear genetic underpinnings (Jacquemont et al., 2014).

The pathophysiology of ASD also remains elusive despite decades of research (Hill & Frith, 2003). There has been a large evolution in understanding the underlying causes and pathophysiology of autism since its original description in the 1940s. In the 1960s, the cause was erroneously believed to be related to parenting. Since the 1970s, however, biology has taken over and appropriately remains the foundation for understanding the causes and pathophysiology of autism. In recent decades of research, many potential causes have been hypothesized, including, without limitation, genetic abnormalities, complications during pregnancy or birth, and exposure to toxins or infection during prenatal, perinatal, and postnatal periods.

Above all, the etiology of autism is known to be highly genetic although environmental factors are also believed to contribute. Family and twin studies demonstrate that up to 90% of variance can be attributed to genetics. Although autism may be the neuropsychiatric disorder most affected by genetic factors, the specifics of these factors remains an area of intense inquiry (Levy, Mandell, & Schultz, 2009). All affected individuals do not have in common "autism genes" that can account for having the condition. Similarly, there have been no definitive aberrant physiological processes that unite all affected individuals. Many body systems have been hypothesized (mainly neurological, gastrointestinal, and immunologic) as potentially abnormal and having a role in the causes and pathophysiology of autism (Hamilton, 2013).

Prevention

Prevention requires sufficient understanding of causes and pathophysiology, which are currently limited. Therefore, a prescription cannot be specifically written for preventing autism. Nevertheless, there are many ideas in the autism community on the topic of prevention (e.g., avoiding certain medication, reducing risk of infections). Because none has demonstrated robust scientific proof either with regard to etiology or in preventing autism, they will not be discussed here. However, it is noteworthy that some of these ideas can actually be harmful and dangerous; therefore, extreme care must be taken before suggesting any preventative measure. Perhaps the most notorious example is the erroneous connection between childhood vaccines and autism. Many studies have repeatedly demonstrated that vaccines do not place children at risk for autism and the original study that suggested the connection was retracted due to lack of legitimacy (Jain et al., 2015).

Presentation

Social disability is the sine qua non of autism; therefore, challenges related to social interaction and communication are common concerns on presentation. Repetitive behaviors and restricted interest play an important role in diagnosis and are also commonly observed on initial presentation. However, many of the signs and symptoms are subtler, encompass a large range of behaviors, and are challenging to understand and operationalize (Lai, Lombardo, Chakrabarti, & Baron-Cohen, 2013). As discussed later in this section, this is part of the reason why professional consultation with an autism specialist is required to make a diagnosis.

It is helpful to think of the diagnostic criteria discussed earlier in this chapter when understanding the clinical manifestation of autism. Abnormalities in social interaction can be assessed through observation of behaviors, including eye contact, attention, directed facial expressions, and sharing (Lord et al., 2000). Abnormalities in communication can be assessed by observing behaviors including vocalization, point, and gestures (Lord et al., 2000). Repetitive behaviors and restricted interests can be assessed by observing behaviors including hand/finger mannerisms, sensory interests, intonation of vocalizations, and pattern of interests (Lord et al., 2000). In addition to core symptoms, it is important to understand other comorbidities that may exist (Lord, Rutter, & Le Couteur, 1994). It is not uncommon for children to exhibit overactivity, agitation, anxiety, tantrums, aggression, or other negative or disruptive behaviors. In fact, some of these comorbid symptoms become the focus of treatment due to their severity and seriousness, which can raise major safety concerns. Medical comorbidities such as seizure disorder, gastrointestinal difficulties, and sleep dysfunction are also common.

The CDC (2015) has identified a number of red flags to guide family members and professionals about autism. It is important to understand that the presence of any of the following aspects does not necessarily constitute a diagnosis of autism:

(1) Unresponsive to calling his or her name before 12 months of age;
(2) does not point at things to show his or her interest by 14 months;
(3) cannot engage in pretend play by 18 months;
(4) maintains poor eye contact and prefers to be alone;
(5) displays poor ability to understand the feelings of self and others;
(6) has impaired or delayed language development;
(7) repeatedly says things he or she hears from the environment;
(8) has abnormally negative reactions to small changes in the environment;
(9) exhibits repetitive behaviors (hand flapping, body rocking, or spinning);
(10) responds abnormally to certain sensations (feel, smell, or taste).

The presence of any of these concerns may warrant consultation with a licensed professional, including specially trained neuropsychologists, because the diagnosis of autism is complex and requires formal clinical assessment to be definitively established. In fact, the gold standards of diagnosis include face-to-face assessments (Lord et al., 2000) and caregiver interviews (Lord et al., 1994) that require specialized training and certification for appropriate clinical and research use (Lord et al., 2012; Rutter, Le Couteur, & Lord, 2003).

Parents commonly bring to the attention of their child's pediatrician concerns about such developmental delays as delayed speech or impaired communication. Another common scenario involves professionals working in daycare, preschool, or elementary school who express behavioral concerns to parents. The child is then referred for an evaluation for early intervention and it is determined whether treatment is needed. There are myriad treatment options, which commonly include a combination of behavioral therapy using principles of applied behavior analysis, occupational therapy, speech therapy, physical therapy, and/or social skills intervention (Volkmar et al., 2014). Medical and psychiatric care is also common, depending on comorbidities. Given the extreme diversity within the autism spectrum, every individual living with autism is unique; therefore, interventions are multidisciplinary and tailored to the individual's specific needs. Similarly, outcomes are also highly diverse and difficult to predict. However, there is a consensus that intensive early intervention invariably benefits all children living with autism. Early intervention models have been developed by researchers and demonstrated to be effective, through ongoing empirical validation. One well-known example is the Early Start Denver Model (Dawson et al., 2010).

What underlies the clinical manifestations of ASD is an area of active research. As mentioned previously, many body systems have been hypothesized to be involved. However, the most compelling arguments are centered around neurodevelopment, which will be briefly reviewed here (Jou et al., 2011). Taken together, the larger body of behavioral, neuropathological, and neuroimaging research literature provide convergent support for abnormal brain connectivity in autism, with possible adverse effects on those temporal lobe structures critical for normal social perception and cognition. Early hints to the neurobiology of ASDs were apparent in Leo Kanner's seminal report, when he noted that some affected children had enlarged heads (Kanner, 1943). Although a tendency toward megacephaly was confirmed in earlier studies (Walker, 1977), this observation only gained considerable attention in the 1990s when it was confirmed by neuroimaging studies, becoming the most consistent structural magnetic resonance imaging (MRI) finding in autism (Piven et al., 1995). Later research suggested that megacephaly was driven more by an increase in white matter rather than gray matter (Courchesne et al., 2001). However, it also appeared that white matter was not uniformly enlarged. More recent volumetric studies in autism found that temporal lobe enlargement is greater than other lobes, with temporal lobe white matter enlarged by about 10% (Schultz et al., 2005). Another consistently reported structural abnormality is a smaller corpus callosum, affecting the typical presence of long-range fiber tracts (Frazier & Hardan, 2009). Investigators have suggested that the white matter abnormality seen in autism consists of an overabundance of short-range fibers (Courchesne & Pierce, 2005; Herbert et al., 2004). These studies are consistent with neuropathological evidence of decreased neuronal cell size in autism (Casanova, Buxhoeveden, Switala, & Roy, 2002), suggesting

a paucity of long-range fibers in areas typically requiring their presence. More specifically, the structural data suggest a paucity of long-range fibers and relative overabundance of short-range fibers, possibly affecting the temporal lobes more so than other lobes of the brain. Other than implicating the temporal lobe, which contains identified components of the "social brain," the structural findings alone do little to explain the social impairment unique to autism. Many behavioral data suggest that individuals with autism have deficits in face perception (Klin et al., 1999), which has been extensively studied using functional MRI (fMRI). In fact, perhaps the best replicated fMRI finding in ASD is hypoactivation of the fusiform face area during face perception tasks (Schultz et al., 2000), which has been replicated by numerous independent laboratories (Schultz, 2005). Other studies have reported hypoactivation of the amygdala (Baron-Cohen et al., 1999) and superior temporal sulcus in autism (Castelli, Frith, Happé, & Frith, 2002). fMRI has also been used to study the presence of abnormal connectivity in autism, which has been implied by structural MRI findings. Multiple studies have reported reduced synchronization and functional connectivity in autism (Castelli et al., 2002; Just, Cherkassky, Keller, & Minshew, 2004). More importantly, there appears to be reduced effective connectivity between the fusiform face area and amygdala in autism (Schultz, Hunyadi, Connors, & Pasley, 2005). Therefore, even without more direct evidence of impaired connectivity, convergent evidence from behavioral, neuropathological, structural MRI, and fMRI findings appear to suggest aberrant brain connectivity within temporal and possibly other cerebral lobes (Jou et al., 2011; Jou, 2012).

Neuropsychological Assessment

ASD is diagnosed through a careful assessment of behavioral presentation, typically through direct observation of the child in a social context (e.g., school setting, one-on-one social interaction with the examiner) as well as through parent or caregiver report of the child's functioning. The gold standard instruments in ASD diagnosis are the Autism Diagnostic Observation Schedule, 2nd Edition (Lord et al., 2012) and the Autism Diagnostic Interview, Revised (Lord et al., 1994). These semistructured measures are designed to be used in conjunction with one another to obtain a standardized observation of the child and caregiver report. Although these are considered the gold standards in autism evaluation, a number of alternative measures are available, including the Diagnostic Interview of Social and Communication Disorders (Wing, Leekam, Libby, Gould, & Larcombe, 2002), the Developmental, Dimensional, and Diagnostic Interview (Skuse et al., 2004), the Childhood Autism Rating Scale (Schopler, Reichler, & Renner, 2002), and the Autism Observational Scale for Infants (Bryson, Zwaigenbaum, McDermott, Rombough, & Brian, 2008). A number of screening questionnaires are also available to help identify children who may be at risk for ASD and who require further evaluation.

Neuropsychological assessment is not critical to the identification or diagnosis of ASD; however, many individuals with ASD have impairments in various domains of neuropsychological functioning. In these cases, a comprehensive neuropsychological assessment battery can be informative in identifying areas of strength and weakness and in informing treatment planning. The following section reviews some of the areas of neuropsychological functioning that can be affected in individuals with ASD, and discusses how assessing these domains may inform treatment planning.

Cognition

Significant discrepancies between verbal and nonverbal domains of cognitive functioning are common in individuals with ASD and appear to occur with greater frequency than in the general population (Nowell, Schanding, Kanne, & Goin-Kochel, 2015). However, no specific direction of discrepancy is associated with ASD; rather, some individuals show relatively stronger verbal abilities and others show relatively stronger nonverbal/perceptual abilities. Deficits in speed of information processing are also common in individuals with ASD, although it should be noted that processing-speed tasks are often confounded with motor demands, and there is some evidence that processing-speed abilities are relatively spared when motor demands are reduced (Kenworthy, Yerys, Weinblatt, Abrams, & Wallace, 2013). Individuals with ASD also commonly have weaknesses in working memory, particularly when working memory tasks are complex, have a high working memory load, or place high demands on other aspects of executive functioning such as cognitive flexibility and planning (Kercood, Grskovic, Banda, & Begeske, 2014; Keehn, Müller, & Townsend, 2013).

Cognitive assessment plays an important role in intervention planning because knowledge of a child's cognitive strengths and weaknesses can inform academic approaches, accommodations, and supports. For example, students with stronger nonverbal/perceptual than verbal abilities may benefit from visually based instruction or visual supports to aid in comprehension. Students with the opposite profile, in turn, may do better with verbally presented material. Students with processing-speed deficits may benefit from academic accommodations such as extended time on exams or assignments, whereas students with working memory challenges may benefit from accommodations to aid in sustaining attention, as described the Language section that follows.

Language

Social communication impairments are a core part of the diagnostic criteria for ASD, and so it is not surprising that individuals with ASD have demonstrated impairments in the pragmatic aspects of language (Simmons, Paul, & Volkmar, 2014). Additionally, some individuals demonstrate impairments in core language functioning. Some highly verbal children may show a pattern in which their expressive language functioning exceeds their receptive functioning, although on the whole, children with ASD appear to have comparable challenges with both the receptive and expressive aspects of language relative to typically developing peers (Kwok, Brown, Smyth, & Cardy, 2015).

A comprehensive speech-language evaluation as part of broader neuropsychological assessment can inform the need for speech-language therapy, as well as identify social communication goals to target within social skills intervention. Additionally, understanding a child's receptive language skills relative to his or her expressive language skills is important in determining how to appropriately "pitch" information to the child's level of understanding. Specifically, when a child's expressive language ability exceeds his or her receptive language ability, adults may erroneously assume that the child's comprehension matches his or her expression and present language with a degree of complexity that in fact exceeds the child's receptive abilities. This behavior may contribute to learning challenges if a child does not comprehend academic material that is pitched too high, or to behavioral escalation if a child does not understand requests or experiences frustration or overwhelm as a result of comprehension difficulties.

Executive Functioning

A number of the diagnostic features of ASD suggest executive functioning impairments, including repetitive behaviors, need for sameness, and difficulty with transitions. Given that, executive functioning in ASD has been widely researched, and deficits have been found in a variety of domains, including planning, cognitive flexibility, inhibition, self-monitoring, and working memory, as noted in the Cognition section. It is unclear, however, the extent to which these impairments are characteristic of ASD per se versus other comorbid deficits (e.g., learning problems, attentional problems) that are commonly associated with ASD (Hill, 2004). Additionally, there have been inconsistencies in the literature, with many of these executive functions found to be impaired in some studies and preserved in others. This may be due to the cognitive functioning of the study samples, with some deficits being secondary to cognitive impairments rather than characteristic of ASD per se (Hill, 2004; Robinson, Goddard, Dritschel, Wisley, & Howlin, 2009). Robinson and colleagues (2009) addressed this concern by investigating executive functioning abilities in children with ASD with average cognitive abilities relative to an age- and IQ-matched typically developing control group. They found that individuals with ASD had a greater tendency toward perseveration and greater difficulties with planning and inhibition (perhaps related to poor self-monitoring), but spared generativity and mental flexibility. There is also evidence that some executive functioning deficits in ASD may remediate or decrease in severity by adulthood (Happé, Booth, Charlton, & Hughes, 2006).

Assessing executive functioning skills can provide data on the types of interventions from which a child may benefit or particular skills that could be targets for intervention; for example, programs are available to address specific areas of deficits (e.g., "Unstuck and On Target" to address difficulties with cognitive flexibility; Cannon, Kenworthy, Alexander, Werner, & Anthony, 2011). Additionally, children with executive functioning impairments may benefit from a variety of organizational supports to help them manage adaptive and academic demands, such as daily schedules, task lists, visual timers, and sequence strips to guide them through tasks. With the widespread use of such technologies as smartphones and tablets, many productivity apps have been developed to aid in these skills, including those designed specifically for the ASD population.

Attention

As reviewed by Keehn et al. (2013), individuals with ASD appear to have deficits across various aspects of attention. With regard to general alertness, there is evidence of both hypo- and hyperarousal, which may reflect different subgroups of individuals. Individuals with ASD may have difficulty regulating their degree of alertness depending on task demands, and in particular their attentional systems may be insensitive to novel information. Additionally, individuals with ASD may exhibit deficits in orienting visual attention, with less frequent or delayed shifting of attention, especially to social information such as gaze shift or other attention-directing cues. Finally, they may show an impaired ability to disengage attention, which may be related to perseverative behaviors.

If a neuropsychological assessment reveals attentional deficits in an individual with ASD, the finding may indicate the need for academic accommodations to aid in the individual's ability to sustain attention to tasks throughout the day. Such strategies may include breaking complex tasks down into smaller component parts, setting interim deadlines, alternating challenging tasks with easier or more enjoyable tasks, assigning preferential seating near a teacher and/or away from potentially distracting stimuli, and providing a quiet environment for test taking.

Memory

There is evidence for impairments in all aspects of memory in individuals with ASD; however, as with working memory, difficulties with memory tasks are most pronounced with high cognitive load or increased stimulus complexity (Southwick et al., 2011). Williams, Goldstein, and Minshew (2006) found that children with ASD had deficits in "memory for complex visual and verbal information and spatial working memory with relatively intact associative learning ability, verbal working memory, and recognition memory." The authors compared this finding in children with ASD to their own prior work in adults with ASD, and found generally parallel results, except that adults with ASD were not impaired in complex verbal memory tasks (sentence and story memory). This finding may reflect increased exposure through learning and/or developmental maturation in this ability with age. Recall ability is also largely spared in ASD, which suggests that it is the organization and encoding of information that is impaired rather than storage and retrieval (Southwick et al., 2011). Thus, the increased difficulty among individuals with ASD with memory tasks associated with increased cognitive load may reflect poor organizational or other strategies to manage and efficiently encode the increased complexity.

Neuropsychological assessment of memory functioning may inform instructional strategies, and the nature of memory impairment may suggest different strategies. For example, children with deficits in recall may benefit from accommodations to provide cueing of learned information. Given that individuals with ASD seem to have most difficulty with the organization and encoding of complex information, they may benefit from instructional strategies to simplify the presentation of information and to break down complex information into component parts, to facilitate learning and encoding. A reduced course load or homework load may also be beneficial.

Sensorimotor Functioning

Impairments in motor functioning have long been noted as an associated feature in ASD, dating back to Asperger's (1944) description of autism. Current research suggests that children with ASD have deficits in both sensory and motor functioning. With regard to motor functioning, motor learning appears to be intact, whereas individuals with ASD have difficulties with fine motor skills and higher level aspects of motor coordination, sequencing, and planning (Hannant, Cassidy, Tavassoli, & Mann, 2016; Gowen & Hamilton, 2013). Likewise, in the sensory domain, the processing of low-level sensory input appears intact, whereas higher-order sensory processing is impaired (Gowen & Hamilton, 2013). Gowen and Hamilton suggest that these higher-order difficulties may be attributable to increased sensorimotor "noise" experienced by individuals with ASD which must be filtered through or to impairments in the integration of sensorimotor information due to "weak central coherence" or a detail-oriented processing style, or both.

Assessing sensorimotor functioning may provide information supporting a need for occupational or physical therapy to remediate areas of deficit. Individuals with fine motor impairments may benefit

from academic accommodations particularly with regard to graphomotor skills. Such accommodations may include use of technology (keyboard, smart pen) for note taking and writing assignments, extended time for writing intensive assignments or exams, advanced provision of lecture outlines to reduce note-taking demands, or the assistance of a note-taking "buddy" or peer.

Intervention

Intervention Approaches for Children with ASD

Intervention for children with ASD has long focused on applied behavior analysis (ABA) and this is the method with the most consistent research support (see Reichow, 2012; Schriebman et al., 2015, for review). ABA is most often viewed as consisting primarily of discrete trial instruction, meaning that the interventionist offers the child a discrete instruction, prompts the child's response if necessary, and provides immediate reinforcement for the correct response. This process is repeated in a series of massed trials, until the skill is mastered. Numerous studies have documented the effectiveness of ABA at improving cognitive skills, language, and adaptive behaviors and have provided support that it is most effective when initiated early, when provided at high levels of intensity (e.g., 25–40 hours weekly), over an extended period of time, and when it includes a specific focus on the generalization of skills to novel environments (Reichow, 2012; Rogers & Vismara, 2008). Despite its effectiveness researchers noted early concerns with ABA, including difficulty engaging children in treatment, some lack of spontaneity in their language, and difficulties generalizing skills to novel settings, all of which prompted efforts to expand on the earliest models. The evolution of behavioral strategies over time was further supported by several developments in the field of ASD. Studies of infant siblings of children with ASD and increased efforts to identify children at risk as early as possible led to a focus on early prerequisites to social and communicative skills. Intervention efforts began to include the integration of behavioral principles with developmental science and its growing literature about how young children learn. First, there was increased recognition that early prelinguistic communication, including gesture, eye gaze, shared affect, and joint attention, is critical to language development, and those skills must be a central focus of early intervention efforts. Second, there was greater appreciation of the fact that young children actively explore their environment and dynamic, child-initiated engagement supports learning. Finally, there was increased attention to the fact that children learn best in the context of reciprocal, affective interactions. (Schriebman et al., 2015; Dawson & Bernier, 2013). Recent theories about the development of ASD suggest that a variety of neurologically based processes including attention and motor development, may interact to preclude typical relationship and learning experiences for infants at risk, and their atypical trajectory may result in the establishment of behavioral patterns characteristic of ASD. Given that model, intervention efforts are less likely to be viewed as efforts to teach skills; instead, intervention is seen as an effort to interrupt negative trajectories and reestablish more typical developmental pathways and experiences.

Second-generation behavioral intervention models focus explicitly on the integration of established behavioral tools and more developmentally sensitive, naturalistic strategies, including the provision of services in natural settings, reliance on naturally occurring contingencies, utilization of child interests and initiative, and a focus on developmentally appropriate and prerequisite skills (Schriebman et al., 2015). Several authors have proposed labeling these models as naturalistic developmental behavioral interventions (Schriebman et al., 2015; Dawson & Bernier, 2013) and note that they have been associated with more rapid skill acquisition in young children, reduced dependence on prompts, and improved generalization of skills. These naturalistic developmental behavioral interventions may be especially useful with young children who benefit from flexible approaches and who have typically not developed entrenched negative behaviors, but they have been increasingly integrated with more traditional ABA approaches for children at all ages. They have also received consistent empirical support in a series of intervention studies.

One of the earliest adaptations of ABA was pivotal response therapy (PRT). PRT adapted traditional behavioral methods to focus on teaching specific "pivotal" behaviors, such as motivation, social initiation and self-regulation that affected multiple areas of functioning. PRT also incorporated natural reinforcers, emphasized child choice and initiation, and

provided instruction in the context of naturally occurring interactions. PRT has a significant base of empirical support and has demonstrated effectiveness in increasing targeted skills such as motivation and in increasing nontargeted skills such as pretend play and imitation (Ingersoll & Schriebman, 2006). In a recent study that used a randomized control trial (RCT) to compare PRT with a more structured ABA approach, the authors report that PRT was significantly more effective in improving both targeted and nontargeted skills after just three months of intervention (Mohammadzaheri, Koegel, Rezaee, & Rafiee, 2014).

Other early adaptations of behavioral treatment focused on early social skills, such as joint attention. Kasari, Paparella, Freeman, and Jahromi (2008) added a specific intervention designed to increase joint attention skills to an existing naturalistic behavioral model for preschool children. In an RCT, they demonstrated significant gains in joint attention and play skills and more rapid language acquisition in the treatment group.

Dawson and colleagues (Dawson et al., 2010) reported on the first randomized controlled trial of a comprehensive intervention program for children with ASD under the age of 3 years, using the Early Start Denver Model (ESDM). ESDM is a manualized treatment that integrates consistent behavioral principles with a focus on child-initiated, affectively positive engagement, in the context of naturally occurring routines. The authors provided 4 hours of intervention daily for up to 2 years to children aged 18–30 months, and compared those children with a group who received community-based services. The authors report significant gains in IQ scores and adaptive behaviors, and marked improvements in ASD symptoms in children in the experimental group. They also note that children who were enrolled in the program earlier and received more intensive services attained better outcomes than children who were enrolled later. Like many integrated behavioral and developmental models, the ESDM also includes parent training, and parents of children in the experimental group provided an average of 16 hours of additional treatment, in the context of daily routines (Dawson et al., 2010).

Parent-implemented intervention involves training parents to develop consistent interactive exchanges, enhance reciprocal communication, and apply behavioral principles. Parents then provide many more hours of intervention daily, largely within the context of naturally occurring routines. The training may also help parents develop more gratifying interactions with their children with ASD, and that fact alone may contribute to alterations in the typical developmental trajectory. Finally, parent-implemented intervention may reduce the cost of services and may make intervention accessible to a broader range of families.

Rogers et al. (2014) tested a short-term, parent-implemented version of ESDM with 7 high-risk infants aged 6–15 months who presented with early signs of ASD (but who did not meet criteria for a diagnosis). At 36 months old, these children had lower rates of ASD diagnosis and of developmental quotients less than 70 than a group of children who had been less severely symptomatic at 9 months and whose families declined to participate in the treatment program. Of the seven infants in the experimental group, only two received a diagnosis of ASD at 36 months. These data, although clearly limited by a small sample size and lack of random assignment, nonetheless suggest that parent-implemented intervention may be helpful and that intervening before a clear diagnosis of ASD is established may indeed alter a negative developmental trajectory.

Wetherby et al. (2014) report on an RCT of the Early Social Interaction Project for children aged 16-20 months with ASD. Children matched on nonverbal development were randomly assigned to individual parent coaching or group coaching. Both models focused on teaching parents to enhance children's efforts at social communication. The results indicated that children in the individual treatment group demonstrated gains on observation-based measures of receptive language and social communication and on parent reports of communication and social skills. Children in the group treatment did not demonstrate comparable changes in skills. The authors suggest that parent-mediated models may have promise as an intervention tool for young children with ASD, provided that parents are provided with sufficient individual coaching and support. Similarly, Steiner et al. (2013) offered pilot evidence of the effectiveness of parent-mediated PRT for 12-month-olds with ASD and report that the intervention was associated with gains in the frequency of infants' functional communication. Brian, Bryson, and Zwaigenbaum (2015) also reported on a 12-week clinical trial of an adapted version of PRT with infants. They provided in-home parent-mediated interaction with coaching from an interventionist. Their results suggest that infants demonstrated gains in language performance and verbalization and increases in imitation, social orienting, and social responsiveness.

Services for children under age 3 years are typically provided through state-funded early intervention systems, and most of those mandate that services be provided in the child's natural environment and involve parental participation. Parent-mediated models are clearly a good fit for that system and seem especially important in the treatment of young children. They also have the potential to expand the reach of intervention efforts for those families who have the resources to participate in intensive parent-mediated intervention. When children reach the age of 3 years, intervention moves to the public school setting. Although behavioral approaches – including those that integrate developmental and naturalistic strategies – remain best practice, they are not always implemented at the level of intensity required.

Reichow and Volkmar (2010) conducted a meta-analysis of 66 studies evaluating the effectiveness of an intervention targeting social skills. Types of interventions included in these studies included interventions based on the principles of ABA, naturalistic interventions in which interventions were delivered in everyday settings, parent-training interventions, interventions involving mediation by a trained peer, social skills groups, visually based interventions (e.g., picture cues, scripts, social stories), and video modeling. Although many of these approaches to intervention had some promising data supporting them, only two intervention types, namely social skills groups and video modeling for school-aged children with ASD, demonstrated sufficient evidence to be considered an evidence-based practice.

With regard to group-based social skills intervention, a number of different specific models exist, but instructional approaches tend to fall into two broad models: experiential and didactic. Experiential models involve having participants engage in games and activities that rely on a variety of social interaction skills, with group facilitators providing feedback and remediation as participants struggle with various aspects of the social interaction. These experiential models tend to have a less prescribed approach, and thus rely on clinical judgment and clinician expertise and talent. Although they may be effective, by nature they cannot easily be manualized and thus do not lend themselves to empirical validation. Didactic models of intervention tend to follow a particular prescription involving didactic teaching of a prescribed skill, modeling use of the skill, allowing participants to role-play the skill, and providing feedback about the participant's performance during the role-play. Of note, while the role-play and feedback provide the participant some opportunity to practice the skill, the context in which this is done tends to be somewhat contrived or scripted, and thus may lack the benefit of practice within naturalistic contexts as offered by more experiential models. To remedy this, many didactic approaches also include homework assignments in which participants are instructed to practice using the skill in naturalistic settings. A number of interventions adopt this basic structure (e.g., Skillstreaming, PEERS) and have some empirical support (e.g., Laugeson, Frankel, Gantman, Dillon, & Mogil, 2012). A meta-analysis of five RCTs of social skills group interventions for individuals with ASD indicated that these interventions are effective, particularly in improving overall social competence and friendship quality (Reichow, Steiner & Volkmar, 2012).

Transition to Adulthood

With the increased incidence of ASDs in recent years (CDC, 2012), more and more individuals with an ASD diagnosis are reaching adulthood. Although supports for young adults are becoming increasingly available, often at the state level in the United States, funding and availability of resources remains an issue that impacts access to care for many adults. As a result, a significant decline in the utilization of services has been demonstrated among individuals with ASD upon exiting high school; furthermore, there are notable socioeconomic and racial disparities in service utilization, with Blacks and those of lower socioeconomic status being less likely to receive services upon the transition to adulthood (Shattuck, Wagner, Narendorf, Sterzing, & Hensley, 2011).

With regard to transition planning, families should work with their child's school personnel as early as possible in the high school career to develop a transition plan as part of the student's individualized education plan. The student should be involved in decision-making to the extent possible. The transition plan should center around the student's goals following completion of high school: i.e., whether they wish to pursue a college degree, or wish to move to employment following graduation. Either way, the high school years should include an emphasis on developing the skills needed for success in college and/or the identified vocation. This includes not only tangible skills related to the area of interest, but also socialization skills needed to function in a work or college setting, organizational skills, communication skills, and adaptive and independent living skills. It may be beneficial to delay high school graduation until age 21 (as afforded by the Individuals with Disabilities Education Act) to have more time to develop these skills.

An important consideration is that after the age of 21 or upon high school graduation, a student is no longer guaranteed a "free and appropriate education" under the law. Thus, if they engage in behaviors that are not tolerated on campus (aggression, stalking, disregard for rules, etc.), colleges have no obligation to continue to provide them an education. College students are, however, entitled to equal rights protections under the Americans with Disabilities Act. This entitles them to certain accommodations that ensure an "equal playing field" with other students (but not an unfair advantage). These accommodations may include extended time on exams, the ability to audio-record lectures, access to syllabi and course materials before the start of the semester, supports to manage the organizational demands of college life, use of technology, and specialized housing arrangements. Accommodations should be tailored to the individual; "blanket" accommodations are not given to all students with an ASD. To be eligible for accommodations, a student must disclose his or her disability to the college disability office, and documentation of disability is required.

In preparing for employment, it is important to first identify a target vocation. This should be based on the student's personal areas of strengths and interest; the student should be actively involved in identifying preferred vocational paths. The match between the student's skills and areas of difficulty should also be considered. For example, a job requiring a high degree of social contact (receptionist, customer service, etc.) is often not a good choice for those with social difficulties. Environmental factors should also be considered; a busy, noisy workplace is not the best choice for those with sensory sensitivities or who are easily distracted. Community-based learning opportunities during the high school years are often critical in assessing goodness of fit, developing relevant skill sets, and teaching the student to function in a "real world" work setting. Other means of obtaining relevant experiences include after-school, summer, volunteer, or temporary employment, formal vocational training programs, and job shadowing or apprenticeships. Many of these can lead to full-time employment opportunities.

When employed, the individual must decide to what extent they wish to disclose their disability and to whom (supervisor, coworkers, etc.). This is a personal decision, but disclosure can facilitate the provision of workplace supports and accommodations. Disclosure can further help the employer understand how to best support the individual; without disclosure, behaviors are often misunderstood and can lead to job loss. Workplace accommodations may include extra training, receiving visual supports, modifications to the work environment, procedures for responding to stress, and provision of adaptations to handle sensory sensitivities (e.g., use of earplugs).

Beyond the specific work required for the job itself, individuals with ASD may need to be explicitly taught information about workplace rules and etiquette. Some examples include when not to interact with coworkers because it might disturb them, how and when to ask for help, accepting feedback and instruction from supervisors, hygiene and appropriate work appearance, punctuality, managing conflict, and understanding such workplace policies and procedures as timesheets, vacation policy, dress code, allowable breaks, organizational hierarchies, and acronyms and abbreviations specific to the workplace. There are also many implicit rules and workplace-specific customs that may not be intuitive to individuals with ASD (e.g., when and where to engage in small talk, how formally or informally to address colleagues, and whether office doors are kept open or closed and under what circumstances).

An often critical component to employment success is the utilization of a job coach. A job coach can assist the individual in identifying and applying for an appropriate job, developing interviewing skills, providing education about ASD to the individual's supervisor and coworkers, developing workplace accommodations, and serving as an ongoing resource to resolve problems as they arise. In most states, job coaching and other services for individuals with disabilities are provided through the state's vocational rehabilitation office.

In addition to supports for college and employment, individuals with ASD may require supports for independent living skills. Utilization of a life coach can be useful in developing these skills. Consideration should be given to appropriate housing arrangements (e.g., living independently, living with family, living in a group home). Guardianship and financial arrangements must also be considered, particularly for those who are unable to attend to their own needs or fully support themselves.

Many individuals with ASD have the cognitive capacity to work and live independently, and yet their significant social disability presents a barrier to achieving this outcome. Transition programs have been developed to meet the needs of these individuals with ASD. These programs are typically residential and are designed to help individuals make the transition to independent living while simultaneously attending college, beginning a career, or engaging in vocational training programs. The programs include instruction on social skills relevant to managing the demands of adult life: adaptive skills, such as managing money and navigating transportation systems, and domestic tasks, such as shopping, cooking, and cleaning, and attending to hygiene and health care. These programs often provide job placement supports and job coaching, and help managing the organizational and social demands of college. These programs offer important education and supports to students in the critical period of transition to adult independence, but tuition tends to be quite expensive, and in the absence of available funding mechanisms, these programs become inaccessible to those without significant means.

Pharmacological Interventions

There is currently no medication approved by health authorities to treat core symptoms of autism. Medications in the atypical antipsychotic class (risperidone and aripiprazole) have received approval for use in autism, but only to treat associated irritability. Despite the limited autism-specific approvals from health authorities, psychotropic medications are commonly used to treat significant psychiatric comorbidities. In a recent review (Jobski, Höfer, Hoffmann, & Bachmann, 2017), median prevalence of psychopharmacotherapy in individuals living with autism was reported to be 41.9% in children and 61.5% in adults. More concerning, however, was polypharmacy being common with reported median of 23.0%. Congruent with the aforementioned health authority approval, antipsychotics were the most frequently used medication. Following antipsychotic medication were agents used to treat inattention, hyperactivity, or both, which was followed by antidepressant medications. Numerous studies have been published assessing the use of psychotropic medications to treat significant psychiatric comorbidities. In a recent update (Ji & Findling, 2015), potential benefits and side effects were highlighted in these different classes of medication. Although atypical antipsychotics were helpful for reducing irritability, stereotypy, and hyperactivity, they were associated with metabolic adverse events such as weight gain and dyslipidemia. Antidepressant medications (selective serotonin reuptake inhibitors) were not recommended due to unfavorable tolerability and effectiveness. Both stimulant and nonstimulant medication can be helpful for reducing inattention or hyperactivity or both, but should be used with greater caution in individuals living with autism. The decision to implement pharmacological interventions requires careful consideration of the pros and cons and alternatives. To assist families in this decision-making process, Autism Speaks' Autism Treatment Network created the Medication Decision Aid, which is freely available (www.autismspeaks.org).

Implications for Clinical Practice

The data reviewed throughout this chapter suggest several implications for clinical practice (Table 3.1). First, it is clear that clinicians can now identify children at risk for ASD and make reliable diagnoses as early as 18 months. In addition, we can identify children with subclinical symptoms of ASD even before 18 months and we have emerging evidence that intervention may be especially helpful to young children. That suggests that aggressive monitoring of high-risk children, including those with genetic vulnerabilities, developmental disorders, and siblings with an ASD diagnosis should be standard practice beginning at 6–9 months. In addition, universal screening for early signs of ASD should also be implemented in well-child-care settings. Several studies have now demonstrated that children can be screened reliably in a variety of settings, and that universal screening has the potential to reduce racial and ethnic disparities in age at diagnosis and access to treatment (Khowaja, Hazzard, & Robins, 2014). Finally, initiating services to high-risk children who demonstrate significant impairments but who may

Table 3.1 Implications for Clinical Practice for ASD Patients

- Increase early monitoring and screening for ASD beginning at age 6–9 months, with a goal toward universal screening by well-child-care practitioners
- Increase training opportunities for clinicians in gold standard autism evaluation measures
- Provide early and ongoing intervention:
  - Include both behavioral and naturalistic strategies
  - Include parent training components
  - Focus early intervention on prerequisite skills such as joint attention, affect sharing, and play
  - Target both core (e.g., social skills, language therapy) as well as associated features of ASD in intervention
  - Give consideration to family's cultural beliefs about intervention in tailoring services
- Increase access to services, including:
  - For infants and toddlers, including those at high risk but not yet diagnosed
  - For adults and those transitioning to adulthood
  - For those of ethnic minority or lower socioeconomic status
- Evaluate and address comorbid psychiatric concerns
- Provide supportive services to parents and other family members

not yet meet full criteria for an ASD diagnosis should be considered.

Assessment of children suspected of ASD should conform to accepted standards of clinical care. Children should be evaluated by clinicians with specific autism-related training, and experience in engaging and evaluating children with complex developmental disorders. Assessment must include parent report using validated measures, such as the Autism Diagnostic Interview, and direct observation of the child's social and communicative behaviors, again using validated measures such as the Autism Diagnostic Observation Schedule. Evaluation should also include a standardized assessment of development or cognition, and language, and the systematic evaluation of sensory concerns that may impact intervention efforts. For older children and adults, evaluation should also include assessment of neuropsychological factors, including attention and executive functioning. Finally, for adolescents and adults, clinicians should assess psychological factors such as anxiety and depression.

Schriebman et al. (2015) and Zwaigenbaum et al. (2015) offer numerous recommendations for intervention with young children, which we summarize briefly here. Intervention should begin as early as possible and should include a blend of behavioral and naturalistic strategies. Intervention efforts should involve parents and caregivers actively and should include systematic training and education for them. Clinicians should consider each family's socioeconomic context and their cultural beliefs about diagnosis and treatment to tailor services as much as possible. Intervention should focus on both core and associated features of ASD, including social communication and emotional regulation, as well as sensory concerns, motor difficulties, and negative behaviors. Early intervention should begin with attention to prerequisite skills such as joint attention, affect sharing, and play.

School-age children should continue to receive intensive behavioral treatment as well as language therapy and social skills training. Although exposure to typically developing peers is important during the school years, children with ASD are likely to require consistent adult support to benefit from that exposure. Ongoing support for social skills and the adaptive behaviors that support independent function in both school and work settings should be provided to children, adolescents, and young adults throughout their development, if we are to address the oft-cited fact that many individuals with ASD struggle to utilize their cognitive abilities because of the limitations imposed by their social concerns. Increasing availability of and access to services for adults with ASD, particularly those of ethnic minority or lower socioeconomic status, is a critical priority. Finally, families of children with ASD report high levels of stress (Kogan et al., 2008). As changes in intervention models place a greater burden on families, there will be a need for more careful assessment of family function and more readily available supportive services.

Future Directions

Despite the enormous progress in the field of ASD research, there are many remaining questions. One of the biggest of those concerns the identification of subcategories of ASD and differing developmental trajectories. The heterogeneity of the disorder is clearly recognized, but there is little clarity about potential subgroups, with the exception of children with known genetic disorders. Large-scale studies that include investigation of behavioral patterns as well as neurological

and neuropsychological findings will be important to disambiguating the complex heterogeneity of the disorder. That effort might support better understanding of mediating variables and moderators that explain individuals' differential response to treatment.

As Zwaigenbaum et al. (2015) note, the rigor of intervention research has improved significantly in recent years. Nonetheless, there is a continued need for clear outcome variables that can detect changes in multiple functional areas rather than in broad diagnostic classifications. Researchers must include careful measures of treatment fidelity, especially as parent-mediated models become more common. The question of intensity of intervention is also unclear. Although early studies suggested that intervention must be very intensive, more recent studies have suggested that less intensive models may also be effective, particularly when they include well-supported parent intervention. The integration of seemingly divergent treatment approaches into comprehensive models has promoted greater flexibility in approaches and more careful tailoring of strategies to the needs of children and families, while retaining the empirically supported strengths of each method. Researchers should continue empirical efforts to describe the critical components of intervention models and to match intervention strategies with client characteristics to promote improved outcomes for all children.

An equally challenging set of problems confronts clinicians in the field. Despite much greater clarity about appropriate assessment and effective intervention, timely assessment and high-quality intervention at appropriate levels of intensity are not available to many families. As Dawson and Bernier (2013) note, there is an immediate need to increase the availability of services for children with ASD both in the United States and abroad. At present, early intervention services are funded largely by state budgets; services for individuals aged 3–21 years are funded by local property taxes. This means that there are enormous disparities in the amount and quality of services available, with the biggest shortfalls affecting children growing up in impoverished settings. Services for adults with ASD are even more scarce despite the large and growing population of adults in need of support. Finally, we need much greater efforts to provide culturally sensitive services and to help families develop an understanding of ASD and an ability to participate in treatment that is consistent with their cultural context.

References

American Psychiatric Association. (2000). Diagnostic and statistical manual of mental disorders-IV-TR. *Washington, DC: American Psychiatric Association.*

American Psychiatric Association. (2013). *Diagnostic and statistical manual of mental disorders* (5th ed.). Washington, DC: Author.

Asperger, H. (1944). Die "Autistischen Psychopathen" im Kindesalter. *European Archives of Psychiatry and Clinical Neuroscience, 117*(1), 76–136.

Baron-Cohen, S., Ring, H. A., Wheelwright, S., Bullmore, E. T., Brammer, M. J., Simmons, A., & Williams, S. C. (1999). Social intelligence in the normal and autistic brain: An fMRI study. *European Journal of Neuroscience, 11*, 1891–1898.

Brian, J., Bryson, S., & Zwaigenbaum, L.(2015) Autism spectrum disorders in infancy: Developmental considerations in treatment targets. *Current Opinion in Neurology, 28*, 117–123.

Bryson, S. E., Zwaigenbaum, L., McDermott, C., Rombough, V., & Brian, J. (2008). The Autism Observation Scale for Infants: Scale development and reliability data. *Journal of Autism and Developmental Disorders, 38*(4), 731–738.

Cannon, L., Kenworthy, L., Alexander, K. C., Werner, M. A., & Anthony, L. (2011). *Unstuck and on target! An executive function curriculum to improve flexibility for children with autism spectrum disorders.* Baltimore, MD: Brookes Publishing Company.

Casanova, M. F., Buxhoeveden, D. P., Switala, A. E., & Roy, E. (2002). Minicolumnar pathology in autism. *Neurology, 58*, 428–432.

Castelli, F., Frith, C., Happé, F., & Frith, U. (2002). Autism, Asperger syndrome and brain mechanisms for the attribution of mental states to animated shapes. *Brain, 125*, 1839–1849.

Centers for Disease Control and Prevention. (2012). Prevalence of autism spectrum disorders autism and developmental disabilities monitoring network, United States, 2008. *MMWR Surveillance Summaries, 61*(3), 1–19.

Centers for Disease Control and Prevention. (2015, Feb 26). *Autism Spectrum Disorder, Signs and Symptoms.* Retrieved from https://www.cdc.gov/ncbddd/autism/signs.html

Centers for Disease Control and Prevention. (2018, April 27). *Autism Spectrum Disorder, Data & Statistics.* Retrieved from https://www.cdc.gov/ncbddd/autism/data.html

Courchesne, E., Karns, C. M., Davis, H. R., Ziccardi, R., Carper, R. A., Tigue, Z. D., … Courchesne, R. Y. (2001). Unusual brain growth patterns in early life in patients with autistic disorder: An MRI study. *Neurology, 57*, 245–254.

Courchesne, E., & Pierce, K. (2005). Why the frontal cortex in autism might be talking only to itself: Local over-connectivity but long-distance disconnection. *Current Opinion in Neurobiology, 15*, 225–230.

Dawson, G. & Bernier, R. (2013). A quarter century of progress on the early detection and treatment of autism spectrum disorder. *Development and Psychopathology, 25*, 1455–1472

Dawson, G., Rogers, S., Munson, J., Smith, M., Winter, J., Greenson, J., Donaldson, A. & Varley, J. (2010). Randomized, controlled trial of an intervention for toddlers with autism: The Early Start Denver Model. *Pediatrics, 125*, e17–e23

Frazier, T. W., & Hardan, A. Y. (2009). A meta-analysis of the corpus callosum in autism. *Biological Psychiatry, 66*, 935–941.

Gowen, E., & Hamilton, A. (2013). Motor abilities in autism: A review using a computational context. *Journal of Autism and Developmental Disorders, 43*(2), 323–344.

Hamilton, A. F. (2013). Reflecting on the mirror neuron system in autism: A systematic review of current theories. *Developmental Cognitive Neuroscience,* doi:10.1016/j.dcn.2012.09.008

Hannant, P., Cassidy, S., Tavassoli, T., & Mann, F. (2016). Sensorimotor difficulties are associated with the severity of autism spectrum conditions. *Frontiers in Integrative Neuroscience, 10*, 28.

Happé, F., Booth, R., Charlton, R., & Hughes, C. (2006). Executive function deficits in autism spectrum disorders and attention-deficit/hyperactivity disorder: Examining profiles across domains and ages. *Brain and Cognition, 61*(1), 25–39.

Herbert, M. R., Ziegler, D. A., Makris, N., Filipek, P. A., Kemper, T. L., Normandin, J. J., … Caviness, V. S., Jr. (2004). Localization of white matter volume increase in autism and developmental language disorder. *Annals of Neurology, 55*, 530–540.

Hill, E. L. (2004). Evaluating the theory of executive dysfunction in autism. *Developmental Review, 24*(2), 189–233.

Hill, E. L., & Frith, U. (2003). Understanding autism: Insights from mind and brain. *Philosophical Transactions of the Royal Society of London. Series B, Biological Sciences, 358*(1430), 281–289.

Ingersoll, B., & Schreibman, L. (2006). Teaching reciprocal imitation skills to young children with autism using a naturalistic behavioral approach: Effects on language, pretend play, and joint attention. *Journal of Autism and Developmental Disorders, 36*(4), 487–505.

Jacquemont, S., Coe, B. P., Hersch, M., Duyzend, M. H., Krumm, N., Bergmann, S., Beckmann, J. S., Rosenfeld, J. A., & Eichler, E. E. (2014). A higher mutational burden in females supports a "female protective model" in neurodevelopmental disorders. *American Journal of Human Genetics,* doi:10.1016/j.ajhg.2014.02.001

Jain, A., Marshall, J., Buikema, A., Bancroft, T., Kelly, J. P., & Newschaffer, C. J. (2015). Autism occurrence by MMR vaccine status among US children with older siblings with and without autism. *Journal of the American Medical Association*, doi:10.1001/jama.2015.3077

Ji, N., & Findling, R. L. (2015). An update on pharmacotherapy for autism spectrum disorder in children and adolescents. *Current Opinion in Psychiatry*, doi:10.1097/YCO.0000000000000132

Jobski, J., Höfer, J., Hoffmann, F., & Bachmann, C. (2017). Use of psychotropic drugs in patients with autism spectrum disorders: a systematic review. *Acta Psychiatrica Scandinavica*, doi:10.1111/acps.12644

Jou, R. J. (2012). *The structural neural phenotype of autism spectrum disorder: Heterogeneous and distributed abnormalities in the social brain and its long-range connectivity* (Doctoral dissertation). Retrieved from ProQuest Dissertations Publishing (Publication No. 3525200).

Jou, R. J., Jackowski, A. P., Papademetris, X., Rajeevan, N., Staib, L. H., & Volkmar, F. R. (2011). Diffusion tensor imaging in autism spectrum disorders: Preliminary evidence of abnormal neural connectivity. *Australian & New Zealand Journal of Psychiatry*, 45(2), 153–162.

Just, M. A., Cherkassky, V. L., Keller, T. A., & Minshew, N. J. (2004). Cortical activation and synchronization during sentence comprehension in high-functioning autism: Evidence of underconnectivity. *Brain*, 127, 1811–1821.

Kanner, L. (1943). Autistic disturbances of affective contact. *Nervous Child*, 2, 217–250.

Kasari, C., Paparella, T., Freeman, S. & Jahromi, L. (2008). Language outcome in autism: Randomized comparison of joint attention and play interventions. *Journal of Consulting and Clinical Psychology*, 76, 125–137.

Keehn, B., Müller, R. A., & Townsend, J. (2013). Atypical attentional networks and the emergence of autism. *Neuroscience & Biobehavioral Reviews*, 37(2), 164–183.

Kenworthy, L., Yerys, B. E., Weinblatt, R., Abrams, D. N., & Wallace, G. L. (2013). Motor demands impact speed of information processing in autism spectrum disorders. *Neuropsychology*, 27(5), 529.

Kercood, S., Grskovic, J. A., Banda, D., & Begeske, J. (2014). Working memory and autism: A review of literature. *Research in Autism Spectrum Disorders*, 8(10), 1316–1332.

Khowaja, M., Hazzard, A. & Robins, D. (2014). Socio-demographic barriers to early detection of autism: Screening and evaluation using the M-CHAT, M-CHAT-R, and follow-up. *Journal of Autism and Developmental Disorders*, 45(6), 1797–1808.

Klin, A., Sparrow, S. S., de Bildt, A., Cicchetti, D. V., Cohen, D. J., & Volkmar, F. R. (1999). A normed study of face recognition in autism and related disorders. *Journal of Autism and Developmental Disorders*, 29, 499–508.

Kogan, M., Strickland, B., Blumberg, S., Singh, G., Perrin, J., van Dyck, P. (2008). A national profile of the healthcare experiences and family impact of autism spectrum disorder among children in the US, 2005-2006. *Pediatrics*, 122(6) e1149–e1158.

Kwok, E. Y., Brown, H. M., Smyth, R. E., & Cardy, J. O. (2015). Meta-analysis of receptive and expressive language skills in autism spectrum disorder. *Research in Autism Spectrum Disorders*, 9, 202–222.

Lai, M. C., Lombardo, M. V., Chakrabarti, B., & Baron-Cohen, S. (2013). Subgrouping the autism "spectrum": Reflections on DSM-5. *PLoS Biology*, doi:10.1371/journal.pbio.1001544

Laugeson, E. A., Frankel, F., Gantman, A., Dillon, A. R., & Mogil, C. (2012). Evidence-based social skills training for adolescents with autism spectrum disorders: The UCLA PEERS program. *Journal of Autism and Developmental Disorders*, 42(6), 1025–1036.

Levy, S. E, Mandell, D. S., & Schultz, R. T. (2009). Autism. *Lancet*, 374(9701), 1627–1638.

Lord, C., Risi, S., Lambrecht, L., Cook, E. H., Leventhal, B. L., DiLavore, P. C., Pickles, A., & Rutter, M. (2000). The autism diagnostic observation schedule-generic: A standard measure of social and communication deficits associated with the spectrum of autism. *Journal of Autism and Developmental Disorders*, 30 (3), 205–223.

Lord, C., Rutter, M., DiLavore, P., Risi, S., Gotham, K., & Bishop, S. (2012). *Autism Diagnostic Observation Schedule* (2nd ed.) (ADOS-2). Los Angeles, CA: Western Psychological Corporation.

Lord, C., Rutter, M., & Le Couteur, A. (1994). Autism Diagnostic Interview-Revised: A revised version of a diagnostic interview for caregivers of individuals with possible pervasive developmental disorders. *Journal of Autism and Developmental Disorders*, 24(5), 659–685.

Lundström, S., Reichenberg, A., Anckarsäter, H., Lichtenstein, P., & Gillberg, C. (2015). Autism phenotype versus registered diagnosis in Swedish children: Prevalence trends over 10 years in general population samples. *British Medical Journal*, doi:10.1136/bmj.h1961

Mohammadzaheri, F., Koegel, L., Rezaee, M., & Rafiee, S. (2014). A randomized clinical trial comparison between pivotal response therapy and structured applied behavior analysis (ABA) intervention for children with autism. *Journal of Autism and Developmental Disorders*, 44, 2769–2777.

Nowell, K. P., Schanding Jr, G. T., Kanne, S. M., & Goin-Kochel, R. P. (2015). Cognitive profiles in youth with autism spectrum disorder: An investigation of base rate discrepancies using the Differential Ability Scales—Second Edition. *Journal of Autism and Developmental Disorders*, 45 (7), 1978–1988.

Piven, J., Arndt, S., Bailey, J., Havercamp, S., Andreasen, N. C., & Palmer, P. (1995). An MRI study of brain size in autism. *American Journal of Psychiatry, 152*, 1145–1149.

Reichow, B. (2012). Overview of meta-analyses of early intensive behavioral intervention for young children with ASD. *Journal of Autism and Developmental Disorders, 42*, 512–520.

Reichow, B., Steiner, A. M., & Volkmar, F. (2013). Cochrane review: Social skills groups for people aged 6 to 21 with autism spectrum disorders (ASD). *Evidence-Based Child Health: A Cochrane Review Journal, 8*(2), 266–315.

Reichow, B., & Volkmar, F. R. (2010). Social skills interventions for individuals with autism: Evaluation for evidence-based practices within a best evidence synthesis framework. *Journal of Autism and Developmental Disorders, 40*(2), 149–166.

Robinson, S., Goddard, L., Dritschel, B., Wisley, M., & Howlin, P. (2009). Executive functions in children with autism spectrum disorders. *Brain and Cognition, 71*(3), 362–368.

Rogers, S. & Vismara, L. (2008) Evidence-based comprehensive treatments for early autism. *Journal of Clinical Child and Adolescent Psychology, 37*, 3–38.

Rogers, S., Vismara, L., Wagner, A., McCormick, C., Young, G., & Ozonoff, S. (2014). Autism treatment in the first year of life: A pilot study of Early Start, a parent-implemented intervention for symptomatic infants. *Journal of Autism and Developmental Disorders, 44*, 2891–2995.

Rutter, M., Le Couteur, A., & Lord, C. (2003). *Autism Diagnostic Interview-Revised. Manual*. Los Angeles, CA: Western Psychological Services.

Schopler, E., Reichler, R. J., & Renner, B. R. (2002). *The Childhood Autism Rating Scale (CARS)*. Los Angeles: Western Psychological Services.

Schreibman, L., Dawson, G., Stahmer, A., Landa, R., Rogers, S., McGee, G., … Halladay, A. (2015). Naturalistic, developmental behavioral interventions: Empirically validated treatments for autism spectrum disorders. *Journal of Autism and Developmental Disorders, 45*, 2411–2428.

Schultz, R. T. (2005). Developmental deficits in social perception in autism: The role of the amygdala and fusiform face area. *International Journal of Developmental Neuroscience, 23*, 125–141.

Schultz, R. T., Gauthier, I., Klin, A., Fulbright, R. K., Anderson, A. W., Volkmar, F., … Gore, J. C. (2000). Abnormal ventral temporal cortical activity during face discrimination among individuals with autism and Asperger syndrome. *Archives of General Psychiatry, 57*, 331–340.

Schultz, R. T., Hunyadi, E., Connors, C., & Pasley, B. (2005, June). *fMRI study of facial expression perception in autism: The amygdala, fusiform face area and their functional connectivity*. Paper presented at the 11th Annual Meeting of the Organization for Human Brain Mapping, Toronto, Canada.

Schultz, R. T., Win, L., Jackowski, A., Klin, A., Staib, L. H., Papademetris, X., … Volkmar, F. (2005, May). *Brain morphology in autism spectrum disorders: An MRI study*. Paper presented at the 4th International Meeting for Autism Research (IMFAR), Boston, MA.

Shattuck, P. T., Wagner, M., Narendorf, S., Sterzing, P., & Hensley, M. (2011). Post–high school service use among young adults with an autism spectrum disorder. *Archives of Pediatrics & Adolescent Medicine, 165*(2), 141–146.

Skuse, D., Warrington, R., Bishop, D., Chowdhury, U., Lau, J., Mandy, W., & Place, M. (2004). The Developmental, Dimensional and Diagnostic Interview (3di): A novel computerized assessment for autism spectrum disorders. *Journal of the American Academy of Child & Adolescent Psychiatry, 43*(5), 548–558.

Simmons, E. S., Paul, R., & Volkmar, F. (2014). Assessing pragmatic language in autism spectrum disorder: The Yale in vivo pragmatic protocol. *Journal of Speech, Language, and Hearing Research, 57*(6), 2162–2173.

Southwick, J. S., Bigler, E. D., Froehlich, A., DuBray, M. B., Alexander, A. L., Lange, N., & Lainhart, J. E. (2011). Memory functioning in children and adolescents with autism. *Neuropsychology, 25*(6), 702.

Steiner, A., Gengoux, G., Klin, A. & Chawarska, K. (2013) Pivotal response treatment for infants at risk for autism spectrum disorder: A pilot study. *Journal of Autism and Developmental Disorders, 43*(1), 91–103.

Volkmar, F., Siegel, M., Woodbury-Smith, M., King, B., McCracken, J., & State, M. (2014). Practice parameter for the assessment and treatment of children and adolescents with autism spectrum disorder. *Journal of the American Academy of Child & Adolescent Psychiatry, 53*(2), 237–257.

Walker, H. A. (1977). Incidence of minor physical anomaly in autism. *Journal of Autism and Childhood Schizophrenia, 7*, 165–176.

Wetherby, A., Guthrie, W., Woods, J., Schatschneider, C., Holland, R. D., Morgan, L., & Lord, C. (2014) Parent-implemented social intervention for toddlers with autism: An RCT. *Pediatrics, 134*(6), 1084–1093.

Williams, D. L., Goldstein, G., & Minshew, N. J. (2006). The profile of memory function in children with autism. *Neuropsychology, 20*(1), 21.

Wing, L., Leekam, S. R., Libby, S. J., Gould, J., & Larcombe, M. (2002). The diagnostic interview for social and communication disorders: Background, inter-rater reliability and clinical use. *Journal of Child Psychology and Psychiatry, 43*(3), 307–325.

Zwaigenbaum, L., Bauman, M. L., Choueiri, R., Kasari, C., Carter, A., Granpeesheh, D., … Pierce, K. (2015). Early intervention for children with autism spectrum disorder under 3 years of age: Recommendations for practice and research. *Pediatrics, 136*(Supplement 1), S60–S81.

Intellectual Disability Syndromes

Kelly Janke and Lisa Jacola

Introduction

Intellectual disability (ID) is characterized by intellectual functioning that is significantly impaired relative to the normative population and significant impairments in one or more areas of adaptive functioning, or those skills needed to independently perform daily activities. Intellectual disability originates during the developmental period (i.e., childhood and adolescence). Typically, this diagnosis is not made until a child is 5 or 6 years old, owing to the normative variability that is present in the development of infants, toddlers, and preschool-age children. Before this age, children with suspected intellectual disability are typically diagnosed with global developmental delay.

Intellectual disability was previously known as "mental retardation." Concerns with negative social stigma and popular language use prompted advocacy for a change in the diagnostic label from families and support organizations. In 2010, a federal law enacted in the United States (Public Law 111–256 [Rosa's Law]) changed the terms "mentally retarded" and "mental retardation" to "intellectual disability" and "intellectually disabled" in federal laws regarding education, employment, and some health programs. The change in terminology is recognized in the most recent version of the *Diagnostic and Statistical Manual of Mental Disorders*, 5th ed. (DSM-5; American Psychiatric Association, 2013) and is commonly used in research journals and by the medical community and advocacy groups, including the American Association of Intellectual and Developmental Disabilities (AAIDD), which was the first organization to define ID (The AAIDD Ad Hoc Committee on Terminology and Classification, 2010). See Tables 4.1 and 4.2 for overviews of the diagnostic criteria and coding for ID. The International Classification of Diseases (ICD) coding is most frequently used globally; a survey conducted by the World Health Organization found that 62% of countries endorse the use of this system (World Health Organization, 2007). Following the ICD, 40% of

countries reported using the DSM. In October 2015, the US Center for Medicare and Medicaid Services mandated that all medical diagnoses and inpatient hospital procedures be coded using the 10th revision of ICD (ICD-10) for reporting and reimbursement purposes.

Changes to the DSM-5 criteria for ID have made these criteria more similar to those used by AAIDD. The previous version of the DSM, the 4th edition, text revision (DSM-IV-TR; American Psychiatric Association, 2000) based classification of severity on intelligence (i.e., IQ); however, the DSM-5 bases this classification on level of adaptive functioning. The DSM-IV-TR specified that an individual had to demonstrate deficits in two or more areas of adaptive functioning; in the DSM-5, an individual may meet criteria with deficits in one or more areas of function. Finally, adaptive functioning used to determine level of support. In contrast to the DSM-5 and AAIDD, the ICD-10 criteria place relative emphasis on the role of intellectual functioning, operationalized as performance on standardized intelligence tests (World Health Organization, 1996). The classification systems also differ with respect to considerations of the level of ID, with the ICD-10 and DSM-5 using a "severity" approach that emphasizes the level of impairment in functioning, whereas the AAIDD system is focused on the level of support needed to meet daily goals and expectations.

Prevalence and Epidemiology. The prevalence of ID in the United States (US) is estimated at 1–3%; two-thirds of these cases are mild in severity (McDermott, Durkin, Schupf, & Stein, 2007). Males are more often affected than females. There is significant public health and societal impact associated with ID. The Centers for Disease Control and Prevention (CDC) estimates the average total lifetime costs to be around $1 million per individual (CDC, 2004). In the United States, lifetime costs are estimated at $50 billion for individuals diagnosed with ID born in 2000 (CDC, 2004). Children with ID are significantly more likely to have comorbid medical conditions or health needs when compared with

Table 4.1 Diagnostic Classification Systems

	ICD-10	DSM-V	AAIDD
Terminology	• Mental retardation	• Intellectual disability	• Intellectual disability
Broad definition	• "Condition of arrested or incomplete development of the mind, which is especially characterized by impairment of skills manifested during the developmental period that contribute to the overall level of intelligence"	• "Disorder with onset during the developmental period that includes both intellectual and adaptive functioning deficits"	• "Disability characterized by significant limitations in both intellectual functioning and in adaptive behavior"
Intellectual functioning	• Based on psychometric test performance and clinical findings • Approximate IQ ranges and mental age estimates are provided • Diagnosis regarded as provisional without the use of standardized tests	• Measured with standardized instruments interpreted with clinical judgment • IQ score ≥ 2 SD below the population mean, including a margin for measurement error (±5 points)	• IQ score of around 70 or as high as 75
Adaptive functioning	• Diminished ability to adapt to the daily demands of the social environment • Diagnosis is regarded as provisional without the use of standardized tests • Recommendations for specific measures	• Deficits in conceptual, social, and practical skills • Failure to meet developmental and cultural standards for personal independence and social responsibility • Deficits limit functioning in one or more areas of daily life • Clinical judgment and standardized measures	• Deficits in conceptual, social, and practical skills • Consider cultural differences in the way people move, communicate, and behave
Onset	• Before age 18	• Developmental period (childhood or adolescence)	• Before age 18
Level	• Level of impairment based on standardized intelligence tests that are supplemented by scales assessing social adaptation • Mild, Moderate, Severe, Profound	• Level of impairment based on adaptive functioning • Mild, Moderate, Severe, Profound	• Level of support needed to meet daily goals and expectations • Intermittent, limited, extensive, pervasive

Note: ICD-10 = International Classification of Diseases, 10th ed.; DSM-5= *Diagnostic and Statistical Manual of Mental Disorders*, 5th ed.; AAIDD = American Association of Intellectual and Developmental Disabilities.

children without ID (US Department of Health and Human Services, 2013). Results of a meta-analysis completed by Maulik and colleagues showed that global prevalence estimates varied significantly by income group of a country, with low, middle, and high income countries reporting 16.41, 15.94, and 9.21 cases per 1,000, respectively (Maulik, Mascarenhas, Mathers, Dua, & Saxena, 2011). Estimates also varied by type of population, with the highest rates found in populations defined as rural (19.88 per 1,000) and mixed urban/rural (21.23 per 1,000).

Etiology. The etiology of ID across development is depicted in Figure 4.1 (McDermott et al., 2007; Klein-Tasman & Janke, 2010). It is important to note that etiology is unknown in 50% of cases, and most of these cases are mild in severity (McDermott et al., 2007). In these cases, there is often a family history of ID, and a

Table 4.2 DSM-5 to ICD-10 Crosswalk

Diagnosis	Severity Level	ICD-10	DSM-V
Intellectual disability	Mild	F 70	317.0
	Moderate	F 71	318.0
	Severe	F 72	318.1
	Profound	F 73	318.2
Unspecified intellectual disability		F 79	319.0
Global developmental delay		F 88	315.8

Note: ICD-10 = International Classification of Diseases, 10th ed.; DSM-5= *Diagnostic and Statistical Manual of Mental Disorders*, 5th ed.

disproportionate number of these cases are identified in families with lower socioeconomic status (SES), suggesting that environmental factors may play a role. Clarification of etiology can be beneficial for prognosis and recurrence risks, symptom management, and treatment planning. For these reasons, the American Academy of Pediatrics recommends genetic screening for all individuals diagnosed with ID of unknown etiology (Moeschler, Shevell, & Committee on Genetics, 2014).

Genetic disorders account for 25–50% of cases with known etiology; these cases are usually severe to profound (Karam et al., 2016; Moeschler, 2008). Genetic disorders most commonly occur at conception and include chromosomal aberrations (e.g., Down syndrome) and single gene disorders (e.g., fragile X syndrome). Other genetic disorders include inborn errors of metabolism, such as such as phenylketonuria (PKU). We focus on several genetic etiologies in the forthcoming Clinical Manifestations section because these are the most common in cases of ID with a known cause.

A full review of other etiologies of ID is beyond the scope of this chapter, and many of these conditions are described elsewhere in this volume. Briefly, other prenatal risk factors include intrauterine exposure to substances and environmental agents. Prenatal alcohol exposure is considered the most common nonhereditary cause of ID in the US, with prevalence rates of fetal alcohol syndrome estimated at 0.2–1.5 cases per 1,000 births (May & Gossage, 2001). In utero exposure to neurotoxic metals including lead and mercury has also been found to affect early

neurodevelopment (Antonelli, Pallarés, Ceccatelli, & Spulber, 2016) and can have long-lasting effects. For example, in utero methylmercury exposure has been found to most strongly impact intellectual functioning during early childhood, but effects on IQ may remain significant into adulthood (Debes, Weihe, & Grandjean, 2016).

Factors associated with ID that manifest in the perinatal period are often related to prematurity or delivery complications. Risk for ID is highest in the most premature (i.e., <29 weeks) or low birthweight (i.e., <1,000 g) babies because these children are more likely to experience medical complications such as hypoxic-ischemic encephalopathy, intraventricular hemorrhage, and periventricular leukomalacia. There is a positive association between IQ scores and gestational age. Cerebral palsy, which can present at birth or up to 3 years of age, is associated with ID in approximately 40% of children, although the incidence varies with the type and generally increases with motor impairment.

Childhood factors are implicated in 3–15% of ID cases with known etiology. The negative impact of lead exposure during childhood has been well documented; studies consistently identify an association between increased exposure and neurobehavioral difficulties across the lifespan, even after controlling for confounding factors. This risk is particularly great for children living in urban environments and those of lower SES (Hornung, Lanphear, & Dietrich, 2009). The developing brain is extremely sensitive to methylmercury exposure, and although this is particularly true during the pre- or perinatal period, the negative impact on development has been identified throughout the lifespan (dos Santos et al., 2016).

There is also an association between intellectual impairment and acquired brain injury. Declines in IQ relate to injury severity and age at the time of injury, with younger children being at a greater risk (Königs, Engenhorst, & Oosterlaan, 2015; Lind et al., 2016). Conversely, ID is a risk factor for trauma and slower recovery after an acquired brain injury (Braden, Swanson, & Di Scala, 2003; Moran et al., 2016).

The environment to which a child is exposed comprises many variables that can affect development and learning. The adverse impact of early environmental deprivation on child development has been well documented. For example, lower SES is predictive of early and persistent deficits in the development of executive

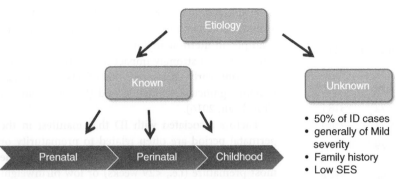

Figure 4.1. Etiology of intellectual disability.

functions (Hackman, Gallop, Evans, & Farah, 2015). Studies have also demonstrated a relationship between environmental variables (i.e., SES) and brain structure and function in typically developing children and adolescents (Ursache, Noble, & Pediatric Imaging, Neurocognition and Genetics Study, 2016). Environmental variables can also impact outcomes after early injury; lower SES is a risk factor for increased behavior problems after pediatric TBI (Max et al., 2005; Schwartz et al., 2003) and family variables (i.e., parent behaviors) are associated with outcomes in children with neurological risk (Landry, Miller-Loncar, Smith, & Swank, 2002).

Prevention. Prevention efforts depend a great deal on the etiology of ID. Genetic and prenatal screenings identify those at risk for various conditions. Families with a history of genetic conditions can be referred to genetic counselors for appropriate guidance and risk assessment; however, many of the genetic anomalies may occur du novo. In some conditions, such as PKU, ID can be prevented by appropriately managing environmental exposure (i.e., omitting foods that contain phenylalanine). Mandatory screening implemented at birth for this condition has increased early identification, thereby limiting these severe consequences.

Research and health initiatives have also focused on prevention strategies for substance and neurotoxin exposure in utero and childhood. Although it is currently unclear what levels of alcohol exposure are required to produce adverse neurodevelopmental effects, the safest approach is to abstain throughout pregnancy. Health-care providers play an important role in educating expectant parents that stopping or reducing alcohol consumption at any time during pregnancy can minimize adverse effects (Alberta Clinical Practice Guidelines, 2003). Much work has also gone into primary prevention of lead exposure through interventions focused on reducing sources of lead in housing, soil, water, and consumer products (American Academy of Pediatrics, 2016).

Clinical Manifestation

Down Syndrome

Epidemiology, Prevalence, and Etiology. Down syndrome (DS) is the most common genetic cause of ID, accounting for two-thirds of cases with genetic etiology. The estimated national prevalence in the United States is 14.47 per 10,000 live births, or 1 in 691 cases per birth (Parker et al., 2010). The syndrome was first recognized as a distinct disorder in 1866 by John Langdon Down. In 1959, Jerome Lejeune identified an extra copy of chromosome 21 (trisomy 21) as the cause.

All cases of DS arise from an overexpression of chromosome 21, and there are three variations: simple trisomy, translocation trisomy, and mosaic trisomy (see Arumugam et al., 2016, for review). Simple trisomy 21 is the most common form and accounts for 90–95% of all cases. Simple trisomy 21 arises during the formation of reproductive cells and is the result of an abnormal chromosome separation that occurs during mitotic division (nondisjunction). Translocation occurs when the additional copy of chromosome 21 is partially or fully translocated to another chromosome. Translocation trisomy 21 accounts for 5–6% of DS cases. Mosaic trisomy occurs when an extra chromosome 21 is present in some, but not all, of an individual's cells. This accounts for 2–3% of cases. DS is not usually inherited; however, some cases of translocation may be associated with genetic risk, and certain families may be more susceptible to nondisjunction and mosaicism. In most cases, the extra copy of trisomy 21 is of maternal origin.

Increased maternal age is the most frequently identified risk factor for giving birth to a child with DS. The most substantial increase in risk is present in mothers who are 35 years and older (Sherman et al., 2007). Data collected on US pregnancy outcomes from 2006 to 2010 documented a pooled prevalence of 11.6 in 10,000 for mothers aged 30–34, 30.3 in 10,000 for mothers aged 35–39, and 94.9 per 10,000 for mothers 40 and older (Mai et al., 2013). Despite the significant age-related increase in the risk for giving birth to a child with DS, most children are born to mothers younger than 35 years of age, given the higher number of overall pregnancies among younger women.

Studies examining differences in the prevalence of DS by maternal race and ethnicity have produced mixed results. One study documented the significantly higher prevalence of live DS births among Hispanics as compared with non-Hispanic Whites (Canfield et al., 2006). Another study found that after accounting for elective terminations, non-Hispanic White mothers have a higher live birth prevalence compared with non-Hispanic Black and Hispanic mothers (Jackson, Crider, Cragan, Rasmussen, & Olney, 2013). Findings regarding maternal race/ethnicity as a risk factor may be confounded by differences across groups in decisions about whether to undergo prenatal testing and decisions about pregnancy after learning the results of prenatal testing.

Physical Phenotype and Medical Comorbidities. The DS phenotype is characterized by anomalies across body systems (see Arumugam et al., 2016, for review). Dysmorphic craniofacial features are present at a higher frequency than the general population and are used to inform diagnosis. These include a flat and round face, narrow and slanted palpebral fissures, epicanthal folds, small white spots on the iris (Brushfield spots), hypertelorism, depressed nasal bridge and constricted nasal passages, small and low-set ears and an overlapping or folding of the helix of the ear, and a protruding tongue. Common musculoskeletal anomalies include short neck, hands, feet, and limbs, although with ligament laxity.

Medical comorbidities have also been reported. The prevalence of congenital cardiac disease ranges between 40% and 76% in this population. Gastrointestinal malformation are common, with a reported overall frequency of 7%. Children are at increased risk for hematological malignancies, celiac disease, and diabetes mellitus. Compared with the general population, children with DS have a 10–20-fold increased risk for acute leukemia (Hasle 2001; Hasle, Clemmensen, & Mikkelsen, 2000). Respiratory problems, obstructive sleep apnea being the most common, occur in 30–50% of individuals. Other medical problems commonly seen include metabolic disorders (e.g., thyroid dysfunction, overweight/obesity). Vision concerns include cataracts, acute keratoconus, and functional vision problems resulting from amblyopia or strabismus. Adults with DS present with accelerated aging and are at increased risk for Alzheimer disease.

Neurobehavioral Profile. Early development of communication and motor skills in infants and toddlers with DS is nearly always delayed. Studies examining milestone attainment in DS have found that skill development progresses in a trajectory that is similar to but slower than that of typically developing populations and populations with other neurodevelopmental disorders (Roberts, Price, & Malkin, 2007). However, as skills become more complex, the variability in the rate of milestone attainment increases in individuals with DS. Comorbid conditions can impact the rate at which skills develop. For example, recurrent ear infections are common in infants and toddlers with DS and can adversely impact speech and language development.

Nearly all individuals with DS present with ID. The severity ranges from mild to severe, although most cases are mild to moderate. In the context of mild to severe ID, the neurocognitive phenotype of DS is characterized by relative weaknesses in linguistic processing, attention, and executive function (Silverman, 2007). Weaknesses in selective and joint attention are evident in early childhood (Breckenridge, Braddick, Anker, Woodhouse, & Atkinson, 2013). School-age children with DS show disproportionate weaknesses in executive function when compared with children with ID from different etiologies (Breckenridge et al., 2013; Costanzo et al., 2013). Attention and behavior regulation problems have been associated with decreased motivation and compliance in early childhood; such deficits may limit participation in early intervention (Gilmore & Cuskelly, 2009). Results from our study showed that adolescents with DS are at increased risk for clinically significant problems with attention and behavior regulation that, in turn, independently and significantly predict deficits in adaptive skills (Jacola, Hickey, Howe, Esbensen, & Shear, 2014). Caregivers of young adults with DS report decreased inhibition, planning, and cognitive flexibility (i.e., executive dysfunction) before the onset of dementia (Ball, Holland, Treppner, Watson, & Huppert, 2008).

Neurological Basis. The neurocognitive phenotype of DS can be understood in the context of a trajectory of atypical neurodevelopment beginning with altered neuronal formation in the perinatal period (Garner & Wetmore, 2012; Haydar & Reeves, 2012). Pervasive cellular abnormalities, including abnormal dendritic branching and reduced synaptic pruning, are evident at birth (Garner & Wetmore, 2012; Haydar & Reeves, 2012). Structurally, the DS brain is characterized by differentially greater volume reductions in cerebellar, frontal cortex, and hippocampal volumes relative to overall brain volume (Pinter, Brown, et al., 2001; Pinter, Eliez, Schmitt, Capone, & Reiss, 2001). Functional magnetic resonance imaging studies demonstrate altered patterns of neural activation during cognitive tasks, including decreased activation in frontal cortical regions relative to age matched controls (Jacola et al., 2011, 2014; Losin, Rivera, O'Hare, Sowell, & Pinter, 2009). Physiological changes associated with cognitive decline (i.e., white matter degeneration) are present in early adulthood (Head, Silverman, Patterson, & Lott, 2012).

Long-Term Prognosis. Survival prognosis for individuals with DS has increased significantly over the past few decades. The survival rate of infants with DS in the United Kingdom was less than 50% in 1942 and 1952; by 1999–2003 the death rate had decreased significantly to 4.4% (Englund et al., 2013). Although the mortality rate is higher in children with DS compared with the general population (Day et al., 2005), longevity in individuals with DS has increased to around 60 years, up from 25 years in 1983, owing to

factors including improved management of comorbid childhood conditions, improved health care, and better nutrition. Many adults with DS live independently, marry, and are gainfully employed. Currently, common causes for mortality in adults with DS include congenital heart disease, respiratory diseases, circulatory disorders, and dementia.

Fragile X Syndrome

Epidemiology, Prevalence, and Etiology. Fragile X syndrome (FXS) is a sex-linked single gene disorder. FXS is the most common inherited cause of ID, with more recent meta-analysis suggesting rates of 1 in 7000 males and 1 in 11,000 females (Hunter et al., 2014). FXS is caused by unstable repetitions of the CGG trinucleotide on the long arm of the X chromosome. A full mutation reduces production of fragile X mental retardation protein (FMRP), which is vital for brain development. Females often experience less severe symptoms because they have one unaffected X chromosome that can compensate for the mutation on the other X chromosome. There is a risk for fragile X-associated tremor/ataxia syndrome in males with premutation status.

Physical Phenotype. FXS often results in classic physical characteristics including facial features (e.g., elongated face, prominent jaw and ears, large head size) and eye problems such as strabismus and nystagmus. Connective tissue abnormalities, including hyperflexible joints, flat feet, and scoliosis as well as hypotonia, often delay motor development. Neuroendocrine issues can include precocious puberty and early-onset menopause. There is an increased risk of cardiac problems (e.g., mitral valve prolapse) and seizures. Some physical features of FXS do not become noticeable until later in childhood, so developmental delays are often the first indication of this syndrome and early detection can be challenging: the mean age of diagnosis is at 36 months for males and higher for females (Tassone, 2014).

Comorbidities. Fragile X is the most common single gene cause of autism spectrum disorder (ASD), and up to half of males with FXS are diagnosed with ASD. Substantially elevated rates of attention-deficit/hyperactivity disorder (ADHD) are also seen, particularly in boys with FXS (Bailey, Raspa, Olmsted, & Holiday, 2008). Emotion regulation difficulties and sleep disorders are also very common. Females may be especially prone to anxiety and mood disorders.

Neurobehavioral Profile. Due to the X-linked transmission of FXS, males are affected more severely than females, and relations between FMRP levels and IQ have been identified. Most males with FXS show impaired intellectual functioning, where only about one-quarter of females with FXS have ID, and most perform in the borderline to low average range. Performance on cognitive tasks may decline with age, likely reflecting a widening gap as demands increase with age rather than a true regression (Huddleston, Visootsak, & Sherman, 2014). Verbal abilities are often stronger than nonverbal skills, although strengths can be seen in more rote skills across domains (e.g., vocabulary, visual matching, recognition memory), whereas weaknesses are seen with increased complexity (e.g., linguistic processing, visuoconstruction). Difficulties with sustained attention, working memory, and executive functioning are particularly pervasive in the FXS population, even after controlling for IQ. Academically, reading and spelling abilities are typically stronger than math skills, particularly with increased demands for working memory and sequential processing. Associated medical complications such as seizures also contribute to cognitive outcomes. Behavioral concerns including aggression and self-injury and co-occurring mental health issues are frequent.

Neurological Basis. Given that FMRP is crucial for dendritic spine maturation and pruning, reduced levels of this regulator result in structural and functional brain changes. The most consistent abnormalities have been in frontal-striatal regions and the cerebellar vermis. Enlargement of the caudate nucleus has been observed in FXS across the lifespan, and is negatively related to both FMRP levels and intellectual functioning. Reduced volume of the cerebellar vermis has also been observed in both males and females across the lifespan, and these reductions are related to lowered FMRP levels, intellectual functioning, visuospatial abilities, and executive functioning. Gothelf and colleagues (2008) found that together, enlarged caudate nucleus and reduced vermis volumes accounted for approximately one-third of the variation in IQ scores. Other neuroanatomical anomalies observed include enlarged ventricles and hippocampi and reduced amygdala and temporal lobe volumes. Widespread and regional connectivity changes have been identified and are consistent with neuroanatomical studies emphasizing the role of subcortical areas (Bruno et al., 2016).

Long-Term Prognosis. More than one-third of females with FXS are able to achieve independent living and a majority are employed. Males tend to have more educational and vocational difficulties, and most require ongoing support. Adaptive skills have been identified as the strongest predictor of independent living for males with FXS, whereas interpersonal skills may be most important for females (Hartley et al., 2011).

Williams Syndrome

Epidemiology, Prevalence, and Etiology. Williams syndrome (WS) is caused by a hemizygous microdeletion of at least 20 genes on chromosome 7q11.23. One of these is the elastin gene, which is used to confirm the diagnosis of WS with a fluorescent in situ hybridization test, and is thought to play a role in the cardiovascular issues often part of the phenotype. The *LIMK1* and *GTF2I* genes likely play a role in the cognitive profile, and the contributions of various other genes are under investigation. A partial phenotype can result from smaller deletions. Most cases occur sporadically, and it follows an autosomal dominant pattern of inheritance. WS is equally prevalent across ethnicities and genders and occurs in about 1 out of 7,500 live births.

Physical Phenotype. Individuals with WS exhibit common physical and medical features that are often identified early, including dysmorphic facial characteristics (e.g., broad brow, upturned nose, small jaw, prominent lips and earlobes), slowed growth, cardiovascular disease, and musculoskeletal problems. Hypotonia can contribute to feeding difficulties and motor delays. Gastrointestinal, endocrine, and sensory (vision, hearing) abnormalities are also common.

Comorbidities. About half of individuals with WS meet criteria for ADHD, typically the predominantly inattentive subtype. Individuals with WS are likely to experience anxiety problems persisting into adulthood, including specific phobias (especially of loud noises), obsessions, and anticipatory anxiety (Leyfer, Woodruff-Borden, Klein-Tasman, Fricke, & Mervis, 2006). Despite often having strong social interest, up to half may experience symptoms overlapping with ASDs, including restricted and repetitive interests and behaviors as well as sociocommunicative impairments (Klein-Tasman, Li-Barber, & Magargee, 2011).

Neurobehavioral Profile. A wide range of intellectual functioning has been observed for children with WS, although most function in the mild range of ID, making it a useful syndrome for studying gene-brain-behavior relations. Despite delays in early childhood, language abilities emerge as a relative strengths with age. Strengths are also seen in face processing and object recognition, while profound weaknesses is seen in visuospatial construction. Difficulties with fine motor coordination and executive skills including attention regulation and inhibitory control are also pervasive. Findings are mixed regarding short- and long-term memory, with some evidence for modality specific performance (verbal>nonverbal), and some finding impairment across domains (Sampaio, Sousa, Férnandez, Henriques, & Gonçalves, 2008). Behaviorally, individuals with WS are often quite sociable, but have sociocommunicative deficits that likely contribute to observed difficulty establishing and maintaining sustained peer friendships.

Neurological Basis. Studies have consistently observed a reduction in overall cortical volume with sparing of cerebellar volume. Reductions are most notable in white matter, with abnormal frontal-striatal connectively and basal ganglia atrophy likely underlying executive and motor difficulties. Gray matter is more preserved, except for posterior brain areas. Functional abnormalities have also been identified, with hypoactivation in parietal regions, consistent with the neuropsychological profile suggesting dorsal stream dysfunction. Increased amygdala activation has been seen in response to threatening scenes, consistent with the high rates of anxiety in WS, whereas reduced activation to threatening faces may be proportional to their level of hypersociability (Thornton-Wells, Avery, & Blackford, 2011).

Long-Term Prognosis. Life expectancy in WS is often normal, unless cardiovascular or other medical complications become severe. Many adults continue needing supervision for day-to-day and vocational tasks. It is currently unclear whether there is an increased risk for accelerated cognitive aging in WS (Cherniske et al., 2004).

Neuropsychological Assessment

Neuropsychologists interpret brain–behavior relationships in the context of ongoing development, contextual factors, and disease or acquired injury, in order to provide tailored recommendations focused on promoting current and future outcomes (Yeates, Ris, Taylor, & Pennington, 2010). Assessments consist of a comprehensive evaluation of strengths and weaknesses, careful integration of behavior observations, test performance, and information from clinical interview with the patient/proxy. This comprehensive, developmental approach can be readily applied to clinical work in the field of ID.

Neuropsychologists are well equipped to address challenges in diagnosis and measurement. Despite increased emphasis on adaptive functioning limitations, deficits in intellectual functioning remain an integral component of the diagnosis of ID. Without a demonstration of significantly impaired intellectual functioning, a diagnosis will not be considered. As shown in Table 4.1, diagnostic criteria specify that intellectual abilities are measured using standardized instruments. Each classification system includes cut-off scores for Full Scale IQ. Equal weight is placed on the relative contributions of component skills that comprise IQ, including verbal and nonverbal reasoning, attention and working memory, and processing speed. This perspective does not account for the individual variability in skill development that is evident during childhood and evident to the phenotype of many genetic syndromes. Studies of typically developing children and adolescents show that nearly half of age-related improvements in IQ can be attributed to developmental improvements in working memory and processing speed (Fry & Hale, 1996). Children with specific learning disabilities frequently have a significant discrepancy between verbal and nonverbal composite scores, such that Full Scale IQ does not accurately represent ability. As discussed previously in this chapter, genetic syndromes of ID (e.g., Down syndrome, Williams syndrome) present with a characteristic pattern of neurocognitive functioning. In these cases, a process-based, comprehensive assessment of neurobehavioral strengths and weaknesses is particularly useful for determining the presence and level of cognitive impairment.

Traditional measures of neurocognitive functioning have limited sensitivity to performance variability in low-functioning populations (i.e., those whose performance falls in the lower extremes of score range); consequently, they have limited utility for detecting change over time and in response to treatment or intervention. Comorbid disabilities, such as vision, hearing, or motor impairments, may further limit

Table 4.3 Clinical Manifestations of Intellectual Disability Syndromes

Syndrome	Common Physical Features	Neuropsychological Profile	Neurological Findings
Down syndrome (see **Janke & Klein-Tasman, in 2018**)	• Facial dysmorphology (e.g., flat face, small nose, upslanting eyes) • Short stature • Heart defects • Hearing, vision problems • Obstructive sleep apnea	Cognitive • Mild-moderate ID • Verbal < visuospatial • Weakness in EF • Declines seen with age Socioemotional • Relative strength in social skills • Risk for co-occurring psychiatric or behavioral issues relatively lower than other causes of ID	• Volume reductions, particularly in frontal, hippocampal, and cerebellar areas • Decreased activation is seen in frontal regions • White matter degeneration is noted in early adulthood
Fragile X syndrome (see **Schwarte, 2008**)	• Facial dysmorphology (e.g., long face, prominent jaw) • Macrocephaly • Connective tissue abnormalities • Neuroendocrine problems • Heart defects • Seizure risk	Cognitive • Moderate ID in males, borderline for females • Verbal > nonverbal; reading/spelling > math • Notable weakness in EF and motor Socioemotional • High rates of ADHD and ASD, particularly in males • Risk for both externalizing and internalizing disorders	• Abnormalities in frontal-striatal regions (particularly enlarged caudate) • Volume reduction in cerebellar vermis • Brain changes related to FMRP levels and IQ
Williams syndrome (see **van der Fluit, Brei, & Klein-Tasman, 2018**)	• Facial dysmorphology (e.g., "elfin" facies) • Connective tissue abnormalities • Cardiovascular problems • Hearing, vision problems	Cognitive • Mild ID • Verbal > visuospatial (with sparing of object recognition) • Weaknesses in EF motor Socioemotional • Hypersociability, but frequent overlapping symptoms with ASD • Chronic anxiety problems	• Volume reductions in posterior regions and basal ganglia • Dorsal stream dysfunction • Atypical amygdala activation
Prader-Willi (see **Kundert, 2008**)	• Facial dysmorphology (e.g., almond almond-shaped eyes, thin upper lip) • Strabismus • Early feeding difficulties, then hyperphagia and obesity • Short stature, small hands and feet	Cognitive • Mild-moderate ID • Verbal < nonverbal, but profile may vary by subtype (deletion vs. uniparental disomy) • Attention and academic problems Socioemotional • Repetitive behaviors (e.g., skin picking)	• Cortical atrophy, enlarged ventricles • Hypothalamic dysfunction • Perisylvian polymicrogyria

Table 4.3 (cont.)

Syndrome	Common Physical Features	Neuropsychological Profile	Neurological Findings
		• Risk for psychiatric disorders, ASD	
Angelman syndrome (see **Dan & Pelc, 2011**)	• Facial dysmorphology (prominent chin, wide mouth) • Microcephaly • Seizure risk • Ataxia • Near average lifespan	Cognitive • Severe ID • Nonverbal or very limited speech Socioemotional • Happy disposition, frequent laughter • Social interest • Hyperactivity & sleep problems • Hand flapping	• Characteristic EEG patterns • Minimal neuroanatomic research, with some indication of reduced cerebellar volumes and perisylvian anomalies
22q11.2 Deletion syndrome (see **Biswas & Furniss, 2016**)	• Facial dysmorphology (long face, narrow eyes) • Cleft palate • Heart problems • Conductive hearing loss • Risk for seizures andautoimmune disorders	Cognitive • 30% with ID, majority borderline range • Verbal > nonverbal; reading > math • Weakness also seen in motor skills, executive functioning, memory and social cognition Socioemotional • Risk for ADHD, anxiety, ASD, psychosis	• Reduced brain volume, particularly posteriorly • White matter more affected than gray matter • Abnormal frontal-subcortical circuitry
Tuberous sclerosis (see **de Vries, 2010**)	• Facial angiofibromas • Seizures in a majority • Risk for SEGA • Cardiac rhabdomyoma • Renal angiomyolipoma • Life expectancy variable depending on medical status	Cognitive • 50–60% with ID • Variable cognitive profile, though deficits in executive functioning particularly common, even with intact IQ Socioemotional • ASD and ADHD common	• Cortical tubers • Subependymal nodules • White matter lesions • Lesion load inconsistently related to cognitive functioning
Sturge-Weber syndrome (see **Suskauer, Trovato, Zabel, & Comi, 2010**)	• Port wine stain • Vascular malformations of eye • Seizures, migraines, stroke-like episodes • Hemiparesis can be indicator for screening cognitive function • Life expectancy may be average depending on medical status	Cognitive: • 50–60% with ID • Cognitive and motor functioning quite variable depending on neurological involvement • Risk for decline Socioemotional • Anxiety, mood disorder	• Vascular malformation of brain (usually same side as port wine stain) causing decreased perfusion • Cortical and subcortical calcification

Note: ADHD = attention-deficit/hyperactivity disorder, ASD = autism spectrum disorder, EEG = electroencephalogram, EF = executive functioning, FMRP = fragile X mental retardation protein, SEGA = subependymal giant cell astrocytoma.

the utility of traditional measures. In these cases, qualitative information, behavior observations, and, in some cases, nonstandardized assessment techniques are particularly useful for gaining meaningful information about an individual's functioning and progress over time and for developing tailored recommendations for intervention.

Intervention

Interventions for ID syndromes have largely been supportive rather than curative. However, for some etiologies, work is underway to modify underlying mechanisms to reduce disease burden (e.g., FXS, tuberous sclerosis; see Table 4.4). Such treatment options will surely have a significant impact on expected outcomes if the focus is shifted to normalizing function more so than mitigating impairments and managing comorbidities. Nonetheless, it is likely that ongoing weaknesses and complications will require remediation, and neuropsychologists are in a unique position to guide treatment planning from a biopsychosocial perspective.

Neuropsychological assessment considers the individual's level of overall functioning, specific phenotypes based on the etiology of ID and individual variability, and the neurological or medical factors contributing to this profile, all of which will affect the expected developmental trajectory and long-term outcomes. The neuropsychologist can provide valuable psychoeducation regarding these expected trajectories, recommendations about how to foster strengths while remediating areas of particular weakness, and service referrals to promote adaptive functioning and quality of life. Research has consistently highlighted the importance of early intervention for optimizing developmental gains. Ongoing assessment and monitoring will guide placement in the least restrictive academic setting, while also ensuring optimal supports and individualization. Particularly for moderate to severe ID, special education supports and related services will almost certainly be required, ideally with a focus on day-to-day skills and transition.

As has been discussed, ID syndromes also carry a high risk for dual diagnoses that may require treatment recommendations. Despite the clear need for treatment options, there is a paucity of research examining the effectiveness of mental health interventions for individuals with specific syndromes. However, there is emerging evidence that interventions

Table 4.4 Interventions and Treatments for Intellectual Disability Syndromes

Domain/Diagnosis	Interventions
Attention	• Psychostimulants (methylphenidate) and α-agonists have been effectively used in children and adults with ID (1), although there may be an increased risk for side effects. • Translational and applied behavioral analysis can be used to shape selective attention, impulse control, and task completion (2).
Motor	• Physical and occupational therapy services are often warranted. Environmental modification can be made in the school setting to improve accessibility, and assistive technology can reduce writing demands. Behavioral strategies (e.g., shaping, chaining, reinforced positive practice) with and without assistive technology can improve motor and adaptive skills (3).
Executive functioning and memory	• Working memory training has not consistently resulted in immediate or longer term transfer effects (4, 5). Baseline abilities and comorbid diagnoses may affect capacity to benefit from such interventions (6). • There is some indication that those with mild to moderate ID can be taught and benefit from metacognitive strategies such as rehearsal, mnemonics, elaboration, and retrieval practice (7–9). Material should be presented multimodally, tailored to specific phenotypes or the individual's profile. • Assistive technology can be used to improve self-management of academic and adaptive tasks by providing multimodal prompts (e.g., paired pictorial and auditory cues, pop-up reminders on devices, alarms) and video modeling (10, 11). • Exercise may promote attention and executive functioning in individuals with DS (12), and may be useful for other populations as well. • The efficacy for using acetylcholinesterase inhibitors to address memory impairment in DS has not yet been established (1).

Table 4.4 (cont.)

Domain/Diagnosis	Interventions
Language and reading	• Reinforcement strategies can be used to increase vocalizations, and alternative communication systems can be used to promote functional communication. • Language interventions must be tailored for specific syndromes and individuals, as the language profile can vary. For example, sign language has successfully been used for those with DS to improve expressive skills (13), but may be less appropriate for those with fine motor impairment (e.g., WS, FXS). • Multimodal interventions for reading and other academic domains is important, particularly for syndromes associated with stronger visuospatial skills (14, 15).
Mood disorders and anxiety	• Dual diagnosis is pervasive, so developmentally appropriate assessment of emotional functioning is critical (for review see [16]). There is also some evidence that behavioral programs can effectively manage mood symptoms, and negative thought processes can be reduced when cognitive strategies are incorporated. Cognitive behavioral strategies including behavioral modeling, relaxation training, gradual exposure to feared stimuli, and social skills training have been successfully implemented to manage anxiety symptoms, although outcomes have mostly been examined on a case-by-case basis. • Exercise may also improve mood and anxiety symptoms (17). • Controlled research examining the efficacy of antidepressants and anxiolytics are sparse and these medications are often associated with side effects including increased agitation (1).
Behavioral disorders	• Functional behavioral analysis and intervention can be used to shape problem behaviors, and there is some evidence that cognitive behavioral therapy modified for developmental level can be effectively used in the ID population (16, 18). • Although lithium can effectively reduce aggression, there is limited evidence for using antiepileptic, antidepressant, and anxiolytic medications for problem behaviors (1).
Disease-modifying treatments (see [19] for review)	• DS: Therapies altering gamma-aminobutyric acid–mediated inhibition to improve hippocampal function are being explored, with trials under way for children and adults. • FXS: Clinical trials are ongoing for therapies that regulate dendritic protein translation, despite the loss of FMRP. • Tuberous sclerosis: mTOR inhibitors (e.g., everolimus) have been used to improve central nervous system integrity and neurocognition. • Angelman syndrome: A pilot study using minocycline to improve language and motor functions has shown some promise and warrants further study. • Prader-Willi syndrome: Use of oxytocin to regulate feeding behaviors has not yet demonstrated significant benefits.

References: (1) Ji & Findling, 2016; (2) Deutsch, Dube, & McIlvane, 2008; (3) Houwen, van der Putten & Vlaskamp, 2014; (4) Dekker, Ziermans, & Swaab, 2016; (5) Perrig, Hollenstein, & Oelhafen, 2009; (6) Söderqvist, Nutley, Ottersen, Grill, & Klingberg, 2012; (7) Chung & Tam 2005; (8) Rinaldi, Hessels, Buchel, Hessels-Schlatter, & Kipfer, 2002; (9) Campione, Nitsch, Bray, Brown, 1980; (10) Browder, Wood, Thompson, & Ribuffo, 2014; (11) Mechling, 2007; (12) Chen & Ringenbach, 2016; (13) Wright, Kaiser, Reikowsky, & Roberts, 2013; (14) Steele, Scerif, Cornish, & Karmiloff-Smith, 2013; (15) Evmenova & Behrmann, 2011; (16) Janke, Schwartz & Klein-Tasman, 2016; (17) Carraro & Gobbi, 2012; (18) Medeiros, 2015; (19) van Karnebeek, Bowden, & Berry-Kravis, 2016.

commonly used and empirically validated in the general population can also be appropriately applied in the ID population if used in a flexible, simplified, and multimodal manner, depending on the individual's level of functioning. Behavioral approaches are the most frequently used, although recent research has examined use of treatment packages incorporating cognitive strategies, including cognitive behavioral therapy,

mindfulness, and dialectical behavioral therapy (see Janke, Schwarz, & Klein-Tasman, 2016, for review).

Table 4.4 summarizes what is known about remediating particular areas of weakness and treating psychiatric or behavioral difficulties for those with ID, which may be useful across specific etiologies. Specific suggestions for providing developmentally appropriate services and recommendations will also be described in the Implications for Clinical Practice section.

Implications for Clinical Practice

General Assessment Considerations

Measurement. Floor effects in standardized tests may limit ability to capture variability in performance in individuals with ID, particularly those with moderate, severe, or profound presentation. Alternate scoring procedures have been recommended for use in this population (Hessl et al., 2008; Orsini, Pezzuti, & Hulbert, 2014)

Comorbid Sensory and Motor Conditions. Individuals with ID are significantly more likely to present with comorbid sensory or motor conditions that may impact their ability to participate in standardized testing. Modifications to the environment and/or assessment material may be warranted to elicit a valid and meaningful estimate of ability. A full discussion of modifications is outside of the scope of this chapter, and some may be addressed in other chapters. Examples of environmental modifications include the use of alternate seating or positioning to promote breath support and avoid excessive fatigue. Assessment materials and procedures can be modified (alternate response modality, enlarged stimuli). Comorbid conditions should be considered when designing a test battery.

Behavior Observation and Management. Noncompliance, inattention, and overactivity can make sustaining effort and motivation during testing challenging. In these cases, it is particularly important to structure the environment to promote success and manage behavior by employing strategies that can be used before testing and to prevent and respond to misbehavior (Herschell, Greco, Filcheck, & McNeil, 2002).

Access to Resources. Eligibility for many programs depends on Medicaid eligibility. Federal and state programs may have chronological age limits for participation (e.g., Early Intervention). Operationalization of adaptive skill deficits may also vary and some programs require the use of specific assessment measures for eligibility determination.

Dual Diagnosis. Diagnostic overshadowing, or the tendency to attribute behavior or mood problems to ID instead of a comorbid condition, is common in this population. Diagnosis and management of comorbid conditions can critically impact individual adaptation to independent living and performance in school or the workplace. Symptom presentation may differ in individuals with ID. Resources available through the National Association for the Dually Diagnosed can be useful in differential diagnosis.

Considerations Specific to Developmental Stage

Infants, Toddlers, and Preschool-Age Children. Early identification of developmental delay ensures access to services, optimizes outcomes, and provides a basis for genetic testing to determine etiology. Studies emphasize the role of parental functioning and parent-child interactions in developmental outcomes. Emotional and behavior regulation (i.e., emerging executive functioning) are predictive of later achievement and adaptive success. Head and Abbeduto provide a systems-based model to use for assessment of these factors (Head & Abbeduto, 2007).

School Age. Academic plans should emphasize skills that will promote independence with activities of daily living (i.e., self-care, money management, reading schedules), acquisition of functional academics, and self-determination (i.e., problem-solving and decision-making; Wehmeyer et al., 2004). Young adolescents transitioning from grade school to high school should complete an updated neuropsychological evaluation in order to gauge progress and modify educational plans to ensure success in an environment with decreased contextual supports. Beginning in high school, educational programming should also include an individualized plan for transition to postsecondary educational or vocational settings.

Transition to Adulthood. Transition planning involves increased emphasis on areas including legal responsibility for decision-making, finances, and health care; independence with self-care and other activities of daily living; management of disruptive behavior; and identification of appropriate living arrangements.

Information regarding neurobehavioral strengths and weakness can be used to inform guardianship decisions and to identify appropriate vocational placements. Guardianship must be obtained through legal procedures; it is not assumed simply because an adult carries a diagnosis of ID. It is important that the student and family work with the educational and health-care teams to assess transition readiness. At the level of transition to vocational training programs, neuropsychologists can work with students and families to evaluate readiness and to educate families and individuals on their rights and responsibilities within a working environment. Repeated neuropsychological evaluations over a student's academic history can serve as critical and comprehensive documentation of a longstanding disability that is often required to gain access to services and programming.

Future Directions

Research is needed to develop valid and reliable assessment tools with adequate sensitivity to variability in low-functioning populations. The availability of psychometrically robust neurocognitive measures will provide clinicians and researchers with a mechanism for quantifying the acute and long-term impact of treatment modifications on neurodevelopmental and functional outcomes and contribute to the development of interventions to promote optimal adaptation and quality of life.

Additional Resources

- **Association of University Centers on Disabilities.** Organization that supports and promotes a network of university-based interdisciplinary programs in advancing policy and practice for and with individuals with disabilities, their families, and communities. Federally funded programs University Centers for Excellence in Developmental Disabilities (67; one in each state), Leadership Education in Neurodevelopmental Disabilities Programs (52; one in each state), and Developmental Disability Research Centers (15). More information can be found at https://www.aucd.org/template/index.cfm
- **National Association of State Directors of Developmental Disabilities Services.** Assists state agencies with the provision of services to children and adults with intellectual and developmental disabilities and their families. State-specific information, including contacts and organizations, can be found at http://www.nasddds.org/
- **Bureau of Vocational Rehabilitation.** Authorized by the Rehabilitation Act, the Bureau of Vocational

Rehabilitation provides individuals with disabilities services and supports needed to attain and maintain employment. Specific services vary by state and/or region, but generally include employer education, job shadowing and coaching programs, assistance with application to vocational/technical schools, and access to rehabilitation technology.
- **Center for Parent Information and Resources – Intellectual Disability.** Central resource of information and resources for parents and community parent centers. Includes information and resources for individuals with ID and their families from infancy to young adulthood. General information can be found at http://www.parentcenterhub.org/ and by searching "intellectual disability".

References

The AAIDD Ad Hoc Committee on Terminology and Classification. (2010). *Intellectual disability: Definition, classification, and systems of supports* (11th ed.). Washington, DC: American Association on Intellectual and Developmental Disabilities.

Alberta Clinical Practice Guidelines. (2003). *Canadian Child and Adolescent Psychiatric Review, 12*(3), 81–86.

American Academy of Pediatrics. (2016). Prevention of childhood lead toxicity. *Pediatrics, 138*(1). doi:10.1542/peds.2016-1493

American Psychiatric Association. (2000). *Diagnostic and statistical manual of mental disorders* (4th ed., text revision) (?DSM-IV-TR). Washington, DC: American Psychiatric Association.

American Psychiatric Association. (2013). *Diagnostic and statistical manual of mental disorders* (5th ed.) (DSM-5). Washington, DC: American Psychiatric Association.

Antonelli, M. C., Pallarés, M. E., Ceccatelli, S., & Spulber, S. (2016). Long-term consequences of prenatal stress and neurotoxicants exposure on neurodevelopment. *Progress in Neurobiology.* doi:10.1016/j.pneurobio.2016.05.005

Arumugam A., Raja K., Venugopalan, M., Chandrasekaran, B., Sampath, K. K., Muthusamy, H., & Shanmugam, N. (2016). Down syndrome – A narrative review with a focus on anatomical features. *Clinical Anatomy, 29*, 568–577. doi:10.002/ca.22672

Bailey, D. B., Raspa, M., Olmsted, M., & Holiday, D. B. (2008). Co-occurring conditions associated with FMR1gene variations: Findings from a national parent survey. *American Journal of Medical Genetics Part A, 146A*(16), 2060–2069. doi:10.1002/ajmg.a.32439

Ball, S. L., Holland, A. J., Treppner, P., Watson, P. C., & Huppert, F. A. (2008). Executive dysfunction and its association with personality and behaviour changes in the development of Alzheimer's disease in adults with Down syndrome and mild to moderate learning disabilities. *British Journal of Clinical Psychology, 47*(Pt 1), 1–29. doi:10.1348/014466507X230967

Biswas, A. B., & Furniss, F. (2016). Cognitive phenotype and psychiatric disorder in 22q11.2 deletion syndrome: A review. *Research in Developmental Disabilities, 53–54*, 242–257. doi:10.1016/j.ridd.2016.02.010

Braden, K., Swanson, S., & Di Scala, C. (2003). Injuries to children who had preinjury cognitive impairment: A 10-year retrospective review. *Archives of Pediatrics & Adolescent Medicine, 157*(4), 336–340.

Breckenridge, K., Braddick, O., Anker, S., Woodhouse, M., & Atkinson, J. (2013). Attention in Williams syndrome and Down's syndrome: Performance on the new early childhood attention battery. *British Journal of Developmental Psychology, 31*(Pt 2), 257–269. doi:10.1111/bjdp.12003

Browder, D. M., Wood, L., Thompson, J., & Ribuffo, C. (2014). *Evidence-based practices for students with severe disabilities* (Document No. IC-3). Retrieved from University of Florida, Collaboration for Effective Educator, Development, Accountability, and Reform Center, http://ceedar.education.ufl.edu/tools/innovation-configurations/

Bruno, J. L., Hosseini, S. M., Saggar, M., Quintin, E., Raman, M. M., & Reiss, A. L. (2016). Altered brain network segregation in fragile X syndrome revealed by structural connectomics. *Cerebral Cortex.* doi:10.1093/cercor/bhw055

Campione, J. C., Nitsch, K., Bray, N., & Brown. A. L. (1980). Improving memory skills in mentally retarded children. Empirical research and strategies for intervention (Technical Report No. 196). Champaign: Center for the Study of Reading, University of Illinois at Urbana-Champaign.

Canfield, M. A., Honein, M. A., Yuskiv, N., Xing, J., Mai, C. T., Collins, J. S., ... Kirby, R. S. (2016) National estimates and race/ethnic variation of selected birth defects in the United States, 1999–2001. *Birth Defects Research Part A: Clinical and Molecular Teratology, 76*, 747–756.

Carraro, A., & Gobbi, E. (2012). Effects of an exercise programme on anxiety in adults with intellectual disabilities, *Research in Developmental Disabilities, 33*, 1221–1226.

Centers for Disease Control and Prevention. (2004). Economic costs associated with mental retardation, cerebral palsy, hearing loss, and vision – United States, 2003. *Morbidity & Mortality Weekly Report. 53*(3): 57–59.

Chen, C. J., & Ringenbach, S. D. (2016). Dose-response relationship between intensity of exercise and cognitive performance in individuals with Down syndrome: A preliminary study. *Journal of Intellectual Disability Research, 60*(6), 606–614.

Cherniske, E. M., Carpenter, T. O., Klaiman, C., Young, E., Bregman, J., Insogna, K., ... Pober, B. R. (2004).

Multisystem study of 20 older adults with Williams syndrome. *American Journal of Medical Genetics, 131A*(3), 255–264. doi:10.1002/ajmg.a.30400

Chung, K. H., & Tam, Y. H. (2005). Effects of cognitive-based instruction on mathematical problem solving by learners with mild intellectual disabilities, *Journal of Intellectual & Developmental Disability, 30*(4), 207–216.

Costanzo, F., Varuzza, C., Menghini, D., Addona, F., Gianesini, T., & Vicari, S. (2013). Executive functions in intellectual disabilities: A comparison between Williams syndrome and Down syndrome. *Research in Developmental Disabilities, 34*(5), 1770–1780. doi:10.1016/j.ridd.2013.01.024

Dan, B., & Pelc, K. (2011). Angelman syndrome. In P. A. Howlin, T. Charman, & M. Ghaziuddin (Eds.), *The SAGE handbook of developmental disorders* (pp. 125–145). London: SAGE Publications.

Dekker, M., Ziermans, T., & Swaab, H. (2016). The impact of behavioural executive functioning and intelligence on math abilities in children with intellectual disabilities. *Journal of Intellectual Disability Research, 60*(11), 1086–1096. doi:10.1111/jir.12276

Debes, F., Weihe, P., & Grandjean, P. (2016). Cognitive deficits at age 22 years associated with prenatal exposure to methylmercury. *Cortex, 74*, 358–369. doi:10.1016/j.cortex.2015.05.017

Dos Santos, A. A., Hort, M. A., Culbreth, M., López-Granero, C., Farina, M., Rocha, J. B., & Aschner, M. (2016). Methylmercury and brain development: A review of recent literature. *Journal of Trace Elements in Medicine and Biology, 38*, 99–107. doi:10.1016/j.jtemb.2016.03.001

Deutsch, C. K., Dube, W. V., & McIlvane, W. J. (2008). Attention deficits, attention-deficit hyperactivity disorder, and intellectual disabilities. *Developmental Disabilities Research Reviews, 14*, 285–292.

de Vries, P. J. (2010). Neurodevelopmental, psychiatric and cognitive aspects of tuberous sclerosis complex. In D. J. Kwiatkowski, V. H. Whittemore, & E. A. Thiele (Eds.), *Tuberous Sclerosis Complex: Genes, Clinical Features and Therapeutics* (pp. 229–267). doi:10.1002/9783527630073.ch12

Donders, J., & Hunter, S. J. (2010). *Principles and practice of lifespan developmental neuropsychology*. Cambridge, UK: Cambridge University Press.

Evmenova, A. S., & Behrmann, M. M. (2011). Research-based strategies for teaching content to students with intellectual disabilities: Adapted videos. *Education and Training in Autism and Developmental Disabilities, 46*(3), 315–325.

Fry, A. S., & Hale, S. (1996). Processing speed, working memory, and fluid intelligence: evidence for a developmental cascade. *Psychological Science, 4*, 237–241.

Garner, C. C., & Wetmore, D. Z. (2012). Synaptic pathology of Down syndrome. *Advances in Experimental Medicine and Biology, 970*, 451–468. doi:10.1007/978-3-7091-0932-8_20

Gilmore, L., & Cuskelly, M. (2009). A longitudinal study of motivation and competence in children with Down syndrome: Early childhood to early adolescence. *Journal of Intellectual Disability Research*, *53*(5), 484–492. doi:10.1111/j.1365-2788.2009.01166.x

Gothelf, D., Furfaro, J. A., Hoeft, F., Eckert, M. A., Hall, S. S., O'Hara, R., … Reiss, A. L. (2008). Neuroanatomy of fragile X syndrome is associated with aberrant behavior and the fragile X mental retardation protein (FMRP). *Annals of Neurology*, *63*(1), 40–51. doi:10.1002/ana.21243

Hackman, D. A., Gallop, R., Evans, G. W., & Farah, M. J. (2015). Socioeconomic status and executive function: Developmental trajectories and mediation. *Developmental Science*, *18*(5), 686–702. doi:10.1111/desc.12246

Hartley, S. L., Seltzer, M. M., Raspa, M., Olmstead, M., Bishop, E., & Bailey, D. B. (2011). Exploring the adult life of men and women with fragile X syndrome: Results from a national survey. *American Journal on Intellectual and Developmental Disabilities*, *116*(1), 16–35. doi:10.1352/1944-7558-116.1.16

Hasle, H. (2001). Pattern of malignant disorders in individuals with Down's syndrome. *The Lancet Oncology*, *2*(7), 429–436.

Hasle, H., Clemmensen, I.H., & Mikkelsen, M. (2000). Risks of leukaemia and solid tumours in individuals with Down's syndrome. *Lance*, *355*(9199), 165–169.

Haydar, T. F., & Reeves, R. H. (2012). Trisomy 21 and early brain development. *Trends in Neuroscience*, *35*(2), 81–91. doi:10.1016/j.tins.2011.11.001

Head, L. S., & Abbeduto, L. (2007). Recognizing the role of parents in developmental outcomes: A systems approach to evaluating the child with developmental disabilities. *Mental Retardation and Developmental Disabilities Research Reviews*, *13*(4), 293–301. doi:10.1002/mrdd.20169

Head, E., Silverman, W., Patterson, D., & Lott, I. T. (2012). Aging and Down syndrome. *Current Gerontology and Geriatrics Research*, 412536. doi:10.1155/2012/412536

Herschell, A. D., Greco, L. A., Filcheck, H. A., & McNeil, C. B. (2002). Who is testing whom?: Ten suggestions for managing the disruptive behavior of young children during testing. *Intervention in School and Clinic*, *37*(3), 140–148. doi:10.1177/105345120203700302

Hessl, D., Nguyen, D. V., Green, C., Chavez, A., Tassone, F., Hagerman, R. J.,… Hall, S. (2008). A solution to limitations of cognitive testing in children with intellectual disabilities: the case of fragile X syndrome. *Journal of Neurodevelopmental Disorders*, *1*(1), 33–45. doi:10.1007/s11689-008-9001-8

Hornung, R. W., Lanphear, B. P., & Dietrich, K. N. (2009). Age of greatest susceptibility to childhood lead exposure: A new statistical approach. *Environmental Health Perspectives*, *117*(8), 1309–1312. doi:10.1289/ehp.0800426

Houwen, S., van der Putten, A., & Vlaskamp, C. (2014). A systematic review of the effects of motor interventions to improve motor, cognitive, and/or social functioning in people with severe or profound intellectual disabilities. *Research in Developmental Disabilities*, *35*(9), 2093–2116. doi:10.1016/j.ridd.2014.05.006

Huddleston, L. B., Visootsak, J., & Sherman, S. L. (2014). Cognitive aspects of Fragile X syndrome. *Wiley Interdisciplinary Reviews: Cognitive Science*, *5*(4), 501–508. doi:10.1002/wcs.1296

Hunter, J., Rivero-Arias, O., Angelov, A., Kim, E., Fotheringham, I., & Leal, J. (2014). Epidemiology of fragile X syndrome: A systematic review and meta-analysis. *American Journal of Medical Genetics Part A*, *164A*, 1648–1658.

Jackson, J. M., Crider, K. S., Cragan, J. D., Rasmussen, S. A., & Olney, R. S. (2013). Frequency of prenatal cytogenetic diagnosis and pregnancy outcomes by maternal race-ethnicity, and the effect on the prevalence of trisomy 21, metropolitan Atlanta, 1996–2005. *American Journal of Medical Genetics Part A*, *164A*, 70–76.

Jacola, L. M., Byars, A. W., Chalfonte-Evans, M., Schmithorst, V. J., Hickey, F., Patterson, B., … Schapiro, M. B. (2011). Functional magnetic resonance imaging of cognitive processing in young adults with Down syndrome., *American Journal on Intellectual and Developmental Disabilities*, *116*(5), 344–359. doi:10.1352/1944-7558-116.5.344

Jacola, L. M., Byars, A. W., Hickey, F., Vannest, J., Holland, S. K., & Schapiro, M. B. (2014). Functional magnetic resonance imaging of story listening in adolescents and young adults with Down syndrome: Evidence for atypical neurodevelopment. *Journal of Intellectual Disability Research*, *58*(10), 892–902. doi:10.1111/jir.12089

Jacola, L. M., Hickey, F., Howe, S. R., Esbensen, A., & Shear, P. K. (2014). Behavior and adaptive functioning in adolescents with Down syndrome: Specifying targets for intervention. *Journal of Mental Health Research in Intellectual Disabilities*, *7*(4), 287–305.

Janke, K. M., & Klein-Tasman, B. P. (in press). Down syndrome. In J. S. Kreutzer, J. DeLuca, & B. Caplan (Eds.), *Encyclopedia of clinical neuropsychology* (2nd ed.). New York: Springer.

Janke, K. M., Schwarz, G. N., & Klein-Tasman, B. P. (2016). Mental health in developmental disabilities. In H. Friedman (Ed.), *Encyclopedia of mental health* (2nd ed., Vol. 3, pp. 99–106). Cambridge, MA: Academic Press.

Ji, N. Y., & Findling, R. L. (2016). Pharmacotherapy for mental health problems in people with intellectual disability. *Current Opinion in Psychiatry*, *29*, 103–125.

Karam, S. M., Barros, A. J., Matijasevich, A., Santos, I. S., Anselmi, L., Barros, F., … Black, M. M. (2016). Intellectual disability in a birth cohort: Prevalence, etiology, and determinants at the age of 4 years. *Public Health Genomics, 19*(5), 290–297. doi:10.1159/000448912

Klein-Tasman, B. P., & Janke, K. M. (2010). Intellectual disability across the lifespan. In S. J. Hunter and J. Donders (Eds.), *Principles and practice of lifespan developmental neuropsychology* (pp. 221–238). New York: Cambridge University Press.

Klein-Tasman, B. P., Li-Barber, K. T., & Magargee, E. T. (2011). Honing in on the social phenotype in Williams syndrome using multiple measures and multiple raters. *Journal of Autism and Developmental Disorders, 41*(3), 341–351. doi:10.1007/s10803-010-1060-5

Königs, M., Engenhorst, P. J., & Oosterlaan, J. (2015). Intelligence after traumatic brain injury: Meta-analysis of outcomes and prognosis. *European Journal of Neurology, 23*(1), 21–29. doi:10.1111/ene.12719

Kundert, D. K. (2008). Prader-Willi syndrome. *School Psychology Quarterly, 23*(2), 246–257. doi:10.1037/1045-3830.23.2.246

Landry, S. H., Miller-Loncar, C. L., Smith, K. E., & Swank, P. R. (2002). The role of early parenting in children's development of executive processes. *Developmental Neuropsychology, 21*(1), 15–41. doi:10.1207/s15326942dn2101_2

Leyfer, O. T., Woodruff-Borden, J., Klein-Tasman, B. P., Fricke, J. S., & Mervis, C. B. (2006). Prevalence of psychiatric disorders in 4 to 16-year-olds with Williams syndrome. *American Journal of Medical Genetics Part B: Neuropsychiatric Genetics, 141B*, 615–622.

Lind, K., Toure, H., Brugel, D., Meyer, P., Laurent-Vannier, A., & Chevignard, M. (2016). Extended follow-up of neurological, cognitive, behavioral and academic outcomes after severe abusive head trauma. *Child Abuse & Neglect, 51*, 358–367. doi:10.1016/j.chiabu.2015.08.001

Losin, E. A., Rivera, S. M., O'Hare, E. D., Sowell, E. R., & Pinter, J. D. (2009). Abnormal fMRI activation pattern during story listening in individuals with Down syndrome. *American Journal on Intellectual and Developmental Disabilities, 114*(5), 369–380.

Mai, C. T., Kuckik, J. E., Isenburg, J., Feldkamp, M. L., Marengo, L. K., Burgenske, E. M., ... for the National Birth Defects Prevention Network. (2013). Selected birth defects data from population-based programs in the United States, 2006 to 2010: Featuring trisomy conditions. *Birth Defects Research Part A: Clinical and Molecular Teratology, 97*, 709–725.

Max, J. E., Schachar, R. J., Levin, H. S., Ewing-Cobbs, L., Chapman, S. B., Dennis, M., ... Landis, J. (2005). Predictors of attention-deficit/hyperactivity disorder within 6 months after pediatric traumatic brain injury. *Journal of the American Academy of Child & Adolescent Psychiatry, 44*(10), 1032–1040. doi:10.1097/01.chi.0000173293.05817.b1

May, P.A., & Gossage, J.P. (2001). Estimating the prevalence of fetal alcohol syndrome. A summary. *Alcohol Res Health, 25*(3), 159–167.

Maulik, P. K., Mascarenhas, M. N., Mathers, C. D., Dua, T., & Saxena, S. (2011). Prevalence of intellectual disability: A meta-analysis of population-based studies. *Research in Developmental Disabilities, 32*(2), 419–436. doi:10.1016/j.ridd.2010.12.018

McDermott, S., Durken, M. S., Schupf, N., & Stein, Z. A. (2007). Epidemiology and etiology of mental retardation. In J. Mulick, J. Rojahn, & J. Jacobson (Eds.), *Handbook of intellectual and developmental disabilities* (pp. 3–40). New York: Springer.

Mechling, L. C. (2007). Assistive technology as a self-management tool for prompting students with intellectual disabilities to initiate and complete daily tasks: A literature review. *Education and Training in Developmental Disabilities, 42*(3), 252–269.

Medeiros, K. (2015). Behavioral interventions for individuals with intellectual disabilities exhibiting automatically reinforced challenging behavior: Stereotypy and self-injury. *Journal of Abnormal Child Psychology 4*(141). doi:10.4172/2329-9525.1000141

Moeschler, J. B., Shevell, M., Committee on Genetics. (2014). Comprehensive evaluation of the child with intellectual disability or global developmental delays. *Pediatrics, 134*(3), e903–e918 doi:10.1542/peds.2014-1839

Moeschler, J. B. (2008). Medical genetics diagnostic evaluation of the child with global developmental delay or intellectual disability. *Current Opinion in Neurology, 21*(2), 117–122. doi:10.1097/wco.0b013e3282f82c2d

Moran, L. M., Babikian, T., Piero, L. D., Ellis, M. U., Kernan, C. L., Newman, N., ... Asarnow, R. (2016). The UCLA study of predictors of cognitive functioning following moderate/severe pediatric traumatic brain injury. *Journal of the International Neuropsychological Society, 22*(5), 512–519. doi:10.1017/s1355617716000175

Orsini, A., Pezzuti, L., & Hulbert, S. (2014). Beyond the floor effect on the Wechsler intelligence scale for children – 4th ed. (WISC-IV): Calculating IQ and indexes of subjects presenting a floored pattern of results. *Journal of Intellectual Disability Research, 59*(5), 468–473. doi:10.1111/jir.12150

Parker, S. E., Mai, C. T., Canfield, M. A., Rickard, R., Wang, Y., Meyer, R. E., ... National Birth Defects Prevention Network. (2010). Updated national birth prevalence estimates for selected birth defects in the United States, 2004-2006. *Birth Defects Research Part A, Clinical and Molecular Teratology, 88*(12), 1008–1016.

Perrig, W. J., Hollenstein, M., & Oelhafen, S. (2009). Can we improve fluid intelligence with training on working memory in persons with intellectual disabilities? *Journal of Cognitive Education and Psychology, 8*(2), 148–164. doi:10.1891/1945-8959.8.2.148

Pinter, J. D., Brown, W. E., Eliez, S., Schmitt, J. E., Capone, G. T., & Reiss, A. L. (2001). Amygdala and hippocampal volumes in children with Down syndrome: A high-resolution MRI study. *Neurology, 56*(7), 972–974.

Pinter, J. D., Eliez, S., Schmitt, J. E., Capone, G. T., & Reiss, A. L. (2001). Neuroanatomy of Down's syndrome: A high-resolution MRI study. *American Journal of Psychiatry, 158*(10), 1659–1665.

Rinaldi, D., Hessels, M. G. P., Büchel, F., Hessels-Schlatter, C., & Kipfer, N. M. (2002). External memory and verbalization in students with moderate mental retardation: Theory and training. *Journal of Cognitive Education and Psychology, 2*(3), 184–227. doi:10.1891/194589502787383272

Roberts, J. E., Price, J., & Malkin, C. (2007). Language and communication development in Down syndrome. *Mental Retardation and Developmental Disabilities Research Reviews, 13*, 26–35.

Sampaio, A., Sousa, N., Férnandez, M., Henriques, M., & Gonçalves, Ó F. (2008). Memory abilities in Williams syndrome: Dissociation or developmental delay hypothesis? *Brain and Cognition, 66*(3), 290–297. doi:10.1016/j.bandc.2007.09.005

Schwarte, A. R. (2008). Fragile X syndrome. *School Psychology Quarterly, 23*(2), 290–300. doi:10.1037/1045-3830.23.2.290

Schwartz, L. (2003). Long-term behavior problems following pediatric traumatic brain injury: Prevalence, predictors, and correlates. *Journal of Pediatric Psychology, 28*(4), 251–263. doi:10.1093/jpepsy/jsg013

Sherman, S. L., Allen, E. G., Bean, L. J., & Freeman, S. B. (2007). Epidemiology of Down syndrome. *Mental Retardation and Developmental Disabilities Research Review, 13*, 221–227.

Silverman, W. (2007). Down syndrome: Cognitive phenotype. *Mental Retardation and Developmental Disabilities Research Review, 13*(3), 228–236. doi:10.1002/mrdd.20156

Söderqvist, S., Nutley, S. B., Ottersen, J., Grill, K. M., & Klingberg, T. (2012) Computerized training of non-verbal reasoning and working memory in children with intellectual disability. *Frontiers in Human Neuroscience, 6*(271). doi: 10.3389/fnhum.2012.00271

Steele, A., Scerif, G., Cornish, K., & Karmiloff-Smith, A. (2013). Learning to read in Williams syndrome and Down syndrome: Syndrome-specific precursors and developmental trajectories. *Journal of Child Psychology and Psychiatry, 54*(7), 754–762.

Suskauer, S. J., Trovato, M. K., Zabel, T. A., & Comi, A. M. (2010). Physiatric findings in individuals with Sturge-Weber syndrome. *American Journal of Physical Medicine & Rehabilitation, 89*(4), 323–330. doi:10.1097/phm.0b013e3181ca23a8

Tassone, F. (2014). Newborn screening for fragile X syndrome. *JAMA Neurology, 71*(3), 355. doi:10.1001/jamaneurol.2013.4808

Thornton-Wells, T. A., Avery, S. N., & Blackford, J. U. (2011). Using novel control groups to dissect the amygdala's role in Williams syndrome. *Developmental Cognitive Neuroscience, 1*(3), 295–304. doi:10.1016/j.dcn.2011.03.003

Ursache, A., Noble, K.G., & Pediatric Imaging, Neurocognition and Genetics Study. (2016). Socioeconomic status, white matter, and executive function in children. *Brain and Behavior, 6*(10), e00531.

US Department of Health and Human Services, Health Resources and Services Administration, Maternal and Child Health Bureau. (2013). *The National Survey of Children with Special Health Care Needs Chartbook 2009–2010.* Rockville, MD: US Department of Health and Human Services.

van der Fluit, F. Brei, N. & Klein-Tasman, B. P. (2018). Williams syndrome. In J. S. Kreutzer, J. DeLuca, & B. Caplan (Eds.), *Encyclopedia of clinical neuropsychology* (2nd ed.). New York: Springer.

van Karnebeek, C. D., Bowden, K., & Berry-Kravis, E. (2016). Treatment of neurogenetic developmental conditions: From 2016 into the future. *Pediatric Neurology, 65*, 1–13. doi:10.1016/j.pediatrneurol.2016.07.010

Wehmeyer, M., Lawrence, M., Kelchner, K., Palmer, S., Garner, N., & Soukup, J. (2004). *Whose future is it anyway? A student-directed transition planning process* (2nd ed.). Lawrence, KS: Beach Center on Disability.

World Health Organization. (1996). ICD-10 Guide for Mental Retardation. http://www.who.int/mental_health/media/en/69.pdf. Accessed 1-6-2017.

World Health Organization. (2007). Atlas – Global Resources for Persons with Intellectual Disabilities. http://www.who.int/mental_health/evidence/atlas_id_2007.pdf. Accessed 1-6-2017.

Wright, C. A., Kaiser, A. P., Reikowsky, D. I., & Roberts, M. Y. (2013). Effects of a naturalistic sign intervention on expressive language of toddlers with down syndrome. *Journal of Speech Language and Hearing Research, 56*(3), 994.

Yeates, K. O., Ris, D. M., Taylor, H. G., & Pennington, B. (Eds.). (2010). *Pediatric neuropsychology: Research, theory, and practice* (2nd ed.). New York: Guilford Press.

Chapter 5

Fetal Alcohol Spectrum Disorders

Israel M. Gross and Doug Bodin

Introduction

Fetal alcohol spectrum disorders (FASD) is an umbrella term describing the range of physical, cognitive, behavioral, and psychosocial effects of prenatal alcohol exposure (PAE). These effects are lifelong and vary in severity. There are several phenotypes (outlined later in this chapter) that have specific criteria. Although FASD is a universal term used to describe the range of effects for PAE it is not a diagnostic label. Currently, there is no universally accepted set of criteria for the phenotypes of FASD, and the nomenclature varies among countries (Cook et al., 2016). With that being said, all diagnostic guidelines focus on facial dysmorphisms and central nervous system (CNS) abnormalities. Diagnostic criteria may vary with respect to the necessity for growth retardation (e.g., microcephaly) and the number of requirements to meet full criteria (e.g., the number of facial dysmorphisms). The phenotypes outlined in this chapter are based on diagnostic guidelines from the National Task Force on Fetal Alcohol Syndrome and Fetal Alcohol Effect (Bertrand et al., 2004) and the National Institute on Alcohol Abuse and Alcoholism consensus guidelines, which were updated in 2016 and largely based on the 1996 Institute of Medicine (IOM) recommended diagnostic guidelines (Hoyme et al., 2016).

Fetal Alcohol Syndrome. At the most severe end of the spectrum, individuals with PAE meet criteria for a diagnosis of fetal alcohol syndrome (FAS) (Mattson, Crocker, & Nguyen 2011). Three main conditions need to be present for a FAS diagnosis: (1) the presence of all three facial dysmorphisms associated with PAE: smooth philtrum, thin vermillion border, and small palpebral fissures; (2) confirmed pre- or postnatal height and/or weight less than the 10th percentile (at any one point), adjusted for appropriate demographics; and (3) confirmed CNS abnormalities, such as structural or neurological abnormalities and/or neurobehavioral deficits.

A diagnosis of FAS can be given with or without the known presence of PAE if an individual meets these three criteria. However, confirmed absence of PAE rules out a FAS diagnosis.

Partial FAS. Most individuals with PAE will not meet full criteria for a FAS diagnosis. Individuals may meet criteria for partial FAS if they have a documented PAE history and at least two of the characteristic facial dysmorphisms accompanied by neurobehavioral deficits. Without a confirmed PAE history there must also be either growth retardation or neurological impairment (Hoyme et al., 2016).

Alcohol-Related Birth Defects and Alcohol-Related Neurodevelopmental Disorder. In 1996 the IOM recommended using the terms alcohol-related birth defects (ARBD) and alcohol-related neurodevelopmental disorder (ARND) for individuals who do not meet the full FAS criteria. Diagnoses of ARBD or ARND require a confirmed history of PAE. ARBD requires at least one congenital structural defect in at least one organ system. People with ARBD are characterized as having normal growth and cognitive/behavioral characteristics. A diagnosis of ARND occurs when individuals have typical growth and structure, but at least one of the following characteristics: head circumference of less than 10% or structural brain abnormalities, or cognitive and/or behavioral deficits not better explained by other neurodevelopmental disorders, genetics, or environment. An ARND diagnosis is not conclusively provided until 3 years of age (Hoyme et al., 2016).

Neurobehavioral Disorder Associated with PAE. Similar to a diagnosis of ARND, the *Diagnostic and Statistical Manual of Mental Disorders*, 5th edition included a set of criteria for neurobehavioral disorder associated with PAE (ND-PAE). These criteria include documented PAE and neurobehavioral impairment with an onset in childhood. Facial dysmorphisms, growth retardation, and CNS involvement may be present, but is not necessary for the diagnosis. Lastly, these deficits and abnormalities are not better explained by other psychiatric, genetic, or neurodevelopmental conditions, or other teratogens (American Psychiatric Association, 2013). There has been some confusion as to the distinction between ND-PAE and ARND because they appear to have overlapping criteria. As articulated by Hoyme and colleagues (2016), however, ARND is a medical diagnosis provided by a multidisciplinary medical team, whereas ND-PAE is a mental health diagnosis provided by clinicians from multiple backgrounds to aid the application of appropriate treatments and interventions, and to facilitate insurance reimbursement.

Clinical Manifestation

Epidemiology

The Centers for Disease Control and Prevention (CDC) has estimated that FAS occurs in only 0.2–1.5 children per 1,000 children and the IOM estimates have been slightly higher, at 0.5–3.0 per 1,000 children (Bertrand et al., 2004). The most recent CDC study analyzing medical records found a FAS prevalence rate of just 0.3 per 1,000 children ages 7–9 years in Arizona, Colorado, and New York (CDC, 2015). The overall prevalence rates for all FASDs are higher, at approximately 10 per 1,000 children (Astley, 2010). However, when active case ascertainment methodology is utilized, higher prevalence rates for FAS and others FASDs have been identified. May and colleagues (2014) used active case ascertainment of a sample of first-grade Midwestern US children and found 6–9 per 1,000 children likely met criteria for FAS and 24–48 per 1,000 children for a FASD. A 2016 meta-analysis of the global prevalence rate of FASDs estimated 23 cases per 1,000 children (Roozen et al., 2016).

Pathophysiology

Alcohol is a well-documented teratogen that has significant negative impact on the CNS of the developing fetus at all stages of gestation (Feldman et al., 2012). There has been no identification of a "safe" level of alcohol consumption during pregnancy. Alcohol quickly crosses the placenta to the developing fetus and the alcohol concentration between fetus and mother is relatively equal (British Medical Association [BMA], 2016). However, part of the increased risk to the fetus is the result of inefficient

alcohol elimination, as well as extended alcohol exposure. Specifically, the activity of alcohol dehydrogenase in the fetal liver is less than 10% of an adult liver. In addition, the amniotic fluid serves as a basin for alcohol, prolonging exposure, because when the fetus eliminates alcohol, it is often "recycled" through intramembranous absorption and/or the fetus swallows amniotic fluid (Heller & Burd, 2014).

The harmful effect of fetal alcohol exposure varies between gestational time periods; however, detrimental neurobehavioral impact may occur at any time during gestation, and in the absence of facial or neuroanatomical abnormalities (Mattson et al., 2011). Notable alcohol exposure during the first trimester is most likely to be associated with facial and structural abnormalities consistent with meeting FAS criteria. Fetal alcohol exposure in the second trimester is associated with spontaneous abortion and exposure in the third trimester is correlated with low weight, reduced length, and lower levels of brain growth (Feldman et al., 2012). Neuroimaging studies have correlated fetal alcohol exposure with reduced brain volume in nearly all areas of the brain, including the frontal lobes, striatum, caudate nucleolus, thalamus, cerebellum, and amygdala (Lebel, Roussotte, & Sowell, 2011). In addition, corpus callosum development disruption, resulting in possible thickening or thinning of the corpus callosum, as well as white matter abnormalities within the cerebellum, have been identified (Bookstein, Streissguth, Sampson, Connor, & Barr, 2002; Wozniak & Muetzel, 2011). The region of the brain with the least amount of impact appears to be the occipital lobes (Lebel et al., 2011).

Prevention

In many Western countries, such as the United Kingdom, the United States, and Canada, alcohol consumption is mainstream and many women of child-bearing age consume alcohol as part of "normal life" (BMA, 2016). According to a 2005 Behavioral Risk Factor Surveillance System report, approximately half of women ages 18–44 years in the United States reported alcohol consumption during the previous month (Floyd, Weber, Denny, & O'Connor, 2009). The harmful effects of PAE are entirely preventable. However, given that nearly 50% of pregnancies in the United States are not planned, early intervention programs must begin before conception occurs (Finer & Henshaw, 2006) because the most severe forms of FAS correlate with alcohol consumption during the first few weeks after conception (Feldman et al., 2012).

As described by Floyd and colleagues (2009), a 2004 US Preventive Services Task Force on FASD postulated that the prevention of PAE requires societies to address alcohol consumption preconception with universal prevention programs. These programs are aimed at reducing the overall risk of PAE in the general population regardless of risk, as well as among populations deemed "at-risk" (Floyd et al., 2009). Universal prevention programs vary greatly, but include the use of alcohol warning labels, media campaigns, warning labels at point of purchase, increased alcohol taxes, and reduced alcohol access. In fact, some have strongly advocated for vastly increasing the cost and limiting access to alcohol, as well as altering the cultural norms around alcohol, as an effective method of reducing the incidence rate of FASD (BMA, 2016). The Task Force has argued for the need to continue to research and evaluate more effective prevention measures, as these strategies alone have not led to notable reductions in FAS incidence rates. Such strategies seem to be more effective for those who have low levels of alcohol consumption preconception than for those who have severe alcohol dependence problems (Chersich et al., 2011).

In addition to universal prevention programs, the Task Force has advocated for selective and indicated prevention strategies (Floyd et al., 2009). Alcohol screening and brief interventions among women of child-bearing age (regardless of pregnancy status) have been found to reduce the rate of alcohol consumption and have been found to be efficacious in multiple settings, such as emergency departments, primary care clinics, and college campuses (Chersich et al., 2011). A 2011 study in South Africa found that when maternal knowledge of the dangers of PAE is low, an intervention utilizing local media and health promotion presentations increased maternal knowledge and greatly reduced the odds for the incidence of FASD in these communities. However, the rates for FAS were unchanged, supporting the notion that education and awareness alone are not enough for FAS prevention (Chersich et al., 2011). For women who might be at greater risk for alcohol consumption during pregnancy (e.g., those who have given birth to a child with a FASD, or who have an alcohol dependence problem) the availability and access to substance abuse treatment is imperative. In the United States, several intensive brief intervention programs specifically targeting at-risk groups have been found to reduce alcohol consumption before and during future pregnancies, resulting in improved birth outcomes (BMA, 2016).

Multifaceted prevention/intervention programs are being established to reduce the incidence rate of FASD. For example, in Canada, a holistic approach to preventing FASD includes four different prevention levels and uses the support of available family members. At the first level, public awareness of the harmful effects of PAE, as well as where to receive help is promoted across all socioeconomic levels. Second, health-care providers are encouraged to have respectful and informed discussions about the risks of alcohol consumption during pregnancy with their female patients (as well as with their support networks when possible). Third, for pregnant women who have alcohol consumption problems, there is access to specialized substance abuse and mental health treatment. Finally, postpartum support is provided for new mothers trying to maintain alcohol consumption reduction (BMA, 2016). At this time, continued research for effective screening and brief interventions is strongly indicated. Furthermore, there is burgeoning research in the area of pharmacological intervention for PAE, which appears promising; however, much of this research has been conducted with animal models (Floyd et al., 2009).

Neuropsychological and Behavioral Profile

PAE is associated with significant cognitive, psychological, and behavioral impairments (see Table 5.1). The severity of such deficits may correlate with facial dysmorphology and physical malformations, but this is not always true (Rasmussen, 2005). Furthermore, neurobehavioral deficits are frequently present among individuals with PAE who do not exhibit the physical features necessary for a FAS diagnosis. Although the physical malformations associated with FAS attenuate with age, neurobehavioral deficits persist into adulthood and commonly result in substance abuse, delinquent behavior, and other adverse life outcomes (Mattson et al., 2011). Not all children with PAE exhibit neurobehavioral deficits. In a 2013 multisite, international study, Mattson and colleagues estimated that approximately 30% of children with heavy PAE exhibit no neurobehavioral deficits when compared with similar matched controls. Factors believed to influence the severity of PAE on neurobehavioral outcomes include gestational timing of maternal alcohol ingestion, genetics, nutrition, chronicity, and volume of alcohol consumed, as well as other demographic factors (Mattson et al., 2013).

Table 5.1 Neurobehavioral Deficits and Neuroanatomical Correlates Among Children with FASD (Lebel et al., 2011)

Neurobehavioral Domain Deficits	Neuroanatomical Correlates
General Intelligence • Significant global cognitive deficits, which are positively correlated with degree of facial dysmorphology • Average FSIQ for FAS ~70 and for other FASDs ~80 • Severity of IQ deficits positively correlated with facial dysmorphology	• Overall brain volume is significantly correlated with IQ (however relationship relatively weak) • Relationship stronger for nonverbal than verbal domains
Attention and Executive Function • Attentional deficits in the areas of information processing, sustained attention, slowed reaction time, sustained attention • Working memory deficits in encoding and shifting focus • EF deficits in the areas of response inhibition, set-shifting, fluency, concept formation, cognitive flexibility, problem-solving, planning, and social cognition	• Reduced size of frontal lobe (more prominent in left hemisphere) • Abnormalities in the dorsal lateral prefrontal cortex • Hyperfusion in right frontal lobe • Reduced size of caudate and relates substructures • Thickening of the corpus callosum
Visual Perceptual and Spatial Processing • Visual perceptual deficits related to specific details • Visual-motor integration deficits	• Abnormal development of hippocampal structures
Language • Initial language delay related to suspected central auditory processing deficits • Receptive and expressive language deficits, with greater deficits in the receptive domain Language deficits may attenuate over time	• Limited neuroimaging studies correlating language (outside of verbal learning tasks and IQ) with neuroanatomical correlates for FASD
Verbal Learning and Memory • Notable encoding deficits • Recall deficits observed, but are no longer present when initial encoding deficits are controlled for	• Reduced hippocampal volume • Corpus callosum displacement • Thickening of dorsal frontal cortex • Cerebellar vemis morphology
Nonverbal Learning and Memory • Encoding inefficiencies • Recall deficits observed; may be the result of poor encoding • Spatial reasoning and visual-motor deficits likely underlying contributors to deficits in this domain	• Reduced hippocampal volume • Corpus Callosum Displacement
Motor Function • Fine and gross motor deficits (at moderate to heavy levels of PAE) • Gross motor deficits inconsistent across studies • Some fine motor deficits in children appear to represent a developmental delay; others may be lifelong deficits	• Volume and size reduction in the areas of cerebellum and caudate nucleus • Thinning of the corpus callosum • Skeletomuscular and peripheral motor nerve damage are notable contributors to motor deficits
Academics • Significant mathematical deficits; basic numerical processing impairment • Deficits increase with age and appear to be dose dependent • Reading and spelling impairments may also be present, but deficits are less than those in mathematics	• Abnormalities medial frontal gyrus and left and right parietal regions

Table 5.1 (cont.)

Neurobehavioral Domain Deficits	Neuroanatomical Correlates
Adaptive Functioning • Impairment in communication, socialization, and daily living skills • Arrest in adaptive functioning skills and level of impairment increases with age	• Limited neuroimaging studies correlating adaptive functioning with neuroanatomical correlates for FASD
Psychosocial, Behavioral Functioning, and Psychopathology • Early attachment issues • Poor self-regulation, impaired social judgment and emotional processing • Environmental factors may mediate the impact of PAE and behavior • Psychosocial and behavioral impairment persist into adult • Externalizing behaviors • Hyperactivity, impulsivity, aggression, social problems, delinquent, and conduct problems • Internalizing behaviors • Negative affect, anxiety, and mood lability • Majority of children with FASD have a comorbid mental health diagnosis • Rates of ADHD, oppositional defiant disorder, conduct disorder, specific phobia, and depressive disorders higher than rates in "healthy" controls. • Increase in substance abuse issues • Increase risk for suicide attempts (lifetime)	• Abnormalities in the medial frontal and orbitofrontal cortex and corresponding networks • Abnormalities in the amygdala and superior temporal sulcus

The negative impact of PAE is not only the direct teratogenic effect on the embryo, but the negative environmental factors associated with PAE. These environmental factors include low socioeconomic status, poor prenatal nutrition and care, other prenatal drug exposures, childhood trauma, parental substance use, neglectful home environments, and/or inconsistent home placement (Crocker, Vaurio, Riley, & Mattson, 2009; Greenbaum, Stevens, Nash, Koren, & Rovet, 2009). These aversive factors contribute to an environment of "toxic stress," which can lead to permanent changes in brain development and structure and subsequent neurobehavioral outcomes (Shonkoff et al., 2012). Moreover, the teratogenic effect of PAE on the brain lays the foundation for greater susceptibility to the environmental factors of toxic stress, which exacerbates their negative impact with respect to neurobehavioral outcomes. Given these known detrimental and often co-occurring environmental factors associated with PAE, much of the neurobehavioral research in this area attempts to control for such factors via well-matched control groups or statistical analysis (Streissguth, 2007).

The next sections outline the most salient cognitive, behavioral, and psychosocial issues associated with FASD. It is important to remain cognizant that individuals with FASD represent a heterogeneous cognitive group and there are notable individual differences with respect to neurobehavioral deficits exhibited (Nash et al., 2013). Overall, children with FASD exhibit intellectual deficits that correlate with severity of facial dysmorphology and have notable executive functioning, visual-spatial, learning and memory, and motor impairments. In addition, clinically significant externalizing behaviors in the areas of hyperactivity, impulsivity, and poor self-regulation, as well as notable social and conduct problems, are reported. Adaptive functioning is an area of significant weakness, which represents an arrest in development, and the level of impairment increases with age. These neurobehavioral deficits are lifelong and often worsen with age in the absence of intervention.

General Intelligence. One of the most consistent neurocognitive findings for individuals with PAE is impaired intellectual functioning. Notably, FAS is the leading recognizable cause of intellectual disability (Mattson et al., 2011). Severity of facial dysmorphology and physical malformation is positively correlated with severity of intellectual disability (Mattson et al., 2011; Nash et al., 2008). However, many individuals with PAE exhibit impaired intelligence without facial dysmorphologies or other physical malformations associated with PAE (Green et al., 2009). As reported by Mattson and colleagues' 2011 review article of neurobehavioral functioning, prior research has identified an average Full Scale Intelligence Quotient (FSIQ) estimate of 70 for those diagnosed with FAS, and higher functioning (average FSIQ estimate of 80) for those without dysmorphic features. In addition, there is often significant discrepancy between verbal and nonverbal intellectual abilities, but not in a consistent manner. Research on low or moderate levels of PAE has exhibited mixed results with respect to overall intelligence, some studies finding declines in intelligence and others finding no deficits (Mattson et al., 2011).

Attention and Executive Functioning. Children with FASD exhibit significant attentional difficulties in the areas of sustained attention, information processing, shifting focus, and reaction time, as well as in the areas related to working memory, such as encoding and shifting attention (Mattson et al., 2010, 2013; Nash et al., 2008). Both parent and teacher report of clinically elevated levels of attentional difficulties is common (Aragon et al., 2008; Nash et al., 2006). Among children with FASD, the comorbidity with attention-deficit/hyperactivity disorder (ADHD) is extremely high. However, unlike children with ADHD, attentional deficits are not uniformly found (Mattson et al., 2011).

Executive functioning (EF) is a set of higher-ordered cognitive abilities, which encompass working memory; planning, sequencing, and organizing information; response inhibition; shifting attention; and cognitive flexibility. In addition, problem-solving and the organization of one's thoughts and behaviors into goal-directed action are critical components of EF (Pennington & Ozonoff, 1996). EF is believed to be divided into "hot" and "cool" processes. Cool EF is believed to be mediated by the dorsolateral prefrontal cortex and encompasses the cognitive components of EF. Hot EF is believed to be mediated by the orbitofrontal cortex and responsible for processing affective states, motivation, and emotional behavior (Zelazo & Muller, 2002).

With respect to FASD, deficits in both cold and hot EF are well documented (Green et al., 2009;

Mattson et al., 2010, 2013; Rasmussen, 2005). In particular, deficits in EF abilities include response inhibition, problem-solving and planning, concept formation and set-shifting, fluency, verbal reasoning, cognitive flexibility, working memory, as well as social cognition emotion-based EF (Green et al., 2009; Mattson et al., 2013). Working memory – the ability to hold and manipulate information – is a critical component of EF and is imperative for performing well on many EF tasks (Ramussen, 2005). Children and adults with PAE have consistently exhibited working memory deficits. Such impairment presents in both verbal and nonverbal working memory domains (Mattson et al., 2010). A study by Green and colleagues (2009) comparing a mix sample of children with FASD to sex- and age-matched controls identified that tasks relying on spatial working memory exhibited the greatest sensitivity to EF deficits.

A number of studies within The Collaborative Initiative on Fetal Alcohol Spectrum Disorders program (see Mattson et al., 2010 for more information on this interdisciplinary project) have identified that EF and spatial processing are most sensitive to PAE (Mattson et al., 2013) and are an integral part of the neurobehavioral profile of FASD. In a large multisite study, Mattson and colleagues (2010) were able to differentiate between children with FASD and healthy controls with a high degree of accuracy mainly based on IQ, EF, and spatial-processing variables. Using logistic regression, these investigators were able to obtain a 75.9% (FAS group) and 73.5% (PAE not meeting full FAS criteria) overall classification accuracy rate for distinguishing children with PAE from healthy controls. When additional neurocognitive variables were included in the model, most containing either a direct or indirect EF component, the overall classification accuracy increased to 92% for distinguishing between healthy controls and children with FAS and 85% for those with PAE, but who did not meet full criteria for FAS.

Several findings within the EF FASD literature are important to highlight. EF impairment has been found to minimally differ between individuals who meet criteria for FAS and for those who do not (Rasmussen, 2005). This is in contrast to other cognitive domains (e.g., learning and memory, IQ), which exhibits a positive correlation between level of cognitive deficits and severity of facial dysmorphisms and physical malformations. Some EF deficits are believed to be mediated by IQ impairment often present among individuals with FASD. However, as highlighted in Rasmussen's 2005 review of EF in FASD, many areas of EF are lower than what would be predicted (based on IQ), as well as when statistically controlling for IQ. Among individuals living with FASD, EF impairment is found across the lifespan. Notable differences between healthy controls and those with PAE are evident as early as 1 year of age (Rasmussen, 2005).

Language. The research on language development among children with PAE has been equivocal. According to Nash and colleagues' review of the neurobehavioral literature, initial delays in language are conceptualized as reflecting central auditory processing deficits (Nash et al., 2008). Language delays may remain evident in the school years and typically there are both receptive and expressive language deficits, with greater impairment within the receptive domain. In their review of the neurobehavioral literature, Mattson and colleagues (2011) highlight consistent language impairment in the areas of word comprehension, grammar and semantic abilities, and expressive and receptive abilities when retrospective studies are utilized. However, in review, these authors found more inconsistent language impairment with prospective study designs. For example, in a prospective study design, O'Leary and colleagues (2009) did not find an association between PAE and parent report of language delays and in a series of prospective studies, deficits in language comprehension at 13 months of age, 2 years, and 3 years were no longer present at the ages of 5 and 6 years. As noted by Nash and colleagues (2008), prospective studies on FASD are often associated with lower levels PAE, which may be partially responsible for the variability of language outcomes in these studies.

Visual Perceptual and Spatial Processing. Children with FASD exhibit both visual-perceptual and visual-spatial deficits (Mattson et al., 2011). In a 1996 study examining visuoperceptual and spatial processing, Mattson and colleagues found that children with PAE exhibit a deficit for processing the details (and not the global feature) of geometric figures compared to typically developing controls. PAE has been found to disrupt healthy development of the hippocampus, a region of the brain imperative for visual-spatial functioning (Lebel et al., 2011). The visual-spatial deficits observed in children with FASD are believed to contribute to their spatial working memory and learning and memory deficits as discussed in the next section (Mattson et al., 2011). Moreover, Mattson and colleagues (2010) found tasks with a spatial-processing component to add incremental classification ability with respect to distinguishing between children with FASD and healthy controls. This finding is consistent with The Seattle Prospective Longitudinal study, which identified spatial-processing deficits among individuals with PAE, even at low levels of exposure (Streissguth, 2007).

Learning and Memory. Children and adults with PAE exhibit notable impairment on tasks of both verbal and nonverbal memory (Coles, Lynch, Kable, Johnson, & Goldstein, 2010; Mattson & Roebuck, 2002). However, in both the verbal and nonverbal domains, these observed deficits are strongest for efficiently acquiring and encoding information. Overall recall and recognition deficits are present to a lesser degree than initial learning impairment, and in some studies retention of verbal information is relatively spared (Mattson & Roebuck, 2002). Learning and memory deficits are present throughout the spectrum of FASD but individuals with the physical features of FAS present with greater overall deficits (Coles et al., 2010; Mattson et al., 2011). The hippocampus, a region of the brain imperative for memory consolidation and retrieval, is believed to be particularly susceptible to the teratogenic effects of alcohol (Willoughby, Sheard, Nash, & Rovet, 2008). These authors reported smaller left hippocampi in children with FASD as well as stunted volume growth compared with healthy controls.

Verbal learning and memory. On list learning tasks, such as the California Verbal Learning Test-Children's Version (CVLT-C), children with PAE exhibit deficits with respect to encoding of information and recall and recognition abilities (Crocker, Vaurio, Riley, & Mattson, 2011). However, other researchers have found retention rates to be commensurate with healthy controls when poor initial encoding is accounted for on the CVLT-C (Mattson & Roebuck, 2002). Support for inefficient encoding of information (both verbal and nonverbal) has been found in other studies as well, and also with young adults (Coles et al., 2010). On verbal tasks presented within a context (e.g., story tasks), children with PAE exhibit improved performance compared with their abilities on list-learning tasks, but still at levels below typically developed controls (Mattson et al., 2011).

Nonverbal learning and memory. Individuals with PAE exhibit inefficient encoding of information, as well as poor retention of information (Aragon et al., 2008; Mattson et al., 2010, 2011; Willoughby et al., 2008). However, given the methodological and task discrepancies among studies, it is unclear whether poor retention of nonverbal information is directly related to poor encoding and consolidation (Mattson et al., 2011). In addition, some research has suggested spatial reasoning and visual-motor deficits may be underlying cognitive contributors to the nonverbal learning and memory deficits exhibited by individuals with PAE (Mattson et al., 2013).

Motor Functioning. PAE is associated with both fine and gross motor impairment, with more consistent deficits in fine motor functioning than in gross motor functioning (Mattson et al., 2011). As summarized in a review by Mattson and colleagues (2011), gross motor deficits with the most support include atypical gait and postural instability, although these gross motor deficits are not consistent among studies. Some areas of fine motor deficits include fine motor speed, bimanual coordination, oculomotor control, weak grasp, hand–eye coordination, and poor sensorimotor functioning (Green et al., 2009; Mattson et al., 2011). The literature is mixed with respect to the persistence of motor deficits. Simmons and colleagues (2006) reported that motor reaction time deficits in childhood are no longer present by adolescence, but other research investigating fine motor control and balance reported data that suggest continued motor deficits into adulthood (Connor, Sampson, Streissguth, Bookstein, & Barr, 2006). Discrepancies with respect to the continuity of motor deficits likely reflects the myriad of motor skills, as well as the possibility that some motor impairments may represent a developmental delay, whereas others represent lifelong impairment (Mattson et al., 2011). Neuroimaging studies have identified notable volume and size reductions in areas of the brain associated with motor movement, such as the cerebellum and caudate nucleus (Lebel et al., 2011). However, a proportion of the motor functioning deficits associated with PAE is related to abnormal peripheral motor development, as well as skeletal malformations of the hands and feet often associated with PAE (Mattson et al., 2011). A review of the fine motor skill literature for children with PAE by Doney and colleagues (2014) suggests that complex fine motor skills such as visual-motor integration, rather than

basic fine motor skills, are more likely to be impaired among those with PAE. In addition, they report few studies that identify fine motor deficits at low levels of PAE, as the majority of studies that documented fine-motor deficits were at moderate to heavy levels of PAE.

Academic Functioning. Mathematics, and in particular, basic numerical skills, has consistently been an area of notable impairment for children with PAE (Mattson et al., 2011; Goldschmidt, Richardson, Stoffer, Geva, & Day, 1996). Neuroimaging studies have documented abnormalities in brain regions believed to be critical for mathematics, such as the medial frontal gyrus and the left and right parietal regions (Lebel et al., 2011). Longitudinal cohort studies controlling for cofounding variables such as postnatal traumatic events and prenatal exposure to other drugs (Streissguth et al., 1994), as well as low socioeconomic status (Howell, Lynch, Platzman, Smith, & Coles, 2006), have documented severe mathematical deficits from childhood to adolescence. Children with FASD may also have academic difficulties in the areas of reading and spelling, but typically to a lesser degree than their mathematic deficits (Streissguth et al., 1994). In another longitudinal study of PAE, Goldschmidt and colleagues (1996) identified a linear dose-respondent relationship with respect to mathematic deficits, whereas deficits in the areas of reading and spelling required meeting a specific threshold of PAE. Furthermore, academic impairments persist when controlling for IQ, although to a lesser degree (Goldschmidt et al., 1996; Howell et al., 2006).

Adaptive Functioning. Children with PAE may exhibit adaptive functioning deficits. Adaptive functioning is the ability to successfully manage tasks of daily living and respond to one's environment appropriately. In a study comparing adaptive functioning among three groups (children with PAE, children with ADHD, and children who are developing typically), the children with PAE and ADHD demonstrated adaptive functioning deficits in the domains of communication, socialization, and daily living skills (Crocker et al., 2009). Furthermore, children with PAE exhibited significantly lower scores than the ADHD group in the area of daily living skills. Moreover, in this study, the adaptive functioning deficits were positively correlated with age for the PAE group of children. In contrast to ADHD there appears to be an arrest in adaptive functioning development for children with FASD, as opposed to a mere delay.

These authors hypothesized that this widening of adaptive functioning abilities represents the continued EF deficits experienced by children with PAE. With increase in age, tasks of daily living increase and increase required EF abilities. As typically developed children age, their EF abilities mature as well, whereas children with PAE experience lifelong EF deficits (Crocker et al., 2009).

Psychosocial and Behavioral Functioning. Children with FASD present with notable psychosocial and emotional difficulties, as well as maladaptive behaviors. These difficulties are first observable in infancy and continue throughout the lifespan. In infancy, there are often feeding problems, sleeping difficulties, and attachment issues (Nash et al., 2008). In early childhood, parent and teacher reports are noteworthy for externalizing behaviors, such as hyperactivity, impulsivity, and aggression (Aragon et al., 2008; Nash et al., 2006), as well as teacher reports of social problems (Greenbaum et al., 2009). In addition, children with FASD frequently exhibit such internalizing symptoms as greater mood lability and negative affect, and are at greater risk for depressive disorders than typically developing children with no PAE (Mattson et al., 2011; Nash et al., 2008). Other research has identified substantial anxiety symptoms among children with PAE (Walthall, O'Connor, & Paley, 2008). In comparison with other children at risk for greater externalizing behaviors (e.g., children with ADHD), children with FASD are reported to have greater delinquent and conduct problems, as well as increased high school dropout rates. However, not all studies have found increases in conduct problems compared with healthy controls (Howell et al., 2006) and might be more reflective of clinical samples than community samples (Greenbaum et al., 2009).

Studies have provided support for impaired social cognition and emotional processing among children with PAE (Greenbaum et al., 2009). Research by Schonfeld, Mattson, and Riley (2005) identified impaired moral reasoning and judgment related to social interactions among children with PAE, which was associated with an increase in stealing and conduct problems. Other investigators have found increases in lying behavior, as well better-developed lying ability at earlier ages (Rasmussen, Talwar, Loomes, & Andrew, 2008). In addition, other interpersonal deficits such as difficulty with perspective taking and accurately reading social cues are also common (Nash et al., 2008). Emotional processing and social cognition deficits, in conjunction with impaired language and EF, are the likely underpinnings for the social emotional difficulties and delinquent behaviors that are often associated with PAE (Greenbaum et al., 2009).

Psychopathology. Compared with typically developing controls with no PAE, children with FASD are at significant risk for developing a mental health disorder (Walthall et al., 2008). In a community sample of children with heavy PAE, 97% of these children met *Diagnostic and Statistical Manual of Mental Disorders*, 4th edition criteria for a mental health disorder (Fryer, Mcgee, Matt, Riley, & Mattson, 2007). For children with FASD, the rates for ADHD, oppositional defiant disorder, conduct disorder, specific phobia, and depressive disorders are substantially higher than nonexposed typically developing controls. Childhood and adolescent behavioral difficulties and psychiatric illness are often lifelong and lead to substance abuse issues during adulthood (Alati et al., 2008). In a follow-up study from birth to 21 years of age, Alati and colleagues (2006) found a 3-fold increase in the rate of alcohol disorders at the age of 21 among young adults with PAE during early pregnancy and small but significant increases for those with PAE in late pregnancy.

Neuropsychological Assessment

Most individuals with PAE do not exhibit the physical features associated with a FAS diagnosis, thus leading to a high rate of individuals with a history of PAE without a FASD diagnosis. Neuropsychological assessment has demonstrated significant potential for identifying individuals who may meet criteria for FASD diagnosis, because the neurobehavioral deficits outlined in the previous sections are critical for a portion of FASD diagnoses (Mattson et al., 2010). Furthermore, the neurobehavioral profile of FASD has been found to be distinguishable from other often comorbid conditions (i.e., ADHD), which further supports the benefit of neuropsychological assessment, to aid in diagnostic accuracy and referrals for appropriate treatment and intervention. It is critical that neuropsychological assessment include a detailed psychosocial history to identify the potential impact of the aforementioned environmental factors that are commonly associated with PAE (Bertrand et al., 2004). In addition, given the extensive heterogeneous nature of neurobehavioral deficits among children with PAE, a comprehensive neuropsychological assessment is warranted, with notable attention paid to the areas of EF and spatial reasoning.

Intervention

The negative effects of PAE on neurobehavioral functioning in children and adolescents are irreversible and static in nature. As a result, the target of interventions is not to seek a "cure" but to ameliorate the functional impairments that result from the neurobehavioral deficits. As described in the previous section, there is extensive literature detailing the cognitive, behavioral, communication, academic, and psychosocial deficits associated with FASD. Interventions are typically undertaken to target one or more of these areas of deficit. Broadly, interventions for the negative effects of PAE can be categorized as either pharmacological or nonpharmacological.

Pharmacological Intervention

There are no federally approved medication treatments specifically for FASD. However, medications are commonly prescribed to manage the negative effects of PAE. Given the high rates of comorbidity between FASD and ADHD (Burd, Klug, Martsolf, & Kerbeshian, 2003), investigators have primarily examined the effectiveness of stimulant medication on managing ADHD symptoms in children with FASD. Snyder, Nanson, Snyder, and Block (1997) and Oesterheld et al. (1998) examined the effectiveness of psychostimulant medication on improving ADHD symptoms in children with FASD and found improvement in hyperactivity-impulsivity symptoms. More recently, Doig, McLenna, and Gibbard (2008) also found that hyperactivity-impulsivity symptoms were more responsive to stimulant medication treatment than were inattention symptoms. O'Malley, Koplin, and Dohner (2000) described a pilot study that found better response rates for dextroamphetamine compared with methylphenidate. Taken together, these studies provide limited support of the use of stimulant medication for managing the hyperactivity-impulsivity symptoms in children with FASD, although certain medications may perform better than others. Further research is clearly needed, especially large-scale double-blind placebo studies examining multiple outcomes.

Nonpharmacological Intervention

Nonpharmacological intervention for children and adolescents with FASD typically targets one or more of the myriad difficulties that these individuals face, such as problems with behavior, academics, socialization, and communication (Paley & O'Connor, 2009). Given the multiple areas of functional impairment attributed to PAE, and the lifelong nature of the impairment (Rangmar, Hjern, Vinnerjung, Stromland, & Aronson, 2015), it is surprising that there is a paucity of intervention studies in this area. Premji, Benzies, Serrett, and Hayden (2006) and Peadon, Rhys-Jones, Bower, and Elliott (2009) published systematic reviews on the intervention literature for children with FASD. Both groups were unable to perform meta-analyses because of the diversity of interventions and outcomes measured. Premji et al. identified ten intervention studies that met inclusion criteria and examined either psychostimulant medication or cognitive control therapy. Only two of these studies utilized randomized control trial (RCT) methodology. Improvement in behavior but not academics or neuropsychological test performance was reported for studies examining cognitive control therapy. Peadon et al. (2009) identified 12 intervention studies that met inclusion criteria. These studies were criticized for numerous methodological weaknesses, such as small sample sizes, poor study design, and lack of longitudinal follow-up. Within that context, studies reviewed documented some support for techniques such as virtual reality training, cognitive control therapy, language therapy, math intervention, rehearsal training for memory, social skills training, and attention process training.

Previous intervention studies largely examined the effectiveness of programs that were adapted to the FASD population but were not designed specifically for children with FASD. In 2001, the CDC provided financial awards for investigators to develop treatment programs specifically designed for children with FASD and their families. Bertrand (2009) summarized the five studies that resulted from these CDC financial awards. *Project Bruin Buddies* is a social skills training program using parents as social skills facilitators and designed to account for the common neuropsychological deficits seen in children with FASD. The treatment group, compared with a delayed treatment control group, showed increased knowledge of appropriate social behavior, improved parent report of social skills, and a decline in behavior problems after the intervention. These improvements were maintained at a 3-month follow-up. The *Georgia Sociocognitive Habilitation Using the Math Interactive Learning Experience (MILE)* program was designed to improve the behavioral and mathematical functioning of children with FASD. The MILE program involved a psychoeducational component to provide compensatory learning strategies directly to the children to facilitate math learning, as well as training for parents and teachers. A subset of the sample also received math tutoring. The parent training component was associated with improvements in behavior and the math tutoring component, in addition to the psychoeducational component, was associated with clinically significant academic gains. The *Neurocognitive Habilitation for Children with FASD* program combined teaching self-regulatory techniques with tools for improving EF. Family education and support was also provided. Significant improvement in executive functions was observed in the treatment group compared with a control group. The fourth study used a *parent-child interaction therapy* paradigm to reduce behavior problems in children with FASD. Improvements in behavior were observed in two different group-based interventions. Finally, the *Families Moving Forward* program was designed to improve caregiver self-efficacy, meet family needs, and reduce behavior problems. Positive effects on parenting attitudes and child behavior were documented in this study.

More recently, Petrenko (2015) provided a review of the empirical support for behavioral interventions and family support programs designed for youth with FASD. That review showed limited support for programs designed to enhance the parent-child relationship for infants and toddlers with FASD. Parent education and training programs were reviewed and demonstrated positive outcomes for both preschool and school-age children with FASD. Petrenko (2015) also reviewed studies that showed some success for attention training and metacognition strategies for children with FASD. Finally, the review yielded no peer-reviewed studies of interventions for adolescents and young adults with FASD although two ongoing trials were noted.

Implications for Clinical Practice

The clinical care of individuals with FASD is complex and requires the health-care provider to be familiar with multiple factors within the individual and within the health-care system (see Table 5.2). During the early childhood years, many children with FASD are involved in the foster care system (Astley, 2010). In addition, mental health comorbidities are common across the lifespan (Burd et al., 2003). As a result, case management services are crucial in this population (Paley & O'Connor, 2009). In addition to adequate case management, providers are encouraged to take a lifespan perspective when working with the FASD population. Most

Table 5.2 Factors to Consider in the Care of Individuals with FASD

- Case management
  - Knowledge of the foster care system
  - Management of multiple comorbidities
  - Lifespan perspective
- Protective factors
  - Early diagnosis
  - Appropriate diagnosis
  - Stable and nurturing home
- Risk factors
  - Delayed diagnosis
  - Violence in the home
  - Exposure to abuse
  - Lower cognitive functioning
  - Male gender

studies examining the outcome of PAE have focused on children and adolescents. However, recent studies have documented poor psychosocial outcomes during adulthood (Rangmar et al., 2015; Streissguth et al., 2004), including problems with completing secondary education, high rates of unemployment, and high rates of disability. Finally, professionals involved in the care of individuals with FASD need to understand the multitude of risk and protective factors related to various outcomes in this population. Receiving an appropriate diagnosis at an early age has been documented as a strong protective factor against negative psychosocial outcomes (Rangmar et al., 2015; Streissguth et al., 2004). An early diagnosis allows families to pursue appropriate early intervention services and provides health-care professionals the opportunity to assist families with setting appropriate and realistic expectations for their child. Additional protective factors against negative outcomes include a stable nurturing home (Streissguth et al., 2004) and an appropriately labeled diagnosis (Paley & O'Connor, 2009; Streissguth et al., 2004). The latter finding represents somewhat of a paradox because children diagnosed using the term *fetal alcohol effects* have been found to be at greater risk than those diagnosed with the more severe FAS because the latter diagnostic label is more likely to result in referrals for appropriate services. Although the diagnostic term *fetal alcohol effects* is not consistent with current nosology, this paradox highlights the importance of recognizing the risks that are inherent across the FASD severity spectrum. Risk factors identified include delayed diagnosis, exposure to violence in the home, abuse, lower cognitive ability, and male gender (Paley & O'Connor, 2009; Streissguth et al., 2004). Knowledge of these various risk and protective factors is crucial for clinical care of individuals with FASD. Treatment programs must be multisystemic and address such environmental risk factors that might contribute to problems as parental substance use, parental stress, and mental health comorbidities (Paley & O'Connor, 2009). Assessment procedures should be comprehensive enough to collect information about potential risk and protective factors at the child, family, and societal levels.

Future Directions

FASD is best viewed from a lifespan perspective with increased risks for difficulties with psychosocial, cognitive, and behavioral functioning from early childhood to adulthood. Previous research has identified numerous risk and protective factors that can be targeted in the course of assessment and intervention efforts. Although the past two decades have witnessed an increase in research on the outcomes of individuals with FASD, methodological weaknesses persist and warrant further investigation. More specifically, few intervention studies in this area employ control groups or use RCT methodology. In addition, most of the literature examining the outcomes in FASD only measure short-term outcomes and do not always control for the various environmental factors that are linked to outcomes. As a result, more longitudinal RCT studies are needed. The bulk of the treatment studies in FASD have examined interventions for school-age children with less attention given to interventions for infants, toddlers, and adults. Intervention studies should also seek to address environmental stressors and to increase protective factors, such as encouraging stable and nurturing home environments during childhood and increasing supports during adolescence and adulthood.

References

Alati, R., Al Mamun, A., Williams, G. M., O'Callaghan, M., Najman, J. M., & Bor, W. (2006). In utero alcohol exposure and prediction of alcohol disorders in early adulthood: A birth cohort study. *Archives of General Psychiatry*, *63*, 1009–1016.

Alati, R., Clavarino, A., Najman, J. M., O'Callaghan, M., Bor, W., Al Mamun, A., ... Williams, G. M. (2008).

The developmental origin of adolescent alcohol use: Findings from the Mater University study of pregnancy and its outcomes. *Drug and Alcohol Dependence*, *98*, 136–143.

American Psychiatric Association. (2013). *Diagnostic and statistical manual of mental disorders* (5th ed.). Arlington, VA: American Psychiatric Publishing

Aragon, A. S., Coriale, G., Fiorentino, D., Kalberg, W. O., Buckley, D., Gossage, J. P., ... May, P. A. (2008). Neuropsychological characteristics of Italian children with fetal alcohol spectrum disorders. *Alcoholism Clinical and Experimental Research*, *32*, 1909–1919.

Astley, S. J. (2010). Profile of the first 1,400 patients receiving diagnostic evaluations for fetal alcohol spectrum disorder at the Washington State Fetal Alcohol Syndrome Diagnostic & Prevention Network. *Canadian Journal of Clinical Pharmacology*, *17*, e132–e164.

Bertrand, J. (2009). Interventions for children with fetal alcohol spectrum disorders (FASDs): Overview of findings for five innovative research projects. *Research in Developmental Disabilities*, *30*, 986–1006.

Bertrand, J., Floyd, R. L., Weber, M. K., O'Connor, M., Riley, E. P., Johnson, K. A., ... National Task Force on Fetal Alcohol Syndrome and Fetal Alcohol Effect. (2004). *Fetal alcohol syndrome: Guidelines for referral and diagnosis.* Atlanta, GA: Centers for Disease Control and Prevention. Available at: www.cdc.gov/ncbddd/fasd/documents/fas_gui delines_accessible.pdf (Accessed on February 16, 2018).

Bookstein, F. L., Streissguth, A. P., Sampson, P. D., Connor, P. D., & Barr, H. M. (2002). Corpus callosum shape and neuropsychological deficits in adult males with heavy fetal alcohol exposure. *Neuroimage*, *1*, 233–251.

British Medical Association. (June 2007, updated February 2016). Alcohol and pregnancy: Preventing and managing fetal alcohol spectrum disorders. Retrieved from http://www.bma.org.uk/workingforchange/improvingandprotec tinghealth/alcohol/alcoholandpregnancy

Burd, L., Klug, M. G., Martsolf, J. T., & Kerbeshian, J. (2003). Fetal alcohol syndrome: Neuropsychiatric phenomics. *Neurotoxicology and Teratology*, *25*, 697–705.

Centers for Disease Control and Prevention (CDC). (2015). Fetal alcohol syndrome among children aged 7–9 years – Arizona, Colorado, and New York, 2010. *MMWR Morbidity and Mortality Weekly Report*, *64*, 54–57. Retrieved from https://www.cdc.gov/mmwr/preview/mmwrhtml/mm6403a2.htm

Chersich, M. F., Urban, M., Olivier, L., Davies, L. A., Chetty, C., & Viljoen, D. (2011). Universal prevention is associated with lower prevalence of fetal alcohol spectrum disorders in northern cape, South Africa: A multicentre before-after study. *Alcohol and Alcoholism*, *47*, 67–74.

Coles, C. D., Lynch, M. E., Kable, J. A., Johnson, K. C., & Goldstein F. C. (2010). Verbal and nonverbal memory in adults prenatally exposed to alcohol. *Alcoholism Clinical and Experimental Research*, *34*, 897–906.

Connor, P. D., Sampson, P. D., Streissguth, A. P., Bookstein, F. L., & Barr, H. M. (2006). Effects of prenatal alcohol exposure on fine motor coordination and balance: A study of two adult samples. *Neuropsychologia, 44*, 744–751.

Cook, J. L., Green, C. R., Lilley, C. M., Anderson, S. M., Baldwin, M. E., Chudley, A. E., ... the Canada Fetal Alcohol Spectrum Disorder Research Network. (2016). Fetal alcohol spectrum disorder: A guideline for diagnosis across the lifespan. *Canadian Medical Association Journal, 188*, 1–7.

Crocker, N., Vaurio, L., Riley, E. P., & Mattson, S. N. (2009). Comparison of adaptive behavior in children with heavy prenatal alcohol exposure or attention-deficit/hyperactivity disorder. *Alcoholism Clinical and Experimental Research, 33*, 2015–2023.

Crocker, N., Vaurio, L., Riley, E. P., & Mattson, S. N. (2011). Comparison of verbal learning and memory in children with heavy prenatal alcohol exposure or attention-deficit/hyperactivity disorder. *Alcoholism Clinical and Experimental Research, 35*, 1114–1121.

Doig, J., McLennan, J. D., & Gibbard, W. B. (2008). Medication effects on symptoms of attention-deficit/hyperactivity disorder in children with fetal alcohol spectrum disorder. *Journal of Child and Adolescent Psychopharmacology, 18*, 365–371.

Doney, R., Lucas, B. R., Jones, T., Howat, P., Sauer, K., & Elliott, E. J. (2014). Fine motor skills in children with prenatal alcohol exposure or fetal alcohol spectrum disorder. *Journal of Developmental and Behavioral Pediatrics, 35*, 598–609.

Feldman, H. S., Jones, K. L., Lindsay, S., Slymen, D., Klonoff-Cohen, H., Kao, K., ... Chambers, C. (2012). Prenatal alcohol exposure patterns and alcohol-related birth defects and growth deficiencies: A prospective study. *Alcoholism Clinical and Experimental Research, 36*, 670–676.

Finer, L. B., & Henshaw, S. K. (2006). Disparities in rates of unintended pregnancy in the United States, 1994 and 2001. *Perspectives on Sexual and Reproductive Health, 38*, 90–96.

Floyd, R. L., Weber, M. K., Denny, C., & O'Connor, M. J. (2009). Prevention of fetal alcohol spectrum disorders. *Developmental Disabilities Research Reviews, 15*, 193–199.

Fryer, S. L., McGee, C. L., Matt, G. E., Riley, E. P., & Mattson, S. N. (2007). Evaluation of psychopathological conditions in children with heavy prenatal alcohol exposure. *Pediatrics, 119*, e733–e741.

Goldschmidt, L., Richardson, G. A., Stoffer, D. S., Geva, D., Day, N. L. (1996). Prenatal alcohol exposure and academic achievement at age six: A nonlinear fit. *Alcoholism Clinical and Experimental Research, 20*, 763–770.

Green, C. R., Mihic, A. M., Nikkel, S. M., Stade, B. C., Rasmussen, C., Munoz, D. P., & Reynolds, J. N. (2009). Executive function deficits in children with fetal alcohol spectrum disorders (FASD) measured using the Cambridge Neuropsychological Tests Automated Battery (CANTAB). *Journal of Child Psychology and Psychiatry, 50*, 688–697.

Greenbaum, R. L., Stevens, S. A., Nash, K., Koren, G., & Rovet, J. (2009). Social cognitive and emotion processing abilities of children with fetal alcohol spectrum disorders: A comparison with attention deficit hyperactivity disorder. *Alcoholism Clinical and Experimental Research, 36*, 670–676.

Heller, M., & Burd, L. (2014). Review of ethanol dispersion, distribution, and elimination from the fetal compartment. *Birth Defects Research Part A: Clinical and Molecular Teratology, 100*, 277–283.

Howell, K. K., Lynch, M. E., Platzman, K. A., Smith, G. H., & Coles, C. D. (2006). Prenatal alcohol exposure and ability, academic achievement, and school functioning in adolescence: A longitudinal follow-up. *Journal of Pediatric Psychology, 31*, 116–126.

Hoyme, H. E., Kalberg, W. O., Elliott, A. J., Blankenship, J., Buckley, D., Marais, A. S., ... May, P. A. (2016). Updated clinical guidelines for diagnosing fetal alcohol spectrum disorders. *Pediatrics, 138*, 1–19.

Lebel, C., Roussotte, F., & Sowell, E. R. (2011). Imaging the impact of prenatal alcohol exposure on the structure of the developing human brain. *Neuropsychology Review, 21*, 102–118.

Mattson, S. N., Crocker, N., & Nguyen, T. T. (2011). Fetal alcohol spectrum disorders: Neuropsychological and behavioral features. *Neuropsychology Review, 21*, 81–101.

Mattson, S. N., & Roebuck, T. M. (2002). Acquisition and retention of verbal and nonverbal information in children with heavy prenatal alcohol exposure. *Alcoholism: Clinical and Experimental Research, 26*, 875–882.

Mattson, S. N., Roesch, S. C., Fagerlund, A., Autti-Rämö, I., Jones, K. L., May, P. A., ... the CIFASD. (2010). Toward a neurobehavioral profile of fetal alcohol spectrum disorders. *Alcoholism: Clinical and Experimental Research, 34*, 1640–1650.

Mattson, S. N., Roesch, S. C., Glass, L., Deweese, B. N., Coles, C. D., Kable, J. A., ... the CIFASD. (2013). Further development of a neurobehavioral profile of fetal alcohol spectrum disorders. *Alcoholism: Clinical and Experimental Research, 37*, 517–528.

May, P. A., Baete, A., Russo, J., Elliott, A. J., Blankenship, J., Kalberg, W. O., ... Hoyme, H. E. (2014). Prevalence and characteristics of fetal alcohol spectrum disorders. *Pediatrics, 134*, 855–866.

Nash, K., Sheard, E., Rovet, J., & Koren, G. (2008). Understanding fetal alcohol spectrum disorders (FASDs): Toward identification of a behavioral phenotype. *The Scientific World Journal, 8*, 873–882.

Nash, K., Rovet, J., Greenbaum, R., Fantus, E., Nulman, I., & Koren, G. (2006). Identifying the behavioural phenotype in fetal alcohol spectrum disorder: Sensitivity, specificity and screening potential. *Archives of Women's Mental Health, 9*, 181–186.

Nash, K., Stevens, S., Rovet, J., Fantus, E., Nulman, I., Sorbara, D., & Koren, G. (2013). Towards identifying a characteristic neuropsychological profile for fetal alcohol spectrum disorders. Analysis of the Motherisk FASD Clinic. *Journal of Population Therapeutics and Clinical Pharmacology, 20*, e44–e52.

Oesterheld, J. R., Kofoed, L., Tervo, R., Fogas, B., Wilson, A., & Fiechtner, H. (1998). Effectiveness of methylphenidate in Native American children with fetal alcohol syndrome and attention deficit/hyperactivity disorder: A controlled pilot study. *Journal of Child and Adolescent Psychopharmacology, 8*, 39–48.

O'Leary, C., Zubrick, S. R., Taylor, C. L., Dixon, G., & Bower, C. (2009). Prenatal alcohol exposure and language delay in 2-year-old children: The importance of dose and timing on risk. *Pediatrics, 123*, 547–555.

O'Malley, K. D., Koplin, B., & Dohner, V. A. (2000). Psychostimulant clinical response in fetal alcohol syndrome. *Canadian Journal of Psychiatry, 45*, 90–91.

Paley, B., & O'Connor, M.J. (2009). Intervention for individuals with fetal alcohol spectrum disorders: Treatment approaches and case management. *Developmental Disabilities Research Reviews, 15*, 258–267.

Peadon, E., Rhys-Jones, B., Bower, C., & Elliott, E.J. (2009). Systematic review of interventions for children with fetal alcohol spectrum disorders. *BMC Pediatrics, 9*, 35.

Pennington, B. F., & Ozonoff, S. (1996). Executive functions and developmental psychopathology. *Journal of Child Psychology and Psychiatry and Allied Disciplines, 37*, 51–87.

Petrenko, C. M. (2015). Positive behavioral interventions and family support for fetal alcohol spectrum disorders. *Current Developmental Disorders Reports, 2*, 199–209.

Premji, S. Benzies, K., Serrett, K., & Hayden, K.A. (2006). Research-based interventions for children and youth with a fetal alcohol spectrum disorder: Revealing the gap. *Child: Care, Health and Development, 33*, 389–397.

Rangmar, J. Hjern, A., Vinnerjung, B., Stromland, K., & Aronson, M. (2015). Psychosocial outcomes of fetal alcohol syndrome in adulthood. *Pediatrics, 135*, e52–e58.

Rasmussen, C. (2005). Executive functioning and working memory in fetal alcohol spectrum disorder. *Alcoholism: Clinical and Experimental Research, 29*, 1359–1367.

Rasmussen C., Talwar, V., Loomes, C., & Andrew, G. (2008). Brief report: Lie-telling in children with fetal alcohol spectrum disorder. *Journal of Pediatric Psychology, 33*, 220–226.

Roozen, S., Peters, G. J., Kok, G., Townend, D., Nijhuis, J., & Curfs, L. (2016). Worldwide prevalence of fetal alcohol spectrum disorders: A systematic literature review including meta-analysis. *Alcoholism: Clinical and Experimental Research, 40*, 18–32.

Schonfeld, A. M., Mattson, S. N., Riley, E. P. (2005). Moral maturity and delinquency after prenatal alcohol exposure. *Journal of Studies on Alcohol, 66*, 545–555.

Shonkoff, J. P., Garner, A. S., & The Committee on Psychosocial Aspects of Child and Family Health, Committee on Early Childhood, Adoption, and Dependent Care, and the Section on Developmental and Behavioral Pediatrics. (2012). The lifelong effects of early childhood adversity and toxic stress. *Pediatrics, 129*, e232–e246.

Simmons, R. W., Thomas, J. D., Levy, S. S., & Riley, E. P. (2006). Motor response selection in children with fetal alcohol spectrum disorders. *Neurotoxicology and Teratology 28*, 278–285.

Snyder, J. Nanson, J., Snyder, R., & Block, G. (1997). A study of stimulant medication in children with FAS. In A. P. Streissguth & J. Kanter (Eds.), *The Challenge of Fetal Alcohol Syndrome: Overcoming Secondary Disabilities* (pp. 64–77). Seattle: University of Washington Press.

Streissguth, A. (2007). Offspring effects of prenatal alcohol exposure from birth to 25 years: The Seattle prospective longitudinal study. *Journal of Clinical Psychology in Medical Settings, 14*, 81–101.

Streissguth, A. P., Bookstein, F. L., Barr, H. M., Sampson, P. D., O'Malley, K., & Young, J. K. (2004). Risk factors for adverse life outcomes in fetal alcohol syndrome and fetal alcohol effects. *Developmental and Behavioral Pediatrics, 25*, 228–238.

Streissguth, A. P., Sampson, P. D., Olson, H. C., Bookstein, F. L., Barr, H. M., Scott, M., … Mirsky, A. F. (1994). Maternal drinking during pregnancy: Attention and short-term memory in 14-year-old offspring – a longitudinal prospective study. *Alcoholism: Clinical and Experimental Research, 18*, 202–218.

Walthall, J. C., O'Connor, M. J., & Paley, B. (2008). A comparison of psychopathology in children with and without prenatal alcohol exposure. *Mental Health Aspects of Developmental Disabilities, 11*, 1–10.

Willoughby, K. A., Sheard, E. D., Nash, K., & Rovet, J. (2008). Effects of prenatal alcohol exposure on hippocampal volume, verbal learning, and verbal and spatial recall in late childhood. *Journal of the International Neuropsychological Society, 14*, 1022–1033.

Wozniak, J. R., & Muetzel, R. L. (2011). What does diffusion tensor imaging reveal about the brain and cognition in fetal alcohol spectrum disorders? *Neuropsychology Review, 21*, 133–147.

Zelazo, P. D., & Muller, U. (2002). Executive function in typical and atypical development. In U. Goswami (Ed.), *Blackwell handbook of childhood cognitive development* (pp. 445–470). Malden, MA: Blackwell Publishers Ltd.

Chapter 6

Attention-Deficit/Hyperactivity Disorder

Jodene G. Fine, David J. Marks, Danielle Wexler, Victoria M. Dahl, and Elizabeth P. Horn

Introduction

Attention-deficit/hyperactivity disorder (ADHD) has been a recognized, diagnosed, and treated syndrome for more than 40 years, but not without considerable controversy. Today, many aspects of ADHD remain unclear, including the heterogeneity and stability of various subtypes, foundational causes, and its developmental trajectory across the lifespan. Previously considered a disorder primarily confined to childhood, ADHD is increasingly diagnosed at later ages, and the prevalence of diagnosis in adulthood has steadily risen over the past decade. Yet, there is some evidence suggesting that adult and pediatric populations may not overlap (Moffitt et al., 2015) and that there may be multiple pathways to the collection of symptoms we call ADHD. And for those who present early in life with symptoms of ADHD, there is also evidence that many symptoms may not be stable across the lifespan (Martel, Levinson, Langer, & Nigg, 2016). Moreover, ADHD may not persist into adolescence and adulthood for all children diagnosed with it as youngsters (Martel et al., 2016), suggesting that the phenotype of ADHD may have multiple genetic/epigenetic, environmental, social, and nutritional influences that require considerably more investigation.

The two core features of ADHD, according to the *Diagnostic and Statistical Manual of Mental Disorders, 5th ed.* (DSM-5) (American Psychiatric Association, 2013), are inattention and hyperactivity/impulsivity, existing within a variety of behavioral symptoms. The degree to which one or the other presents divides the syndrome into subtypes: predominantly inattentive, predominantly hyperactive/impulsive, and combined inattention and hyperactive/impulsive. Impairment in functioning is captured as mild, moderate, or severe. The DSM-5 attempted to recognize that symptoms may not be evident until environmental demands (e.g., schooling) exceed coping, allowing a diagnosis as long as symptoms emerged before age 12 years, rather than age 7 years in DSM 4th ed., text revision (DSM-IV-TR) (American Psychiatric Association, 2000). Adult ADHD has also been explicitly incorporated, and requires the presence of one fewer symptom (five) in each domain compared with six for children younger than age 17 years (American Psychiatric Association, 2013).

Epidemiology and Pathophysiology

Epidemiology

ADHD is among the most common neurodevelopmental disorders of childhood, with worldwide prevalence rates estimated to range from 5% to 7% (Polanczyk & Rohde, 2007; Thomas, Sanders, Doust, Beller, & Glasziou, 2015; Willcutt, 2012) or higher (9.5%) based on parental reports (Visser, Bitsko, Danielson, Perou, & Blumberg, 2010). Although a diagnosis of ADHD in childhood does not signify lifespan persistence, there is considerable continuity from childhood to adolescence (50–80%) and to adulthood (35–65%; Owens, Cardoos, & Hinshaw, 2015). Of the ADHD subtypes, the predominantly inattentive presentation (ADHD-PI) is the most prevalent (3–5%), followed by the combined presentation (ADHD-C; 2%), and the hyperactive/impulsive presentation (ADHD-HI; 1–3%) (Froehlich et al., 2007; Merikangas et al., 2010; Willcutt, 2012). Yet within and across subtypes, prevalence rates have been found to range from <1% to 20% and have varied as a function of geographic location, sample (i.e., community vs. clinically referred), diagnostic criteria, and assessment procedures. Thus, a consensus regarding the exact prevalence of ADHD has not been conclusively established.

Despite a lack of consensus, the prevalence of ADHD has been shown to vary by age, gender, and race/ethnicity. Research suggests that younger children have a higher prevalence of ADHD symptoms relative to adults (5% vs. 2.5%; American Psychiatric Association, 2013). Generally, as children with ADHD age, hyperactive/impulsive symptoms decrease, and inattentive symptoms become more prevalent or remain steady (Hinshaw, Owens, Sami, & Fargeon, 2006; Lahey & Wilcutt, 2010; Larsson, Lichtenstein, & Larsson, 2006). For preschool-aged children, more meet criteria for ADHD-HI and ADHD-C versus ADHD-PI (Egger, Kondo, & Angold, 2006).

Among children, boys are more likely to be diagnosed with ADHD. Recent community and epidemiological studies suggest a male-female ratio of approximately 2:1 (Bauermeister et al., 2007; Froehlich et al., 2007; Polanczyk & Rohde, 2007; Ramtekkar, Reiersen, Todorov, & Todd, 2010), whereas studies of clinically referred youth have documented more robust male-female ratios (American Psychiatric Association, 1994; MTA Cooperative Group, 1999; Owens et al., 2015). In addition, boys are more likely to be diagnosed with ADHD-HI and ADHD-C than are girls (Ramtekkar et al., 2010; Rucklidge, 2008), who primarily manifest inattentive features (American Psychiatric Association, 2013). Although studies have attempted to find gender differences in outcomes, impairment, and treatment responses, few differences have been identified (Bauermeister et al., 2007; Biederman, Kwon, et al., 2005; Graetz, Sawyer, & Baghurst, 2005; Owens et al., 2015). For reasons that are not entirely clear, the gender distribution hews more equitably among adults, as do levels of functional impairment (Biederman, Faraone, Monuteaux, Bober, & Cadogen, 2004; Owens et al., 2015); however, subtype variations earlier in development coupled with gender differences in comorbidity profiles result in significant phenotypic heterogeneity.

Recent studies examining prevalence rates of ADHD by race/ethnicity indicate that White children are more frequently diagnosed with ADHD than are Black and Latino children (Morgan, Staff, Hillemeier, Farkas, & Maczuga, 2013; Pastor & Reuben, 2008). Some contradictory research suggests that disparities in ADHD exist only between White and Latino children, whereas prevalence rates are nearly equivalent between White and Black children (Froehlich et al., 2007; Visser et al., 2014). Although there are mixed findings related to racial/ethnic disparities in diagnosis of ADHD, Black and Latino children are often undertreated.

Functional Consequences

ADHD affects many domains of functioning throughout the lifespan. Among children, ADHD has been associated with academic underachievement; however, such findings are at least partially confounded by elevated rates of co-occurring learning disorders (DuPaul & Langberg, 2015). Relative to their peers, children with ADHD are more likely to require tutoring, repeat a grade, and be enrolled in at least one special education classroom (DuPaul & Langberg, 2015). Notably, research has linked academic problems to ADHD in childhood, and the coexistence of ADHD and disruptive behavior disorders to school-based disciplinary actions (DuPaul & Langberg, 2015). Adolescents with ADHD are more likely to be suspended from school and drop out of high school completely (Fischer, Barkley, Edelbrock, & Smallish, 1990), both of which are often exacerbated by concurrent conduct disorder (CD) (Barkley, Fischer, Smallish, & Fletcher, 2006). Academic difficulties often persist into adulthood because individuals with ADHD perform less well academically (Able, Johnston, Adler, & Swindle, 2007) and are less likely to enroll in college (Barkley et al., 2006).

A diagnosis of ADHD in childhood or adulthood has also been linked to problems in occupational functioning, including diminished professional status, fewer hours worked per week, and compromised workplace adjustment. Adverse relational outcomes have also been associated with ADHD, including less productive communication styles and impoverished romantic satisfaction (Barkley, Murphy, & Fischer, 2008: Eakin et al., 2004). As adults, children with ADHD have higher divorce rates and financial management problems (e.g., impulse buying, extreme use of credit, low credit ratings; Barkley, 2015a). In adulthood, deficits in areas of executive functioning (e.g., response inhibition, working memory, set-shifting) might contribute to impairments in academic, occupational, and financial domains because these areas require self-management (Barkley, 2012; Solanto, 2015). Adults with ADHD often find it difficult to initiate and/or execute future plans (Barkley, 2012) and are frequently motivated by proximal versus distal rewards (Antrop et al., 2006; Scheres, Tontsch, Thoeny, & Kaczkurkin, 2010).

As might be expected, aspects of functional impairment among individuals with ADHD often occur as a result of comorbid psychiatric disorders. Children and adults with ADHD, especially those who are clinic-referred, are likely to meet the criteria for one or two, if not more, other disorders (Barkley, 2015b, Pliszka, 2015). Research has found that 76–87% of adults with ADHD have a lifetime prevalence of another disorder (Sobanski et al., 2008). Externalizing disorders, such as oppositional defiant disorder (ODD) and CD, are the most commonly seen comorbid disorders in children and adults with ADHD (American Psychiatric Association, 2013). Previous research indicates that 45–84% of youth with ADHD will be diagnosed with ODD, with or without CD, and 15–56% will meet criteria for CD (Pliszka, 2015; Wilens et al., 2002). The presence of ODD or CD, in combination with ADHD, place children and adults at heightened risk for additional psychiatric diagnoses, including personality disorders (Pliszka, 2015).

Comorbid internalizing disorders, such as major depressive disorder, dysthymia, and anxiety disorders, are also common in individuals with ADHD. Anxiety affects approximately 25% of children with ADHD, and 32–41% of adults with ADHD have at least one internalizing disorder (Miller, Nigg, & Faraone, 2007; Pliszka, 2015; Tannock, 2000). Among children, the coexistence of ADHD and anxiety can result in diminished impulsivity, but also more impoverished working memory (Pliszka, 2015). In clinically referred adults, rates of major depressive disorder (13–45%) and dysthymia (19–37%) closely parallel rates of anxiety (Barkley et al., 2008; Cumyn, French, & Hechtman, 2009; Klein et al., 2012; Michielsen et al., 2013; Murphy, Barkley, & Bush, 2002).

Teenagers and adults with ADHD frequently engage in increased risk-taking behaviors, including use of psychoactive substances and high-risk sexual behavior (Barkley et al., 2006). Relative to their peers, individuals with ADHD are more likely to use both legal and nonlegal substances (Barkley et al., 2008); however, comorbid CD has been shown to at least partially mediate elevated rates of substance abuse among adolescents with ADHD (Pliszka, 2015). In addition, risky sexual behaviors, such as early initiation, more partners, and less likely utilization of contraception, have been linked with elevated rates of teenage pregnancy and sexually transmitted diseases among individuals with ADHD (Barkley et al., 2006). Finally, among children and adults, females have been shown to be at higher risk for internalizing disorders, and boys at elevated risk for externalizing behaviors (e.g., substance abuse) (Bauermiester et al., 2007; Hinshaw, 2002; Rasmussen & Levander, 2009).

Pathophysiology

ADHD has been recognized as a highly heritable disorder in which there is a high incidence in siblings and parents. Familial research and twin studies have demonstrated heritability estimates approximating 80% (Larsson, Dilshad, Lichtenstein, & Barker, 2011; Lichtenstein, Carlström, Rastam, Gilberg, & Anckarsäter, 2010). Research from twin studies also suggests that shared environmental factors (e.g., socioeconomic status, home environment, parenting practices) contribute minimal individual variation (0–5%) in ADHD traits (Burt, Larsson, Lichtenstein, & Klump, 2012; Nikolas & Burt, 2010).

Due to the extremely high heritability of ADHD, extensive research has focused on identifying specific gene variants that transmit the risk for the disorder and account for symptom variation. Although genome-wide linkage scans have implicated chromosome 16 (16q22-16q24), candidate gene association studies and the established phenotypic heterogeneity of the disorder implicate a role for several genes in the expression of ADHD, rather than a single gene or chromosome. Consistent with this assertion, researchers have identified several important genes associated with ADHD, including the serotonin transporter gene (*5HTT*), the dopamine transporter gene (*DAT1*), the D4 dopamine receptor gene (*DRD4*), the D5 dopamine receptor gene (*DRD5*), the serotonin 1B receptor gene (*HTR1B*), and a gene coding for a synaptic vesicle-regulating protein (*SNAP25*) (Gizer, Ficks, & Waldman, 2009). Although there have only been a few genes consistently detected across studies, researchers have recognized many more candidates that may be involved in the development of ADHD, and researchers are now identifying groups of genes that contribute to affected pathways underlying ADHD symptoms within the brain. For example, Poelmans, Pauls, Buitelaar, and Franke (2011) found that 45 of the 85 top ADHD candidate genes fit into a network that is involved in neurite outgrowth. Additional research on networks or groups of genes is needed to fully understand the extent to which genes interact and work together to produce the diverse ADHD phenotype.

Along with genetic risk factors, research indicates that impairments in neurological structure and functioning are associated with the development of ADHD. Neuroimaging research has revealed structural brain differences between those with and without ADHD, including volumetric reductions in the frontal lobes and basal ganglia (caudate nucleus, globus pallidus) (Casey et al., 1997; Filpek et al., 1997; Yeo et al., 2003). More recently, these findings have been supported across several meta-analytic studies. For example, in their analysis of 21 studies, Valera, Faraone, Murray, and Seidman (2007) found significant volumetric reductions in cerebellar regions, the splenium of the corpus callosum, and the right caudate, as well as total cerebral volume. Another meta-analysis reported significant gray matter reductions in areas of the basal ganglia (putamen, globus pallidus, and caudate nucleus) along with more robust gray matter volumes in the left posterior cingulate/precuneus (Nakao, Radua, Rubia, & Mataix-Cols, 2011). In addition, Frodl and Skokauskas (2012) documented reduced volume in the right globus pallidus and putamen, and bilaterally in the caudate, whereas Ellison-Wright, Ellison-Wright, and Bullmore (2008) identified significantly reduced volumes in the right putamen and globus pallidus. Taken together, these meta-analytic studies have identified volumetric reductions in cerebellar and basal ganglia regions among individuals with ADHD and have implicated such perturbations as structural markers for dysfunction in frontostriatal circuits that mediate cognitive control (Ellison-Wright et al., 2008).

Within the past several years, investigators have suggested that structural/volumetric abnormalities do not constitute a permanent deficiency, but instead represent a maturational lag. In an attempt to detect small cortical changes over time, Shaw et al. (2006, 2007) measured the cortical thickness across the entire cerebrum of 163 children with ADHD and 166 typically developing children over 10 years. Results indicated that children with ADHD reached cortical maturation (i.e., when cortical points reached their peak thickness) significantly later relative to controls (7.5 years vs. 10.5 years), and that the prefrontal cortex showed the greatest delay in development (Shaw et al., 2006, 2007).

Along with these findings, recent research using diffusion tensor imaging, which examines brain white matter, has indicated similar results. In a meta-analysis of diffusion tensor imaging studies, researchers found deficits in several white matter regions and tracts, including the inferior and superior longitudinal fasciculus, anterior corona radiata, corticospinal tract, cingulum, corpus callosum, internal capsule, caudate nucleus, and cerebellum (van Ewijk, Heslenfeld, Zwiers, Buitelaar, & Oosterlaan, 2012). Results also indicated differences in the basal ganglia as well as the frontal, temporal, parietal, and occipital lobes (van Ewijk et al., 2012). Collapsing across studies, the investigators identified five clusters that were consistent across studies: right anterior corona radiata, forceps minor near the corpus callosum, right and left internal capsule, and left cerebellar white matter (van Ewijk et al., 2012). Collectively, the results (e.g., delayed myelination) were deemed consistent with other findings indicating delayed brain maturation among children with ADHD.

Functional magnetic resonance imaging (fMRI) studies have documented functional differences compared with neurotypical controls in regions suspected to subserve attention, impulse control, and executive functioning. The frontal lobes, especially the prefrontal cortex, has been implicated in the pathophysiology of ADHD. In studies of children with ADHD, brain regions such as the inferior, middle, and superior frontal gyri, precentral gyrus, insula, and caudate have shown decreased blood-oxygen-level dependent (BOLD) response during response inhibition tasks (Lei et al., 2015; McCarthy, Skokauskas, & Frodl, 2014), whereas other research has shown increased activation (Lei et al., 2015; McCarthy et al., 2014). These discrepancies may be related to specific scanner tasks (Simmonds, Pekar, & Mostofsky, 2008), statistical thresholding, and small sample sizes (Bennet & Miller, 2017), all of which have rendered poor replication of fMRI findings in neurodevelopmental disorders overall. Nonetheless, the findings align with research suggesting altered connectivity in frontostriatal, frontoparietal, and frontocerebellar networks (Hart, Radua, Mataix-Cols, & Rubia, 2012; Hart, Radua, Nakao, Mataix-Cols, & Rubia, 2013; Tian et al., 2006; Yu-Feng et al., 2007). In addition, sensorimotor regions and the cerebellum have been implicated in ADHD in fMRI research (Tian et al., 2006; Yu-Feng et al., 2007). Thus, converging lines of evidence indicate that, as a group, youth with ADHD present with perturbations in brain activity that incorporate regions of the frontal cortex, basal ganglia, anterior cingulate, and cerebellum, and that such disruptions in broad networks likely underpin reported deficiencies in neuropsychological functioning.

Within the past decade, Halperin and Schulz (2006) proposed a model of ADHD that, in many respects, challenged the prevailing zeitgeist and stipulated distinct mechanisms of symptom emergence and recovery. Per the model, the ADHD phenotype derives from dysfunction in subcortical mechanisms and remains static throughout development irrespective of symptom remission. Symptom reduction/recovery is proposed to be related to prefrontal cortex maturation counteracting the effects of unremitting subcortical dysfunction. Consistent with this model, Rajendran and colleagues found that the magnitude of change in neuropsychological functioning from preschool (age 4.19 years) to latency (age 7.35 years) was linearly associated with the trajectory of ADHD, such that individuals with increased neurocognitive development showed the most significant reduction in ADHD severity and impairment (Rajendran, Trampush, et al., 2013). Moreover, indications emerged to suggest that improved neuropsychological functioning temporally preceded the attenuation of symptoms (Rajendran, Rindskopf, et al., 2013).

Key tenets of the model were also supported using an independent sample of school-age youth who were followed into adolescence. Although adolescents and young adults diagnosed with ADHD in childhood were found to demonstrate broad-based neurocognitive deficits relative to controls, both persisters and remitters of ADHD symptoms had more motor activity, poorer perceptual sensitivity, and greater response variability relative to controls. In contrast, persisters performed significantly less well than controls on measures of executive/effortful processing. Applying neuroimaging methodology to the same cohort, adult probands initially diagnosed with ADHD in childhood exhibited diminished functional connectivity between the right thalamus and brain stem regardless of adult status. Relative to persisters, those with remitted ADHD symptoms exhibited greater connectivity between right thalamic and prefrontal regions, suggesting that functional enhancement of the thalamocortical network may be instrumental to symptom recovery.

In addition to heritable neurodevelopmental occurrences, many biological and environmental factors have been correlated with ADHD symptoms. Studies have suggested that low birth weight is causally related to attentional difficulties (Groen-Blokhuis, Middeldorp, van Beijsterveldt, & Boomsma, 2011), and that this relation persists into young adulthood (Elgen, Holsten, & Odberg, 2013). Research also suggests that prenatal exposure to toxins (e.g., tobacco, alcohol) (Banerjee, Middleton, & Faraone, 2007; Freitag et al., 2012) and maternal stress during pregnancy (Glover, 2011; Grizenko, Shayan, Polotskaia, Ter-Stepanian, & Joober, 2008) increases susceptibility to ADHD. Postnatal exposure to certain toxins (e.g., lead) has been found to increase the risk of ADHD (Braun, Kahn, Froehlich, Auinger, & Lanphear, 2006; Froehlich et al., 2009; Nigg, Nikolas, Mark Knowttnerus, Cavanagh, & Friderici, 2010). Although the relation between ADHD risk and these biological and environmental factors has not been fully determined, they are extremely important considerations, especially as prevention efforts are developed. Please see Table 6.1 for a summary of the neuropsychological findings of ADHD across the lifespan.

Neuropsychological Assessment

One of the most important aspects of assessing for ADHD is the process of ruling out everything else that looks like it. Although there are uncountable neural connections that can be disrupted or altered as the brain organizes, there are more limited ways in which people, especially children, can behave. Thus, a great many potential developmental conditions manifest with impulsivity, distraction, and inattention as part of their profile, and these conditions may easily be mistaken for ADHD. In addition, many social and environmental pressures can lead children and adults to present with challenges that resemble ADHD symptoms. Careful consideration of data within the context of home and family, school and learning, work functioning, medical and psychiatric concerns, and developmental progress in language, social maturity, and motor functioning are critical when ruling in ADHD. Nevertheless, although rating scales and structured interviews capture reported evidence of behaviors associated with ADHD, they do so with some insensitivity. Standardized instruments yield direct observations of specific symptoms of ADHD in controlled testing environments, yet are consistently identified as being insensitive to specific clinical diagnosis (Lange, 2014).

Table 6.1 Summary of Neuropsychological Findings in ADHD

Neuropsychological Findings	Moderating Variables/Correlates	Implications
Epidemiology		
Variation in prevalence by age, gender, race	Age: younger children have higher prevalence relative to adults	ADHD does not impact all groups equally
	Gender differences: 2:1 male-female ratio in epidemiological studies of children, but more equitable distribution among adults	
	Race/ethnicity: contradictory findings as to whether White children are diagnosed more frequently than Black and Latino children	
Functional Consequences		
Childhood: academic underachievement	Co-occurring learning disorders	Academic support or special education classification may be necessary
	Comorbid externalizing disorders (e.g., ODD; CD)	
	Deficits in executive functioning (e.g., response inhibition, working memory, set-shifting)	Lower college enrollment
Adulthood: occupational, financial, and relational problems	Deficits in executive functioning (e.g., response inhibition, working memory, set-shifting, which are important for self-management)	Difficulty maintaining employment, managing finances, and intimate relationships
Pathophysiology		
Heritability estimates around 80%	Several potential gene variants: *5HTT, DAT1, DRD4, DRD5, HTR1B, SNAP25*	Genetic factors play a large role in development of ADHD, more so than shared environmental factors
	Continued research on networks of genes	
Biological/environmental factors correlated with ADHD symptoms	Prenatal exposure to tobacco and alcohol	Relation between ADHD risk and these factors has not entirely been determined but are important to consider as prevention efforts are developed
	Maternal stress during pregnancy	
	Low birth weight	
	Postnatal exposure to lead	
Structural brain differences	Volumetric reductions in gray matter in basal ganglia (putamen, globus pallidus, and caudate nucleus) and in left posterior cingulate/precuneus	Structural markers for dysfunction in frontostriatal circuits that mediate cognitive control
Functional brain differences	Decreased and increased BOLD response in prefrontal cortex (inferior, middle, and superior frontal gyri, precentral gyrus, insula, and caudate)	Disruptions in broad networks that are suspected to be responsible for attention, impulse control, and executive functioning
	Sensorimotor regions and cerebellum have been implicated in ADHD	
Slowed cortical maturation	Delayed myelination in five consistent brain regions: right anterior corona radiata, forceps minor near the corpus callosum, right and left internal capsule, and left cerebellar white matter	Structural/volumetric abnormalities may represent a maturational lag, as opposed to permanent deficiency

Table 6.1 (cont.)

Neuropsychological Findings	Moderating Variables/Correlates	Implications
Slowed prefrontal cortex maturation related to symptom reduction/recovery	Linear and temporal relationship between neurocognitive development and reduction in ADHD symptom severity	The thalamocortical network may be influential in ADHD symptom recovery
	Greater connectivity between right thalamic and prefrontal regions in adults with remitted ADHD symptoms	

Note: BOLD = blood-oxygenation-level dependent

Rating Scales and Multi-informant Assessment

Because the diagnostic criteria for ADHD are behavioral and linked to performance in multiple environments (e.g., home, work, school), the tools used most often to assess for it are rating scales completed by parents and teachers for children, and self-report, and/or another informant for adults. There are a variety of rating scales, and most appear to be generally equivalent for both children and adults (Rodriguez & Simon-Dack, 2013) as long as the raters are responding regarding similar environments (De Los Reyes et al., 2015). Most rating scales are based on the diagnostic criteria in both DSM-IV-TR and DSM-5, but some have scales for inattention and hyperactivity embedded in broad-spectrum psychosocial assessment measures. In many cases, a broader measure is preferable when ruling out or in symptoms of ADHD against the background of other symptoms that may look similar, such as sleep disorders, anxiety, depression, functional communication problems, personality disorders, and oppositional defiant behaviors.

The validity of rating scales using the multi-informant approach for diagnostic assessment consistently has been criticized in the literature. Agreement between raters and across environments has been notably poor (Antrop, 2002; Goodman, De Los Reyes, & Bradshaw, 2010), yielding low to moderate correlations across ratings in the United States and other parts of the world (Rescorla et al., 2013). Recently, it has been more actively considered that the discrepancies between informants and across environments can be clinically informative (see, for example, De Los Reyes, Henry, Tolan, & Wakschlag, 2009). Discrepant ratings between parents and their adolescents may signal maladjustment (Goodman et al., 2010), or parent's ratings of child behaviors relative to teachers may reflect a more limited understanding of normative child development (De Los Reyes et al., 2009), differential reference points, and/or legitimate situational fluctuation. Although teacher informant data have been shown to be influenced by oppositional and/or defiant behaviors (Antrop, 2002), such data are considered to be stronger than parent data as indicators of future functioning for ADHD (Aitken, Martinussen, & Tannock, 2016; Johnson, Hollis, Marlow, Simms, & Wolke, 2014).

In addition to rating scales designed specifically for ADHD diagnosis and the broad-spectrum measures, several rating scale measures of executive functioning are believed to be helpful in confirming a diagnosis of ADHD. For example, one can observe whether there is consistency across emotional and cognitive regulation using a measure such as the Behavior Rating Inventory of Executive Functioning (Gioia, Isquith, Guy, & Kenworthy, 2015). If, for example, a child is emotionally dysregulated but shows few cognitive symptoms associated with ADHD, other diagnoses may be important to pursue before endorsing ADHD, even if behavioral symptoms on a DSM-based rating scale meet criteria.

Despite improvement in the breadth of rating scales for the diagnosis of ADHD, there remains the concern that these measures are a subjective assessment of a disorder recognized as highly heterogeneous. Lengthy interviews, additional psychosocial and academic measures, as well as direct observations of behaviors at home and school are often required to convincingly confirm the diagnosis. There are also methods for directly observing some cognitive symptoms of ADHD in a testing environment, most notably with continuous performance tests (CPTs), which have been used in the research on ADHD since the 1950s (Albrecht, Uebel-von Sandersleben, Wiedmann, & Rothenberger, 2015) and are considered to be a more objective measure of some aspects of ADHD symptomology.

Continuous Performance Tests

CPTs vary in their conceptual premise, with some (e.g., Conners CPT [Conners, 2004]; Test of Variables of Attention [Greenberg, 1989]) based on a go/no-go paradigm in which an examinee executes frequent responses but must periodically inhibit responses to a rare target stimulus, and others pulling more for selective attention and vigilance by embedding a target response within a group of nontarget stimuli. Among commercial CPT instruments, some use stimuli that are purely auditory, visual abstract or alphabetic, or of mixed modalities. Most types of CPT instruments are considered to be good indicators of sustained attention/vigilance and impulsivity/cognitive control within the research literature (Albrecht et al., 2015). Although ADHD is characterized as involving inattention and hyperactivity without regard to modality, some researchers have found that for hyperactivity some persons may demonstrate problems with either auditory or visual stimuli, but not both, whereas inattention is more consistently found across modalities (Schmidt, Simões, & Novais Carvalho, 2016).

Although many studies have demonstrated utility with CPTs when distinguishing persons with ADHD from those without (Ogundele, Ayyash, & Banerjee, 2011), there is less ability to distinguish between subtypes and specific symptoms (Epstein et al., 2006). The classical interpretations of CPT data, such as that commission errors are related to hyperactivity/impulsivity and omission errors signal inattention, have been challenged in recent years. Instead, faster reaction time (RT) (Hervey et al., 2006) and greater RT variability in ADHD are more strongly correlated with ADHD symptoms and psychopharmacological treatment, with moderate to large effect sizes (Epstein et al., 2006).

The research is mixed regarding the clinical utility of neuropsychological measures in predicting ADHD subtype. In one of the largest studies to date, stop-task RT variability and CPT signal detection (d') were found to contribute unique variance in subtype membership and best predicted parent and teacher ratings (Nikolas &

Nigg, 2013). Signal detection, thought to reference arousal, and RT variability were both higher in individuals with ADHD-C compared with those with ADHD-PI.

An enhanced CPT measure, the QbTest (QBtech AB, Stockholm, Sweden), integrates the CPT with an infrared motion detector to capture head movements. The instrument provides the usual CPT data (e.g., d', RT variation, omissions, commissions) along with five activity variables (time active, distance traveled, score area, number of microevents, and motion simplicity) and has shown promise in distinguishing ADHD from autism spectrum disorder and healthy controls in a sample of adults (Groom, Young, Hall, Gillott, & Hollis, 2016) and children (Vogt & Shameli, 2011). Classification accuracy was improved over rating scales alone. Nonetheless, it remains under investigation as a potentially useful tool with ADHD diagnosis.

Executive Functioning

In some studies, measures of executive functioning, including set-shifting, planning, response inhibition, working memory, and cognitive flexibility, have been only loosely tied to clinical symptoms in ADHD (see, for example, Coghill, Hayward, Rhodes, Grimmer, & Matthews, 2014), although differences in executive functioning between ADHD and typical groups have been well established in the research literature (Willcutt, Doyle, Nigg, Faraone, & Pennington, 2005). In a study of children with and without ADHD, the discriminant validity of selected subtests of executive functioning from the Delis-Kaplan Executive Function System (Delis, Kaplan, & Kramer, 2001) and the Test of Everyday Attention for Children (TEA-Ch) (Manly, Robertson, Anderson, & Nimmo-Smith, 1999) along with the Conners CPT (Conners, 2004) was conducted (Holmes et al., 2010). Classification accuracy was high using all of the tests, although the time involved, more than 90 minutes, may be prohibitive for standard clinical practice. However, even the one single best predictor, the Walk-Don't Walk test of the TEA-Ch (Manly et al., 1999), correctly predicted ADHD group membership for 83% of the children with ADHD. Although these measures may provide potential utility in confirming ADHD, more research into how children with other psychosocial and/or neurodevelopmental disorders perform differentially is needed.

Among the most important tasks for neuropsychological assessment of ADHD is to understand how an adult or child arrives at behaviors consistent with an ADHD diagnosis. Despite the lack of a specific "test for ADHD," neuropsychological assessment has been shown to improve outcomes by enhancing parent participation in behavior management, access to special education services, and increased initiation of medication management (Pritchard, Koriakin, Jacobson, & Mahone, 2014). Because functional challenges are idiopathic and span multiple academic, social, and executive domains, careful evaluation provides points of support and intervention that are not informed by rating scales alone. Direct measures are encouraged within a multi-informant comprehensive evaluation to provide specific feedback to families and schools.

Intervention

Interventions to support children with ADHD include pharmacotherapy and psychosocial interventions that are implemented at home and at school. Stimulant medications are currently the first-line treatment option for ADHD (Chacko et al., 2015); however, pharmacological approaches are not always sufficient, and a variety of individual differences may limit the effectiveness of drug treatment for any given individual (Vidal-Estrada, Bosch-Munso, Nogueira-Morais, Casas-Brugue, & Ramos-Quiroga, 2012). Psychosocial treatment typically reflects principles of behavior modification and includes school-based and/or parent-mediated interventions (e.g., behavioral parent training). In addition, researchers have recently examined whether cognitive training constitutes an effective, empirically supported treatment for children with ADHD.

Beyond pharmacological treatment, only cognitive behavioral therapy (CBT)-oriented treatments, both individual and group, can be considered evidence-based for adults with ADHD (Ramsay & Rostain, 2007). Other interventions, such as individual or group counseling, family and couples therapy, vocational counseling, coaching, use of technological aids, and advocacy, although potentially beneficial on an individual level, are not presently considered empirically validated and have therefore been excluded from review.

Pharmacological Intervention

Most treatment guidelines recommend medication as a front-line intervention (Vaughan & Kratochvil,

2012; Wolraich, 2011). Stimulant medications, methylphenidate and amphetamine, are most commonly prescribed for ADHD. Several randomized controlled trials (RCTs) have shown this class of drug to be effective, safe, and well tolerated in school-age children, adolescents, and adults with ADHD, although they have had reduced effects in samples of adolescents and adults relative to younger children (Chacko et al., 2015). Research suggests that 65–75% of children with ADHD respond to the first stimulant medication prescribed, and for those who do not respond to the first, 80–90% will respond to a second stimulant (Greenhill, Pliszka, & Dulcan, 2002; Pliszka, 2007).

Although stimulant medication is generally prescribed first, up to 30% of children and adolescents may have an insufficient response to stimulants or experience untoward effects that preclude continued treatment (Pliszka, 2007); in such instances, such nonstimulant alternatives as guanfacine (Intuniv) and atomoxetine (Strattera) may be prescribed. Large RCTs of children, adolescents, and adults with ADHD have shown atomoxetine to be superior to placebo on measures of ADHD symptoms and related impairments (Brown et al., 2011; Kratochvil et al., 2011; Wilens et al., 2006); however, for children and adults, stimulants have been shown to have greater efficacy than nonstimulants like atomoxetine (Bitter, Angyalosi, & Czobor, 2012; Wigal, 2009). Notably, despite the established efficacy of pharmacotherapy, medication adherence has been a challenge with adolescents and adults (Chacko, Newcorn, Feirsen, & Uderman, 2010).

In more recent years, research has expanded to include preschoolers, adolescents, and adults with ADHD. For preschool children, stimulant medication demonstrated significant positive effects on ADHD symptoms; however, compared with older children on the same medication, effect sizes for preschoolers with ADHD were smaller, and side effects more prevalent (Greenhill et al., 2006). Thus, close monitoring of very young children with ADHD taking stimulant medication is warranted, along with regular monitoring of medication treatment in all children with ADHD (Vaughan & Kratochvil, 2012).

To our knowledge, there are no systematic evaluations of combined pharmacological and psychosocial treatments for adolescents or adults with ADHD. Van der Oord, Prins, Oosterlaan, and Emmelkamp's (2008) meta-analysis revealed no significant differences between pharmacological intervention and combined treatment in improving ADHD symptoms, social behavior, and academic functioning; both had large effect sizes. Still, psychosocial interventions alone have been found to have moderate effects on ADHD symptoms, social behavior, and academic functioning in adolescents (Van der Oord et al., 2008). Moreover, psychosocial interventions have added value in mitigating the effects of comorbidity, enhancing the application of management strategies across contexts, and providing coverage beyond the window conferred by medication.

Practitioners and researchers have asserted that pharmacological treatment is most holistically effective when combined with behavioral intervention. Forness, Freeman, and Paparella (2006) contend that treatment of ADHD with stimulant medication in communities is often substandard, and behavioral interventions are critical for school-based interventions. Rostain and Ramsay (2006) assert that, due to the severity and pervasiveness of the symptoms of ADHD, pharmacotherapy alone is insufficient treatment for upward of 50% of adult patients, and therefore should be combined with some form of psychosocial intervention. Furthermore, pharmacological interventions may lead to adverse side effects, and families, as well as individuals with ADHD themselves, may be less open to using medication as a treatment. Importantly, pharmacological intervention does not explicitly target functional impairments, such as academic difficulties, that result from ADHD; rather, medication targets ADHD symptoms (DuPaul, 2007; Jensen et al., 2007). Nonetheless, these functional impairments often precipitate treatment seeking, which further illustrates the importance of research on psychosocial and behaviorally based interventions used concurrently with pharmacotherapies.

School-Based Interventions

Research suggests that the most effective interventions for improving school performance in children with ADHD are those employed consistently within the school setting. There are three areas that school-based interventions must target: (1) reducing off-task and disruptive behaviors, (2) increasing positive social interactions and reducing verbal and physical aggression, and (3) enhancing work completion.

Accordingly, a number of interventions have demonstrated effectiveness in either one or more than one of these areas.

Classroom-Based Behavioral Interventions. Many classroom-based interventions are based on principles of behavior modification and include preventive, or antecedent-based, strategies as well as reactive, or consequence-based, strategies. Empirical support for classroom-based behavioral interventions has been well documented across single-subject studies (e.g., Gormley & DuPaul, 2015), group research (e.g., Fabiano et al., 2007), systematic literature reviews (e.g., Evans, Owens, & Bunford, 2014; Pelham & Fabiano, 2008), and meta-analyses (e.g., DuPaul, Eckert, & Vilardo, 2012). Based on this research, classroom interventions meet criteria as a well-established treatment because they have been shown to be effective in comparison with alternative interventions or control conditions across multiple studies. The information that follows describes a number of evidence-based classroom-based behavioral interventions.

Antecedent or preventive strategies include altering the classroom and school environment as well as individual accommodations to reduce the incidence of problem behaviors. Modifications to the classroom environment include preferential seating, clear behavioral and instructional expectations, and visual aids. The goal of these strategies is to create a classroom that is organized, structured, and predictable, so students know what is expected of them. In addition, teachers can prevent problem behavior by using abundant positive praise (ideally in a ratio of four positive statements for each negative statement or reprimand) and judicious ignoring. In combination, positive praise can lead to increases in desirable behavior, and ignoring to reductions in undesirable behavior.

To supplement positive praise, contingency management (e.g., token reinforcement/response-cost systems) can be developed and implemented. Generally, research indicates that contingency management has moderate to large effects on behavioral and academic outcomes (DuPaul et al., 2012; Trout, Lienemann, Reid, & Epstein, 2007). Token reinforcement and response-cost systems were found to be effective in increasing the rate of responding, work completion, and overall accuracy for students with ADHD (Trout et al., 2007). Moreover, the combination of token reinforcement and response-cost systems was found to produce greater behavioral gains than stimulant medication between similar classrooms (Fabiano et al., 2007). Accordingly, contingency management is a central component of school-based interventions for ADHD.

Additionally, daily report cards combine preventive and positive reinforcement strategies to provide students with feedback about their behavior via communication between school and home. Daily report cards include explicitly defined target behaviors (e.g., leaves seat fewer than five times) and a method for rating the designated target behavior (e.g., frequency, percentage, duration). Research suggests that daily report cards produce positive changes in teacher-rated symptoms of ADHD and conduct problems, parent-rated daily functioning across multiple domains, and teacher-rated classroom functioning (Owens, Murphy, Richerson, Girio, & Himawan, 2008). Although Fabiano et al. (2010) found that daily report cards did not result in significant improvements in teacher-rated ADHD symptoms, academic achievement, or the student-teacher relationship, positive effects were found for overall classroom functioning as well as teacher ratings of academic productivity and disruptive classroom behavior. Moreover, there is evidence to suggest that interventions that incorporate communication and involvement between the home and school are more effective than those that are implemented only in the school (Vannest, Davis, Davis, Mason, & Burke, 2010).

Self-Regulatory Interventions. Self-regulatory interventions, also referred to as self-monitoring or self-management strategies, target skills believed to be affected by key deficits underlying ADHD. This intervention involves teaching students to identify a specific behavior and record a response when the target behavior occurs (e.g., leaving seat). Self-regulation interventions also teach students to reinforce their own behavior. Teachers simultaneously monitor the student's behavior to ensure that the student's self-evaluation matches the teacher's; once the ratings are in alignment, teacher ratings are reduced and the student's ratings used. A meta-analysis found that self-regulation interventions had large positive effects on increasing on-task behavior and academic productivity and accuracy as well as reducing disruptive behavior in students with ADHD (Reid, Trout, & Schartz, 2005).

In addition, self-monitoring of homework completion and preparedness has been shown to improve organizational skills in students with ADHD (Gureasko-Moore, DuPaul, & White, 2007). Thus, self-regulatory interventions may produce changes in ADHD symptoms as well as functional improvements in the classroom.

Academic Interventions. Because children with ADHD often experience academic skill deficits and performance difficulties, accommodations can help address related problems. This includes shortening the length of the assignments, allowing the child to dictate answers, having someone read the assignment to the child, and providing the child with a computer or keyboard to record responses. Explicit instruction is an additional intervention to support the learning of students with ADHD and involves providing clear information about what will be learned, teaching in small steps with many concrete examples, continuously evaluating student understanding, and emphasizing active student participation. Although the principles of explicit instruction have strong evidence in behavioral analytic research, little research is available to support the use of academic interventions, such as explicit instruction, for students with ADHD. Nonetheless, considerable research that indicates that explicit instruction is effective for students with emotional and behavioral disorders, who often display similar academic difficulties (see Nelson, Brenner, & Bohaty, 2015, for review). Finally, although computer-assisted instruction and peer tutoring may be effective academic interventions for students with ADHD, research has not yet extended to RCTs or large-scale single-case design studies specifically for students with ADHD. Consequently, additional research in this area is warranted.

Parent-Mediated Interventions

Parent-mediated interventions, such as behavioral parent training (BPT), have a long-standing history of success for children with ADHD. Systematic reviews and meta-analyses have demonstrated that BPT meets criteria for a well-established treatment for ADHD (Evans et al., 2014; Pelham & Fabiano, 2008; Fabiano et al., 2009). Research studies on the efficacy of BPT indicate significant improvements in parent ratings of child symptoms and/or impairment in comparison with wait-list or care-as-usual conditions as well as active alternative treatments (see

Evans et al., 2014). Therefore, BPT is a viable treatment option for families of children with ADHD, especially for those who demonstrate more challenging behaviors that impact family functioning and increase parental stress.

According to Chacko et al. (2014), BPT should be used with families of children with ADHD who experience difficulties in coping with their child's behavior, have significant challenges in maintaining positive parent-child relationships, and experience parental stress. Parent-mediated interventions, such as BPT, emphasize training or coaching parents to improve the child's behavior and the parent-child relationship. Although numerous BPT manuals are available, the core components of BPT have been identified. These components commonly include (1) psychoeducation about ADHD and related disorders (e.g., ODD) and how social learning theory views child misbehavior, (2) positive strategies to increase appropriate child behavior (e.g., praise, positive attending, child-directed quality time), (3) planned ignoring of mildly annoying behaviors, (4) preventive positive strategies to increase positive behavior (e.g., reinforcement systems, behavior contracts, effective commands, transition planning), (5) reactive discipline strategies (e.g., time-out, response-cost), and (6) training parents in behavioral problem-solving (Chacko et al., 2014). Most manuals recommend that these components be implemented across at least 12, 1-hour weekly sessions, although clinician flexibility is also important. That is, although it is important to adhere to following the treatment manual, BPT treatment should be prescribed based on the family's main concerns, by changing the order of content delivery and by altering the depth of coverage of certain concepts in BPT. Overall, given that BPT is deemed a well-established treatment for children with ADHD, parents may choose this treatment option to help improve behavior and relationships within the family.

Skill-Based Interventions

Impairments in organization, time management, and planning (OTMP) are commonly observed among individuals with ADHD and exact an increasing functional burden through late childhood, adolescence, and adulthood with increased scholastic and executive demands (Abikoff et al., 2012). Consequently, several interventions have been designed, for both children and adults, to facilitate the implementation of strategies to organize their lives, manage their time, and enhance self-motivation. Organizational skills training (Gallagher, Abikoff, & Spira, 2014) is a manualized treatment designed to expose children with ADHD to tools and methods for recording assignments, organizing academic materials, monitoring the time required to complete assignments, and dismantling larger tasks into smaller, more manageable ones. For adults, manualized skills-based cognitive behavioral approaches have recently become available for group and individual applications, the efficacy of which have been supported by several randomized trials (Safren et al., 2010; Solanto et al., 2010).

Organizational Skills Training

For many youth with ADHD, compromised organizational effectiveness (e.g., forgetting or losing materials, failing to record assignments or due dates) can significantly hamper academic performance. Without these skills, children – especially those with ADHD – are at risk for school disengagement, school failure, and subsequent related negative outcomes (Barkley et al., 2006). In addition, difficulties with OTMP can lead to conflicts with parents, teachers, and even peers (Abikoff & Gallagher, 2009). Despite the pervasive negative impact of their difficulties with OTMP, few systematic efforts have attempted to target these problems through interventions for elementary school-age children with ADHD. One such effort to target these problems has been the development of Organizational Skills Training (OST), an intervention that operates on the theory that OTMP difficulties primarily reflect skills deficits in children's ability to organize materials, track assignments, manage time, and plan tasks (Abikoff et al., 2012). OST has been developed for elementary and middle-school youth for use in clinic and school settings. Although it seems like this type of intervention would be more important for older school-age youth – because they often require a greater organizational capacity for developmentally relevant tasks – theoretically, the impact of such an intervention would be greater for elementary school-age children because they are encountering expectations that they independently organize their behaviors at home and at school for the first time (Newcorn, Ivanov, & Chacko, 2015).

In 2014, Gallagher, Abikoff, and Spira published an empirically supported treatment manual for using OST specifically with children – in third to fifth grade – with ADHD. Their manual is based on a programmatic body of clinical research that spanned more than a decade, and included a pilot study and randomized clinical trial of the manualized intervention. The pilot study of OST provided evidence to support their theory that OTMP difficulties result primarily from a skill deficit; they found that training children with ADHD in organizational skills significantly improved organizational behaviors at home and in school, and reduced family conflicts related to homework problems (Abikoff & Gallagher, 2008). The randomized clinical trial provided extensive support for the efficacy of the intervention: those children treated with OST improved substantially at home and in school in their OTMP skills compared with those children in both wait-list and active control groups (Abikoff et al., 2012). OST also yielded significant improvements in key aspects of school, homework, and family functioning. Parents reported significant reductions in homework problems and family conflict resulting from the child's organizational functioning, and significant improvements in family relationships (Gallagher et al., 2014). Additionally, the gains achieved in family relations, children's academic performance and productivity, and organizational functioning in school, as well as the reduction in OTMP-related family conflict, were sustained at the 12-month follow-up (Abikoff et al., 2012).

Skills-Based CBT

Like their child counterparts, adults with ADHD struggle with disorganization, procrastination, and planning due to skill deficits and functional problems caused by the symptoms of their disorder (Ramsey & Rostain, 2007). As a result, adults with ADHD can benefit from individual and group CBT, which is based on behavior modification principles and strategies similar to those utilized in OST with children (Murphy, 2015). The CBT model of adult ADHD is centered on the premise that ADHD's core symptoms impact executive functioning and sensitivity to reinforcement; over time, this interaction of core symptoms with the environment results in functional impairment in the individual's life. Skills-based CBT is intended to disrupt this cycle by teaching clients compensatory strategies to organize their lives, manage their time, motivate themselves, and recognize and counteract the thought patterns that lead to avoidance of skill use (Knouse, 2015). Within the

past 15 years, several manualized treatments have become available, and their efficacy has been supported by large RCTs (Safren et al., 2010; Solanto et al., 2010). From these empirically supported treatments, two specific approaches to adapting CBT for ADHD become apparent: individual CBT treatment and group metacognitive therapy.

Individual CBT. Safren, Perlman, Sprich, and Otto (2005) recognized that many adults who take medication for ADHD continue to experience difficulties, not only with symptom-related functioning impairments, but in other domains of functioning as well. To address this gap, they developed a CBT-based treatment to be utilized with adults with ADHD, in addition to treating them with medication. Their treatment comprises three core skills modules: organization and planning skills, distractibility reduction skills, and skills to address dysfunctional thought patterns. In addition, there are two optional modules; one that involves the patient's partner, and another that addresses procrastination (Knouse, 2015). Each session is individual and follows the structure of a typical CBT session: The therapist and client set an agenda together, review self-reported ADHD symptoms from the previous week, review any assigned homework (typically practice with any previously learned skills), learn new skills, and discuss the next homework assignment (Safren, Otto, et al., 2005). The clinical efficacy of this treatment is supported by a large RCT, which compared the CBT treatment to an attention-matched control group (relaxation training applied to ADHD symptoms) in 86 patients who were receiving concurrent pharmacological treatment (Safren et al., 2010). Relative to controls, those who received CBT experienced significantly greater reductions in ADHD symptoms that were maintained at 6 and 12 months follow-up (Vidal-Estrada et al., 2012).

Group Metacognitive Therapy. Solanto and colleagues have developed a metacognitive therapy group based on cognitive behavioral strategies to help patients develop executive self-management skills and learn how to implement them in their daily lives (Solanto et al., 2008, 2010). Patients attend weekly 2-hour group sessions, where they receive five sessions of training in each skill category: time-planning strategies, motivation maintenance, and management of automatic thoughts (particularly those that block skill application). Additionally, a full hour of each session is dedicated to generalizing the skills learned during treatment to daily life by reviewing the at-home practice assignment from the previous week (Solanto, 2011). Patients are also encouraged to address their own motivation to actively engage in treatment by using self-reward. Initial evidence of the treatment's efficacy was first demonstrated by an open trial (Solanto et al., 2008), and then by a large RCT (Solanto et al., 2010) that compared group CBT with a psychoeducation control condition. Those patients in the metacognitive therapy group achieved a significantly greater reduction in inattentive symptoms compared with the psychoeducation group.

Cognitive Training Interventions

Cognitive training interventions, also known as facilitative intervention training, were initially developed to address deficits in executive functions and/or their component processes that are frequently observed in children with ADHD. Cognitive training interventions, initially introduced in the early 2000s, were designed to promote the development of these skills in children with ADHD (Rapport, Orban, Kofler, Friedman, & Bolden, 2014). These interventions have been largely computer based and utilize repetition, practice, and feedback on activities that children progress through at increasing levels of difficulty.

Most cognitive training interventions are commercially available and proclaim improvements in attention, impulse control, interpersonal functioning, academic performance, and complex reasoning for children with ADHD (Rapport et al., 2014). Cogmed and BrainTrain's Captain's Log MindPower are among the most popular interventions and emphasize working memory (Cogmed) or a combination of executive processes, including working memory, attention, and problem-solving (BrainTrain's Captain's Log MindPower). Research investigating the effectiveness of these programs has emphasized two primary questions of interest: (1) To what extent do the programs target the executive functions they were designed to target? (2) Do the programs lead to functional gains for children with ADHD? These questions correspond to the examination of near-transfer improvements (i.e., performance on identical but untrained tasks), the maintenance of near-transfer improvements over time, and the acquisition and maintenance of far-transfer improvements on tasks less related to the training tasks (e.g., ADHD symptoms and/or impairment, academic achievement).

Although some researchers argue that cognitive training interventions results in near- and far-transfer effects for children with ADHD, recent meta-analyses (Cortese et al., 2015; Evans et al., 2014; Melby-Lervåg & Hulme, 2013; Rapport, Orban, Kofler, & Friedman, 2013; Shipstead, Redick, & Engle, 2012) have revealed short-term improvements in specific executive functions (i.e., working memory) that do not typically generalize to other areas of functioning (e.g., behavioral and academic). For example, Rapport et al.'s (2013) meta-analysis of 25 studies involving cognitive training intervention programs for children with ADHD indicated that studies that utilized working memory training alone had moderate near-transfer effects ($d = 0.63$), whereas studies that trained attention alone or emphasized an amalgam of executive functions had a negligible impact on the executive functions under study. Long-term near-transfer effects of working memory were maintained for 3–6 months; however, this finding was based on only three studies.

With respect to far-transfer effects, meta-analytic reviews have failed to find long-term improvements (Cortese et al., 2015; Melby-Lervåg & Hulme, 2013; Rapport et al., 2013). For instance, Rapport et al.'s (2013) findings indicated that the cognitive training interventions resulted in nonsignificant or negligible effects on academic functioning, blinded ratings of behavior, and cognitive tests. Accordingly, unblinded raters reported significantly larger effects of the intervention in comparison with objective tests and blinded raters, which suggests biased ratings. Cortese et al. (2015) reported similar findings, such that unblinded raters indicated more improvements than blinded raters. Ultimately, the results of these meta-analyses signify little to no benefit of cognitive training interventions vis-à-vis core ADHD symptoms and impairments or dimensions of academic performance. One possible explanation for the lack of far-transfer to behavioral and/or scholastic outcomes is the fact that only a subset of ADHD youth randomized into cognitive training programs present with deficiencies targeted by the intervention(s). Thus, only a subgroup of individuals with ADHD enrolled into working memory training studies may present with deficits in working memory. It is therefore conceivable that individuals with baseline deficiencies will be most effectively positioned to benefit from the intervention. This distinction is important and should be more closely investigated. Overall, cognitive training interventions should be considered experimental and not used as primary treatments for ADHD (Evans et al., 2014; Shipstead et al., 2012).

Physical Activity Interventions

Based on a promising line of basic research, several researchers have evaluated the role of physical activity as a potential intervention for youth with ADHD (Halperin, Berwid, & O'Neill, 2014; Hoza, Martin, Pirog, & Shoulberg, 2016). In their recent review, Hoza and colleagues (2016) characterized physical activity as a promising treatment for ADHD symptoms, executive function, and motor skills and noted that it may confer additional benefit vis-à-vis social-emotional and behavioral functioning. Although not assessed with sufficient methodological rigor to function as a stand-alone intervention, evidence supports its application as an adjunctive strategy for ADHD youth.

Attempting to integrate findings from the literature on cognitive remediation, early intervention, and physical exercise, investigators have also employed cognitively stimulating activities with preschool youth to enhance inhibitory control, working memory, attention, visuospatial abilities, planning, and motor skills. In a 5-week, open-trial, proof-of-concept study, Halperin and colleagues (Halperin et al., 2013) found that children and families who participated in scaffolded game-based activities and physical exercise (30–45 min/day) experienced significant reductions in parent- and teacher-rated ADHD symptoms immediately post-treatment and 3 months later. These findings were replicated in an independent study (Healey & Halperin, 2015), which reported improvements in parent-rated hyperactivity, aggression, and attention problems that were effectively maintained at 12-month follow-up. Although promising, more methodologically rigorous (randomized controlled) trials will be necessary to gauge the feasibility of the above interventions.

Implications for Clinical Practice

ADHD is a chronic neurodevelopmental disorder that typically emerges early in ontogeny and persists into adolescence and adulthood for a significant proportion of affected individuals. By definition, individuals with ADHD experience impairment in multiple functional domains, and a significant majority present with one or more co-occurring psychiatric disorders.

Although the precise etiology of ADHD has yet to be determined, the disorder is highly heritable and has been associated with perturbations in neural structure and function. Within the past decade, investigators have suggested that structural/volumetric abnormalities do not constitute a permanent deficiency, but instead represent a maturational lag. Future efforts should emphasize use of large-scale imaging databases or networks (e.g., 1000 Functional Connectomes Project's International Neuroimaging Data-Sharing Initiative; http://fcon_1000.projects.nitrc.org/) to enhance statistical power; however, variations in inclusion criteria (e.g., comorbidity, medication history) may get lost in big data initiatives.

To date, no consensus exists regarding evaluation methodology for individuals with ADHD; however, given the phenotypic heterogeneity of the disorder, prevalence of psychiatric comorbidity (both of which may have significant treatment implications), and the role played by primary care professionals in evaluation and treatment (particularly in rural communities), standardized assessment practices should be established and disseminated.

Given the lack of definitive assessment procedures, and reliance on behavioral reports that have poor multirater concordance, inclusion of direct observations of ADHD symptoms within a controlled testing environment may be helpful in diagnosis. Inclusion of assessment for sustained attention and response control (e.g., CPTs) and executive functions can confirm behavioral reports and provide additional information as to best treatment, as can measures of school (academic) and work functioning.

Treatment for ADHD in children and adults has primarily consisted of pharmacological treatment and behavioral/cognitive behavioral interventions.

For adults, stimulants or other pharmacological treatments are most often used, but skills-based interventions have been shown to be effective as well. Recent work also suggests that CBT in adults is effective for reducing symptoms of ADHD and overall functioning, particularly in combination with pharmacotherapy.

Cognitive remediation efforts have yielded near/proximal benefits, but have conferred limited benefit vis-à-vis ADHD symptoms and impairment, particularly when rated by informants blind to treatment.

Recent research has also demonstrated the positive effects of exercise on ADHD symptoms; however, it remains an adjunctive intervention and not a stand-alone treatment.

References

Able, S. L., Johnston, J. A., Adler, L. A., & Swindle, R. W. (2007). Functional and psychosocial impairment in adults with undiagnosed ADHD. *Psychological Medicine, 37*(1), 97–107.

Abikoff, H. A., & Gallagher, R. (2008). Assessment and remediation of organizational skills deficits in children with ADHD. In K. McBurnett & L. Pfiffner (Eds.), *Attention deficit hyperactivity disorder: Concepts, controversies, new directions* (pp. 137–152). New York, NY: Information Healthcare USA.

Abikoff, H., & Gallagher, R. (2009). *The Children's Organizational Skills Scales: Technical Manual*. North Tonawanda, NY: Multi-Health Systems.

Abikoff, H., Gallagher, R., Wells, K. C., Murray, D. W., Huang, L., Feihan, L., & Petkova, E. (2012). Remediating organizational functioning in children with ADHD: Immediate and long-term effects from a randomized controlled trial. *Journal of Counseling and Clinical Psychology, 81*, 113–128.

Aitken, M., Martinussen, R., & Tannock, R. (2016). Incremental validity of teacher and parent symptom and impairment ratings when screening for mental health difficulties. *Journal of Abnormal Child Psychology, 45*, 827–837. doi:10.1007/s10802-016-0188-y

Albrecht, B., Uebel-von Sandersleben, H., Wiedmann, K., & Rothenberger, A. (2015). ADHD history of the concept: The case of the continuous performance test. *Current Developmental Disorders Reports, 2*(1), 10–22. doi:10.1007/s40474-014-0035-1

American Psychiatric Association. (1994). *Diagnostic and statistical manual of mental disorders* (4th ed.). Washington, DC: Author.

American Psychiatric Association. (2000). *Diagnostic and statistical manual of mental disorders* (4th ed., text revision). Washington, DC: Author.

American Psychiatric Association. (2013). *Diagnostic and statistical manual of mental disorders* (5th ed.). Arlington, VA: Author.

Antrop, I. (2002). Agreement between parent and teacher ratings of disruptive behavior disorders in children with clinically diagnosed ADHD. *Journal of Psychopathology and Behavioral Assessment, 24*(1), 67–73. doi:10.1023/A:1014057325752

Antrop, I., Stock, P., Verté, S., Wiersema, J. R., Baeyens, D., & Roeyers, H. (2006). ADHD and delay aversion: The influence of non-temporal stimulation on choice for delayed rewards. *Journal of Child Psychology and Psychiatry, 47*(11), 1152–1158.

Banerjee, T. D., Middleton, F., & Faraone, S. V. (2007). Environmental risk factors for attention-deficit hyperactivity disorder. *Acta Paediatrica, 96*, 1269–1274.

Barkley, R. A. (2015a). *Educational, occupational, dating and marital, and financial impairments in adults with ADHD*. In R. A. Barkley, *Attention-deficit hyperactivity disorder: A handbook for diagnosis and treatment* (pp. 314–342). New York, NY: Guilford Press.

Barkley, R. A. (2015b). *Comorbid psychiatric disorders and psychological maladjustment in adults with ADHD*. In R. A. Barkley, *Attention-deficit hyperactivity disorder: A handbook for diagnosis and treatment* (pp. 343–355). New York, NY: Guilford Press.

Barkley, R. A. (2012). *Executive functions: What they are, how they work, and why they evolved*. New York, NY: Guilford Press.

Barkley, R. A., Fischer, M., Smallish, L., & Fletcher, K. (2006). Young adult outcome of hyperactive children: Adaptive functioning in major life activities. *Journal of the American Academy of Child & Adolescent Psychiatry, 45*(2), 192–202.

Barkley, R. A., Murphy, K. R., & Fischer, M. (2008). *Adult ADHD: What the science says*. New York, NY: Guilford.

Bauermeister, J. J., Shrout, P. E., Chávez, L., Rubio-Stipec, M., Ramírez, R., Padilla, L., … Canino, G. (2007). ADHD and gender: Are risks and sequela of ADHD the same for boys and girls? *Journal of Child Psychology and Psychiatry, 48*, 831–839.

Bennett, C. M., & Miller, M. B. (2013). fMRI reliability: Influences of task and experimental design. *Cognitive, Affective & Behavioral Neuroscience, 13*(4), 690–702.

Biederman, J., Faraone, S. V., Monuteaux, M. C., Bober, M., & Cadogen, E. (2004). Gender effects on attention-deficit/hyperactivity disorder in adults, revisited. *Biological psychiatry, 55*(7), 692–700.

Biederman, J., Kwon, A., Aleardi, M., Chouinard, V. A., Marino, T., Cole, H., … Faraone, S. V. (2005). Absence of gender effects on attention deficit hyperactivity disorder: findings in nonreferred subjects. *American Journal of Psychiatry, 162*(6), 1083–1089.

Bitter, I., Angyalosi, A., & Czobor, P. (2012). Pharmacological treatment of adult ADHD. *Current Opinion in Psychiatry, 25*, 529–534.

Braun, J. M., Kahn, R. S., Froehlich, T., Auinger, P., & Lanphear, B. P. (2006). Exposures to environmental toxicants and attention deficit hyperactivity disorder in U.S. children. *Environmental Health Perspectives, 114*, 1904–1909.

Brown, T. E., Holdnack, J., Saylor, K., Adler, L., Spencer, T., Williams, D. W., … Kelsey, D. (2011). Effect of atomoxetine on executive function impairments in adults with ADHD. *Journal of Attention Disorders, 15*, 130–138.

Burt, S. A., Larsson, H., Lichtenstein, P., & Klump, K. L. (2012). Additional evidence against shared environmental contributions to attention-deficit/hyperactivity problems. *Behavior Genetics, 42*, 711–721.

Casey, B. J., Castellanos, X. F., Giedd, J. N., Marsh, W. L., Hamburger, S. D., Schubert, A., ... Rapoport, J. (1997). Implication of right frontostriatal circuitry in response inhibition and attention-deficit/hyperactivity disorder. *Journal of the American Academy of Child and Adolescent Psychiatry, 36*, 374–383.

Chacko, A., Allan, C. C., Uderman, J., Cornwell, M., Anderson, L., & Chimiklis, A. (2014). Training parents of youth with ADHD. In R. A. Barkley (Ed.), *Attention-deficit hyperactivity disorder: A handbook for diagnosis and treatment* (pp. 513–536). New York, NY: Guilford Press.

Chacko, A. K., Feirsen, N., Rajwan, E., Zwilling, A., Pelham, W. E., & Kapalka, G. M. (2015). Attention-deficit hyperactivity disorder. In G. M. Kapalka (Ed.), *Treating disruptive disorders* (pp. 71–98). New York, NY: Routledge.

Chacko, A., Newcorn, J. H., Feirsen, N., & Uderman, J. Z. (2010). Improving medication adherence in chronic pediatric health conditions: A focus on ADHD in youth. *Current Pharmaceutical Design, 16*(22), 2416–2423.

Coghill, D. R., Hayward, D., Rhodes, S. M., Grimmer, C., & Matthews, K. (2014). A longitudinal examination of neuropsychological and clinical functioning in boys with attention deficit hyperactivity disorder (ADHD): Improvements in executive functioning do not explain clinical improvement. *Psychological Medicine, 44*(5), 1087–1099. doi:10.1017/S0033291713001761

Conners, C. K. (2004). *Conners' Continuous Performance Test*. North Tonawanda, NY: Multi-Health Systems.

Cortese, S., Ferrin, M., Brandeis, D., Buitelaar, J., Daley, D., Dittmann, R. W., ... Sonuga-Barke, E. (2015). Cognitive training for attention-deficit/hyperactivity disorder: Meta-analysis of clinical and neuropsychological outcomes from randomized controlled trials. *Journal of the American Academy of Child & Adolescent Psychiatry, 54*, 164–174.

Cumyn, L., French, L., & Hechtman, L. (2009). Comorbidity in adults with attention-deficit hyperactivity disorder. *The Canadian Journal of Psychiatry, 54*(10), 673–683.

Delis, D. C., Kaplan, E., & Kramer, J. H. (2001). *Delis-Kaplan executive function system (D-KEFS)*. San Antonio, TX: Psychological Corporation.

De Los Reyes, A., Augenstein, T. M., Wang, M., Thomas, S. A., Drabick, D. A. G., Burgers, D. E., & Rabinowitz, J. (2015). The validity of the multi-informant approach to assessing child and adolescent mental health. *Psychological Bulletin, 141*(4), 858–900. doi:10.1037/a0038498

De Los Reyes, A., Henry, D. B., Tolan, P. H., & Wakschlag, L. S. (2009). Linking informant discrepancies to observed variations in young children's disruptive behavior. *Journal of Abnormal Child Psychology, 37*(5), 637-652. doi:10.1007/s10802-009-9307-3

DuPaul, G. J. (2007). School-based interventions for students with attention deficit hyperactivity disorder: Current status and future directions. *School Psychology Review, 36*, 183.

DuPaul, G. J., Eckert, T. L., & Vilardo, B. (2012). The effects of school-based interventions for attention deficit hyperactivity disorder: A meta-analysis 1996–2010. *School Psychology Review, 41*, 387.

DuPaul, G. J., & Langberg, J. M. (2015). Educational impairments in children with ADHD. In R. A. Barkley (Ed.), *Attention-deficit hyperactivity disorder: A handbook for diagnosis and treatment* (pp. 169–190). New York, NY: Guilford Press.

Eakin, L., Minde, K., Hechtman, L., Ochs, E., Krane, E., Bouffard, R., ... Looper, K. (2004). The marital and family functioning of adults with ADHD and their spouses. *Journal of Attention Disorders, 8*(1), 1–10.

Egger, H. L., Kondo, D., & Angold, A. (2006). The epidemiology and diagnostic issues in preschool attention-deficit/hyperactivity disorder: A review. *Infants & Young Children, 19*, 109–122.

Elgen, I. B., Holsten, F., & Odberg, M. D. (2013). Psychiatric disorders in low birthweight young adults. Prevalence and association with assessments at 11 years. *European Psychiatry, 28*, 393–396.

Ellison-Wright, I., Ellison-Wright, Z., & Bullmore, E. (2008). Structural brain change in Attention Deficit Hyperactivity Disorder identified by meta-analysis. *BMC Psychiatry, 8*. Retrieved from http://bmcpsychiatry.biomedcentral.com/articles/10.1186/1471-244X-8-51

Epstein, J. N., Conners, C. K., Hervey, A. S., Tonev, S. T., Arnold, L. E., Abikoff, H. B., ... Group, M. T. A. C. S. (2006). Assessing medication effects in the MTA study using neuropsychological outcomes. *Journal of Child Psychology and Psychiatry, 47*(5), 446–456. doi:10.1111/j.1469-7610.2005.01469.x

Evans, S. W., Owens, J. S., & Bunford, N. (2014). Evidence-based psychosocial treatments for children and adolescents with attention-deficit/hyperactivity disorder. *Journal of Clinical Child & Adolescent Psychology, 43*, 527–551.

Fabiano, G. A., Pelham, W. E., Jr., Gnagy, E. M., Burrows-MacLean, L., ... Robb, J. A. (2007). The single and combined effects of multiple intensities of behavior modification and methylphenidate for children with attention deficit hyperactivity disorder in a classroom setting. *School Psychology Review, 36*, 195–216.

Fabiano, G. A., Pelham, W. E., Coles, E. K., Gnagy, E. M., Chronis-Tuscano, A., & O'Connor, B. C. (2009). A meta-analysis of behavioral treatments for attention-deficit/hyperactivity disorder. *Clinical Psychology Review, 29*, 129–140.

Fabiano, G. A., Vujnovic, R. K., Pelham, W. E., Waschbusch, D. A., Massetti, G. M., Pariseau, M. E., ... Volker, M. (2010). Enhancing the effectiveness of special education programming for children with attention deficit hyperactivity disorder using a daily report card. *School Psychology Review, 39*, 219–239.

Filipek, P. A., Semrud-Clikeman, M., Steingard, R. J., Renshaw, P. F., Kennedy, D. N., & Biederman, J. (1997). Volumetric MRI analysis comparing subjects having attention-deficit hyperactivity disorder with normal controls. *Neurology, 48*, 589–601.

Fischer, M., Barkley, R. A., Edelbrock, C. S., & Smallish, L. (1990). The adolescent outcome of hyperactive children diagnosed by research criteria: II. Academic, attentional, and neuropsychological status. *Journal of Consulting and Clinical Psychology, 58*(5), 580.

Forness, S. R., Freeman, S. F., & Paparella, T. (2006). Recent randomized clinical trials comparing behavioral interventions and psychopharmacologic treatments for students with EBD. *Behavioral Disorders, 31*, 284–296.

Freitag, C. M., Hänig, S., Schneider, A., Seitz, C., Palmason, H., Retz, W., & Meyer, J. (2012). Biological and psychosocial environmental risk factors influence symptom severity and psychiatric comorbidity in children with ADHD. *Journal of Neural Transmission, 119*, 81–94.

Frodl, T., & Skokauskas, N. (2012). Meta-analysis of structural MRI studies in children and adults with attention deficit hyperactivity disorder indicates treatment effects: Meta-analysis of structural MRI ADHD studies. *Acta Psychiatrica Scandinavica, 125*, 114–126.

Froehlich, T. E., Lanphear, B. P., Auinger, P., Hornung, R., Epstein, J. N., Braun, J., & Kahn, R. S. (2009). Association of tobacco and lead exposures with attention-deficit/hyperactivity disorder. *Pediatrics, 124*, e1054–e1063.

Froehlich, T. E., Lanphear, B. P., Epstein, J. N., Barbaresi, W. J., Katusic, S. K., & Kahn, R. S. (2007). Prevalence, recognition, and treatment of attention-deficit/hyperactivity disorder in a national sample of US children. *Archives of Pediatrics & Adolescent Medicine, 161*, 857–864.

Gallagher, R., Abikoff, H., & Spira, E. G. (2014). *Organizational skills training for children with ADHD: An empirically supported treatment.* New York, NY: Guilford.

Gioia, G. A., Isquith, P. K., Guy, S. C., & Kenworthy, L. (2015). *Behavior Rating Inventory of Executive Function* (2nd ed.) (BRIEF-2). Lutz, FL: PAR, Inc.

Gizer, I. R., Ficks, C., & Waldman, I. D. (2009). Candidate gene studies of ADHD: A meta-analytic review. *Human Genetics, 126*, 51–90.

Glover, V. (2011). Annual research review: Prenatal stress and the origins of psychopathology: An evolutionary perspective. *Journal of Child Psychology and Psychiatry, 52*, 356–367.

Goodman, K. L., De Los Reyes, A., & Bradshaw, C. P. (2010). Understanding and using informants' reporting discrepancies of youth victimization: A conceptual model and recommendations for research. *Clinical Child and Family Psychology Review, 13*(4), 366–383. doi:10.1007/s10567-010-0076-x

Gormley, M. J., & Dupaul, G. J. (2015). Teacher-to-teacher consultation: Facilitating consistent and effective intervention across grade levels for students with ADHD. *Psychology in the Schools, 52*, 124–138.

Graetz, B. W., Sawyer, M. G., & Baghurst, P. (2005). Gender differences among children with DSM-IV ADHD in Australia. *Journal of the American Academy of Child & Adolescent Psychiatry, 44*(2), 159–168.

Greenberg, L. M. (1989). Test of Variables of Attention (TOVA). Los Alamitos, CA: Universal Attention Disorders, Inc.

Greenhill, L., Kollins, S., Abikoff, H., Mccracken, J., Riddle, M., Swanson, J., … Vitiello, B. (2006). Efficacy and safety of immediate-release methylphenidate treatment for preschoolers with ADHD. *Journal of the American Academy of Child & Adolescent Psychiatry, 45*, 1284–1293.

Greenhill, L. L., Pliszka, S., & Dulcan, M. K. (2002). Practice parameter for the use of stimulant medications in the treatment of children, adolescents, and adults. *Journal of the American Academy of Child & Adolescent Psychiatry, 41*, 26S–49S.

Grizenko, N., Shayan, Y. R., Polotskaia, A., Ter-Stepanian, M., & Joober, R. (2008). Relation of maternal stress during pregnancy to symptom severity and response to treatment in children with ADHD. *Journal of Psychiatry & Neuroscience, 33*, 10–16.

Groen-Blokhuis, M. M., Middeldorp, C., van Beijsterveldt, C., & Boomsma, D.I. (2011). Evidence for a causal association of low birth weight and attention problems. *Journal of the American Academy of Child & Adolescent Psychiatry, 50*, 1247–1254.

Groom, M. J., Young, Z., Hall, C. L., Gillott, A., & Hollis, C. (2016). The incremental validity of a computerised assessment added to clinical rating scales to differentiate adult ADHD from autism spectrum disorder. *Psychiatry Research, 243*, 168–173. doi:10.1016/j.psychres.2016.06.042

Gureasko-Moore, S., Dupaul, G. J., & White, G. P. (2007). Self-management of classroom preparedness and homework: Effects on school functioning of adolescents with attention deficit hyperactivity disorder. *School Psychology Review, 36*, 647–664.

Halperin, J. M., Berwid, O. G., O'Neill, S. (2014). Healthy body, healthy mind?: The effectiveness of physical activity to treat ADHD in children. *Child and Adolescent Psychiatric Clinics of North America, 23*, 899–936.

Halperin, J. M, Marks, D. J., Bedard, A. C., Chacko, A., Curchack, J. T., Yoon, C. A., & Healey, D. M. (2013).

Training executive, attention, and motor skills: A proof-of-concept study in preschool children with ADHD. *Journal of Attention Disorders, 17*, 711–721.

Halperin, J. M., & Schulz, K. P. (2006). Revisiting the role of the prefrontal cortex in the pathophysiology of attention-deficit/hyperactivity disorder. *Psychological Bulletin, 132*, 560–581.

Hart, H., Radua, J., Mataix-Cols, D., & Rubia, K. (2012). Meta-analysis of fMRI studies of timing in attention-deficit hyperactivity disorder (ADHD). *Neuroscience & Biobehavioral Reviews, 36*, 2248–2256.

Hart, H., Radua, J., Nakao, T., Mataix-Cols, D., & Rubia, K. (2013). Meta-analysis of functional magnetic resonance imaging studies of inhibition and attention in attention-deficit/hyperactivity disorder: Exploring task-specific, stimulant medication, and age effects. *JAMA Psychiatry, 70*, 185.

Healey, D. M. & Halperin, J. M. (2015). Enhancing neurobehavioral gains with the aid of games and exercise (ENGAGE): Initial open trial of a novel early intervention fostering the development of preschoolers' self-regulation. *Child Neuropsychology, 21*, 465–480.

Hervey, A. S., Epstein, J. N., Curry, J. F., Tonev, S., Eugene Arnold, L., Keith Conners, C., … Hechtman, L. (2006). Reaction time distribution analysis of neuropsychological performance in an ADHD sample. *Child Neuropsychology, 12*(2), 125–140. doi:10.1080/09297040500499081

Hinshaw, S. P. (2002). Preadolescent girls with attention-deficit/hyperactivity disorder: I. Background characteristics, comorbidity, cognitive and social functioning, and parenting practices. *Journal of Consulting and Clinical Psychology, 70*(5), 1086.

Hinshaw, S. P., Owens, E. B., Sami, N., & Fargeon, S. (2006). Prospective follow-up of girls with attention-deficit/hyperactivity disorder into adolescence: Evidence for continuing cross-domain impairment. *Journal of Consulting and Clinical Psychology, 74*, 489–499.

Holmes, J., Gathercole, S. E., Place, M., Alloway, T. P., Elliott, J. G., & Hilton, K. A. (2010). The diagnostic utility of executive function assessments in the identification of ADHD in children. *Child and Adolescent Mental Health, 15*(1), 37–43. doi:10.1111/j.1475-3588.2009.00536.x

Hoza, B., Martin, C. P., Pirog, A., & Shoulberg, E. K. (2016). Using physical activity to manage ADHD symptoms: The state of the evidence. *Current Psychiatry Reports, 18*, 113.

Jensen, P. S., Arnold, L. E., Swanson, J. M., Vitiello, B., Abikoff, H. B., Greenhill, L. L., … Hur, K. (2007). 3-Year follow-up of the NIMH MTA study. *Journal of the American Academy of Child & Adolescent Psychiatry, 46*, 989–1002.

Johnson, S., Hollis, C., Marlow, N., Simms, V., & Wolke, D. (2014). Screening for childhood mental health disorders using the Strengths and Difficulties Questionnaire: The validity of multi-informant reports. *Developmental Medicine and Child Neurology, 56*(5), 453–459. doi:10.1111/dmcn.12360

Klein, R. G., Mannuzza, S., Olazagasti, M. A. R., Roizen, E., Hutchison, J. A., Lashua, E. C., & Castellanos, F. X. (2012). Clinical and functional outcome of childhood attention-deficit/hyperactivity disorder 33 years later. *Archives of General Psychiatry, 69*(12), 1295–1303.

Knouse, L. E. (2015). Cognitive-behavioral therapies for ADHD. In R. A. Barkley (Ed.), *Attention-deficit hyperactivity disorder: A handbook for diagnosis & treatment* (pp. 757–773). New York, NY: Guilford.

Kratochvil, C. J., Vaughan, B. S., Stoner, J. A., Daughton, J. M., Lubberstedt, B. D., Murray, D. W., … March, J. S. (2011). A double-blind, placebo-controlled study of atomoxetine in young children with ADHD. *Pediatrics, 127*, e862–868.

Lahey, B. B., & Willcutt, E. G. (2010). Predictive validity of a continuous alternative to nominal subtypes of attention-deficit/hyperactivity disorder for DSM-V. *Journal of Clinical Child & Adolescent Psychology, 39*, 761–775.

Lange, K. W. (2014). Utility of cognitive neuropsychological assessment in attention-deficit/hyperactivity disorder. *Attention Deficit and Hyperactivity Disorders, 6*(4), 241–248. doi:10.1007/s12402-014-0132-3

Larsson, H., Dilshad, R., Lichtenstein, P., & Barker, E. D. (2011). Developmental trajectories of DSM-IV symptoms of attention-deficit/hyperactivity disorder: Genetic effects, family risk and associated psychopathology: Developmental trajectories of DSM-IV symptoms of ADHD. *Journal of Child Psychology and Psychiatry, 52*, 954–963.

Larsson, H., Lichtenstein, P., & Larsson, J.O. (2006). Genetic contributions to the development of ADHD subtypes from childhood to adolescence. *Journal of the American Academy of Child & Adolescent Psychiatry, 45*, 973–981.

Lei, D., Du, M., Wu, M., Chen, T., Huang, X., Du, X., … Gong, Q. (2015). Functional MRI reveals different response inhibition between adults and children with ADHD. *Neuropsychology, 29*, 874–881.

Lichtenstein, P., Carlström, E., Råstam, M., Gillberg, C., & Anckarsäter, H. (2010). The genetics of autism spectrum disorders and related neuropsychiatric disorders in childhood. *The American Journal of Psychiatry, 167*, 1357–1363.

Manly, T., Robertson, I. H., Anderson, V., & Nimmo-Smith, I. (1999). *TEA-Ch: The Test of Everyday Attention for Children Manual*. Bury St. Edmunds, UK: Thames Valley Test Company Limited.

Martel, M. M., Levinson, C. A., Langer, J. K., & Nigg, J. T. (2016). A network analysis of developmental change in ADHD symptom structure from preschool to adulthood. *Clinical Psychological Science, 4*, 988–1001.

McCarthy, H., Skokauskas, N., & Frodl, T. (2014). Identifying a consistent pattern of neural function in attention deficit hyperactivity disorder: A meta-analysis. *Psychological Medicine*, *44*, 869–880.

Melby-Lervåg, M., & Hulme, C. (2013). Is working memory training effective? A meta-analytic review. *Developmental Psychology*, *49*, 270–291.

Merikangas, K. R., He, J. P., Brody, D., Fisher, P. W., Boturdon, K., & Koretz, D. S. (2010). Prevalence and treatment of mental disorders among US children in the 2001–2004 NHANES. *Pediatrics*, *125*, 75–81.

Michielsen, M., Comijs, H. C., Semeijn, E. J., Beekman, A. T., Deeg, D. J., & Kooij, J. S. (2013). The comorbidity of anxiety and depressive symptoms in older adults with attention-deficit/hyperactivity disorder: A longitudinal study. *Journal of Affective Disorders*, *148*(2), 220–227.

Miller, T. W., Nigg, J. T., & Faraone, S. V. (2007). Axis I and II comorbidity in adults with ADHD. *Journal of Abnormal Psychology*, *116*(3), 519.

Moffitt, T. E., Houts, R., Asherson, P., Belsky, D. W., Corcoran, D. L., Hammerle, M., ... Poulton, R. (2015). Is adult ADHD a childhood-onset neurodevelopmental disorder? Evidence from a four-decade longitudinal cohort study. *American Journal of Psychiatry*, *172*, 967–977.

Morgan, P. L., Staff, J., Hillemeier, M. M., Farkas, G., & Maczuga, S. (2013). Racial and ethnic disparities in ADHD diagnosis from kindergarten to eighth grade. *Pediatrics*, *132*, 85–93.

MTA Cooperative Group. (1999). A 14-month randomized clinical trial of treatment strategies for attention-deficit/hyperactivity disorder. *Archives of General Psychiatry*, *56*, 1073–1086.

Murphy, K. R., Barkley, R. A., & Bush, T. (2002). Young adults with attention deficit hyperactivity disorder: Subtype differences in comorbidity, educational, and clinical history. *The Journal of Nervous and Mental Disease*, *190*(3), 147–157.

Nakao, T., Radua, J., Rubia, K., & Mataix-Cols, D. (2011). Gray matter volume abnormalities in ADHD: Voxel-based meta-analysis exploring the effects of age and stimulant medication. *The American Journal of Psychiatry*, *168*, 1154–1163.

Nelson, J.R., Benner, G.J., & Bohaty, J., (2015). Addressing the academic problems and challenges of students with emotional and behavioral disorders. In J. M. Kauffman, H. M. Walker, & F. M. Gresham (Eds.), *Handbook of evidence-based practices for emotional and behavioral disorders: Applications in schools* (pp. 363–377). New York, NY: Guilford.

Newcorn, J. H., Ivanov, I., & Chacko, A. (2015). Recent progress in psychosocial and psychopharmacological treatments for ADHD. *Current Treatment Options in Psychiatry*, *2*, 14–27.

Nigg, J. T., Nikolas, M., Knottnerus, M., Cavanagh, K., & Friderici, K. (2010). Confirmation and extension of association of blood lead with attention-deficit/hyperactivity disorder (ADHD) and ADHD symptom domains at population-typical exposure levels: ADHD and blood lead. *Journal of Child Psychology and Psychiatry*, *51*, 58–65.

Nikolas, M. A., & Burt, S. A. (2010). Genetic and environmental influences on ADHD symptom dimensions of inattention and hyperactivity: A meta-analysis. *Journal of Abnormal Psychology*, *119*, 1–17.

Nikolas, M. A., & Nigg, J. T. (2013). Neuropsychological performance and attention-deficit hyperactivity disorder subtypes and symptom dimensions. *Neuropsychology*, *27*(1), 107–120. doi:10.1037/a0030685

Ogundele, M. O., Ayyash, H. F., & Banerjee, S. (2011). Role of computerised continuous performance task tests in ADHD. *Progress in Neurology and Psychiatry*, *15*, 8–13. doi:10.1002/pnp.198

Owens, E. B., Cardoos, S. L., & Hinshaw, S. P. (2015). Developmental progression and gender differences among individuals with ADHD. In R. A. Barkley (Ed.), *Attention-deficit hyperactivity disorder: A handbook for diagnosis and treatment* (pp. 223–255). New York, NY: Guilford.

Owens, J. S., Murphy, C. E., Richerson, L., Girio, E. L., & Himawan, L. K. (2008). Science to practice in underserved communities: The effectiveness of school mental health programming. *Journal of Clinical Child & Adolescent Psychology*, *37*, 434–447.

Pastor, P. N., & Reuben, C. A., (2008). Diagnosed attention deficit hyperactivity disorder and learning disability, United States, 2004–2006. National Center for Health Statistics. *Vital and Health Statistics*, *10*(237), 1–14.

Pelham, W. E., & Fabiano, G. A. (2008). Evidence-based psychosocial treatments for attention-deficit/hyperactivity disorder. *Journal of Clinical Child & Adolescent Psychology*, *37*, 184–214.

Pliszka, S. (2007). Practice parameter for the assessment and treatment of children and adolescents with attention-deficit/hyperactivity disorder. *Journal of the American Academy of Child & Adolescent Psychiatry*, *46*, 894–921.

Pliszka, S. R. (2015). Comorbid psychiatric disorders in children with ADHD. In R. A. Barkley (Ed.), *Attention-deficit hyperactivity disorder: A handbook for diagnosis and treatment* (pp. 140–168). New York, NY: Guilford.

Poelmans, G., Pauls, D. L., Buitelaar, J. K., & Franke, B. (2011). Integrated genome-wide association study findings: Identification of a neurodevelopmental network for attention deficit hyperactivity disorder. *The American Journal of Psychiatry*, *168*, 365–377.

Polanczyk, G., & Rohde, L. A. (2007). Epidemiology of attention-deficit/hyperactivity disorder across the lifespan. *Current Opinion in Psychiatry*, *20*, 386–392.

Pritchard, A. E., Koriakin, T., Jacobson, L. A., & Mahone, E. M. (2014). Incremental validity of neuropsychological assessment in the identification and treatment of youth with ADHD. *Clinical Neuropsychology*, *28*(1), 26–48. doi:10.1080/13854046.2013.863978

Rajendran, K., Rindskopf, D., O'Neil, S., Marks, D. J., Nomura, Y., & Halperin, J. M. (2013). Neuropsychological functioning and severity of ADHD in early childhood: a four-year cross-lagged study. *Journal of Abnormal Psychology*, *122*, 1179–1188.

Rajendran, K., Trampush, J. W., Rindskopf, D., Marks, D. J., O'Neil, S., & Halperin, J. M., (2013). Association between variation in neuropsychological development and trajectory of ADHD severity in early childhood. *American Journal of Psychiatry*, *170*, 1205–1211.

Ramsay, J. R., & Rostain, A. L. (2007). Psychosocial treatments for attention-deficit/hyperactivity disorder in adults: Current evidence and future directions. *Professional Psychology: Research and Practice*, *38*(4), 338–346.

Ramtekkar, U. P., Reiersen, A. M., Todorov, A. A., & Todd, R. D. (2010). Sex and age differences in attention-deficit/hyperactivity disorder symptoms and diagnoses: Implications for DSM-V and ICD-11. *Journal of the American Academy of Child & Adolescent Psychiatry*, *49*, 217–228.

Rapport, M. D., Orban, S. A., Kofler, M. J., & Friedman, L. M. (2013). Do programs designed to train working memory, other executive functions, and attention benefit children with ADHD? A meta-analytic review of cognitive, academic, and behavioral outcomes. *Clinical Psychology Review*, *33*, 1237–1252.

Rapport, M. D., Orban, S. A., Kofler, M. J. Friedman, L. M., & Bolden, J. (2014). Executive function training for children with ADHD. In R. A. Barkley (Ed.), *Attention-deficit hyperactivity disorder: A handbook for diagnosis and treatment* (pp. 641–665). New York, NY: Guilford.

Rasmussen, K., & Levander, S. (2009). Untreated ADHD in adults: Are there sex differences in symptoms, comorbidity, and impairment? *Journal of Attention Disorders*, *12*(4), 353–360.

Rescorla, L. A., Ginzburg, S., Achenbach, T. M., Ivanova, M. Y., Almqvist, F., Begovac, I., ... Verhulst, F. C. (2013). Cross-informant agreement between parent-reported and adolescent self-reported problems in 25 societies. *Journal of Clinical Child & Adolescent Psychology*, *42*(2), 262–273. doi:10.1080/15374416.2012.717870

Reid, R., Trout, A. L., & Schartz, M. (2005). Self-regulation interventions for children with attention deficit/hyperactivity disorder. *Exceptional Children*, *71*, 361–377.

Rodriguez, P. D., & Simon-Dack, S. L. (2013). Factor analysis of five adult ADHD self-report measures: Are they all the same? *Journal of Attention Disorders*, *17*(1), 64–69. doi:10.1177/1087054711423627

Rostain, A. L., & Ramsay, J. R. (2006). A combined treatment approach for adults with ADHD – Results of an open study of 43 patients. *Journal of Attention Disorders*, *10*(2), 150–159.

Rucklidge, J. J. (2008). Gender differences in ADHD: implications for psychosocial treatments. *Expert Review of Neurotherapeutics*, *8*, 643–655.

Safren, S.A., Otto, M., Sprich, S., Winett, C. L., Wilens, T., & Biederman, J. (2005). Cognitive-behavioral therapy for ADHD in medication-treated adults with continued symptoms. *Behavior Research and Therapy*, *43*(7), 831–842.

Safren, S. A., Perlman, C. A., Sprich, S., & Otto, M. W. (2005). *Mastering your adult ADHD: A cognitive-behavioral treatment program, therapist guide*. New York, NY: Oxford University Press.

Safren, S. A., Sprich, S., Mimiaga, M. J., Surman, C., Knouse, L. E., Groves, M., & Otto, M. W. (2010). Cognitive behavioral therapy vs. relaxation with educational support for medication-treated adults with ADHD and persistent symptoms: A randomized controlled trial. *Journal of the American Medical Association*, *304*(8), 857–880.

Scheres, A., Tontsch, C., Thoeny, A. L., & Kaczkurkin, A. (2010). Temporal reward discounting in attention-deficit/hyperactivity disorder: the contribution of symptom domains, reward magnitude, and session length. *Biological Psychiatry*, *67*(7), 641–648. doi: 10.1016/j.biopsych.2009.10.033

Schmidt, S. L., Simões, E. N., & Novais Carvalho, A. L. (2016). Association between auditory and visual continuous performance tests in students with ADHD. *Journal of Attention Disorders*. doi: 10.1177/1087054716679263

Shaw, P., Eckstrand, K., Sharp, W., Blumenthal, J., Lerch, J. P., Greenstein, D., ... Rapoport, J. L. (2007). Attention-deficit/hyperactivity disorder is characterized by a delay in cortical maturation. *Proceedings of the National Academy of Sciences*, *104*, 19649–19654.

Shaw, P., Lerch, J., Greenstein, D., Sharp, W., Clasen, L., Evans, A., ... Rapoport, J. (2006). Longitudinal mapping of cortical thickness and clinical outcome in children and adolescents with attention-deficit/hyperactivity disorder. *Archives of General Psychiatry*, *63*, 540–549.

Shipstead, Z., Redick, T. S., & Engle, R. W. (2012). Is working memory training effective? *Psychological Bulletin*, *138*, 628–654.

Simmonds, D. J., Pekar, J. J., & Mostofsky, S. H. (2008). Meta-analysis of go/no-go tasks demonstrating that fMRI activation associated with response inhibition is task-dependent. *Neuropsychologia*, *46*(1), 224–232. doi:10.1016/j.neuropsychologia.2007.07.015

Sobanski, E., Brüggemann, D., Alm, B., Kern, S., Philipsen, A., Schmalzried, H., ... Rietschel, M. (2008). Subtype differences in adults with attention-deficit/hyperactivity disorder (ADHD) with regard to ADHD symptoms, psychiatric comorbidity and psychosocial adjustment. *European Psychiatry, 23*(2), 142–149.

Solanto, M. V. (2011). *Cognitive-behavioral therapy for adult ADHD: Targeting executive dysfunction.* New York, NY: Guilford Press.

Solanto, M. V. (2015). Executive function deficits in adults with ADHD. In R. A. Barkley, *Attention-deficit hyperactivity disorder: A handbook for diagnosis and treatment* (pp. 256–266). New York, NY: Guilford.

Solanto, M. V., Marks, D. J., Mitchell, K. J., Wasserstein, J., & Kofman, M. (2008). Development of a new psychosocial treatment for adult ADHD. *Journal of Attention Disorders, 11*, 728–736.

Solanto, M. V., Marks, D. J., Wasserstein, J., Mitchell, K., Abikoff, H., Alivir, J. M. J., & Kofman, M. D. (2010). Efficacy of meta-cognitive therapy (MCT) for adult ADHD. *American Journal of Psychiatry, 167*, 958–968.

Tannock, R. (2000). Attention deficit disorders with anxiety disorders. In T. E. Brown (Ed.), *Attention-deficit disorders and comorbidities in children, adolescents and adults* (pp. 125–175). New York, NY: American Psychiatric Press.

Thomas, R., Sanders, S., Doust, J., Beller, E., & Glasziou, P. (2015). Prevalence of attention-deficit/hyperactivity disorder: A systematic review and meta-analysis. *Pediatrics, 135*, e994–e1001.

Tian, L., Jiang, T., Wang, Y., Zang, Y., He, Y., Liang, M., ... Zhuo, Y. (2006). Altered resting-state functional connectivity patterns of anterior cingulate cortex in adolescents with attention deficit hyperactivity disorder. *Neuroscience Letters, 400*, 39–43.

Trout, A. L., Lienemann, T. O., Reid, R., & Epstein, M. H. (2007). A review of non-medication interventions to improve the academic performance of children and youth with ADHD. *Remedial and Special Education, 28*, 207–226.

Valera, E. M., Faraone, S. V., Murray, K. E., & Seidman, L. J. (2007). Meta-analysis of structural imaging findings in attention-deficit/hyperactivity disorder. *Biological Psychiatry, 61*, 1361–1369.

Van der Oord, S., Prins, P. J. M., Oosterlaan, J., & Emmelkamp, P. M. G. (2008). Efficacy of methylphenidate, psychosocial treatments and their combination in school-aged children with ADHD: A meta-analysis. *Clinical Psychology Review, 28*, 783–800.

van Ewijk, H., Heslenfeld, D. J., Zwiers, M. P., Buitelaar, J. K., & Oosterlaan, J. (2012). Diffusion tensor imaging in attention deficit/hyperactivity disorder: A systematic review and meta-analysis. *Neuroscience & Biobehavioral Reviews, 36*, 1093–1106.

Vannest, K. J., Davis, J. L., Davis, C. R., Mason, B. A., & Burke, M. D. (2010). Effective intervention for behavior with a daily behavior report card: A meta-analysis. *School Psychology Review, 39*, 654–672.

Vaughan, B., & Kratochvil, C. J. (2012). Pharmacotherapy of pediatric attention-deficit/hyperactivity disorder. *Child and Adolescent Psychiatric Clinics of North America, 21*, 941–955.

Vidal-Estrada, R., Bosch-Munso, R., Nogueira-Morais, M., Casas-Brugue, M., & Ramos-Quiroga, J. A. (2012). Psychological treatment of attention deficit hyperactivity disorder in adults: A systematic review. *Actas Españolas de Psiquiatría, 40*(3), 147–154.

Visser, S. N., Bitsko, R. H., Danielson, M. L., Perou, R., & Blumberg, S. J. (2010). Increasing prevalence of parent-reported attention-deficit/hyperactivity disorder among children—United States, 2003 and 2007. *Morbidity and Mortality Weekly Report, 59*, 1439–1443.

Visser, S. N., Danielson, M. L., Bitsko, R. H., Holbrook, J. R., Kogan, M. D., Ghandour, R. M., ... Blumberg, S. J. (2014). Trends in the parent-report of health care provider-diagnosed and medicated attention-deficit/hyperactivity disorder: United States, 2003–2011. *Journal of the American Academy of Child & Adolescent Psychiatry, 53*, 34–46.

Vogt, C., & Shameli, A. (2011). Assessments for attention-deficit hyperactivity disorder: Use of objective measurements. *The Psychiatrist, 35*(10), 380–383. doi:10.1192/pb.bp.110.032144

Wigal, S. B. (2009). Efficacy and safety limitations of attention-deficit hyperactivity disorder pharmacotherapy in children and adults. *CNS Drugs, 23*, Suppl 1, 21–31.

Willcutt, E. G. (2012). The prevalence of DSM-IV attention-deficit/hyperactivity disorder: A meta-analytic review. *Neurotherapeutics, 9*, 490–499.

Willcutt, E. G., Doyle, A. E., Nigg, J. T., Faraone, S. V., & Pennington, B. F. (2005). Validity of the executive function theory of attention-deficit/hyperactivity disorder: A meta-analytic review. *Biol Psychiatry, 57*(11), 1336–1346. doi:10.1016/j.biopsych.2005.02.006

Wilens, T. E., Biederman, J., Brown, S., Tanguay, S., Monuteaux, M. C., Blake, C., & Spencer, T. J. (2002). Psychiatric comorbidity and functioning in clinically referred preschool children and school-age youths with ADHD. *Journal of the American Academy of Child & Adolescent Psychiatry, 41*(3), 262–268.

Wilens, T. E., Newcorn, J. H., Kratochvil, C. J., Gao, H., Thomason, C. K., Rogers, A. K., ... Levine, L. R. (2006). Long-term atomoxetine treatment in adolescents with attention-deficit/hyperactivity disorder. *Journal of Pediatrics, 149*, 112–119.

Wolraich, M. L. (2011). Pharmacological interventions for individuals with attention deficit hyperactivity disorder. In S. W. Evans & B. Hoza (Eds.), *Treating attention deficit hyperactivity disorder: Assessment and intervention in developmental context* (pp. 1–21) Kingston, NJ: Civic Research Institute.

Yeo, R. A., Hill, D. E., Campbell, R. A., Vigil, J., Petropoulos, H., Hart, B., … Brooks, W. M. (2003). Proton magnetic resonance spectroscopy investigation of the right frontal lobe in children with attention-deficit/hyperactivity disorder. *Journal of the American Academy of Child & Adolescent Psychiatry, 42*, 303–310.

Yu-Feng, Z., Yong, H., Chao-Zhe, Z., Qing-Jiu, C., Man-Qiu, S., Meng, L., … Yu-Feng, W. (2007). Altered baseline brain activity in children with ADHD revealed by resting-state functional MRI. *Brain and Development, 29*, 83–91.

Chapter 7

Learning Disabilities

Richard Boada, Robin L. Peterson, and Robert L. Mapou

Introduction

A learning disability (LD) is a neurodevelopmental disorder that results in unexpected academic under-achievement in the presence of adequate intelligence and instruction (Fletcher, Lyon, Fuchs, & Barnes, 2007; Pennington, 2009). Although initially viewed as a childhood disorder, LDs can persist across the lifespan; however, their manifestations may change as a function of developmental demands (American Psychiatric Association, 2013; Mapou, 2009).

Achieving consensus on the definition of an LD has been difficult, due, in part, to the many stakeholders who have had an interest in this construct over the years. LD was initially defined in a legal context in the late 1960s and was subsequently included in the 1975 Education for All Handicapped Children Act (Public Law 94–142). This law mandated identification of, and service delivery to, children with LDs in public education. Although there has been considerable research since then, this federal definition has remained essentially unchanged. It was written into the 1990 Individuals with Disabilities Education Act (IDEA, 1990) and its revisions in 1997 and 2004. It is helpful for clinicians to be familiar with the definition, because it is used when developing individualized education programs and 504 Plans for children in public schools. It states:

> Specific learning disability means a disorder in one or more of the basic psychological processes involved in understanding or in using language, spoken or written, that may manifest itself in an imperfect ability to listen, think, speak, read, write, spell, or do mathematical calculations. The term includes such conditions as perceptual handicaps, brain injury, minimal brain dysfunction, dyslexia, and developmental aphasia. The term does not include children who have learning problems that are primarily the result of visual, hearing, or motor handicaps; of mental retardation; of emotional disturbance; or of environmental, cultural, or economic disadvantage. (IDEA, 1990)

This definition is relatively broad in scope, and introduces the idea that psychological processes underlie the behavioral phenotypes, although these are not specified further. It assumes that mathematical deficits are also caused by language dysfunction, and does not recognize the persistence of learning disabilities into adulthood. The definition also includes acquired neurological disorders (i.e., brain injury), which are different from developmental disorders. However, it was written in this manner due to the initial focus of special education law on identification and service delivery for children with all types of cognitive disabilities. Over the years, refinements to the definition of LD have occurred, including one proposed by The National Joint Committee on Learning Disabilities in 1981 (revised in 1987 and 1990), which acknowledged that learning disabilities are intrinsic to the individual, presumed to be due to central nervous system dysfunction, and may occur across the lifespan (National Joint Committee on Learning Disabilities, 1990). Although the committee's definition did not include problems in self-regulatory behaviors, social perception, or social interaction as core features of the LD definition, other attempts to broaden the scope of an LD exist. For example, in 1985, the Rehabilitation Services Administration established a definition of specific LD where its manifestation could be due to a deficit in one or more of the following areas: attention, reasoning, processing, memory, communication, reading, writing, spelling, calculation, coordination, social competence, and emotional maturity (Rehabilitation Services Administration, 1985). This definition was written shortly after the agency accepted learning disorders as a medically recognized disability.

It should be increasingly clear that definitions of LD have evolved over time in response to scientific advances in the field, as well as the potential policy implications for educational and medical communities. Defining who has an LD, what counts as a potential etiology, and how it manifests across the lifespan all have significant implications for how school districts allocate resources, whether treatments will be covered under medical insurance, and how accommodations are written into laws to protect adults in the workforce. Scientists studying LDs have also had philosophical differences in how much to weigh various factors in determining what constitutes an LD. Some argue that the academic skill deficit should occur in the presence of intact skills in most other areas, whereas others allow for more variable presentations across domains. Researchers have debated the nature, quantity, and severity of core deficits and to what extent environmental factors can also be considered primary causes of an LD (e.g., drug exposure in utero, lead exposure in the environment). In response to the increasing recognition that LDs continue to manifest in adulthood, Mapou (2009) offered a definition highlighting that the impact of LDs may not become fully obvious until later in life. He also stipulated that an LD has to substantially limit functioning in one or more areas of a person's life (e.g., school, work, home, social), to be consistent with the definition of a disability under the 1990 Americans with Disabilities Act (ADA) and the 2008 ADA Amendments Act. In addition, his definition includes a broad range of cognitive effects (i.e., spoken language, attention, executive functions, visuospatial skills, memory) that might stem from having an LD. As in most other previous definitions, LD should not be diagnosed if academic weaknesses are due to cultural or linguistic differences, psychiatric impairment, or lack of appropriate education.

Possibly due to the inherent difficulties that come from heterogeneity in a definition, but also likely due to the need for more carefully defined phenotypes for advancing research, the field has converged on three main areas of achievement deficit – reading, writing and math – and the underlying cognitive processes that are involved in the development of these skills. Dyslexia, a specific LD in reading, has been the best studied of these deficits and has the only evidence-based definition. It states:

> Dyslexia is a specific LD that is neurobiological in origin. It is characterized by difficulties with accurate and/or fluent word recognition and by poor spelling and decoding abilities. These difficulties typically result from a deficit in the phonological component of language that is often unexpected in relation to

other cognitive abilities and the provision of effective classroom instruction. Secondary consequences may include problems in reading comprehension and reduced reading experience that can impede growth of vocabulary and background knowledge. (Lyon, Shaywitz, & Shaywitz, 2003)

There are no comparable evidence-based definitions of specific LDs in mathematics or written expression. Nonetheless, researchers and clinicians have achieved some level of consensus on the underlying cognitive processes and academic skill deficits that characterize these other LDs, and these are now enumerated in the Specific Learning Disorder category of the *Diagnostic and Statistical Manual of Mental Disorders*, 5th ed. (DSM-5) (American Psychiatric Association, 2013), under the more general heading of Neurodevelopmental Disorders. Individuals are given a diagnosis of a Specific Learning Disorder with a specifier identifying the area of impairment. It should be noted that DSM-5 nomenclature uses "disorder," consistent with other terminology for other psychiatric/medical conditions, whereas the term "disability" is used more frequently in the education literature. Under each specified area of impairment, the DSM-5 identifies core areas of weakness that are supported by the research literature as being characteristic of that LD diagnosis (c.f., Fletcher et al., 2007; Pennington, 2009). The criteria are as follows:

- 315.00 (F81.0) With impairment in reading:
  - Difficulty with word reading accuracy
  - Difficulty with reading rate or fluency
  - Difficulty with reading comprehension

- 315.2 (F81.81) With impairment in written expression:
  - Difficulty with spelling accuracy
  - Difficulty with the use of grammar and punctuation accuracy
  - Difficulty with clarity or organization of written expression

- 315.1 (F81.2) With impairment in mathematics:
  - Difficulty with number sense
  - Difficulty with memorization of arithmetic facts
  - Difficulty with accurate or fluent calculation
  - Difficulty with accurate math reasoning

It is important to note that, as opposed to the Lyon, Shaywitz, and Shaywitz (2003) definition, the

DSM-5 does not specify any underlying neurocognitive or etiological mechanisms that lead to the expressed academic dysfunction. In addition, there have been some important conceptual shifts that occurred in the DSM-5 relative to prior versions of the manual. First, the DSM-5 places all the specific LDs under one heading, rather than in discrete specific LD categories, as in the DSM-IV-TR (4th edition, text revision). This shift is consistent with considerable epidemiological research that demonstrates substantial comorbidity among specific LDs (on the order of 25–40%). However, as described by Peterson and Pennington (2015), there are problems with this approach. Some subtypes of LDs (i.e., reading disorder and mathematics disorder) have more support for their diagnostic validity than others (i.e., written expression), so practitioners should be wary of ascribing the same level of syndrome validity to each one. Furthermore, there is utility in keeping the specific LDs separate, because treatments will vary depending on which one is diagnosed.

The second significant change in the DSM-5 is that it embodies a distinction between basic and complex academic skills that has been the focus of more recent research in the area of LDs. In the past, basic deficits were emphasized, such as reading decoding, handwriting and spelling, and number sense/math calculation. In the medical literature, these deficits have traditionally been called dyslexia, dysgraphia, and dyscalculia, respectively. As described in Pennington and Peterson (2015), basic academic skills have to be learned, practiced, and automatized to provide the foundation for higher level academic tasks such as reading comprehension, written composition, and math problem-solving. When an individual has difficulty with an area of academic achievement, especially as they get older and the complexity of the required task increases (i.e., in higher grades or at work), failure to perform adequately may be due to a deficit at the level of the basic skill, a deficit at the level of the higher level process, or both. Complex academic tasks require an integration of basic academic skills and additional nonacademic cognitive and linguistic abilities; the latter include listening comprehension, narration (i.e., oral language composition), and fluid reasoning. The implication of this conceptual framework is that the practitioner now has to identify whether a deficit exists at the level of a basic skill or at the level of a more complex skill; for many individuals, deficits exist at both levels. Differential diagnosis among these possibilities is important for treatment. A child whose reading problem is restricted to reading comprehension, called a "poor comprehender" in the research literature (Cain, Oakhill, & Lemmon, 2004; Nation, 2005) needs a different intervention than a child whose reading problem is mainly at the level of single-word reading accuracy and fluency. Lastly, it should be noted that there is limited research currently on the validity of "complex learning disabilities" as stand-alone disorders. Some initial cognitive models of complex LDs are discussed in the following section.

The third major shift in the DSM-5 criteria for specific LD is the exclusion of an IQ discrepancy requirement to meet criteria for a diagnosis. In the DSM-IV, the requirement was for a child's academic deficit to be discrepant from both age *and* IQ expectations. This shift in criteria came about as a result of research showing little external validity for the distinction between an IQ and age discrepancy definitions of dyslexia (Fletcher et al., 2007). Although elimination of this requirement allows children with borderline IQ and academic scores to still receive an appropriate diagnosis and intervention for an LD, it also means that a child with a very high IQ (i.e., Full Scale IQ > 120) but only average reading or mathematical ability (e.g., standard score of 90–109 on an appropriate academic achievement test) would not qualify for a diagnosis. The latter issue has generated controversy. For example, proponents argue that a relative weakness should not define an LD; individuals with such discrepancies but average academic skills will unfairly receive accommodations, but individuals who are average in all areas will not. Also, neuropsychological research has shown that variability in test scores is the rule and not the exception in both adults and children (Binder, Iverson, & Brooks, 2009;; Brooks, 2010; Brooks, Iverson, Sherman, & Holdnack, 2009; Schretlen, Munro, & Anthony, 2003; Schretlen, Testa, Winicki, Pearlson, & Gordon, 2008).

On the other hand, the DSM-5 section on Specific Learning Disorder (American Psychiatric Association, 2013, p. 69) acknowledges that "Specific learning disorder may also occur in individuals identified as intellectually gifted." However, if a gifted child (IQ > 130) is also required to meet the age discrepancy criterion, then he or she would have to score over 3.5 SDs below their IQ level, whereas a child with a mean IQ of 100 would have to score only 1.5 SDs below their IQ level.

This makes it much harder for a gifted child to meet diagnostic criteria than for a nongifted child. Therefore, an alternate view is that a child should be able to meet diagnostic criteria for a specific LD with an age discrepancy *or* an IQ discrepancy (Gregg, Coleman, Lindstrom, & Lee, 2007; Pennington & Peterson, 2015). The issue of functional impairment becomes a point of debate in the latter approach, since one might argue that reading skills that are generally in the average range do not hinder an individual's ability to function or constitute a disability under the ADA; but if the frame of reference is a gifted person's accelerated curriculum or the high-level reading demands of a particular career, then documenting functional impairment may not be as difficult. Elbro (2010) refers to this issue by differentiating between dyslexia as a disability (poor ability) versus a handicap (i.e., the consequences of poor ability). For individuals with higher IQ but relatively weaker reading skills, their handicap may predominantly lie in the discrepancy between their literacy level and the difficulty of the texts they are supposed to be able to read based on their intelligence. But, even then, the law has been fairly clear in the definition of a disability as requiring skills below the level of most people. So, the comparison standard from a legal standpoint is the general population and not one's educational or vocational peer group (Lovett & Lewandowski, 2015). This is important when advising individuals who plan to attend law or medical school.

Clinical Manifestation

Epidemiology, Etiology, and Pathophysiology

The rest of this chapter focuses primarily on specific reading and math disorders, dyslexia and dyscalculia, respectively, because these are the best validated learning disorders in the literature. Reading comprehension and math problem-solving deficits are not discussed per se, except in the context of reading and math disorders. Lastly, not much time is spent on the specific LD of written expression, due to the limited research on this LD.

Reading Disorder

The prevalence rate of reading disorder (RD) depends on the definition used. Because reading skill is normally distributed, a deficit requires one to impose a cutoff along the lower end of the skill distribution; the degree of severity required for classification of RD varies to some extent among researchers and educational professionals. This variability is compounded by the fact that clinicians also have to consider the effects of socioeconomic status, adequacy of educational instruction, and possible cultural and linguistic factors that may influence a child's performance. Nevertheless, scores on standardized achievement tests are still the primary assessment method to determine academic proficiency. A score of 1.3 *SD*s below the mean, which identifies approximately the bottom 9% of the population, is often used as a cutoff. More conservative cutoffs will result in lower prevalence and vice versa. Researchers generally report prevalence rates of 5–17%. RD has been found in every culture studied, and mounting evidence underscores cross-linguistic similarity in its neurobiological and neurocognitive bases. Population-based studies have found a small male predominance for RD (approximately 1.5:1; Rutter et al., 2004). The gender difference is even higher in referred samples, from about 3- to 6-fold (Smith, Gilger, & Pennington, 2002), which suggests that girls are referred for evaluation less often than boys. This referral bias is related to a higher rate of comorbid externalizing disorders in boys (Willcutt & Pennington, 2000), mostly attention-deficit/hyperactivity disorder (ADHD). In contrast, girls more commonly present with comorbid dysthymia. In a longitudinal study of RD by Boetsch (1996), children at high family risk for RD showed higher rates of ADHD symptoms before kindergarten, whereas dysthymia emerged only after the beginning of reading instruction. This finding suggests that internalizing symptoms may be secondary to reading difficulties, whereas ADHD is a primary comorbidity. This finding also is consistent with other research showing that RD and ADHD share both cognitive and genetic risk factors (McGrath et al., 2011; Willcutt et al., 2010).

As has been mentioned previously, RD is comorbid with other neurodevelopmental disorders, including language disorder, speech sound disorder, and math disorder. In a longitudinal study of children with speech and language impairment (Peterson, Pennington, Shriberg, & Boada, 2009), 75% of children with a history of language impairment were subsequently diagnosed with RD. There is also evidence that the comorbidity with RD is mediated by shared etiological and neurocognitive risk factors

(Smith, Pennington, Boada, & Shriberg, 2005; Willcutt et al., 2010). The extensive comorbidity of RD with other disorders means that a thorough assessment for these comorbid conditions is necessary to inform treatment.

The etiology of LDs is multifactorial and involves multiple genes and environmental risk factors. RD is familial and moderately heritable (Pennington & Olson, 2005) and has been linked to nine risk loci through replicated linkage studies (Carrion-Castillo, Franke, & Fisher, 2013; Raskind, Peter, Richards, Eckert, & Berninger, 2013). Recently, several candidate genes for dyslexia have been identified, and results from animal models suggest that some of these genes may influence neuronal migration, although more research is still needed (Kere, 2011). Although RD segregates in families, no highly penetrant causal mutations have been identified. Intriguingly, four of the most replicated genes, *DYX1C1*, *DCDC2*, *KIAA0319*, and *ROBO1*, are all involved in neuronal or axonal migration (Meng et al., 2005; Paracchini et al., 2006). This finding is consistent with a study of white matter tracts using diffusion tensor imaging (Carter et al., 2009), which leads to the speculation that specific networks of genes could affect the development and/or maintenance of certain central nervous system tracts or circuits.

RD is associated with aberrant activation of a distributed left hemisphere language and reading network. In particular, consistent underactivations have been reported in two posterior left hemisphere regions: a temporoparietal region believed to be critical for phonological processing and letter–sound conversion, and an occipitotemporal region believed to participate in whole-word recognition. In addition, many studies have reported abnormal activation of the left inferior frontal gyrus. Abnormal cerebellar activation has also sometimes been found, as has over-activation of homologous right hemisphere regions (hypothesized to reflect compensatory processes). Recent research controlling for reading experience suggests that characteristic brain differences are a cause rather than a result of dyslexia, although further work is still needed on this question. Structural differences in dyslexia have also been reported across a widely distributed set of brain regions. The most consistent findings correspond with the functional results and include gray matter decreases in left hemisphere reading and language regions. Furthermore, substantial diffusion tensor imaging work implicates local white matter changes in left temporoparietal regions and left inferior frontal gyrus, consistent with the notion that dyslexia represents a disconnection syndrome, at least in part. Finally, both seminal and recent research highlights problems with neuronal migration, which is particularly interesting given the possibility that some of the dyslexia risk genes may be implicated in this process.

The heritability of dyslexia is greater for children from more enriched environments than for children from less enriched environments, which is called a bioecological gene-by-environment interaction (Friend, DeFries, & Olson, 2008). In essence, if a child were raised in an optimal environment, the main reason he or she would have difficulties with reading would be a genetically related risk. On the other hand, there are multiple possible reasons why a child might have difficulties with reading if raised in a suboptimal environment. Some of these reasons might still be genetic, but environmental factors are likely to account for some of the variance as well. As the relative proportion of explanatory variance that is genetic decreases, so does the heritability. It should be noted that the risk factors that affect children in each environment are likely to be the same, it is just the relative contribution of each to individual differences in outcome that differs. Furthermore, we do not know which specific environmental factors underlie this interaction. Reasonable possibilities include the language and preliteracy environments that parents provide for their children, but these hypotheses have not yet been tested directly.

Math Disorder

The prevalence rate of math disorder (MD) is also going to be affected by the need to impose a categorical cutoff on a normal distribution, and the other educational opportunity and cultural factors explained in the previous section for RD. Standardized tests of math achievement, usually measuring a combination of calculation and math problem-solving skills, are commonly used. A population study in Israel found a prevalence rate of 4.6% (Shalev & Gross-Tsur, 2001). The male-to-female ratio was 1.1: 1. This is consistent with the other few population studies that exist, which report a rate between 3% and 6.5% (Badian, 1983; Lewis, Hitch, & Walker, 1994). Interestingly, prevalence rate of MD in clinical samples, as reported by the DSM-IV-TR, was 1%, which means that disproportionately fewer children are referred for MD than exist in the population. The explanation for this discrepancy could be that isolated MD is less impairing than isolated RD, because reading is such a foundational educational skill that cuts across curricular areas (Geary, 2013).

Comorbidity is also quite common in children with MD. As is the case with RD, MD is comorbid with ADHD, RD, and language impairment. In the Badian (1983) and Lewis et al. (1994) studies, respectively, 43% and 64% of children with MD also had RD. This is in line with more recent studies that have shown that RD and MD co-occur in 30–70% of individuals with either disorder (Kovas et al., 2007; Landerl & Moll, 2010). Twin studies suggest that some of the same genetic influences contribute to both disorders (Light & DeFries, 1995; Plomin & Kovas, 2005). However, relatively few studies have examined possible shared cognitive predictors. In the aforementioned Israeli study, 26% of children with MD also had ADHD. Capano and colleagues (2008) found a similar prevalence rate of 18.1%. Although these comorbidity percentages are high, they do suggest that there are children with isolated MD. Studies have found that some of these children have spatial and nonverbal reasoning difficulties.

Previous behavioral genetic studies have found MD to be heritable. A twin study by Alarcon et al. (1997) found an overall group deficit heritability estimate of 0.38. Significant bivariate heritability for RD and MD was found in the same twin sample, and the association was found to be largely genetically mediated by phonological and broader language skills. These bivariate heritability results have since been replicated by Haworth et al. (2007). It should be noted that MD also appears as a common characteristic in two genetic disorders, Turner syndrome and fragile X syndrome. The neuropsychological profile of these two syndromes includes spatial and attention/executive functioning deficits, respectively. This factor suggests the possibility of subtypes of MD, one that is mediated by verbal deficits and is comorbid with RD, and others that are mediated by spatial and/or executive dysfunction. More research is needed to validate MD subtypes and to see how they may map on to the DSM-5 subcategories of MD (i.e., number sense, memorization of math facts, calculation, or math reasoning). Less is currently understood about the molecular genetics of MD. To date one study identified genes implicated in neuronal migration and neurite outgrowth – similar to RD (Docherty

et al., 2010). Another study found pleiotropic effects of RD risk genes *DCDC2* and *DYX1C1* on math abilities (Marino et al., 2011).

Limited research has explored brain mechanisms in developmental MD. Reasonable candidates include the networks that support mathematics skill in adults, which appear to include a distributed bilateral cortical network involving portions of the parietal and frontal lobes (Dehaene, 2003). One key brain region in this network appears to be the left inferior parietal region posterior to the angular gyrus. As reviewed by Dehaene (2003), this region is activated in normal adults performing arithmetic calculations or comprehending the magnitude of a number, regardless of input or output modality, or even awareness of a numerical stimulus. Moreover, activity is proportional to difficulty of the task. The one patient with developmental dyscalculia or MD who has been studied with neuroimaging had a localized abnormal signal overlapping this inferior parietal region in the left hemisphere (Levy, Reis, & Grafman, 1999). The importance of bilateral parietal structures for arithmetic is also supported by neuroimaging studies of females with Turner syndrome. These studies have found abnormalities in bilateral parieto-occipital areas using both structural (Reiss et al., 1993; Reiss, Mazzocco, Greenlaw, Freund, & Ross, 1995) and functional (Clark et al., 1990) scans. The other brain region identified by Dehaene (2003) is the inferior frontal cortex on both sides. It is more activated by larger exact language-dependent calculations, such as multiplication, whereas the inferior parietal site is more important for approximation.

Disorder of Written Expression

Although there are undoubtedly individuals with clinically disabling writing difficulties, the validity of an LD in writing that is distinct from existing neurodevelopmental diagnoses (e.g., RD, language disorder) has not been well established. The only two existing epidemiologic studies of specific LD of written expression (Katusic, Colligan, Weaver, & Barbaresi, 2009; Yoshimasu et al., 2011) reported that 75% of children meeting criteria also had RD, and of the remaining 25%, nearly 30% had ADHD. Thus, there may be very few children with writing problems not explained by another diagnosis. As one would expect given this finding, the prevalence rate was similar to that of RD (6.9–14.7%) and there was a male predominance in the gender ratio (2–3: 1).

Wagner et al. (2011) modeled the development of written composition skill in children from first to fourth grade. They found that the complex skill of written composition is predicted by the simple skill of handwriting automaticity and a more general language skill involving productivity (i.e., ability to generate words to express ideas).

Prevention

It has been well established that early identification and intervention are key in preventing LDs or minimizing their impact (Fletcher et al., 2007). If a child with RD has not been identified or had intervention by second or third grade, there is a greater likelihood that their reading impairment will affect achievement in other academic domains, because accumulation of knowledge becomes more text driven as a child moves to higher grades. Additionally, children with RD engage in reading less often, causing continued vocabulary acquisition to occur at a slower rate. As spelling deficits hinder the amount of written output that is typically generated by children with RD, there is less experience and practice developing skills in the use of written conventions, punctuation, and written language organization. Similarly, early math deficits will compound, given the hierarchical nature of math curricula, slowing not only the pace and facility of learning higher level math concepts but also their use in related domains, especially science. Unfortunately, the later that intervention begins, the less likely the these broader academic skills can be fully remediated.

Clinical Manifestations

Reading Disorder

A large body of research makes it clear that RD is a language-based disorder the primary underlying deficit of which involves problems in phonological processing (i.e., processing of sounds in language; Peterson & Pennington, 2012). Phonological processing deficits have been documented even before the start of formal literacy instruction and persist in many adults with RD. Further, the same pattern has been observed across cultures and languages that vary in orthographic systems and educational practices (Laasonen, Lehtinen, Leppämäki, Tani, & Hokkanen, 2010; Paulesu et al., 2001). Although the phonological account of RD is compelling in many ways, it is incomplete. An important caveat is that the

relationship between phonological skills and reading is bidirectional, so that over time, poor reading also causes poor phonological processing (Nation & Hulme, 2011). Further, a single phonological deficit is neither necessary nor sufficient to cause RD. Some children with reading difficulties have intact phonological processing (Pennington et al., 2012), whereas some children with phonological problems go on to develop normal reading (Bishop et al., 2009; Peterson et al., 2009). Many researchers have adopted a multiple cognitive deficit framework in which a phonological deficit interacts with other neurocognitive risk and protective factors to determine reading outcome (Pennington, 2006). Additional risk factors that have received research support include problems in broader language skill (e.g., vocabulary knowledge), rapid automatized naming, processing speed, and visual attention.

In their recent review of reading development, Hulme and Snowling (2014) also highlight the importance of oral language skills in reading acquisition. Although they agree that difficulty with decoding is predicted by deficits in phonological awareness, letter–sound knowledge, and rapid naming, as other researchers have reported, they found that difficulty with reading comprehension is associated with deficits in vocabulary knowledge, grammatical and morphological skills, and pragmatic ability.

Although RD manifests in childhood and persists into adulthood, the degree and nature of the deficits that manifest can change over time based on a variety of factors (e.g., initial severity, intervention, amount of practice). One common theme of reading studies in adults is that brighter individuals with dyslexia compensate more effectively for reading difficulties. For example, when IQ is controlled, differences in phonological measures are larger, but differences on reading measures are smaller. Although some adults show both orthographic and phonologic deficits, the latter make a more significant contribution to reading problems (Birch & Chase, 2004). Those with stronger phonological skills were better readers, but orthographic skills did not predict better reading. There also does not appear to be a pure orthographic deficit group in adults. Rather, Osmon, Braun, and Plambeck (2005) found a group with both deficits or a group with only phonologic deficits. Birch (2016) recently extended these findings and found that phonological deficits were primary in college students with RDs. Although there is some support for a double deficit in phonological awareness and rapid naming in children with dyslexia, there is less support in adolescents and adults (Nelson, 2015).

Deficits in spoken language, auditory-verbal attention, working memory, vocabulary, spoken language comprehension, and general knowledge are common in adults with RDs (Birch & Chase, 2004; Braze, Tabor, Shankweiler, & Mencl, 2007; Isaki & Plante, 1997; Katz, Goldstein, & Beers, 2001; Ransby & Swanson, 2003). Furthermore, phonological awareness appears to be more important for reading acquisition than for reading comprehension. Rather, higher level language skills and general knowledge make a larger contribution to reading comprehension difficulties (cf. Hulme & Snowling, 2014). When these skills are stronger, adults with RD can compensate more effectively for difficulties with phonological awareness. Similarly, Stothers and Klein (2010) found that phonological deficits persist in adults with reading disabilities and affect reading speed, but not necessarily comprehension. They also found that stronger vocabulary and stronger simultaneous nonverbal processes (i.e., Perceptual Organization Index) are associated with better reading comprehension, providing avenues for compensation.

A study by Laasonen, Leppämäki, Tani, and Hokkanen (2009) in Finland showed that adults with RD have broader weaknesses in processing speed that go beyond naming speed, similar to what Pennington (2009) has found in children. Smith-Spark et al. (2016) found that adults with dyslexia also had deficits in executive functioning, similar to what Cutting and Denckla (2003) reported in children. These deficits can make it harder to apply academic skills effectively. Although there is evidence that some individuals with dyslexia have weaknesses in visual perceptual skills, visual hemiattention, and orthographic skills (Gabay, Gabay, Schiff, Ashkenazi, & Henik, 2013; Mano & Osmon, 2008; Osmon et al., 2005), researchers have found no evidence that a deficit in visual skills is causal (Vellutino, Fletcher, Snowling, & Scanlon, 2004) or that remediation of visual skills improves reading (Handler et al., 2011).

Finally, Swanson (2012) completed a meta-analysis of 52 studies of adults with and without reading disabilities. There were 1,793 adults with reading disabilities and 1,893 normal adult readers, ranging in age from 18 to 44 years. Fifty-five percent were male. Looking at all measures, the overall effect size was 0.72, with normal readers performing better.

Table 7.1 Meta-analysis of Deficits in Academic Skills and Cognitive Skills in Adults With and Without RDs

Deficit Area	Effect Size
Academic Skills	
Spelling	1.57
Reading recognition	1.37
Word attack	1.33
Reading comprehension	1.20
Math	0.75
Writing	0.72
Cognitive Skills	**Effect Size**
Processing speed, including rapid naming	0.96
Phonological processing	0.87
Vocabulary	0.71
Verbal intelligence	0.63
Verbal memory	0.62
General information (long-term memory)	0.47
Cognitive monitoring	0.27
General intelligence	0.20
Visual perceptual	0.13
Problem-solving and reasoning	0.11
Social and personal skills	0.10
Perceptual motor skills	-0.13
Auditory perceptual	-0.18
Visuospatial memory	-0.39

Note: Adapted from Table 2 in "Adults with reading disabilities: Converting a meta-analysis to practice," by H. L. Swanson, 2012. *Journal of Learning Disabilities, 45*, pp. 17–30. Reprinted with permission.

Of more interest, the weighted effect sizes for the individual domains, shown in Table 7.1, nicely paralleled what has been found in the individual studies. As expected for a group with RD, effect sizes were largest for word attack, reading recognition, reading comprehension, and spelling. However, effect sizes also were large for writing and math. On measures of the underlying component skills important for reading, the effect sizes were largest for phonological processing, processing speed including rapid naming, vocabulary, verbal intelligence, general information, and verbal memory. Effect sizes for skills commonly associated with executive functioning (problem-solving and reasoning, cognitive monitoring) were small.

Mathematics Disorder

A foundational developmental precursor of the academic skill of mathematics is what the DSM-5 calls "number sense" or, more properly, the "approximate number system." The approximate number system (ANS) is also called the nonsymbolic number system and is contrasted with the exact or cardinal number system, which depends on spoken and written symbols for integers (Feigenson, Dehaene, & Spelke, 2004). The ANS is measured by tasks on which an individual has to decide rapidly which of two simultaneously presented (and sometimes intermixed) displays has more items. The accuracy and speed of this judgment vary systematically as a function (i.e., the Weber function) of how different the two displays are in numerosity (called "ratio-dependent number discrimination"), which would not be the case if the participant counted the items in each display. This Weber function accurately describes performance across humans of different ages and across species, although the accuracy and speed of this judgment vary across development and across individuals of the same age. Although the ANS may be partly innate, its development in humans is protracted, with individual differences persisting at least until high school (Halberda & Feigenson, 2008). Preschool individual differences in the ANS predict mathematics achievement in early elementary school (Mazzocco, Feigenson, & Halberda, 2011a). A deficit in the ANS is specific to MD (Mazzocco, Feigenson, & Halberda, 2011b; Piazza et al., 2010), because it remains when IQ, verbal short-term memory, and rapid naming speed are accounted for. In addition to being specific to MD, the relation between the ANS and mathematics achievement across the whole distribution shrinks but remains significant (still accounting for 15% of the variance) when other general cognitive correlates of mathematics achievement (i.e., IQ and rapid naming speed) are controlled statistically (Halberda & Feigenson, 2008).

Symbolic number skill builds on the earlier developing ANS, and so a deficit in the ANS would be expected to have repercussions at later stages of mathematical development. A normative developmental framework has been used to analyze the performance of children with MD (Butterworth, 2005; Geary et al., 2004). Although children with MD have often learned number names and some aspects of counting procedures, they are impaired in the ANS, and that affects their understanding of the exact number system and how counting is a procedure for finding the exact, cardinal number of a set of objects. This impairment in the core understanding of numerosity would be expected to undermine later development of counting and calculation strategies, and the evidence is consistent with that view.

Problems with an understanding of numerosity and counting principles would lead to problems with arithmetic. Typical children initially solve simple sums by counting all the items in both addends, then learn to count up from the larger addend, and then start to solve harder sums by reducing them to simpler ones (6 + 5 = 5 + 5 plus one). This sequence reflects an increasing understanding of the relations among number facts and also increased use of memory-based strategies for remembering. Eventually, typical children master all their number facts and do not have to rely on counting. As reviewed in Geary et al. (2004), it has been found in several countries that children with MD make more counting errors in simple calculations and persist in simpler counting strategies (e.g., counting all). Most dramatically, children with MD are much worse than typical controls at learning their math facts and applying them automatically, a deficit that is still present at the end of elementary school.

Where there is less agreement in the field of MD is whether MD is primary, namely due to a core deficit in numerosity per se (e.g., Butterworth, 2005) or in the ANS (Mazzocco et al., 2011b) or is secondary to a more general deficit in verbal working memory or spatial cognition (Geary, 2013; Geary et al., 2004). A plausible resolution to this debate is a multiple-deficit model of MD (and mathematics skill across the distribution) in which both specific (i.e., ANS skill) and general (verbal working memory, rapid naming speed, and IQ) cognitive predictors play a role. Although they did not test ANS skills specifically, Peterson et al. (2017) did test a multiple-deficit model using various general cognitive predictors to predict RD, MD, and ADHD and their comorbidity. Interestingly, verbal conceptual ability, verbal working memory, and processing speed accounted for 88% of the variance in mathematical ability in a cohort of 636 children ages 8 to 16 years.

There is less research on MD in adults. Several studies have shown deficits in visuospatial constructional skills, motor skills, nonverbal reasoning, and attention (Ashkenazi & Henik, 2012; Ashkenazi, Rubinstein, & Henik, 2009; Greiffenstein & Baker, 2002). A study by Rubinstein and Henik (2005) examining attention and numerical processing in college students using a numerical Stroop paradigm showed that those with MD had smaller interference effects when judging numerical value versus physical size of digits. This was interpreted as evidence of a lack of automatic activation of numerical value. Follow-up studies by the same group showed that participants with MD had specific difficulty recruiting attention to numerical information (Ashkenazi et al., 2009) and had broader deficits in networks mediating alertness and executive functioning (Ashkenazi & Henik, 2010b). However, Ganor-Stern (2017) found that deficits in estimation were more prominent than deficits in activation of magnitude. He concluded that there may be subtypes of MD in adults.

Cirino, Morris, and Morris (2002, 2007) studied college students referred for assessment of learning disabilities. They found that semantic knowledge retrieval, executive functioning, and visuospatial skills predicted written calculation and math problem-solving skills. Osmon, Smerz, Braun, and Plambeck (2006) found that college students with mathematics disabilities showed impairment in visuospatial skills and executive functioning. Those who were impaired in both areas (double deficit) had the most impaired skills. Proctor (2012) found that processing speed and working memory predicted math calculation. However, math problem-solving was predicted by measures of language/semantic knowledge, reasoning, and working memory. Taken together, these studies show that attention, speed, reasoning, and semantic knowledge all make contributions to math skills.

Overall, results of cognitive studies of MD in both children and adults support a multiple-deficit model, with both skill-based predictors and more dynamic cognitive processes (i.e., working memory, processing speed). Discrepancies in the identified set of predictors between adult and child cognitive models may be due to various factors, including test battery selection, whether higher order math problem-solving skills were emphasized over lower-level math calculation skills, and exclusion of potential comorbidities (RD, ADHD) in the participants.

Test Limitations

In general, assessment of basic reading and math computation skills is well validated and psychometrically sound. Measures such as the Test of Word Reading Efficiency–2nd edition and the Gray Oral Reading Test-5th edition are considered gold standards in assessing reading accuracy and fluency under timed conditions. The more general achievement batteries commonly administered in the schools (i.e., Wechsler Individual Achievement Test-III, Woodcock-Johnson Achievement Test-IV) have robust measures of untimed word and nonword reading, spelling, math calculations, and math fluency. However, there is more difficulty assessing reading comprehension. The main criticism is that the passage dependency of the questions used to assess comprehension is relatively poor. That is, many questions can be answered without reading the passages. This has been found to be the case for both the Nelson-Denny Reading Test and the Gray Oral Reading Test–4th edition (Coleman, Lindstrom, Nelson, Lindstrom, & Gregg, 2010; Keenan & Betjemann, 2006). Researchers in these studies suggested that the test was measuring knowledge, oral language skills, and reasoning ability and not just reading comprehension. Ready, Chaudhry, Schatz, and Strazzullo (2013) confirmed and extended these findings by showing that passage-independent comprehension on the Nelson-Denny was at least double what was expected by chance. Several indices from the Wechsler Adult Intelligence Scale, 4th edition (Verbal Comprehension, Working Memory, Processing Speed) and the Broad Reading score from the Woodcock-Johnson had a strong positive correlation with the passage-independent comprehension score. There have been research tasks that have been devised to control for the issue of passage dependency as well as the confound of prior knowledge on reading comprehension. The Barnes Task (Barnes, Dennis, & Haefele-Kalvaitis, 1996) is one such measure, where passages involve learning new vocabulary (i.e., stories involve children on a make-believe planet), knowledge is pretested and posttested, and questions are rated as requiring either factual or inferential skill to be answered correctly. Unfortunately, this type of approach has not been incorporated by general assessments of reading comprehension in educational or clinical settings.

Neuropsychological Assessment

There are several models for LD diagnosis. Some rely on discrepancies between aptitude and achievement, or between different cognitive skills believed to be associated with academic achievement. Other models rely solely on documenting low achievement in the academic domain, or how the skill deficit responds to intervention. An excellent detailed discussion of these models and associated research can be found in Chapter 3 (Classification, Definition, and Identification of Learning Disabilities) of Fletcher et al. (2007). These models are best established for dyslexia, although there is some support for MD. There is little or no work examining these models in disorders of written expression. Finally, these models have been tested primarily in children, so evidence for their validity and utility in adults is limited. We describe the low achievement model first because it has become the preferred method of arriving at a diagnosis, and then we briefly describe the other models.

Low Achievement Model. A preferred model for diagnosis is the low achievement model, in which an LD is diagnosed based on a below-average (typically 80 or lower) score on an achievement measure. This model has validity, because children identified as low achieving but not intellectually disabled typically differ on other cognitive variables associated with the LD. It is important to note that the achievement measure used plays a key role in this model, and not all will be equally sensitive across development. For example, an untimed single-word reading measure may identify a child with RD in first or second grade, but the same child may obtain an adequate score when tested with the same measure in fifth grade. Whether this occurs may depend on various factors, including the initial severity of the LD, protective factors (i.e., good language skills), how much reading practice the child has engaged in spontaneously, and how much informal remediation he or she has received (from parents, teachers, etc.). Measures of reading fluency in connected text, which capture deficits in accuracy and rate, are considered the gold standard instruments for determining whether there is low achievement that meets criteria for a diagnosis of RD. As is the case in general neuropsychological practice, the clinician is well served to look for convergence across multiple measures (e.g., reading fluency, nonword decoding, spelling), and for a consistent history of early difficulties

(e.g., slow acquisition of letter–name and letter–sound knowledge, poor use of sound–letter correspondence rules to decode words, family history of reading difficulties), especially when assessing adolescents or adults.

The low achievement model is frequently used to define learning-disabled groups in research (Fletcher et al., 2007; Mahone & Mapou, 2014) and is now used more often in school systems. However, because low achievement can be due to intellectual disability or other environmental factors (e.g., English as a second language, poor instruction), other causes must be ruled out before concluding that low achievement is due to an LD (Fletcher et al., 2007).

Intraindividual Differences Model. In this model, learning disabilities are diagnosed based on a profile of cognitive strengths and weaknesses that are presumed to be associated with academic underachievement. In some instances, variability on the cognitive measures may be seen as sufficient to indicate the presence of an LD ("test scatter"); however, because variability is ubiquitous, the face validity of this definition is poor. More commonly, the presence of a specific profile of weaknesses is used to diagnose a specific LD (Fletcher et al., 2007; Mahone & Mapou, 2014). This model would seem to have some content validity, because weaknesses in specific cognitive skills (i.e., phonemic awareness, rapid naming, auditory working memory) have been found to be associated with specific learning disabilities (Fletcher et al., 2007; Mapou, 2009; Pennington, 2009).

However, this approach has been criticized by Fletcher et al. (2007) and, more recently, by Fletcher and Miciak (2017). They noted that there is little support for the premise that identifying the cognitive weaknesses underlying the academic skill deficit will lead to treatment that is targeted more effectively. There is also no clear evidence that remediating an underlying cognitive weakness will improve the academic deficit more effectively than working specifically on that deficit. In addition, Fletcher and colleagues noted that the more severe the LD, the flatter the neuropsychological profile will be, because many skills are affected. This is supported by the logic of the multiple-deficit model of learning disabilities; because severity is likely to be correlated with the number of underlying cognitive deficits that a child has, increased severity will result in a flatter profile. The latter problem is compounded further by the fact that children often have comorbid learning disabilities, so cognitive skills that one might have expected to be a relative strength if the child had only one LD are also affected. Overall, this situation makes detection of a specific pattern of strengths and weaknesses more difficult in children who are more severely affected.

Lastly, there are difficulties in implementing this model that result from the fact that cut points must now be imposed on multiple cognitive domains, all of which are normally distributed. The result is that most students with clinically impairing literacy problems do not meet a "pattern of strengths and weaknesses" criteria, and even a relatively small change in diagnostic criteria results in a large shift in which specific children are identified (Miciak, Fletcher, Stuebing, Vaughn, & Tolar, 2014; Stuebing, Fletcher, Branum-Martin, & Francis, 2012). These problems make using this model for individual diagnosis impractical and potentially harmful. Even those who have supported this model for LD diagnosis have acknowledged that support is limited and that more research is needed (Schneider & Kaufman, 2017).

Aptitude–Achievement Discrepancy Model. The most familiar model is the one based on an aptitude–achievement discrepancy, but this model has slowly fallen out of favor both in the research community and clinically (for example, it is no longer part of the DSM-5 criteria). The model is based on the concept that an LD is defined by a discrepancy between aptitude, as measured by an intelligence test (IQ) and achievement in a specific academic skill, as measured by an academic achievement test. Many states have adopted this in their legal definition of an LD when considering whether a child qualifies for special education. Typically, a 1-*SD* difference (15 points) is defined as significant. However, the definition is not consistent across clinical, school, or research settings, and sometimes a 1.5 or 2 *SD* discrepancy has been used. Changing the discrepancy necessary would invariably identify different numbers of students as having an LD, which was advantageous when attempting to match students to available resources.

A significant number of problems with this model have been identified, and the extensive research summarized, in Fletcher et al. (2007). The arguments against the use of this model are both theoretical and practical. First, the model assumes that IQ, as a proxy for aptitude, imposes an upper limit on achievement. Second, there is the problem of selecting the most appropriate measure of aptitude. Because IQ and achievement scores are correlated, it is impossible to select an IQ score that is not going to reflect, in part, its association with the affected academic skill. With the expansion of index scores on the newer IQ measures, it is even more difficult to know which one to select (e.g., Full Scale IQ, General Ability Index, Fluid Reasoning Index, Verbal Comprehension Index). Third, there is little evidence that poor readers identified using an aptitude discrepancy model and those selected using a low achievement model differed significantly in terms of their underlying cognitive weaknesses. When reading level is low, the underlying cognitive correlates are the same, regardless of IQ level. Furthermore, children selected by these two methods do not differ significantly in how they respond to intervention or in their long-term reading development (Vellutino, Scanlon, & Lyon, 2000). Fourth, the diagnoses based on aptitude–achievement discrepancy are not stable over time. Children identified based on this model in one grade do not always show the necessary discrepancy in a later grade. This is partly because difference scores are less reliable than a single score. Thus, children on either side of the discrepancy cut point are more alike than they are different in terms of their reading skill. Lastly, there is little evidence that this discrepancy model identifies a unique neurobiological group, as indexed by genetic or neuroimaging studies.

Regression to the Mean. This is a modification of the aptitude–achievement discrepancy model and was originally proposed by Rutter and Yule (1973). It takes into account that, from a statistical standpoint, a smaller difference between aptitude and achievement is needed at low IQ to be statistically significant, but a larger difference is needed at a high IQ. Because of this, low functioning children may be missed when a discrepancy model is used, but higher functioning children may be overdiagnosed (Fletcher et al., 2007). Consequently, the required discrepancy is computed based on the IQ score, rather than being fixed. However, this model has many of the same limitations as the discrepancy model and has been challenged on a statistical basis (Cahan, Fono, & Nirel, 2012). Although one study showed the differential benefit of this model for Black college students when compared with a strict discrepancy model (Warner, Dede, Garvan, & Conway, 2002), these authors concluded that a team-based clinical model was still more effective in identifying students who needed support services.

Response to Intervention. In contrast to the models discussed in the previous sections, which are based on a single initial assessment that leads to a diagnosis, response to intervention (or instruction; RTI) is based on a model that is dynamic rather than static and that is modified over time (Fletcher et al., 2007). Although there is no single RTI model, the approach typically consists of initial screening, monitoring the response to standard instruction, and initiating more intervention when needed. Special education placement is made only in cases in which these earlier interventions are not effective. In the best implementation of this model, all students are screened at the start of school. Those who show an academic deficit are immediately given more intensive intervention to improve that academic skill. However, all students continue to be tested periodically, and those who do not progress with normal instruction are given more intensive intervention. The model requires curriculum-based assessments that are reliable, valid, and repeatable. Intervention focuses on the academic skill (e.g., decoding, sight reading, reading fluency, spelling, automaticity of math fact retrieval) and not on an underlying cognitive weakness. Those students who do not respond adequately may be identified as learning disabled and placed in special education. Research has shown that those who do not respond are much more likely to show abnormalities on functional neuroimaging and to have more severe deficits in a range of skills than those who do respond to intervention (Fletcher et al., 2007). However, the primary goal of the model is not diagnosis, but rather improving the deficit so that the student can benefit from his or her education, similar to students without such deficits.

Some difficulties with this model have been identified. Although there are validated approaches to improving specific academic skills (Fletcher et al., 2007), there is variability in how well intervention programs are implemented, or even which treatment approaches are used. So assuming that a child who is not responding to intervention is more likely to have an LD and should be eligible for more intensive special education services may not be correct, if the initial interventions are of variable efficacy. Second, there is little consensus regarding what constitutes an appropriate response to intervention (Mahone & Mapou,

2014). For example, how much improvement is considered sufficient to move the child into a standard instruction environment? Another potential downside to the RTI model is that comprehensive evaluation and intensive intervention are often delayed, because a child with difficulties must pass through several levels of curriculum-based instruction first, each of which takes time. Further evaluation with an appropriate expert could be especially important for a student whose academic difficulties are not due solely to an isolated LD, but who might have an undiagnosed autism spectrum disorder, intellectual disability, language disorder, psychiatric disorder, or ADHD. As we have already seen, comorbidity among learning disorders is the rule rather than the exception, but the RTI model emphasizes limited assessment of academic domains, typically by individuals who do not have the appropriate training to evaluate for these comorbid disorders. Finally, Fletcher and Miciak (2017) acknowledged that RTI cannot be used to diagnose LDs in adults and that this is one circumstance in which comprehensive assessment (e.g., Mapou 2009, 2013) is appropriate.

Hybrid Model. To address the limitations of the various models, Fletcher et al. (2007) proposed an integrated hybrid model for children that combines features of the RTI and low achievement models. First, all students are monitored using curriculum-based instruction. Second, if a child is not responding adequately to standard instruction, then a brief, standard norm-referenced assessment is completed, focusing on the academic skill of concern (i.e., reading, spelling, expressive writing, math), to help target more intensive intervention. In addition, other causes for the problem are assessed, including possible intellectual disability, speech/language impairment, ADHD, emotional/behavioral disturbance, and environmental factors (e.g., socioeconomic disadvantage, primary language, home literacy level). Those students who do not respond to the more intensive intervention would then undergo limited neuropsychological assessment of the abilities important to the academic skill (e.g., phonological awareness and rapid naming for dyslexia), which may contribute to modifying the intervention program. The goal of this hybrid approach is to isolate the group of inadequate responders, for which the integrity of instruction is assured, and that epitomize the construct of unexpected underachievement.

Discrepancy Approaches Used to Diagnose LD in Adults. Although the field has moved away from using a discrepancy approach in the diagnosis of LD in children, it is still used widely in college-age adults. This makes theoretical sense, given that students attending college are likely to be a higher functioning subgroup than the general population. Unfortunately, there has been significant inconsistency in how models of LD diagnosis have been applied in this population. For example, Lovett and Sparks (2010) reviewed documentation of college students classified as learning disabled and receiving accommodations. They used several different models of LD definition and found that the number of students classified by these models as learning disabled varied from 7% with the most conservative definition (requiring impairment and an LD diagnosis before college) to 45% with the most liberal IQ-achievement discrepancy definition (i.e., 1 *SD*). Furthermore, 54% of these students did not meet any of the LD criteria.

In a second study, Lovett and Sparks (2013) reviewed 46 studies of college students with learning disabilities and found that 23 different criteria had been used to classify participants as learning disabled, with discrepancy approaches being used most frequently. Students classified as having an LD had lower IQ and academic achievement scores than those not classified as learning disabled. Nevertheless, mean academic scores for students with an LD were still in the average range, with the lowest scores on writing/spelling measures. Students who had been identified by a discrepancy model had higher scores on achievement tests and college entrance exams than students identified as learning disabled using nondiscrepancy-based models. Overall, they concluded that classification of college students as learning disabled is not based on consistent, objective criteria, and that accommodations and support may be granted to average students, based purely on a discrepancy. They noted that some college students diagnosed in this way may simply lack college-level academic skills rather than being disabled, and require intervention rather than accommodation.

Intervention

Successful interventions for RD have primarily emphasized phonics instruction. Treatment elements that have also been helpful include training in phonemic awareness, supported reading of increasingly difficult connected text, writing exercises, and teaching comprehension strategies (Scammacca, Vaughn, Roberts, Wanzek, & Torgesen, 2007; Vaughn et al., 2003). Intervention has been most effective when provided in a one-to-one or small group setting. Much more is known about effective remediation of reading problems in younger than in older children, and gains from phonologically based treatment are greater, on average, for younger than for older children (Suggate, 2010). In addition, it appears to be easier to treat accuracy than fluency problems, in part because fluency is so dependent on reading experience. However, there is some evidence that fluency problems can be prevented with appropriate early intervention, at least over the short term (Torgesen, 2005). Although there is a solid evidence base for treatments emphasizing direct instruction in reading and phonological training, several alternative therapies either lack sufficient evidence or have been shown to be ineffective for dyslexia and, therefore, should not be recommended (Handler & Fierson, 2011; Pennington, 2011). Most of these therapies are based on sensorimotor theories and include various visual treatments (colored lenses, vision therapy), training in rapid auditory processing, and exercise/movement-based treatment.

There has been less research on treatment for MD. One pilot study (Kaufmann, Handl, & Thony, 2003) found that a treatment program focused on basic understanding of the numerical concepts discussed earlier benefited the calculation skills of children with MD. Two adaptive computerized training tools have been developed as well, targeting students with MD. The first, "The Number Race" is designed to improve the precision of numerical magnitude representations (Wilson, Revkin, Cohen, Cohen, & Dehaene, 2006). The second program, "Graphogame," focuses on exact numerosities, and seeks to link those with number symbols (Arabic digits). Although both programs target cognitive processes believed to be crucial for the development of math skills, and both result in improvements in number-comparison performance, neither program results in training effects that generalize to counting and arithmetic (Räsänen, Salminen, Wilson, Aunio, & Dehaene, 2009). At a curriculum level, the JUMP Math program developed in Canada has shown evidence of helping a broad set of students in various countries, including those with lower math proficiency (Solomon et al., 2011). An intervention based on this curriculum led to gains in math performance in college students requiring math remediation (Gula, Hessler, & Maciejewski, 2015).

There is limited work to guide intervention for adults with learning disabilities. Eden et al. (2004), using a phonologically targeted training program for adults with dyslexia, found improvement in phonological awareness and reading, normalization on functional magnetic resonance imaging activation in brain regions important for reading, and reports of increased everyday reading skills. Some evidence-based programs used to improve reading in children with dyslexia can be applied to adults (Shaywitz, 2003; Shaywitz & Shaywitz, 2005). Similarly, programs for illiterate adults can be helpful (Shaywitz, 2003). However, if adults have not developed effective decoding and fluency as children, intervention is much more difficult, and it is unlikely they will ever become fully fluent readers.

There is some limited work on helping college students and adults with learning disabilities function more effectively. Chiba and Low (2007) found that a class for college students with LDs that educated them about LDs, reviewed the importance of assessment, and taught self-advocacy, compensatory strategies, and the use of assistive technology had a positive impact on the students' acceptance and understanding of their LDs and their transition and adjustment to college.

In addition to intervention, accommodations are frequently used for children and adults with LDs. Notably, although some people believe that accommodations are designed to help a person "perform up to his or her potential" or "at the level of his or her intellect," this is not the purpose. Rather, the purpose of an accommodation is to enable to the person to access the material, but not to guarantee a particular level of performance (Lovett & Lewandowski, 2015). The most common testing accommodations involve changes in timing (e.g., extended time, extra breaks), setting (e.g. reduced distraction), presentation (e.g., audio), response format (e.g., no Scantron, word processor), and scheduling (e.g., extra breaks, testing over several days, only one final a day). However, there is limited research on the effectiveness of accommodations and even less on how test results can be used to determine the most appropriate and reasonable accommodation.

The most common accommodation is extended time on tests. Gregg and Nelson (2012) completed a meta-analysis of studies that used extended time in high school students transitioning to college. Of 132 eligible studies of extended time on high school

graduation tests, only nine met their inclusion criteria. There were typically only two conditions in these studies, and so it was not possible to assess the interaction of LD status (disabled, nondisabled) and test administration type (standard time, extended time). Keeping these limitations in mind, the findings made sense. First, learning-disabled students had lower scores on the tests than nondisabled students, regardless of the testing condition. However, the effect size was largest when both groups completed the test under standard testing time conditions. Second, both student groups showed higher scores when given extended time. However, the effect size was larger for the learning-disabled students than the nondisabled students. Gregg and Nelson concluded that extended time did not appear to provide an unfair advantage to learning-disabled students, but acknowledged that much more research was needed.

Implications for Clinical Practice

There has been much progress over the past decades in our understanding of the etiological, cognitive, and environmental factors that influence individual differences in reading and math skills, yet clinicians and researchers continue to debate which is the best method to use for individual diagnosis. There are empirical arguments for not relying solely on a discrepancy approach, even when correcting for regression to the mean. In early childhood, there is increased consensus that low achievement is required, although the applicability of this in adults is debated, especially when it is likely that there have been remediation efforts along the way, and a greater amount of practice leading to (partial) compensation. Severity of the LD, the high degree of comorbidity with other neurodevelopmental disorders, the added impact of emotional factors over time as students struggle with school and potentially develop negative attitudes toward or avoidance of academic challenges, and the influence of protective factors (both genetic and environmental) also complicate the diagnostic formulation across development and into adulthood.

The concept of unexpected underachievement has been a consistent and core aspect of the definition of LD. This is why some experts argue strongly that an aptitude–achievement discrepancy approach should be allowed to be one of the methods of arriving at an LD diagnosis, as long as the developmental and early academic history is consistent, and there is evidence of functional impairment given the particular context in which the individual finds himself (i.e., college or other high-functioning environment). Work by Ferrer et al. (2010) is consistent with this view: they showed that in typical readers, reading and IQ development are dynamically linked over time. In contrast, dyslexic readers do not show such mutual interrelationships, suggesting a developmental uncoupling between cognition and reading in those with RD. A recent imaging study also lends support to this approach. Hancock Gabrieli and Hoeft (2016), using functional magnetic resonance imaging, showed that children with IQ-discrepant, yet average, reading skills had patterns of reduced activation in left temporoparietal neocortex similar to what was observed when children with RD were compared with typical controls.

As studies have pointed out, there is much inconsistency in how diagnoses are made, especially in college-age adults. There should be greater weight placed on an appropriate early academic history and a previous diagnosis in addition to discrepancy and current functional impairment. In the study by Lovett and Sparks (2010), only 40% of students had been diagnosed with an LD before entering college, indicating that there is room for improvement in the application of even basic criteria. There is an ascertainment bias for who gets into college; individuals must have at least passable academic skills in most cases, so the low achievement model is likely too stringent, and would exclude individuals who struggle with reading-related skills in relation to the cognitive level at which they are asked to function. Additionally, an LD such as dyslexia has a complex phenotype, often including reduced working memory and processing speed. So even if word decoding is now in the average range, these associated difficulties may still render impairment. It is also important to keep in mind that the aspects of the behavioral phenotype that are most prominent change with development. In preschool and kindergarten, children with RD often (but not always) exhibit speech or language delay, poor emerging phonemic awareness, and poor letter knowledge. In early elementary school, poor decoding accuracy for words and nonwords is most prevalent, along with poor spontaneous spelling. Adolescents and adults, especially those who have protective factors (i.e., good vocabulary, an enriched print environment, a cognitive and personality profile that facilitates learning and persistence, etc.), may

only demonstrate reduced reading fluency and comprehension. Thus, for college-age students, measures that focus on reading fluency and reading comprehension at the passage level should be included in the assessment battery. Comparison of timed and extended time formats is also essential (Mapou, 2013).

In the context of early schooling, we are in agreement with Fletcher et al. (2007) that the hybrid model discussed earlier is likely to be the most appropriate way to identify a cohort of children with unexpected underachievement, for whom there is a critical need to apply prompt evidenced-based intervention. However, there is debate regarding the best timing of a more thorough evaluation of academic and related cognitive skills. Once a child has shown little progress in the first phase of RTI, assuming instruction practices have been appropriately applied, delaying assessment until further failure is documented may just be delaying specialized intervention and appropriate accommodation. The hybrid model provides for more formal assessment of academic abilities using norm-referenced procedures, ruling out intellectual disability or language disorder, and determining whether there are other environmental or psychological causes that might be contributing to inadequate progress. These, in fact, are fundamental components of a psychoeducational or abbreviated neuropsychological evaluation.

With regard to the use of an intraindividual differences approach, requiring a specific pattern of strengths and weaknesses at the level of cognitive endophenotypes (i.e., phonological processing or rapid naming deficit) is no longer a very tenable position, at least for RD. Many practitioners have required evidence of a phonological processing deficit for a diagnosis of dyslexia, on the basis of many decades of group studies showing that phonological deficits appear causal in the disorder. However, it turns out that there is considerable variability at the individual level. As shown by Pennington et al. (2012), using a version of the multiple case study approach in two large samples ($N > 800$ each), less than 15% of children with poor basic literacy skills were best characterized by a single phonological deficit. The remaining children were relatively evenly distributed among the following categories: single deficit in another area (such as naming speed or vocabulary), multiple deficits, or no clear-cut deficits. Thus, requiring a deficit in phonological processing (or any other specific cognitive skill) for diagnosis is inappropriate and would unfairly exclude some individuals with clinically impairing literacy difficulties.

That is not to say that understanding the particular profile of a person with LD cannot be useful in other ways. Especially when one finds convergence across tests, so as to avoid overinterpretation of normal variability (Binder et al., 2009; Schretlen et al., 2008), analysis of a neuropsychological profile can likely aid teachers in setting appropriate curriculum expectations and implementing appropriate interventions and supports. For example, a child who has comorbid language impairment, an attentional disorder, and an LD will likely require increased support across academic domains relative to a child who only has one of those conditions. Because comorbidity is more the rule than the exception in neurodevelopmental disorders, the likely yield of complex presentations in a thorough evaluation is high. This is even more important for adults, who have a longer history and are more likely to have compounding emotional factors (Mapou, 2009).

It is not disputed that environmental factors can significantly negatively affect academic achievement. However, by maintaining that "environmental" and "neurobiological" factors are separate, there is a danger of reifying a false dichotomy that affects both diagnosis and intervention. For example, using cognitive endophenotypes as markers for a neurobiological etiology of an RD denies the fact that there is a dynamic and bidirectional relationship between changes to the behavioral phenotype (reading) via environmentally applied remediation and practice, and changes to underlying cognitive processes such as phonological awareness. Bidirectional effects are even observed at the level of brain imaging (Eden et al., 2004; Shaywitz et al., 2003). Thus, there are no levels of analysis that are immune to feedback effects. Furthermore, as explained by Pennington (2006), the full multiple-deficit model has genetic and environmental etiologies interacting and likely producing nonadditive effects at the cognitive and behavioral levels. Cases where learning deficits are solely due to extreme environmental disadvantage are fortunately rare. It is far more likely that when a child is referred for evaluation, the presenting difficulties are the end result of a complex developmental process that has included multiple genetic and environmental risk factors interacting for many years. Thus, it may be too simplistic to think that the presence of adverse environmental factors should

exclude a child from a "medical model" diagnosis of LD. In fact, doing so may lead to children who are already disadvantaged being disproportionately denied services from which they could benefit.

An underlying assumption of the RTI model is that learning deficits that stem from environmental causes are more easily remediated; hence, the first phase of the program is instituted to attempt to level the environmental playing field (at least in regard to instruction). This helps to identify those children for whom the deficit is likely to be neurobiological in origin (i.e., those who fail initial stages of RTI). However, this assumption may be false. The extent to which a deficit is sensitive to remediation does not tell one about its etiology. Some problems that are entirely genetic are easily remediated by specific environmental treatments, and some problems that are mostly environmental may be very difficult to treat. The fact that the child does not respond well to initial interventions may in fact be more of a marker for severity than etiology per se. This brings us back to the need to identify comorbid conditions in these children (i.e., language impairment, coexisting learning disabilities, ADHD, and psychological, cultural, and environmental factors), because those will likely increase the severity of symptoms, require more integrated and higher intensity treatment, and place the child at risk for poorer adjustment and negative secondary behaviors.

Future Directions

There are a number of important questions that will undoubtedly continue to be the focus of research in the coming years. Some have already been alluded to in previous sections of this chapter. First, there is a paucity of research regarding the validity of a disorder of written expression as a separate and unique type of LD. Spelling deficits are part of RD, and other aspects of written expression are influenced to a significant extent by fine motor, language, and attentional skills. Studies are needed to investigate whether there is unexplained variance to be accounted for once the aforementioned components are controlled, and if so, to establish the internal and external validity of the disorder.

Second, questions remain regarding the potential heterogeneity of MD. Are there discrete subtypes? To what extent do linguistic, spatial, and executive function deficits identify subgroups of children with significantly different pathways to the same common outcome? Common composite measures of math achievement (i.e., broad math index of the Woodcock-Johnson Achievement Test-IV) are a blend of subtests that measure efficiency of math fact retrieval, math computation procedures, linear and spatial aspects of math, and math problem-solving. These different components of math may be influenced by different underlying deficits, so careful selection and understanding of what composes outcome measures used in cognitive models is necessary.

The DSM-5's characterization of LDs has led researchers to begin investigating the validity of complex LDs and their relation to more basic levels of academic deficit. Cognitive models of complex LDs are currently being investigated to establish potential predictive cognitive endophenotypes. Genetic and brain bases for complex LDs will also need to be explored, once the behavioral phenotype is adequately defined. As the level of complexity and abstraction increases in more complex academic endeavors, there is also the question of being able to differentiate these skills from IQ. There will also need to be a concerted effort, at both the research and clinical levels, to refine models of intervention for children with complex LDs.

Finally, much progress has been made in understanding genetic and environmental factors that influence academic achievement, but there is a need to identify and refine our models to account for gene–environment interactions and correlations. Findings that the heritability of RD varies as a function of environmental enrichment (and IQ) are likely to lead to the discovery of more nuanced interactions, some of which may be more amenable to intervention. These goals will also need to be expanded to include individuals who are bilingual/bicultural, given that this portion of the population is increasing significantly in the United States and in other countries.

References

Alarcon, M., DeFries, J. C., Light, J. G., & Pennington, B. F. (1997). A twin study of mathematics disability. *Journal of Learning Disability*, *30*(6), 617–623.

American Psychiatric Association. (2013). *Diagnostic and statistical manual of mental disorders* (5th ed.). Arlington, VA: Author.

Ashkenazi, S., & Henik, A. (2010a). A dissociation between physical and mental number bisection in developmental dyscalculia. *Neuropsychologia*, *48*, 2861–2868.

Ashkenazi, S., & Henik, A. (2010b). Attentional networks in developmental dyslexia. *Behavioral and Brain Functions*, *6*(2), 1–12.

Ashkenazi, S., & Henik, A. (2012). Does attentional training improve numerical processing in developmental dyscalculia? *Neuropsychology*, *26*, 45–56.

Ashkenazi, S., Rubinstein, O., & Henik, A. (2009). Attention, automaticity, and developmental dyscalculia. *Neuropsychology*, *23*, 535–540.

Badian, N. A. (1983). Arithmetic and nonverbal learning. In H. R. Myklebust (Ed.), *Progress in learning disabilities* (Vol. 5, pp. 253–264). New York, NY: Grune and Stratton.

Barnes, M. A., Dennis, M., & Haefele-Kalvaitis, J. (1996). The effects of knowledge availability and knowledge accessibility on coherence and elaborative inferencing inchildren from six to fifteen years of age. *Journal of Experimental Child Psychology*, *61*, 216–241.

Binder, L. M., Iverson, G. L., & Brooks, B. L. (2009). To err is human: "Abnormal" neuropsychological scores and variability are common in healthy adults. *Archives of Clinical Neuropsychology*, *24*, 31–46.

Birch, S. L. (2016). Prevalence and profile of phonological and surface subgroups in college students with a history of reading disability. *Journal of Learning Disabilities*, *49*, 339–353.

Birch, S., & Chase, C. (2004). Visual and language processing deficits in compensated and uncompensated college students with dyslexia. *Journal of Learning Disabilities*, *37*, 389–410.

Bishop, D. V., McDonald, D., Bird, S., & Hayiou-Thomas M. E. & (2009). Children who read words accurately despite language impairment: Who are they and how do they do it? *Child Development*, *80*(2), 593–605.

Braze, D., Tabor, W., Shankweiler, D. P., & Mencl, W. E. (2007). Speaking up for vocabulary: Reading skill differences in young adults. *Journal of Learning Disabilities*, *40*, 226–243.

Brooks, B. L. (2010). Seeing the forest for the trees: Prevalence of low scores on the Wechsler Intelligence Scale for Children, Fourth Edition (WISC-IV). *Psychological Assessment*, *22*, 650–656.

Brooks, B. L., Iverson, G. L., Sherman, E. M. S., & Holdnack, J. A. (2009). Healthy children and adolescents obtain some low scores across a battery of memory tests. *Journal of the International Neuropsychological Society*, *15*, 613–617.

Boetsch, E. A. (1996). *A longitudinal study of the relationship between dyslexia and socioemotional functioning in young children* (Unpublished PhD thesis). University of Denver, Denver, CO.

Butterworth, B. (2005). Developmental dyscalculia. In Campbell, J. I. D. (Ed.), *Handbook of mathematical cognition* (pp. 455–469). New York, NY: Psychology Press.

Cahan, S., Fono, D., & Nirel, R. (2012). The regression-based definition of learning disability: A critical appraisal. *Journal of Learning Disabilities, 45*, 170–178.

Cain, K., Oakhill, J., & Lemmon, K., (2004). Individual differences in the inference of word meanings from context. *Journal of Educational Psychology, 96*, 671–681.

Capano, L., Minden, D., Chen, S. X., Schacher, R., & Ickowicz, A. (2008). Mathematical learning disorder in school-age children with attention-deficit hyperactivity disorder. *Canadian Journal of Psychiatry. Revue Canadienne de Psychiatrie, 53*(6), 392–399.

Carrion-Castillo, A., Franke, B., & Fisher, S. E. (2013). Molecular genetics of dyslexia: An overview. *Dyslexia, 19*, 214–240.

Carter, J. C., Lanham, D.C., Cutting, L. E., Clements-Stephens, A. M., Chen, X., Hadzipasic, M., Kim, J., Denckla, M. B., & Kaufmann, W. E. (2009). A dual DTI approach to analyzing white matter in children with dyslexia. *Psychiatry Research 172*, 215–219.

Chiba, C., & Low, R. (2007). A course-based model to promote successful transition to college for students with learning disorders. *Journal of Postsecondary Education and Disability, 20*(1), 40–53.

Cirino, P. T., Morris, M. K., & Morris, R. D. (2002). Neuropsychological concomitants of calculation skills in college students referred for learning difficulties. *Developmental Neuropsychology, 21*, 201–218.

Cirino, P. T., Morris, M. K., & Morris, R. D. (2007). Semantic, executive, and visospatial abilities in mathematical reasoning of referred college students. *Assessment, 14*, 94–104.

Clark, C., Klonoff, H., & Hayden, M. (1990). Regional cerebral glucose metabolism in Turner syndrome. *Canadian Journal of Neurological Science, 17*, 140–144.

Coleman, C., Lindstrom, J., Nelson, J., Lindstrom, W., & Gregg, K. N. (2010). Passageless comprehension on the Nelson-Denny Reading Test: Well above chance for university students. *Journal of Learning Disabilities, 43*, 244–249.

Cutting, L. E., & Denckla, M. B. (2003). Attention: Relationships between attention-deficit hyperactivity disorder and learning disabilities. In H. L. Swanson, K. R. Harris, & S. Graham (Eds.), *Handbook of learning disabilities* (pp. 125–139). New York: Guilford Press.

Dehaene S (2003). Acalculia and number processing disorders. In T. E. Feinberg & M. J. Farah (Eds.), *Behavioral neurology and neuropsychology* (2nd ed., pp. 207–215). New York, NY: McGraw-Hill.

Docherty, S. J., Davis, O. S. P., Kovas, Y., Meaburn, E. L., Dale, P. S., Petrill, S. A., … Plomin, R. (2010). A genome-wide association study identifies multiple loci associated with mathematics ability and disability. *Genes, Brain and Behavior 9*, 234–247.

Eden, G. F., Jones, K. M., Cappell, K., Gareau, L., Wood, F. B., Zeffiro, T. A., … Flowers, D. L. (2004). Neuronal changes following remediation in adult developmental dyslexia. *Neuron, 44*, 411–422.

Elbro, C. (2010). Dyslexia as a disability or handicap: When does vocabulary matter? *Journal of Learning Disabilities, 43* (5), 469–78.

Feigenson, L., Dehaene, S., & Spelke, E. (2004). Core systems of number. *Trends in Cognitive Sciences, 8*(7), 307–314.

Ferrer, E., Shaywitz, B.A., Holahan, J. M., Marchione, K., & Shaywitz, S. E. (2010). Uncoupling of reading and IQ over time: Empirical evidence for a definition of dyslexia. *Psychological Science, 21*(1), 93–101.

Fletcher, J. M., Lyon, G. R., Fuchs, L. S., & Barnes, M. A. (2007). *Learning disabilities: From identification to intervention.* New York: Guilford Press.

Fletcher, J. M., & Miciak, J. (2017). Comprehensive cognitive assessments are not necessary for the identification and treatment of learning disabilities. *Archives of Clinical Neuropsychology, 32*, 2–7.

Friend, A., DeFries, J. C., & Olson, R.K. (2008). Parental education moderates genetic influences on reading disability. *Psychological Science, 19*, 1124–30.

Gabay, Y., Gabay, S., Schiff, R., Ashkenazi, S., & Henik, A. (2013). Visuospatial attention deficits in developmental dyslexia: evidence from visual and mental number line bisection tasks. *Archives of Clinical Neuropsychology, 28*(8), 829–36.

Ganor-Stern, D. (2017). Can dyslexics estimate the results of arithmetic problems? *Journal of Learning Disabilities, 50*, 23–33.

Geary, D. C. (2013). Early foundations for mathematics learning and their relations to learning disabilities. *Psychological Science, 22*(1), 23–27.

Geary, D. C., Hoard, M. K., Byrd-Craven, J., Geary, D. C., Hoard, M. K., Byrd-Craven, J., & DeSoto, M. C. (2004). Strategy choices in simple and complex addition: contributions of working memory and counting knowledge for children with mathematical disability. *Journal of Experimental Child Psychology, 88*(2), 121–151.

Gregg, N., Coleman, C., Lindstrom, J., & Lee, C. (2007). Who are most, average, or high-functioning adults? *Learning Disabilities Research and Practice, 22*, 264–274.

Gregg, N., & Nelson, J. M. (2012). Meta-analysis on the effectiveness of extra time as a test accommodation for transitioning adolescents with learning disabilities: More questions than answers. *Journal of Learning Disabilities, 45*, 128–138.

Greiffenstein, M. F., & Baker, W. J. (2002). Neuropsychological and psychosocial correlates of adult arithmetic deficiency. *Neuropsychology, 16*, 451–458.

Gula, T., Hoessler. C., & Maciejewski, W. (2015). Seeking mathematics success for college students: A randomized field trial of an adapted approach. *International Journal of Mathematical Education in Science and Technology, 46,* 1130–1148.

Halberda, J., & Feigenson, L. (2008). Developmental change in the acuity of the "number sense": The approximate number system in 3-, 4-, 5-, and 6-year olds and adults. *Developmental Psychology, 44*(5), 1457–1465.

Hancock, R., Gabrieli, J. D. E., & Hoeft, F. (2016). Shared temporoparietal dysfunction in dyslexia and typical readers with discrepantly high IQ. *Trends in Neuroscience and Education, 5*(4), 173–177.

Handler, S. M., & Fierson, W. M. & the American Academic of Pediatrics, Section on Ophthalmology, Council on Children with Disabilities, American Society of Ophthalmology, American Academy of Ophthalmology, American Association for Pediatric Ophthalmology and Strabismus, & American Association for Certified Orthoptists. (2011). Joint Technical Report–Learning disabilities, dyslexia, and vision. *Pediatrics, 127,* e818–e856.

Haworth, C. M., Kovas, Y., & Petrill, S. A., & Plomin, R. (2007). Developmental origins of low mathematics performance and normal variation in twins from 7 to 9 years. *Twin Research and Human Genetics, 10*(1), 106–117.

Hulme, C., & Snowling, M. J. (2014). The interface between spoken and written language: Developmental disorders. *Philosophical Transactions of the Royal Society B-Biological Sciences, 369,* 20120395. doi:dx.doi.org/10.1098/rstb.2012.3095

Individuals with Disabilities Educational Act of 1990, Public Law 101–476, 104 Stat. 1142 (1990).

Isaki, E., & Plante, E. (1997). Short-term and working memory differences in language/learning disabled and normal adults. *Journal of Communication Disorders, 30,* 427–437.

Katusic, S. K., Colligan, R. C., Weaver, A.L., & Barbaresi, W. J. (2009). The forgotten learning disability: Epidemiology of written-language disorder in a population-based birth cohort (1976–1982), Rochester, Minnesota. *Pediatrics, 123*(5), 1306–1313.

Katz, L. J., Goldstein, G., & Beers, S. R. (2001). *Learning disabilities in older adolescents and adults.* New York: Kluwer Academic/Plenum Publishers.

Kaufmann, L., Handl,P., & Thony, B. (2003). Evaluation of a numeracy intervention program focusing on basic numerical knowledge and conceptual knowledge: A pilot study. *Journal of Learning Disabilities, 36*(6), 564–573.

Keenan, J. M., & Betjemann, R. S. (2006). Comprehending the Gray Oral Reading Test without reading it: Why comprehension tests should not include passage-independent items. *Scientific Studies of Reading, 10,* 363–380.

Kere, J. (2011). Molecular genetics and molecular biology of dyslexia. *WIREs Cognitive Science, 2,* 441–448.

Kovas, Y., Haworth, C., Harlaar, N., Petrill, S. A., Dale, P. S., & Plomin, R. (2007). Overlap and specificity of genetic and environmental influences on mathematics and reading disability in 10-year-old twins. *Journal of Child Psychology and Psychiatry, 48*(9), 914–922.

Landerl, K., & Moll, K. (2010). Comorbidity of learning disorders: Prevalence and familial transmission. *Journal of Child Psychology and Psychiatry 51,* 287–294.

Laasonen, M., Lehtinen, M., Leppämäki, S., Tani, P., & Hokkanen, L. (2010). Project DyAdd: Phonological processing, reading, spelling, and arithmetic in adults with dyslexia or ADHD. *Journal of Learning Disabilities, 43*(1), 3–14.

Laasonen, M., Leppämäki, S., Tani, P., & Hokkanen, L. (2009). Adult dyslexia and attention deficit disorder in Finland—Project DyADD. *Journal of Learning Disabilities, 42,* 511–527.

Levy, L. M., Reis, I. L., & Grafman, J. (1999). Metabolic abnormalities detected by 1H-MRS in dyscalculia and dysgraphia. *Neurology, 53*(3), 639–641.

Lewis, C., Hitch, G. J., & Walker, P. (1994). The prevalence of specific arithmetic difficulties and specific reading difficulties in 9- to 10-year-old boys and girls. *Journal of Child Psychology and Psychiatry, 35*(2), 283–292.

Light, J. G., & DeFries, J. C. (1995). Comorbidity of reading and mathematics disabilities: Genetic and environmental etiologies. *Journal of Learning Disabilities, 28* (2), 96–106.

Lovett, B. J., & Lewandowski, J. (2015). *Accommodations for students with disabilities: Research-based practice.* Washington, DC: American Psychological Association.

Lovett, B. J., & Sparks, R. L. (2010). Exploring the diagnosis of "gifted/LD": Characterizing postsecondary students with learning disability diagnoses at different IQ levels. *Journal of Psychoeducational Assessment, 28,* 91–101.

Lovett, B. J., & Sparks, R. L. (2013). The identification and performance of gifted students with learning disability diagnoses: A quantitative synthesis. *Journal of Learning Disabilities, 46,* 304–316.

Lyon, G. R., Shaywitz, S. E., & Shaywitz, B. A. (2003). A definition of dyslexia. *Annals of Dyslexia, 53,* 1–14.

Mahone, E. M., & Mapou, R. L. (2014). Learning disabilities. In K. Stucky, M. Kirkwood, & J. Donders (Eds.), *American Academy of Clinical Neuropsychology neuropsychology study guide and board review* (pp. 184–201). New York: Oxford University Press.

Mano, Q. R., & Osmon, D. C. (2008). Visuoperceptual-orthographic reading abilities: A confirmatory factor analysis study. *Journal of Clinical and Experimental Neuropsychology, 2008,* 421–434.

Mapou, R. L. (2009). *Adult learning disabilities and ADHD: Research-informed assessment*. New York: Oxford University Press.

Mapou, R. L. (2013). Process focused assessment of learning disabilities and ADHD in adults. In L. Ashendorf, R. Swenson, & D. J. Libon (Eds.), *The Boston Process approach to neuropsychological assessment: A practitioner's guide* (pp. 329–354). New York: Oxford University Press.

Marino, C., Mascheretti, S., Riva, V., Cattaneo, F., Rigoletto, C., Rusconi, M., … Molteni, M. (2011). Pleiotropic effects of DCDC2 and DYX1C1 genes on language and mathematics traits in nuclear families of developmental dyslexia. *Behavioral Genetics, 41*, 67–76.

Mazzocco, M. M., Feigenson, L., & Halberda, J. (2011a). Preschoolers' precision of the approximate number system predicts later school mathematics performance. *PLoS One, 6* (9), e23749.

Mazzocco, M. M., Feigenson, L., & Halberda, J. (2011b). Impaired acuity of the approximate number system underlies mathematical learning disability (dyscalculia). *Child Development, 82*(4), 1224–1237.

McGrath, L., Pennington, B. F., Shanahan, M. A., Santerre-Lemmon, L. E., Barnard, H. D., Willcutt, E. G., … Olson, R. K. (2011). A multiple deficit model of reading disability and attention-deficit/hyperactivity disorder: Searching for shared cognitive deficits. *Journal of Child Psychology and Psychiatry, 52*, 547–557.

Meng, H., Smith, S. D., Hager, K., Held, M., Liu, J., Olson, R. K., … Gruen, J. R. (2005). DCDC2 is associated with reading disability and modulates neuronal development in the brain. *Proceedings of the National Academy of Sciences of the United States of America, 102*, 17053–17058.

Miciak, J., Fletcher, J. M., Stuebing, K., Vaughn, S., & Tolar, T. D. (2014). Patterns of cognitive strengths and weaknesses: Identification rates, agreement, and validity for learning disabilities identification. *School Psychology Quarterly : The Official Journal of the Division of School Psychology, American Psychological Association, 29*(1), 21–37.

Nation, K. (2005). Children's reading comprehension difficulties. In M. J. Snowling & C. Hulme (Eds.), *The science of reading: A handbook* (pp. 248–265). Oxford, UK: Blackwell Publishing.

Nation, K., & Hulme, C. (2011). Learning to read changes children's phonological skills: evidence from a latent variable longitudinal study of reading and nonword repetition. *Developmental Science, 14*(4), 649–659.

National Joint Committee on Learning Disabilities (NJCLD). (1990). Operationalizing the NJCLD definition of learning disabilities for ongoing assessment in schools: A report from the National Joint Committee on Learning Disabilities. *Perspectives: The International Dyslexia Association, 23*(4), 29.

Nelson, J. M. (2015). Evaluation of the double-deficit hypothesis in adolescents and young adults with dyslexia. *Annals of Dyslexia, 65*, 159–177.

Osmon, D. C., Braun, M. M., & Plambeck, E. A. (2005). Processing abilities associated with phonologic and orthographic skills in adult learning disability. *Journal of Clinical and Experimental Neuropsychology, 27*, 544–554.

Osmon, D. C., Smerz, J. M., Braun, M. M., & Plambeck, E. A. (2006). Processing abilities associated with math skills in adult learning disability. *Journal of Clinical and Experimental Neuropsychology, 28*, 84–95.

Paracchini, S., Thomas, A., Castro, S., Lai, C., Paramasivam, M., Wang, Y., … Monaco, A. P. (2006). The chromosome 6p22 haplotype associated with dyslexia reduces the expression of KIAA0319, a novel gene involved in neuronal migration. *Human Molecular Genetics, 15*, 1659–1666.

Paulesu, E., Demonet, J. F., Fazio, F., McCrory, E., Chanoine, V., Brunswick, N., … Frith, U. (2001). Dyslexia: Cultural diversity and biological unity. *Science, 291*, 2165–2167.

Pennington, B. F. (2006). From single to multiple deficit models of developmental disorders. *Cognition, 101*(2), 385–413.

Pennington, B. F. (2009). *Diagnosing learning disorders: A neuropsychological framework* (2nd ed.). New York: Guilford Press.

Pennington, B. F. (2011). Controversial therapies for dyslexia. *Perspectives on Language and Literacy* (Winter), 7–8.

Pennington, B. F., & Olson, R. K. (2005). Genetics of dyslexia. In M. Snowling & C. Hulme (Eds.), *The science of reading: A handbook* (pp. 453–472.). Oxford, UK: Blackwell Publishing.

Pennington, B. F., & Peterson, R. L., (2015). Neurodevelopmental disorders: Learning disorders. In A. Tasman, J. Kay, J. A. Lieberman, M. B. First, & M. B. Riba (Eds.), *Psychiatry* (4th ed., pp. 765–778). Hoboken, NJ: Wiley-Blackwell.

Pennington, B. F., Santerre-Lemmon, L., Rosenberg, J., MacDonald, B., Boada, R., Friend, A., … Olson, R. K. (2012). Individual prediction of dyslexia by single versus multiple deficit models. *Journal of Abnormal Psychology, 121*, 212–224.

Peterson, R. L., & Pennington, B. F. (2012). Developmental dyslexia. *The Lancet, 379* (9830), 1997–2007.

Peterson, R. L., & Pennington, B. F. (2015). Developmental dyslexia. *Annual Review of Clinical Psychology, 11*, 283–307.

Peterson, R. L., Pennington, B. F., Shriberg, L. D., & Boada, R. (2009). What influences literacy outcome in children with speech sound disorder? *Journal of Speech Language Hearing Research, 52*, 1175–1188.

Peterson, R. L., Boada, R., McGrath, L., Willcutt, E. G., Olson, R. K., & Pennington, B. F. (2017). Cognitive prediction of reading, math, and attention: Shared and unique influences. *Journal of Learning Disabilities*, **50**(4), 408–421.

Piazza, M., Facoetti, A., Trussardi, A. N.,Bertelletti, I., Conte, S., Lucangeli, D., … Zorzi, M. (2010). Developmental trajectory of number acuity reveals a severe impairment in developmental dyscalculia. *Cognition*, **116**(1), 33–41.

Plomin, R., & Kovas, Y. (2005). Generalist genes and learning disabilities. *Psychological Bulletin*, **131**(4), 592.

Proctor, B. (2012). Relationships between Cattell-Horn-Carroll (CHC) cognitive abilities and math achievement within a sample of college students with learning disabilities. *Journal of Learning Disabilities*, **45**, 278–287.

Ransby, M. J., & Swanson, H. L. (2003). Reading comprehension skills of young adults with childhood diagnoses of dyslexia. *Journal of Learning Disabilities*, **36**, 538–555.

Räsänen, P., Salminen, J., Wilson, A. J., Aunio, P., & Dehaene, S. (2009). Computer- assisted intervention for children with low numeracy skills. *Cognitive Development*, **24**(4), 450–472.

Raskind, W. H., Peter, B., Richards, T. L., Eckert, M. A., & Berninger, V. W. (2013). The genetics of reading disabilities: From phenotypes to candidate genes. *Frontiers in Psychology*, **3**.

Ready, R. E., Chaudhry, M. F., Schatz, K. C., & Strazzullo, S. (2013). "Passageless" administration of the Nelson-Denny Reading Comprehension Test: Associations with IQ and reading skills. *Journal of Learning Disabilities*, **46**, 377–384.

Rehabilitation Services Administration. (1985, January 24). *Program policy directive*. Washington, DC: US Office of Special Education and Rehabilitation Services.

Reiss, A. L., Freund, L., Plotnick, L., Baumgartner, T., Green, K., Sozer, A. C., … Denckla, M. B. (1993). The effects of X monosomy on brain development: Monozygotic twins discordant for Turner's syndrome. *Annals of Neurology*, **34**(1), 95–107.

Reiss, A. L., Mazzocco, M. M., Greenlaw, R.,Freund, L. S., & Ross, J. L. (1995). Neurodevelopmental effects of X monosomy: A volumetric imaging study. *Annals of Neurology*, **38**(5), 731–738.

Rubinstein, O., & Henik, A. (2005). Automatic activation of internal magnitudes: A study of developmental dyscalculia. *Neuropsychology*, **19**, 641–648.

Rutter, M., Caspi, A., Fergusson, D., Horwood, L. J., Goodman, R., Maughan, B., … Carroll, J. (2004). Sex differences in developmental reading disability: New findings from 4 epidemiological studies. *JAMA*, **291**, 2007–12.

Rutter, M., & Yule, W. (1973). Specific reading retardation. In L. Mann & D. Sabatino (Eds.), *The first review of special education* (pp. 1–50). Philadelphia: JSE Press.

Scammacca, N,. Vaughn, S., Roberts, G., Wanzek, J., & Torgesen, J. K. (2007). *Extensive reading interventions in grades K–3: From research to practice.* Portsmouth, NH: RMC Research Corporation, Center on Instruction.

Schneider, W. J., & Kaufman, A. S. (2017). Let's not do away with cognitive assessments just yet. *Archives of Clinical Neuropsychology*, **32**, 8–20.

Schretlen, D. J., Munro, C. A., Anthony, J. C., & Pearlson, G. D. (2003). Examining the range of normal intraindividual variability in neuropsychological test performance. *Journal of the International Neuropsychological Society*, **9**, 864–870.

Schretlen, D. J., Testa, S. M., Winicki, J. M., Pearlson, G. D., & Gordon, B. (2008). Frequency and bases of abnormal performance by healthy adults on neuropsychological testing. *Journal of the International Neuropsychological Society*, **14**, 436–445.

Shalev, R. S., & Gross-Tsur, V. (2001). Developmental dyscalculia. *Pediatric Neurology*, **24**(5), 337–342.

Shaywitz, S. (2003). *Overcoming dyslexia*. New York: Alfred A. Knopf.

Shaywitz, S. E., & Shaywitz, B. A. (2005). Dyslexia (specific reading disability). *Biological Psychiatry*, **57**, 1301–1309.

Shaywitz, S.E., Shaywitz, B. A., Fulbright, R. K., Skudlarski, P., Mencl, W. E., Constable, R. T., … Gore, J. C. (2003). Neural systems for compensation and persistence: Young adult outcome of childhood reading disability. *Biological Psychiatry* **54**, 25–33.

Smith, S. D., Gilger, J.W., & Pennington, B. F. (2002). Dyslexia and other specific learning disorders. In D. L. Rimoin, J. M. Conner, R. E. Pyeritz, & B. Korf (Eds.), *Emery and Rimoin's principles and practice of medical genetics* (4th ed., pp. 2827–2865). New York, NY: Churchill Livingstone.

Smith, S. D., Pennington, B. F., Boada, R. & Shriberg, L. D. (2005). Linkage of speech sound disorder to reading disability loci. *Journal of Child Psychology and Psychiatry*, **46**, 1057–1066.

Smith-Spark, J. H., Henry, L. A., Messer, D. J., Edvardsdottir, E., & Zięcik, A. P. (2016). Executive functions in adults with developmental dyslexia. *Research in Developmental Disabilities*, **53**, 323–341.

Solomon, T., Martinussen, R., Dupuis, A., Gervan, S., Chaban, P., Tannock, R., & Ferguson, B. (2011, March–April) *Investigation of a cognitive science based approach to mathematics instruction.* Peer-reviewed data presented at the Society for Research in Child Development Biennial Meeting, Montreal, Canada.

Stothers, M., & Klein, P. D., (2010). Perceptual organization, phonological awareness, and reading comprehension in adults with and without learning disabilities. *Annals of Dyslexia, 60*(2), 209–237.

Stuebing, K. K., Fletcher, J. M., Branum-Martin, L., & Francis, D. J. (2012). Evaluation of the technical adequacy of three methods for identifying specific learning disabilities based on cognitive discrepancies. *School Psychology Review, 41*(1), 3–22.

Suggate, S. P. (2010). Why what we teach depends on when: Grade and reading intervention modality moderate effect size. *Developmental Psychology, 46*(6), 1556–1579.

Swanson, H. L. (2012). Adults with reading disabilities: Converting a meta-analysis to practice. *Journal of Learning Disabilities, 45*, 17–30.

Torgesen, J. K. (2005). Recent discoveries on remedial interventions for children with dyslexia. In M. Snowling & C. Hulme (Eds.), *The science of reading: A handbook* (pp. 521–537). Oxford, UK: Blackwell Publishing.

Vaughn, S., Linan-Thompson, S., Kouzeanani, K., Pedrotty Bryant, D., Dickson, S., & Blozis, S. A. (2003). Reading instruction grouping for students with reading difficulties. *Remediation Research Quarterly, 24*, 301–315.

Vellutino, F. R., Fletcher, J. M., Snowling, M. J., & Scanlon, D. M. (2004). Specific reading disability (dyslexia): What have we learned in the past four decades? *Journal of Child Psychology and Psychiatry, 45*, 2–40.

Vellutino, F. R., Scanlon, D. M., & Lyon, G. R. (2000). Differentiating between difficult-to-remediate and readily remediated poor readers: More evidence against the IQ-achievement discrepancy definition of reading disability. *Journal of Learning Disabilities, 33*, 223–238.

Wagner, R. K., Puranik, C. S., Foorman, B., Foster, E., Gehron Wilson, I., Tschinkel, E., & Thatcher Kantor, P. l. (2011). Modeling the development of written language. *Reading and Writing, 24*(2), 203–220.

Warner, T. D., Dede, D. E., Garvan, C. W., & Conway, T. W. (2002). One size still does not fit all in specific learning disability assessment across ethnic groups. *Journal of Learning Disabilities, 35*, 501–509.

Willcutt, E. G. & Pennington, B. F. (2000). Comorbidity of reading disability and attention-deficit/hyperactivity disorder: Differences by gender and subtype. *Journal of Learning Disabilities, 33*(2), 179–191.

Willcutt, E. G., Pennington, B. F., Duncan, L., Smith, S. D., Keenan J. M., Wadsworth, S., ... Olson, R. K. (2010). Understanding the complex etiologies of developmental disorders: Behavioral and molecular genetic approaches. *Journal of Developmental Behavioral Pediatrics, 31*, 533–544.

Wilson, A. J., Revkin, S. K., Cohen, D., Cohen, L., & Dehaene, S. (2006). Principles underlying the design of "The Number Race", an adaptive computer game for remediation of dyscalculia. *Behavior Brain Functions, 30*, 2–19.

Yoshimasu, K., Barbaresi, W. J., Colligan, R. C., Killian, J. M., Voigt, R. G., Weaver, A. L., & Katusic, S. K. (2011). Written-language disorder among children with and without ADHD in a population-based birth cohort. *Pediatrics, 128*(3), 605–612.

Chapter 8

Traumatic Brain Injury

Tresa Roebuck-Spencer, Naddley Désiré, and Miriam Beauchamp

Introduction

Traumatic brain injury (TBI), as defined by the Centers for Disease Control and Prevention (CDC), is an injury to the head that involves alteration of consciousness, memory loss, skull fracture, objective neurological or neuropsychological abnormality, or intracranial lesion (Marr & Coronado, 2004). Severity of TBI is based on initial neurological signs and symptoms and is classified on a continuum from mild to moderate to severe. Severity is most commonly determined by depth of coma (e.g., via scores on the Glasgow Coma Scale: <3–8 for severe TBI, 9–12 for moderate TBI, 13–15 for mild TBI [interchangeably referred to as "concussion"]), duration of altered consciousness (e.g., loss of consciousness [LOC] or time to follow commands), or duration of confusion after injury (e.g., length of posttraumatic amnesia [PTA]). Most definitions of mild TBI require scores on the Glasgow Coma Scale to be at least 13; LOC and PTA, if present, to be brief (e.g., <30 minutes and <24 hours, respectively); and neuroimaging to have no abnormal findings (Carroll, Cassidy, Holm, et al., 2004). The term "complicated mild TBI" has been used to indicate an injury that meets the mild TBI definition with the presence of abnormal neuroimaging findings. TBI commonly results in disturbance of cognitive, behavioral, emotional, and physical functioning, which in turn can affect social, psychological, and occupational domains. These effects may be transient, long-lasting, or permanent depending on injury characteristics and severity, which then dictate treatment, recovery course, and ultimate outcome. Thus, neuropsychology plays a significant contributory role in management and treatment of TBI at all severity levels.

Epidemiology

TBI is a leading cause of death and disability worldwide. As of 2010, the CDC estimated that TBI accounted for 2.5 million emergency department visits, hospitalizations, and deaths in the United States; of these, 11% of individuals were hospitalized and 2% died (CDC, 2015). In children, annual population estimates of TBI are 691 per 100,000 children in the United States. Worldwide estimates range from 47 to 280 per 100,000 children, with the lowest rates reported in North-European countries and the highest rates in New Zealand (McKinlay et al., 2008). Increases in emergency department visits for TBI have been documented, particularly for children age 0–4 years and for those 13–18 years old (CDC, 2015; Zemek, Grool, et al., 2016). This effect may be related to increased public awareness of concussion. Rates of TBI-related hospitalizations and deaths are highest for those older than 65 years. Notably, documented rates of TBI likely underestimate the actual occurrence of TBI because they do not account for individuals who do not present to clinics or hospitals, are treated on an outpatient basis, or receive care in federal facilities, such as a Veterans Affairs hospital. Military service members are at significant risk for TBI: there have been more than 352,000 cases of TBI since the year 2000, most of which were mild in severity (Defense and Veterans Brain Injury Center, 2016).

It is estimated that at least 3.2–5.3 million Americans are living with disability due to TBI (Langlois, Rutland-Brown, & Wald, 2006). Although TBI occurs in all demographic groups, particular risk factors for sustaining TBI include age (i.e., very young or aging individuals), male gender, lower socioeconomic status, minority race/ethnic group, history of alcohol or other substance abuse, and prior history of TBI (Centers for Disease Control and Prevention, 2015; Corrigan, Bogner, & Holloman, 2012; Langlois, Rutland-Brown, & Thomas, 2006; Saunders et al., 2009). Falls and motor vehicle accidents are the most common causes of TBI overall, but causes vary across the lifespan (Centers for Disease Control and

Prevention, 2015; Dewan, Mummareddy, Wellons, & Bonfield, 2016). In the very youngest age group (0–2 years) nonaccidental trauma ("inflicted TBI") is prevalent and should be differentiated from other, accidental etiologies. Falls are the most common cause of accidental TBI in the youngest (0–4 years; 72.8%) and oldest (65+ years; 81.8%). Similarly, children and young adolescents (5–14 years) are most likely to sustain a TBI as a result of falls (35.1%) or being struck by/against an object (34.9%), whereas rates of TBI due to motor vehicle accidents increase between ages 15 and 64.

Pathophysiology

Pathology resulting from TBI is heterogeneous and can be categorized as focal or diffuse. Focal injuries most often occur from direct impact to the head or brain (e.g., blunt force, being struck by an object) and may include cortical or subcortical contusions and lacerations, as well as intracranial bleeding (e.g., subarachnoid hemorrhage and subdural hematoma). Diffuse brain injury is commonly seen following acceleration/deceleration injuries (e.g., motor vehicle accidents) and refers to widespread stretching and tearing of brain tissue, as well as hemorrhages throughout the brain. The main form of diffuse injury after TBI is diffuse axonal injury and involves shearing of neuronal axons. The extent of diffuse axonal injury may account for decreased arousal levels and the broad range of neurological deficits after TBI (Gennarelli & Graham, 2005). Acceleration/deceleration injuries also often include tearing of bridging veins resulting in intracranial bleeding. Intracranial hematomas, which include subarachnoid, epidural, and subdural hematomas, are the most common cause of clinical deterioration in patients who initially present well (Rockswold, Leonard, & Nagib, 1987).

Contusions to the brain after TBI are common and occur in a characteristic distribution involving the frontal and temporal poles, the lateral and inferior aspects of the frontal and temporal lobes, and less commonly the inferior aspects of the cerebellum. This pattern of injury is most likely due to abrasion of the brain against the bony ridges on the surface of the skull. Contusions and intracranial hematomas are primary contributors to the early focal cognitive signs and symptoms seen after TBI. Secondary or delayed complications can also occur after TBI and include edema, hypoxia/ischemia, raised intracranial pressure, associated vascular changes, seizures, and less commonly meningitis and abscess (Gennarelli & Graham, 2005).

Children present with specific pathophysiological risks and are more likely than adults to suffer from diffuse injuries, posttraumatic brain swelling and hypoxic-ischemic insults after TBI (Levin, Shum, & Chan, 2014). This is due to different biomechanical characteristics, less myelinated brains, greater cerebral fluid and blood volumes, and higher head-to-body ratio in children compared with their adult counterparts. Pediatric patients are also at higher risk for epilepsy, with early seizures occurring within the first week post-TBI and posttraumatic epilepsy commonly diagnosed in children with penetrating, inflicted, or depressed skull fractures (Christensen et al., 2009).

Despite clear transient cognitive and behavioral changes, brain injury resulting from mild TBI is typically not observable on conventional structural neuroimaging. There is no dispute, however, that mild TBI results in metabolic alteration of the brain and possibly diffuse microscopic trauma that is only observable using advanced neuroimaging techniques (Beauchamp, Ditchfield, et al., 2011; Hunter, Wilde, Tong, & Holshouser, 2012). The initiating event is believed to be stretching and disruption of neuronal and axonal cell membranes, resulting in abrupt and indiscriminate release of neurotransmitters and ionic shifts. Enhanced release of excitatory neurotransmitters, particularly glutamate, results in a cascade of neurochemical reactions that can lead to a generalized cellular crisis due to a prompt decrease in glucose supply. This is coupled with decreased cerebral blood flow and increased demand for glucose consumption as membrane pumps increase activity to restore ionic balance (Barkhoudarian, Hovda, & Giza, 2011). This overall process is transient with an ultimate return to homeostasis believed to occur within a few days.

"Blast" injury refers to physical trauma from exposure to detonation of explosions and has been described as a new mechanism of brain injury (Magnuson, Leonessa, & Ling, 2012). Blast injuries are commonly described in military samples but also occur in civilians exposed to explosion events. Primary injuries from explosive blasts result from the direct effects of high-force pressure waves. Blast waves are known to affect air-filled organs, such as the ears and lungs. Animal research suggests that these waves may also affect organs within fluid-filled cavities, such as the brain and spinal cord; however, the nature of the effects on the human central nervous system remain a controversial topic. Blasts may also result in mechanical injuries, including secondary injuries caused by flying debris or shrapnel that impact and penetrate the body; tertiary injuries caused when the body is thrown and collides with another object, such as a structure or the ground; and quaternary injuries, such as burns, toxic inhalation, and radiation exposure. Effects from the mechanical aspects of blast-related TBI would be expected to be similar to blunt-force and acceleration/deceleration TBI. Although some studies show similar cognitive profiles between blast and other mechanisms of TBI (Belanger, Kretzmer, Yoash-Gantz, Pickett, & Tupler, 2009), individuals with blast TBI may have different clinical presentations due to high rates of sensory impairment, pain, polytrauma, and emotional comorbidities (French, 2010).

Clinical Manifestations

Like the pathophysiology of TBI, clinical manifestations are broad and heterogeneous. Of most relevance to neuropsychologists are the effects of TBI on cognition, emotions, behavior/personality, and social skills (see Table 8.1 for a summary of characteristic cognitive and neurobehavioral impairments after TBI and proposed neuroanatomical correlates). The magnitude and pattern of impairments resulting from TBI vary according to many factors, the most important of which are severity of injury, time since injury, and age. Magnitude of impairment typically

Table 8.1 Cognitive and Neurobehavioral Characteristics of TBI and Neuroanatomical Correlates

TBI-Related Characteristic	Neuroanatomical Correlates
Cognitive Impairment	
Impaired alertness/arousal	Diffuse axonal injury and/or brain stem injuries with greater severity associated with depth of coma
Slowed cognitive processing	Diffuse axonal injury; white matter lesions, particularly frontal and corpus callosum microstructural lesions
Attentional impairment	Diffuse cerebral contusions and/or diffuse axonal injury
Learning and memory impairment	Frontal and/or temporal lobe contusions; diffuse axonal injury; lesions to extrafrontoparietal areas, limbic structures
Working memory impairment	Diffuse axonal injury; white matter lesions; frontal lobe dysfunction
Executive functioning impairment	Contusions to the prefrontal cortex, frontal and temporal poles, the lateral and inferior aspects of the frontal and temporal lobes, and less commonly to the inferior aspects of the cerebellum; damage to frontal/subcortical loops
Aphasia	Focal injury to left hemisphere or left subcortical structures through hematomas or cerebral contusions. Rare in the pediatric TBI but may occur with lesions in perisylvian area in severe TBI cases.
Limb apraxia	Focal injury to left hemisphere from hematoma or cerebral contusion
Social functioning impairment	Frontal lobe injury; disruption of social brain network
Neurobehavioral Syndromes	
Disinhibition syndromes	Loss of inhibition by the orbitofrontal system, often through damage to the orbital frontal cortex and its associative connections
Impairments in initiation	Lack of integration between drive-related behaviors and cognitive mediators of behavioral expression, often through damage to the medial frontal cortex and its associative connections
Impairments in self-awareness	Poorly understood, but frequently associated with damage to the prefrontal cortex and temporal poles
Neuropsychiatric disorders	Disruption of distributed neurotransmitter systems (particularly early in recovery). Psychosocial factors may play an increasing role in later recovery.

increases with greater levels of injury severity in a dose-response fashion. These impairments are greatest initially after injury with expected neurologic recovery over time (Schretlen & Shapiro, 2003). Age at time of injury is also significant, given that presenting problems and subsequent expectations for recovery may be complicated in geriatric patients or may follow a different trajectory in children due to interruptions of typical brain development and cognitive maturation.

Individuals who sustain mild TBI typically experience transient cognitive (e.g., mild confusion, difficulty maintaining attention, and forgetfulness), emotional (e.g., tearfulness, irritability), and physical (e.g., headaches, sensitivity to light, blurred vision) symptoms that begin immediately or shortly after the injury and improve over a period of days to weeks. Most available research, particularly prospective and meta-analytic studies, shows that both children and adults with uncomplicated mild TBI typically recover to baseline levels of cognitive functioning within 1–3 months postinjury and are expected to have favorable long-term outcome (Belanger & Vanderploeg, 2005; Carroll, Cassidy, Peloso, et al., 2004; Zemek, Barrowman, et al., 2016).

Prolonged or atypical recovery course after mild TBI has been associated with acute injury indicators, such as presence of LOC or PTA, severity of initial symptoms, findings on computed tomography scans, and repeated mild TBI (Dagher, Richard-Denis, Lamoureux, de Guise, & Feyz, 2013; Guskiewicz et al., 2003; McCrea et al., 2013). It has long been recognized that atypical recovery of clinical symptoms after mild TBI may be associated with preexisting or comorbid psychiatric, medical, psychosocial, or litigation factors (McCrea, 2008; Yeates, 2010). More recently, noninjury factors such as coping styles and history of stressful life events have also been shown to be predictive of outcome (Maestas et al., 2013; van Veldhoven et al., 2011). Further, recent multicenter TBI research initiatives have confirmed that factors such as older age, lower education, and premorbid neuropsychiatric conditions predict unfavorable outcomes in adult mild TBI (Lingsma et al., 2015), combined with contrasting findings that magnetic resonance imaging and diffusion tensor imaging parameters may be better predictors of outcome at 3 and 6 months post-TBI than clinical and psychosocial factors (Yuh et al., 2014).

Findings regarding preinjury and injury variables as prognostic factors for mild TBI extend to children and adolescents. Poor outcome 1 month postinjury is associated with being female, being between 13 and 18 years old, history of migraine, history of prior concussion with symptoms lasting more than 1 week, and a number of acute clinical indicators (e.g., experiencing sensitivity to noise, fatigue, headaches, answering questions slowly, and poor balance) (Zemek, Barrowman, et al., 2016). There is also evidence that preexisting child and family factors (e.g., learning disabilities, parental stress) may be more associated with persistent postconcussive symptoms over time than injury characteristics (Bernard, Ponsford, McKinlay, McKenzie, & Krieser, 2016).

In contrast to mild TBI, individuals with moderate to severe TBI are more likely to have persisting or even chronic impairments that limit their ability to return to previous levels of functioning. These individuals are more likely to require hospitalization or inpatient or postacute rehabilitation and to have worse functional outcomes. The early recovery period after moderate to severe TBI includes a series of predictable stages. Impaired consciousness, when present, is typically seen immediately after injury, with coma and persistent vegetative state representing the most extreme end of the spectrum. Resolution of coma and persistent vegetative state is typically followed by a period of PTA, in which the individual is responsive, but markedly confused and amnestic. After resolution of PTA, most individuals with moderate to severe TBI typically evolve to have some combination of cognitive and neurobehavioral impairments that vary depending on severity and specifics of injury, premorbid functioning, comorbid neurological and psychiatric status, and time since injury (see Table 8.2 summarizing the course of impairments after TBI across the severity spectrum).

Cognitive Outcome. Cognitive functioning typically improves over time with the most recovery seen in the first 6 months after moderate to severe TBI. Improvement in basic cognitive skills, such as immediate attention and orientation, precedes improvement in more complex cognitive skills, such as problem-solving and executive functioning. In large-scale studies, more than half of individuals with moderate or severe TBI and almost all individuals with very severe TBI had residual cognitive impairments after 1 year (Dikmen, Machamer, Winn, & Temkin, 1995; Dikmen, Reitan, & Temkin,

Table 8.2 Course of Impairments Over Time

TBI Severity	Age	Onset of Symptoms	Primary Cognitive Effects	Primary Neurobehavioral Effects	Course	Risk Factors
Mild	Adult	Immediate	Mild effects seen in attention, processing speed, short-term memory	Minimal; transient emotional lability	Recovery within days to weeks	Persisting symptoms often accounted for by psychiatric comorbidities, psychosocial factors, and compensation-seeking scenarios
	Pediatrics	Immediate	Reduced speed of information processing, decreased executive control, poor memory and attention	Very mild to moderate effects	Variable recovery within days to 2 months; subsample of patients recover within a year	Young age at injury; sex; history of concussion, preinjury behavioral or cognitive problems; premorbid learning problems; lower parental education
Moderate to severe	Adult	Immediate	Global cognitive effects most pronounced in attention, processing speed, memory, executive functioning	Often pronounced and may include decreased awareness, disinhibition, impaired social skills, poor judgment, and others	Recovery over months to years; possible chronic effects	Comorbid medical and psychiatric factors, previous TBI, poor family support or coping
	Pediatrics	Immediate	Global intellectual impairment when injury occurs at early age (<3 years), pronounced effects in attention, processing speed, memory and learning; expressive and receptive language; executive functioning; social cognition	Moderately to severely impaired social adjustment and interaction, adaptive functioning; externalizing behaviors	Variable and unpredictable recovery over years; persistent long-term effects; dependent on developmental stage and trajectory	Preinjury learning and behavioral problems; adjustment difficulties, family burden, and stress, social disadvantage

1983). Recovery of cognitive functioning usually reaches a plateau at 18–24 months, but some patients improve beyond this point whereas others may show late decline. In adults, older age at time of injury and increased levels of depression may be associated with increased risk of late decline (Millis et al., 2001). In children, environmental factors such as family functioning and parental mental health play a substantial role in recovery after early moderate to severe TBI (Yeates et al., 2002).

Characteristic cognitive impairments are diffuse and include impaired fine motor speed, attention, cognitive processing speed, learning and memory, complex language and discourse, and executive functions. Circumscribed or localized cognitive impairments, such as language or visual-spatial impairment (i.e., aphasia, apraxia, attentional neglect), may be seen in individuals with focal injuries, but tend to be observed in the very early course of injury and are generally superimposed on global cognitive dysfunction resulting from diffuse injury. Typically, studies of children and adults find that intellectual level is only minimally affected and when premorbid functioning is accounted for, the greatest impairments are typically seen on tests of information processing speed and cognitive flexibility, followed by immediate and delayed memory (Anderson, Brown, Newitt, & Hoile, 2011). In contrast, moderate to severe injury before 3 years of age may result in intellectual decline, suggesting that significant insult to the brain incurred in very early childhood is detrimental to cognitive development (Anderson, Catroppa, Morse, Haritou, & Rosenfeld, 2009; Ewing-Cobbs et al., 2006).

Behavioral/Emotional Outcome. A broad range of neurobehavioral and emotional changes are seen after TBI. For those with mild TBI, the most notable of these changes are emotional lability and irritability. It is unclear to what extent these changes are related to direct brain injury versus accompanying stress of the injury and its disruption of daily routines and responsibilities. The presence of anxiety after mild TBI may pose an additional risk factor for persistent symptoms over time (Segev et al., 2016). Expected recovery of behavioral and emotional symptoms typically mirrors recovery of cognitive symptoms (Ponsford et al., 1999).

When compared with adults with mild TBI, young children are at higher risk of developing persisting behavioral and emotional problems. In particular, mild TBI sustained before school entry is associated with poorer psychosocial development, with children at higher risk for oppositional and conduct problems (McKinlay, Grace, Horwood, Fergusson, & MacFarlane, 2010). Persistent behavioral deficits such as poor self-control, aggression, social disinhibition, and discipline problems are also typical after pediatric TBI more generally, as are mood and anxiety disorders (Luis & Mittenberg, 2002).

After moderate to severe TBI, neurobehavioral changes and impairments are particularly common and are often persistent, posing a significant challenge to recovery of preinjury functional status. Disinhibition syndromes and emotional dysregulation are common and are believed to be related to damage to the orbitofrontal cortex, which is vulnerable to acceleration/deceleration injuries. Such behaviors include aggression/agitation, social disinhibition, impulsivity, risk-taking behavior, and affective lability. Impairments in initiation of behavior, ranging from extreme apathy and avolition to more subtle impairments in initiating and persisting with goal-directed activities, are also typical and believed to be related to medial frontal injury, particularly the cingulate gyrus and its subcortical connections (Cohen et al., 1999; Middleton & Strick, 2000). Impaired awareness of cognitive and behavioral deficits is common and can evolve to include poor awareness of the functional implications of deficits or impaired ability to correctly judge one's abilities on future tasks. The neuroanatomic substrates of self-awareness are not well understood, and studies show that they likely involve broadly distributed networks (Sherer, Hart, Whyte, Nick, & Yablon, 2005).

Finally, emotional disruption and psychiatric disorders are common after moderate to severe TBI, with depression and anxiety being the most widespread (Kim et al., 2007; Rogers & Read, 2007). Disruption of distributed neurotransmitter systems is one hypothesized cause of depression after TBI, particularly earlier in recovery. Depression later in recovery may be more strongly related to psychosocial stressors and emerging awareness of deficits. Depression after TBI is associated with poorer psychosocial outcome, with risk factors including preinjury depression, psychosocial stress, and social isolation. Anxiety after TBI is often generalized in nature. Posttraumatic stress disorder (PTSD) remains a point of controversy because amnesia for the traumatic event is typical after moderate to severe TBI. PTSD symptoms are more common in milder injuries, where recall of the event is common, although there is evidence that PTSD symptoms in more severe injuries may develop secondary to the trauma of hospitalization, medical procedures, and pain (Bryant, 2001; Bryant, Marosszeky, Crooks, Baguley, & Gurka, 2001). TBI encountered in military service members is frequently associated with PTSD and other psychiatric conditions, making it important to account for and address comorbidities in this population (Tanielian & Jaycox, 2008). These comorbidities are particularly important to consider in blast-related mild TBI, given that PTSD and depression have been found to be important mediators between mild TBI and long-term postconcussion symptoms (Hoge et al., 2008).

In children, more severe instances of TBI can lead to the emergence of new psychological or psychiatric syndromes such as depression, anxiety and obsessive-compulsive disorder. For instance, Max et al. (2011) found that development of anxiety disorder was associated with concurrent depression and personality changes due to TBI and proposed that anxiety after pediatric TBI may be the outcome of affective dysregulation related to damage to the dorsal frontal lobe. Accordingly, children and adolescents with TBI frequently endorse lower rates on scales of adaptive functioning and quality of life, in part related to the presence of psychiatric disorder. Furthermore, a recent study investigating the prevalence and predictors of externalizing behaviors in survivors of pediatric TBI found that 25% of young adults having sustained a TBI before age 12 demonstrated some level of externalizing behaviors such as aggression, rule-breaking, and conduct problems (Ryan et al., 2015). They also found that persistent and frequent disruptive behaviors were associated with poorer preinjury adaptive functioning, lower global intellectual functioning, and reduced social communication skills, regardless of injury severity.

Psychosocial/Functional Outcome. The psychosocial impact of TBI is immense and difficult to quantify. Cognitive, emotional, and behavioral changes after TBI frequently result in changes in interpersonal roles and relationships and decreased engagement in community activities such as work, school, driving, and leisure activities. This impact is particularly significant for young adult TBI survivors, who are just beginning to establish social, vocational, and family roles. Return to employment is a common area of poor psychosocial outcome, with recent postinjury unemployment rates reported at just over 60% at 2 years postinjury (Cuthbert et al., 2015). Factors such as older age, lower educational levels, stability of preinjury work history, and injury severity are all strongly related to return to work after TBI (Dikmen et al., 1994). As expected, individuals with milder injuries return to work more frequently and sooner than those with more severe injuries. In addition, persisting behavioral and cognitive effects of moderate to severe TBI result in many individuals facing decreased personal independence (many live with parents at 1 year postinjury) and a markedly increased risk for institutional placement (usually a nursing home) (Dikmen, Machamer, & Temkin, 1993; Kersel, Marsh, Havill, & Sleigh, 2001).

Personal and family roles are frequently strained by personality and behavioral changes after TBI. Aggression and disinhibition, as well as impaired social skills, poor self-awareness, and impaired social problem-solving can negatively affect interpersonal relationships. Caregiver subjective burden has been reported to have higher associations with TBI-related behavioral disruption than with physical impairments (Liss & Willer, 1990; Riley, 2007). Adjustment to the caregiver role is often more difficult for spouses than for parents, given the specific strains that are placed on marriages due to personality changes, increasing dependence, and increasing social isolation. Also common after TBI is attrition of friendships and leisure activities, which can result in TBI survivors becoming increasingly dependent on their primary caregivers to meet their social needs, further increasing caregiver burden and social isolation.

In pediatric TBI, environmental factors such as parenting behaviors have a considerable influence on recovery from brain injury in young children. For instance, the family environment accounts for significant variance in psychosocial outcomes after TBI in young children and predicts behavioral adjustment and social competence at 18 months postinjury (Yeates, Taylor, Walz, Stancin, & Wade, 2010). Additionally, parenting behaviors such as parental negativity have been shown to result in higher levels of externalizing problems and symptoms of attention-deficit/hyperactivity disorder, and may impede behavioral recovery after early TBI (Wade et al., 2011).

Adult Outcomes of Childhood TBI. The evolution of pediatric TBI into adulthood remains poorly understood, particularly in cases of milder brain injuries because only a small number of longitudinal studies have followed survivors of childhood TBI into their adult years. Evidence of residual impacts of mild TBI into adulthood has been scarce due to methodological limitations of longitudinal research (e.g., sample attrition, changes in the diagnosis and definition of TBI over the years). Results from studies to date appear to suggest that pediatric mild TBI is rarely associated with significant long-term neurobehavioral consequences (Hessen, Nestvold, & Anderson, 2007); however, some studies also suggest that subjective reports of psychological problems appear more common in individuals who sustained complicated mild TBI in childhood (Hessen, Anderson, & Nestvold, 2008).

There is increasing evidence that after severe TBI sustained in childhood, some cognitive, social, and psychological difficulties do persist into adulthood and have an unfavorable impact on daily functioning. Specifically, long-term problems in cognitive domains such as attention, memory, executive functioning, and processing speed are more likely to be identified in survivors of childhood TBI (Beauchamp, Catroppa, et al., 2011), whereas overall intellectual functioning has been noted to improve slightly over a span of 10 years, indicating that children with TBI do make developmental gains (Anderson, Catroppa, Godfrey, & Rosenfeld, 2012). In addition, a growing body of research demonstrates that injuries sustained during childhood mostly impact social and psychological functioning. For instance, adolescent and young adult survivors of early childhood TBI are at elevated risks for developing internalizing symptoms such as depression, anxiety, and withdrawal (Rosema et al., 2014). Social maladjustment, poor quality of life, and family problems are also often reported after child TBI (Anderson et al., 2011; Hoofien, Gilboa, Vakil, & Donovick, 2001). It has also been suggested that survivors of pediatric TBI are at higher risk for exhibiting and developing maladaptive behaviors because there appears to be a high prevalence of child TBI survivors among individuals in detention centers (Kenny & Lennings, 2007; Ryan et al., 2015); however, there has been limited investigation into the factors that contribute to such outcomes.

Overall, it is important to bear in mind that multiple factors come into play and can contribute to outcomes from childhood TBI such as age at injury, injury severity, psychosocial factors, premorbid characteristics, and child and family adjustment (Hessen et al., 2007). There is clearly a need for more longitudinal research to better understand the interplay of preinjury and postinjury factors implicated in the adult outcomes of childhood TBI.

TBI and Dementia Risk. There is substantial evidence for increased risk of later-life dementia after history of at least one moderate to severe TBI (Bazarian, Cernak, Noble-Haeusslein, Potolicchio, & Temkin, 2009; Institute of Medicine, 2009). Animal models and autopsy studies indicate that TBI initiates a trigger for inflammation and amyloid-beta accumulation in the brain reminiscent of Alzheimer-type dementia (Johnson, Stewart, & Smith, 2010). Some studies indicate that moderate to severe TBI may lead to earlier onset of dementia (Nordström, Michaëlsson, Gustafson, & Nordström, 2014) and that those who sustain injuries later in life may be at particular risk for developing dementia (Gardner et al., 2014). However, consensus is not complete, given a large number of studies that fail to show an association between TBI and later dementia (Dams-O'Connor et al., 2013). Of particular relevance is a study that followed TBI patients over a 30-year period and showed only mild cognitive decline over time (Himanen et al., 2006), with men and those with injury later in life at greatest risk for decline. However, semantic memory improved over time, indicating that changes seen were not consistent with an Alzheimer-type dementia.

Risk for dementia after mild TBI has not been supported. Evidence from prospective studies and systematic reviews has concluded no increased risk for later-life dementia after mild TBI without LOC (Albrecht, Masters, Ames, Foster, & Group, 2016; Bazarian et al., 2009; Institute of Medicine, 2009). However, it is now proposed that *repeated* mild TBI may result in accumulated neuropathology, chronic neurological problems, and ultimate dementia (Blennow, Hardy, & Zetterberg, 2012). Dementia pugilistica has long been described in boxers who, by the nature of their sport, sustain repeated blows to the head. More recently, a series of autopsy reports in athletes has shown neuropathological changes, including accumulated neurofibrillary tangles, believed to result from repeated mechanical and rotational forces on the brain (McKee et al., 2009). These neuropathological changes are believed to be associated with separately described chronic cognitive and neurobehavioral problems in athletes with history of repeated mild TBI. The term chronic traumatic encephalopathy (CTE) is being used to describe these findings, with CTE believed by some to be a chronic neurodegenerative condition clinically manifested by irritability, impulsivity, aggression, depression, cognitive changes, and heightened suicidality (McKee et al., 2009, 2013). However, the clinical course and symptoms reported in patients believed to have CTE are variable; there are no generally accepted guidelines for clinical diagnosis or for how to distinguish it from other types of dementias, and there are, to date, no prospective or case-controlled studies to verify causal relationships between the behavioral syndrome and underlying neuropathological findings.

Neuropsychological Assessment After TBI

Information from neuropsychological evaluations is invaluable and can be used to provide feedback to the patient, caregivers, and attending medical staff regarding treatment and discharge planning, effectiveness of drug trials and other interventions, supervision needs, decision-making capacity, driving capacity, and readiness to return to work, school, or other independent activities. The focus and goals of neuropsychological assessment after TBI are also determined by severity of injury, stage of recovery, and return to school/work or rehabilitation guidelines and objectives.

Assessment After Mild TBI. Individuals with mild TBI typically recover from their symptoms before ever needing a neuropsychological assessment. Some individuals, particularly children and adolescents with sports-related concussion, may be seen in specialized concussion clinics for screening evaluations, whereas others may be seen for more extensive neuropsychological testing to assess cognitive abilities and make recommendations regarding return to functional activities and treatment needs. For evaluations of individuals with mild TBI, it is essential to consider the expected duration of TBI-related symptoms, given that clinical symptoms related to mild injuries have been empirically shown to resolve within 1–3 months after injury in most individuals. Comorbidities with mild TBI can be high, particularly for military service members. Thus, potential etiological factors other than TBI should be considered for individuals reporting symptoms outside the expected window of recovery, or for individuals reporting excessive or atypical complaints. Individuals with complicated mild TBI may perform somewhat worse on cognitive testing than those with uncomplicated mild TBI, although evidence suggests that long-term outcome for most individuals with complicated mild TBI is still good overall (Iverson, 2006).

In some settings, particularly those treating sports-related concussions, initial neuropsychological testing after mild TBI or concussion can occur within hours or days after injury. Some concussion management protocols call for neuropsychological testing once subjective symptoms have resolved in order to assist with return to play/school/work (Echemendia & Cantu, 2003; Moser et al., 2007). This testing can take the form of serial assessments using sensitive measures of attention, processing speed, and symptom report with the goal of tracking recovery from injury (McCrea et al., 2003). Although there is controversy regarding incremental validity, sensitivity, and reliability of computerized testing after concussion (Randolph, McCrea, & Barr, 2005), these testing procedures have been shown to document recovery of cognitive functioning over 1–2 weeks after concussion and to have incremental validity over and above symptom report and other measures tracking concussion recovery (Brooks, Khan, Daya, Mikrogianakis, & Barlow, 2014; McCrea et al., 2005).

Assessment After Moderate to Severe TBI. For individuals with moderate to severe TBI, early neuropsychological assessment may focus on determining level of responsiveness and tracking cognitive status and recovery. With responsive but confused patients, measures of orientation are well suited to determine when a patient has recovered basic cognitive skills. Traditionally, administration of formal neuropsychological tests has been contingent on PTA resolution; however, administration of selected neuropsychological tests to patients still in PTA can result in useful prognostic data (Pastorek, Hannay, & Contant, 2004). Key domains to target when evaluating an individual with TBI should include orientation, fine motor skills, attention, cognitive speed, learning and memory, language skills, visual-perceptual skills, and executive functions. Despite compelling evidence of a TBI, some individuals may either consciously or unconsciously exaggerate symptoms when seen for follow-up evaluations, particularly those engaged in litigation or presenting with other potential secondary gain issues (e.g., return to school/work). Thus, performance and symptom validity measures should be included in assessment batteries when appropriate.

It is also essential to assess neurobehavioral status, given the possibility of impairments in this area even when cognition is within normal limits. Further, evaluation of emotional status is imperative given high rates of psychopathology after TBI and the association of poor outcome with emotional distress.

Results from neuropsychological evaluations are generally predictive of personal safety, independent living, driving safety, and return to school/work. A brief battery of neuropsychological tests administered early in the recovery course has been shown to be predictive of handicap, supervision needs, and employability at 1 year (Hanks et al., 2008) with test results predicting functional outcome above and beyond injury severity variables. Early neuropsychological evaluation is also predictive of long-term functional disability at 1–2 years postinjury after considering demographic variables, injury severity, and computed tomography findings (Williams, Rapport, Hanks, Millis, & Greene, 2013).

In addition to what has been discussed in previous sections concerning neuropsychological assessment post-TBI, a few considerations should also be taken into account when assessing neuropsychological effects of TBI in children. For one, such assessments occur in a dynamic period of brain and functional development and, as such, provide an accurate profile for only a brief period. This limitation has implications for determining long-term recovery, because evolving postinjury recovery must be considered in the context of rapidly developing abilities and it may not always be possible to differentiate the two. In addition, both injury pathology and resulting cognitive impairments tend to be more diffuse in children than in adults, causing a greater range in variability in expected outcome. A study evaluating the predictive value of neuropsychological assessment with respect to special education placement at 12 and 24 months after pediatric brain injury indicates that neuropsychological test scores are sensitive to acute injury severity and predict educational outcome above and beyond demographic and clinical variables (Miller & Donders, 2003), thus indicating the incremental role of neuropsychology in TBI. A further distinction concerns the role of parents and other caregivers in the evaluation process, whereby children are often subject to environmental influence more so than adults. Assessment should therefore rely on collateral reports of child functioning whenever possible, while remaining aware of the potential biases these introduce.

Prevention

The implementation of legislative policies and preventive strategies has helped alleviate the incidence of TBI by reducing the number of deaths and severe injuries and by improving parents' and caregivers' ability to recognize and respond appropriately to incidents that may cause TBI. For instance, to prevent severe injuries associated with motor vehicle accidents, seatbelt laws and child passenger safety policies (e.g., appropriate use of child car seats and boosters) have been adopted in most developed countries and are proven to be effective in reducing the risk for serious and fatal injuries in infants (<1 year), toddlers (aged 1–4 years), and older children (>13 years) by up to 71% (Sauber-Schatz, Thomas, & Cook, 2015). National campaigns against drunk driving have also successfully contributed to reducing the incidence of moderate to severe TBI while alleviating death rates in both older adolescents and adults. Drivers between 16 and 19 years of age are at higher risk of being involved in severe motor vehicle accidents. As a result, graduated driver licensing programs requiring lengthier and supervised learning periods and limiting teenagers to driving only under stringent conditions (e.g., restricting driving at night and/or with young passengers) have been adopted in multiple countries and are associated with substantially lower rates of severe injuries and crashes in teenage drivers (Masten, Foss, & Marshall, 2011).

Recreational and sports-related injuries (e.g., bicycling, snowboarding, skiing) have benefited from helmet use legislation, which has been shown to prevent and decrease head injury rates in both children and adults (Macpherson & Spinks, 2008). Within organized sports, education programs about mild TBI or concussion, such as the CDC's Heads Up initiative (Sawyer et al., 2010), have become mandatory in the United States for coaches and trainers involved in youth sports. The objectives of these types of educational prevention tools are to thoroughly inform caregivers on the symptoms associated with concussion to help prevent, recognize, and swiftly respond to sports-related brain injuries. Because of the observation that individuals with a history of one or more concussions are more likely to sustain future head injuries, and evidence that repetitive TBIs may lead to cumulative persistent consequences in athletes across the lifespan, multiple governments have implemented laws to remove concussed athletes from play or have adopted clear return-to-play guidelines to minimize residual or serial consequences after injury.

Prevention efforts have also targeted groups more vulnerable to inflicted TBI. For instance, education programs delivered to new parents via assigned nurses, instructive videos, or public education campaigns teach new parents about the dangers of violently shaking a baby and are effective in reducing the occurrence and serious long-term deficits associated with inflicted TBI (formerly referred to as "shaken baby syndrome") (Barr et al., 2009). Although there has been an important effort in developing methods to prevent TBI, more controlled and randomized research designs are needed to fully assess the efficiency of protective gear legislations, driving policies, and educational strategies on TBI incidence and injury severity across age groups.

Intervention

Some degree of improvement in clinical symptoms is the expectation after TBI due to spontaneous neurological recovery. There is evidence that interventions can further enhance this recovery process, lead to improved outcomes, and improve overall quality of life (see Table 8.3 for a summary of empirically supported treatments for TBI). Interventions benefit both children and adults with TBI and vary based on severity of injury, time since injury, and treatment goals.

Table 8.3 Empirically Supported Treatments for TBI

Target Problems	Treatment(s)
Mild TBI	
Neuropsychological effects of mild TBI	Single-session psychoeducational treatment
	Return-to-play/activity protocols
Cognition	
Language/communication Impairments	Cognitive linguistic therapies; group communication treatment
Visual-spatial; unilateral neglect	Training of compensatory visual scanning strategies
Apraxia	Gestural or strategy training
Attentional Impairment	Self-management attention processing strategies (for postacute periods only)
	Medication (e.g., methylphenidate)
Learning and memory	Internal compensatory strategies (e.g., visual imagery; memory logs/diaries (mild impairment)
	External memory aids such as pagers or phone alarms (moderate to severe impairment)
	Errorless learning strategies
	Medication (e.g., donepezil)
Executive dysfunction	Formal metacognitive and problem-solving training (e.g., self-monitoring and self-regulation strategies)
	Medication (e.g., bromocriptine)
Neurobehavioral Deficits	
Impairment in language pragmatics	Group communication treatment
	Psychotherapeutic approaches
Poor self-awareness	Awareness training interventions
	Real-world/occupational training including teaching awareness of errors
Aggression	Behavioral and environmental modification
	Medication (e.g., beta-blockers)

Table 8.3 (cont.)

Target Problems	Treatment(s)
Depression/Anxiety	Psychotherapy (individual and group)
	Medication (tricyclic antidepressants and serotonin reuptake inhibitors)
Psychosis	Medication (e.g., olanzapine)
Psychosocial	
Coping skills	Individual and group-based supportive therapy
Family	Psychoeducation about impairments, coping, and behavioral/environmental modifications
	Caregiver support
	Traditional family therapy
Community reintegration	Comprehensive-integrated postacute rehabilitation programs
	Psychotherapeutic approaches
Return to work	Supported employment
	Comprehensive-integrated postacute rehabilitation programs
	Compensatory and adaptive strategy implementation
Return to school/learning environments	Educational plans; individualized education plans
	Behavior and environment modification
	Compensatory and adaptive strategy implementation

Common goals of intervention after TBI are to manage or reduce symptoms, provide support/education to the individual with TBI and their caregivers, develop and maintain compensatory strategies, reduce personal and environmental barriers to progress, and to promote independence and return to previous activities or functional levels.

Interventions and Return-to-play Guidelines in Mild TBI. Although the effects of mild TBI are expected to be transient, they can limit an individual's return to school or work. Additionally, misinformation about the effects and prognosis of mild TBI, hypervigilance to normally occurring cognitive errors, or misattribution of comorbid symptoms to TBI can complicate recovery (McCrea, 2008; Waldron-Perrine, Tree, Spencer, Suhr, & Bieliauskas, 2015). Empirical evidence supports the notion that early single-session treatment providing education about the effects and recovery of mild TBI, in conjunction with reassurance and appropriate attribution of symptoms, improves outcome after mild TBI (Mittenberg, Canyock, Condit, & Patton, 2001; Waldron-Perrine et al., 2015). Single-session treatments have been shown to be as effective as

more extensive assessment and treatment, with effects lasting up to 1 year postinjury (Paniak, Toller-Lobe, Reynolds, Melnyk, & Nagy, 2000).

After mild TBI, return-to-play or -school protocols are a form of intervention that may impact the course of recovery. A number of consensus groups have put forward protocols providing health-care professionals with guidelines and recommendations for mild TBI management (Marshall, Bayley, McCullagh, Velikonja, & Berrigan, 2012; McCrory et al., 2013); however, their downward extension to younger children remains unclear and may require models that are developmentally sensitive and include individual youth, family, teacher, and school input. A balanced evidence-based protocol for return to school for children and youth after mild TBI has been proposed by the National Institutes of Health (NIH) (DeMatteo et al., 2015). This five-stage protocol focuses on adapting and modifying school attendance, curriculum, environment, and activities until children are symptom free (see Table 8.4 for a summary of the NIH protocol).

Cognitive rest is commonly prescribed after concussion; there is some evidence that it is beneficial for symptom resolution (Moser et al., 2015). However,

Table 8.4 Return-to-School Protocol for Children and Youth with Concussion

Rehabilitation Stage	Global Objective	Specific Recommendations
Stage 1	Brain rest, no school	No school for up to 1 week
		Cognitive rest (limits on TV, video games, texting, reading)
Stage 2	Getting ready to go back	Begin gentle activity guided by symptoms
Stage 3	Back to school, modified academics	Constant sleep routine and hygiene
		Academic modifications: less stressful classes first, no tests, regular breaks
		Gradual school attendance
Stage 4	Nearly normal routine	Possible back to full days of school
		Maximum of one test per week
Stage 5	Fully back to school	Gradual return to normal routines, including attendance, homework, tests, and extracurricular activities

Note: Adapted from "A balanced protocol for return to school for children and youth following concussive injury," by C. DeMatteo, K. Stazyk, L. Giglia, W. Mahoney, S. K. Singh, R. Hollenberg, … D. McCauley, 2015, *Clinical Pediatrics*, 54, pp. 783–792.

emerging evidence suggests that prolonged physical and cognitive rest could lead to protracted recovery (DiFazio, Silverberg, Kirkwood, Bernier, & Iverson, 2016) and recent research indicates improved outcomes with the inclusion of moderate levels of exercise in concussion management protocols (Grool et al., 2016). Patients with associated cervical spine or vestibular dysfunction may benefit from interventions specifically targeted toward those symptoms (Sawyer, Vesci, & MacLeod, 2016).

There are no recognized pharmacological treatment guidelines for mild TBI, given that symptoms are generally transient and self-limited. When utilized, pharmacological interventions typically target posttraumatic symptoms such as headaches, nausea, and sleep disturbances. For instance, medications such as amitriptyline and melatonin, have been shown to reduce the severity and frequency of posttraumatic headaches or sleep difficulties, respectively, in a subset of children presenting with persistent symptoms (Kuczynski, Crawford, Bodell, Dewey, & Barlow, 2013). Regarding emerging treatments, long-term clinical improvement has also been reported after the use of advanced brain stimulation techniques such as repetitive transcranial magnetic stimulation (Koski et al., 2015) and transcranial direct current stimulation

(Pinchuk, Pinchuk, Sirbiladze, & Shuhgar, 2013) to target posttraumatic symptoms after mild TBI. More research on the clinical effectiveness and feasibility of such treatments is needed.

Interventions in Moderate to Severe TBI. Persisting impairments after moderate to severe TBI often impact ability to return to work, school, and previous levels of functioning. Patients with moderate to severe TBI are much more likely than patients with mild injuries to require inpatient rehabilitation. Upon discharge from inpatient rehabilitation, many individuals with moderate to severe TBI still require some level of supervision within the home and often are not ready to return to work, school, or other previous levels of independent functioning. Many are referred for further outpatient rehabilitation treatments, including some combination of speech, occupational, and physical therapy.

Comprehensive-integrated postacute rehabilitation programs (often referred to as day-treatment programs) are designed to treat persons with TBI with cognitive and behavioral difficulties that may render them less likely to benefit from single-treatment (nonintegrated) outpatient therapies. Postacute rehabilitation programs should provide all aspects of rehabilitation treatment in an integrated format with health professionals from various disciplines creating collaborative goals related to the client's individual needs, such as work reentry, school reentry, or independence. There is evidence of improved functional outcome related to participation in such programs, including improvements in independent living, participation in household activities, productive activity, and vocational reentry, with further evidence of maintained gains up to 4 years postinjury (Sander, Roebuck, Struchen, Sherer, & High, 2001). There is also evidence that these programs result in improved functional outcome even for individuals more than a year postinjury (High, Roebuck-Spencer, Sander, Struchen, & Sherer, 2006).

In the months and years after moderate to severe injury, specific interventions can be useful in facilitating recovery and improving long-term outcome. Although evidence-based intervention programs are limited, a variety of intervention approaches have been implemented in research protocols (Bryck & Fisher, 2012). Direct approaches aim to retrain, stimulate, and improve cognitive and social difficulties. These approaches have also been referred to as "restitution training," defined as the direct attempt to restore underlying impaired function. Direct approaches tend to be most effective in cognitive domains such as attention and working memory (Mateer, Kerns, & Eso, 1996). Unfortunately, however, there is little evidence supporting the effectiveness or generalization of direct methods to daily functions (Park & Ingles, 2001).

In contrast, indirect approaches or "strategy training" are defined as development of strategies and use of practical tools to compensate for residual cognitive deficits, alleviate functional impairment, and improve psychological and behavioral difficulties. For instance, behavioral compensation or behavior modification strategies are used to teach individuals to perform various tasks using alternative or compensatory strategies and to train behaviors in ways to improve daily functioning and attain goal behavior. Similarly, modifying an individual's environment and offering support through external aids, adapted school/work materials and tasks, and task-specific partial assistance are often beneficial for promoting optimal levels of functioning in children and adults. Families and school personnel may collaborate to simplify tasks by allowing a child with TBI more time to complete tasks or by reducing noise or distractions. In vocational settings, adults with TBI can benefit from workload or workstation adaptations.

Reviews of the effectiveness of cognitive rehabilitation (Cicerone et al., 2011) show that cognitive linguistic therapies are effective for language-based impairments, compensatory visual scanning strategies are helpful for unilateral neglect, and self-management strategies improve attention in postacute periods of recovery. Remediation of memory impairments typically focuses on compensatory strategies and use of assistive technology. Individuals with relatively mild memory impairments and intact self-management abilities may benefit from internal compensatory strategies (such as visual imagery) and external strategies (such as memory logs or diaries). Those with moderate to severe memory problems may benefit from external memory aids, such as paging devices. Additionally, for those with severe injuries, errorless learning techniques have been shown to be beneficial for learning specific skills and knowledge, although there is limited transfer to novel tasks or reduction of overall functional memory problems. Effective remediation of executive functioning includes training of metacognitive (e.g., self-monitoring and self-regulation) and formal problem-solving strategies and their application to everyday situations and functional activities. Notably, these cognitive rehabilitation methods have been shown to be effective in postacute periods, years postinjury.

An evidence-based review of cognitive and behavioral intervention studies in children with acquired brain injury (Laatsch et al., 2007) has developed three evidence-based recommendations for treatment, and proposes that (1) comprehensive rehabilitation programs should consider involving family members as active treatment providers as part of the rehabilitation treatment plan, (2) the use of informational booklets in the acute phase of TBI rehabilitation is beneficial for children with mild TBI and should be integrated in more comprehensive approaches to treatment, and (3) rehabilitation programs should consider providing attention remediation to assist recovery because there is sufficient evidence to support the development of a practice guideline for this intervention in children with TBI. According to Laatsch et al. (2007), effective remediation and rehabilitation programs are also incumbent upon the development of psychometrically sound cognitive and behavioral assessment tools adapted for children and adolescents, as they will facilitate the measurement of functional gains postintervention. When investigating difficulties in the areas of executive functioning and attention, Sohlberg, Harn,

MacPherson, and Wade (2014) put forth an evidence-based cognitive intervention program, the Attention Intervention and Management program, with the goal of improving attention and reducing executive functioning difficulties in children with a history of TBI. Through an innovative combination of online home-based practice sessions and face-to-face clinical session, the authors used computerized attention tasks and instructions in metacognitive strategies that targeted the specific attention and executive function impairment profile of each child, which extended previous interventions. It was shown that children with TBI demonstrated significant improvement postintervention on a neuropsychological measure of attention, as well as on a parent report questionnaire of executive functioning, indicating that improvements in everyday life and cognitive functioning are possible with the Attention Intervention and Management program (Treble-Barna, Sohlberg, Harn, & Wade, 2016). Cognitive intervention programs such as those discussed in the preceding paragraphs are promising, but maintenance of gains achieved by these treatments needs further study, given evidence that initial improvements seen for some forms of cognitive rehabilitation, specifically memory training, are not seen at 6 months posttreatment (Milders, Deelman, & Berg, 1998).

Neurobehavioral and emotional changes after TBI are often the most challenging to treat and the most distressing to families and caregivers. For instance, by its very nature, poor self-awareness is resistant to treatment, given that individuals do not consistently acknowledge their own difficulties and do not realize when behavioral or compensatory strategies need to be employed. Interventions including feedback regarding performance, education about impairments, and implementation of self-performed prediction and goal-setting exercises have been explored in the literature. Awareness training interventions have been shown to improve performance on functional tasks and self-regulation (Cheng & Man, 2006; Goverover, Johnston, Toglia, & Deluca, 2007). One study demonstrated growth in awareness of injury-related changes after occupation-based, goal-directed rehabilitation efforts (Doig, Kuipers, Prescott, Cornwell, & Fleming, 2014). Studies of social communication skills training showed improved communication and improved overall life satisfaction for individuals with TBI (Dahlberg et al., 2007). Group-based supportive therapy has been found to be successful for improving coping skills and adjustment

after TBI (Anson & Ponsford, 2006). Vocational rehabilitation, and more specifically supported employment, has been shown to increase return to work rates and job stability in survivors of TBI (e.g., Wehman et al., 1991).

Pharmacological interventions after moderate to severe TBI typically target cognition, aggression, and affective disorders. A comprehensive literature review (Warden et al., 2006) did not find empirical support for standards of pharmacological treatment, but a number of guidelines were generated supporting the use of classes of medications for specific symptoms after TBI. The review indicated the use of stimulants for treatment of attention and speed of processing deficits, cholinesterase inhibitors for treatment of attention and memory function, and dopamine agonists for treatment of executive dysfunction. Aggression and agitation benefit from treatment with beta-blockers and benzodiazepines. Mood disorders may be treated with tricyclic antidepressants and serotonin reuptake inhibitors and atypical antipsychotics have been used to treat psychosis. Although pharmacological management of TBI-related symptoms is common, combining multiple approaches and tailoring them to an individual's strengths and weaknesses in an integrated comprehensive plan should be encouraged and studied in the years to come.

Implications for Clinical Practice

Clinical Implications for Adults and Children with Mild TBI

Early psychoeducation regarding expected symptoms, coping with and managing symptoms, expected recovery, risk factors for symptom exacerbation, and gradual reintegration to daily activities is beneficial and has been shown to improve outcome after mild TBI.

Neuropsychological screening, evaluation, and management of mild TBI should take certain factors into account:

- time since injury
- atypical recovery patterns
- comorbid medical and psychiatric factors
- history of previous concussions or brain injuries
- history of learning, attention, or mood disorders
- environmental factors
- potential sources of secondary gain.

Return-to-activity guidelines should be adapted based on persisting symptoms, concomitant emotional distress and psychosocial stressors, and should further take into account an individual's daily needs and strengths and weaknesses. Clinicians should stay abreast of and adapt into their clinical practice emerging empirical evidence regarding cognitive rest and introduction of therapeutic exercise into concussion management protocols.

Clinical Implications for Adults and Children with Moderate to Severe TBI

Comprehensive neuropsychological assessment should be used to establish the magnitude and pattern of persisting cognitive/neurobehavioral impairments, to document cognitive strengths and capabilities, to determine presence of impaired capacities and need for supervision in targeted areas (e.g., supervision of financial or medical decision-making), and to recommend tailored interventions and compensatory strategies.

Interventions should include direct or indirect approaches of cognitive rehabilitation and promotion of coping skills to assist with adjustment to and reintegration into previous roles/responsibilities. Family members, caregivers, and educators should be included in interventions and facilitation of strategy implementation.

Moderate to severe TBI significantly impacts an individual's daily functioning in multiple domains, including physical, behavioral, emotional, and cognitive spheres. The involvement of a multidisciplinary team is therefore fundamental during rehabilitation. Care providers from each discipline (e.g., physiotherapy, occupational therapy, speech/language pathology, neuropsychology, social work, educational consultation) can help identify specific impairments that will affect the individual's daily life and should collaborate to propose a more integrated plan for recovery.

Neuropsychologists are uniquely suited to assist multidisciplinary treatment teams with treatment planning of patients with moderate to severe TBI, given their understanding of brain–behavior relationships, the impact of cognitive and behavioral impairments on real-world functioning, and potential interactions between treatment goals and emotional, psychosocial, family, and environmental factors.

Future Directions

Research aimed at fine-tuning our understanding of TBI and its assessment, management, and evolution has gained substantial ground and momentum in the past decade. However, a need remains for compelling evidence-based guidelines for effective TBI diagnosis, intervention, and determination of long-term prognosis. TBI continues to represent a serious and increasing public health issue with direct and indirect costs estimated to be exceeding the billion dollar range in the United States alone. According to unsettling projections from the World Health Organization, TBI will become the second most common cause of death and disability in industrialized countries by 2020 (World Health Organization, 2006); a prediction that is likely to fuel TBI research and clinical practice change in the years to come.

High-quality research is needed to bridge persisting gaps in the current TBI literature. For example, TBI research methodology often presents with limitations associated with recruitment methods and potential sample bias, with participants being selected retrospectively from clinic-based samples or recruited from single sites as opposed to multicenter university and hospital centers. Furthermore, attrition over time can be a challenge, necessitating collection of detailed demographic information for individuals who drop out of studies to understand and prevent bias in sample selection (Sherer, Roebuck-Spencer, & Davis, 2010). The use of clinically relevant control groups is needed to facilitate interpretations of clinical assessment tools, predictors, treatment, and interventions as well as outcome measures (Mathias, Dennington, Bowden, & Bigler, 2013). Perhaps one of the most problematic methodological shortcomings of TBI studies is the lack of consensus in TBI definition, diagnostic and prognostic tools, and outcomes assessed, making it difficult to compare results and effects across studies. Parameters such as injury characteristics, diagnostic measures and outcome variables, and research designs are highly heterogeneous and account for the considerable variability of findings in TBI literature. Epidemiology studies are of great value and are essential to better understand causes, risk factors, and underlying mechanisms of TBI that can lead to better guidelines for prevention, assessment, and management of TBI. They can also facilitate the creation and implementation of preventive programs to appropriate populations and regions.

In terms of management and rehabilitation, the effectiveness of intervention programs for physical, cognitive, behavioral, and psychosocial symptoms after TBI often lack a strong evidence base. Evaluating the effects of an intervention is complex and must overcome obstacles such as accounting for the confound of spontaneous recovery, delivery of multiple interventions simultaneously, limited availability and use of appropriate and well-validated outcome measures, differing study methodologies, small sample sizes, and lack of information about maintenance of gains and generalization to novel tasks and situations. Multiple methods and models incorporating diverse comprehensive approaches to intervention should be integrated to determine the best outcome for the individual. Of note, many of these challenges are currently being addressed by multicenter, international, multidisciplinary task forces, consensus groups, and large-scale research endeavors, as exemplified by the TBI Model Systems (Hammond & Malec, 2010), NIH Common Data Elements workgroups (Hicks et al., 2013), the TRACK-TBI initiative (Yue et al., 2013), and by organizations such as the International Initiative for Traumatic Brain Injury Research (InTBIR). Such programs will support further collaborative research cutting across multiple domains and levels of analysis, with the hopes of establishing evidence-based diagnostic guidelines and interventions.

References

Albrecht, M. A., Masters, C. L., Ames, D., Foster, J. K., & Group, A. R. (2016). Impact of mild head injury on neuropsychological performance in healthy older adults: Longitudinal assessment in the AIBL cohort. *Frontiers in Aging Neuroscience*, 8, 105. doi:10.3389/fnagi.2016.00105

Anderson, V., Brown, S., Newitt, H., & Hoile, H. (2011). Long-term outcome from childhood traumatic brain injury: Intellectual ability, personality, and quality of life. *Neuropsychology*, 25(2), 176–184.

Anderson, V., Catroppa, C., Godfrey, C., & Rosenfeld, J. V. (2012). Intellectual ability 10 years after traumatic brain injury in infancy and childhood: What predicts outcome? *Journal of Neurotrauma*, 29(1), 143–153.

Anderson, V., Catroppa, C., Morse, S., Haritou, F., & Rosenfeld, J. V. (2009). Intellectual outcome from preschool traumatic brain injury: A 5-year prospective, longitudinal study. *Pediatrics*, 124(6), e1064–e1071.

Anson, K., & Ponsford, J. (2006). Evaluation of a coping skills group following traumatic brain injury. *Brain Injury*, 20(2), 167–178.

Barkhoudarian, G., Hovda, D. A., & Giza, C. C. (2011). The molecular pathophysiology of concussive brain injury. *Clinics in Sports Medicine*, 30(1), 33–48, vii–iii. doi:10.1016/j.csm.2010.09.001

Barr, R. G., Rivara, F. P., Barr, M., Cummings, P., Taylor, J., Lengua, L. J., & Meredith-Benitz, E. (2009). Effectiveness of educational materials designed to change knowledge and behaviors regarding crying and shaken-baby syndrome in mothers of newborns: A randomized, controlled trial. *Pediatrics*, 123(3), 972–980.

Bazarian, J. J., Cernak, I., Noble-Haeusslein, L., Potolicchio, S., & Temkin, N. (2009). Long-term neurologic outcomes after traumatic brain injury. *Journal of Head Trauma Rehabilitation*, 24(6), 439–451. doi:10.1097/HTR.0b013e3181c15600

Beauchamp, M. H., Catroppa, C., Godfrey, C., Morse, S., Rosenfeld, J. V., & Anderson, V. (2011). Selective changes in executive functioning ten years after severe childhood traumatic brain injury. *Developmental Neuropsychology*, 36(5), 578–595.

Beauchamp, M. H., Ditchfield, M., Maller, J. J., Catroppa, C., Godfrey, C., Rosenfeld, J. V., … Anderson, V. A. (2011). Hippocampus, amygdala and global brain changes 10 years after childhood traumatic brain injury. *International Journal of Developmental Neuroscience*, 29(2), 137–143.

Belanger, H. G., & Vanderploeg, R. D. (2005). The neuropsychological impact of sports-related concussion: A meta-analysis. *Journal of the International Neuropsychological Society*, 11(4), 345–357.

Belanger, H. G., Kretzmer, T., Yoash-Gantz, R., Pickett, T., & Tupler, L. A. (2009). Cognitive sequelae of blast-related versus other mechanisms of brain trauma. *Journal of the International Neuropsychological Society*, 15(01), 1–8.

Bernard, C. O., Ponsford, J. A., McKinlay, A., McKenzie, D., & Krieser, D. (2016). Predictors of post-concussive symptoms in young children: Injury versus non-injury related factors. *Journal of the International Neuropsychological Society*, 22(8), 793–803. doi:10.1017/S1355617716000709

Blennow, K., Hardy, J., & Zetterberg, H. (2012). The neuropathology and neurobiology of traumatic brain injury. *Neuron*, 76(5), 886–899. doi:10.1016/j.neuron.2012.11.021

Brooks, B. L., Khan, S., Daya, H., Mikrogianakis, A., & Barlow, K. M. (2014). Neurocognition in the emergency department after a mild traumatic brain injury in youth. *Journal of Neurotrauma*, 31(20), 1744–1749.

Bryant, R. A. (2001). Posttraumatic stress disorder and mild brain injury: Controversies, causes and consequences. *Journal of Clinical and Experimental Neuropsychology*, 23(6), 718–728.

Bryant, R. A., Marosszeky, J. E., Crooks, J., Baguley, I. J., & Gurka, J. A. (2001). Posttraumatic stress disorder and psychosocial functioning after severe traumatic brain injury. *Journal of Nervous and Mental Disease*, *189*(2), 109–113.

Bryck, R. L., & Fisher, P. A. (2012). Training the brain: Practical applications of neural plasticity from the intersection of cognitive neuroscience, developmental psychology, and prevention science. *American Psychologist*, *67*(2), 87–100.

Carroll, L. J., Cassidy, J. D., Holm, L., Kraus, J., Coronado, V. G., & Injury, W. H. O. C. C. T. F. o. M. T. B. (2004). Methodological issues and research recommendations for mild traumatic brain injury: the WHO Collaborating Centre Task Force on Mild Traumatic Brain Injury. *Journal of Rehabilitation Medicine* (43 Suppl), 113–125.

Carroll, L. J., Cassidy, J. D., Peloso, P. M., Borg, J., von Holst, H., Holm, L., ...Pepin, M. (2004). Prognosis for mild traumatic brain injury: Results of the WHO Collaborating Centre Task Force on Mild Traumatic Brain Injury. *Journal of Rehabilitation Medicine* (43 Suppl), 84–105.

Centers for Disease Control and Prevention. (2015). *Report to Congress on traumatic brain injury in the United States: Epidemiology and rehabilitation*. Atlanta, GA: Author.

Cheng, S. K., & Man, D. W. (2006). Management of impaired self-awareness in persons with traumatic brain injury. *Brain Injury*, *20*(6), 621–628.

Christensen, J., Pedersen, M. G., Pedersen, C. B., Sidenius, P., Olsen, J., & Vestergaard, M. (2009). Long-term risk of epilepsy after traumatic brain injury in children and young adults: A population-based cohort study. *The Lancet*, *373*(9669), 1105–1110.

Cicerone, K. D., Langenbahn, D. M., Braden, C., Malec, J. F., Kalmar, K., Fraas, M., ...Bergquist, T. (2011). Evidence-based cognitive rehabilitation: Updated review of the literature from 2003 through 2008. *Archives of Physical Medicine and Rehabilitation*, *92*(4), 519–530.

Cohen, R. A., Kaplan, R. F., Zuffante, P., Moser, D. J., Jenkins, M. A., Salloway, S., & Wilkinson, H. (1999). Alteration of intention and self-initiated action associated with bilateral anterior cingulotomy. *Journal of Neuropsychiatry and Clinical Neuroscience*, *11*(4), 444–453.

Corrigan, J. D., Bogner, J., & Holloman, C. (2012). Lifetime history of traumatic brain injury among persons with substance use disorders. *Brain Injury*, *26*(2), 139–150. doi:10.3109/02699052.2011.648705

Cuthbert, J. P., Harrison-Felix, C., Corrigan, J. D., Bell, J. M., Haarbauer-Krupa, J. K., & Miller, A. C. (2015). Unemployment in the United States after traumatic brain injury for working-age individuals: Prevalence and associated factors 2 years postinjury. *The Journal of Head Trauma Rehabilitation*, *30*(3), 160–174.

Dagher, J. H., Richard-Denis, A., Lamoureux, J., de Guise, E., & Feyz, M. (2013). Acute global outcome in patients with mild uncomplicated and complicated traumatic brain injury. *Brain Injury*, *27*(2), 189–199. doi:10.3109/02699052.2012.729288

Dahlberg, C. A., Cusick, C. P., Hawley, L. A., Newman, J. K., Morey, C. E., Harrison-Felix, C. L., & Whiteneck, G. G. (2007). Treatment efficacy of social communication skills training after traumatic brain injury: A randomized treatment and deferred treatment controlled trial. *Archives of Physical Medicine and Rehabilitation*, *88*(12), 1561–1573.

Dams-O'Connor, K., Gibbons, L. E., Bowen, J. D., McCurry, S. M., Larson, E. B., & Crane, P. K. (2013). Risk for late-life re-injury, dementia and death among individuals with traumatic brain injury: A population-based study. *Journal of Neurology, Neurosurgery and Psychiatry*, *84*(2), 177–182. doi:10.1136/jnnp-2012-303938

Defense and Veterans Brain Injury Center. (2016). DoD Numbers for traumatic brain injury worldwide — Totals. 2000–2016 (Q1-Q2) Retrieved December 8, 2016, from http://dvbic.dcoe.mil/files/tbi-numbers/DoD-TBI-Worldwide-Totals_2000-2016_Q1-Q2_Aug-12-2016_v1.0_508_2016-09-20.pdf

DeMatteo, C., Stazyk, K., Giglia, L., Mahoney, W., Singh, S. K., Hollenberg, R., ...McCauley, D. (2015). A balanced protocol for return to school for children and youth following concussive injury. *Clinical Pediatrics*, *54*(8), 783–792.

Dewan, M. C., Mummareddy, N., Wellons, J. C., 3rd, & Bonfield, C. M. (2016). Epidemiology of global pediatric traumatic brain injury: Qualitative review. *World Neurosurgery*, *91*, 497–509 e491. doi:10.1016/j.wneu.2016.03.045

DiFazio, M., Silverberg, N. D., Kirkwood, M. W., Bernier, R., & Iverson, G. L. (2016). Prolonged activity restriction after concussion: Are we worsening outcomes? *Clinical Pediatrics*, *55*(5), 443–451. doi:10.1177/0009922815589914

Dikmen, S., Machamer, J., & Temkin, N. (1993). Psychosocial outcome in patients with moderate to severe head injury: 2-year follow-up. *Brain Injury*, *7*(2), 113–124.

Dikmen, S., Machamer, J., Winn, R., & Temkin, N. R. (1995). Neuropsychological outcome at 1-year post head injury. *Neuropsychology*, *9*, 80–90.

Dikmen, S., Reitan, R. M., & Temkin, N. R. (1983). Neuropsychological recovery in head injury. *Archives of Neurology*, *40*(6), 333–338.

Dikmen, S., Temkin, N. R., Machamer, J. E., Holubkov, A. L., Fraser, R. T., & Winn, H. R. (1994). Employment following traumatic head injuries. *Archives of Neurology*, *51*(2), 177–186.

Doig, E., Kuipers, P., Prescott, S., Cornwell, P., & Fleming, J. (2014). Development of self-awareness after severe traumatic brain injury through participation in occupation-based rehabilitation: Mixed-methods analysis of a case series. *American Journal of Occupational Therapy*, *68*(5), 578–588.

Echemendia, R. J., & Cantu, R. C. (2003). Return to play following sports-related mild traumatic brain injury: The role for neuropsychology. *Applied Neuropsychology*, *10*(1), 48–55.

Ewing-Cobbs, L., Prasad, M. R., Kramer, L., Cox Jr, C.S., Baumgartner, J., Fletcher, S., ...Swank, P. (2006). Late intellectual and academic outcomes following traumatic brain injury sustained during early childhood. *Journal of Neurosurgery*, *105*(4 Suppl), 287–296.

French, L. M. (2010). Military traumatic brain injury: An examination of important differences. *Annals of the New York Academy of Sciences*, *1208*(1), 38–45.

Gardner, R., Burke, J., Nettiksimmons, J., Kaup, A., Barnes, D., & Yaffe, K. (2014). Dementia risk after traumatic brain injury vs nonbrain trauma: The role of age and severity. *JAMA Neurology*, *71*(12), 1490–1497.

Gennarelli, T. A., & Graham, D. I. (2005). Neuropathology. In J. M. Silver, T. W. McAllister, & S. C. Yudofsky (Eds.), *Textbook of traumatic brain injury* (pp. 27–50). Washington, DC: American Psychiatric Publishing, Inc.

Goverover, Y., Johnston, M. V., Toglia, J., & Deluca, J. (2007). Treatment to improve self-awareness in persons with acquired brain injury. *Brain Injury*, *21*(9), 913–923.

Grool, A. M., Aglipay, M., Momoli, F., Meehan, W. P., Freedman, S. B., Yeates, K. O., ...Zemek, R. (2016). Association between early participation in physical activity following acute concussion and persistent postconcussive symptoms in children and adolescents. *Journal of the American Medical Association*, *316*(23), 2504–2514.

Guskiewicz, K. M., McCrea, M., Marshall, S. W., Cantu, R. C., Randolph, C., Barr, W., ...Kelly, J. P. (2003). Cumulative effects associated with recurrent concussion in collegiate football players: The NCAA Concussion Study. *Journal of the American Medical Association*, *290*(19), 2549–2555. doi:10.1001/jama.290.19.2549

Hammond, F. M., & Malec, J. F. (2010). The Traumatic Brain Injury Model Systems: A longitudinal database, research, collaboration and knowledge translation. *European Journal of Physical and Rehabilitation Medicine*, *46*(4), 545–548.

Hanks, R. A., Millis, S. R., Ricker, J. H., Giacino, J. T., Nakese-Richardson, R., Frol, A. B., ...Gordon, W. A. (2008). The predictive validity of a brief inpatient neuropsychologic battery for persons with traumatic brain injury. *Archives of Physical Medicine and Rehabilitation*, *89*(5), 950–957.

Hessen, E., Anderson, V., & Nestvold, K. (2008). MMPI-2 profiles 23 years after paediatric mild traumatic brain injury. *Brain Injury*, *22*(1), 39–50.

Hessen, E., Nestvold, K., & Anderson, V. (2007). Neuropsychological function 23 years after mild traumatic brain injury: A comparison of outcome after paediatric and adult head injuries. *Brain Injury*, *21*(9), 963–979.

Hicks, R., Giacino, J., Harrison-Felix, C., Manley, G., Valadka, A., & Wilde, E. A. (2013). Progress in developing common data elements for traumatic brain injury research: Version two–the end of the beginning. *Journal of Neurotrauma*, *30*(22), 1852–1861.

High, W. M., Jr., Roebuck-Spencer, T., Sander, A. M., Struchen, M. A., & Sherer, M. (2006). Early versus later admission to postacute rehabilitation: Impact on functional outcome after traumatic brain injury. *Archives of Physical Medicine and Rehabilitation*, *87*(3), 334–342.

Himanen, L., Portin, R., Isoniemi, H., Helenius, H., Kurki, T., & Tenovuo, O. (2006). Longitudinal cognitive changes in traumatic brain injury: A 30-year follow-up study. *Neurology*, *24*(66 (2)), 187–192. doi: 10.1212/01.wnl.0000194264.60150.d3

Hoge, C. W., McGurk, D., Thomas, J. L., Cox, A. L., Engel, C. C., & Castro, C. A. (2008). Mild traumatic brain injury in US soldiers returning from Iraq. *New England Journal of Medicine*, *358*(5), 453–463.

Hoofien, D., Gilboa, A., Vakil, E., & Donovick, P. J. (2001). Traumatic brain injury (TBI) 10-20 years later: A comprehensive outcome study of psychiatric symptomatology, cognitive abilities and psychosocial functioning. *Brain Injury*, *15*(3), 189–209.

Hunter, J. V., Wilde, E. A., Tong, K. A., & Holshouser, B. A. (2012). Emerging imaging tools for use with traumatic brain injury research. *Journal of Neurotrauma*, *29*(4), 654–671.

Institute of Medicine. (2009). *Gulf War and health, Volume 7: Long-term consequences of traumatic brain injury*. Washington, DC: The National Academies Press.

Iverson, G. L. (2006). Complicated vs uncomplicated mild traumatic brain injury: Acute neuropsychological outcome. *Brain Injury*, *20*(13-14), 1335–1344.

Johnson, V. E., Stewart, W., & Smith, D. H. (2010). Traumatic brain injury and amyloid-beta pathology: A link to Alzheimer's disease? *Nature Review Neurosciences*, *11*(5), 361–370. doi:10.1038/nrn2808

Kenny, D. T., & Lennings, C. J. (2007). The relationship between head injury and violent offending in juvenile detainees. *BOCSAR NSW Crime and Justice Bulletins*, *107*, 1–15.

Kersel, D. A., Marsh, N. V., Havill, J. H., & Sleigh, J. W. (2001). Psychosocial functioning during the year following severe traumatic brain injury. *Brain Injury*, *15*(8), 683–696. doi:10.1080/02699050010013662

Kim, E., Lauterbach, E. C., Reeve, A., Arciniegas, D. B., Coburn, K. L., Mendez, M. F., ...Coffey, E. C. (2007). Neuropsychiatric complications of traumatic brain injury: A critical review of the literature (a report by the ANPA Committee on Research). *Journal Neuropsychiatry and Clinical Neurosciences*, *19*(2), 106–127.

Koski, L., Kolivakis, T., Yu, C., Chen, J.-K., Delaney, S., & Ptito, A. (2015). Noninvasive brain stimulation for persistent postconcussion symptoms in mild traumatic brain injury. *Journal of Neurotrauma*, *32*(1), 38–44.

Kuczynski, A., Crawford, S., Bodell, L., Dewey, D., & Barlow, K. M. (2013). Characteristics of post-traumatic headaches in children following mild traumatic brain injury and their response to treatment: A prospective cohort. *Developmental Medicine & Child Neurology*, *55*(7), 636–641.

Laatsch, L., Harrington, D., Hotz, G., Marcantuono, J., Mozzoni, M. P., Walsh, V., & Hersey, K. P. (2007). An evidence-based review of cognitive and behavioral rehabilitation treatment studies in children with acquired brain injury. *The Journal of Head Trauma Rehabilitation*, *22*(4), 248–256.

Langlois, J. A., Rutland-Brown, W., & Thomas, K. E. (2006). *Traumatic brain injury in the United States: Emergency department visits, hospitalizations, and deaths*. Atlanta, GA: Centers for Disease Control and Prevention, National Center for Injury Prevention and Control.

Langlois, J. A., Rutland-Brown, W., & Wald, M. M. (2006). The epidemiology and impact of traumatic brain injury: a brief overview. *Journal of Head Trauma Rehabilitation*, *21*(5), 375–378.

Levin, H. S., Shum, D., & Chan, R. C. K. (2014). *Understanding traumatic brain injury: Current research and future directions*. New York, NY: Oxford University Press.

Lingsma, H. F., Yue, J. K., Maas, A. I. R., Steyerberg, E. W., Manley, G. T., Cooper, S. R., ...Mukherjee, P. (2015). Outcome prediction after mild and complicated mild traumatic brain injury: External validation of existing models and identification of new predictors using the TRACK-TBI pilot study. *Journal of Neurotrauma*, *32*(2), 83–94.

Liss, M., & Willer, B. (1990). Traumatic brain injury and marital relationships: A literature review. *International Journal of Rehabilitation Research*, *13*(4), 309–320.

Luis, C. A., & Mittenberg, W. (2002). Mood and anxiety disorders following pediatric traumatic brain injury: A prospective study. *Journal of clinical and experimental neuropsychology*, *24*(3), 270–279.

Macpherson, A., & Spinks, A. (2008). Bicycle helmet legislation for the uptake of helmet use and prevention of head injuries (review). *Cochrane Database of Systematic Reviews*, *2*, 1–15.

Maestas, K. L., Sander, A. M., Clark, A. N., van Veldhoven, L. M., Struchen, M. A., Sherer, M., & Hannay, H. J. (2013). Preinjury coping, emotional functioning, and quality of life following uncomplicated and complicated mild traumatic brain injury. *Journal of Head Trauma Rehabilitation*. doi:10.1097/HTR.0b013e31828654b4

Magnuson, J., Leonessa, F., & Ling, G. S. F. (2012). Neuropathology of explosive blast traumatic brain injury.

Current Neurology and Neuroscience Reports, *12*(5), 570–579.

Marr, A., & Coronado, V. (Eds.). (2004). *Central nervous system injury surveillance data submission standards-2002*. Atlanta, GA: Centers for Disease Control and Prevention, National Center for Injury Prevention and Control.

Marshall, S., Bayley, M., McCullagh, S., Velikonja, D., & Berrigan, L. (2012). Clinical practice guidelines for mild traumatic brain injury and persistent symptoms. *Canadian Family Physician*, *58*(3), 257–267.

Masten, S. V., Foss, R. D., & Marshall, S. W. (2011). Graduated driver licensing and fatal crashes involving 16- to 19-year-old drivers. *JAMA*, *306*(10), 1098–1103. doi:10.1001/jama.2011.1277

Mateer, C. A., Kerns, K. A., & Eso, K. L. (1996). Management of attention and memory disorders following traumatic brain injury. *Journal of Learning Disabilities*, *29*(6), 618–632.

Mathias, J. L., Dennington, V., Bowden, S. C., & Bigler, E. D. (2013). Community versus orthopaedic controls in traumatic brain injury research: How comparable are they? *Brain Injury*, *27*(7–8), 887–895.

Max, J. E., Keatley, E., Wilde, E. A., Bigler, E. D., Levin, H. S., Schachar, R. J., ...Dennis, M. (2011). Anxiety disorders in children and adolescents in the first six months after traumatic brain injury. *The Journal of Neuropsychiatry and Clinical Neurosciences*, *23*(1), 29–39.

McCrea, M. (2008). *Mild traumatic brain injury and postconcussion syndrome: The new evidence base for diagnosis and treatment*. New York: Oxford University Press.

McCrea, M., Barr, W. B., Guskiewicz, K., Randolph, C., Marshall, S. W., Cantu, R., ...Kelly, J. P. (2005). Standard regression-based methods for measuring recovery after sport-related concussion. *Journal of the International Neuropsychological Society*, *11*(1), 58–69.

McCrea, M., Guskiewicz, K., Randolph, C., Barr, W. B., Hammeke, T. A., Marshall, S. W., ...Kelly, J. P. (2013). Incidence, clinical course, and predictors of prolonged recovery time following sport-related concussion in high school and college athletes. *Journal of the International Neuropsychological Society*, *19*(1), 22–33. doi:10.1017/S1355617712000872

McCrea, M., Guskiewicz, K. M., Marshall, S. W., Barr, W., Randolph, C., Cantu, R. C., ...Kelly, J. P. (2003). Acute effects and recovery time following concussion in collegiate football players: The NCAA Concussion Study. *Journal of the American Medical Association*, *290*(19), 2556–2563.

McCrory, P., Meeuwisse, W. H., Aubry, M., Cantu, B., Dvořák, J., Echemendia, R. J., ...Raftery, M. (2013). Consensus statement on concussion in sport: The 4th International Conference on Concussion in Sport held in Zurich, November 2012. *British Journal of Sports Medicine*, *47*(5), 250–258.

McKee, A. C., Cantu, R. C., Nowinski, C. J., Hedley-Whyte, E. T., Gavett, B. E., Budson, A. E., ...Stern, R. A. (2009). Chronic traumatic encephalopathy in athletes: Progressive tauopathy after repetitive head injury. *Journal of Neuropathology & Experimental Neurology*, *68*(7), 709–735. doi:10.1097/NEN.0b013e3181a9d503

McKee, A. C., Stein, T. D., Nowinski, C. J., Stern, R. A., Daneshvar, D. H., Alvarez, V. E., ...Cantu, R. C. (2013). The spectrum of disease in chronic traumatic encephalopathy. *Brain*, *136*(Pt 1), 43–64. doi:10.1093/brain/aws307

McKinlay, A., Grace, R., Horwood, L., Fergusson, D., Ridder, E. M., & MacFarlane, M. (2008). Prevalence of traumatic brain injury among children, adolescents and young adults: Prospective evidence from a birth cohort. *Brain Injury*, *22*(2), 175–181.

McKinlay, A., Grace, R. C., Horwood, L. J., Fergusson, D. M., & MacFarlane, M. R. M. e. a., 2010. (2010). Long-term behavioural outcomes of pre-school mild traumatic brain injury. *Child: Care, Health and Development*, *36*(1), 22–30.

Middleton, F. A., & Strick, P. L. (2000). Basal ganglia and cerebellar loops: Motor and cognitive circuits. *Brain Research. Brain Research Reviews*, *31*(2-3), 236–250.

Milders, M., Deelman, B., & Berg, I. (1998). Rehabilitation of memory for people's names. *Memory*, *6*(1), 21–36.

Miller, L. J., & Donders, J. (2003). Prediction of educational outcome after pediatric traumatic brain injury. *Rehabilitation Psychology*, *48*(4), 237–241.

Millis, S. R., Rosenthal, M., Novack, T. A., Sherer, M., Nick, T. G., Kreutzer, J. S., ...Ricker, J. H. (2001). Long-term neuropsychological outcome after traumatic brain injury. *Journal of Head Trauma Rehabilitation*, *16*(4), 343–355.

Mittenberg, W., Canyock, E. M., Condit, D., & Patton, C. (2001). Treatment of post-concussion syndrome following mild head injury. *Journal of Clinical and Experimental Neuropsychology*, *23*(6), 829–836.

Moser, R. S., Iverson, G. L., Echemendia, R. J., Lovell, M. R., Schatz, P., Webbe, F. M., ...Broshek, D. K. (2007). Neuropsychological evaluation in the diagnosis and management of sports-related concussion. *Archives of Clinical Neuropsychology*, *22*(8), 909–916.

Moser, R. S., Schatz, P., Glenn, M., Kollias, K. E., & Iverson, G. L. (2015). Examining prescribed rest as treatment for adolescents who are slow to recover from concussion. *Brain Injury*, *29*(1), 58–63. doi:10.3109/02699052.2014.964771

Nordström, P., Michaëlsson, K., Gustafson, Y., & Nordström, A. (2014). Traumatic brain injury and young onset dementia: A nationwide cohort study. *Annals of neurology*, *75*(3), 374–381.

Paniak, C., Toller-Lobe, G., Reynolds, S., Melnyk, A., & Nagy, J. (2000). A randomized trial of two treatments for mild traumatic brain injury: 1 year follow-up. *Brain Injury*, *14*(3), 219–226.

Park, N. W., & Ingles, J. L. (2001). Effectiveness of attention rehabilitation after an acquired brain injury: A meta-analysis. *Neuropsychology*, *15*(2), 199–210.

Pastorek, N. J., Hannay, H. J., & Contant, C. S. (2004). Prediction of global outcome with acute neuropsychological testing following closed-head injury. *Journal of the International Neuropsychological Society*, *10*(6), 807–817.

Pinchuk, D., Pinchuk, O., Sirbiladze, K., & Shuhgar, O. (2013). Clinical effectiveness of primary and secondary headache treatment by transcranial direct current stimulation. *Frontiers in Neurology*, *4*(25), 1–7.

Ponsford, J., Willmott, C., Rothwell, A., Cameron, P., Ayton, G., Nelms, R., ...Ng, K. T. (1999). Cognitive and behavioral outcome following mild traumatic head injury in children. *The Journal of Head Trauma Rehabilitation*, *14*(4), 360–372.

Randolph, C., McCrea, M., & Barr, W. B. (2005). Is neuropsychological testing useful in the management of sport-related concussion? *Journal of Athletic Training*, *40*(3), 139–152.

Riley, G. A. (2007). Stress and depression in family carers following traumatic brain injury: The influence of beliefs about difficult behaviours. *Clinical Rehabilitation*, *21*(1), 82–88.

Rockswold, G. L., Leonard, P. R., & Nagib, M. G. (1987). Analysis of management in thirty-three closed head injury patients who "talked and deteriorated." *Neurosurgery*, *21*(1), 51–55.

Rogers, J. M., & Read, C. A. (2007). Psychiatric comorbidity following traumatic brain injury. *Brain Injury*, *21*(13-14), 1321–1333.

Rosema, S., Muscara, F., Anderson, V., Godfrey, C., Eren, S., & Catroppa, C. (2014). Young adults' perspectives on their psychosocial outcomes 16 years following childhood traumatic brain injury. *Social Care and Neurodisability*, *5*(3), 135–144.

Ryan, N. P., Hughes, N., Godfrey, C., Rosema, S., Catroppa, C., & Anderson, V. A. (2015). Prevalence and predictors of externalizing behavior in young adult survivors of pediatric traumatic brain injury. *The Journal of Head Trauma Rehabilitation*, *30*(2), 75–85.

Sander, A. M., Roebuck, T. M., Struchen, M. A., Sherer, M., & High, W. M., Jr. (2001). Long-term maintenance of gains obtained in postacute rehabilitation by persons with traumatic brain injury. *Journal of Head Trauma Rehabilitation*, *16*(4), 1–19.

Sauber-Schatz, E. K., Thomas, A. M., & Cook, L. J. (2015). Motor vehicle crashes, medical outcomes, and hospital charges among children aged 1-12 years-Crash Outcome Data Evaluation System, 11 states, 2005-2008. *MMWR: Surveillance Summaries*, *64*(8), 1–32.

Saunders, L. L., Selassie, A. W., Hill, E. G., Nicholas, J. S., Horner, M. D., Corrigan, J. D., & Lackland, D. T. (2009). A population-based study of repetitive traumatic brain injury among persons with traumatic brain injury. *Brain Injury, 23*(11), 866–872. doi:10.1080/02699050903283213

Sawyer, Q., Vesci, B., & McLeod, T. C. (2016). Physical activity and intermittent postconcussion symptoms after a period of symptom-limited physical and cognitive rest. *Journal of Athletic Training, 51*(9), 739–742. doi:10.4085/1062-6050-51.12.01

Sawyer, R. J., Hamdallah, M., White, D., Pruzan, M., Mitchko, J., & Huitric, M. (2010). High school coaches' assessments, intentions to use, and use of a concussion prevention toolkit: Centers for Disease Control and Prevention's Heads Up: Concussion in high school sports. *Health Promotion Practice, 11*(1), 34–43.

Schretlen, D. J., & Shapiro, A. M. (2003). A quantitative review of the effects of traumatic brain injury on cognitive functioning. *International Review of Psychiatry, 15*(4), 341–349. doi:10.1080/09540260310001606728

Segev, S., Shorer, M., Rassovsky, Y., Pilowsky Peleg, T., Apter, A., & Fennig, S. (2016). The contribution of posttraumatic stress disorder and mild traumatic brain injury to persistent post concussive symptoms following motor vehicle accidents. *Neuropsychology, 30*(7), 800–810.

Sherer, M., Hart, T., Whyte, J., Nick, T. G., & Yablon, S. A. (2005). Neuroanatomic basis of impaired self-awareness after traumatic brain injury: Findings from early computed tomography. *The Journal of Head Trauma Rehabilitation, 20*(4), 287–300.

Sherer, M., Roebuck-Spencer, T., & Davis, L. C. (2010). Outcome assessment in traumatic brain injury clinical trials and prognostic studies. *The Journal of Head Trauma Rehabilitation, 25*(2), 92–98.

Sohlberg, M. M., Harn, B., MacPherson, H., & Wade, S. L. (2014). A pilot study evaluating attention and strategy training following pediatric traumatic brain injury. *Clinical Practice in Pediatric Psychology, 2*(3), 263–280.

Tanielian, T., & Jaycox, L. H. (Eds.) (2008). *Invisible wounds of war : Psychological and cognitive injuries, their consequences, and services to assist recovery.* Santa Monica, CA: RAND.

Treble-Barna, A., Sohlberg, M. M., Harn, B. E., & Wade, S. L. (2016). Cognitive intervention for attention and executive function impairments in children with traumatic brain injury: A pilot study. *The Journal of Head Trauma Rehabilitation, 31*(6), 407–418.

van Veldhoven, L. M., Sander, A. M., Struchen, M. A., Sherer, M., Clark, A. N., Hudnall, G. E., & Hannay, H. J. (2011). Predictive ability of preinjury stressful life events and post-traumatic stress symptoms for outcomes following mild traumatic brain injury: Analysis in a prospective emergency room sample. *Journal of Neurology, Neurosurgery and Psychiatry, 82*(7), 782–787. doi:10.1136/jnnp.2010.228254

Wade, S. L., Cassedy, A., Walz, N. C., Taylor, H. G., Stancin, T., & Yeates, K. O. (2011). The relationship of parental warm responsiveness and negativity to emerging behavior problems following traumatic brain injury in young children. *Developmental Psychology, 47*(1), 119–133.

Waldron-Perrine, B., Tree, H., Spencer, R., Suhr, J., & Bieliauskas, L. (2015). Informational literature influences symptom expression following mild head injury: An analog study. *Brain Injury, 29*(9), 1051–1055. doi:10.3109/02699052.2015.1004742

Warden, D. L., Gordon, B., McAllister, T. W., Silver, J. M., Barth, J. T., Bruns, J., …Zitnay, G. (2006). Guidelines for the pharmacologic treatment of neurobehavioral sequelae of traumatic brain injury. *Journal of Neurotrauma, 23*(10), 1468–1501.

Wehman, P. H., Revell, W. G., Kregel, J., Kreutzer, J. S., Callahan, M., & Banks, P. D. (1991). Supported employment: An alternative model for vocational rehabilitation of persons with severe neurologic, psychiatric, or physical disability. *Archives of Physical Medicine and Rehabilitation, 72*(2), 101–105.

Williams, M. W., Rapport, L. J., Hanks, R. A., Millis, S. R., & Greene, H. A. (2013). Incremental validity of neuropsychological evaluations to computed tomography in predicting long-term outcomes after traumatic brain injury. *Clinical Neuropsychologist, 27*(3), 356–375. doi:10.1080/13854046.2013.765507

World Health Organization. (2006). *Neurological disorders: Public health challenges:* Geneva: Author.

Yeates, K. O. (2010). Mild traumatic brain injury and postconcussive symptoms in children and adolescents. *Journal of the International Neuropsychological Society, 16*(6), 953–960. doi:10.1017/S1355617710000986

Yeates, K. O., Taylor, H. G., Wade, S. L., Drotar, D., Stancin, T., & Minich, N. (2002). A prospective study of short- and long-term neuropsychological outcomes after traumatic brain injury in children. *Neuropsychology, 16*(4), 514–523.

Yeates, K. O., Taylor, H. G., Walz, N. C., Stancin, T., & Wade, S. L. (2010). The family environment as a moderator of psychosocial outcomes following traumatic brain injury in young children. *Neuropsychology, 24*(3), 345–356.

Yue, J. K., Vassar, M. J., Lingsma, H. F., Cooper, S. R., Okonkwo, D. O., Valadka, A. B., …Yuh, E. L. (2013). Transforming research and clinical knowledge in traumatic brain injury pilot: multicenter implementation of the common data elements for traumatic brain injury. *Journal of Neurotrauma, 30*(22), 1831–1844.

Yuh, E. L., Cooper, S. R., Mukherjee, P., Yue, J. K., Lingsma, H. F., Gordon, W. A., …Vassar, M. J. (2014). Diffusion tensor imaging for outcome prediction in mild traumatic brain injury: A TRACK-TBI study. *Journal of Neurotrauma, 31*(17), 1457–1477.

Zemek, R., Barrowman, N., Freedman, S. B., Gravel, J., Gagnon, I., McGahern, C., ... for the Pediatric Emergency Research Canada (PERC) Concussion Team. (2016). Clinical risk score for persistent postconcussion symptoms among children with acute concussion in the ED. *JAMA*, *315*(10), 1014–1025. doi:10.1001/jama.2016.1203

Zemek, R., Grool, A. M., Rodriguez Duque, D., DeMatteo, C., Rothman, L., Benchimol, E. I., ... Macpherson, A. K. (2016). Annual and seasonal trends in ambulatory visits for pediatric concussion in Ontario between 2003 and 2013. *Journal of Pediatrics.* doi:10.1016/j.jpeds.2016.10.067

Cancer

Iris Paltin, Darcy E. Burgers, Marsha Gragert, and Chad Noggle

Introduction

Cancer involves a number of diseases characterized by abnormal cell division and proliferation. Benign tumors (neoplasms) are not cancerous; they are abnormal tissue growths that do not invade other structures. The greatest risk associated with benign neoplasms is their location, because they may impact vital structures and vessels. Malignant neoplasms are cancerous and can spread to other parts of the body. Malignant neoplasms are divided into low grade and high grade. The three broad groups of cancer include central nervous system (CNS) tumors, liquid tumors, and non-CNS solid tumors.

CNS tumors involve the brain and spinal cord. Children generally develop primary CNS tumors, which arise directly from the brain and spinal cord. Adults often develop CNS tumors via the metastatic process of cancerous cells being carried through the blood to the nervous system from another primary site, such as the lungs. CNS tumors are further classified by location and type. CNS tumor locality can be divided into (1) the skull, (2) the meninges, (3) the cranial nerves, (4) the supporting tissue, (5) the pituitary or pineal body, (6) congenital origin, and (7) supratentorial versus infratentorial. Brain tumor types are gliomas, meningiomas, schwannomas, pituitary adenomas, primary CNS lymphoma, and metastatic tumors. Gliomas are further divided into astrocytomas, ependymomas, glioblastomas, medulloblastomas, and oligodendrogliomas. Although the histology of gliomas is the same between children and adults, the incidence of tumor types and location is radically different.

Liquid tumors are cancers that involve the blood and lymphatic systems, and include leukemia and lymphoma. Leukemia is a cancer that causes abnormal blood cell production. Abnormal production of lymphoid white blood cells is called lymphocytic leukemia, and abnormal myeloid white blood cell production is called myelogenous leukemia. The four primary types of leukemia include acute lymphocytic leukemia (ALL), chronic lymphocytic leukemia, acute myeloid leukemia, and chronic myeloid leukemia. The two most prevalent forms of lymphoma, which is cancer of the lymphocytes of the immune system, are Hodgkin lymphoma and non-Hodgkin lymphoma.

Solid tumors within the adult population most frequently include carcinomas (tumors of the skin, organs, and glands such as lung, breast, and prostate, along with colorectal cancers) and sarcomas (tumors of the bone, muscle, fat, and connective tissue). Solid tumors within the pediatric population most frequently include neuroblastoma, Wilms tumor (kidneys), rhabdomyosarcoma (soft tissues such as muscle), osteosarcoma (bone), and retinoblastoma (eye). As is detailed in the Epidemiology and Pathophysiology section, the prevalence of cancer types is dramatically different in pediatric versus adult populations.

Epidemiology and Pathophysiology

In 2016, more than 1.6 million new cases of cancer were diagnosed in the United States, and more than 15,000 of these involved children and adolescents (US Cancer Statistics Working Group, 2016). Currently, the most common adult cancers are breast cancer, lung and bronchus cancer, prostate cancer, colon and rectum cancer, bladder cancer, melanoma of the skin, non-Hodgkin lymphoma, thyroid cancer, kidney and renal pelvis cancer, leukemia, endometrial cancer, and pancreatic cancer. With respect to pediatric cancers, ALL is the most common, accounting for approximately 20% of all cancers, followed by CNS tumors (18%), Hodgkin disease (8%), non-Hodgkin lymphoma (7%), acute myeloid leukemia (5%), neuroblastoma (5%), bone tumors, and other cancers each accounting for 3% or less (American Cancer Society, 2014).

Sixty percent of children who survive cancers (of all diagnoses) experience late effects, such as infertility, heart failure, secondary cancers, and neuropsychological sequelae. Chemotherapy-related cognitive dysfunction is reported in 15–70% of adult patients (Bender et al., 2006), with approximately 30% of patients reporting long-term residual chemotherapy-associated deficits (Ferguson & Ahles, 2003). Neurocognitive difficulties can be transient during treatment or can also be longer lasting, with late-emerging and long-term cognitive deficits (termed "late effects") particularly prevalent in childhood cancer survivors. Increased survival rates achieved through development of more effective cancer treatments have led to increased attention to such late effects. At the same time, disparities in pediatric cancer survival exist, with African American children and those from the West and South of the United States demonstrating higher mortality rates (Lindley & Oyana, 2016). Higher mortality rates have also been reported in African American adults and those from lower socioeconomic strata (O'Keefe, Meltzer, & Bethea, 2015).

Disease and Treatment Factors Impacting Functioning

The neuropsychological late effects of pediatric cancer that extend into adolescence and adulthood, as well as the neurocognitive impact of cancer when diagnosed in adulthood, are associated with location, treatment- and nontreatment-related factors. Brain tumors and ALL are the most studied conditions with respect to neuropsychological late effects due to the direct impact of disease and treatment on the CNS.

Location results in variability of neuropsychological presentation and outcome. Brain tumors carry the potential for virtually any neurological or neuropsychological sign. Prediagnosis symptoms result from regional infiltration of the tumor, mass effect, and increased intracranial pressure caused by tumor growth and blockage of the flow of cerebrospinal fluid through the ventricles. In some cases the tumor presses upon or destroys parts of the brain, gradually increasing effects as the tumor grows. Consequently, common symptoms of intracranial tumors include headaches, especially after lying flat, increased by coughing or stooping; vomiting, which usually occurs at the peak of the headache; diplopia; blurred vision when moving the head; slowing of the pulse; increased

drowsiness, which progresses to coma; dilation of the pupils, which fail to react to light; and papilledema. Convulsive seizures, focal or generalized, occur with cerebral hemisphere tumors and may precede other symptoms by months or years. Treatment-related factors including surgical interventions, chemotherapies, and cranial radiotherapy (CRT), contribute to neuropsychological sequelae.

Surgical interventions for CNS tumors include biopsy, resection, and procedures to address associated neurologic complications (e.g., shunt placements and revisions, ventriculostomy). It is important to note that the contribution of postsurgical cerebellar mutism to neuropsychological outcomes has likely been underappreciated in the existing literature, although increased emotional lability, ataxia, and hypotonia, as well as protracted cognitive, academic, and psychosocial impacts, are described.

Research evaluating cancer-related cognitive impairment (CRCI) in the adult population has more traditionally focused on neurotoxicity associated with chemotherapy, a phenomenon often referred to as "chemobrain." These CRCIs include problems in attention, concentration, memory, and executive functioning and they have has also been documented in the absence of chemotherapy, leading to hypothesized associations with cancer itself (Debess, Riis, Pedersen, & Ewertz, 2009), surgery (Chen, Miaskowski, Liu, & Chen, 2012), and other adjuvant therapies (Schilder et al., 2010). Longitudinal studies evaluating neuropsychological outcomes in patients with cancer suggest that up to 30% of patients experience CRCIs before any treatment (Janelsins et al., 2011). Up to 75% of patients experience CRCI during active treatment and up to 35% experience CRCI months or years after completion of treatments for cancer (Janelsins et al., 2011). As noted by Wefel, Kesler, Noll, and Schagen (2015), the pattern of CRCI differs across patients and disease course, and severity typically qualifies as mild to moderate (i.e., performances that are from −1.5 to −2 SDs below population normative means). CRCI also varies in domains affected; may be subtle or dramatic, temporary or permanent, stable or progressive; can onset acutely or in a latent fashion; and can resolve quickly or persist for 20 years posttreatment (Ahles, Root, & Ryan, 2012; Koppelmans et al., 2012). These cognitive symptom are associated with fatigue, depression, and perceived health status (Li, Yu,

Long, Li, & Cao, 2015; Vardy et al., 2014) and are negatively related to job performance, work ability, productivity, and sustainable work (Munir, Burrows, Yarker, Kalawsky, & Bains, 2010; Von, Habermann, Carpenter, & Schnieder, 2013).

Chemotherapy in adults has in one way or another been associated with mild reductions in cognitive functioning compared with controls across most cognitive domains. However, the most common pattern of cognitive deficits associated with chemotherapy suggests preferential dysfunction of frontal subcortical networks, including changes in working memory, executive functions, and processing speed (Janelsins, Kesler, Ahles, & Morrow, 2014).

Certain factors have been associated with increased risk of chemotherapy-induced neurotoxicity. These include but are not limited to (1) additive or synergistic effects of multimodality therapy that includes administration of chemotherapy either concurrently with or subsequent to CRT, (2) additive or synergistic effects of multiagent chemotherapy, (3) exposure to higher dosing due to either planned use of high-dose regimens or higher concentrations of the parent drug and/or its metabolite secondary to disrupted systemic clearance and/or pharmacogenetic modulation of drug pharmacokinetics, (4) intraarterial administration with blood–brain barrier disruption, and (5) intrathecal administration (Noggle & Dean, 2013; Sul & DeAngelis, 2006; Taphoorn & Klein, 2004). In the case of chemotherapy, these deficits arise through both direct and indirect neurotoxic routes. The latter includes those cognitive issues that arise from physiological states such fatigue, anemia, and metabolic abnormalities.

The literature to date has demonstrated both structural and functional changes in the brain in relation to chemotherapy. Cross-sectional studies indicate that adult patients treated with previous chemotherapy have more gray matter and white matter volume loss than controls, reduced white matter integrity, and altered brain activation (Janelsins et al., 2014). Findings of reduced overall gray matter volume appear to be most pronounced in the prefrontal lobe; however, reduced temporal (e.g., thalamus, hippocampus, parahippocampal region), parietal and occipital (e.g., precuneus), and cerebellar cortical volume have also been found via magnetic resonance imaging (MRI) techniques (McDonald, Conroy, Ahles, West, & Saykin, 2010). Decreased white matter integrity and diffusivity have also been noted in widespread brain

regions using diffusion tensor imaging (de Ruiter et al., 2012; Deprez et al., 2011).

Although chemotherapy is generally believed to be less toxic than CRT within pediatric cohorts, the addition of chemotherapy with CRT may confer declines in cognition (e.g., learning and memory) beyond those associated with CRT alone (Di Pinto, Conklin, Li, & Merchant, 2012). With respect to non-CNS cancers, the strongest evidence for adverse neuropsychological effects of chemotherapy alone has been documented in survivors of ALL who receive intrathecal and high-dose intravenous methotrexate for standard-risk disease (Hearps et al., 2016). However, studies have also documented adverse neuropsychological effects of corticosteroids (Mrakotsky et al., 2011), and the inclusion of vincristine and platinum-based agents is associated with peripheral neuropathy and ototoxicity, respectively, which can increase risk for cognitive and academic difficulties during survivorship.

Hematopoietic stem cell transplant (HSCT) is another treatment-related risk factor that has received empirical attention in the pediatric cancer outcome literature. There is mixed evidence of its contribution to cognitive outcomes above and beyond that conferred by other known risk factors (Willard, Leung, Huang, Zhang, & Phipps, 2014), but the evidence generally suggests a relatively benign outcome. There are physiological and psychological demands of HSCT that have potential to affect health-related quality of life. Evidence does support an early effect on health-related quality of life after HSCT, but the longer term outcomes are not well studied and likely vary based upon a host of methodological (e.g., instrumentation) as well as child-related (e.g., age, gender) and family-based (parent emotional distress) risk factors.

In cases of HCST within the adult population, Friedman and colleagues (2009) revealed that there is a high rate of cognitive impairment (39%) before HSCT. Approximately one-quarter of the sample participated in serial evaluations, with a subset of patients demonstrating worsening cognitive performance up to 28 weeks after HSCT. Cognitive decline was not accounted for by either baseline or concurrent measures of quality of life, depression, or anxiety but lower education and older age were predictive of baseline impairment (Friedman et al., 2009). In another study, Jones and colleagues (2013) found that 47% of their sample exhibited cognitive impairment postinduction. Impairment continued to be high over time: nearly 49% of patients at 1 month and 48% at 3 months post-HSCT exhibited deficits on one or more measures. Learning/memory showed the greatest vulnerability to impairment at all three time points. Executive function showed greater vulnerability at the pre-HSCT time point, motor function at 1 month post-HSCT, and psychomotor speed at 3 months post-HSCT.

The evidence for neuropsychological impact of surgery, chemotherapy, and HSCT notwithstanding, CRT has been associated with the greatest risks, although much variance in outcomes remains unaccounted for in the existing literature. In pediatric cancer, long-term neuropsychological effects related to CRT appear to be mitigated by CRT dose, volume, and type. Younger age at treatment and increased time since treatment are risk factors for adverse neuropsychological sequelae (de Ruiter, van Mourik, Schouten-van Meeteren, Grootenhuis, & Oosterlaan, 2013; Palmer et al., 2013). See Tables 9.1 and 9.2 for additional information regarding radiation's impact on structural and functional aspects of cognitive functioning including attention, working memory, verbal fluency, processing speed, memory, and vocational abilities.

Other factors that may moderate neuropsychological outcomes include CNS tumor histology and location, neurologic/medical complications (e.g., hydrocephalus, seizures, endocrine dysfunction), child-specific factors (e.g., higher baseline cognitive functioning, female gender), and family factors (e.g., lower socioeconomic status [SES], higher parent stress) (Kullgren, Morris, Morris, & Krawiecki, 2003; Palmer et al., 2013; Reddick et al., 2014).

Effects on the microglial and microvasculature environments, neurogenesis, neuroinflammatory responses, and apoptosis constitute potential underlying mechanisms in the pathophysiology of CRT-induced neuropsychological sequelae. These effects can culminate in cortical and subcortical white matter changes, which have received the most attention in the literature (Mabbott, Noseworthy, Bouffet, Rockel, & Laughlin, 2006), with increased treatment intensity associated with reduced white matter volumes (Reddick et al., 2014). Direct correlations between normal-appearing white matter and neurocognitive outcomes, including IQ, math, and verbal working memory, have also been reported (Jacola et al., 2014; Mabbott et al., 2006).

Adults who receive radiation therapy also experience neurocognitive deficits and structural changes on imaging. In the case of both neurocognitive functioning and structural changes, a dose-dependent pattern is also observed in adults, with total dose and dose per fraction influencing the severity of outcomes. Adjuvant chemotherapy also increases the burden on patients. Effects can be minimized, however, by keeping the radiation dosing below 2 GY per fraction. Even when taking these factors into consideration, acute and chronic impairments are commonly reported, with some deficits (e.g., attention, memory, information processing, executive functioning, and motor coordination) developing in a latent fashion, over the course of a few weeks, to months, to even years after treatment (Habets et al., 2016). Functionally, within the adult population, memory has demonstrated particular susceptibility to the effects of CRT.

In addition to CRT and chemotherapy, endocrine/hormonal therapy has also been associated with neurocognitive deficits. Such treatments include the use of estrogen deprivation treatment within the breast cancer population and testosterone deprivation within the prostate cancer population. In the case of prostate cancer, testosterone has been linked with the development and growth of the disease. As a result, androgen deprivation therapy (ADT) has proven effective in treating prostate cancer, particularly in cases postradiation. Although the antineoplastic benefits of ADT are unquestionable, the treatment has been associated with cognitive deficits and even psychiatric manifestation for which anxiety and depression are the most commonly reported. Research evaluating the cognitive effects of androgen deprivation in patients with prostate cancer has produced mixed results, with some studies showing no effect (Joly et al., 2006), others demonstrating impaired function (Jenkins, Bloomfield, Shilling, & Edginton, 2005), and a mixed effect with patients showing an improved performance on some tests and a deterioration on others (Salminen et al., 2003). Functional MRI showed that compared with participants who did not receive ADT, patients with prostate cancer undergoing ADT did not differ in cognitive performance, but they showed altered prefrontal cortical activation during cognitive control (Chao et al., 2012). Chao and colleagues (2013) observed a decrease in gray matter volumes in frontal and prefrontal cortical structures associated with the use of ADT. The decrease in gray matter volume of the

Table 9.1 Clinical Manifestations of Cancer and Neuroanatomical Correlates

Neuropsychological Domain	Clinical Manifestation	Neuroanatomical Correlates and Moderating Factors

Intellectual functioning	• Lower global, verbal, and visuospatial intellectual abilities[1,2,3,4,5,6,7]	• Associated with
		  • reduced temporal-occipital connectivity[6]
		  • increased activation of the left inferior frontal gyrus[6]
		  • NOS3 894 T homozygosity[5]
		• [a]Reduced white matter volume[1,46]

Attention and executive functions	• Reduced attention and processing speed on performance-based and parent/teacher report and slower reaction time[1,8,13,18,19]
	• [a]Reduced attention[14]
	• [a]Working memory deficits[5,10,11,13,17]
	• [a]Reduced attention, verbal fluency, and motor speed[5]
		• Attention deficits associated with:
		  • Leukoencephalopathy and reduced caudate volume[6]
		  • [a]White matter changes
		• Working memory deficits associated with
		  • leukoencephalopathy[6,31]
		  • increased activation in left superior/middle frontal gyri and left parietal lobe[6,12]
		  • decreased BOLD signal in bilateral frontal regions
		  • greater BOLD signal in left cingulate regions[15]
		  • increased dorsolateral prefrontal cortex and anterior cingulate cortex activation during working memory tasks[3,4,16,15]
		  • COMT gene[5]
		  • [a]increased RT dose more impactful than brain metastases[43]
		  • [a]dysfunction of frontal subcortical networks[47]
		• Disrupted folate pathways of MTHFR 1298AC/CC[5]
		• Worse executive function associated with microbleeds[25]
		• [a]COMT enzyme Val158 Met variant associated with weaker performance[5]
		• [a]Genetic polymorphisms of inflammation, DNA repair and metabolism pathways[20]

Processing speed and motor skills	• Lower processing speed and motor abilities compared to estimated IQ[1,2,3,17,18,19,28,22,23,24] • [a]Reduced motor and psychomotor speed[44]	• [a]Genetic polymorphisms of inflammation, DNA repair, and metabolism pathways[20] • [a]Decrease in gray matter volume of primary motor cortex[51]

Memory	• Verbal and visual memory impairments[4,14,21,26,28]
	• [a]Verbal and visual memory impairments[4,14,21,26,28,43,45,]
		• Weaker verbal memory associated with
		  • reduced amygdala and caudate volume[6]
		  • increased activation in left inferior frontal gyrus[6]
		  • smaller right hippocampus[27]

Table 9.1 (cont.)

Neuropsychological Domain	Clinical Manifestation	Neuroanatomical Correlates and Moderating Factors
		• [a]cortical hypometabolism on PET and MRI, when compared with scans in women not taking tamoxifen[52]
		• Weaker visual memory associated with
		• abnormal and inefficient activation and deactivation of the anterior rostral medial prefrontal cortex and thalamus[28]
		• [a]Apo E genotype[5]
		• [a]Significant decline in neurogenesis in the subgranular zone[53]
		• [a]Increased hippocampal dose associated with reduced memory[45]
Academic and vocational functioning	• Poorer performance on reading, spelling, and math tasks[1,4] • Reduced job performance, productivity, and sustainable work[48,49]	• Reading deficits may be associated with reduced white matter volume[29,30,31]
Behavioral, adaptive, and psychosocial functioning, and fatigue	• Mixed findings; some support for higher internalizing and externalizing symptoms[31,32] • Increased risk for PTSD symptoms and suicidal ideation[33,34] • Increased anxiety, depression, global distress[35,38] • Reduced adaptive skills[36] • Reduced educational/vocational attainment[37] • Increased social problems[39,40] • [a]Increased depression and anxiety[50] • [a]Fatigue is the most common reported symptom among adults[42]	• Lower SES associated with reduced adaptive functioning and increased behavioral symptoms[41] • Homozygosity of the GSTM1 null genotype[5] • [a]Androgen deprivation therapy associated with decreased gray matter volume in frontal and prefrontal cortical structures[54]

Note: BOLD = blood-oxygen-level dependent, PET = positron emission tomography, PTSD = posttraumatic stress disorder.
[a] Denotes finding in adults.

[1] Reddick et al., 2014; [2] de Ruiter et al., 2013; [3] Iyer et al., 2015; [4] Peterson et al., 2008; [5] Wefel et al., 2016; [6] Hearps et al., 2016; [7] Mabbott et al., 2006; [8] Moyer et al., 2012; [9] Gurney et al., 2009; [10] Palmer et al., 2013; [11] Knight et al., 2014; [12] King et al., 2015; [13] Kayl et al., 2006; [14] Pusztai et al., 2014; [15] Robinson et al., 2014; [16] Campbell et al., 2007; [17] Hiniker et al., 2014; [18] Kanellopoulous et al., 2016; [19] Wolfe et al., 2012; [20] Liu et al., 2015; [21] Robinson et al., 2010; [22] Kahalley et al., 2013; [23] Palmer et al., 2013; [24] Annett et al., 2015; [25] Roddy et al., 2016 [26] Nagel et al., 2006; [27] Riggs et al., 2014; [28] Ozyurt et al., 2014; [29] Palmer et al., 2010; [30] Fouladi et al., 2004; [31] Jacola et al., 2014; [32] Buizer et al., 2006; [33] Brinkman et al., 2013; [34] Kazak et al., 2004; [35] Brackett et al., 2012; [36] Papazoglou et al., 2008; [37] Gurney et al., 2009; [38] Respini et al., 2003; [39] Willard et al., 2014; [40] Wolfe et al., 2013; [41] Robinson et al., 2015; [42] Hayes et al., 2013; [43] Chang et al., 2009; [44] Jones et al., 2002; [45] Gondi et al., 2012; [46] Mabbott et al., 2006; [47] Janelsins et al., 2014; [48] Munir et al., 2010; [49] Von et al., 2013; [50] Li et al., 2015; [51] Chao et al., 2013; [52] Eberling et al., 2004; [53] Monje et al., 2002); [54] Chao et al., 2013.

primary motor cortex correlated with increased response time on an N-back task, suggesting processing insufficiency.

Tamoxifen is a selective estrogen receptor modulator that is commonly used in the breast cancer population. Although tamoxifen can reduce recurrence and mortality, it has been linked with neurocognitive deficits and complaints. In comparison studies between groups of patients treated with chemotherapy and those treated with hormonal

Table 9.2 Implications of Cancer-Related Neuropsychological Conditions for Clinical Practice

Developmental Period	Assessment	Intervention
Childhood	• Clinical surveillance and consultation with medical team regarding patient risk factors and potential evaluation • Neuropsychological screening of at-risk patients (e.g., standardized self-/family report measures, computerized assessments) • Targeted or comprehensive neuropsychological assessment, including performance-based assessment and self, family, and teacher reports on functioning to identify late effects and provide specific home, community and school recommendations • Psychosocial screening and support for at-risk patients and families	• Pharmacologic interventions (e.g., methylphenidate) may improve attention, behavior, and social skills • Neurocognitive intervention involving acetylcholinesterase inhibitors may attenuate cognitive late effects • Utilization of school liaison programming to increase knowledge about the survivor's medical condition • Cognitive remediation programming • Social skills training • Encourage exercise • Implement family-based cognitive interventions, including maternal problem-solving intervention • Link to social work and resource supports
Adolescence/ Young Adulthood	• Assessment and planning for transition readiness • Consideration of other risk factors that may impact likelihood of assessing follow-up care • Assessment and monitoring of anxiety and depression symptoms	• Provide education about importance of lifelong medical surveillance • Individual therapy to address issues of mood and identity • Link to social work and resource supports • Telehealth opportunities
Adulthood	• Baseline and sequential assessment to monitor disease status • Comprehensive neuropsychological evaluations to identify late effects of treatment • Distress thermometer screening tool to assess psychosocial stressors	• Individual and/or family therapy • Utilization of support groups • Structured exercise programs and dietary plans • Complementary services (e.g., yoga, meditation) • Pharmacological intervention to address pain, sleep, fatigue, appetite, cognition, and mood • Telehealth opportunities

therapies, both groups show declines compared with healthy controls suggesting that hormone therapies can also lead to CRCI (Ahles et al., 2012). Research has also demonstrated that combined treatment of tamoxifen and chemotherapy leads to greater difficulties than chemotherapy alone (Palmer, Trotter, Joy, & Carlson, 2008). One prospective study found deterioration in verbal memory and executive function in postmenopausal patients taking tamoxifen for at least a year compared with healthy controls; those taking the aromatase inhibitor, exemestane, did not have significant deficits compared with controls

(Schilder et al., 2010). This research also showed that women with breast cancer taking tamoxifen demonstrated widespread cortical hypometabolism on positron emission tomographic and MRI scans, when compared with scans of women not taking tamoxifen (Eberling, Wu, Tong-Turnbeaugh, & Jagust, 2004).

Beyond the neurotoxic effects of primary cancer therapy, the use of supportive medications (e.g., steroids, immunosuppressive agents, anticonvulsants) has also been tied to alterations in cognitive function. Glucocorticoids, certain anticonvulsants (topiramate, phenobarbital), and analgesics used for pain control can all correspond with cognitive complaints and deficits.

Regarding nontreatment factors, there are broader social factors that impact outcomes. SES is an identified moderator of neurocognitive outcome after pediatric ALL treatment, with SES associated with behavioral functioning 3–4 years after brain tumor diagnosis (Kullgren et al., 2003). For pediatric brain tumor survivors, among other variables, lower family income and lower parental education are associated with increased behavioral symptoms and reduced aspects of adaptive functioning (Robinson et al., 2015). Similar findings have been noted in adults. Minority ethnic groups and those of low SES are less likely to pursue recommended cancer screenings (e.g., colorectal cancer screening, mammogram) and to receive cancer-reducing vaccinations (e.g., human papillomavirus vaccination), all factors that, in the end, also contribute to higher cancer mortality rates (O'Keefe et al., 2015).

Prevention

Attempts to prevent or minimize neuropsychological sequelae for pediatric patients with cancer have largely focused on reducing treatment-related neurotoxicity. CRT has been eliminated from treatment protocols for patients with standard-risk ALL. With respect to pediatric brain tumor (PBT) treatment, efforts have focused on limiting the dose and volume of CRT, or on delaying CRT, to avoid the increased neurocognitive risk associated with younger age at treatment. Reduced craniospinal radiotherapy (RT) doses have been shown to be associated with attenuated yet significant cognitive and academic decline (Ris et al., 2013). Other RT techniques (hyperfractionation) and chemoprotectants have been utilized to effectively increase the CRT dose delivered to the tumor without increasing the associated toxicity. Conformal CRT techniques reduce the volume of brain tissue exposed to radiotherapy. These techniques do not entirely prevent healthy tissue surrounding the target from being exposed to entrance and exit radiation doses, and significant neuropsychological sequelae continue to be documented, although attenuation of impairment has been reported in some PBT studies.

Recently, proton beam RT (PBRT) has replaced conventional photon radiation in PBT treatment protocols at specialized treatment centers because it involves a lower entrance dose and no exit dose and is thus considered to hold promise for reducing treatment-related neurocognitive sequelae. Although over the past decade PBRT availability for pediatric patients has become much more widespread, the number of patients who would be considered long-term survivors at risk for late effects remains small. Most available studies directly examining the cognitive risks associated with PBRT are hampered by methodological limitations, including small sample sizes and/or lack of control group. These studies document outcomes ranging from no declines in Full Scale IQ to declines that are attenuated relative to those documented after conventional RT, although with similar moderating factors (i.e., increased risk for decline with young age and higher baseline performance) (Pulsifer et al., 2015; Yock et al., 2016). The one available study to date to directly compare the cognitive effects of conventional RT and PBRT also failed to provide clear evidence of cognitive sparing after PBRT because significant IQ decline was found in the conventional RT group but not the PBRT group, yet the IQ slopes over time did not differ between the two groups (Kahalley et al., 2016).

Pharmacological prevention techniques, particularly those aimed at reversing treatment effects on the microglial and microvasculature environments, neurogenesis, chronic inflammation, and apoptosis, may also hold promise based upon animal models. Lastly, engagement in physical exercise has well-documented physical and emotional benefits that are important for pediatric cancer survivors, who as a group are at risk for cardiac and pulmonary late effects as well as socioemotional difficulties. Given preliminary findings of a relationship between cardiorespiratory fitness and executive functioning in survivors of PBT, exercise may prove promising in attenuating cognitive late effects (Wolfe et al., 2013). Exercise could also counteract the pathophysiological effects of RT because of its ability to increase growth hormone and reduce inflammation. Rodent studies have shown that exercise can ameliorate RT-induced deficits in both neurogenesis and cognition. However, the evidence in the pediatric oncology literature is limited in that it primarily relies on descriptive, pilot studies rather than randomized trials. Within that context, there is preliminary evidence that exercise-based interventions, typically conducted during cancer treatment, are generally without adverse effects and positively affect physical fitness and health-related quality of life outcomes in pediatric oncology (primarily ALL) sample groups. Cognitive and motor skill outcomes have not received empirical attention. Adult oncology studies have also documented that exercise has a positive impact on physical outcomes (i.e., fatigue, fitness, and strength) and quality of life (Mishra, Scherer, Snyder, Geigle, & Gotay, 2016).

Within the adult population, cancer prevention includes limiting risk factors. This includes not using tobacco products, eating a healthy diet, maintaining a low body mass index, engaging in regular exercise, limiting exposure to ultraviolet light, and avoiding environmental carcinogens. At the same time, regular screenings for certain cancer types are important. Although such screenings do not prevent cancer, they increase the likelihood of early identification, which is often associated with treatment at a lower grade and stage, which, itself, has been associated with improved mortality and morbidity. Such screenings include mammograms for women, prostate exams for men, and colonoscopies for both men and women. These medical examinations are in addition to self-exams that are encouraged: women checking regularly for lumps in their breast and men checking for lumps or nodules in their testicles.

Clinical Manifestations

The reader is directed to Table 9.1 for additional information and references describing structural and functional associations of neuropsychological abilities within the oncology population. This includes attention and executive functions, processing speed, motor abilities, memory, social-emotional and adaptive functioning, and academic and vocational abilities.

Neuropsychological Functioning Among Pediatric Patients with Cancer

The late effects of pediatric cancer and treatment affect global intellect, executive functions, attention, processing speed, memory, motor skills, academic achievement, and behavioral and psychosocial functioning (Palmer, 2008).

Intellectual Functioning. Compared with the normative population, multiple meta-analyses highlight that survivors of PBT (treated by a variety of modalities) demonstrate lower global, verbal, and visuospatial intellectual abilities, especially if treated before the age of 7 years (Reddick et al., 2014; de Ruiter et al., 2013). Patients with ALL who received total body

irradiation plus cranial boost (average 25 Gy) before HSCT demonstrated average cognitive abilities approximately 5 years after treatment completion, although processing speed and working memory were relatively impaired (Hiniker et al., 2014).

Meta-analytic findings demonstrated that youth with ALL treated with chemotherapy only (including intrathecal methotrexate) had significantly lower verbal, performance, and Full Scale IQ scores relative to control groups (Iyer, Balsamo, Bracken, & Kadan-Lottick, 2015; Peterson et al., 2008). A systematic review of imaging studies revealed that ALL survivors treated with chemotherapy only demonstrated reduced attention, working memory, verbal memory, visual memory and IQ, which was associated with leukoencephalopathy; reduced amygdala, hippocampal, and caudate volumes; and increased activation of the left inferior frontal gyrus and reduced connectivity between the temporal and occipital lobes (Hearps et al., 2016).

Attention, Working Memory, and Executive Functions. Survivors of PBT and ALL demonstrated worse attention on performance and parent and teacher report measures, including slower reaction time (de Ruiter et al., 2013; Moyer et al., 2012; Reddick et al., 2014). Among survivors of ALL and PBT, parent-reported attention problems contributed to social functioning difficulties (Moyer et al., 2012), suggesting that neuropsychological deficits can also affect other realms of functioning and adjustment posttreatment. Despite preserved IQ, ALL survivors treated exclusively with chemotherapy and survivors of posterior fossa tumors demonstrated deficits in processing speed, executive functions, and working memory compared with peers (Kanellopoulous et al., 2016; Wolfe, Madan-Swain, & Kana, 2012). Less efficient working memory is a consistent finding among survivors of PBT and ALL and is one of the more studied areas of neuroanatomical underpinnings (Iyer et al., 2015; Palmer et al., 2013).

Processing Speed and Motor Skills. Survivors of ALL and PBT demonstrated significantly slower processing speed and motor abilities compared with their estimated IQ, with contributing factors including high-risk disease, craniospinal irradiation, male gender, younger age at diagnosis, and increased time since diagnosis (Annett, Patel, & Phipps, 2015; Iyer et al., 2015; Palmer et al., 2013).

Memory. Children treated for medulloblastoma (necessitating CRT) and those treated for ALL treated with chemotherapy only demonstrated verbal memory impairments (Peterson et al., 2008). Survivors of craniopharyngioma revealed abnormal and inefficient activation and deactivation of the anterior rostral medial prefrontal cortex and thalamus when asked to recognize neutral and emotional faces (Ozyurt et al., 2014).

Academic Functioning. Compared with controls, survivors of PBT and ALL treated with chemotherapy only performed significantly worse on reading, spelling, and math tasks (Peterson et al., 2008; Reddick et al., 2014), with visual-spatial and visual and verbal short-term memory abilities predicting performance (Moore et al., 2016). Reading deficit in survivors of PBT who received CRT has been associated with reduced white matter volume, particularly in the areas of the pons, internal capsule, and occipital and temporal lobes (Palmer et al., 2010). In a cohort of children who received allogenic HSCT (diagnoses including ALL, acute myeloid leukemia, and nonmalignant hematological disorders), weaknesses in processing speed and memory accounted for significant variance in mathematics and reading abilities (Lajiness-O'Neill et al., 2015). However, approximately 12 years after a cohort of patients with ALL who received total body irradiation before HSCT, a majority had attended 2- or 4-year degree programs (Hiniker et al., 2014).

Another likely underidentified risk group is children with non-CNS solid tumors. Specifically, approximately one-third of children with Wilms tumor diagnosed before the age of 6 years reported academic difficulties, including failed grades, weakness on neuropsychological evaluation, and utilization of formal individualized education plans (Mohrmann, Henry, Hauff, & Hayashi, 2015).

Inclusion of academic functioning measures should be considered not only for children and adolescents, but also young adults exploring postsecondary education (e.g., vocational, college, or graduate education) who may require academic supports, resources, and intervention.

Emotional, Behavioral, and Psychosocial Functioning

There are mixed findings regarding emotional functioning of pediatric patients with cancer. Those treated for ALL have higher parent-reported internalizing and externalizing symptoms and teacher-reported levels of externalizing symptoms (Buizer, de Sonneville, van den Heuvel-Eibrink, & Veerman, 2006). Survivors of PBT are at risk for increased posttraumatic stress symptoms (Kazak et al., 2004) and report higher levels of suicidal thoughts compared with the general population (Brinkman et al., 2013). PBT survivors also experience increased social difficulties, which may be associated with cognitive difficulties, including executive function weakness (Willard et al., 2014; Wolfe et al., 2013). For survivors of cerebellar tumors, attention span predicted communication skills, whereas verbal memory predicted socialization skills among youth with third-ventricle tumors (Papazoglou, King, Morris, & Krawiecki, 2008). No indications of emotional or behavioral difficulties were noted among children with a history of Wilms tumor (Buizer et al., 2006). Adolescent cancer survivors may be particularly at risk for adjustment difficulties given the typical stressors of this developmental period in addition to the late effects emerging at this time. Specifically, social and academic pressures may make coping with changes in physical appearance and academic abilities particularly difficult.

Longitudinal Outcomes. Longer term consequences of pediatric cancer to consider include educational achievement, employment, financial independence, relationships, and independent living. Almost one-quarter of participants in the Childhood Cancer Survivor Study Cohort reported a history of receiving special education services, with survivors at greatest risk of using services if diagnosed at age 5 years or younger; diagnosed with brain tumor, leukemia, or Hodgkin disease; or if treated with intrathecal chemotherapy and/or CRT (Gurney et al., 2009). Survivors of pediatric cancer are also at risk for not completing secondary and postsecondary education or having full-time employment, with survivors of brain tumors least likely to complete college (Gurney et al., 2009).

Relationships in adulthood are also affected by pediatric cancer. Adult survivors of pediatric cancer are less likely to be married, participate in social activities, and live independently, particularly if they experience physical limitations associated with diagnosis and treatment (Gurney et al., 2009), with an increased risk of never having married among leukemia survivors and female patients treated with CRT (Gurney et al., 2009). Taken together, longer term educational, employment, and social outcomes of adult survivors of childhood cancer emphasize the effect of diagnosis and treatment across the transition from childhood to adulthood. Such outcomes are important to consider among the adult survivor population.

Genetics. Emerging evidence suggests the importance of genetic moderators of neuropsychological outcome. Genome wide association studies looking at single nucleotide polymorphisms (SNPs) in pediatric cancer survivors may help to identify patients at increased risk for poor neurocognitive outcomes. This is of particular importance because children have developing CNSs, and are especially vulnerable to treatment-associated effects on cognition. Primary focus has been on evaluating SNPs of genes already believed to directly affect neural repair such as the ApoE ε4 allele, which is associated with an increased risk of late-onset Alzheimer disease (Wefel, Noll, & Scheurer, 2016). A study looking at 109 adult survivors of childhood medulloblastoma using their healthy siblings as controls identified association of homozygosity of the GSTM1 null genotype with increased anxiety, depression, and global distress (Brackett et al., 2012). The *COMT* gene involved in the neurotransmitter pathway has also been associated with decreased verbal working memory in a cross-sectional analysis of survivors of childhood ependymoma and craniopharyngioma (Wefel et al., 2016). Analysis of survivors of non-CNS cancers has also implicated genes associated with neurocognitive function. Children with leukemia with nitric oxide synthase 3 894 T homozygosity who are treated with CRT may be more susceptible to intellectual functioning decline (Wefel et al., 2016). Survivors of pediatric leukemia with disrupted folate pathways of MTHFR 1298AC/CC genotypes may be at greater risk for executive dysfunction (Wefel et al., 2016). In summary, genome wide association-based studies have identified specific genotypes of interest that might associate with decreased neuropsychological outcomes in pediatric cancer survivors.

Neuropsychological Functioning Among Adult Patients with Cancer

In cases when cancer first develops in adulthood, cognitive deficits are common complaints of survivors. Interestingly, as suggested previously, cognitive deficits have been noted across all phases of care, including pretreatment, active treatment, and posttreatment phases with attention, processing speed, executive functioning, and memory constituting the most common difficulties at all time points. Yet such deficits are often not fully appreciated because commonly employed screening measures such as the Mini-Mental State Examination lack the sensitivity to detect these residuals. As a result, a comprehensive, standardized neuropsychological approach, while being mindful of fatigue, is recommended. This approach also has the benefit of addressing individual variability, particularly for those with direct CNS involvement, Inclusion of subjective report measures is also critical because patients may report greater impairments in everyday functioning than is revealed on objective assessment. Self-report measures pertaining to everyday executive functioning, fatigue, and pain are highly recommended. Fatigue is particularly important to assess via self-report given its direct influence on emotional, physical, and cognitive well-being. Such measures may include the fatigue scales of the Patient-Reported Outcomes Measurement Information System, the Fatigue Questionnaire, Fatigue Severity Scale, or Multidimensional Assessment of Fatigue Scale.

The neurological and neuropsychological impairment resulting from metastatic lesions are similar to those arising from primary brain tumors. In many instances, cognitive features are seen later, as unrecognized tumors continue to grow. Interestingly, subtle changes in cognition can predict recurrence and/or tumor growth before the tumor is recognized on imaging. Still, data suggests that non-specific neurocognitive deficits are present in upwards of 90% of patients (Tucha, Smely, Preier, & Lange, 2000). Approximately 91% of patients with primary brain tumors will present with at least one area of cognitive dysfunction at baseline and roughly 70% will present with at least three areas of dysfunction (Tucha et al., 2000). The frequency of cognitive deficits emphasizes the role of neuropsychological assessment in the care of patients. In fact, neuropsychological assessment in some ways is more powerful then neuroimaging. Meyers and Hess (2003) performed a baseline neuropsychological assessment on 80 patients with recurrent glioblastoma or anaplastic astrocytoma before beginning a clinical trial for recurrence. They found that 61% of patients demonstrated measurable neurocognitive change on assessment before imaging modalities, demonstrating significant change. This has been noted in low-grade and high-grade gliomas as well as brain metastases (Meyers et al., 2004).

Genetics. Investigation of the ApoE ε4 allele in a large cohort of adults with brain tumors revealed an association of the Apo E genotype with neurocognitive performance, specifically in learning, memory, and executive function (Wefel et al., 2016). Other SNPs have been implicated in neurocognitive outcomes. For example, the catechol-O-methyltransferase (COMT) enzyme Val158 Met variant has been associated with weaker performance on measures of attention, verbal fluency, and motor speed in chemotherapy-treated breast cancer survivors. Those adults with brain tumors with specific DNA repair pathway genes may have weaker processing speed and executive functions. In adults with high-grade glioma, decreased neurocognitive function in the areas of processing speed and executive functions has been associated with genetic polymorphisms of inflammation, DNA repair, and metabolism pathways (Liu et al., 2015). The limitation of these studies to date has been heterogeneity in tumor histopathology, different treatment modalities, and lack of prospective longitudinal cohort study design.

Role of Assessment

As described in earlier sections, pediatric assessment allows for monitoring of changing neurocognitive abilities over the course of development; allows planning for home, school, and community supports; and informs the research literature about the extent of neurotoxicity of different treatment modalities (e.g., intrathecal chemotherapy, steroid use, photon vs. proton radiation). Assessment can include evaluation near to diagnosis, and repeated evaluations during treatment and in the years after treatment completion. Within adult settings, practitioners must be mindful of the timing of assessment in conjunction with the intended purpose. In the research setting, with most studies focusing on either the impact of the disease itself or the treatment, pretreatment assessment is always critical. Depending on the additional research interests, further assessments may be utilized. This could involve assessment during treatment, immediately after the completion of active therapy, and at key time points following treatment. This may even include assessments out to 1 year or more after treatment, given that latency effects have been reported. Again, given the potential impact of factors such as fatigue and sleep disturbance, mood, medicinal changes and, anemia, these factors should be examined at the same time as the various assessments to offer some control over their potential confounding effects.

When the purpose of the assessment is purely clinical, pretreatment assessment may still be strongly warranted, and it depends on the specifics of the case. Neuropsychological assessment has proven effective in monitoring disease status. Consequently, this form of clinical tracking relies critically on baseline assessment. When assessment is carried out during treatment, just as in research, professionals should be mindful of fatigue, mood, medicinal changes, anemia, and other factors because they may have a direct influence on performance.

Intervention in a Pediatric Population

Pharmacologic interventions are the most extensively studied of the interventions available for survivors of CNS-involved pediatric cancers, and methylphenidate has been the primary focus of this literature to date. The published studies have generated predominantly from two independent, randomized, double-blind, placebo-controlled trials and document positive, short-term outcomes on direct measures of attention and parent/teacher ratings of behavior at intervals up to 3 weeks after medication initiation (Conklin, Helton, et al., 2010). Two nonrandomized studies have since collectively demonstrated that improvements are maintained at 12 months, with specific evidence of improvement on direct measures of attention, parent ratings of social skills and behavioral problems, and parent, teacher, and self-report (adolescent subsample) ratings of attention (Conklin, Reddick et al., 2010; Netson et al., 2011).

Neurocognitive intervention involving acetylcholinesterase inhibitors (Donepezil, Sunitinib) have been the focus of various studies. Overall, these studies have provided initial evidence that these agents may improve cognition, health-related quality of life, and mood in adults with cancer (Castellino et al., 2012; Shaw et al., 2006). In comparison, studies evaluating the effectiveness of other psychoactive medications (i.e., antidepressants, anticonvulsants, CNS stimulants, and neuroleptic medications) are not readily available in the literature even though their use in the cancer population does appear to be on the rise (Brinkman et al., 2013).

Beyond pharmacological interventions, various cognitive and educational interventions have been adopted in the clinical care of survivors of pediatric cancer. Two sets of published guidelines, including one by the Children's Oncology Group, recommend neuropsychological evaluation after completion of treatment or upon entry into long-term follow-up at 2 years posttreatment, and follow-up evaluations as clinically indicated thereafter (Annett et al., 2015; Noll et al., 2013). However, empirical studies documenting the efficacy of neuropsychological evaluation in pediatric cancer are limited. Anderson, Godber, Smibert, Weiskop, and Ekert (2000) reported improved reading and spelling skills in survivors of ALL between initial neuropsychological evaluation at 2 years posttreatment and a follow-up evaluation 3 years later when the initial evaluation was accompanied by verbal feedback to parents and provision of written information to both parents and school. Most recommendations in neuropsychological reports were not implemented.

Children's Oncology Group guidelines also recommend school liaison programming for survivors of pediatric cancer with educational needs, and many specialized pediatric cancer centers utilize such programs to facilitate school reentry, communication of information between the medical and educational teams, and implementation of educational recommendations. However, although various formal educational interventions were the subject of several, methodologically limited, empirical investigations more than a decade ago, no recent studies are available. Within this context, the available studies documented preliminary evidence of increased participant knowledge about the survivor's medical condition, increased peer interest in interacting with a classmate who is a cancer survivor, and decreased personal worry about cancer. A more recent study of a direct math intervention in a sample of survivors of ALL who received only chemotherapy documented specific improvements in calculation and applied math skills that were not evident in reading and spelling and were maintained 1 year after the intervention (Moore, Hockenberry, Anhalt, McCarthy, & Krull, 2012).

Cognitive remediation programs have also been the focus of empirical research for survivors of pediatric cancer. Preliminary studies provided empirical support for a cognitive remediation program involving a tripartite model of rehabilitation techniques, metacognitive strategies, and clinical psychology techniques for survivors with CNS-involved disease or treatments, but the results of a follow-up, multicenter, randomized controlled trial were mixed (Butler, 1998; Butler et al., 2008), with small to medium effect sizes on measures of academic achievement, self-reported metacognitive strategy use, and parent (not teacher) ratings of attention. There was no improvement on direct measures of neurocognitive functioning.

In contrast to time- and resource-heavy clinic-based interventions, online, computerized cognitive training programs have been the focus of more recent investigations. Kesler, Lacayo, and Jo (2011) demonstrated significant improvements in processing speed, cognitive flexibility, and visual and verbal declarative memory as well as changes in functional MRI (fMRI) activation patterns in the dorsolateral prefrontal cortex in a small sample of survivors of ALL and PBT immediately after completing an online cognitive rehabilitation program developed by Lumos Labs (www.lumosity.com; San Francisco, CA). Another online program to remediate working memory, Cogmed (www.cogmed.com, Pearson Education, New York, NY), has been found to be feasible and acceptable in samples of children ALL and PBT who have a history of CNS-directed therapies (Cox et al., 2015; Hardy, Willard, Allen, & Bonner, 2013). In a randomized, single-blind, wait-list–controlled trial of the 5- to 9-week Cogmed program in these samples (Conklin et al., 2015), the intervention was associated with benefit on direct measures of working memory, attention, and processing speed as well as on caregiver ratings of inattention and executive dysfunction. Training-related neuroplasticity was documented in the left lateral prefrontal, left cingulate, and bilateral medical frontal areas on fMRI. However, fMRI activation changes were not associated with the cognitive changes, and improvements in processing speed did not generalize to measures of academic fluency. Thus, although the research highlights the potential promise of cognitive remediation techniques in children who have CNS disease or CNS treatment histories, studies investigating the maintenance and generalization of the associated benefits and their superiority to direct academic interventions are an essential next step before clinical adoption can be recommended. Similarly, neurofeedback was not supported as efficacious for survivors of PBT in a double-blind, randomized, placebo-controlled trial (de Ruiter et al., 2016).

With respect to socioemotional interventions that do not involve pharmacological agents, the pediatric cancer literature focuses primarily in three areas: maternal problem-solving, posttraumatic stress, and child social functioning. The efficacy of a maternal problem-solving intervention for mothers of children newly diagnosed with cancer has been established in multiple randomized controlled trials (most recently Sahler et al., 2013). A randomized wait-list control trial of a family intervention based in cognitive behavioral and family systems theory targeting posttraumatic stress symptoms among adolescent cancer survivors, their parents, and their adolescent siblings documented significant reduction of intrusive thoughts among fathers and arousal among survivors (Kazak et al., 2004). Finally, investigations of survivor-directed social skills training in mixed cancer groups have documented preliminary evidence of their benefit on parent and child ratings of behavior problems, parent ratings of school and social competence, patient ratings of social competence, and patient perceptions of peer and teacher social support, and on direct social performance behaviors such as maintaining eye contact with peers, social conversations with peers, and cooperative play (Schulte, Vannatta, & Barrera, 2014). An emerging area of investigation is social interventions that involve peer-mediated training in the classrooms of survivors, with available evidence demonstrating initial feasibility and acceptability of a classroom-based intervention that modeled appropriate ways to include, sustain interactions with, and befriend isolated children. Preliminary evidence has documented a trend toward increased peer-based friend nominations for PBT survivors but not other (social acceptance, rejection, victimization) outcomes, and larger trials are warranted to better elucidate the efficacy of such peer-mediated interventions (Devine et al., 2016).

Intervention in an Adult Population

Focused intervention within the adult oncology setting is multifaceted. Attention should be placed on providing psychosocial support and symptom relief. Within the clinical setting, once patients have a confirmed diagnosis, they may experience a wide range of emotions that are constantly changing as they proceed through their treatment and even into survivorship. Depression and anxiety are by far the two most common psychiatric symptoms experienced within the cancer population. As with other medical ailments, the experience of prominent psychological distress in cancer has been linked with poorer outcomes in terms of mortality and morbidity. Functionally, the negative impact of depression, anxiety, as well as other such features has been extensively described, including within the cancer population. The most effective way to address these issues is through psychosocial support in the form of individual counseling for patients and loved ones, family counseling, and access to support groups. Cognitive behavioral therapy has been indicated in the treatment of many of the physical and emotional sequelae of cancer and its treatment. Cognitive behavioral therapy has demonstrated utility in treating depression, anxiety, insomnia, quality of life, and even fatigue (Marcus, 2013). Structured exercise programs and dietary plans have also demonstrated substantial utility in improving depression, reducing anxiety and stress, and improving fatigue (Vicari & Anton, 2013). Finally, complementary services such as yoga, meditation, and massage therapy have all proven effective in enhancing patient well-being.

These intervention options are in addition to the symptom relief provided through more traditional medicinal intervention. A detailed discussion of the full spectrum of medications used within the cancer population for symptom relief is well beyond the scope of this chapter. Interested readers are encouraged to see Sutton and Altomare (2013).

Medicinal interventions may focus on reducing pain and nausea or improving appetite, sleep, energy, and cognition. Pharmacological interventions to improve psychiatric status have also been discussed extensively in the literature. Professionals working with the population are encouraged to educate themselves about not only these medicinal options, but also their contraindications within this population. Some antidepressants, for example, interfere with the activity of chemotherapeutic agents, and vice versa.

Implications for Clinical Practice

Pediatrics

As discussed, multiple factors contribute to risk for neuropsychological impairment, including diagnosis (brain tumor, leukemia), treatment and complications (radiation, chemotherapy, shunts), individual factors (age at diagnosis, time since treatment, gender), family factors (stress), and demographic characteristics (SES). There are key areas of vulnerability that require follow-up and monitoring, including IQ, attention and executive functions (particularly working memory), processing speed, memory, academic functions, and social-emotional well-being.

At the same time, as the number of survivors of childhood cancer grows there are limited resources (neuropsychologists) and practical pressures (insurance preauthorization and cost) that influence the ability to provide the "right" type of service. Consequently, multiple groups have outlined standards and recommendations for monitoring survivors of childhood cancer, including the Children's Oncology Group, Psychosocial Standards of Care Project for Childhood Cancer, and National Comprehensive Cancer Network. A clinical collaborative of pediatric neuropsychologists recently published guidelines regarding different options for levels of care that would provide appropriate access for patients (Baum et al., 2017). Neuropsychologists should consider their role within multidisciplinary teams, and how to maximize access and meet patient needs appropriately. The following is a summary of the collaborative's suggestions.

First, all patients can benefit from clinical surveillance, which can be accomplished by multiple members of a medical team throughout treatment and survivorship to explore perceived cognitive or academic problems and investigate the need for neuropsychologist involvement. Next, consultation can occur between a neuropsychologist and the medical team members and/or family members regarding potential risks, evaluations, and interventions that could benefit a patient. Third, neuropsychological screening can occur with identified at-risk patients (due to medical team member observations, parent or self-report, known risk factors) and includes standardized self- or family report measures or computerized assessments administered by a range of medical team members that would indicate the need for additional assessment or intervention (e.g., neuropsychological evaluation, psychosocial involvement, alteration to school supports). Fourth, targeted evaluation can occur based on screening results and includes administration and interpretation of performance-based measures by a neuropsychologist to answer specific questions about cognitive functioning, and then generate tailored recommendations. The most in-depth and time-intensive option would be a comprehensive neuropsychological evaluation that would describe a patient's broad profile of strengths and weaknesses by including performance-based measures as well as self-, family, and possibly teacher reports to implement broad recommendations at home, school, and in the community. Individuals who require targeted or comprehensive evaluations will likely be monitored by a neuropsychologist every several years throughout childhood and into adulthood.

As there are tiered levels of neuropsychological involvement, there are also tiered levels of psychosocial screening and support for patients and their families. According to the Pediatric Psychosocial Preventative Health Model psychologists should provide consultation and intervention for those patients and families with the highest risk factors and vulnerabilities, least resources, and greatest distress. An example of an at-risk subset would include those survivors with reduced cognitive abilities, specifically executive functions, because poor behavioral control is associated with increased parental stress (Patel, Wong, Cuevas, & Van Horn, 2013). At the same time, because parental distress is a predictor of overall survivor functional status, psychologists and neuropsychologists could include discussion and screening of parental distress and family functioning during clinical interviews in addition to questions targeting cognitive and academic performance.

More than 60,000 adolescents and young adults age 15 to 39 years are diagnosed with cancer in the United States each year (American Cancer Society, 2014). Psychologists and neuropsychologists must pay particular attention to this population because they are at specific risk for difficulties with adjustment (if diagnosed in adolescents or young adulthood), as well as demonstrating increased neurocognitive, behavioral, and psychosocial sequelae due to treatment (if treated in earlier childhood). Consequently, the transition to independence in adolescence and adulthood, including the transition to adult care, requires understanding of a person's cognitive abilities, monitoring of anxiety and depression symptoms, assessment and planning for transition readiness, and education about the importance of life-long medical surveillance (Nathan, Hayes-Lattin, Sisler, & Hudson, 2011). This also includes awareness of risk factors such as reduced educational and employment attainment, lower SES, lack of private insurance, difficulty with travel, and being non–White are associated with reduced likelihood of accessing follow-up care.

Adults

Within the adult population, attention is placed on the methods used in the assessment of cognitive functioning and ongoing assessment of psychosocial needs. Practitioners are encouraged to remain mindful of the fact that patient functioning is constantly changing. Within the realm of cognitive functioning, as previously noted, screening tools such as the Mini-Mental State Examination are not adequately sensitive to detect many of the cognitive sequelae that develop secondary to various forms of cancer and its treatment. Self-report measures that assess subjective cognitive complaints can be useful from an identification standpoint, although such measures often overestimate the extent of cognitive impairment. Sequential assessment can prove useful not only in tracking cognitive status over time, but also in some cases noticing significant changes that indicate disease progression before it is fully appreciated on imaging (Janelsins et al., 2014). Research protocols are still needed to expand our understanding of the full utility of assessment in the ongoing care and assessment of patients with cancer.

As to ongoing assessment of psychosocial needs, the National Comprehensive Cancer Network has spoken on the importance of regular, ongoing assessment of psychosocial needs. The National Comprehensive Cancer Network Distress Thermometer is a screening tool that assesses psychosocial stressors ranging from physical complaints (pain, fatigue, insomnia), to emotional complaints (depression, anxiety), to issues pertaining to social stressors such as financial burden or childcare concerns. The measure directs patients to rate their level of acute distress and identify areas of concern. Because these issues can change over time, repeated assessment is recommended over the course of care, which emphasizes to patients that the focus of care extends beyond antineoplastic care, thus they are more willing to discuss such issues with their oncology health-care providers. Establishing such an alliance is critical within the oncology setting. Establishing such close and trusting relationships with their providers, in and of itself, is therapeutic for patients. Consequently, when patients are forced

to switch providers or as they transition in their care to less regular checkups, it is not uncommon to observe fluctuations in their emotional status.

Although within the clinical setting comprehensive assessment is more essential, within the parameters of a clinical study the desired end points may direct assessment in a more focused direction. In both instances, the practicing clinician is encouraged to avoid lengthy assessment that extends beyond 2 hours, given that this population is already susceptible to fatigue, which will inevitably skew results.

For a summary of assessment and intervention recommendations presented according to developmental stage (childhood, adolescence/young adult, adult) the reader is referred to Table 9.2. Key areas to assess or follow up with are IQ, attention and executive functions, processing speed, motor skills, memory, academic functions, adaptive functioning, social-emotional well-being, and fatigue.

Future Directions

Future directions should focus on *who* should receive increased attention, *how* neuropsychological functioning should be assessed, *what* to include in assessments, *when* to conduct assessments, and *identifying* possible interventions with survivors and families. An empirically validated model would allow for "rightsizing" neuropsychology services and provide appropriate access to a larger number of patients and survivors (Baum et al., 2017). To facilitate this clinical care, and to streamline research, it will be important to develop and implement validated screening tools that can identify at risk patients based on treatment risk factors, personal and family characteristics, emotional well-being, SES, vocational/educational attainment, fatigue, physical activity, sleep, and other factors so that both assessment and intervention resources are most effectively deployed.

In our diverse society it is essential that care be culturally competent and language appropriate so that information is accurately communicated, and support and interventions engage wide support networks (e.g., parents and extended family/community) to attain functional survivor improvements (Bava, Johns, Freyer, & Ruccione, 2016). Additional research is needed across all points of care, including prevention, as it pertains to health disparities across different groups. Similarly, clinical and research questions need to more rigorously incorporate family factors, such as family functioning and SES, to better understand how these variables impact survivor outcomes, and how these factors can be incorporated in interventions. This is needed within both the pediatric and adult populations.

Increasing emotional functioning screening, to be employed by a wide range of medical team members, could also provide important information about patient functional status. Emotional adjustment is known to influence morbidity and mortality, and should be evaluated within both pediatric and adult populations. Over the course of treatment, the emotional well-being of patient, caregivers, and family may all go through significant shifts. Continued refinement is needed of the process by which these outcomes are monitored, and how that information is used by the broader medical team. At the same time, the benefits of specialized care are well known but not always readily available. Consequently, research should look into the feasibility, utility, and efficacy of telehealth services to address the emotional needs of patients with cancer.

Professionals trained in fields such as health psychology may not be readily available to patients in rural settings. Teletherapeutic services could create an avenue by which these patients and their families can be reached. Within the psychosocial realm this has been seen in the development of the Patient-Reported Outcomes Measurement Information System, which permits practitioners to collect a wide array of clinical data pertaining to a patient's physical, social, and emotional well-being, is feasible for adults and young children with cancer to complete, and has been translated into many languages to increase patient access. As a result of the program employing item-response theory as an underlying statistical tenant, the task is not time-consuming for the patient.

Currently neurocognitive cancer research is hampered by the wide range of measures employed, particularly in pediatric cancer research. Uniform administration of a consistent battery (e.g., National Institutes of Health NIH Toolbox for the Assessment of Neurological and Behavioral Function [Gershon et al., 2013]; Children's Oncology Group Protocol ALTE 07C1: Neuropsychological, Social, Emotional, and Behavioral Outcomes in Children with Cancer) enables comparisons of findings that can describe impact of treatment and changes over time across the developmental trajectory. A broadly accepted abbreviated battery that is feasible to administer and

samples from the domains of highest risk, while mindful of the impact of fatigue on functioning, would accrue important data. It is imperative that standardized research batteries include measures beyond IQ (e.g., attention, executive functions, processing speed, memory, mood), particularly because imaging and genetic studies have found correlations with attention, executive function, and memory, to better understand survivor needs and possible methods and times to intervene.

Another option for standardized and widely available assessment is employment of computerized assessments. These techniques must be comprehensive, abbreviated, and administered in a sequential fashion without prominent practice effects. Several computerized neuropsychological batteries have been employed in the assessment of individuals with cancer, including Cambridge Neuropsychological Test Automated Battery (CANTAB; Cambridge Cognition, Cambridge, UK, www.cantab.com), Immediate Post-Concussion Assessment and Cognitive Test (ImPACT; Lovell, 2016), and, more prolifically, Cogstate (Cogstate Ltd., Melbourne, Australia, www.cogstate.com). Cogstate is increasing in popularity and accessibility across multiple disease groups and age ranges (particularly in elderly populations). It has demonstrated acceptable sensitivity and neuroimaging correlations compared to traditional neuropsychological batteries (Maruff et al., 2009). It is currently used in treatment (high-risk ALL) and neurocognitive intervention trials within the Children's Oncology Group due to its demonstrated validity, reliability, time limits, portability (laptop), limited training required to administer, and ease of multisite administration. Cogstate is also incorporated into an on-study ALL trial at the Dana-Farber Cancer Institute (Boston) and has shown correlations with biomarkers in hopes of identifying those at risk for cognitive impairment and informing when to initiate intervention (Sands et al., 2016). For both pediatric and adult populations, it is imperative that within the research setting, initial assessments are undertaken at the earliest possible point, before any treatment intervention and tracked over time, permitting between-group and within-group comparisons.

At the same time, in nononcology settings there have been concerns about Cogstate's unsatisfactory reliability and validity estimates compared with conventional neuropsychological assessments (Fratti, Bowden, & Cook, 2016). There are also concerns related to the strong emphasis of reaction time and speed and the reliance on a purely visual assessment. Assertions that visual reasoning, response rate, and executive functions are predictive of risk and/or long-term cognitive functioning ignores the potentially separate and unique relationship of verbal functioning during and after cancer treatment.

There are two patient groups that could specifically benefit from increased access to neuropsychological services. First, young children treated for solid non-CNS tumors (Sleurs, Deprez, Emsell, Lemiere, & Uyttebroeck, 2016) may demonstrate greater functional impairment (e.g., failed grades) than has previously been appreciated. Second, survivors of treatment including HSCT may face unique impacts of treatment such as prolonged school or vocational absences.

Practitioners can also adapt and increase the frequency of conversations they have with adolescents and young adults regarding transition from pediatric to adult care in survivorship. Awareness of unique stressors and concerns of adolescents and young adults (including appearance, fertility, cognitive impact, social isolation) is essential and will allow for the bridging of care between child and adult treatment teams.

An additional path that must be taken moving forward is understanding the variability of response across patients to disease processes and interventions, including the development of cognitive deficits. This should include research on genetic and other biological markers that correspond with patient response and susceptibility. Preliminary research has been undertaken such as determining subsets of patients who are more sensitive to CRT. Such information can be critical to treatment decision-making in the future. For example, in cases where adult patients are identified as being radiation sensitive, a hippocampal-sparing approach may be taken that could reduce residual cognitive burden (although, admittedly, treatment effectiveness could also be diminished in some cases). Identifying vulnerabilities also holds promise for identifying and implementing interventions earlier (either on treatment or soon after completion) to stave off negative neurocognitive outcomes. Longitudinal trials are required to explore and answer these questions.

Intervention research, particularly in pediatrics, may want to focus on more consistent accrual of "real-world" long-term outcomes (e.g., grades, employment,

relationships) in conjunction with traditional assessment to better understand functional outcomes. Several areas of emerging intervention research in pediatric care are promising. They include timing and extent of cognitive interventions, including cognitive remediation, to both prevent possible late effects and to ameliorate deficits that have emerged. In addition, a better understanding of how the family understands neuropsychological reports is essential so a family can translate findings into effective support and intervention strategies in the home, school, and community. Ongoing research into the role of family management and functioning in supporting survivor growth (as is explored in the medical/traumatic brain injury and behavioral health/schizophrenia literature) is also warranted. When attempting to maximize professional resources and survivor outcomes, it is important to discover whether a school liaison increases survivor academic success. Early literature also suggests that targeting social skills and social cognition may improve quality of life.

Both children and adults will benefit from finding ways to improve sleep hygiene and sleep quality during and after treatment completion. This would be one important component of increasing quality of life by reducing fatigue. Improving ways in which treatment-induced fatigue is addressed is critical given its ramifications for overall well-being and quality of life for those with cancer. Other avenues where new interventions could mitigate the effects of fatigue may include increased physical activity and/or the use of medication. In particular, more focus should be placed on nonpharmacological interventions such as yoga and resistance training. Such interventions affect other aspects of physical well-being and functioning, ranging from immune response to return-to-school and/or work issues. Overall, ongoing research that identifies specific at-risk populations and maximizes the timing of interventions is an important next step.

References

Ahles, T. A., Root, J. C., & Ryan E. L. (2012). Cancer- and cancer treatment-associated cognitive change: An update on the state of the science. *Journal of Clinical Oncology*, *30* (30), 3675–3686.

American Cancer Society (2014). *Cancer facts & figures*. Atlanta, GA: Author.

Anderson, V. A., Godber, T., Smibert, E., Weiskop, S., & Ekert, H., (2000). Cognitive and academic outcome following cranial irradiation and chemotherapy in children: A longitudinal study. *British Journal of Cancer*, *82*(2), 255–262.

Annett, R. D., Patel, S. K., & Phipps, S. (2015). Monitoring and assessment of neuropsychological outcomes as a standard of care in pediatric oncology. *Pediatric Blood Cancer*, *62*(S5), S460–513.

Baum, K. T., Powell, S. K., Jacobson, L. A., Gragert, M. N., Janzen, L. A., Paltin, I., … Wilkening, G. N. (2017). Implementing guidelines: Proposed definitions of neuropsychology services in pediatric oncology. *Pediatric Blood & Cancer*, *64*(8). doi: 10.1002/pbc.26446

Bava, L., Johns, A., Freyer, D. R., & Ruccione, K. (2016). Development of a culturally competent service to improve academic functioning for Latino survivors of acute lymphoblastic leukemia: Methodological considerations. *Journal of Pediatric Oncology Nursing*, 1–8. doi: 10.1177/1043454216676837

Bender, C. M., Sereika S. M., Berga, S. L., Vogel, V. G., Brufsky, A. M., Paraska, K. K., & Ryan, C.M. (2006). Cognitive impairment associated with adjuvanttherapy in breast cancer. *Psychooncology*, *15*, 422–430.

Brackett, J., Krull, K., Scheurer, M. E., Liu, W., Srivastava, D. K., Stovall, M., … Okcu, M. F. (2012). Antioxidant enzyme polymorphisms and neuropsychological outcomes in medulloblastoma survivors: A report from the childhood cancer survivor study. *Neuro-Oncology*, *14*(8), 1018–1025.

Brinkman, T. M., Ullrich, N. J., Zhang, N., Green, D. M., Zeltzer, L. K., Lommel, K. M., … Krull, K. R. (2013). Prevalence and predictors of prescription psychoactive medication use in adult survivors of childhood cancer: A report from the childhood cancer survivor study. *Journal of Cancer Survivorship*, *7*(1), 104–114.

Butler, R. W. (1998). Attentional processes and their remediation in childhood cancer. *Medical and Pediatric Oncology*, *30*(S1), 75–78.

Butler, R. W., Copeland, D. R., Fairclough, D. L., Mulhern, R. K., Katz, E. R., Kazak, A. E., … Sahler, O. J. (2008). A multicenter, randomized clinical trial of a cognitive remediation program for childhood survivors of a pediatric malignancy. *Journal of Consulting and Clinical Psychology*, *76*(3), 367–378.

Buizer, A. I., de Sonneville, L. M., van den Heuvel-Eibrink, M. M., & Veerman, A. J. (2006). Behavioral and educational limitations after chemotherapy for childhood acute lymphoblastic leukemia or Wilms tumor. *Cancer*, *106*(9), 2067–2075.

Campbell, L. K., Scaduto, M., Sharp, W., Dufton, L., Van Slyke, D., Whitlock, J. A., & Compas, B. (2007). A meta-analysis of the neurocognitive sequelae of treatment for childhood acute lymphocytic leukemia. *Pediatric Blood Cancer*, *49*, 65–73.

Castellino, S. M., Tooze, J. A., Flowers, L., Hill, D. F., McMullen, K. P., Shaw, E. G., & Parsons, S. K. (2012). Toxicity and efficacy of the acetylcholinesterase (AChe) inhibitor donepezil in childhood brain tumor survivors: A pilot study. *Pediatric Blood Cancer*, *59*(3), 540–7.

Chang, G., Meadows, M.-E., & Orav, E. J. (2009). Mental status changes after hematopoietic stem cell transplantation. *Cancer*, *15*(19), 4625–4635.

Chao, H. H., Hu, S., Ide, J. S., Uchio, E., Zhang, S., Rose, M., Concato, J., &. Li, C. (2013). Effects of androgen deprivation on cerebral morphometry in prostate cancer patients: An exploratory study. *PLOS One*, *8*(8), e72302.

Chao, H. H., Uchio, E., Zhang, S., Hu, S., Bednarski S. R., Xi, L., … Chiang-shan, R. L. (2012). Effects of androgen deprivation on brain function in prostate cancer patients: A prospective observational cohort analysis. *BMC Cancer*, *12*, 371–378.

Chen, M. L., Miaskowski, C., Liu, L. N., & Chen S. C. (2012). Changes in perceived attentional function in women following breast cancer surgery. *Breast Cancer Research and Treatment*, *13*, 599–606.

Conklin, H. M., Helton, S., Ashford, J., Mulhern, R. K., Reddick, W. E., Brown, R., … Khan, R. B. (2010). Predicting methylphenidate response in long-term survivors of childhood cancer: A randomized, double-blind, placebo-controlled, crossover trial. *Journal of Pediatric Psychology*, *35*(2), 144–155.

Conklin, H. M., Ogg, R. J., Ashford, J. M., Scoggins, M. A., Ping, Z., Clark, K. N., … Zhang, H. (2015). Computerized cognitive training for amelioration of cognitive late effects among childhood cancer survivors: A randomized controlled trial. *Journal of Clinical Oncology*, *33*(33), 3894–902.

Conklin, H. M., Reddick, W. E., Ashford J., Ogg, S., Howard, S. C., Brannon Morris, E., … Khan, R. B. (2010). Long-term efficacy of methylphenidate in enhancing attention regulation, social skills, and academic abilities of childhood cancer survivors. *Journal of Clinical Oncology*, *28*(29), 4465–4472.

Cox, L. E., Ashford, J. M., Clark, K. N. Martin-Elbahesh, K., Hardy, K. K., Merchant, T. E., … Conklin, H. M. (2015). Feasibility and acceptability of a remotely administered computerized intervention to address cognitive late effects among childhood cancer survivors. *Neuro-Oncology Practice Journal*, *2*(2), 78–87.

de Ruiter, M. A., Oosterlaan, J., Schouten-van Meeteren, A. Y., Maurice-Stam, H., van Vuurden, D. G., Gidding, C., … Grootenhuis, M. A. (2016). Neurofeedback ineffective in paediatric brain tumour survivors: Results of a double-blind randomised placebo-controlled trial. *European Journal of Cancer*, *64*, 62–73.

de Ruiter, M. B., Reneman, L., Boogerd, W., Veltman, D. J., Caan, M., Douaud, G., & Schagen, S.B. (2012). Late effects of high-dose adjuvant chemotherapy on white and gray matter in breast cancer survivors: Converging results from multimodal magnetic resonance imaging. *Human Brain Mapping, 33*(12), 2971–2983.

de Ruiter, M. A., van Mourik, R., Schouten-van Meeteren, A. Y., Grootenhuis, M. A., & Oosterlaan, J. (2013). Neurocognitive consequences of a paediatric brain tumour and its treatment: A meta-analysis. *Developmental Medicine & Child Neurology, 55*(5), 408–417.

Debess, J., Riis, J. O., Pedersen, L., & Ewertz, M. (2009). Cognitive function and quality of life after surgery for early breast cancer in North Jutland, Denmark. *Acta Oncologica, 48*, 532–540.

Deprez, S., Amant, F., Yigit, R., Porke, K., Verhoeven J., van den Stock, J., & Sunaert, S. (2011). Chemotherapy induced structural changes in cerebral white matter and its correlation with impaired cognitive functioning in breast cancer patients. *Human Brain Mapping, 32*(3), 480–493.

Devine, K. A., Bukowski, W. M., Sahler, O.J. Ohman-Strickland, P., Smith, T. H., Lown, E. A., ... Noll, R. B. (2016). Social competence in childhood brain tumor survivors: feasibility and preliminary outcomes of a peer-mediated intervention. *Journal of Developmental and Behavioral Pediatrics, 37*(6), 475–482.

Di Pinto, M., Conklin, H. M., Li, C., & Merchant, T. E., (2012). Learning and memory following conformal radiation therapy for pediatric craniopharyngioma and low-grade glioma. *International Journal of Radiation Oncology, Biology, Physics, 84*(3), e363–e369.

Eberling, J. L., Wu, C., Tong-Turnbeaugh, R., & Jagust, W. J. (2004). Estrogen- and tamoxifen-associated effects on brain structure and function. *NeuroImage, 21*, 364–371.

Ferguson, R. J., & Ahles, T. A. (2003). Low neuropsychologic performance among adult cancer survivors treated with chemotherapy. *Current Neurology and Neuroscience Reports, 3*, 215–222.

Fouladi, M., Chintagumpala, M., Laningham, F. H., Ashley, D., Kellie, S. J., Langston, J. W., ... Gajjar, A. (2004). White matter lesions detected by magnetic resonance imaging after radiotherapy and high-dose chemotherapy in children with medulloblastoma or primitive neuroectodermal tumor. *Journal of Clinical Oncology, 22* (22), 4551–4560.

Friedman, M. A., Fernandez, M., Wefel, J. S., Myszka, K. A., Champlin, R. E., & Meyers, C. A. (2009). Course of cognitive decline in hematopoietic stem cell transplantation: A within-subjects design. *Archives of Clinical Neuropsychology, 24*, 689–698.

Fratti, S., Bowden, S. C., & Cook, M. J. (2016). Reliability and validity of the CogState computerized battery in patients with seizure disorders and healthy young adults: comparison with standard neuropsychological tests. *The Clinical Neuropsychologist, 31*(3), 569–586. http://dx .doi.org/10.1080/13854046.2016.1256435

Gershon, R. C., Wagster, M. V., Hendrie, H. C., Fox, N. A., Cook, K. F., & Nowinski, C. J. (2013). NIH toolbox for assessment of neurological and behavioral function. *Neurology, 80*(11 Suppl 3), S2–6. doi: 10.1212/ WNL.0b013e3182872e5f

Gondi, V., Hermann, B. P., Mehta, M. P., & Tome, W. A. (2012). Hippocampal dosimetry predicts neurocognitive function impairment after fractionated stereotactic radiotherapy for benign or low-grade adult brain tumors. *International Journal of Radiation Oncology Biology Physics, 85*, 348–354.

Gurney, J. G., Krull, K. R., Kadan-Lottick, N., Nicholson, H. S., Nathan, P. C., Zebrack, B., ... Ness, K. K. (2009). Social outcomes in the childhood cancer survivor study cohort. *Journal of Clinical Oncology, 10*(14), 2390–2395.

Habets, E. J.,Dirven, L., Wiggenraad, R. J., Verbeek-de Kanter, A., Lycklama À Nijeholt, G.J., Zwinkels, H., ... Taphoorn, M. J. B. (2016). Neurocognitive functioning and health-related quality of life in patients treated with stereotactic radiotherapy for brain metastases: A prospective study. *Neuro-Oncology 18*(3), 435–444.

Hardy, K. K., Willard, V. W., Allen, T. M., & Bonner, M. J. (2013). Working memory training in survivors of pediatric cancer: A randomized pilot study. *Psychooncology, 22*(8), 1856–1865.

Hayes, S. M., Hayes, J. P., Cadden, M., & Verfaellie, M. (2013). A review of cardiorespiratory fitness-related neuroplasticity in the aging brain. *Frontiers in Aging Neuroscience, 5*,31.

Hearps, S., Seal, M., Anderson, V., McCarthy, M., Connellan, M., Downie, P., & De Luca, C. (2016). The relationship between cognitive and neuroimaging outcomes in children treated for acute lymphoblastic leukemia with chemotherapy only: A systematic review. *Pediatric Blood & Cancer, 64*(2), 225–233.

Hiniker, S. M., Agarwal, R., Modlin, L. A., Gray, C. C., Harris, J. P., Million, L., ... Donaldson, S. S. (2014). Survival and neurocognitive outcomes after cranial or craniospinal irradiation plus total-body irradiation before stem cell transplantation in pediatric leukemia patients with central nervous system involvement. *International Journal of Radiation Oncology, Biology, Physics, 89*(1), 67–74.

Iyer, N. S., Balsamo, L. M., Bracken, M. B., & Kadan-Lottick, N. S. (2015). Chemotherapy-only treatment effects on long-term neurocognitive functioning in childhood ALL survivors: A review and meta-analysis. *Blood Journal, 126* (3), 346–353. doi: https://doi.org/10.1182/blood-2015-02-627414

Jacola, L. M., Ashford, J. M., Reddick, W. E., Glass, J. O., Ogg, R. J., Merchant, T. E., & Conklin, H. M. (2014). The relationship between working memory and cerebral white matter volume in survivors of childhood brain tumors treated with conformal radiation therapy. *Journal of Neuro-Oncology, 119*(1), 197–205.

Janelsins, M. C., Kesler, S. R., Ahles, T. A., & Morrow, G. R. (2014). Prevalence, mechanisms, and management of cancer-related cognitive impairment. *International Review of Psychiatry, 26*(1), 102–113.

Janelsins, M. C., Kohli, S., Mohile, S. G., Usuki, K., Ahles, T. A., & Morrow, G. R. (2011). An update on cancer- and chemotherapy-related cognitive dysfunction: Current status. *Seminars in Oncology, 38*(3), 431–438.

Jenkins, V. A., Bloomfield, D. J., Shilling. V. M., & Edginton, T. L. (2005). Does neoadjuvant hormone therapy for early prostate cancer affect cognition? Results from a pilot study. *BJU International, 96*, 48–53.

Joly, F., Alibhai, S. M., Galica, J., Park, A., Yi, Q.L., & Tannock, I. F. (2006) Impact of androgen deprivation therapy on physical and cognitive function, as well as quality of life of patients with nonmetastatic prostate cancer. *Journal of Urology, 176*, 2443–2447.

Jones, D, Vichaya, E. G., Wang, X. S., Sailors, M. H., Cleeland, C. S., & Wefel, J. S. (2013). Acute cognitive impairment in patients with multiple myeloma undergoing autologous hematopoietic stem cell transplant. *Cancer, 119* (23), 4188–4195.

Kahalley, L. S., Ris, M. D., Grosshans, D. R. Okcu, M. F., Paulino, A. C., Chintagumpala, M., ... Mahajan, A. (2016). Comparing intelligence quotient change after treatment with proton versus photon radiation therapy for pediatric brain tumors. *Journal of Clinical Oncology, 34*(10), 1043–1049.

Kanellopoulos, A., Anderson, S., Zeller, B., Tamnes, C. K., Fjell, A. M., Walhovd, K. B., & Ruud, E. (2016). Neurocognitive outcome in very long-term survivors of childhood acute lymphoblastic leukemia after treatment with chemotherapy only. *Pediatric Blood Cancer, 63*, 133–138.

Kazak, A. E., Alderfer, M. A., Streisand, R. Simms, S., Rourke, M. T., Barakat, L. P., ... Cnaan, A. (2004). Treatment of posttraumatic stress symptoms in adolescent survivors of childhood cancer and their families: A randomized clinical trial. *Journal of Family Psychology, 18* (3), 493–504.

Kesler, S. R., Lacayo, N. J., & Jo, B. (2011). A pilot study of an online cognitive rehabilitation program for executive function skills in children with cancer-related brain injury. *Brain Injury, 25*(1), 101–112.

King, T. Z., Na, S., & Mao, H. (2015). Neural underpinnings of working memory in adult survivors of childhood brain tumors. *Journal of the International Neuropsychological Society, 21*(7), 494–505. doi: 10.1017/ S135561771500051

Koppelmans, V., Breteler, M. M., Boogerd, W., Seynaeve, C., Gundy, C., & Schagen, S. B. (2012). Neuropsychological performance in survivors of breast cancer more than 20

years after adjuvant chemotherapy. *Journal of Clinical Oncology, 30*(10), 1080–1086.

Kullgren, K. A., Morris, R. D., Morris, M. K., & Krawiecki, N. (2003). Risk factors associated with long-term social and behavioral problems among children with brain tumors. *Journal of Psychosocial Oncology, 21*(1), 73–87.

Lajiness-O'Neill, R., Hoodin, F., Kentor, R., Heinrich, K., Colbert, A., & Connelly, J. A. (2015). Alterations in memory and impact on academic outcomes in children following allogeneic hematopoietic cell transplantation. *Archives of Clinical Neuropsychology, 30*(7), 657–669.

Li, J., Yu, L., Long, Z., Li, Y., & Cao F. (2015). Perceived cognitive impairment in Chinese patients with breast cancer and its relationship with posttraumatic stress disorder symptoms and fatigue. *Psychooncology, 24*(6), 676–82.

Lindley, L. C., & Oyana, T. J. (2016). Geographic variation in mortality among children and adolescents diagnosed with cancer in Tennessee. Does race matter? *Journal of Pediatric Oncology Nursing, 33*(2), 129–136. doi: 10.1177/ 1043454215600155

Liu, Y., Zhou, R., Sulman, E. P., Scheurer, M. E., Boehling, N., Armstrong, G. N., ... Wefel, J. S. (2015). Genetic modulation of neurocognitive function in glioma patients. *Clinical Cancer Research, 21*(14), 3340–3346.

Lovell, M. (2016). *ImPACT administration and interpretation manual.* San Diego, CA: ImPACT Applications, Inc.

Mabbott, D. J., Noseworthy, M. D., Bouffet, E., Rockel, C., & Laughlin, S. (2006). Diffusion tensor imaging of white matter after cranial radiation in children for medulloblastoma: Correlation with IQ. *Neuro-Oncology, 8* (3), 244–252.

Marcus, J. (2013). Psychosocial functioning. In C. A. Noggle & R. S. Dean (Eds.), *The neuropsychology of cancer and oncology* (pp. 343–362). New York: Springer Publishing Company.

Maruff, P., Thomas, E., Cysique, L., Brew, B., Collie, A., Snyder, P., & Pietrzak, R. H. (2009). Validity of the cogstate brief battery: Relationship to standardized tests and sensitivity to cognitive impairment in mild traumatic brain injury, schizophrenia, and AIDS dementia complex. *Archives of Clinical Neuropsychology, 24*, 165–178.

McDonald, B. C., Conroy, S. K., Ahles, T. A., West, J. D., & Saykin, A. J. (2010). Gray matter reduction associated with systemic chemotherapy for breast cancer: A prospective MRI study. *Breast Cancer Research and Treatment, 123*, 819–828.

Meyers, C. A., & Hess, K. R. (2003). Multifaceted end points in brain tumor clinical trials: cognitive deterioration precedes MRI progression. *Neuro-Oncology, 5*, 89–95.

Meyers, C. A., Smith, J. A., Bezjak A, Mehtra, M. P., Liebmann, J., Illidge, T.,... Renschler, M. F. (2004). Neurocognitive function and progression in patients with brain metastases treated with whole-brain radiation and motexafin gadolinium: Results of a randomized phase III trial. *Journal of Clinical Oncology, 22*, 157–165.

Mishra, S. I., Scherer, R. W., Snyder, C., Geigle, P., & Gotay, C., (2016). Are exercise programs effective for improving health-related quality of life among cancer survivors? A systematic review and meta-analysis. *Oncology Nursing Forum, 41*(6), E326–342.

Mohrmann, C., Henry, J., Hauff, M., & Hayashi, R. J. (2015). Neurocognitive outcomes and school performance in solid tumor cancer survivors lacking therapy to the central nervous system. *Journal of Personalized Medicine, 5*(2), 83–90.

Monje, M. L., Mizumatsu, S., & Fike, J. R. (2002). Irradiation induces neural precursor-cell dysfunction. *Nature Medicine, 8*, 955–962.

Moore, I. M., Hockenberry, M. J., Anhalt, C., McCarthy, K., & Krull, K. R. (2012) Mathematics intervention for prevention of neurocognitive deficits in childhood leukemia. *Pediatric Blood Cancer, 59*(2), 278–284.

Moore, I. M., Lupo, P. J., Insel, K., Harris, L. L., Pasvogel, A., Koerner, K. M., ... Hockenberry, M. J. (2016). Neurocognitive predictors of academic outcomes among childhood leukemia survivors. *Journal of Cancer Nursing, 39* (4), 255–262. doi: 10.1097/NCC.0000000000000293

Moyer, K. H., Willard, V. W., Gross, A. M., Netson, K. L., Ashford, J. M., Kahalley, L. S., ... Conklin, H. M. (2012). The impact of attention on social functioning in survivors of pediatric acute lymphoblastic leukemia and brain tumors. *Pediatric Blood & Cancer, 15*(7), 1290–1295.

Mrakotsky, C. M., Silverman, L. B., Dahlberg, S. E., Alyman, M. C. A., Sands, S. A., Queally, J. T., ... Waber, D. P. (2011). Neurobehavioral side effects of corticosteroids during active treatment for acute lymphoblastic leukemia in children are age-dependent: report from dana-farber cancer institute ALL consortium protocol 00–01. *Pediatric Blood Cancer, 57*(3), 492–498.

Munir, F., Burrows, J., Yarker, J., Kalawsky, K., & Bains, M. (2010). Women's perceptions of chemotherapy-induced cognitive side effects on work ability: A focus group study. *Journal of Clinical Nursing, 19*, 1362–1370.

Nathan, P. C., Hayes-Lattin, B., Sisler, J. J., & Hudson, M. M. (2011). Critical issues in transition and survivorship for adolescents and young adults with cancers. *Cancer, 117*(10 Suppl), 2335–2341.

Netson, K. L., Conklin, H. M., Ashford, J. M., Kahalley, L. S., Shengie, S., & Xiong, X. (2011). Parent and teacher ratings of attention during a year-long methylphenidate trial in children treated for cancer. *Journal of Pediatric Psychology, 36*(4), 438–450.

Noggle, C. A., & Dean, R. S. (Eds.). (2013). *The neuropsychology of cancer and oncology.* New York, NY: Springer Publishing Company.

Noll, R. B., Patel, S. K., Embry, L., Hardy, K., Pelletier, W., Annett, R. D., ... Barakat, L. P. (2013). Children's Oncology Group's 2013 blueprint for research: Behavioral science. *Pediatric Blood and Cancer, 60*(6), 1048–1054.

O'Keefe, E. B., Meltzer, J. P., & Bethea, T. N. (2015). Health disparities and cancer: Racial disparities in cancer mortality in the United States, 2000–2010. *Frontiers in Public Health, 3*, 1–15.

Ozyurt, J., Lorenzen, A., Gebhardt, U., Warmuth-Metz, M., Muller, H. L., & Thiel, C. M., (2014). Neuropsychological outcome in patients with childhood craniopharyngioma and hypothalamic involvement. *The Journal of Pediatrics, 164*, 876–881.

Palmer, S. L. (2008). Neurodevelopmental impact on children treated for medulloblastoma: A review and proposed conceptual model. *Developmental Disabilities Research Reviews, 14*, 203–210.

Palmer, S. L., Armstrong, C., Onar-Thomas, A., Wu, S., Wallace, D., Bonner, M. J., ... Gajjar, A. (2013) Processing speed, attention, and working memory after treatment for medulloblastoma: An international, prospective, and longitudinal study. *Journal of Clinical Oncology, 31*(28), 3494–3500.

Palmer, S., Reddick, W., Glass, J., Ogg, R., Patay, Z., Wallace, D., & Gajjar, A. (2010). Regional white matter anisotropy and reading ability in patients treated for pediatric embryonal tumors. *Brain Imaging and Behavior, 4* (2), 132–140. doi: 10.1007/s11682-010-9092-1.

Palmer, J. L., Trotter, T., Joy, A. A., & Carlson, L. E. (2008). Cognitive effects of tamoxifen in premenopausal women with breast cancer compared to healthy controls. *Journal of Cancer Survivorship: Research and Practice, 2*(4), 275–282. doi: 10.1007/s11764-008-0070-1.

Papazoglou, A., King, T. Z., Morris, R. D., & Krawiecki, N. S. (2008). Cognitive predictors of adaptive functioning vary according to pediatric brain tumor location. *Developmental Neuropsychology, 33*, 505–520.

Patel, S. K., Wong, A. L., Cuevas, M., & Van Horn, H. (2013). Parenting stress and neurocognitive late effects in childhood cancer survivors. *Psychooncology, 22*(8), 1774–1782. doi: 10.1002/pon.3213.

Peterson, C. C., Johnson, C. E., Ramirez, L. Y., Huestis, S., Pai, A. L., Demaree, H. A., & Drotar, D. (2008). A meta-analysis of the neuropsychological sequelae of chemotherapy-only treatment for pediatric acute lymphoblastic leukemia. *Pediatric Blood & Cancer 51*(1), 99–104.

Pulsifer, M. B., Sethi, R. V., Kuhlthau, K. A., MacDonald, S. M., Tarbell, N. J., & Yock, T. I. (2015). Early cognitive outcomes following proton radiation in pediatric patients with brain and central nervous system tumors. *International Journal of Radiation Oncology, Biology, Physics, 93*(2), 400–407.

Pusztai, L., Mendoza, T. R., Reuben, J. M., Martinez, M. M., Willey, J. S., Lara, J., & Hortobagyi, G. N. (2004). Changes in plasma levels of inflammatory cytokines in response to paclitaxel chemotherapy. *Cytokine*, *25*(3), 94–102.

Reddick, W. E., Taghipour, D. J., Glass, J. O. Ashford, J., Xiong, X., Wu, S., ... Conklin, H. M. (2014). Prognostic factors that increase the risk for reduced white matter volumes and deficits in attention and learning for survivors of childhood cancers. *Pediatric Blood Cancer*, *61*(6), 1074–1079.

Respini, D., Jacobsen, P. B., Thors, C., Tralongo, P., & Balducci, L. (2003). The prevalence and correlates of fatigue in older cancer patients. *Critical Reviews in Oncology/Hematology*, *47*(3), 273–279. doi:https://doi.org/10.1016/S1040-8428(02)00176-2

Riggs, L., Bouffet, E., Laughlin, S., Laperriere, N., Liu, F., Skocic, J., ... Mabbott, D. J. (2014) Changes to memory structures in children treated for posterior fossa tumors. *Journal of the International Neuropsychological Society*, *20*(2), 168–180. doi: 10.1017/S135561771300129.

Ris, M. D., Walsh K., Wallace, D., Armstrong, F. D., Homes, E., Gajjar, A., ... Packer, R. J. (2013). Intellectual and academic outcome following two chemotherapy regimens and radiotherapy for average-risk medulloblastoma: COG A9961. *Pediatric Blood Cancer*, *60*(8):1350–1357.

Robinson, K. E., Pearson, M. M., Cannistraci, C. J., Anderson, A. W., Kuttesch, J. F., Wymer, K., ... Compas, B. E., (2014). Functional neuroimaging of working memory in survivors of childhood brain tumors and healthy children: Associations with coping and psychosocial outcomes. *Child Neuropsychology: A Journal on Normal and Abnormal Development in Childhood and Adolescence*, *21*(6), 779–802. doi: 10.1080/09297049.2014.924492.

Robinson, K. E., Wolfe, K. R., Yeates, K. O., Mahone, E. M., Cecil, K. M., & Ris, M. D. (2015). Predictors of adaptive functioning and psychosocial adjustment in children with pediatric brain tumor: A report from the brain radiation investigative study consortium. *Pediatric Blood Cancer*, *62*, 509–516.

Roddy, E., Sear, K., Felton, E., Tamrazi, B., Gauvain, K., Torkildson, J., ... Mueller, S. (2016). Presence of cerebral microbleeds is associated with worse executive function in pediatric brain tumor survivors. *Neuro-Oncology*, *18*(11), 1548–1558. doi: 10.1093/neuron/now163.

Sahler, O. J., Dolgin, M. J., Phipps, S., Faiclough, D. L., Askins, M. A., Katz, E. R., ... Butler, R. W. (2013). Specificity of problem-solving skills training in mothers of children newly diagnosed with cancer: Results of a multisite randomized clinical trial. *Journal of Clinical Oncology*, *1*(10), 1329–1335.

Salminen, E., Portin, R., Korpela, J., Backman, H., Parvinen, L. M., Helenius, H., & Nurmi, M. (2003). Androgen deprivation and cognition in prostate cancer. *British Journal of Cancer*, *89*, 971–976.

Sands, S. A., Hare, B. T., Savone, M., Kelly, K., Vijayanathan, V., Welch, J. G., ... Cole, P. D. (2016). Feasibility of baseline neurocognitive assessment using Cogstate during the first month of therapy for childhood leukemia. *Support Care Cancer*, *25*(2), 449–457. doi: 10.1007/s00520-016-3422-9

Schilder, C. M., Seynaeve, C., Beex, L. V., Booger, W., Linn, S. C., Gundy, C. M., ... Schagen, S. B. (2010). Effects of tamoxifen and exemestane on cognitive functioning of postmenopausal patients with breast cancer: Results from the neuropsychological side study of the tamoxifen and exemestane adjuvant multinational trial. *Journal of Clinical Onoclogy*, *28*, 1294–1300.

Schulte, F., Vannatta, K., & Barrera, M. (2014). Social problem solving and social performance after a group social skills intervention for childhood brain tumor survivors. *Psychooncology*, *23*(2), 183–189.

Shaw, E. G., Rosdhal, R., D'Agostino R. B., Jr., Lovato, J., Naughton, M. J., Robbins, M. E., & Rapp, S. R. (2006). Phase II study of donepezil in irradiated brain tumor patients: Effect on cognitive function, mood, and quality of life. *Journal of Clinical Oncology*, *24*(9), 1415–1420.

Sleurs, C., Deprez, S., Emsell, L., Lemiere, J., & Uyttebroeck, A. (2016). Chemotherapy-induced neurotoxicity in pediatric solid non-CNS tumor patients: An update on current state of research and recommended future directions. *Critical Reviews in Oncology/Hematology*, *103*, 37–48.

Sul, J. K., & DeAngelis, L. M. (2006). Neurological complications of cancer chemotherapy. *Seminars in Oncology*, *33*(3), 324–332.

Sutton, L. M. & Altomare, I. (2013). Pharmacological interventions: Addressing residuals and outcomes. In C. A. Noggle & R. S. Dean (Eds.), *The neuropsychology of cancer and oncology* (pp. 399–412). New York, NY: Springer Publishing Company.

Taphoorn, M. J. B., & Klein, M. (2004). Cognitive deficits in adult patients with brain tumors. *Lancet Neurology*, *3*, 159–168.

Tucha, O., Smely, C., Preier, M., & Lange, K. W. (2000). Cognitive deficits before treatment among patients with brain tumors. *Neurosurgery*, *47*, 324–333.

US Cancer Statistics Working Group. (2016). *United States cancer statistics: 1999–2013 incidence and mortality web-based report*. Atlanta, GA: US Department of Health and Human Services, Centers for Disease Control and Prevention and National Cancer Institute. Available at: www.cdc.gov/uscs.

Vardy, J., Dhillon, H. M., Pond, G. R., Xu, W., Rourke, S. B., Dodd A., ... Tannock, I. F. (2014). Cognitive function and fatigue after diagnosis of colorectal cancer. *Annals of Oncology*, *25*, 2404–2412.

Vicari, S. & Anton, P. (2013). Complementary practices: Fatigue, stress, exercise, & diet. In C. A. Noggle & R. S. Dean (Eds.), *The neuropsychology of cancer and oncology* (pp. 413–424). New York, NY: Springer Publishing Company.

Von A. D., Habermann, B., Carpenter, J. S., & Schnieder, B. (2013). Impact of perceived cognitive impairment in breast cancer survivors. *European Journal of Oncology Nursing*, *17*, 236–241.

Wefel, J., Kesler, S. R., Noll, K. R., & Schagen, S. B. (2015). Clinical characteristics, pathophysiology, and management of noncentral nervous system cancer-related cognitive impairment in adults. *A Cancer Journal for Clinicians*, *65*(2), 123–138.

Wefel, J. S., Noll, K. R., & Scheurer, M. E. (2016). Neurocognitive functioning and genetic variation in patients with primary brain tumours. *The Lancet Oncology*, *17*, 97–108.

Willard, V. W., Leung, W., Huang, Q., Zhang, H., & Phipps, S. (2014). Cognitive outcome after pediatric stem-cell transplantation: impact of age and total-body irradiation. *Journal of Clinical Oncology*, *2*(35), 3982–3988.

Wolfe, K. R., Madan-Swain, A., & Kana, R. K. (2012). Executive dysfunction in pediatric posterior fossa tumor survivors: A systematic literature review of neurocognitive deficits and interventions. *Developmental Neuropsychology*, *37*, 153–175.

Wolfe, K. R., Madan-Swain, A., Hunter, G. R., Reddy, A. T., Banos, J., & Kana, R. K. (2013). An fMRI investigation of working memory and its relationship with cardiorespiratory fitness in pediatric posterior fossa tumor survivors who received cranial radiation therapy. *Pediatric Blood Cancer*, *60*(4), 669–675.

Yock, T. I., Yeap, B. Y., Ebb, D. H., Weyman, E., Eaton, B. R., Sherry, N.A., ... Tarbell, N. J. (2016). Long-term toxic effects of proton radiotherapy for paediatric medulloblastoma: A phase 2 single-arm study. *Lancet Oncology*, *17*(3), 287–298.

Chapter 10

Epilepsy

Julie Janecek, Klajdi Puka, Evan Schulze, and Mary Lou Smith

Introduction

Epilepsy is one of the most common neurological disorders worldwide, defined by an enduring predisposition to generate epileptic seizures that can lead to neurobiological, cognitive, and psychosocial consequences. Epileptic seizures are brief periods of altered behavior, including alterations of consciousness and involuntary motor, sensory, autonomic, cognitive, and psychiatric effects, accompanied by abnormal excessive or synchronous neuronal activity in the brain. The International League Against Epilepsy (ILAE) revised the practical definition of epilepsy in 2014 to include (1) at least two unprovoked (or reflex) seizures occurring >24 hours apart, (2) one unprovoked (or reflex) seizure and a probability of further seizures similar to the general recurrence risk (at least 60%) after two unprovoked seizures, occurring over the next 10 years, or (3) diagnosis of an epilepsy syndrome (Fisher et al., 2014).

Historically, the neuropsychological evaluation of individuals with epilepsy has contributed to our understanding of brain–behavior relationships, including hippocampal models of memory, language organization, and lateralization of cognitive functions. Neuropsychology continues to play a critical role as the characterization of epilepsy evolves to include increased understanding of biomarkers for epileptogenesis (i.e., the underlying process that results in the development of epilepsy and the progression of the disease once established) and patterns of neuronal network connectivity. The combination of increased understanding of the heterogeneous pathophysiology of the epilepsies, neuropsychological evaluation, and advanced neuroimaging methods (e.g., functional magnetic resonance imaging [fMRI], diffusion tensor imaging) is essential for the management of individuals with epilepsy, yielding important information about the effects of disease and treatment on cognition and behavior.

Epidemiology and Pathophysiology

Seizures are paroxysmal, transient surges of excitatory or synchronous signals within a network of neurons and result from an imbalance of excitatory and inhibitory signals. The affected neurons determine the clinical manifestation or the subjective experience of the seizure. Seizures have been traditionally divided in two types: generalized and focal. The onset of generalized seizures involves all, or most, of the brain, and are believed to involve alterations to the normal excitatory/inhibitory oscillatory rhythm of the thalamocortical circuit (Kramer & Cash, 2012). In contrast, focal seizures originate from a defined region and arise from decreased inhibition or increased activation in a group of neurons leading to a net excitatory signal that may then propagate to other brain regions (Kramer & Cash, 2012). Antiepileptic drugs (AEDs) reduce the propensity for seizures by enhancing inhibitory and decreasing excitatory neurotransmission, and by these same mechanisms can produce cognitive side effects.

More than 65 million people worldwide are living with epilepsy; however, the large majority of these individuals live in low-income and lower middle income countries (Ngugi, Bottomley, Kleinschmidt, Sander, & Newton, 2010). A recent meta-analysis (Ngugi et al., 2010) found that the median lifetime prevalence of epilepsy in developed countries is 5.8 per 1,000, compared with 15.4 and 10.3 per 1,000 in rural and urban areas of developing countries, respectively. The median prevalence of active epilepsy (having experienced a seizure in the previous 5 years and/or being treated) is 4.9 per 1,000 in developed countries and 12.7 and 5.9 per 1,000 in rural and urban areas of developing countries, respectively. A similar socioeconomic-based disparity is also found in developed countries. There is also a stark difference in the incidence rate among developed and developing countries; in developed countries, the incidence rate follows a bimodal curve peaking at early childhood and in later life (over the age of 65 years), whereas in developing countries the incidence is increased in older children and young adults. This difference in prevalence and incidence is believed to be associated with epilepsy etiologies that are more common in developing countries, namely traumatic brain injuries and central nervous system infections (Ngugi et al., 2010). Other factors that may drive the disparity in prevalence are believed to include malnutrition, poor prenatal and perinatal care, poor access to treatment, and classification or record-keeping differences. Common risk factors in developed and developing countries include family history and gender, with the rate being slightly higher among males.

Prevention

The importance of epilepsy prevention is emphasized by its frequency of occurrence in the general population across the lifespan, and its associated cognitive, psychiatric, and psychosocial consequences. Despite this recognition, the prevention of epilepsy in individuals of all ages remains a major unmet medical need, of critical importance for the nearly 40% of those with acquired epilepsy as a result of brain insult. Prevention efforts have historically focused on reducing the common causes of acquired epilepsy (e.g., traumatic brain injury, cerebral vascular accident, and neuroinfection) or the use of early prophylaxis intervention in those known to be at risk for developing epilepsy. With advances in neuroscience and epigenetics, the field has shifted research efforts to the identification of biomarkers, particularly for the process of epileptogenesis. This new emphasis could provide clear targets for preventive, or potentially curative, therapies that span all age groups and etiologies of epilepsy. The search for antiepileptogenic targets and mechanisms is ongoing, and the current state of prevention efforts for the most common acquired epilepsies are reviewed in this section.

Early Prevention. Strategies for the prevention of epilepsy can begin as early as in utero. During prenatal development, maintaining the health of the mother, taking measures to limit opportunity for infection by completing vaccinations, and preventing fetal toxic exposure and injury are essential for healthy neurodevelopment and limiting opportunities for epileptogenesis. Further, early detection and diagnosis of infection and genetic and metabolic abnormalities allow parents and the medical team the

opportunity for early intervention and management when possible to prevent the occurrence of seizures. Additionally, prenatal measures to prevent premature birth and perinatal asphyxia, and the utilization of neuroprotective agents in cases of hypoxic-ischemic encephalopathy have been demonstrated effective for the prevention of postneonatal epilepsy (Lai & Yang, 2011).

Infection. Certain public health measures are highly effective in preventing infectious causes of epilepsy. Timely vaccination for protection against microorganisms such as measles, rubella, haemophilus influenzae or pneumococcus that cause neuroinfection is important in epilepsy prevention. In cases of infection-related encephalitis or meningioencephalitis, early detection and empirical medical treatment to limit the degree and duration of inflammation can reduce the risk of first seizure and subsequent recurrent seizures. Good hygiene, food safety, and responsible farming practices are effective in preventing parasitic infections, including neurocysticercosis, which is a leading cause of acquired epilepsy in the developing world.

Traumatic Brain Injury. The precise percentage of individuals who develop posttraumatic epilepsy (PTE) after a traumatic brain injury (TBI) is not known, but it is estimated that TBI is an etiological factor in up to 20% of the symptomatic epilepsies in the general population (Agrawal, Timothy, Pandit, & Manju, 2006). Risk factors for PTE include injury severity (e.g., duration of loss of consciousness, diffuse cerebral contusions, intracerebral hemorrhage, and neurosurgical intervention for subdural hematoma), penetrating injury, and increased age. It is well established that moderate and severe TBI confers increased risk for PTE, but the relationship between mild TBI and PTE is less clear. Studies generally rely on samples of hospital-treated mild TBI, which likely represents mild TBIs of greater severity and does not account for the unknown number of mild TBIs that go unreported and/or unrecognized. This factor underestimates the true incidence of mild TBI, thus affecting estimates of risk of PTE after mild TBI.

Research focused on identifying the cause and process of epileptogenesis has suggested the presence of a "latent" period from the time of initial injury to the clinical presentation of recurrent seizures during which epileptogenesis is active. Targeted intervention during the latent period may provide opportunity to abort the process of epileptogenesis. However, review of all randomized clinical trials to date evaluating various AEDs for their potential in preventing PTE has indicated that there exists low evidence that early treatment with AEDs compared with placebo or usual care can reduce the risk of early posttraumatic seizures, and no evidence to support a reduction in risk of late seizures (Thompson, Pohlmann-Eden, Campbell, & Abel, 2015). An area of potentially promising research is the targeting of inflammation, a possible mechanism in epileptogenesis after brain trauma, with initial animal models showing encouraging long-term results (D'Ambrosio, Eastman, Fattore, & Perucca, 2013).

Cerebral Vascular Accident. Poststroke seizures have been observed in 5–20% of patients with stroke; a smaller subset develops poststroke epilepsy, and stroke is the most common cause of seizures in the elderly (Silverman, Restrepo, & Mathews, 2002). After ischemic stroke, greater stroke severity or stroke disability predicts development of seizures, whereas risk factors for seizures after subarachnoid hemorrhage include middle cerebral artery aneurysms, intraparenchymal hematoma, cerebral infarction, and history of hypertension (Silverman et al., 2002). At present, there exists insufficient evidence to support routine prophylactic AED use to prevent epileptogenesis in newly diagnosed stroke. However, recent class III evidence found that statin use, especially in the acute phase, may reduce the risk of postischemic stroke seizures and may prevent the progression of initial poststroke neurodegeneration into chronic epilepsy (Guo et al., 2015).

Clinical Manifestation

Understanding the cognitive, psychiatric, and psychosocial issues associated with epilepsy requires consideration of disease variables (e.g., etiology, pathophysiology, syndrome, duration, seizure frequency, age at onset), treatment variables (e.g., antiepileptic drug effects, surgical intervention), and sociocultural factors (e.g., cultural background, socioeconomic status). The evaluation of individuals with epilepsy is best completed by a multidisciplinary team that includes an epileptologist, neurosurgeon, neuroradiologist, neuropsychologist, psychiatrist, and social worker. Comprehensive assessment may include specialized techniques including electroencephalography (EEG), structural magnetic resonance imaging (MRI),

intracarotid anesthetic testing, task-related functional MRI (fMRI) and resting-state fMRI, magnetoencephalography, and neuropsychological evaluation. Ambulatory and video EEG monitoring are diagnostic tests used to identify seizure type, syndrome, and location, and to distinguish epileptic from nonepileptic events. Structural MRI is commonly used to identify underlying etiologies for seizure disorders (e.g., malformations of cortical development). Intracarotid anesthetic procedures (sometimes referred to as Wada testing) have been used for more than 50 years to provide information about language and memory laterality. More recently, fMRI and magnetoencephalography protocols have been developed to identify patterns of language and memory organization and characterize patterns of neural network dysfunction. In conjunction with these methods, neuropsychological evaluation is used to identify functional deficits, confirm seizure laterality or location, and predict postsurgical language and memory outcome in cases of intractable epilepsy that proceed to neurosurgical intervention.

Table 10.1 is both a summary of the key neuropsychological aspects of epilepsy and a summary of evidence for their neuroanatomical correlates and moderating variables.

Cognitive Manifestations in Children. Most children with active epilepsy – up to 80% – have a behavioral disorder and/or a cognitive impairment (IQ < 85) (Reilly et al., 2014b). Some childhood-onset epilepsy syndromes are characterized by marked developmental delays and behavioral disturbance (see Table 10.2). Although there is a huge range of variability in terms of intellectual function – where some children score at >99th percentile – population-based studies find that up to 40% of children with epilepsy have an intellectual disability (IQ <70), and an additional 15% score in the borderline range (IQs 70–84) (Reilly et al., 2015). Such impairments may be particularly deleterious in children, where they may interfere with the development and attainment of other cognitive, behavioral, and social skills essential for long-term educational, vocational, psychosocial, and quality-of-life outcomes. Impairments in cognition and deficits in multiple aspects of life may also persist after seizure control, so it is essential that children be evaluated, and receive support, for cognitive and psychosocial deficits to improve the quality of life of the child and family.

Table 10.1 Key Neuropsychological Aspects of Epilepsy and Moderating Variables

Epilepsy Focus	Prominent Cognitive/Behavioral Deficits		References
	Dominant Hemisphere	Nondominant Hemisphere	
Temporal lobe	• Naming • Verbal fluency • Verbal skills • Verbal memory • Working memory • Executive functioning, especially set-shifting	• Visuospatial skills • Visual memory • Working memory • Facial recognition • Facial emotional processing • Executive functioning, especially set-shifting	Drane (2015) Hermann, Lin, Jones, & Seidenberg (2009) MacAllister & Sherman (2015) Stretton & Thompson (2012)
Frontal lobe	• Verbal fluency • Naming if inferior frontal gyrus is implicated • Learning and retrieval memory deficits with relatively spared recognition • Proactive interference on memory tasks • Primary and complex attention • Constructional/drawing tasks requiring planning • Response inhibition • Problem-solving • Perseverative errors • Contralateral motor dexterity and grip strength if motor/premotor cortex implicated	• Figural fluency • Learning and retrieval memory deficits with relatively spared recognition • Proactive interference on memory tasks • Primary and complex attention • Constructional/drawing tasks requiring planning • Response inhibition • Problem-solving • Perseverative errors • Contralateral motor dexterity and grip strength if motor/premotor cortex implicated	Drane (2015) Lee (2010) MacAllister & Sherman (2015) Smith (2016)
Parietal lobe	• Naming • Repetition • Comprehension • Reading • Writing • Mathematical calculations • Sensory discrimination	• Constructional abilities • Spatial reasoning • Visuospatial abilities • Attention • Sensory discrimination	Drane (2015) Lee (2010) MacAllister & Sherman (2015)
Occipital lobe	• Basic visual-perceptual abilities • Facial processing • Object recognition • Possible visual illusory phenomenon • Possible visual field cut	• Basic visual-perceptual abilities • Facial processing • Object recognition • Possible visual illusory phenomenon • Possible visual field cut	Drane (2015) Lee (2010) MacAllister & Sherman (2015) Schoenberg, Werz, & Drane (2011)
Generalized	• Intellectual functioning • Attention • Executive functioning • Memory • Verbal fluency • Processing speed		Hermann & Seidenberg (2007) Loughman, Bowden, & D'Souza (2014) MacAllister & Sherman (2015)

Table 10.1 (cont.)

Epilepsy Focus	Prominent Cognitive/Behavioral Deficits		References
	Dominant Hemisphere	Nondominant Hemisphere	
Moderators			
AEDs	Common side effects include alterations in: • Processing speed • Attention • Language • Memory • Mood and behavior		Loring, Marino, & Meador 2007
Age at onset	Earlier age of onset is associated with greater degree of cognitive deficits		Witt & Helmstaedter (2015)
Seizure variables	In general, more significant cognitive deficits are associated with: • Greater seizure frequency • More episodes of status epilepticus • More frequent generalized tonic-clonic seizures • Longer duration of seizure disorder • Refractory epilepsy		Hermann, Meador, Gaillard, & Cramer (2010) Witt & Helmstaedter (2015)
Structural abnormalities	In general, more significant cognitive deficits are associated with: • Mesial temporal lobe sclerosis • Tumor • Stroke • Brain trauma Specific relationships between neuroanatomical structures and cognition have been identified in the context of temporal lobe epilepsy: • Atrophy or sclerosis of the hippocampus has been associated with memory performance, with abnormalities in the language-dominant hemisphere associated with reduced verbal memory, naming, and fluency • Atrophy of the thalamus has been associated with reduced memory and intellectual functioning in left temporal lobe epilepsy • Decreased volume of the basal ganglia has been associated with affective flattening, alogia and avolition, anergia, apathy, anhedonia, and loss of social drive • Amygdala abnormalities have been associated with psychopathology • Decreased volume of the prefrontal cortex has been associated with executive dysfunction • Atrophy of the cingulate and orbitofrontal cortex has been associated with reduced memory performance • Greater differences in T2 values between left and right fusiform gyrus and hippocampus have been associated with worse immediate, but not delayed memory • Left, but not right, temporal pole abnormality identified with fluorodeoxyglucose positron emission tomography has been associated with semantic retrieval of knowledge of famous persons • Cerebellar atrophy has been associated with reduced implicit associative learning		De Reuck, De Clerck, & Van Maele (2006) Hermann et al. (2009) Hermann et al. (2010) Klein, Levin, Duchowny, & Llabre (2000) Widjaja et al. (2013) Widjaja, Zamyadi, Raybaud, Snead, & Smith (2014)

Table 10.1 (cont.)

Epilepsy Focus	Prominent Cognitive/Behavioral Deficits		References
	Dominant Hemisphere	Nondominant Hemisphere	

	• Cortical surface abnormalities in curvature, area, and thickness have been associated with reduced performance IQ, verbal and visual memory, psychomotor processing, speeded fine motor dexterity
	• Corpus callosum volume has been associated with measures of nonverbal problem-solving, immediate memory, complex psychomotor processing, speeded fine motor dexterity
	• In children with nonlesional localization-related epilepsy:
	  · Widespread white matter abnormalities that are correlated with neuropsychological impairment
	  · Smaller hippocampal volumes
	• In left hemisphere-onset epilepsy, left hippocampal volume associated with verbal memory		

Table 10.2 Epilepsy Syndromes of Childhood Characterized by Marked Cognitive and/or Behavioral Dysfunction

Syndrome	Neuropsychological Features
Infantile spasms (West syndrome)	• Onset within first year of life. • Development may be normal or abnormal before onset; deterioration in development commonly, although not inevitably, follows onset of seizures. • Most children develop intellectual disabilities, with such adverse outcome related to the underlying etiology (e.g., genetic disorders, cortical malformations).
Severe myoclonic epilepsy in infancy (Dravet syndrome)	• Onset in first year of life, with prior normal development. • When seizures persist, developmental delay (cognitive and motor) is usually evident by the second or third year of life.
Lennox-Gastaut syndrome	• Onset usually in second year of life but may be later with majority before age 7 years. • Characterized by cognitive, motor, and behavioral disturbances, which may be evident before onset of seizures. • Cognitive function deteriorates progressively over time such that most cases eventually have marked intellectual disabilities.
Epilepsy with continuous spikes and waves during slow wave sleep	• Onset 2 months to 12 years with peak at 4–5 years. • Cognitive and motor decline and behavioral disturbance emerge over time. • With seizure remission, there may be improvement in cognition and behavior but recovery is usually not complete.
Myoclonic-astatic epilepsy (Doose syndrome)	• Typical onset between the ages of 7 months and 5 years. • Developmental outcomes relate to seizure control, but up to 20% have borderline or mild developmental delay; another 20% have moderate to severe delay.
Landau-Kleffner syndrome	• Onset typically occurs at between 3 and 7 years of age, with presentation of receptive language impairment which may eventually also affect expressive language. • May occur in children in whom language development has been significantly delayed before onset of seizures. • Lack of cognitive progression may occur, resulting in intellectual disability. • Behavior may be disturbed, either as a primary feature of the seizure disorder or secondary to the frustration imposed by the language impairments.

Cognitive difficulties are a main area of concern for children with epilepsy and their parents. Although cognitive deficits may be more likely among children with medically refractory epilepsy, impairments in multiple cognitive domains are also found in syndromes previously believed to be benign with respect to cognitive comorbidities (Jackson et al., 2013). Furthermore, cognitive impairments are found in children with epilepsy before the onset of clinical seizures or antiepileptic medications (Jackson et al., 2013). These findings suggest that the underlying neural substrate predisposes patients to both seizures and cognitive morbidities. In addition, frequent epileptic activity, especially early in life, may increase the risk for seizures later in life and exacerbate the underlying neural substrate, cognitive functioning and behavioral disorders (see Figure 10.1). Indeed, recurrent seizures affect neural development and white matter tracts, but it is not clear whether these neural changes arise as a result of neural damage or as an adaptive mechanism to compensate for the hyperexcitability of epilepsy.

Children with new-onset and medically refractory epilepsy have been found to have widespread structural and functional changes in comparison with healthy controls in brain imaging studies (Bonilha et al., 2014; Smith, 2016). Although such changes are present at the onset of seizures, some studies have related connectivity changes to the duration of epilepsy, suggesting that recurrent seizures may further disrupt network organization. Children with epilepsy show alternations in the volume of various cortical and subcortical regions as well as connectivity differences, including impaired white matter integrity and suboptimal topological organization with enhanced network segregation and reduced global integration. Importantly, these widespread differences have been linked to, and are more prominent, among children with cognitive impairments. Such differences extend beyond the seizure onset zone and have been found in both cerebral hemispheres even in children with localization-related epilepsy. These findings are in line with the new proposed framework suggesting that underlying networks, as opposed to isolated regions, play a role in epileptogenesis and comorbidities (Smith, 2016). Therefore, although some specific cognitive impairments are typically associated with specific syndromes or seizure foci, various cognitive impairments are possible in all epilepsy syndromes.

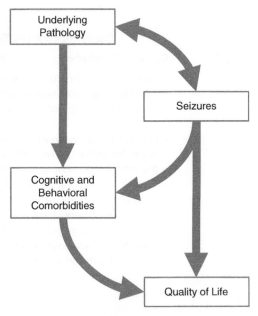

Figure 10.1. Schematic representation of the relationship between the underlying pathology, recurrent seizures, and cognitive and behavioral comorbidities. The underlying etiology predisposes patients to seizures and comorbidities. In turn, recurrent seizures lead to structural and functional changes and may in addition contribute to or act synergistically with the underlying pathology to negatively affect development and cognition. Cognitive and behavioral comorbidities and recurrent seizures are two of the most important determinants of quality of life in children with epilepsy.

Children with epilepsy – even those with normal intelligence – show cognitive impairments in a number of domains, particularly in attention, memory, executive functioning, and academic achievement. Deficits in attention are particularly important as they can affect other cognitive functions and many tasks in life. Although attention deficits are more prevalent among patients with lower IQs, they can be distinguished from generalized cognitive impairments and have been documented in children with normal IQ. Moreover, such deficits may be common in a third of children with new-onset epilepsy before the initiation of AEDs. Diagnosis of attention deficit hyperactivity disorder (ADHD) may also precede or follow the onset of clinical seizures and is prevalent in up to 40% of children with epilepsy (Salpekar & Mishra, 2014). Children with epilepsy and ADHD differ from other samples of children with ADHD by an equal male-to-female ratio and a predominance of the inattentive subtype of ADHD. In addition, children with epilepsy are less likely to be diagnosed with ADHD or receive psychostimulant treatment. It is important to note that there is no evidence that stimulant medications for the treatment of ADHD exacerbates seizures in children with epilepsy (Salpekar & Mishra, 2014).

Memory problems are also commonly identified in children with epilepsy and may present as abnormally rapid forgetting or impairments in episodic, semantic, or autobiographical memory. Most of these studies find that children with epilepsy score significantly below the test norms and in comparison with healthy peers; in addition, up to 58% of children with epilepsy have been found to have poorer performance in at least one type of memory task than would be expected based on their IQ (Reilly et al., 2015). Studies evaluating memory deficits in children with epilepsy have traditionally focused among those with temporal lobe seizures; however, memory dysfunction is common in children with frontal lobe epilepsy, and has also been documented in other epilepsy syndromes. Memory impairments in these groups may arise as a result of the anatomical and functional connections to the temporal lobes. Unlike adults, children do not always show hemispheric lateralization of memory function but this may emerge with further development; when memory function is lateralized, verbal memory deficits are associated relatively more with left-sided temporal lobe epilepsy, and nonverbal memory deficits are associated with right-sided temporal lobe epilepsy.

Impairments in executive function – the set of cognitive processes involving attentional control, working memory, planning, categorization, mental flexibility, inhibitory control, reasoning, comprehension, concept formation, and motor coordination – are most commonly observed in children with frontal lobe epilepsy (Smith, 2016). In these patients, impairments have not been linked to the laterality or localization of the epileptogenic foci within the frontal lobes. However, executive dysfunctions are also found in children with extrafrontal lobe epilepsy, likely as a result of anatomical and functional networks propagating to the frontal lobes (Smith, 2016). Additionally, few differences in executive function have been found among children with temporal and frontal lobe epilepsy in studies that have directly compared these groups.

Lastly, academic problems, in reading, spelling, and/or arithmetic, are common in children with epilepsy and have been found in up to 72% of children (Reilly et al., 2014a). In children with epilepsy, cognitive deficits may interfere with the development and attainment of academic skills; however, academic problems go beyond, and can be distinguished from, overall cognitive impairments.

Although some specific cognitive impairments are typically associated with specific syndromes or seizure foci, epilepsy is a network disorder and various cognitive impairments are possible in all epilepsy syndromes. Investigating the child and epilepsy-related predictors of cognitive impairment, studies typically find poorer outcomes associated with an earlier age of seizure onset, a longer duration of life with seizures, more frequent seizures, symptomatic etiology, and a greater number of antiepileptic medications. Improved cognitive functioning after seizure control and deteriorated functioning with recurrent seizures have also been reported. However, not all studies find these associations; consequently, the impact of recurrent seizures and the duration of epilepsy on cognitive functioning continue to be debated. It may be that the epilepsy syndrome and the type and frequency of seizures are important moderators in reconciling these differences in studies. The impact of antiepileptic medications is also not ubiquitous and depends on the medication used. (This is further discussed in the Intervention section.) There is also evidence that family factors may also play an important role in cognitive development among some children with epilepsy.

Overall, most children with epilepsy experience some degree of cognitive impairment, even before the onset of seizures or antiepileptic medication. Children with epilepsy have widespread structural and functional abnormalities with reduced global integration and increased connectivity to the epileptogenic zone. These widespread differences have been associated with cognitive impairment; consequently, a variety of possible cognitive impairments can be found in in all epilepsies. Recurrent seizures may in addition contribute to, or act synergistically with, the underlying aberrant network. This in turn may lead to greater structural and functional changes and exacerbated cognitive development. Early identification and intervention for cognitive impairments may be essential in children with epilepsy because there may be a window of opportunity for early intervention in some children.

Cognitive Manifestations in Adults. Cognitive deficits of adults with epilepsy mirror those of children in that they are highly variable, given the heterogeneity of the epilepsies, but may include abnormalities in intelligence, language, visuoperception, learning and memory, executive function, and/or processing speed. Cognitive deficits often precede or are present at the onset of epilepsy and may be related to developmental or acquired structural abnormalities that can cause both epilepsy and cognitive impairment. However, cognitive impairment has been described in adults with newly diagnosed epilepsy without evidence of brain pathology as well, believed to be primarily related to epileptic dysfunction and secondarily related to behavioral and psychiatric problems that may also precede the first seizure. The cognitive course associated with epilepsy is affected by age at onset, seizure variables (e.g., type, duration, and frequency), AED effects, psychiatric comorbidities, cognitive reserve, and age- and gender-dependent neural plasticity (Witt & Helmstaedter, 2015). Factors that have been associated with poorer cognitive functioning in adulthood include earlier age at onset or first risk for seizures, greater exposure to AEDs (e.g., higher doses, rapid titration, and the cumulative effects of multiple AEDs), longer duration of seizure disorder, greater seizure frequency, greater lifetime total of generalized seizures, more frequent episodes of status epilepticus, presence of mesial temporal sclerosis and hippocampal volume loss, and refractory epilepsy (Hermann et al., 2010).

Cognitive deficits can be characteristic of a particular epilepsy syndrome (e.g., executive dysfunction associated with frontal lobe epilepsy, verbal memory impairment associated with dominant hemisphere temporal lobe epilepsy). However, there is significant overlap between syndromes, which is likely due to the presence of widespread structural abnormalities and neural network dysfunction, regardless of seizure focus. For example, mesial temporal lobe epilepsy is the most common localization-related epilepsy in adults. This condition is associated with mesial temporal sclerosis, and therefore memory impairment is common, which can be material-specific; adults with left temporal lobe seizure foci and typical language organization often demonstrate verbal memory deficits. However, volumetric studies have demonstrated structural abnormalities that lie both within and outside the epileptogenic focus in the hippocampus, amygdala, entorhinal and perirhinal cortices, fornix, mammillary bodies, and the thalamus, as well as bilateral cortical thinning. Any of these abnormalities can disrupt complex neural

networks, resulting in widespread cognitive abnormalities in the areas of attention, processing speed, intellectual functioning, language, visuoperceptual skills, verbal and nonverbal memory, executive functioning, and motor skills. Volumetric abnormalities at time of diagnosis and lower intellectual functioning have been shown to predict progressive cognitive deficits (Hermann et al., 2010). In addition to these structural abnormalities, increased use of functional neuroimaging in recent years has advanced our understanding of neural network dysfunction associated with epilepsy, which is consistent with the widespread and variable cognitive deficits that can be observed. For example, in both focal and generalized epilepsy syndromes, resting-state fMRI data indicate widespread neural network abnormalities that are often seen bilaterally, with some commonalities across syndromes such as disruption of the default mode network (Centeno & Carmichael, 2014).

The cognitive assessment of older adults with chronic or new-onset epilepsy requires special consideration due to unique risks for comorbidities and complications in the elderly. For example, older adults are more likely to have comorbid health conditions that affect cognition (e.g., cerebrovascular disease, hypertension, diabetes), are more susceptible to adverse effects of AEDs and medication interactions due to polypharmacy, and may be at greater risk for postoperative cognitive decline if they undergo neurosurgical intervention (Chapin & Naugle, 2015). The percentage of individuals with epilepsy who are at risk for cognitive decline in older adulthood and the type of cognitive decline (i.e., focal deficits vs. global decline; gradual decline vs. acute decline) has not been adequately characterized. This is likely due to the wide variety in the etiology, course, and treatment of epilepsy. The impact of epilepsy on cognition in older adults is not well understood but there is some evidence that supports a bidirectional relationship between epilepsy and dementia, such that individuals with epilepsy may be at increased risk of developing dementia and individuals with dementia may be at increased risk of developing seizure disorders. Moreover, there is some evidence that seizures may be associated with accelerated cognitive aging. Two models that have been proposed are the "chronic accumulation model" and the "second hit model" (Breuer et al., 2016). The chronic accumulation model has previously been referred to as "epileptic dementia" and suggests that there is a gradual cognitive decline in excess of that associated with normal aging over the lifespan due to disease and treatment factors. The second hit model suggests that cerebral reserve is diminished by a "first hit" (e.g., TBI, vascular disease, epilepsy) with incomplete recovery, followed by a subsequent "second hit" that results in acute cognitive decline that does not return to baseline. Several risk factors for cognitive decline in older adults with epilepsy have been identified, including early or late age at onset (i.e., early onset associated with abnormal neurodevelopment, late onset associated with decreased cognitive and brain reserve), disease duration, seizure type and frequency, epileptic encephalopathy, coexisting diseases (e.g., vascular disease, Alzheimer disease), and the use of multiple AEDs (Breuer et al., 2016).

Psychosocial Clinical Features in Children. The psychosocial comorbidities in children with epilepsy comprise psychiatric and psychological disorders and social difficulties. The interested reader is directed to the recent detailed report on psychiatric and behavioral disorders in children with epilepsy by the ILAE Child Neuropsychiatry Task Force (Besag et al., 2016), and the review in this section is largely based on that report. Epidemiological studies from around the world indicate that the rates of psychiatric disorder range from around 35% to 50%; in children with complicated epilepsy, usually implying structural brain abnormality and accompanying intellectual disability, the rate is even higher, well over 50%. The varying rates reflect the differences in methods used for assessment, recruitment settings (community setting vs. tertiary care vs. population-based), the chronicity of the epilepsy, and whether the study is cross-sectional or longitudinal in design. Even with this variance, it is clear that children with epilepsy are at 3–9 times higher risk for mental health disorders than are healthy children and children with non–central nervous system chronic illness. Although these problems are well recognized, there has been a lack of systematic assessment of psychosocial comorbidities at the clinical care level, and only about one-third of children who experience such distress receive treatment. Studies of long-term psychosocial outcomes have demonstrated that those with intellectual disability usually have a lifetime of dependence; those with intelligence within normal limits are often undereducated, under- or unemployed, have a higher risk of psychiatric disorders, and are at risk for social adversity such as isolation or inadvertent

pregnancy. These risk factors remain even in those who achieve seizure remission.

The most common forms of psychopathology in children with epilepsy are ADHD (covered in the earlier section), anxiety (15–36%) and depression (8–35%). The presence of anxiety and depression may be related to the epilepsy or to treatment factors, such as side effects of AEDs, or the anxiety that children may feel due to the unpredictability of the seizures, or the development of social phobias due to avoidance of social situations where they may have seizures. Children with symptomatic epilepsy or epilepsy syndromes have high rates of developmental delay, hyperactivity, and autism.

There is little consistent evidence for the role of seizure variables (e.g., age of seizure onset, frequency of seizures) in psychopathology; however, it is clear that psychiatric and behavioral problems predate the onset of seizures and have a relationship with seizure recurrence, thus suggesting a bidirectional relationship between epilepsy and psychopathology. Neuroimaging studies have identified functional and structural abnormalities associated with psychiatric and behavioral symptoms, suggesting that these mental health and behavioral disorders arise from the underlying neuropathology that is causative in the epilepsy.

At all ages, children and adolescents with epilepsy report problems with social function, including difficulties in peer interaction and social isolation. Furthermore, it has recently been recognized that children with epilepsy have impairments in social cognition, specifically in aspects of theory of mind such as the understanding of false belief and intentional lying, even in the face of parental report of adequate social skills per se (Raud, Kaldoja, & Kolk, 2015).

Psychosocial Clinical Features in Adults. Adults with epilepsy have a higher rate of mental health disorders compared with the general population. In a Canadian population-based analysis using a standardized mental health interview, adults with epilepsy had higher rates of major depressive disorder and anxiety disorders, with lifetime prevalence rates at 17.4% and 22.8%, respectively, and almost twice the lifetime prevalence of any mental health disorder (Tellez-Zenteno, Patten, Jette, Williams, & Wiebe, 2007). As with cognitive dysfunction, psychiatric disturbances may precede or be present at the onset of seizure disorders. Thus, a bidirectional relationship has been proposed between epilepsy and various psychiatric disorders including depression, ADHD, schizophrenia, psychosis, and suicidality. Although there are core psychiatric deficits associated with particular epilepsy syndromes, there are more commonly shared psychiatric symptoms across syndromes. For example, temporal lobe epilepsy has been associated with depression and anxiety, whereas frontal lobe epilepsy has been associated with behavioral and personality changes. However, mood disorders that co-occur with temporal lobe epilepsy are not limited to depression and anxiety, and have been associated with widespread structural abnormalities in orbital frontal cortex, cingulate gyrus, subcortical regions, and the brain stem. Among adults with epilepsy, psychiatric comorbidities are associated with greater limitation and disability and greater health-care utilization cost. Although individuals with epilepsy can experience psychiatric disorders in a similar fashion to their counterparts without epilepsy, there are factors that have the potential to influence the expression of psychiatric symptoms including underlying brain disorder, behavioral changes that precede or follow seizures, psychiatric syndromes such as interictal dysphoric disorder, and the psychotropic effect of seizure medications (Lin, Mula, & Hermann, 2012).

The psychological functioning of older adults with epilepsy is understudied and poorly understood. Assessment tools specifically designed to measure emotional symptoms in this population are limited, but critically important because there can be overlap between psychiatric symptoms and epilepsy symptoms. Moreover, atypical presentations are possible, and it has been suggested that depression in elderly adults may be characterized by weight loss, fewer feelings of guilt and worthlessness, and "subsyndromal" presentations in which symptoms are reported that do not meet diagnostic criteria for major depressive disorder (Chapin & Naugle, 2015).

Epilepsy significantly affects many aspects of psychosocial functioning, including quality of medical care and quality of life. According to the Centers for Disease Control and Prevention's Behavioral Risk Surveillance Study (Kobau et al., 2008), adults with a history of epilepsy compared with those without epilepsy have lower rates of educational attainment (40.9% with less than a high school education vs. 26.3%), higher rates of unemployment (6.8% vs. 5%) or inability to work (23.7% vs. 4.8%), and lower annual household incomes (annual incomes < $25,000, 40.9% vs. 26.3%). Lower socioeconomic status has significant ramifications for health-care access; 23.7% of adults with epilepsy reported cost as a barrier to seeking care from a doctor within the past year and 34.9% reported that they had not seen a neurologist or epileptologist. Stigma and shame associated with the presence of the disease have frequently been reported and many individuals with epilepsy reported rarely or never getting the emotional support they needed. In addition, approximately 40% of adults with active epilepsy (i.e., having a seizure in the past 3 months or taking medication for epilepsy) reported that epilepsy or its treatment limited their activities during the past month, and overall health-related quality of life is rated lower among individuals with epilepsy compared with individuals without epilepsy. Greater seizure severity has been frequently correlated with lower quality of life, but a number of studies have demonstrated that depression is an independent determinant of quality of life above and beyond seizure control. In addition, being able to drive and employment status have been shown to be highly related to quality of life, and regaining driving privileges is often a main treatment goal (Jehi, Tesar, Obuchowski, Novak, & Najm, 2011). A systematic review of predictors of health-related quality of life in adults with epilepsy revealed relationships between increased seizure frequency, and comorbid conditions such as depression and anxiety and reduced quality of life. Although other factors such as unemployment, lower educational status, age at onset of epilepsy, and AED polytherapy have also been reported as predictors of quality of life, when adjusted for gender, socioeconomic status, and poor seizure control, these factors were no longer statistically predictive (Taylor, Sander, Taylor, & Baker, 2011). Mixed findings have been reported regarding quality of life in older adults with epilepsy, and unique factors related to the psychosocial impact of epilepsy in older adulthood remains relatively unexplored. Typically, older adults with epilepsy report concerns similar to those of their younger adult counterparts, including driving/transportation, medication side effects, personal safety, AED costs, employment, social embarrassment and lack of social support, mood symptoms, and memory loss (Chapin & Naugle, 2015).

Cultural Considerations Across the Lifespan. The experience and treatment of epilepsy are heavily influenced by cultural background and beliefs. Throughout the world, epilepsy is attributed to various folk, religious, or spiritual causes, including possession by a demon, a test from a religious figure, or a punishment, and is frequently accompanied by considerable stigma. Symptom reporting is influenced by culture, knowledge, beliefs, and fear of potential repercussions due to stigma. Moreover, cultural background is often associated with socioeconomic status, and both are factors that are related to access to health care and acceptance and trust of medical professionals. For example, when compared with English-speaking US-born persons with epilepsy, Spanish-speaking immigrant persons with epilepsy living in the United States had less access to comprehensive health insurance coverage and were receiving significantly fewer AEDs. In addition, this group reported higher levels of anxiety and depression, but was receiving less treatment for depression (Myers et al., 2015).

Longitudinal Development and Longer Term Outcomes. Population-based studies find an overall favorable outcome in terms of seizure control; prospective studies evaluating patients over decades find that prolonged periods of seizure remission occur in up to 80% of patients, and up to 50% continue to be seizure free after treatment discontinuation (Beghi, Giussani, & Sander, 2015). However, despite a favorable prognosis for most patients, rates of remission are lower for patients with symptomatic etiology, and epilepsy carries a greater risk of premature mortality as a result of the underlying neurological disorder (Beghi et al., 2015). In addition, up to 30% of patients continue to have poorly controlled seizures despite maximal medical management and require surgical management, a vagal nerve stimulator, or placement on the ketogenic diet. Beyond seizure-related variables patients often face debilitating cognitive and psychosocial deficits that often persist after seizure remission. Consequently, long-term outcomes with respect to education, employment, income, and social relations are often poor in those with a history of epilepsy.

Studies evaluating long-term life outcomes consistently identify neurological, cognitive, and psychiatric problems as key determinants of poor outcomes (Camfield & Camfield, 2014). Nonetheless, poor outcomes are also found among adults with uncomplicated epilepsy and normal intelligence. Seizure control has been associated with improved outcomes in some studies; however, even individuals who enter adulthood seizure and medication free are found to have poor outcomes. A number of studies find that adults with a history of childhood-onset epilepsy achieve lower levels of educational attainment, income, and marriage or long-term relationships relative to healthy peers, whereas their unemployment rate and likelihood of living alone are higher (Camfield & Camfield, 2014). Although not all population studies find deficits in all life outcomes, it is evident that the course of childhood epilepsy, even when seizures remit, continues to have negative consequences on patients' lives. This is particularly important because children may be lost to follow-up in the transition to adult care, particularly when seizures are well controlled. Consequently, patients may be left with myriad comorbidities and may find it difficult to access appropriate services.

Psychogenic Nonepileptic Seizures

Psychogenic nonepileptic seizures (PNES) resemble epileptic seizures but are not caused by abnormal neuronal electrical discharges and arise as a result of psychological distress. These are not factitious events consciously feigned by patients. PNES is classified as a psychiatric disorder (specifically, conversion disorder) falling under the diagnostic category of somatic symptom disorders in the *Diagnostic and Statistical Manual of Mental Disorders*, 5th edition. Patients with PNES often have a misdiagnosis of epilepsy; on average the diagnostic delay has been 7 years, although more recently, in dedicated PNES clinics, this delay has been reduced to 2 years. The gold standard for diagnosis is video EEG monitoring of the typical events, which show no evidence of associated epileptiform discharges. The American Epilepsy Society has recently published a Clinical Information Sheet for PNES, which details the characteristics, risk factors, and management strategies, which may be found at: https://www.aesnet.org/sites/default/files/file_attach/ClinicalResources/PracticeTools/42981132_pnes_information_sheet-2016–062216.pdf.

Adults and children with PNES differ in terms of risk factors and treatment approaches. PNES is less prevalent among children, presenting in 3.5–9% admitted for prolonged video EEG – compared with 20% in adult series – likely related to the effects of chronic epilepsy in older patients (Lortie, 2013). Although most children with PNESs are older than

13 years of age, children as young as 5 years have been diagnosed. Girls are also more likely to be diagnosed, although this is less clear in younger populations. Psychological stressors are more frequent than psychiatric problems among children; consequently, psychological adverse events such as bullying, social difficulties, family dysfunction, and unrealistic parent expectations are risk factors among youth. In addition, epilepsy, history of medically unexplained symptoms, and history of psychopathology present additional risk factors. The first and one of the most important interventions is to clearly, and in a nonjudgmental, positive manner, present the diagnosis, which should be presented separately to parents and children. Patients and families should be provided with educational material before discharge and followed by a mental health professional. Unless there is comorbid epilepsy and PNES, AEDs should not be continued and their use may worsen symptoms. The long-term treatment goal for children is to use adaptive problem-solving strategies developed through comprehensive psychotherapy with the child and parallel work with the parents. Prognosis is better in children in comparison with adults, where 73% and 81% are seizure free at 1- and 3-year follow-up, respectively (Lortie, 2013).

In cases of adult onset, PNES typically manifests in the second or third decade of life, with 75% of adults with PNESs in most epilepsy center series identifying as female. The gender disparity diminishes when the onset is later in life, which may be related to the common gender-neutral etiological factor of health-related traumatic experiences in older adults (Reuber, 2008). Generally, research investigating predisposing factors for the development of PNESs have demonstrated that around 90% of adults with PNESs report significant traumatic experiences in their past, commonly child physical and sexual abuse (Reuber, 2008). Although the presence of trauma is hypothesized to be an important predisposing factor, the interaction with other psychosocial factors, including childhood maltreatment and familial dysfunction, personality factors especially borderline personality traits, tight emotional control, a hostile or avoidant coping style, and more severe levels of psychopathology may play a role in the manifestation of PNES and underlie the importance of taking a comprehensive psychosocial history (Bodde et al., 2009; Reuber, 2008). Investigations of neurobiological underpinnings of PNES using neuroimaging techniques have suggested that dysfunction of emotion processing areas (e.g., insula), dysregulation of executive control regions (e.g., dorsal lateral prefrontal cortex, inferior frontal gyrus), dysregulation of the parietal cortex, and an increased focus on somatic function attributed to insula, parietal cortex, and anterior cingulate gyrus function may be involved in the pathophysiology of PNES (Asadi-Pooya, 2015).

A significant concern for the treating clinician is the comorbid presentation of epilepsy and PNES, which poses a diagnostic challenge. The prevalence of comorbid epilepsy and PNES is unknown, with reported rates ranging from 5.3% to 50% (Baroni et al., 2016). A recent review of the literature by Baroni et al. (2016) revealed that the available research to date provides insufficient data to delineate demographic, epileptological, and psychiatric variables that can reliably distinguish individuals with comorbid epilepsy and PNES from those with PNES alone or those with epilepsy alone, highlighting the need for further research in this area. Notably, the manifestation of PNES is commonly preceded by epilepsy in the comorbid condition, and can manifest when epileptic seizures have been controlled by AEDs. Such a scenario may increase the likelihood for addition of AEDs, which in turn may hinder the treatment and prognosis of PNES.

Opportunity for intervention in adults with PNES begins by communicating the diagnosis to the patient and family members. It is important to recognize that many patients have endured stigma and psychosocial consequence associated with their seizures, many with a previous diagnosis of epilepsy, which can make the delivery of a PNES diagnosis challenging for the patient and clinician. Presenting the diagnosis as a team, with the neurologist or epileptologist accompanied by a consulting psychologist or neuropsychologist may assist in delivering the message that the diagnosis is agreed upon based on the medical and psychological workup. Further, the ruling out of epilepsy is not simply a negative diagnosis; the positive diagnosis of PNES needs to be conveyed along with a plan for treatment. Early psychoeducation regarding PNES with informational handouts provided to the patients may facilitate a good prognosis. To aid in the management of psychiatric distress often underlying the manifestation of PNES, the utilization of empirically based psychotherapy (e.g., cognitive behavioral therapy, interpersonal therapy, dialectical behavioral therapy) is generally recommended, as is the treatment of underlying psychiatric disorders with medication. In their review of the literature, Bodde et al. (2009) highlight factors believed to be associated with favorable prognosis: no or a mild psychiatric history; short history of PNES or an early diagnosis; identifiable acute psychological trauma preceding onset of PNES; living independently; absence of comorbid epilepsy; intact cognitive functioning; higher socioeconomic class; less dramatic seizure presentation; younger age; no history of violence; no ongoing use of AEDs; lower scores on personality measures of inhibition, emotional dysregulation, and compulsiveness; and being female. The current outcome data is limited by lack of well-controlled studies of long-term outcome; however, it has been noted that simply making the diagnosis of PNES can lead to cessation of seizures in a substantial number of patients, although long-term remission rates tend to be <50% with relapse common (Langfitt & Watson, 2016). Health-related quality of life in adults with PNES has been found to be most associated with depressive symptoms, the presence of dissociation, somatic symptoms, escape-avoidance coping strategies, and family dysfunction, which may serve as therapeutic targets. Importantly, psychological and interpersonal factors, not seizure reduction, were found to be associated with health-related quality of life in PNES, and these factors should be primary targets of treatment (Jones, Reuber, & Norman, 2016).

Neuropsychological Assessment

A variety of neurophysiological (e.g. EEG, magnetoencephalography) and neuroimaging (e.g., MRI, fMRI, positron emission tomography) techniques are widely used in diagnosing and monitoring patients with epilepsy. The unique contribution of neuropsychology is its ability to detect the functional consequences of epilepsy, and the potential effects of the medical or surgical treatment of epilepsy (Jones-Gotman et al., 2010). The contribution of neuropsychologists in epilepsy has been well recognized in a number of published guidelines for specialized epilepsy centers and recommendations for practice (Jayakar et al., 2014; Labiner et al., 2010).

Multiple roles for neuropsychological assessment have been identified (Wilson et al., 2015). At times, the purpose of the assessment is diagnostic because deficits in cognition or behavior can provide lateralizing or localizing information about the nature or extent of the seizure network, or the nature of the

epilepsy syndrome. Assessment results can also delineate the neurological, psychological, and social processes affecting a patient's clinical presentation, and thus contribute to the identification and provision of optimal treatment. A third role is prognostic, with assessment results used to monitor and estimate the impact of ongoing seizures or a particular treatment on the future cognitive and behavioral functioning of an individual. Finally, providing information about the nature and implications of the assessment results is a form of education to those affected epilepsy, in that it can address the impact of epilepsy on the patient and family, management of cognitive or behavioral comorbidities, and any educational, vocational or psychosocial difficulties.

The key role of neuropsychology in the comprehensive diagnostic workup of patients for epilepsy surgery and their postsurgical management is well recognized (Jayakar et al., 2014; Labiner et al., 2010). Neuropsychological evaluation establishes a cognitive and psychological baseline before surgical intervention. Although video EEG monitoring is the gold standard method used to localize seizure focus, neuropsychological assessment can be used to confirm the lateralization and location of seizure focus, because the convergence of neurophysiological, neuroimaging, and neuropsychological data has been shown to predict postoperative cognitive and seizure outcomes. Moreover, preoperative naming and verbal memory scores combined with language lateralization data can be used to predict postoperative naming and verbal memory outcome (Swanson, Binder, Raghavan, & Euler, 2015).

The ILAE Neuropsychology Task Force recently developed recommendations to address expectations for assessment in routine epilepsy care (Wilson et al., 2015). First, it recommended that all patients undergo a brief screening for cognitive and psychosocial comorbidities at the time of epilepsy onset, to identify those people who require a more intensive neuropsychological assessment and to provide a minimal baseline against which to evaluate potential progression of the disease or the effects of treatment. Second, it recommended assessment when there are signs or symptoms of a focal cognitive impairment, because such symptoms can provide critical diagnostic information about the syndrome, lesion location, or seizure network underpinning the patient's epilepsy, and may help to distinguish between ictal and interictal deficits. Third, assessment is warranted when there is a question of neurodevelopmental delay, behavioral or learning difficulties which have not previously been documented with psychological assessment, or when the patient undergoes cognitive decline. Fourth, repeated assessments provide a means for evaluating the effects of the disorder and its treatment, and in detecting clinically meaningful changes in cognition or behavior associated with medication changes or after neurosurgery in adult and pediatric populations.

Considerations for the neuropsychological assessment of culturally diverse individuals with epilepsy have recently been reviewed by Bender (2015). It is important to recognize the potential for test bias when using tests that were developed and normed in a country different than the individual's country of origin, to complete testing in primary and secondary languages, and to consider culture-specific experiences such as years of education, level of acculturation, and degree of bilingualism when interpreting test results. In addition, when evaluating bilingual or multilingual individuals, cognitive assessment should be conducted in all languages spoken because most cortical mapping studies indicate separate as well as common cortical areas supporting each language in the case of bilingual individuals. The culture of the client may also have an impact on the perception of the clinician-patient relationship. As such there may be an influence on the interactions that occur during the assessment, the test-taking behavior (which could affect the test results), and the nature of the feedback provided on the test results. Cultural differences in the meaning or perception of time may influence performance on timed tests (Jones-Gotman et al., 2010).

The neuropsychological evaluation of individuals with epilepsy should include a broad battery of tests to fully assess the highly variable focal and diffuse effects of seizures and treatment. Cognitive domains of interest include general intellectual functioning, academic skills, attention and speed of processing, language, nonverbal skills, memory, executive functions, sensory and motor functions, personality, mood, and behavior. Specific tests recommended for the assessment of individuals with epilepsy have been reviewed by Jones-Gotman et al. (2010) and particular considerations for the presurgical neuropsychological evaluation have been reviewed by Drane (2015). In addition, the National Institute of Neurological Disorders and Stroke (NINDS) commissioned a group to develop recommendations for neuropsychological testing in epilepsy, which can be found on the NINDS Common Data Elements website: https://www.commondataelements.ninds.nih.gov.

In general, it is important to assess intellectual functioning because, although a wide range of intellectual functioning has been documented, individuals with epilepsy are at risk for reduced intellectual functioning and IQ scores are good predictors of educational, vocational, and economic outcome. In addition, assessment of academic skills is of particular importance for individuals who are in the educational system and may require academic accommodations. Attention and processing speed should be assessed as well, because problems in these domains are common sequelae of seizures and treatment with AEDs, or may co-occur as a result of underlying pathology (e.g., ADHD occurs with greater frequency in this population). Reduced attention and processing speed may also interfere with performance in other cognitive domains (e.g., memory), thus influencing the interpretation of the entire test battery. Numerous tests of attention and processing speed exist, and may be brief or sustained, visual or auditory, with or without a motor component, and of varied complexity. In addition, symptoms of inattention to sensory stimuli can also be assessed through tests of double simultaneous presentation.

Comparisons of nonverbal skills and language can be used to identify lateralized cognitive dysfunction. Nonverbal cognitive functions should be assessed, beginning with basic visual perception which, if impaired, may preclude higher level nonverbal testing. Additional assessment of nonverbal skills may include visuospatial and construction skills, nonverbal reasoning, and visuoperception. Language testing is also essential, and comprehensive language assessment may include naming, comprehension, fluency, repetition, and reading. Assessment of visual confrontation naming is especially critical for the presurgical epilepsy patient because visual naming decline is commonly seen after dominant hemisphere anterior temporal lobectomy, and confrontation naming preoperative score combined with fMRI language laterality indices has been used to develop a published regression equation designed to predict naming decline after left temporal lobectomy (Swanson et al., 2015).

Epilepsy often arises from the temporal lobe, and so memory assessment is critically important, and should be assessed in both the verbal and visual modality. The tests should be as similar as possible to maximize the ability to provide information regarding material-specific memory deficits. However, this comparison has proven difficult due to the challenges of developing nonverbal analogs to verbal memory tests, and a consistent relationship between right temporal seizure foci and nonverbal memory deficits has not been reported. In general, multiple trial list learning verbal memory tests have been recommended, including learning trials, recall, and recognition trials. In the presurgical epilepsy evaluation, verbal memory assessment is critical because verbal memory decline has been reported in a portion of patients who undergo left hemisphere anterior temporal lobectomy. Single trial story memory tasks may appear to be the more ecologically valid choice because new learning is frequently contextual with a single exposure, but because list learning tests have been shown to be more sensitive to decline after dominant hemisphere anterior temporal lobectomy than story memory tasks, a list learning test is the preferred choice for presurgical candidates. In addition, list learning preoperative score has been combined with fMRI language laterality indices to develop a published regression equation designed to predict verbal memory decline after left temporal lobectomy (Swanson et al., 2015).

Executive functions including initiation, planning, inhibition of overlearned responses, problem-solving, mental flexibility, abstract reasoning, generative fluency, complex attention, and working memory should be assessed routinely, and a more extensive assessment may be useful for individuals with a frontal lobe seizure focus and/or those planning to undergo resection of a portion of the frontal lobe. Motor and sensory testing have been recommended to assess for motor slowing and lateralizing motor and sensory effects of focal seizure disorders.

In addition to cognitive testing, mood symptoms and quality of life should be routinely assessed. Psychological disorders such as depression and anxiety co-occur with epilepsy at a higher rate than in the general population and, if symptoms are present, are targets for intervention. Thus, measures of depressive and anxious symptomatology should be routinely included. Assessment of personality characteristics can provide insight into additional areas for cognitive behavioral intervention, and so a more comprehension personality inventory may be beneficial as well. Finally, optimal quality of life is a treatment goal and so assessment of quality of life, with both epilepsy-specific and general scales may be included.

As with adults, neuropsychological assessment in children with epilepsy should target a wide range of cognitive and behavioral functions. The process and interpretation may be more difficult for a variety of reasons (Jones-Gotman et al., 2010). Infants and preschoolers may present with developmental delays that preclude finding focal patterns of impairment, even when the underlying neuropathology or seizure focus is focal. Assessment should include measures that are sensitive to developmental differences and to theoretically expected stages of development for emerging or established skills. With continued development, the patterns of intact and impaired skills may change over time, and reassessment at key developmental or academic milestones may be needed.

Intervention

Regardless of the epilepsy syndrome or etiology, most patients with a diagnosis of epilepsy begin treatment with AEDs. Important for the caregivers and patient alike is the understanding that AEDs may be associated with cognitive or behavioral side effects. A recent review by the ILAE Task Force on the adverse cognitive and behavioral effects of AEDs in children indicated that phenobarbital, phenytoin, topiramate, and zonisamide are associated with negative cognitive effects, whereas phenobarbital, valproate, gabapentin, topiramate, levetiracetam, and zonisamide seem to be associated with negative behavioral effects (Aldenkamp et al., 2016). Across the lifespan, of the newer AEDs, topiramate is particularly effective in seizure treatment, but also has a higher rate of negative effects on cognitive functioning, including executive dysfunction and reductions in reaction time, memory, and language skills such as word-finding and verbal fluency. Often the clinician prescribing AEDs has the task of balancing need to minimize seizure and limit the number of AEDs used in treatment because polypharmacy is a major factor in contributing to cognitive difficulties (Loring et al., 2007). In the elderly, changes in pharmacokinetics associated with aging can make elderly patients more susceptible to the side effects of AEDs. Given that, AED monotherapy with newer drugs and lower doses may be necessary in those of advanced age (Burakgazi & French, 2016). Although the cognitive side effects associated with many AEDs may lead to patient dissatisfaction with treatment, and in some cases poor medication adherence, education regarding the likely more pronounced and expected cognitive decline associated with uncontrolled seizures should be provided.

Between 30% and 40% of individuals with epilepsy have intractable seizures, meaning they will experience failure of seizure control after an appropriate trial of two or more medications (Kwan, Schachter, & Brodie, 2011). In such cases, especially for patients with focal epilepsy and identifiable structural abnormities (e.g., mesial temporal lobe sclerosis, focal cortical dysplasia, vascular malformations, or neoplasms), surgery may be a treatment option. The recommendation for early surgical intervention after failure of AED trials is driven by neuroimaging studies that have shown functional abnormalities extending beyond the initial region of epileptic activity, resulting in the development of more widespread neural dysfunction in chronic epilepsy (Centeno & Carmichael, 2014). When epileptogenesis becomes more widespread, surgical intervention may no longer be advisable and treatment options become more limited. With proper screening and presurgical preparation, epilepsy surgery has been demonstrated effective, with 60–80% of surgical patients achieving seizure freedom after resection of the epileptic focus (Chang, Englot, & Vadera, 2015). To limit the resection of otherwise healthy brain tissue and to reduce cognitive morbidity, especially when resecting aspects of the language-dominant hemisphere, some epilepsy centers are utilizing more tailored (e.g., selective amygdalohippocampectomy) or minimally invasive techniques including laser ablation when appropriate.

When AEDs fail and surgery is undesirable or not an option, the implantation of brain stimulation devices may be considered. The vagal nerve stimulator (VNS) system is one commonly used device that consists of an electrical pulse generator that is implanted below the clavicle and a bipolar electrode wire that runs underneath the skin and is implanted typically into the left vagus nerve of the neck. The VNS mechanism of action is not entirely understood, but it is hypothesized that activation of ascending vagal nerve fibers to the locus coeruleus and dorsal raphe nucleus may modulate its effect on seizure activity. Analysis of efficacy and predictors of VNS response indicated that in general, seizure frequency was reduced by an average of 45%, with a 36% reduction occurring at 3–12 months after implantation and a 51% reduction after more than 1 year of VNS therapy. The same analysis indicated that PTE and tuberous sclerosis were positive predictors of a favorable

outcome in VNS studies, and cognitive side effects are rarely reported (Englot, Chang, & Auguste, 2011). A more recently developed focal brain stimulation device is the RNS System developed by NeuroPace (Mountain View, CA), which provides stimulation directly to the seizure focus when abnormal neuronal discharge is detected to abort the synchronous build resulting in seizure. An initial efficacy study has demonstrated that the RNS device can reduce seizures by 44% at 1 year and up to 66% by year 6 after implantation, with minimal impact on cognition or mood (Morrell & Halpern, 2016).

A nonpharmacological and noninvasive complimentary therapy to AED treatment is adherence to a ketogenic diet. The ketogenic diet is a high-fat, low-carbohydrate diet based on a ratio of 3–4 g of fat for every 1 g of carbohydrate and protein. The result is shifting the body to a state of ketosis, a metabolic state in which the body's energy comes from ketone bodies produced by the liver, instead of the typical state of glycolysis, in which blood glucose serves as the major energy supply. A meta-analysis of 12 studies investigating the efficacy of the complimentary use of the ketogenic diet in adults with epilepsy revealed that 42% of adults on the diet experienced 50% or greater reduction of seizures, which is similar to the pediatric literature suggesting 30–60% of children and adolescents show a similar reduction in seizure frequency (Ye, Li, Jiang, Sun, & Liu, 2015).

Individuals with epilepsy have almost twice the lifetime prevalence of mental health disorders compared with those without epilepsy (Tellez-Zenteno et al., 2007) and, when present, mood symptoms are a critical target for intervention. Emotional distress associated with epilepsy or epilepsy treatment is often associated with disability and significant reductions in quality of life. The ability to manage one's medical care and maintain medication or treatment compliance is affected by emotional and cognitive status. Additionally, research on epilepsy-related quality of life has demonstrated that the presence of depression is a greater predictor than epilepsy factors (including seizure frequency) in overall health-related quality of life for individuals with epilepsy (Meldolesi et al., 2006). Cognitive behavioral therapy, which is founded in empirical study, has proven effective when used to treat depression and anxiety in those with epilepsy. The detailed consensus statement on the evaluation and treatment of people with epilepsy and affective disorders provides an excellent set of guidelines and treatment algorithms to adequately address this quality of life issue for children and adults, and dispels the notion that antidepressant treatment necessarily lowers seizure threshold (Barry et al., 2008).

Cognitive rehabilitation attempts for individuals with epilepsy have tended to focus on attention and memory. Although the literature related to cognitive rehabilitation and epilepsy is limited, there is preliminary evidence to suggest that such services may aid in addressing specific cognitive concerns, which in turn may reduce distress in daily life and improve overall quality of life for those with epilepsy. Several studies have attempted to investigate the benefit of various methods of cognitive rehabilitation (e.g., use of mental imagery, keeping a diary, computer-based and interpersonal cognitive training including retraining and compensation methods, and education about epilepsy) on outcomes including aspects of neuropsychological functioning (e.g., word list learning, memory, attention), and quality of life with mixed results. Eighteen such studies were reviewed by Farina, Raglio, and Giovagnoli (2015), who concluded that there is limited evidence of efficacy for cognitive rehabilitation in epilepsy, noting that findings to date are limited by the presence of few experimental studies with methodological concerns including lack of randomization and small sample sizes. In addition, standardized evidence-based cognitive rehabilitation methods to improve aspects of cognition or behavior have not yet been established, and interventions and outcome measures vary greatly across studies. It has been recommended that future studies include larger samples recruited from multiple centers, the use of standardized high-quality interventions, the use of randomized controlled studies, and long-term follow-ups, with suggested outcome measures including neuropsychological tests, measures of perceived ability, autonomy, and quality of life (Farina et al., 2015).

Transition to Adult Health Care. It is important for clinicians to consider how the patient's age and development factor into managing care for the treatment of epilepsy. It is well understood that adolescence is a critical and vulnerable period in life, and having a chronic illness like epilepsy adds challenge and complexity when transitioning into adulthood. It is noted that successful treatment of seizures in childhood does not solve many of the social difficulties in adulthood. Furthermore, it has been demonstrated that adolescents with chronic medical illness transitioning into adulthood are prone to becoming lost to the medical system and missing opportunity for later intervention. Optimally, transition of health care involves an ongoing process of preparing youth and their caregivers for the adult health-care system. The goal is to prepare youth to function as independently as possible as adults in advocating, planning, and decision-making about their medical care, to maintain healthy behaviors, and to use health-care resources properly. The transition plan should be individualized, and should address education about epilepsy and its treatment, the individual's needs and concerns, the educational and vocational goals of the youth, a health-care plan from the perspective of all providers, and legal guardianship (if appropriate).

The transition from pediatric to adult care can be challenging for families because they may feel abandoned by their long-term health-care team. In addition, the adult system may not provide as many supports for the comorbidities of epilepsy, and those patients who have relatively well-controlled seizures may still continue to have significant psychosocial challenges (Carrizosa, An, Appleton, Camfield, & Von Moers, 2014). Perhaps the most challenging patients for transition are those with specific childhood-onset epilepsy syndromes characterized by difficult-to-control seizures, marked developmental delays, and at times significant behavioral challenges (for example, see Table 10.2). Adult neurologists are not necessarily trained in how to manage these features, and in addition, the epilepsy in some of these syndromes may change over time.

A number of different models of transition in epilepsy care exist in different countries (Carrizosa et al., 2014). Many places have established specific clinics, whereas in others the transition plan consists of only a letter detailing the developmental and medical history. Existing differences across models include whether there is a specific transition clinic within either the pediatric or the adult hospital, or in both; whether both the pediatric and adult neurologist (or in some cases the nurse) attend the clinic; and the age at which the transition process begins (ranging from age 12 through to the early 20s). None of these models of transition in epilepsy care have been rigorously tested for their efficacy, and it is recognized that the optimal model may differ across settings (Carrizosa et al., 2014).

Implications for Clinical Practice

Epilepsy is a disorder that may develop at any age. Seizure onset during childhood may have significant impact on early development, educational attainment, and transition into adulthood, whereas onset later in life may shift the trajectory of occupational goals and complicate the clinical presentation and management of other neurological or medical conditions. Because epilepsy is a lifespan disorder that is prevalent worldwide, it is important that neuropsychologists maintain lifespan knowledge of the disorder through a culturally sensitive lens. When working with culturally diverse populations, assessment of the patient's level of acculturation is important for test selection and to provide context for case conceptualization. Neuropsychologists must be aware of the cultural limitations inherent in many standard neuropsychological tests and the level of normative data available for culturally appropriate comparison. In addition, an effort must be made to use tests with the closest available normative data (e.g., country of origin, linguistic background, level of education, age), with assessment conducted in the patient's native or primary language. For patients who are bilingual or multilingual, the clinician should consider administering language-based tasks in each language which the patient is proficient.

In line with the ILAE Neuropsychology Task Force recommendations, all patients should undergo neuropsychological screening for cognitive and psychosocial comorbidities at the time of epilepsy onset (Wilson et al., 2015). Although the initial screening may be a focused evaluation, it is important for the clinician to assess the major domains of cognitive ability (attention, processing speed, language, visuospatial/constructional, verbal and visual memory, sensory/motor, and executive functioning) regardless of the area of seizure focus because widespread neuronal abnormalities may affect many aspects of cognition. The screening evaluation can be used as a baseline for comparison to assess the potential progression of cognitive change secondary to disease and treatment. The use of measures with multiple equivalent forms, or use of reliable change indices and standard regression-based change score norms to control for test-retest effects and measurement error, is recommended for repeat evaluations. The screening should also be used to identify individuals who will require more comprehensive neuropsychological assessment, including academic achievement testing to evaluate for need of academic accommodations, or more clearly addressing the need for occupational accommodations or career transition. Because mental health disorders are more prevalent in individuals with epilepsy, all neuropsychological evaluations need to assess psychosocial comorbidities, including depression, anxiety, and suicidal ideation. Early identification and treatment of psychosocial comorbidities are indicated for all ages because psychotropic medication use and/or psychotherapeutic services can improve overall quality of life. Whether by clinical interview or formal self-report measure, neuropsychologists should assess lifestyle factors (e.g., alcohol and other substance use, sleep, environmental stressors and irritants, and general stress management) often implicated in reducing seizure threshold, but also amenable to change once identified and intervention provided.

It is recognized that AEDs may impact brain functioning, so knowledge of common AED cognitive and behavioral side effects is essential. Neuropsychologists can aid in assessing the presence and degree of AED-related cognitive and behavioral effects by evaluating patients before beginning AEDs and again once titrated to a therapeutic range. Repeat evaluations may allow the treating clinician to discern medication effects from the underlying disease, which may assist in the selection of AEDs and drug levels that achieve seizure relief while minimizing the negative cognitive and behavioral effects. In circumstances when only a single evaluation is permitted, it will be important to consider the possible effects of the patient's AED regimen on their overall cognitive and behavioral profile. This is of particular importance in the preoperative context, where AEDs may suppress cognitive performance in areas unrelated to the underlying seizure focus that can be a confounding factor when attempting to confirm seizure focus, and may ultimately underestimate the patient's risk for postoperative decline.

When neurosurgical intervention is being considered, comprehensive neuropsychological evaluation should be used to assist in identifying lateralized cognitive dysfunction, given that the convergence of neurophysiological, neuroimaging, and neuropsychological data has been shown to predict postoperative cognitive and seizure outcomes. Preoperative neuropsychological testing in conjunction with specialized assessment for language and memory lateralization and localization (e.g., Wada testing, fMRI) before pursuing surgery may be used to predict postoperative cognitive morbidity. The use of regression equations such as one published by Swanson et al. (2015) can aid in quantifying predicted postoperative cognitive change at the individual patient level. Postoperatively, repeat evaluation for comparison against the patient's preoperative performances can assist the patient and caregivers in understanding the presence of any cognitive or psychiatric changes, and provide timely and targeted recommendations to maximize psychosocial functioning and postoperative treatment adherence, and to assist with strategies or accommodations for cognitive deficits.

Neuropsychologists can serve a key role in the transition phases of epilepsy care across the lifespan by identifying early any cognitive or behavioral factors that may reduce independent functioning, impede adherence to medical plans, and diminish a patient's participation in his or her medical care. It is a major clinical responsibility for the neuropsychologist working with patients with epilepsy to communicate these concerns to the treatment team and caregivers, and to provide informed recommendations on the basis of

evaluation results to address any concerns and assist in timely initiation of interventions. For example, relating the degree of one's memory impairment to need for assistance in medication management and appointment reminders may result in simple interventions (e.g., pillbox prefilled by the pharmacy and appointment phone call reminders by scheduling staff) to help maintain treatment adherence and independent functioning.

Key points arising from the review in this chapter that are pertinent to clinical practice are presented in Table 10.3.

Future Directions

Early identification of cognitive and psychosocial comorbidities is recognized as an important step in the optimal care of people with epilepsy, and the ILAE Neuropsychology Task Force (Wilson et al., 2015) has recommended screening at the time of epilepsy onset. Such screening requires the identification of brief, valid measures with demonstrated sensitivity, and the education of a wide variety of mental health professionals on what steps to take for further in-depth

Table 10.3 Implications of Epilepsy for Clinical Practice

General Assessment Considerations

- Screening evaluations should be completed for all patients at the time of epilepsy onset.
- Assess all major domains of cognitive ability regardless of seizure focus.
- Be aware of cultural limitations inherent in many standard neuropsychological tests and make every effort to use tests with the most appropriate normative data when working with diverse populations.
- All assessments should include evaluation of psychosocial difficulties and other lifestyle factors that may reduce quality of life or seizure threshold.
- Consider selecting tests with multiple forms or the use of reliable change indices and standard regression-based change scores to account for test-retest effects when repeat evaluations are anticipated.
- More comprehensive evaluation may be necessary to address questions of academic accommodations, occupational planning and accommodations, preoperative planning, or to better address individual needs.
- Recommended tests have been reviewed by Jones-Gotman et al. (2010) and Drane (2015).
- The NINDS commissioned a group to develop recommendations for neuropsychological testing in epilepsy which can be found on the NINDS Common Data Elements website: https://www.commondataelements.ninds.nih.gov.

AED Considerations in Assessment

- Testing before and after AED titration may help identify medication-related cognitive and/or behavioral changes.
- Always consider possible effects of AEDs on cognitive and behavioral profile.
- Titrating off AEDs before preoperative evaluation may aid in more clearly lateralizing or localizing seizure focus and predictions of risk for declines.
- Phenobarbital, phenytoin, topiramate, and zonisamide are associated with negative cognitive effects; phenobarbital, valproate, gabapentin, topiramate, levetiracetam, and zonisamide seem to be associated with negative behavioral effects.
- Polypharmacy is a major factor contributing to cognitive difficulties.
- Elderly patients may be more susceptible to AED cognitive side effects.

Table 10.3 (cont.)

Preoperative Assessment Considerations

- Comprehensive neuropsychological assessment can be used to confirm the lateralization and location of seizure focus; convergence of neurophysiological, neuroimaging, and neuropsychological data has been shown to predict postoperative cognitive and seizure outcomes.
- Children with epilepsy show more generalized patterns of impairment, which can make it more difficult to use the neuropsychological assessment results in a lateralizing and localizing manner.
- Preoperative naming and verbal memory performance combined with patient's language lateralization can assist in predicting risk for postoperative declines in those areas.
- Postoperative assessment allows for comparison against preoperative performance for identifying surgery-related changes needing interventions or accommodations.

Interventions and Transitions

- Interventions to address psychosocial comorbidities should be implemented as soon as possible for children, adolescents, and adults to improve quality of life.
- Cognitive behavioral therapy for depression in patients with epilepsy is effective in improving quality of life beyond epilepsy-related factors including seizure frequency.
- Cognitive and behavioral deficits that may reduce independence or participation in patient's own medical care need to be communicated to the care team and caregivers, and interventions implemented especially when transitioning from pediatric to adult medical management.

assessment and management of those in whom the screening reveals potential problems. In addition, it will be essential for the field of neuropsychology to continue to develop more culturally sensitive measures with improved normative comparison groups to better serve our culturally diverse population.

There has been research on the nature of the neuropsychological profile in both children and adults at the time of epilepsy onset and the tracking of performance patterns over time. Most of this research has involved samples with well-controlled epilepsy, and it will be important to extend this work to identify whether those patients who develop intractable epilepsy show different trajectories. Moreover, the discovery of biomarkers of epileptogenesis, integrated with advances in neuroimaging techniques and neuropsychological assessment, may lead to better classification of the cognitive and behavioral manifestations associated with epilepsies of various etiologies and improved treatment outcomes. Multicenter studies are needed to identify new therapeutic targets and reduce the risk for cognitive morbidity after intervention.

There is a need for further development and validation of cognitive and psychological treatments, with emphasis on programs that are cost efficient and can be provided by telephone or the Internet so that they are readily accessible to patients who do not live near major treatment centers or who are not able to drive because of their epilepsy. Increased awareness of and support

for the comorbidities may lead to improvements in quality of life, education, employment, and social integration.

References

Agrawal, A., Timothy, J., Pandit, L., & Manju, M. (2006). Post-traumatic epilepsy: An overview. *Clinical Neurology and Neurosurgery, 108*, 433–439.

Aldenkamp, A., Besag, F., Gobbi, G., Caplan, R., Dunn, D. W., & Sillanpää, M. (2016). Psychiatric and behavioural disorders in children with epilepsy (ILAE Task Force Report): Adverse cognitive and behavioral effects of antiepileptic drugs in children. *Epileptic Disorders, 18* (Suppl. 1), S55–S67.

Asadi-Pooya, A. A. (2015). Neurobiological origin of psychogenic nonepileptic seizures: A review of imaging studies. *Epilepsy & Behavior, 52*, 256–259.

Baroni, G., Piccinini, V., Martins, W. A., de Paola, L., Paglioli, E., Margis, R., & Palmini, A. (2016). Variables associated with co-existing epileptic and psychogenic nonepileptic seizures: A systematic review. *Seizure, 37*, 35–40.

Barry, J. J., Ettinger, A. B., Friel, P., Gilliam, F. G., Harden, C. L., Hermann, B.,... Jones, J. (2008). Consensus statement: The evaluation and treatment of people with epilepsy and affective disorders. *Epilepsy & Behavior, 13*, S1–S29.

Beghi, E., Giussani, G., & Sander, J. W. (2015). The natural history and prognosis of epilepsy. *Epileptic Disorders, 17*(3), 243–253.

Bender, H. A. (2015). The neuropsychological assessment of culturally and linguistically diverse epilepsy patients. In W. B. Barr & C. Morrison (Eds.), *Handbook on the neuropsychology of epilepsy* (pp. 317–344). New York, NY: Springer.

Besag, F., Aldenkamp, A., Caplan, R., Dunn, D. W., Gobbi, G., & Sillanpää, M. (2016). Psychiatric and behavioural disorders in children with epilepsy: An ILAE Task Force Report. *Epileptic Disorders, 18* (Suppl 1), 1–86.

Bodde, N. M. G., Brooke, J. L., Baker, G. A., Boon, P. A. J. M., Hendriksen, J. G. M., Mulder, O. G., & Aldenkamp, A. P. (2009). Psychogenic non-epileptic seizures-Definition, etiology, treatment and prognostic issues: A critical review. *Seizure, 18*, 543–553.

Bonilha, L., Tabesh, A., Dabbs, K., Hsu, D. A., Stafstrom, C. E., Hermann, B. P., & Lin, J. J. (2014). Neurodevelopmental alterations of large-scale structural networks in children with new-onset epilepsy. *Human Brain Mapping, 35*(8), 3661–3672.

Breuer, L. E. M., Boon, P., Bergmans, J. W. M., Mess, W. H., Besseling, R. M. H., de Louw, A.,... Aldenkamp, A. P. (2016). Cognitive deterioration in adult epilepsy: Does accelerated cognitive ageing exist? *Neuroscience and Biobehavioral Reviews, 64*, 1–11.

Burakgazi, E., & French, J. A. (2016). Treatment of epilepsy in adults. *Epileptic Disorders, 18*(3), 228–239.

Camfield, P. R., & Camfield, C. S. (2014). What happens to children with epilepsy when they become adults? Some facts and opinions. *Pediatric Neurology, 51*, 17–23.

Carrizosa, J., An, I., Appleton, R., Camfield, P., & Von Moers, A. (2014). Models for transition clinics. *Epilepsia, 55*, 46–51.

Centeno, M., & Carmichael, D. W. (2014). Network connectivity in epilepsy: Resting state fMRI and EEG-fMRI contributions. *Frontiers in Neurology, 5*, 1–19.

Chang, E. F., Englot, D. J., & Vadera, S. (2015). Minimally invasive surgical approaches for temporal lobe epilepsy. *Epilepsy & Behavior, 47*, 24–33.

Chapin, J., & Naugle, R. (2015). Geriatric patients with epilepsy. In W. B. Barr & C. Morrison (Eds.), *Handbook on the neuropsychology of epilepsy* (pp. 63–86). New York, NY: Springer.

D'Ambrosio, R.,Eastman, C. L.,Fattore, C., & Perucca, E. (2013). Novel frontiers in epilepsy treatments: Preventing epileptogenesis by targeting inflammation. *Expert Review of Neurotherapeutics, 13*, 615–625.

De Reuck, J., De Clerck, M., & Van Maele, G. (2006) Vascular cognitive impairment in patients with late-onset seizures after an ischemic stroke. *Clinical Neurology and Neurosurgery, 108*(7), 632–637.

Drane, D. (2015). Neuropsychological evaluation of the epilepsy surgical candidate. In W. B. Barr & C. Morrison (Eds.), *Handbook on the neuropsychology of epilepsy* (pp. 87–122). New York, NY: Springer.

Englot, D. J., Chang, E. F., & Auguste, K. I. (2011). Vagus nerve stimulation for epilepsy: A meta-analysis of efficacy and predictors of response. *Journal of Neurosurgery, 115*(6), 1248–1255.

Farina, E., Raglio, A., & Giovagnoli, A. R. (2015). Cognitive rehabilitation in epilepsy: An evidence-based review. *Epilepsy Research, 109*, 210–218.

Fisher, R. S., Acevedo, C. A., Arzimanoglou, A., Bogacz, A., Cross, H., Elger, C. E.,... Wiebe, S. (2014). ILAE official report: A practical definition of epilepsy. *Epilepsia, 55*, 475–482.

Guo, J., Guo, J., Li, J., Zhou, M., Qin, F., Zhang, S.,... Zhou, D. (2015). Statin treatment reduces the risk of poststroke seizures. *American Academy of Neurology, 85*, 701–707.

Hermann, B. P., Lin, J. J., Jones, J. E., & Seidenberg, M. (2009). The emerging architecture of neuropsychological impairment in epilepsy. *Neurologic Clinics, 27*, 881–907.

Hermann, B., Meador, K. J., Gaillard, W. D., & Cramer, J. A. (2010). Cognition across the lifespan: Antiepileptic drugs, epilepsy, or both? *Epilepsy & Behavior, 17*, 1–7.

Hermann, B. P., & Seidenberg, M. (2007). Epilepsy and cognition. *Epilepsy Currents, 1*, 1–6.

Jackson, D. C., Dabbs, K., Walker, N. M., Jones, J. E., Hsu, D. A., Stafstrom, C. E., ... Hermann, B. P. (2013). The neuropsychological and academic substrate of new/recent-onset epilepsies. *Journal of Pediatrics, 162*(5), 1047–1053.

Jayakar, P., Gaillard, W. D., Tripathi, M., Libenson, M. H., Mathern, G. W., & Cross, J. H. (2014). Task Force for Paediatric Epilepsy Surgery, Commission for Paediatrics, and the Diagnostic Commission of the International League Against Epilepsy. Diagnostic test utilization in evaluation for resective epilepsy surgery in children. *Epilepsia, 55*, 507–518.

Jehi, L., Tesar, G., Obuchowski, N., Novak, E., & Najm, I. (2011). Quality of life in 1931 adult patients with epilepsy: Seizures do not tell the whole story. *Epilepsy & Behavior, 22*, 723–727.

Jones, B., Reuber, M., & Norman, P. (2016). Correlates of health-related quality of life in adults with psychogenic nonepileptic seizures: A systematic review. *Epilepsia, 57*(2), 171–181.

Jones-Gotman, M., Smith, M. L., Risse, G. L., Westerveld, M., Swanson, S. J., Giovagnoli, A. R., ... Piazzini, A. (2010). The contribution of neuropsychology to diagnostic assessment in epilepsy. *Epilepsy & Behavior, 18*, 3–12.

Klein, B., Levin, B. E., Duchowny, M.S., & Llabre, M. M. (2000). Cognitive outcome of children with epilepsy and malformations of cortical development. *Neurology, 55,* 230–235.

Kobau, R., Zahran, H., Thurman, D. J., Zack, M. M., Henry, T. R., Schachter, S. C., & Prince, P. H. (2008). Epilepsy surveillance among adults -19 states, behavioral risk factor surveillance system, 2005. *MMWR Surveillance Summaries, 57,* 1–20.

Kramer, M. A., & Cash, S. S. (2012). Epilepsy as a disorder of cortical network organization. *Neuroscientist, 18*(4), 360–372.

Kwan, P., Schachter, S. C., & Brodie, M. J. (2011). Drug-resistant epilepsy. *New England Journal of Medicine, 365* (10), 919–926.

Labiner, D. M., Bagic, A. I., Herman, S. T., Fountain, N. B., Walczak T. S., & Gumnit, R. J. (2010). Essential services, personnel, and facilities in specialized epilepsy centers – Revised 2010 guidelines. *Epilepsia, 51,* 2322–2333.

Lai, M. C. & Yang, S. N. (2011). Perinatal hypoxic-ischemic encephalopathy. *Journal of Biomedicine and Biotechnology, 2011,* 1–6.

Langfitt, J. T., & Watson, W. Evaluation and management of psychogenic nonepileptic attacks. (2016). In W. B. Barr & C. Morrison (Eds.), *Handbook on the neuropsychology of epilepsy* (pp. 257–274). New York, NY: Springer.

Lee, G. P. (2010). *Neuropsychology of epilepsy and epilepsy surgery.* New York, NY: Oxford University Press.

Lin, J. J., Mula, M., & Hermann, B. P. (2012). Uncovering the lifespan neurobehavioral comorbidities of epilepsy. *Lancet, 380,* 1180–1192.

Loring, D. W., Marino, S., & Meador, K. J. (2007). Neuropsychological and behavioral effects of antiepilepsy drugs. *Neuropsychology Review, 17*(4), 413–425.

Lortie, A. (2013). Psychogenic nonepileptic seizures. In O. Dulac, M. Lassonde, & H. B. Sarnat (Eds.), *Handbook of clinical neurology, Vol. 112; Pediatric neurology part II* (pp. 875–879). Amsterdam: Elsevier.

Loughman, A., Bowden, S. C., & D'Souza, W. (2014). Cognitive functioning in idiopathic generalized epilepsies: A systemic review and meta-analysis. *Neuroscience & Behavioral Reviews, 43,* 20–34.

MacAllister, W. S., & Sherman, E. M. S. (2015). Evaluation of children and adolescents with epilepsy. In W. B. Barr & C. Morrison (Eds.), *Handbook on the neuropsychology of epilepsy* (pp. 37–62). New York, NY: Springer.

Meldolesi, G. N., Picardi, A., Quarato, P. P., Grammaldo, L. G., Espositio, V., Mascia, A.,… DiGennaro, G. (2006). Factors associated with generic and disease-specific quality of life in temporal lobe epilepsy. *Epilepsy Research, 69*(2), 135–146.

Morrell, M. J. & Halpern, C. (2016). Responsive direct brain stimulation. *Neurosurgery Clinics of North America, 27*(1), 111–121.

Myers, L., Lancman, M., Vazquez-Casals, G., Bonafina, M., Perrine, K., & Sabri, J. (2015). Depression and quality of life in Spanish-speaking immigrant persons with epilepsy compared with those in English-speaking US-born persons with epilepsy. *Epilepsy & Behavior, 51,* 146–151.

Ngugi, A. K., Bottomley, C., Kleinschmidt, I., Sander, J. W., & Newton, C. R. (2010). Estimation of the burden of active and life-time epilepsy: A meta-analytic approach. *Epilepsia, 51*(5), 883–890.

Raud, T., Kaldoja, M.L., & Kolk, A. (2015). Relationship between social competence and neurocognitive performance in children with epilepsy. *Epilepsy & Behavior, 52*(Pt. A), 93–110.

Reuber, M. (2008). Psychogenic nonepileptic seizures: Answers and questions. *Epilepsy & Behavior, 12,* 622–635.

Reilly, C., Atkinson, P., Das, K. B., Chin, R. F., Aylett, S. E., Burch, V.,… Neville, B. G. (2014a). Academic achievement in school-aged children with active epilepsy: A population-based study. *Epilepsia, 55*(12), 1910–1917.

Reilly, C., Atkinson, P., Das, K. B., Chin, R. F., Aylett, S. E., Burch, V.,… Neville, B. G. (2014b). Neurobehavioral comorbidities in children with active epilepsy: A population-based study. *Pediatrics, 133*(6), e1586–1593.

Reilly, C., Atkinson, P., Das, K. B., Chin, R. F., Aylett, S. E., Burch, V.,… Neville, B. G. (2015). Cognition in school-aged children with "active" epilepsy: A population-based study. *Journal of Clinical and Experimental Neuropsychology, 37* (4), 429–438.

Salpekar, J. A., & Mishra, G. (2014). Key issues in addressing the comorbidity of attention deficit hyperactivity disorder and pediatric epilepsy. *Epilepsy & Behavior, 37,* 310–315.

Schoenberg, M. R., Werz, M. A., & Drane, D. L. (2011). Epilepsy and seizures. In M. R. Schoenberg & J. G. Scott (Eds.), *The little black book of neuropsychology: A syndrome-based approach* (pp. 423–520). New York, NY: Springer.

Silverman, I. E., Restrepo, L., & Mathews, G. C. (2002). Poststroke seizures. *Archives of Neurology, 59,* 195–201.

Smith, M. L. (2016). Rethinking cognition and behavior in the new classification for childhood epilepsy: Examples from frontal lobe and temporal lobe epilepsies. *Epilepsy & Behavior,* pii: **S1525**–5050(16)30072–5.

Stretton, J., & Thompson, P. J. (2012). Frontal lobe function in temporal lobe epilepsy. *Epilepsy Research, 98,* 1–13.

Swanson, S. J., Binder, J. R., Raghavan, M., & Euler, M. (2015). Functional MRI in the presurgical epilepsy evaluation. In W. B. Barr & C. Morrison (Eds.), *Handbook on the neuropsychology of epilepsy* (pp. 169–194). New York, NY: Springer.

Taylor, R. S., Sander, J. W., Taylor, R. J., & Baker, G. A. (2011). Predictors of health-related quality of life and costs in adults with epilepsy: A systematic review. *Epilepsia, 52,* 2168–2180.

Tellez-Zenteno, J. F., Patten, S. B., Jette, N., Williams, J., & Wiebe, S. (2007). Psychiatric comorbidity in epilepsy: A population-based analysis. *Epilepsia*, *48*, 2336–2344.

Thompson, K., Pohlmann-Eden, B., Campbell, L. A., & Abel, H. (2015). Pharmacological treatments for preventing epilepsy following traumatic brain injury. *Cochrane Database of Systematic Reviews*, *8*, 1–85.

Widjaja, E., Skocic, J., Go, C., Snead, O. C., Mabbott, D., & Smith, M. L. (2013). Abnormal white matter correlates with neuropsychological impairment in children with localization-related epilepsy. *Epilepsia*, *54*(6), 1065–1073.

Widjaja, E., Zamyadi, M., Raybaud, C., Snead, O. C., & Smith, M. L. (2014). Volumetric changes in hippocampal subregions and their relation to memory in pediatric nonlesional localization-related epilepsy. *Epilepsia*, *55*(4), 519–527.

Wilson, S. J., Baxendale, S., Barr, W., Hamed, S., Langfitt, J., Samson, S.,… Smith, M. I. (2015). Indications and expectations for neuropsychological assessment in routine epilepsy care: Report of the ILAE Neuropsychology Task Force, Diagnostic Methods Commission, 2013–2017. *Epilepsia*, *56*, 674–681.

Witt, J., & Helmstaedter, C. (2015). Cognition in the early stages of adult epilepsy. *Seizure*, *26*, 65–68.

Ye, F., Li, X. J., Jiang, W. L., Sun, H. B., & Liu, J. (2015). Efficacy of and patient compliance with a ketogenic diet in adults with intractable epilepsy: A meta-analysis. *Journal of Clinical Neurology*, *11*(1), 26–31.

Human Immunodeficiency Virus

Steven Paul Woods, Kelli L. Sullivan, Sharon Nichols, and Scott J. Hunter

Introduction

Over the past 35 years, there have been significant challenges posed across multiple domains of medical and clinical science regarding the impact of infection with the human immunodeficiency virus (HIV) and the subsequent development of acquired immune deficiency syndrome (AIDS). The epidemic of HIV/AIDS has affected individuals across the lifespan and is worldwide in its scope. It is known as a disease that targets individuals when they are young adults, with infection most commonly seen in men and women during their late teens to their late 20s, and disease intervention becomes lifelong. But HIV has a wide age range of vulnerability, beginning in infancy with maternal transmission perinatally, and postbirth, in exposure through breast milk or blood transfusions; continuing through adolescence and adulthood, typically secondary to behavioral transmission; and with aging populations who are infected living longer, as well as older adults who are having unprotected sexual activity with partners who are HIV-positive (HIV+), extending into senescence.

Medical science has been remarkable in its ability to move from identification of the virus that led to the appearance of a series of confounding illnesses in gay men in the early 1980s, to the development of antiretroviral (ARV) treatments that have allowed infected individuals to fight back against the range of secondary illnesses that define AIDS. Nevertheless, HIV seroconversion and AIDS continue as a serious epidemic across the globe. Western countries, including North America, Europe, and Australia, have seen greater levels of control over both infection rates and the development of illness across time. Yet many countries, including those across South America, the Caribbean, the former Soviet states, Africa, and Asia, have had much less success at controlling HIV infection and the development of AIDS, due in part to a troubling mix of political, socioeconomic, and sociocultural constraints. Such conditions result in the continued reality that HIV infection remains a serious, pernicious risk, with a range of physical, neurocognitive, and psychosocial implications (The Henry J. Kaiser Family Foundation, 2017).

Although it is beyond the scope of this chapter to review the history of HIV identification and the complex steps that have been taken over time to reach a point where we are able to classify HIV infection as a chronic treatable disease, it is important to point out several key considerations. Of note is the recognition that HIV has been around for a very long time, likely since the early part of the 20th century, and was first present within several nonhuman primate species across Africa (Lemey et al., 2003; Santiago et al., 2005). That HIV was able to jump from animals to humans, and to then become principally a sexually transmitted disease affecting mostly, but not exclusively, individuals of minority status (e.g., gay men, people of color, individuals who are drug users sharing needles, sex workers, and children born to infected women), with its greatest impact seen in very low income populations, argues that this virus is one of particular challenge to treat, with multiple factors influencing its spread and effect. The history of HIV/AIDS is still today one of discrimination, that has as a result affected both how it has been understood, in terms of risk factors and continued vulnerabilities, and to availability of treatment for those infected. This has meant that many individuals have acquired HIV/AIDS and its associated potential devastation to the body and brain secondary to a lack of support for prevention and treatment.

Simultaneously, many heroic individuals have been at the center of research and intervention with regard to HIV/AIDS despite the discrimination this disease holds. Their efforts toward identifying the virus, understanding how it leads to infection, and then developing pharmacological approaches to managing its impact across multiple systems have allowed for significant steps toward lessening negative outcomes. Apart from scientists addressing the biological implications of the disease, neuropsychologists, clinical psychologists, and other mental health professionals have been actively engaged in identifying, tracking, and then developing interventions for the neurocognitive and behavioral effects of HIV infection, with important guidance made toward supporting medical and holistic approaches to treatment. This chapter addresses those findings, from infancy through older adulthood, and encourages considerations for future efforts.

It is the goal of this chapter therefore to address what has been learned about the pathophysiology of HIV infection and how both the disease and its treatment affect neuropsychological and behavioral functioning across the lifespan. We also hope to guide the reader in understanding where research and clinical practice need to go forward. With the introduction of preexposure prophylaxis (or PrEP, as it is commonly known) in particular, and given the success of ARVs in addressing vulnerability to AIDS, there is a new horizon opening up that argues for the continuation of an interdisciplinary approach to addressing infection risk and effect. Additionally, because current treatments for HIV infection are not curative, and even when controlled, there are a range of negative effects taking place on the neurological and broader biological systems, recognizing that individuals with HIV remain vulnerable across the lifespan is a critical need.

Epidemiology and Pathophysiology

According to recent estimates from the Joint United Nations Programme on HIV/AIDS (2016), approximately 36.7 million individuals worldwide are currently living with HIV, and 2.1 million new infections occur each year, across all ages. HIV is a lentivirus, and it primarily infects immune cells, particularly $CD4^+$ lymphocytes and macrophages (Ellis, Calero, & Stockin, 2009). If left untreated, the immune system can become severely compromised, which can lead to opportunistic infections that may damage the central nervous system (CNS). However, HIV can also cause primary CNS damage. HIV is highly neurovirulent and crosses the blood–brain barrier in the early stages of infection. Although antiretroviral medications are effective at reducing systemic HIV replication and improving immune functioning, neuroAIDS is multifactorial and not easily treated. In fact, the brain can serve as a reservoir for persistent HIV infection even after systemic viral suppression has been achieved (Saylor et al., 2016).

Although HIV does not directly infect neurons, the HIV genome codes for neurotoxic proteins including gp120, which disrupts glutamate signaling, and Tat, which can cause dendritic loss and neuronal cell death (Ellis et al., 2009). Additionally, HIV can indirectly cause CNS damage through cytokines and chemokines. These chemicals, which mediate inflammation and immunity, are upregulated in HIV infection and lead to neuronal damage (Ellis, Langford, & Masliah, 2007). Through these mechanisms, HIV can cause synaptodendritic injury and reduced white matter volume, which are strongly related to neurocognitive impairment (Ellis et al., 2009). Although this synaptodendritic injury affects all brain systems, HIV-associated neurocognitive deficits primarily reflect damage to the frontostriatothalamocortical circuits (Ellis et al., 2007). In addition, HIV+ individuals with comorbid substance use or hepatitis C coinfection may be particularly susceptible to CNS damage and resulting neurocognitive impairment (Ellis et al., 2009). Therefore, HIV-associated neurocognitive disorders (HAND) can develop as a result of multiple processes after HIV infection.

The neuropathogenesis of HIV acquired before, during, or shortly after birth may differ from that acquired in adults due to immaturity of the blood–brain barrier, greater susceptibility to chemokines, and impact on neural progenitor cells (Crowell, Malee, Yogev, & Muller, 2014). The effects of perinatal infection on brain development and functioning vary depending on the extent and timing of greatest disease severity. The most severe effects, including acquired microcephaly, or brain atrophy and basal ganglia calcifications, are seen with prenatal infection and lack of viral suppression during the first 3 years of life (Crowell et al., 2014; Smith & Wilkins, 2015). However, recent neuroimaging studies demonstrate abnormalities in white matter development and brain volume differences even in the context of long-term viral suppression (Cohen et al., 2016; Hoare et al., 2014; Uban et al., 2015). In addition, evidence suggests differences in functional connectivity with perinatal HIV acquisition (Herting et al., 2015). Developmental neurotoxicity of antiretroviral agents and interactions with known susceptibility of the developing brain to substances of abuse (Squeglia &

Gray, 2016) are additional considerations specific to children.

Among adults, aging with HIV disease creates its own unique set of challenges to brain structure and function. Additive effects of HIV disease and typical aging processes have been observed on structural volumes of both cortical and deep gray matter, as well as the integrity of white matter tracts, primarily in frontal and temporal circuits. Resting state functional magnetic resonance imaging data also point to independent, additive effects of HIV and aging on baseline brain functioning (e.g., default mode network and associated connectivity). The underlying pathology of such changes in the aging HIV brain remains uncertain, but biomarker research points to a variety of candidates, including chronic inflammatory processes, immunovirologic neurotoxicity, neuroaxonal injury (e.g., tau), and deposition of amyloid beta. Rigorous clinicopathological studies are needed to draw more reliable conclusions about the mechanisms of brain injury in older HIV+ adults, particularly as this cohort reaches the ages at which the most common dementias (e.g., Alzheimer disease) typically emerge in later life.

Prevention

Approximately 25–50% of HIV-infected adults meet criteria for HAND (Saylor et al., 2016). Unfortunately, little is known about the factors that allow some HIV-infected individuals to remain neurocognitively normal while others develop this disorder. Some studies (Foley et al., 2012; Sheppard et al., 2015) suggest that cognitive reserve or resiliency and early HIV treatment are two protective factors against the development of HAND.

Cognitive reserve refers to the ability to withstand brain damage and delay the onset of neurocognitive impairment due to participation in cognitively stimulating activities. Although there is no consensus on how to measure cognitive reserve, it is typically operationalized as a combination of intelligence, education, and occupational achievement. Several studies have found an association between high cognitive reserve scores and better overall neuropsychological functioning (e.g., Foley et al., 2012). This association persists among HIV-infected older patients, who are at an increased risk of neurocognitive decline. Longitudinal studies have also linked cognitive reserve scores with a lower 1-year incidence of HAND, providing the strongest evidence for cognitive reserve as a protective factor in HIV infection (e.g., Sheppard et al., 2015).

Among children with HIV, sociodemographic and educational factors are associated with resilience in neurodevelopmental functioning. Along with familial psychiatric and learning disorders, and birth and early life risks common to this population such as prematurity, prenatal substance exposure, early chronic stress and trauma, and poverty, identification of factors that contribute to risk for impact versus resilience are currently under active study. As the first cohorts of youth treated for perinatal infection are reaching adulthood, research is now focusing on identifying those protective and potential intervening factors that can promote a more successful transition into independence.

The literature, across ages of infection, suggests that early treatment of HIV with combination antiretroviral therapy (cART) may protect against neurocognitive disruption and decline. Medication adherence, as well as viral suppression, is associated with better neurocognitive functioning and lower risk of neurocognitive decline over time (Heaton et al., 2015). Neurocognitive functioning tends to improve when individuals begin taking cART, but some research has found that long-term neurocognitive outcomes may be associated with the level of impairment at cART initiation (Tozzi et al., 2007). These findings provide support for early initiation of treatment, to prevent neurocognitive decline before it begins. However, studies comparing the effects of early versus late treatment initiation have yielded inconsistent results in adolescents and adults (Nichols, Bethel, et al., 2016; Saylor et al., 2016) and this issue is still being studied in those who experienced infection earlier in their lives. Thus, further research is necessary to determine the nature of early HIV treatment as a protective factor for HAND. In the context of perinatal HIV infection, earlier treatment and prevention of immune suppression appear to be protective for neurodevelopment (Crowell et al., 2015), leading to recommendations for immediate treatment initiation in infants younger than 12 months of age (Panel on Antiretroviral Therapy and Medical Management of HIV-Infected Children, 2015).

Clinical Manifestation

Adults

Cognition. Neurocognitive impairment in adults with HIV is evident across many domains. Executive functions are some of the most commonly impaired ability areas in HIV infection and are also the strongest neurocognitive predictors of everyday functioning. Research has documented HIV-related impairments in a wide range of executive functions such as abstraction, problem-solving, inhibition, set-shifting, planning, and decision-making (Woods, Moore, Weber, & Grant, 2009). In contrast, the literature on visuoperceptual abilities in HIV infection has yielded mixed findings. If present, visuoperceptual deficits appear to be secondary to frontostriatoparietal network dysregulation rather than exclusively posterior damage (Weber et al., 2010; Woods et al., 2009). Speech and language abilities are not typically affected in adults with HIV, although mild to moderate deficits in verbal fluency have been reported (Iudicello et al., 2007) and are likely driven by executive dysfunction rather than language-specific difficulties.

Although severe motor difficulties are rare, decreased psychomotor speed and coordination are fairly common and may affect performance on neuropsychological tests of other domains (Woods et al., 2009). Additionally, speed of information processing is frequently impaired, especially in tasks that are more demanding. Both verbal and visual episodic memory deficits are prominent in HAND. Rapid forgetting is fairly uncommon, but higher level encoding and retrieval deficits are often responsible for episodic memory issues and may be a result of damage to the frontostriatal loop (Gongvatana et al., 2007). These encoding and retrieval deficits can also cause impairment in prospective memory (i.e., "remembering to remember"), which plays a crucial role in everyday functioning. Impairment in working memory and attention tends to emerge in later stages of HIV disease, although the underlying neuropsychological mechanisms of these deficits remain unclear (Woods et al., 2009).

HIV-associated neurocognitive deficits increase risk for everyday functioning impairment. Although basic activities of daily living (ADLs) are typically spared in adults with HIV, deficits in instrumental ADLs are more common. Medication adherence, which is crucial for effective HIV treatment, is associated with motor skills, attention, prospective memory, and executive function, and such relationships are likely bidirectional (e.g., Ettenhofer et al., 2010). Unemployment is common in adults with HIV and is related to prospective memory and executive function. Automobile driving, which requires a complex set of neurocognitive processes, is also related to visuospatial abilities and attention in older patients

with HIV (Foley et al., 2013). Additionally, research has demonstrated that neurocognitive decline, including motor deficits and prospective memory impairment, negatively affects health-related quality of life. Therefore, for many HIV+ adults, neurocognitive impairment is clinically relevant and may cause significant strain in their everyday lives.

Behavior and Emotional Functioning. Anxiety and mood disorders are common among adults living with HIV disease (Brandt et al., 2016; O'Cleirigh et al., 2015). Approximately one-quarter to one-third of adults with HIV experience an anxiety disorder (e.g., generalized anxiety, panic), which is notably higher than the general population estimates. Similarly, mood disorders, including both depression and bipolar disorder, are common among HIV+ adults, with population rates estimated at around 50% (e.g., Brandt et al., 2016). Across these emotional disorders, risk factors include stigma, health worries, disclosure concerns, and psychosocial stressors. Apathy also commonly occurs among persons living with HIV disease and is present in about 40% of the population (Bryant et al., 2015). Importantly, all of these behavioral and emotional disturbances are associated with higher rates of everyday functioning problems, including instrumental ADLs such as medication nonadherence. However, there is no strong or reliable evidence linking their presence or severity to HIV-associated neurocognitive impairment.

Infants and Children

Cognition. Although a large percentage of infants with perinatally acquired HIV (PHIV) experienced CNS morbidity and death within infancy and toddlerhood early in the HIV epidemic, severe sequelae are now preventable with ART and viral suppression. Studies during the era of effective ART demonstrate global as well as domain-specific neurocognitive impairment primarily among children who experienced immunosuppression of sufficient severity to qualify for a diagnosis of AIDS (Class C), particularly if accompanied by diagnosed encephalopathy (Martin et al., 2006; Smith et al., 2012). Impairments remain despite immune reconstitution with ART and persist at least into young adulthood (Willen, Cuadra, Arheart, Post, & Govind, 2016); longer term outcomes are as yet unknown because the first generation of PHIV survivors are currently young adults. Although conflicting findings exist, most recent studies in high-resource countries demonstrate comparable global neurocognitive functioning in children and youth with PHIV and no history of Class C diagnosis and those perinatally HIV-exposed but uninfected (PHEU), with both groups obtaining mean scores in the low-average to average range (Smith et al., 2012), whereas studies comparing PHEU and unexposed children vary (Jahanshad et al., 2015; Le Doare, Bland, & Newell, 2012). Sociodemographic (e.g., poverty) and pre- or perinatal risk factors (e.g., low birth weight) that are relatively common among women with HIV may contribute to lower neurocognitive performance in both PHIV and PHEU groups.

A 2016 meta-analysis (Phillips et al., 2016) suggested that among domain-specific neurocognitive functions, the largest differences between children with and without PHIV occur in executive function (EF), processing speed, and working memory (note however, that this analysis was limited to studies that did not use PHEU children as a comparison group). As with adults, studies on EF figure prominently in the literature due to both the vulnerability of this area to HIV and to its importance for functional outcomes, particularly as youth become more independent. Studies have used both performance EF tests and questionnaires regarding everyday EF problems. The results vary, with some large recent studies suggesting that EF functioning in HIV-exposed youth in general is affected by sociodemographic risk factors (Llorente et al., 2014), with additional deficits in those with PHIV occurring primarily in the context of prior Class C diagnoses. These differences may be explained in part by slower processing speed rather than being isolated to inhibition or other primarily EF-specific functions (Nagarajan et al., 2012; Nichols, Chernoff, Malee, Sirois, Woods, et al., 2016; Nichols et al., 2015). Questionnaires reporting everyday EF functioning have shown persistent problems in school-age youth with PHIV compared with PHEU or unexposed youth in Uganda (Ezeamama et al., 2016), and self-reported problems in metacognition among youth with Class C diagnoses in the United States (Nichols et al., 2015). However, some studies comparing everyday EF in PHIV and PHEU children have shown no differences (Llorente et al., 2014) or even greater problems among the youth with PHEU, particularly in behavioral regulation (Nichols et al., 2015). In general, although both PHIV and PHEU children

may show reduced EF compared with unexposed children, the role of underlying cognitive components and the contribution of HIV require further study.

Processing speed has shown particular vulnerability to the effects of HIV in children and youth, as in adults (Nichols et al., 2015; Ruel et al., 2012; Smith et al., 2012). It is associated with measures of vascular functioning (Kapetanovic et al., 2014) and with neuroimaging indicators of CNS impact such as magnetic resonance spectroscopy (Nagarajan et al., 2012) and functional connectivity (Herting et al., 2015), suggesting it may be useful as a marker of ongoing CNS effects of HIV. Its role in performance of other cognitive tasks and a variety of everyday functions, such as driving, further argues for its importance. Although motor impairments were a prominent feature of HIV encephalopathy before cART, it currently receives less attention, although studies of HIV in lower resource countries in particular continue to note motor impairments relative to uninfected children (Ruel et al., 2012).

Impairments in working memory, or temporary storage and management of information, are described among children and youth with PHIV (Phillips et al., 2016; Smith et al., 2012) and are associated with brain white matter microstructure (Uban et al., 2015). Although episodic memory is relatively less studied than among adults, evidence suggests that youth with PHIV are at risk for impairments in both verbal and nonverbal learning and memory (Nichols, Chernoff, Malee, Sirois, Williams, et al., 2016). Their pattern of performance on memory tasks suggests that verbal memory deficits lie in encoding and learning, rather than retention, of information; although associations of verbal memory performance with CD4% at cognitive evaluation suggests the possibility of ongoing effects of HIV on memory, children with PHIV did not differ from those with PHEU once demographic and other confounding factors were taken into account. Consistent with literature showing visual processing impairment in PHIV (Phillips et al., 2016), visual memory continued to show an impact of HIV even after adjustment for demographic risks.

In contrast to adult-acquired HIV, PHIV has been associated with deficits in language acquisition and performance and in academic functioning. Language impairments, although a striking feature of HIV encephalopathy in young children, appear in the context of global cognitive impairment in the era of effective ART (Rice et al., 2012); longitudinal changes are associated with HIV disease severity and treatment (Redmond et al., 2016). Children exposed to HIV perinatally are, in general, at high risk of language impairment, with risk affected by familial history of language impairment and demographic factors. Academic functioning is an area of significant concern for youth with HIV due to known relationships between literacy and health suggesting that low academic functioning may complicate health-care self-management in these youth (Berkman et al., 2011). Both children with PHIV and PHEU have low academic performance compared with normative standards; however, those with PHIV and a history of encephalopathy have a greater discrepancy between their achievement and the performance predicted by their cognitive functioning (Garvie et al., 2013).

The impact of PHIV on daily functioning, including medication adherence, has been less clear. Caregiver reports of adaptive functioning in perinatally HIV-exposed children with and without HIV infection were comparable according to a large study in the United States (Smith et al., 2012), although differences may emerge among older adolescents and young adults (Pearlstein et al., 2014). Significant contributions of cognitive functioning to both adaptive and, as expected, academic functioning (Sirois et al., 2016) suggest that remediation of specific cognitive skills may improve outcomes. In contrast to the adult literature, relationships of cognitive functioning with medication adherence have been inconsistent (Malee et al., 2009; Nichols et al., 2012), with some studies suggesting better adherence in youth with impairments possibly as the result of greater support, and particular risk for those with mild and possibly unrecognized difficulties (Malee et al., 2009). Cognitive and academic factors, including related functions such as health literacy, warrant greater attention as youth with HIV move into adulthood and assume independent management of their health care along with other responsibilities.

Behavior and Emotional Functioning. Existing studies are inconclusive regarding risk for psychiatric disorders and behavior problems among children with perinatally acquired HIV, with studies showing higher or no difference in rates compared to the general population. The literature includes studies using both psychiatric diagnostic tools and behavioral symptom checklists, and spans low- to high-income countries (Louw, Ipser, Phillips, & Hoare, 2016). Rates of substance use in this population appear to be at least as high as typical youth as they age through adolescence. The origin of mental health and substance use problems is likely multifactorial, including socioeconomic, demographic, family history and mental health, and environmental factors in addition to HIV; the role of HIV is unclear because studies show both increased and decreased rates of behavioral symptoms compared with children perinatally exposed to HIV but uninfected (Mellins & Malee, 2013). Protective factors related to relationships with caregivers and support from peers and teachers have been demonstrated. Regardless of the origin of behavioral symptoms, a significant concern for this population is evidence suggesting that they may affect medication adherence (Kacanek et al., 2015). In addition, both adherence and tendency to engage in sexual activity, with resulting higher risk of HIV transmission, have the potential to be affected by substance use. Targeted, evidence-based services for prevention and treatment of mental health and substance use concerns among youth with PHIV infection, as well as structural changes to decrease non–HIV-related contributing causes, have the potential for both individual quality of life and public health impact.

Adolescence

Cognition. The acquisition of HIV during adolescence has been a topic of growing consideration, given the increased awareness regarding the significant brain development that occurs during this period through emerging adulthood. Like with adults, most adolescents seroconvert in response to behavioral choices, including unprotected sexual activity or use of drugs. A small number, mostly outside of the first-world countries, may also acquire HIV through medical procedures or disease management with infected blood products. Cognitive impact is broadly similar to what has been described for adults, although not uniformly so; the greatest effects of infection are seen with regard to memory and learning, motor and processing speed, and EF (Malee, Smith, & Mellins, 2016; Sherr, Croome, Parra Castaneda, Bradshaw, & Herrero Romero, 2014; Smith et al., 2012). Two factors are particularly important when considering cognition and its disruption secondary to HIV infection in adolescence: (1) that treatment with ARVs is a key component to lessening potential long-term effect of infection on the brain and nervous system, and (2) compliance with treatment is a significant challenge, with poor medication adherence leading to both greater development of drug resistance to HIV and to decreasing opportunity to assist with fighting cognitive and behavioral impact of the infection (Malee et al., 2016).

Because adolescence is a primary period of transition, challenges from infection secondary to not knowing one has seroconverted, and with the normal impulsivity that comes developmentally at this time, raise serious concerns regarding educational and social success. Teens experiment with ideas and opportunities; they make rash choices and vary often between uncertain reluctance and headstrong jumps into risky options (Hunter & Sparrow, 2012). These are a by-product of a developing network of behavioral controls neurologically. That the virus has a particular affinity for affecting just this system highlights the need to be particularly responsive to vulnerabilities that infection can extend. Additionally, it is just these vulnerabilities that contribute to challenges with medication compliance, as well as with making poor choices about self-care, that can exacerbate the risk toward AIDS-related illnesses. And with illness, comes the greater likelihood of more significant deficits in attention, memory, and EF (cf. Malee et al., 2016).

Behavior and Emotional Functioning. HIV has been shown to directly impact decision-making, which leads to challenges with behavioral regulation (Nichols, 2012). Poorer self-control contributes to challenges with social and emotional functioning. During adolescence, a period when greater risk for emotion regulation variability occurs as a course of normal developmental changes, it is noted that greater potential for anxiety and mood difficulties arises in adolescents who are HIV+ (Brandt et al., 2016; Malee et al., 2016). Sociocultural and socioeconomic factors serve to influence this vulnerability, given the likelihood for adverse experiences among those adolescents who are at highest risk for exposure and illness. As has been discussed with both children and adults, it appears that a mix of challenges with coping, self-efficacy, and self-esteem influences the likelihood of developing a behavioral or emotional disorder in response to infection. Similarly, a lack of compliance with medication management, both in regard to ARVs, but also if accompanying medications are required to treat such concerns as depression, anxiety, or posttraumatic stress disorder, increases the risk for greater behavioral challenge (Mellins & Malee, 2013). At present, research is focusing directly on ways to provide both more effective social support and guidance regarding self-care and self-efficacy, as well as promoting greater adherence.

Longitudinal Development

Neuropsychological development in children and adolescents has improved significantly since the introduction of ARV, both for those exposed prenatally and for those who are behaviorally infected in adolescence (Malee et al., 2016; Sherr et al., 2014). Additionally, because guidelines for assessment, diagnosis, and treatment for HAND (Antinori et al., 2007) highlight the appropriateness of assessing neurocognitive functioning in all patients with HIV, not just those who are symptomatic, as part of their regular medical and developmental follow-up, there has been an improved effort to more effectively identify deterioration or change in clinical status, allowing for the implementation of interventions that can support improved functioning. This is particularly important given the vulnerabilities regarding language, attention, and EF development that emerge early on with infection and continue to be of concern even with ongoing developmental support (Malee et al., 2016).

Upon reaching adulthood, patient concerns focus on developing sufficient academic skills and attaining both behavioral and vocational independence. Currently, studies are taking place that follow large cohorts of youth as they progress from treatment for their HIV exposure as children and adolescents into adulthood, where expectations for adherence, ongoing monitoring of health-care needs, maintenance of connections to appropriate physical and mental health-care providers, and adaptive functioning consistent with positive self-care are potentially significant challenges (Tassiopoulos et al., 2016). Although findings regarding these youth will vary, given many socioeconomic and epidemiological factors discussed previously that serve to influence how treatment and support unfold, there is expectation that environment, parenting, health care, and opportunity will intersect significantly. Studies indicating greater risk for developing executive capabilities are of key interest in understanding what potential interventions may be required to support the move toward vocational and behavioral opportunity.

Similarly, due to cART's effectiveness at reducing mortality rate, there is an increased number of older adults living with HIV disease. Because older age confers a greater risk of neurocognitive impairment and a greater prevalence of medical risk factors such as cardiovascular disease, older adults with HIV may have a higher risk of developing HAND. Both aging and HIV disease are also independently associated with changes in brain structure (e.g., Ances, Ortega, Vaida, Heaps, & Paul, 2012). Despite these risk factors, the literature regarding the effects of age and HIV disease on the prevalence of neurocognitive deficits is inconsistent, and the presence of HAND may be moderated by comorbid medical or psychiatric factors. Similarly, although a recent study did not find an effect of older age on incidence of HAND (Sheppard et al., 2015), other studies have reported greater rates of neurocognitive decline among HIV+ older adults. Older adults with HIV disease are also at greater risk for everyday functioning impairment. Age and HIV appear to have synergistic effects on basic and instrumental ADL functioning and additive effects on some aspects of health-related quality of life (Morgan et al., 2012). Interestingly, older adults tend to have better cART adherence than younger individuals, although the reason for this effect is unknown (e.g., Hinkin et al., 2002). Whether HIV infection early in life confers additional risk for aging-associated declines due to aberrant brain development and reduced cognitive reserve remains unknown but is a significant concern.

Neuropsychological Assessment

Adults

The most widely used criteria for research diagnosis of HAND, commonly referred to as the Frascati criteria, designate three subtypes of neurocognitive impairment: asymptomatic neurocognitive impairment (ANI), mild neurocognitive disorder, and HIV-associated dementia (Antinori et al., 2007). For a diagnosis of ANI, an individual must demonstrate mild cognitive impairment, as evidenced by performance at least 1 SD below the demographically adjusted mean in at least two cognitive domains, but no interference with everyday functioning. A diagnosis of mild cognitive disorder requires mild cognitive impairment in addition to mild functional difficulties. The most severe subtype of HAND, HIV-associated dementia, involves marked cognitive impairment, as evidenced by performance at least 2 SD below the demographically adjusted mean in at least two

cognitive domains, in addition to marked functional impairment. The inclusion of ANI in these criteria has been controversial because it does not require functional impairment; however, research has shown that when HAND diagnoses include an asymptomatic subtype, the diagnosis is more strongly associated with HIV encephalitis at autopsy (Cherner et al., 2007). To assess cognitive impairment, the Frascati group recommends administering at least two neuropsychological tests in each of seven cognitive domains: verbal/language, attention/working memory, abstraction/executive, memory (including learning and recall), speed of information processing, sensory/perceptual, and motor skills. The authors also include suggestions for specific neuropsychological tests in each of these domains (see Antinori et al., 2007).

In addition to a diagnosis of HAND, neuropsychological assessment can be instrumental in identifying comorbid medical and psychiatric conditions that may be responsible for, or contributing to, neurocognitive impairment in patients with HIV. The Frascati criteria include supplementary guidelines for identifying some common confounds to HAND, namely depression, developmental disability, traumatic brain injury, substance use disorder, HIV-related opportunistic CNS disease, non–HIV-related neurologic condition, systemic disease, and hepatitis C coinfection (see Antinori et al., 2007). In these cases, a referral for treatment of the comorbid condition(s) may be indicated.

Neuropsychological assessment can also be beneficial in identifying patients at risk for noncompliance with treatment. Executive dysfunction, attentional difficulties, and memory impairment are associated with medication nonadherence in patients with HIV (Hinkin et al., 2002). Among HIV+ older adults, neurocognitive impairment is also associated with poorer retention in care (Jacks et al., 2015). Therefore, a neuropsychological assessment can be useful not only for diagnosis of HAND, but also for informing the treatment-planning process.

Children and Adolescents

Neuropsychological assessment of infants, children, and adolescents who are affected by HIV is based on the recognition that what is at question is the impact of infection on a developing brain and nervous system. Importantly, HAND diagnosis and reliance on a specific system of classification regarding the impact of the disease are not typical in pediatric HIV management. However, similar to assessing for HAND, a comprehensive battery that details capacities in all the domains of potential vulnerability (attention, EF, memory for visual and verbal information, expressive and receptive language, visuospatial analysis, and sensorimotor functioning) is recommended, due to variability related to both the effect of HIV and the numerous other risks facing this population of children. Additionally, understanding cognitive effect and behavioral outcomes requires attention to typical developmental trajectories and the effect of both HIV and antiretroviral treatment at different points in development. Before the advent of ART, severe effects of HIV on the developing nervous system seen in some infants and children included frank loss of milestones as well as focal neurological and motor sequelae. A slower pattern of progression was also seen with more subtle CNS symptoms early in the disease course and the development of encephalopathy in the end stages. In the era of ART, detecting the more subtle cognitive problems that may occur requires careful assessment and comparison with known developmental patterns through use of age- and demographically adjusted instruments. Although cognitive and behavioral effects may be less severe, the possibility remains that they will affect the development of independence as youth are faced with more complex educational and social tasks and required to learn occupational skills.

Neuropsychological assessment allows for the identification of both significant impairment and potential subtle challenges, cognitively and behaviorally, that affect developmental opportunity and success with learning. Specific areas of functioning that have been identified as being directly and more subtly affected in children and youth with HIV include expressive and receptive language, the speed and efficiency of information processing, memory for visual and verbal information, sustaining attention across time, and EF (Allison, Wolters, & Brouwers, 2009). Additionally, children across developmental periods have been shown to experience problems with emotional and behavioral functioning, including symptoms of anxiety, hyperactivity, depression, and other psychiatric concerns (Mellins, Brackis-Cott, Dolezal, & Abrams, 2006). Importantly, as Nichols (2013) has stated, research has shown that the key issue with addressing the impact of HIV on development "is disentangling the effects of HIV from other developmental risks children face, including poverty and stress, educational disadvantage, family disruption and loss due to HIV, and family history of psychiatric or learning disorders." Additionally, symptoms related to both HIV infection and the side effects of drugs used to control the illness are an important variable to consider as part of the assessment because they can readily affect learning and adaptive functioning. Finally, there are a significant number of complicating issues that require consideration, as they intersect with HIV in childhood and adolescence. These include important developmental history factors like challenges during pregnancy including preeclampsia; prematurity; low birth weight; prenatal exposure to teratogens, including a variety of drugs, tobacco, alcohol, and other environmental toxins; and other infections that can accompany HIV in the mother, such as syphilis, chlamydia, and cytomegalovirus. As noted previously, medications such as ART used to treat HIV or accompanying concerns also continue to be investigated for important potential effects on development.

Pediatric research with children who were prenatally infected and those exposed prenatally to HIV but uninfected has shown that they perform about the same on tests of intellectual functioning, generally falling in the average to low-average range. Additionally, they have not been shown to present with a risk for behavioral disorders greater than those of children without HIV (Malee et al., 2011; Smith et al., 2012).

The presence of neurocognitive and behavioral problems in children and youth with HIV has implications for adaptive functioning and developmental outcomes across time. Given this, a foremost goal of neuropsychological evaluation is to detect potential problems with learning, attention, academic skills, and other broader cognitive areas, and to identify the presence and impact of emotional issues such as depression or anxiety. The results of the evaluation allow the clinician to describe the child or adolescent's strengths as well as weaknesses, and to guide ongoing approaches to intervention and support, both medically and with regard to the learning and home environments.

With infants and young children, developmental evaluation serves to principally identify lags in their attainment of developmental milestones and outline their potential risk for further delays as they mature. The neuropsychologist uses the findings from the evaluation to make recommendations to parents and treating clinicians for appropriate interventions, including developmental, speech/language, or occupational therapies, special education services, and/or parent training. In addition, with the implementation of serial assessment, emergent impairments that are suspected to be due to HIV or such things as medication side effects can be followed up to determine whether treatment changes are indicated, and further accommodations and interventions warranted.

As has been discussed previously, children and youth with HIV have been shown to have significant obstacles to ongoing success with learning that may be the result of cognitive difficulties like memory and attentional challenges, but also reflects such issues as a loss of consistent educational time due to illness and medical treatment; the impact of family disruption, including homelessness; living in areas with disadvantaged school systems that often contribute to high dropout rates; and a lack of basic nutritional and adaptive supports, given the variability of available funds (Nichols, 2013). Neuropsychological evaluation therefore serves as an important component of intervention for these youths; it facilitates for the medical and social support team, as well as the parent and educational setting, an understanding of the interplay of infection-related considerations and the accompanying psychosocial and environmental factors that affect learning success. Ultimately, the findings as discussed in the report, when shared with clinicians and case managers, can help direct parents and educators toward necessary educational and accommodation support services, with the goal of further assisting the family in accessing them. Additionally, serial assessment of youths serves to provide an ongoing understanding of the impact of the disease process and medication adherence, and the effects of interventions and accommodations on the individual's academic and psychosocial attainment. Knowledge acquired from the assessments across time can provide direction toward appropriate secondary and postsecondary educational and vocational training options, fostering a more successful transition to adulthood (Smith et al., 2012; Nichols, 2013).

Nichols and Farley (2009) have highlighted that medication adherence is a critical issue for children and youth with HIV. This is another realm where assessment can prove quite meaningful. Because many families begin transitioning the responsibility for medication adherence from the caregiver to the child before or during adolescence, issues with comprehension of the demands involved in daily medication management, and the capacity to take on this responsibility, often unfold. It has been shown that even adolescents without cognitive impairment can have difficulty taking medications properly; their organizational and self-monitoring abilities are still developing, leading to inefficiencies with the necessary problem-solving adherence requires (Mellins & Malee, 2013; Williams, Storm, & Montepiedra, 2006). Additionally, because it is not unusual that adolescents seek to avoid thinking about their HIV status (as is seen with most chronic illnesses during adolescence), emotional responses serve to impact adherence as well (Mellins & Malee, 2013). Because medical advances have now turned HIV into a chronic condition, consistent medication adherence is required to ensure that resistance to medications does not develop, leading to limits both on treatment options and increased risk for illness and potential death. Additionally, because "the likelihood of transmitting HIV to another person is lower if viral load is kept low through good adherence" (Nichols, 2013), an important public health issue exists for adolescents and young adults, who are more likely to engage in high-risk behaviors such as unsafe sex and self-care. Therefore, neuropsychological assessment assists in identifying youth who are at risk for showing adherence challenges, specifically related to inefficiencies in executive skill development. As a result, it can provide the basis for effective recommendations for adherence interventions, within the context of supporting a gradual level of independence in collaboration with their multidisciplinary adherence team.

Methods of Pediatric Neuropsychological Assessment

Assessment of infants and toddlers who have been infected with HIV has been important for identifying possible alterations in cognitive and motor development, and as a guide toward initiating early intervention approaches, including physical, occupational, and developmental therapies. Both research studies and clinical programs with infants and young children have typically utilized such developmental batteries as the Bayley Scales of Infant Development, 3rd edition (Bayley, 2006) to address broad domains of developing engagement and orientation, attention, discrimination of verbal and visual information, memory, and sensorimotor control. The principle use of these measures has been to describe specific areas of weakness in relationship to typically developing capacities. Similar approaches have been utilized both clinically and in research when working with infants who have been treated in utero with ARVs. Research has demonstrated the reliability and usefulness of this approach for supporting our understanding of developmental gains and to highlight areas of difficulty and for documenting the success which early intervention, including cART both pre- and postdelivery, has had on allowing more typical neuropsychological development to unfold (Linn et al., 2015; Prasad, 2015; Nozyce et al., 2014; Walker, Pierre, Christie, & Chang, 2013; and see Sherr et al., 2014, for a systematic review).

During the toddler to early elementary period, assessment of language skill development has been identified as particularly important. Studies have shown that delays in expressive and receptive language are more common in children exposed to HIV (Coplan et al., 1998; Rice et al., 2012; Sherr, Mueller, & Varrall, 2009; Sherry et al., 2014). Therefore, in addition to the use of broad-based intellectual batteries, assessment of language development is a key focus. Consideration of broader neuropsychological domains, including direct assessment of developing executive skills, is considered important beginning from this age. Attentional and executive difficulties serve to undermine early learning; by identifying and then recommending appropriate accommodations, support for better educational outcomes can be provided. During the elementary to middle school years, considerations regarding attention, memory, language, and growing executive control remain pertinent. Assessment of general cognitive development is typically supplemented with measures addressing visual and verbal memory, and a broader assessment of language, attention and EF, and sensorimotor control, is useful for addressing a wider range of cognitive status (Smith et al., 2012).

Assessment with adolescents and emerging adults requires the recognition that the brain continues to develop into the early to mid-20s (Hunter & Sparrow, 2012). This highlights not only that we need to consider that effects of HIV on the brain in adolescents may be different from that in adults, but it also reminds us that the consolidation of EF ability may be a particularly important domain of consideration. Assessing neurocognitive and behavioral capacities typically involves administration of a combination of broad-based and more specific batteries of tests, with comparisons made with the standardized normative sample. It is important to recognize that cognitive performance in adolescents can be affected by such factors as depression, anxiety, other psychiatric issues, the impact of learning disabilities, and such risks as poverty and environmental stress. This emphasizes the importance of standardized questionnaires addressing mood, behavior, and adaptive functioning (Mellins & Malee, 2013). Because considerations regarding the transition to adulthood are particularly important during this age period, the neuropsychological evaluation requires attention to such capabilities as personal and community living awareness (Smith et al., 2012). Use of money, awareness of means of transport and how to utilize available resources, and the capability to make effective decisions regarding school, peers, and behavioral choice are domains requiring attention.

An additional concern during adolescence, particularly with individuals who are HIV-infected, is the awareness of a high level of substance use among many youth with HIV (Nichols, 2013). Our understanding of how HIV and recreational substances commonly used by adolescents, such as alcohol and marijuana, might interact to affect the brain remains weak at this time. Although careful studies are required, to best understand the interplay of factors affecting cognitive development in adolescents affected by HIV, there are hints in the current literature that encourage the open discussion with patients, as part of rapport building, taking into account better awareness of individual differences in behavior and cognitive skill.

Intervention

cART, which emerged in the mid-1990s, has drastically altered the course and management of HIV infection. cART has led to greatly reduced mortality, and HIV is now largely seen as a chronic disease. Although previous recommendations suggested initiating cART only at advanced stages of HIV disease, cART is currently the recommended standard of care at all stages of infection. When taken as prescribed, cART is highly effective at suppressing HIV RNA in plasma and improving immune functioning, which reduces the risk of developing opportunistic infections and enhances longevity and quality of life. In addition, viral suppression with cART can prevent secondary transmission of HIV either behaviorally or from a pregnant mother to her infant in most cases. However, the beneficial effects of cART on the CNS have been less impressive, and research on the neuropsychological effects of cART shows mixed findings.

Surprisingly, the overall prevalence of HAND in adults remains stable in the cART era, despite a substantial decrease in the incidence of HAD. Possible explanations for discrepant research findings regarding neuropsychological benefits of cART include differences in study design and variability among antiretroviral medications, which may differentially penetrate the CNS (Weber, Blackstone, & Woods, 2013). A 2011 meta-analysis found modest effect sizes for improvements in attention (mean d = 0.17), EF (mean d = 0 .18), and motor function (mean d = 0.24) with cART, but no significant improvements in other cognitive domains (Al-Khindi, Zakzanis, & van Gorp, 2011). These improvements in neurocognitive function were strongly correlated with increases in CD4 cell count and younger age. Therefore, it appears that cART may have mild neurocognitive benefits for some individuals, but it is not sufficient for treating HAND. Even among those with prescribed cART regimens, medication nonadherence may prevent some neurocognitively impaired individuals from experiencing any potential benefits of these treatments. Prevention of significant immune suppression (Class C diagnosis) in children through the use of cART has reduced the risk of HIV-related cognitive impairment according to some studies, although other notable neurodevelopmental impacts are common in this population.

Preliminary research has also investigated the neurocognitive effects of nonantiretroviral medications in HIV. Some studies have reported neuropsychological benefits of psychiatric medications, including lithium, serotonin reuptake inhibitors, methylphenidate, selegiline, and memantine (Weber et al., 2013). However, other studies of these medications have failed to find any significant neuropsychological effects (Weber et al., 2013). As of now, no medications have been proven effective for treating HAND.

Cognitive rehabilitation, therefore, may be a beneficial addition to standard medical treatment of HIV for patients with HAND. Several intervention studies have reported improved neuropsychological test performance after consistent use of computerized cognitive training programs, which are aimed at restoring neurocognitive functions through repeated practice. Although these results are promising, most studies have failed to compare these experimental effects against an active control group (Weber et al., 2013). However, a recent study of HIV+ individuals with substance use disorder found that participants who were trained on a compensatory goal-management strategy performed significantly better on a multitasking test compared with an active control group (Casaletto et al., 2016). More extensive studies are therefore needed to determine whether restorative and compensatory cognitive rehabilitation programs could significantly improve HAND symptoms, either alone or in combination with cART. Although few studies of cognitive intervention in children with HIV exist, promising findings have been observed in Africa (Boivin, Nakasujja, Sikorskii, Opoka, & Giordani, 2016).

Implications for Clinical Practice

Evidence-Based Guidelines for Adult HIV

Positive health outcomes in HIV are most reliably tied to active engagement in care and adherence to prescribed treatment regimens, most notably ARVs. Evidence-based clinical neuropsychological practice therefore may focus on issues related to the identification and remediation of established risk factors for dropping out of care or nonadherence to prescribed treatment regimens. This might include differential diagnosis of HAND using established guidelines, behavioral and emotional disorders (e.g., depression, anxiety, apathy), and other comorbid factors (e.g., substance abuse), all of which might increase risk of poor health outcomes. Neuropsychologists might also work to identify potential protective factors, such as self-efficacy and psychosocial supports, which may help to bolster positive health outcomes. At present, there are no empirically supported treatments for HAND.

Evidence-Based Guidelines for Pediatric HIV

What has been most clearly demonstrated to date is that the key to promoting a more effective outcome for children and youth affected by HIV is early and sustained treatment with cART. Differentiating between the needs of children who were prenatally infected, who through their mother's use of ARVs are most typically born negative, and whose experience of development is more consistent with that of their uninfected peers, and those who acquired HIV perinatally or during later childhood or adolescence, is a key consideration. Regardless of HIV status, however, is the need to address key questions through diagnostic assessment, including neuropsychological evaluation, and the understanding of sociocultural and socioeconomic factors that are at play with regard to daily life. For those children who are infected with HIV, emphasis should be on maintaining their medication regimen, coupled with ongoing understanding of the challenges that emerge across time, both developmentally and in terms of their economic, educational, and cultural experiences and needs. Addressing, through appropriate treatment referrals, emotional and behavioral concerns, and promoting the development of an individualized education plan or Section 504 Plan, to address learning concerns and accommodation needs, is a principal outcome from assessment. Recognizing too that identification of HIV status is a particularly difficult consideration, due to ongoing stigma and likely negative responses

in some communities, also requires attention. Promoting ongoing awareness of transition needs, across childhood and adolescence, toward adulthood, and connecting youth to appropriate resources for fostering the best path toward seamless continual intervention, is an ongoing challenge.

Future Directions

At present, the greatest challenge within pediatric HIV is to best understand what fosters the greatest opportunity for a successful move toward independence and productive adulthood. Addressing the difficulties with adherence, ensuring opportunities for obtaining needed educational and vocational supports, and promoting social competence are principal goals. Key areas of research are better understanding how effective EF can be fostered, across a range of developmental milestones, and assisting youth and their caregivers in accessing appropriate supports to better ensure successful development across time. With regard to neuropsychological development in particular, addressing the interaction between adversity and developmental risk, and understanding how such choices as substance use and abuse influence this vulnerable period from

Table 11.1 Clinical Manifestations of HIV Disease

Domain	Children and Adolescents	Adults
Neurocognitive	• Attention • Language • Memory • EFs • Psychomotor speed • Motor coordination	• Attention/working memory • Episodic memory • EFs • Psychomotor speed • Motor coordination
Behavioral	• Depression • Anxiety • Substance use disorders (adolescence) • ADHD	• Depression • Anxiety • Apathy • Substance use disorders
Everyday functioning	• Medication nonadherence • School failure • Health-related quality of life	• Medication nonadherence • Unemployment • Household activities • Automobile driving • Health-related quality of life

Note. ADHD = attention-deficit/hyperactivity disorder.

Table 11.2 Evidence-based Guidelines for HIV

Diagnosis	• Assess neurocognitive functioning of adults according to the Frascati guidelines for diagnosis of HAND (Antinori et al., 2007) • In children, focus on attention, developing EF and language specifically • Assess for behavioral and emotional disorders, including depression, anxiety, and substance use • In children, consider risk for ADHD and LD • Assess for possible comorbid medical conditions
Treatment	• Emphasize the importance of early and sustained use of ARVs • Address psychological and sociocultural risk factors for treatment nonadherence and dropping out of care • Provide referrals for treatment of comorbid behavioral and medical conditions • Provide resources for ongoing care during the transition from childhood to adulthood • Promote the development of a plan for educational accommodations, if applicable

Note. HAND = HIV-associated neurocognitive disorders, ADHD = attention-deficit/hyperactivity disorders, LD = learning disablity, ARVs = antiretrovirals.

childhood to emerging adulthood, is a necessary focus. Associated with this is understanding the intersection of economic and cultural challenge that underlie adversity, and addressing means to improve self-efficacy and choice through effective supportive interventions remains a needed domain.

With regard to working with adults with HIV, the key challenge that remains is understanding both the interrelationship that exists between aging and HIV infection, and how this is both mediated and exacerbated by long-term medication use to manage the vulnerability to disease. Similarly, identifying effective integrated care approaches, that simultaneously address HIV as a chronic illness and its impact on how life is experienced, both psychologically and physically, is an area requiring continued attention. As efforts are made to diminish HIV infection, given broader accessibility of such approaches as preexposure prophylaxis, there remains a population of individuals who still require significant attention to ensure that their health and neurocognitive functioning are able to sustain ongoing independence. As the focus moves toward earlier efforts at intervention, with infected adolescents and with preventing infection in adolescents and emerging adults, taking what has been learned across time regarding prevention and treatment is key. Neuropsychologists are in a particular position to guide this, given the ability to identify options for individualized approaches to management and disease prevention within a neurocognitive framework.

References

Allison, S., Wolters, P., & Brouwers, P. (2009). Youth with HIV/AIDS: Neurobehavioral consequences. In R. H. Paul, N. Sacktor, V. Valcour, & K. T. Tashima (Eds.), *HIV and the brain: New challenges in the modern era* (pp. 187–211). New York, NY: Humana Press.

Al-Khindi, T., Zakzanis, K. K., & van Gorp, W. G. (2011). Does antiretroviral therapy improve HIV-associated cognitive impairment? A quantitative review of the literature. *Journal of the International Neuropsychological Society, 17,* 956–969.

Ances, B. M., Ortega, M., Vaida, F., Heaps, J., & Paul, R. (2012). Independent effects of HIV, aging, and HAART on brain volumetric measures. *Journal of Acquired Immune Deficiency Syndromes, 59,* 469–477.

Antinori, A., Arendt, G., Becker, J. T., Brew, B. J., Byrd, D. A., Cherner, M., … Wojna, V. E. (2007). Updated research nosology for HIV-associated neurocognitive disorders. *Neurology, 69,* 1789–1799.

Bayley, N. B. (2006). *Bayley Scales of Infant and Toddler Development* (3rd ed.). San Antonio, TX: Pearson Assessment.

Berkman, N. D., Sheridan, S. L., Donahue, K. E., Halpern, D. J., & Crotty, K. (2011). Low health literacy and health outcomes: An updated systematic review. *Annals of Internal Medicine, 155,* 97–107.

Boivin, M. J., Nakasujja, N., Sikorskii, A., Opoka, R. B. & Giordani, B. (2016). A randomized controlled trial to evalute if computerized cognitive rehabilitation improves neurocognition in Ugandan children with HIV. *AIDS Research and Human Retroviruses, 32,* 743–755.

Brandt, C. P., Sheppard, D. P., Zvolensky, M. J., Morgan, E. E., Atkinson, J. H., & Woods, S. P. (2016). Does age influence the frequency of anxiety symptoms and disorders in HIV disease? *Journal of HIV and Social Services*, **15**, 380–403.

Bryant, V. E., Whitehead, N. E., Burrell, L. E., Dotson, V. M., Cook, R. L., Malloy, P., … Cohen, R. A. (2015). Depression and apathy among people living with HIV: Implications for treatment of HIV associated neurocognitive disorders. *AIDS and Behavior*, **19**, 1430–1437. http://doi.org/10.1007/s10461-014-0970-1

Buchanan, D., Kee, R., Sadowski, L.S., & Garcia, D. (2009). The health impact of supportive housing for HIV-positive homeless patients: A randomized controlled trial. *American Journal of Public Health*, **99**, S675–S680. doi: 10.2105/AJPH.2008.137810.

Casaletto, K. B., Umlauf, A., Moore, D. J., Woods, S. P., Scott, J. C., & Heaton, R. K. (2016). Abbreviated goal management training shows preliminary evidence as a neurorehabilitation tool for HIV-associated neurocognitive disorders among substance users. *The Clinical Neuropsychologist*, **30**, 107–130.

Cherner, M., Cysique, L., Heaton, R. K., Marcotte, T. D., Ellis, R. J., Masliah, E. … the HNRC Group. (2007). Neuropathologic confirmation of definitional criteria for human immunodeficiency virus-associated neurocognitive disorders. *Journal of NeuroVirology*, **13**, 23–28.

Cohen, S., Caan, M. W., Mutsaerts, H. J., Scherpbier, H. J., Kuijpers, T. W., Reiss, P., … Pajkrt, D. (2016). Cerebral injury in perinatally HIV-infected children compared to matched healthy controls. *Neurology*, **86**, 19–27. doi:10.1212/wnl.0000000000002209.

Coplan J., Contello K. A., Cunningham C. K., Weiner L. B., Dye T. D., Roberge L., … Kirkwood, K. (1998). Early language development in children exposed to or infected with human immunodeficiency virus. *Pediatrics*, **102**, e8.

Crowell, C. S., Huo, Y., Tassiopoulos, K., Malee, K. M., Yogev, R., Hazra, R., … Muller, W. J. (2015). Early viral suppression improves neurocognitive outcomes in HIV-infected children. *AIDS*, **29**, 295–304.

Crowell, C. S., Malee, K. M., Yogev, R., & Muller, W. J. (2014). Neurologic disease in HIV-infected children and the impact of combination antiretroviral therapy. *Review of Medical Virology*, **24**, 316–331. doi: 10.1002/rmv.1793

Ellis, R. J., Calero, P., & Stockin, M. D. (2009). HIV infection and the central nervous system: A primer. *Neuropsychology Review*, **19**, 144–151.

Ellis, R., Langford, D., & Masliah, E. (2007). HIV and antiretroviral therapy in the brain: Neuronal injury and repair. *Nature Reviews Neuroscience*, **8**, 33–44.

Ettenhofer, M. L., Foley, J., Castellon, S. A., & Hinkin, C. H. (2010). Reciprocal prediction of medication adherence and neurocognition in HIV/AIDS. *Neurology*, **74**(15), 1217–1222.

Ezeamama, A. E., Kizza, F. N., Zalwango, S. K., Nkwata, A. K., Zhang, M., Rivera, M. L., … Whalen, C. C. (2016).

Perinatal HIV status and executive function during school-age and adolescence: A comparative study of long-term cognitive capacity among children from a high HIV prevalence setting. *Medicine (Baltimore)*, **95**, e3438. doi: 10.1097/md.0000000000003438

Foley, J. M., Ettenhofer, M. L., Kim, M. S., Behdin, N., Castellon, S. A., & Hinkin, C. H. (2012). Cognitive reserve as a protective factor in older HIV-positive patients at risk for cognitive decline. *Applied Neuropsychology. Adult*, **19**, 16–25. http://doi.org/10.1080/09084282.2011.595601

Foley, J. M., Gooding, A. L., Thames, A. D., Ettenhofer, M. L., Kim, M. S., Castellon, S. A., … Hinkin, C. H. (2013). Visuospatial and attentional abilities predict driving simulator performance among older HIV-infected adults. *American Journal of Alzheimer's Disease and Other Dementias*, **28**, 185–194. http://doi.org/10.1177/1533317512473192

Garvie, P. A., Zeldow, B., Malee, K., Nichols, S. L., Wilkins, M. L., Smith, R. E., … PHACS. (2013). *Concordance of cognitive and academic achievement outcomes in youth with perinatal HIV exposure.* Paper presented at the National Conference on Pediatric Psychology (NCPP), New Orleans, LA.

Gongvatana, A., Woods, S. P., Taylor, M. J., Vigil, O., Grant, I., & the HNRC Group. (2007). Semantic clustering inefficiency in HIV-associated dementia. *Journal of Neuropsychiatry and Clinical Neurosciences*, **19**, 36–42.

Heaton, R. K., Franklin, D. R., Deutsch, R., Letendre, S., Ellis, R. J., Casaletto, K., … Teshome, M. (2015). Neurocognitive change in the era of HIV combination antiretroviral therapy: The longitudinal CHARTER study. *Clinical Infectious Diseases*, **60**, 473–480. http://doi.org/10.1093/cid/ciu862

Henry J. Kaiser Family Foundation. (2017). *The Global HIV/AIDS Epidemic Fact Sheet.* Retrieved from http://kff.org/global-health-policy/fact-sheet/the-global-hivaids-epidemic/

Herting, M. M., Uban, K. A., Williams, P. L., Gautam, P., Huo, Y., Malee, K., … Sowell, E. R. (2015). Default mode connectivity in youth with perinatally acquired HIV. *Medicine (Baltimore)*, **94**, e1417. doi: 10.1097/md.0000000000001417

Hinkin, C. H., Castellon, S. A., Durvasala, R. S., Hardy, D. J., Lam, M. N., Mason, K. I., … Stefaniak, M. (2002). Medication adherence among HIV+ adults: Effects of cognitive dysfunction and regimen complexity. *Neurology*, **59**, 1944–1950.

Hoare, J., Ransford, G. L., Phillips, N., Amos, T., Donald, K., & Stein, D. J. (2014). Systematic review of neuroimaging studies in vertically transmitted HIV positive children and adolescents. *Metabolic Brain Disorders*, **29**, 221–229. doi: 10.1007/s11011-013-9456-5

Hunter, S. J., & Sparrow, E. P. (2012). *Executive function and dysfunction: Identification, assessment, and treatment.* Cambridge, UK: Cambridge University Press.

Iudicello, J. E., Woods, S. P., Parsons, T. D., Moran, L. M., Carey, C. L., & Grant, I. (2007). Verbal fluency in HIV infection: A meta-analytic review. *Journal of the International Neuropsychological Society, 13*(01), 183–189.

Jacks, A., Wainwright, D., Salazar, L., Grimes, R., York, M., Strutt, A. M. … Hasbun, R. (2015). Neurocognitive deficits increase risk of poor retention in care among older adults with newly diagnosed HIV infection. *AIDS, 29*(13), 1711–1714.

Jahanshad, N., Couture, M. C., Prasitsuebsai, W., Nir, T. M., Aurpibul, L., Thompson, P. M., … Valcour, V. G. (2015). Brain imaging and neurodevelopment in HIV-uninfected Thai children born to HIV-infected mothers. *Pediatric Infectious Disease Journal, 34*, e211–216.

Joint United Nations Programme on HIV/AIDS. (2016). *Global AIDS Update 2016*. NY: UNAIDS. Retrieved from: http://www.unaids.org/sites/default/files/media_asset/global-AIDS-update-2016_en.pdf

Kacanek, D., Angelidou, K., Williams, P. L., Chernoff, M., Gadow, K. D., & Nachman, S. (2015). Psychiatric symptoms and antiretroviral nonadherence in US youth with perinatal HIV: A longitudinal study. *AIDS, 29*, 1227–1237. doi: 10.1097/qad.0000000000000697

Kapetanovic, S., Griner, R., Zeldow, B., Nichols, S., Leister, E., Gelbard, H. A., … Williams, P. L. (2014). Biomarkers and neurodevelopment in perinatally HIV-infected or exposed youth: a structural equation model analysis. *AIDS, 28*, 355–364. doi: 10.1097/qad.0000000000000072

Le Doare, K., Bland, R., & Newell, M. L. (2012). Neurodevelopment in children born to HIV-infected mothers by infection and treatment status. *Pediatrics, 130*, e1326–1344.

Lemey, P., Pybus, O. G., Wang, B., Saksena, N. K., Salemi, M., & Vandamme, A. M. (2003) Tracing the origin and history of the HIV-2 epidemic. *Proceedings of the National Academy of Science, 100*, 6588–6592. doi:10.1073/pnas.0936469100

Linn, K., Fay, A., Meddles, K., Isbell, S., Lin, P. N., Thair, C., … Mar, S. S. (2015). HIV-related cognitive impairment of orphans in Myanmar with vertically transmitted HIV taking antiretroviral therapy. *Pediatric Neurology, 53*, 485–490. doi: 10.1016/j.pediatrneurol.2015.08.004

Llorente, A. M., Brouwers, P., Leighty, R., Malee, K., Smith, R., Harris, L., … Chase, C. (2014). An analysis of select emerging executive skills in perinatally HIV-1-infected children. *Applied Neuropsychology: Child, 3*, 10–25. doi: 10.1080/21622965.2012.686853

Louw, K. A., Ipser, J., Phillips, N., & Hoare, J. (2016). Correlates of emotional and behavioural problems in children with perinatally acquired HIV in Cape Town, South Africa. *AIDS Care, 28*, 842–850. doi: 10.1080/09540121.2016.1140892

Malee, K., Williams, P. L., Montepiedra, G., Nichols, S., Sirois, P. A., Storm, D., … Kammerer, B. (2009). The role of cognitive functioning in medication adherence of children and adolescents with HIV infection. *Journal of Pediatric Psychology, 34*, 164–175. doi: 10.1093/jpepsy/jsn068

Malee, K. M., Smith, R. A., & Mellins, C. A. (2016). Brain and cognitive development among US youth with perinatally acquired human immunodeficiency virus infection. *Journal of the Pediatric Infectious Diseases Society, 5*(Suppl 1), S1–S5. doi:10.1093/jpids/piwo41

Malee, K. M., Tassiopoulos, K., Huo, Y., Siberry, G., Williams, P. L., Hazra, R., … Mellins, C. A. (2011). Mental health functioning among children and adolescents with perinatal HIV infection and perinatal HIV exposure. *AIDS Care, 23*, 1533–1544. doi: 10.1080/09540121.2011.575120

Martin, S. C., Wolters, P. L., Toledo-Tamula, M. A., Zeichner, S. L., Hazra, R., & Civitello, L. (2006). Cognitive functioning in school-aged children with vertically acquired HIV infection being treated with highly active antiretroviral therapy (HAART). *Developmental Neuropsychology, 30*, 633–657. doi: 10.1207/s15326942dn3002_1

Mellins, C. A., Brackis-Cott, E., Dolezal, C., & Abrams, E. J. (2006). Psychiatric disorders in youth with perinatally acquired Human Immunodeficiency Virus infection. *The Pediatric Infectious Disease Journal, 25*, 432–437. doi: 10.1097/01.inf.0000217372.10385.2a

Mellins, C. A., & Malee, K. M. (2013). Understanding the mental health of youth living with perinatal HIV infection: Lessons learned and current challenges. *Journal of the International AIDS Society, 16*, 18593.

Morgan, E. E., Iudicello, J. E., Weber, E., Duarte, N. A., Riggs, K. P., Delano-Wood, L., … the HNRP. (2012). Synergistic effects of HIV infection and older age on daily functioning. *Journal of Acquired Immune Deficiency Syndromes, 61*, 341–348.

Nagarajan, R., Sarma, M. K., Thomas, M. A., Chang, L., Natha, U., Wright, M., … Keller, M. A. (2012). Neuropsychological function and cerebral metabolites in HIV-infected youth. *Journal of Neuroimmune Pharmacology, 7*, 981–990. doi: 10.1007/s11481-012-9407-7

Nichols, S. L. (2012). Executive functions in HIV. In S. J. Hunter & E. P. Sparrow (Eds)., *Executive function and dysfunction: Identification, assessment, and treatment* (pp. 168–173). Cambridge, UK: Cambridge University Press.

Nichols, S. L. (2013). Neuropsychology of HIV in children and adolescents. *Psychology and AIDS Exchange Newsletter, 1*. Retrieved from: http://www.apa.org/pi/aids/resources/exchange/2013/01/neuropsychology-children.aspx

Nichols, S. L., Bethel, J., Kapogiannis, B. G., Li, T., Woods, S. P., Patton, E. D., … Garvie, P. A. (2016). Antiretroviral treatment initiation does not differentially alter neurocognitive functioning over time in youth the behaviorally acquired HIV. *Journal of Neurovirology, 22*, 218–230.

Nichols, S. L., Brummel, S. S., Smith, R. A., Garvie, P. A., Hunter, S. J., Malee, K. M., … Mellins, C. A. (2015). Executive functioning in children and adolescents with perinatal HIV infection. *Pediatric Infectious Diseases Journal, 34*, 969–975. doi: 10.1097/inf.0000000000000809

Nichols, S. L., Chernoff, M. C., Malee, K., Sirois, P. A., Williams, P. L., Figueroa, V., & Woods, S. P. (2016). Learning and memory in children and adolescents with perinatal HIV infection and perinatal HIV exposure. *Pediatric Infectious Diseases Journal, 35*, 649–654. doi: 10.1097/inf.0000000000001131

Nichols, S. L., Chernoff, M. C., Malee, K. M., Sirois, P. A., Woods, S. P., Williams, P. L., … Kammerer, B. (2016). Executive functioning in children and adolescents with perinatal HIV infection and perinatal HIV exposure. *Journal of the Pediatric Infectious Diseases Society, 5*(suppl 1), S15–S23. doi: 10.1093/jpids/piw049

Nichols, S. L., & Farley, J. J. (2009). Human immunodeficiency virus infection in children. In W. B. Carey, A. C. Crocker, E. R. Elias, A. M. Feldman, & W. L. Coleman (Eds.), *Developmental-behavioral pediatrics* (4th ed., pp. 269–276). St. Louis, MO: Elsevier Publishing.

Nichols, S. L., Montepiedra, G., Farley, J. J., Sirois, P. A., Malee, K., Kammerer, B., … Naar-King, S. (2012). Cognitive, academic, and behavioral correlates of medication adherence in children and adolescents with perinatally acquired HIV infection. *Journal of Developmental and Behavioral Pediatrics, 33*, 298–308. doi: 10.1097/DBP.0b013e31824bef47

Nozyce, M. L., Huo, Y., Williams, P.L., Kapetanovic, S., Hazra, R., Nichols, S., … Sirois P. A. (2014). Safety of in utero and neonatal antiretroviral exposure: cognitive and academic outcomes in HIV-exposed, uninfected children 5-13 years of age. *Pediatric Infectious Disease Journal, 33*, 1128–1133. doi: 10.1097/INF.0000000000000410.

O'Cleirigh, C., Magidson, J. F., Skeer, M. R., Mayer, K. H., & Safren, S. A. (2015). Prevalence of psychiatric and substance abuse symptomatology among HIV-infected gay and bisexual men in HIV primary care. *Psychosomatics, 56*, 470–478.

Panel on Antiretroviral Therapy and Medical Management of HIV-Infected Children. (2015). *Guidelines for the use of antiretroviral agents in pediatric HIV infection*. Retrieved from: https://aidsinfo.nih.gov/contentfiles/lvguidelines/PediatricGuidelines.pdf

Pearlstein, S. L., Mellins, C. A., Dolezal, C., Elkington, K. S., Santamaria, E. K., Leu, C. S., … Abrams, E. J. (2014). Youth in transition: Life skills among perinatally HIV-infected and HIV-exposed adolescents. *Journal of Pediatric Psychology, 39*, 294–305. doi: 10.1093/jpepsy/jst077

Phillips, N., Amos, T., Kuo, C., Hoare, J., Ipser, J., Thomas, K. G. F., & Stein, D. J. (2016). HIV-associated cognitive impairment in perinatally infected children: A meta-analysis. *Pediatrics, 138*, e20160893.

Prasad, R. (2015). HIV primary care. In J. E. South-Paul, S. C. Matheny, & E. L. Lewis (Eds.), *Lange current diagnosis and treatment: Family medicine* (4th ed., pp. 582–597). NY: McGraw-Hill.

Redmond, S. M., Yao, T. J., Russell, J. S., Rice, M. L., Hoffman, H. J., Siberry, G. K., … Williams, P. L. (2016). Longitudinal evaluation of language impairment in youth with perinatally acquired human immunodeficiency virus (HIV) and youth with perinatal HIV exposure. *Journal of the Pediatric Infectious Diseases Society, 5*(Suppl 1), S33–S40. doi: 10.1093/jpids/piw045

Rice, M. L., Buchanan, A. L., Siberry, G. K., Malee, K. M., Zeldow, B., Frederick, T., … Williams, P. L. (2012). Language impairment in children perinatally infected with HIV compared to children who were HIV-exposed and uninfected. *Journal of Developmental and Behavioral Pediatrics, 33*, 112–123. doi: 10.1097/DBP.0b013e318241ed23

Ruel, T. D., Boivin, M. J., Boal, H. E., Bangirana, P., Charlebois, E., Havlir, D. V., … Wong, J. K. (2012). Neurocognitive and motor deficits in HIV-infected Ugandan children with high CD4 cell counts. *Clinical Infectious Diseases, 54*, 1001–1009. doi: 10.1093/cid/cir1037

Santiago, F., Range, B. F., Keele, Y., Li, E., Bailes, F., Bibollet-Ruche, C., … Hahn, B. H. (2005). Simian immunodeficiency virus infection in free-ranging sooty mangabeys (Cercocebus atys atys) from the Taï Forest, Côte d'Ivoire: Implications for the origin of epidemic human immunodeficiency virus type 2. *Journal of Virology, 79*, 12515–12527. doi.org/10.1128/JVI.79.19.12515–12527.2005

Saylor, D., Dickens, A. M., Sacktor, N., Haughey, N., Slusher, B., Pletnikov, M., … McArthur, J. C. (2016). HIV-associated neurocognitive disorder – Pathogenesis and prospects for treatment. *Nature Reviews Neurology, 12*, 234–248.

Sheppard, D. P., Woods, S. P., Bondi, M. W., Gilbert, P. E., Massman, P. J., Doyle, K. L., & the HNRP Group. (2015). Does older age confer an increased risk of incident neurocognitive disorders among persons living with HIV disease? *Clinical Neuropsychology, 29*, 656–677.

Sherr, L., Croome, N., Parra Castaneda, K., Bradshaw, K., & Herrero Romero, R. (2014). Developmental challenges in in HIV infected children – An updated systematic review. *Children and Youth Services Review, 45*, 74–89.

Sherr, L., Mueller, J., & Varrall, R. (2009). A systematic review of cognitive development and child human immunodeficiency virus infection. *Psychology, Health, & Medicine, 14*, 387–404.

Sirois, P. A., Chernoff, M. C., Malee, K. M., Garvie, P. A., Harris, L. L., Williams, P. L., … Nichols, S. L. (2016). Associations of memory and executive functioning with academic and adaptive functioning among youth with perinatal HIV exposure and/or infection. *Journal of the Pediatric Infectious Diseases Society, 5*(suppl 1), S24–S32. doi: 10.1093/jpids/piw046

Smith, R., Chernoff, M., Williams, P. L., Malee, K. M., Sirois, P. A., Kammerer, B., … Rutstein, R. (2012). Impact of HIV severity on cognitive and adaptive functioning during childhood and adolescence. *Pediatric Infectious Diseases Journal*, *31*, 592–598. doi: 10.1097/INF.0b013e318253844b

Smith, R., Malee, K., Leighty, R., Brouwers, P., Mellins, C., Hittelman, J., ... Blasini, I. (2006). Effects of perinatal HIV infection and associated risk factors on cognitive development among young children. *Pediatrics*, *117*, 851–862. doi: 10.1542/peds.2005-0804

Smith, R., & Wilkins, M. (2015). Perinatally acquired HIV infection: Long-term neuropsychological consequences and challenges ahead. *Child Neuropsychology*, *21*, 234–268. doi: 10.1080/09297049.2014.898744

Squeglia, L. M., & Gray, K. M. (2016). Alcohol and drug use and the developing brain. *Current Psychiatry Reports*, *18*, 46. doi: 10.1007/s11920-016-0689-y

Tassiopoulos K., Patel K., Alperen J., Kacanek D., Ellis A., Berman C., ... Seage G. R., III. (2016). Pediatric HIV/AIDS cohort study following young people with perinatal HIV infection from adolescence into adulthood: The protocol for PHACS AMP Up, a prospective cohort study. *British Medical Journal:Open*, *6*, e011396. doi: 10.1136/bmjopen-2016-011396.

Tozzi, V., Balestra, P., Bellagamba, R., Corpolongo, A., Salvatori, M. F., Visco-Comandini, U., ... Narciso, P. (2007). Persistence of neuropsychologic deficits despite long-term highly active antiretroviral therapy in patients with HIV-related neurocognitive impairment: Prevalence and risk factors. *Journal of Acquired Immune Deficiency Syndromes*, *45*, 174–182.

Uban, K. A., Herting, M. M., Williams, P. L., Ajmera, T., Gautam, P., Huo, Y., ... Sowell, E. R. (2015). White matter microstructure among youth with perinatally acquired HIV is associated with disease severity. *AIDS*, *29*, 1035–1044. doi: 10.1097/qad.0000000000000648

Walker, S. Y., Pierre, R. B., Christie, C. D. C., & Chang, S. M. (2013). Neurocognitive function in HIV-positive children in a developing country. *International Journal of Infectious Diseases*, *17*, e862–867.

Weber, E., Blackstone, K., & Woods, S. P. (2013). Cognitive neurorehabilitation of HIV-associated neurocognitive disorders: A qualitative review and call to action. *Neuropsychology Review*, *23*, 81–98.

Weber, E., Woods, S. P., Cameron, M. V., Gibson, S., Grant, I., & the HNRC Group (2010). Mental rotation of hands in HIV infection: Neuropsychological evidence of dysfunction in fronto-striato-parietal networks. *Journal of Neuropsychiatry and Clinical Neurosciences*, *22*, 115–122.

Williams, P. L., Storm, D., & Montepiedra, G. (2006). Predictors of adherence to antiretroviral medications in children and adolescents with HIV infection. *Pediatrics*, *118*, 1745–1757.

Willen, E. J., Cuadra, A., Arheart, K. L., Post, M. J., & Govind, V. (2016). Young adults perinatally infected with HIV perform more poorly on measures of executive functioning and motor speed than ethnically matched healthy controls. *AIDS Care*, *29*, 387–393. doi: 10.1080/09540121.2016.1234677

Woods, S. P., Moore, D. J., Weber, E., & Grant, I. (2009). Cognitive neuropsychology of HIV-associated neurocognitive disorders. *Neuropsychology Review*, *19*, 152–168.

Chapter 12

Multiple Sclerosis

Lana Harder, Julie A. Bobholz, and William S. MacAllister

Introduction

Multiple sclerosis (MS) is an immune-mediated central nervous system (CNS) demyelinating disorder characterized by the production of widespread lesions, or plaques, in the brain and spinal cord, which lead to the destruction of the myelin sheaths of the nerves and axons, impacting axonal signal transmission (Chiaravalloti & DeLuca, 2008). Individuals diagnosed along the spectrum of demyelinating conditions, including MS, acute disseminated encephalomyelitis, neuromyelitis optica, and transverse myelitis, are considered to be at risk for adverse neuropsychological outcomes (Tan, Hague, Greenberg, & Harder, 2017). MS is the most common and well-studied demyelinating condition and has historically been viewed as a disease of young adults; however, recent research has raised awareness that this disease can affect individuals across the lifespan. Literature suggests that individuals with MS, at any age, are at risk for motor, cognitive, and psychological problems. Given that lesions may emerge anywhere in the CNS, individuals with MS present with a wide range of symptoms, and neuropsychological profiles vary considerably, presenting challenges for researchers working to characterize a neuropsychological phenotype of the disease. This chapter reviews the recent literature regarding clinical manifestation of this disease across the lifespan, current neuropsychological assessment approaches, intervention, implications for clinical practice, and suggested future directions for the study of MS from a neuropsychological perspective.

Epidemiology and Pathophysiology

The onset of MS usually occurs in early adulthood (between 20 and 30 years of age) and is 2–3 times more common in women. The peak age of onset for most patients with MS is between 20 to 40 years of age. However, as noted, there has been a recent increase in MS as it pertains to younger individuals. About 3% of individuals with MS have disease onset before the age of 18 years (Chitnis, Glanz, Jaffin, & Healy, 2009), with a far smaller number of cases seen with onset before puberty (i.e., 0.2–0.7% of cases). This said, MS has been seen in infancy and "late-onset" cases have been seen as old as 72.

In adult MS, the onset is estimated to be approximately 5 years earlier for women. Further, the prevalence and incidence of MS appears to be growing, especially in women (Koch-Henriksen & Sørensen, 2010). MS is a disease that occurs predominantly in the Caucasian population, with the overall prevalence of the disease ranging between 2 and 150 per 100,000, depending on the country or specific population. Adult MS is more common among persons of Northern European heritage. It is also more common among people who live in northern latitudes during childhood. With this observation, MS has historically been more common in the northern states of the United States, although it is worth highlighting that the latitude gradient has lessened over time, and increased incidences of MS cases are seen further south (Alonso & Hernan, 2008).

MS is an immune-mediated disease in which the individual's immune system attacks the CNS, leading to demyelination. In the acute phases of an MS attack in both adults and children, there are infiltrates of T cells, some B cells, and lipid-laden macrophages in the brain and spinal cord lesions. The foundation of the MS diagnosis in both children and adults is the dissemination of inflammatory lesions in both space and time. More specifically, clinical symptoms of the disease must localize to different regions of the CNS (e.g., optic nerve inflammation/optic neuritis vs. paresthesias of the lower extremities) and manifest over time. Whereas earlier diagnostic criteria required evidence of disease activity based on neurological examination, subsequent revisions allowed for the establishment of dissemination of lesions in space and time based on other clinical tools, such as evidence of new lesions on magnetic resonance imaging (MRI) or cerebrospinal fluid findings (Polman et al., 2011). The applicability of these criteria to pediatric populations has been established by The International Pediatric Multiple Sclerosis Study Group (Krupp et al., 2013). Complicating the diagnostic process in children, however, is the fact that there are several diseases with similar initial clinical manifestations, most notably acute disseminated encephalomyelitis.

MRI lesions are characteristic of MS, with the diagnostic criteria incorporating specific features such as (1) one or more gadolinium enhancing lesions or nine or more T2-hyperintense lesions, (2) three or more periventricular lesions, (3) one or more infratentorial lesions, and/or (4) one or more juxtacortical lesions. The MRI characteristics of adults and children with MS are similar, although children tend to show more lesions in the brain stem, pons, and cerebellum, likely due to the caudal to rostral sequence of myelination. Further, in the youngest patients with MS (e.g., those below age 10 years) diffuse, ill-defined, bilateral lesions are more common in comparison with the more well-defined ovoid lesions seen in older individuals (Yeh, Weinstock-Guttman, et al., 2009). Cerebrospinal fluid findings in MS typically include the presence of elevated white blood cell count, elevated immunoglobulin G index, and oligoclonal bands, although younger children are less likely to show the latter (Chabas et al., 2010).

In 2013, the International Advisory Committee on Clinical Trials of MS proposed labeling of new disease courses: (1) Clinically isolated syndrome, identified as the initial clinical presentation of MS but without meeting full criteria for MS; and (2) radiologically isolated syndrome, which consists of imaging findings of possible demyelination without the signs of symptoms of MS (Lublin et al., 2014).

Although no definitive cause of MS has been identified, the etiology is widely believed to involve a genetic susceptibility coupled with environmental risk factors that lead to a dysregulated immune system. A common hypothesis is that a viral infection, or retroviral reactivation, primes a genetically susceptible immune system, leading to an abnormal reaction later in life. Another theory is that MS is a response to a chronic infection, such as Epstein-Barr virus, spirochetal bacteria infection, *Chlamydophila pneumoniae*, or varicella zoster. Interestingly, recent work has suggested a link between mode of delivery and

prenatal exposures to pesticides and increased rates on pediatric MS (Graves et al., 2017). Smoking has also been noted to increase risk for developing MS in adults (Hedström, Olsson, & Alfredsson, 2016). In children, research suggests that having a parent who smokes increases the risk for developing pediatric MS (Mikaeloff, Caridade, Tardieu, Suissa, & KIDSEP Study Group, 2007).

In addition to environmental factors, genetics relate to the risk of developing MS. For example, a 30% concordance rate has been found for identical twins, as compared with 3–5% for dizygotic twins. Further, first-degree relatives of patients with MS have a 2–5% risk of developing the disease, in comparison with the 0.1% risk seen in the general population (Gourraud, Harbo, Hauser, & Baranzini, 2012).

Interestingly, the demographic factors associated with pediatric MS are somewhat different. In the largest sample of pediatric patients with MS to date ($N = 490$), drawing from the data collected from the US Network of Pediatric MS and Other Demyelinating Diseases Database, the racial and ethnic profile of this young sample differed from what is typically seen in adult MS. Specifically, nearly 21% of this sample self-identified as African American, 30% identified as Latino. Further, there was a high number of second-generation Americans (39%), i.e., children born to foreign-born parents (Belman et al., 2016). It is worth noting that, in pediatric MS samples from Canada, higher proportions of Asian, Middle Eastern, and Caribbean ancestry have been documented (Kennedy et al., 2006). Although the exact reason for these racial/ethnic differences is not clear, a combination of both genetic and environmental factors are likely at play. With respect to gender ratios, in adolescents with MS, like in adult-onset MS, girls tend to outnumber boys. However, this is not true in younger onset cases; with onset below age 10 years, the gender ratio is essentially equal (Belman et al., 2016).

Prevention

Unfortunately, given our limited understanding of the exact causal mechanisms of MS, we are certainly in no position to definitively prevent the disease. However, there are some lifestyle factors that are related to higher rates of the disease that are worth some commentary. First, cigarette smoking and exposure to secondhand smoke have been linked to increased rates of MS (Hedström et al., 2016); given this correlation, then, an important lifestyle change that can be made is to cease tobacco use and limit exposure to smokers. Likewise, low levels of vitamin D are associated with higher rates of MS (Mokry et al., 2015), and vitamin D supplementation has been recommended for pregnant mothers to reduce the likelihood of MS in offspring (Nielsen et al., 2017). Interestingly, breastfeeding infants may also have a protective effect on the development of MS (Langer-Gould et al., 2017).

Clinical Manifestation

The most common presenting symptoms of MS include sensory disturbance in limbs, visual loss (i.e., optic neuritis), and motor disturbance. About 14% of MS begins with a polysymptomatic presentation (Olek, 2005). Sensory changes that can occur in MS include numbness in one or more limbs, paresthesia (tingling) in the limbs, and Lhermitte's sign, which involves an electric shock–like sensation in the back and limbs upon flexing the neck. Optic neuritis,

internuclear ophthalmoplegia, diplopia, and changes in visual acuity can also occur in MS. Common MS-related motor changes include gait disturbance, weakness, balance problems, limb ataxia, slurred speech, decreased coordination, and swallowing difficulty. Spasticity, vertigo, pain, sexual dysfunction, and bladder disturbance are also common symptoms of MS. Paraparesis or hemiparesis can also occur.

The clinical presentation in children is similar to that seen in adults, but about half have multifocal presentations. Further, about 5% of children with MS have seizures, although this is more commonly seen in the youngest of patients. Younger children are also more likely to have experienced a prodromal event (e.g., infection, trauma, or vaccination) before their first MS attack and are more likely to experience encephalopathy at initial presentation (Belman et al., 2016).

The clinical manifestations of MS, including physical, cognitive, and psychological symptoms, observed variation across the lifespan, and treatment considerations, are detailed in Table 12.1.

Table 12.1 Clinical Manifestations of MS

Manifestation	Comment	Adult MS vs. Pediatric MS	Treatment Considerations
Common Symptoms			
Fatigue	Related to dysregulated immune system, neuroendocrine factors, sleep disruption, etc.	About 80% of adults report significant fatigue versus about 50% of children/adolescents.	Medications such as amantadine or modafinil; exercise/physical therapy; cooling programs
Numbness, tingling, weakness	Commonly seen in arms, legs, and face.	Common in adults and children.	Corticosteroids used in acute phases. If weakness persists, physical therapy recommended.
Visual symptoms	Optic neuritis cause by inflammation of the optic nerve. Diplopia, and nystagmus related to brainstem or cerebellar lesions.	Common in adults and children.	Corticosteroids used in acute phases. If double vision persists, prism glasses can be used or, in extreme cases, surgery.
Dizziness/vertigo	Can be caused by brainstem or cerebellar lesions.	Common in adults and children.	Antinausea agents may be prescribed.
Bowel/bladder dysfunction	Constipation and urinary retention or incontinence can be seen.	Common in adults and children.	Bowel symptoms typically treated with dietary considerations. Urinary issues can be treated with medications or catheterization.

Table 12.1 (cont.)

Manifestation	Comment	Adult MS vs. Pediatric MS	Treatment Considerations
Gait abnormalities	Related to many factors including general weakness, spasticity, fatigue, balance problems, and numbness. Falls are common in those with MS, as many as 70% of individuals reporting falls in the past 2–6 months.	Although gait abnormalities can be seen in both children and adults, because children/adolescents have a slower overall disease progression, they tend to progress more slowly to wheelchair dependence.	Typically treated with physical therapy or assistive devices (e.g., orthotics, cane, walker, wheelchair). Medications such as dalfampridine can be used in mild cases.
Pain, spasticity	Pain can be seen in more than half of individuals with MS, but is more commonly reported by females. Pain may include trigeminal neuralgia, Lhermitte's sign, or burning sensations. Pain is commonly seen with spasticity in general.	Common in adults and children.	Pain can be treated with medications such as gabapentin, amitriptyline. When associated with spasticity, baclofen, tizanidine or similar medications can be used. Further, alternative approaches are also helpful (e.g., stretching, yoga).
Less Common Symptoms			
Speech or swallowing problems	Both dysarthric speech and dysphagia can be seen.	More commonly seen in later stages of the disease, so children/adolescents may be less commonly affected.	Speech/language therapy can be helpful for both speech difficulties, as well as swallowing difficulties. In severe cases of swallowing dysfunction, dietary changes may be necessary.
Breathing problems	Can be related to loss of muscle strength and endurance in MS.	More commonly seen in later stages of the disease, so children/adolescents may be less commonly affected.	Physical therapists with specialized training are typically involved in the assessment/treatment of breathing problems. In severe cases, ventilator support may be required.
Tremor	The rates of reported tremor vary considerably across studies, but severity often only mild and may go unreported by patients themselves (but detected on examination). Intention tremor is most common in MS.		Tremors in MS are difficult to treat, but treatment may involve medications such as beta-blockers. Deep brain stimulation and medical marijuana have been studied as treatment for tremor in MS, with mixed results.
Seizures	Incidence of seizures in MS is slightly higher than seen in the general population.	Not common in MS, but more common in the youngest individuals with MS.	Standard anticonvulsant medications are used to treat seizures in MS.

Table 12.1 (cont.)

Manifestation	Comment	Adult MS vs. Pediatric MS	Treatment Considerations
Cognitive Impairment			
Overall cognitive impairment	Definitions of impairment vary from study to study, but impairment is seen across all studies.	Approximately half of adults experience cognitive impairment compared with one-third of pediatric patients.	Treatment varies based on individual's cognitive profile.
IQ	May be more vulnerable at earlier age of onset.	Tends to be spared in adults compared with pediatric samples, although findings are variable.	Curriculum modification may be indicated.
Memory	One of the most common cognitive symptoms. Episodic or explicit memory tends to be most impacted.	Initial learning or encoding of information is problematic. Both short- and long-term memory problems noted.	Consider stimulant medication. Cognitive rehabilitation utilizing imagery and compensatory strategies. Aerobic exercise is also helpful. Children and adolescents may require academic accommodations.
Attention	One of the most common symptoms. Complex attention is most impacted.	Simple attention tends to be spared in adults. Simple and complex attention are often reduced in pediatric cohorts.	Consider stimulant medication. School- and work-related accommodations such as seating near the front of the room, reduced distraction environment.
Information processing speed	One of the most common cognitive deficits. Likely to undermine performance in other areas.	Deficits noted in pediatric and adult samples.	Consider stimulant medication and school- or work-related accommodations such as extended time to complete tasks.
Executive function	Problems with working memory, abstract reasoning, problem-solving, cognitive flexibility, planning, organization, verbal fluency.	Executive function deficits are common and have been noted across adult and pediatric samples.	Interventions may include tools to increase skills in planning and organization (e.g., use of a planner or electronic calendar) and accommodations to manage problems with working memory (e.g., lists).
Language	May be more vulnerable at earlier age of onset.	Tends to be spared in adults compared to pediatric patients. In youth, problems with verbal fluency, receptive language, expressive language and verbal knowledge have been noted.	Speech/language therapy can be helpful.

Table 12.1 (cont.)

Manifestation	Comment	Adult MS vs. Pediatric MS	Treatment Considerations
Visual-motor and psychomotor speed	Likely to undermine performance in other areas.	Impacted in both pediatric and adult patients.	Occupational therapy warranted. Individual supports including note-taking assistance and access to keyboarding.
Psychological Factors			
Internalizing symptoms	Depression symptoms are believed to relate to the disease process (i.e., lesions and inflammation).	Lifetime prevalence of approximately 50% for depression for adults. In pediatric patients, estimates of affective disorders range from approximately 30–50% and are consistent with depression and/or anxiety. Likely contributes to medications adherence/compliance.	Individual psychotherapy and/or family therapy warranted. Consider medication consultation as well.
Sleep disruption	Sleep can be disrupted secondary to other MS symptoms (e.g., pain, spasticity), but problems with sleep onset, maintenance, and early waking being reported by individuals with MS; women experience more sleep problems than men.	About half of adults with MS report sleep disturbance versus about 26% of children/adolescents.	Proper sleep hygiene essential. Consider recommending a formal sleep study.

Disease Course. The first clinical presentation of MS is known as clinically isolated syndrome (CIS) (Lublin et al., 2014). CIS is diagnosed when a first event of inflammation is believed to be MS, but has yet to fulfill diagnostic criteria (i.e., dissemination of symptoms across time). Subtypes of MS are distinguished by the clinical pattern of disease activity and include relapsing-remitting, primary progressive, secondary progressive, and progressive relapsing (Vollmer, 2007).

The majority of cases of MS begin with a relapsing-remitting course and account for approximately 85% of cases in the early stage (Vollmer, 2007). Although the relapsing-remitting form of the disease is the most common subtype at all ages, this is particularly true for pediatric MS cases, with nearly all pediatric MS cases presenting with this form of the disease. The relapsing-remitting course is characterized by clearly defined relapses, or unpredictable attacks, followed by periods of remission or complete recovery of symptoms. Secondary progressive MS emerges following a relapsing-remitting presentation and is marked by progressive worsening of symptoms with or without occasional relapses and minor remissions (Lublin et al., 2014). Of note, individuals with pediatric-onset MS typically progress to this course at a slower rate (i.e., 16–28 years) compared with that of those with adult-onset (i.e., 7–19 years); however, those with pediatric onset tend to be younger when they reach secondary progression (Yeh, Chitnis, et al., 2009). A third type of MS is known as primary progressive and refers to progressive accumulation of disability from onset with or without minor remission. Finally, progressive relapsing MS is characterized by progressive neurologic deterioration with distinct relapses (Lublin et al., 2014). In all subtypes, a neurologic dysfunction can accumulate over time; neurologists typically track the progression of neurologic dysfunction with the Expanded Disability Status Scale. Unfortunately, although MS is less common in racial and ethnic minorities, there is evidence to suggest that, when they get MS, they often experience a more severe disease course.

Cognitive Functioning in Adults. Approximately half of patients with MS experience cognitive impairment (Benedict et al., 2006), which can be seen even in the earliest phases of MS (Amato et al., 2010). Although cognitive outcomes vary widely across patients, the most commonly described areas of impairment include memory, information processing speed, complex attention, and executive functioning. In contrast, general intelligence, simple attention, and language generally tend to be spared in adults with MS (Chiaravalloti & DeLuca, 2008).

Long-term memory deficits have been consistently reported in approximately 40–60% of patients with MS (Rao et al., 1993). Episodic or explicit memory tends to be most affected, whereas implicit, semantic, and autobiographical memory are typically spared or deficits in such may emerge later in the disease course. Memory disruption appears to stem from initial learning or encoding of information; however, with repetition, individuals with MS reach levels of retention and recognition of information commensurate with controls (Chiaravalloti & DeLuca, 2008). Of note, one study found that patients with MS demonstrated increased brain activation during the recognition trial of a memory task compared with controls, suggesting that retrieval processes are more affected by the disease (Bobholz et al., 2006).

Patients diagnosed with MS are at risk for problems with complex attention, whereas simple attention tends to be spared. Executive skills including abstract reasoning, problem-solving, cognitive flexibility, planning, organization, and verbal fluency (letter fluency and semantic fluency) have also been noted (Amato et al., 2010; Chiaravalloti & DeLuca, 2008). Deficits in processing speed are the most common MS-related cognitive deficit and are believed to be closely related to other cognitive deficits observed in MS, such as working memory, long-term memory, attention, and executive functioning (Chiaravalloti & DeLuca, 2008). Similarly, psychomotor speed may undermine one's performance on tasks of processing speed and these domains should be carefully assessed. It should also be noted that fatigue and depression, which are commonly associated with MS, may adversely impact performance in the aforementioned areas.

Research on longitudinal outcomes is sparse and findings have been mixed. Although it has been found that all subtypes of MS may be associated with cognitive decline, impairment tends to increase with disease duration and is most pronounced in progressive MS subtypes (Planche, Gibelin, Cregut, Pereira, & Clavelou, 2016). Existing longitudinal studies have shown greater decline in working memory and processing speed over time relative to memory and fluency, with many showing no significant cognitive change (Chiaravalloti & DeLuca, 2008).

Cognitive Functioning in Children and Adolescents. The study of cognitive functioning in pediatric MS has lagged behind literature focused on adults. That said, pediatric MS is well studied in comparison with other CNS-demyelinating conditions of childhood. Many have speculated that pediatric MS is associated with greater cognitive deficits given the impact of the disease process on the developing brain (MacAllister et al., 2013). Over the last decade, research on the neuropsychological manifestations of pediatric MS has emerged and suggests that approximately one-third of patients experience cognitive impairment (Amato et al., 2008; Julian et al., 2013); however, no clear cognitive profile has emerged, likely given the heterogeneity of the condition, as well as varying research methodology across studies. Importantly, research regarding cognitive function in pediatric patients with MS varies widely with respect to test battery and domains assessed, definitions of impairment, and sample sizes. Nevertheless, studies have fairly consistently documented deficits in language, attention and information processing, memory, executive functions, and visual-motor and visual-spatial skills, but IQ findings vary (Suppiej & Cainelli, 2014).

Notably, in contrast to what is observed in the adult literature, pediatric patients with MS appear to be more vulnerable to language deficits, likely because language skills in the child brain are still developing (Tan et al., 2017). Specifically, deficits have been noted in verbal fluency, receptive language, expressive language, and verbal knowledge (Amato et al., 2008; Pastò et al., 2016; Portaccio et al., 2009). More consistent with the adult literature, research indicates that youth diagnosed with MS are at risk for problems with simple and complex attention as well efficient processing of information (Portaccio et al., 2009; Till et al.,

2011). Memory impairment has also been reported in the areas of both immediate and delayed visual and verbal memory (Amato et al., 2008; Portaccio et al., 2009). Previous research has also identified deficits in visual-motor integration (Charvet et al., 2014; MacAllister et al., 2005; MacAllister, Christodoulou, Milazzo, & Krupp, 2007) and fine motor coordination (Julian et al., 2013).

Given that frontal systems mature later in the developmental sequence, impaired executive functions are not surprising, although it has been noted that slow processing speed may undermine skills in this area (MacAllister et al., 2013). Impairment has been documented in several areas of executive functioning including working memory, cognitive flexibility, as well as parent-reported executive skills (Amato et al., 2008; Charvet et al., 2014; Holland, Graves, Greenberg, & Harder, 2014; MacAllister, 2010; Till et al., 2012).

Research on longitudinal outcomes in pediatric MS is quite limited and existing research is mixed. For instance, some research has shown declines in cognitive functioning over time (Till et al., 2013), whereas other studies have shown no declines at follow-up (Charvet et al., 2014). Amato and colleagues followed pediatric patients with MS through serial assessment across time and at 5-year follow-up; they described a range of outcomes including decline, improvement, and stability of cognitive functioning in their sample (Amato et al., 2014). In this study, male gender, younger age at disease onset, and lower education level were associated with cognitive loss over time. However, other investigations have highlighted the protective value of cognitive reserve (Pastò et al., 2016). Such results highlight the varied neuropsychological outcomes associated with pediatric MS.

Psychosocial Impact. In addition to cognitive impairment, MS is frequently associated with depression, fatigue, and sleep disturbance. These problems are described across pediatric and adult MS populations. Moreover, these symptoms often relate to symptoms of cognitive dysfunction. As such, these areas should be carefully assessed, and their potential impact on neuropsychological function and overall quality of life should be considered carefully in overall treatment planning.

Mood disturbance is commonly associated with MS, typically characterized by internalizing symptoms. In fact, in adults with MS, there is an estimated lifetime prevalence of approximately 50% for major depression; the rate of depression in MS exceeds that of any other chronic illness group (Pucak, Carroll, Kerr, & Kaplin, 2007). Further, depression is associated with increased morbidity and mortality and is a significant factor related to cognition, interpersonal relationships, treatment adherence, and overall quality of life (Feinstein, 2011). Importantly, symptoms of depression are largely believed to be directly related to the MS disease process (i.e., lesions and cytokine effects), rather than based solely the psychosocial consequences of living with a chronic medical condition (Pucak et al., 2007). Among pediatric patients, a similar trend is observed: several studies have shown that a significant portion of these patients meet criteria for an affective disorder such as depressive and anxiety disorders (Goretti et al., 2010; Weisbrot et al., 2010).

Fatigue is one of the most commonly reported symptoms in patients with MS, with as many as 75% of adult patients reporting prominent fatigue during the disease. Notably, fatigue is often described as the most debilitating symptom of the disease, adversely affecting quality of life, and is a major factor related to employment status (i.e., need to reduce work hours, retirement). Further, patients diagnosed with MS are at increased risk for sleep problems and sleep-related disorders (e.g., sleep-disordered breathing, restless leg syndrome), which further contribute to fatigue in MS (Braley & Chervin, 2010). Fatigue and sleep problems are also prominent in pediatric MS: the largest study examining fatigue in pediatric MS to date revealed that one-fourth to one-third of participants reported mild and severe fatigue, respectively (MacAllister et al., 2009). Importantly, in both children and adults, the experience of fatigue may be variable throughout the day and exacerbated by physical exertion and heat.

Neuropsychological Assessment

The extent of neuropsychological assessment varies depending on the reason the patient is being referred. Neuropsychological evaluation is a critical component of overall clinical care of patients with MS. Specifically, evaluations are useful for determining the functional impact of MS on daily life, informing needs for educational or work-related support services, as well as other interventions to address difficulties frequently associated with MS (e.g., individual therapy to address depression). Evaluations may be requested to establish a baseline level of function before treatment initiation or to monitor cognitive functioning in the context of disease progression over time. Other times, patients may be referred for a neuropsychological screening evaluation to determine whether additional testing is needed. Therefore, the length and depth of the evaluation may differ based on the purpose of the assessment.

Over time, brief cognitive batteries have been developed and validated to screen cognitive functioning in adults with MS and are often a useful starting point in the evaluation process. The most well-known screening batteries are the Minimal Assessment of Cognitive Function in MS (MACFIMS) and the Brief Repeatable Battery of Neuropsychological Tests (BRB). Both batteries limit requirements for motor skills and maximize use of measures with alternative forms. The MACFIMS is a 90-minute battery composed of seven tests designed to assess the cognitive domains commonly affected in MS, which has subsequently been validated (Benedict et al., 2006). The battery includes measures of working memory, processing speed, verbal memory, visual memory, visuospatial perception, verbal fluency, and problem-solving (see Table 12.2). Interestingly, Benedict and colleagues (2006) showed that most of the MACFIMS tests discriminated between disabled and employed patients, with tests of verbal memory and executive function as the most predictive of vocational status. The BRB is a 40-minute battery administered to screen for cognitive deficits in adults with MS in clinical settings and longitudinal trials. The battery assesses verbal memory, spatial memory, attention, and verbal fluency. Prior research has shown the comparability of these batteries (Strober et al., 2009).

Research on assessment tools for pediatric MS has been limited compared with that focused on adult MS; however, neuropsychologists from six pediatric National MS Society Centers of Excellence reached a consensus on a "core" battery on which to build. Given overlap between cognitive outcomes associated with pediatric and adult MS, recommended batteries overlap considerably across the lifespan; however, pediatric assessment should also include assessment of language and IQ. The proposed battery includes a brief IQ screener and measures of processing speed, attention, confrontation naming, verbal fluency, visual-motor integration, fine motor speed and dexterity, and verbal learning and memory as well as caregiver standardized rating forms to assess executive function, psychological functioning, and fatigue

Table 12.2 Minimal Assessment of Cognitive Function in MS (MACFIMS) Battery

Test	Function
Controlled Oral Word Association Test	Language
Judgment of Line Orientation Test	Spatial processing
California Verbal Learning Test, 2nd ed.	New learning and memory
Brief Visuospatial Memory Test – Revised	New learning and memory
Symbol Digit Modalities Test	Processing speed and working memory
Paced Auditory Serial Addition Test	Processing speed and working memory
Delis-Kaplan Executive Function System – Sorting Test	Executive function

(see Table 12.3). In terms of screening tools for use in pediatric patients, the Brief Neuropsychological Battery for Children (BNBC) has been proposed by Portaccio and colleagues (2009) as a screening tool for this population in Italy. The BNBC includes measures of memory, processing speed, simple and complex attention, and vocabulary knowledge. The BNBC has shown sensitivity of 96% and specificity of 76% (Portaccio et al., 2009).

A brief cognitive screening evaluation is cost-effective, but there are limitations to this approach and many patients will require a more comprehensive evaluation. For example, referral questions related to the individual's ability to work or perform academic functions are likely to warrant a full evaluation to adequately explore cognitive difficulties and to formulate an appropriate treatment plan. There are clinical challenges to assessing cognitive dysfunction in MS that should be considered. For example, clinicians should consider that patients with MS often fatigue easily and may have difficulty tolerating testing sessions that last several hours. For some individuals, evaluations may need to be divided into more than one session. Other issues such as depression and sleep problems must also be considered when conceptualizing a patient's current neuropsychological status and developing treatment recommendations.

Table 12.3 National MS Society Pediatric Centers of Excellence Neuropsychological Core Battery

Test	Function
Wechsler Abbreviated Scale of Intelligence	IQ
Wechsler Coding, Symbol Digit Modalities Test	Processing speed
Wechsler Digit Span	Auditory attention and working memory
California Verbal Learning Test, Children's Version	Verbal learning and memory
Beery Buktenica Test of Visual Motor Integration	Visuomotor skills
Grooved Pegboard	Fine motor speed and dexterity
Contingency Naming Test	Simple and complex attention
Trail-Making Test	
Conners' Continuous Performance Test, 2nd ed.	Sustained attention
Expressive One-Word Vocabulary Test	Confrontation naming
Controlled Oral Word Association	Verbal fluency
Brief Rating Inventory of Executive Function	Rating of executive function in the last 6 months
Behavior Assessment System for Children, 2nd ed.	Rating of behavioral and emotional functioning in the last several months
PedsQL Multidimensional Fatigue Scale	Rating of fatigue in the last 4 weeks

Intervention

A comprehensive discussion of the treatment of MS from a neurological perspective is outside the scope of this chapter, but it is important for neuropsychologists to be somewhat familiar with general approaches to disease management. Generally speaking, the overall treatment of MS involves three main components: treatment of acute relapses, overall disease modification, and treatment of specific symptoms.

In the acute phases of a relapse, corticosteroids are used. The goal at this stage is to both reduce the severity of symptoms in this acute phase and to shorten the overall duration of the event. Both intravenous steroids (e.g., intravenous methylprednisolone) and oral agents (e.g., oral prednisone) can be used in children and adults. Neuropsychologists working with patients with MS should be aware of the side effects of such medications, because steroids can be associated with the temporary side effects of irritability, sleep disruptions, and related cognitive changes. Intravenous immunoglobulins can also be used in individuals who do not respond to steroids.

To alter the overall course of the MS progression (e.g., reduce the number of relapses, reduce accrual of neurological dysfunction, reduce lesion burden on MRI), "disease-modifying therapies" are used. Historically, therapies have involved injectable medications, and by and large these are still considered the first-line therapies. They include glatiramer acetate, interferon beta-1a, and interferon beta-1b. The most common side effects of these agents are injection site reactions, but the interferons can also be associated with flulike symptoms.

More recently, natalizumab, a human monoclonal antibody, was released, and this infusion medication is presently considered the most effective medication for relapsing-remitting MS. Unfortunately, it has also been associated with a severe potential side effect, namely progressive multifocal leukoencephalopathy, an opportunistic brain infection associated with the JC virus. Given this association, the use of this agent requires special considerations. Other monoclonal antibodies recently approved for use in MS include rituximab, alemtuzumab, and daclizumab.

A recent advance in the treatment of MS has been the introduction of several oral medications, including fingolimod, teriflunomide, and dimethyl fumarate. Although these may be more preferred by patients because they do not require injection or infusion, unfortunately they have been associated with such potentially serious side effects as teratogenicity, hepatic failure, and leukopenia.

In addition to disease-modifying therapies, other more aggressive therapies are occasionally used in particularly pernicious cases. An example is mitoxantrone, a chemotherapy agent. Although it has shown effectiveness in severe cases of relapsing-remitting MS, secondary progressive MS, and primary progressive MS, it is generally used cautiously given the potential cardiotoxic effects. Detailed reviews of disease-modifying therapies in adult MS and pediatric MS are available elsewhere (see Comi, Radaelli, & Sørensen, 2017; Narula, Hopkins, & Banwell, 2015).

Beyond treatment of the disease process itself, many medications and interventions are available to target associated features of the disease. For example, in those with comorbid mood disorders, selective serotonin reuptake inhibitors have shown effectiveness (Fiest et al., 2016), although cognitive behavioral therapy appears to be as effective (Hind et al., 2014). Given that mobility impairment is common in MS, patients are often referred for traditional physical therapy, and complementary/alternative approaches such as yoga are also quite helpful. Additionally, there is some support for the medication dalfampridine to improve walking speed in those with motor skills impairment (Applebee et al., 2015). Fatigue is often treated pharmacologically with medications such as modafinil or amantadine. However, given the association between heat and fatigue, "cooling programs" are also helpful. Moreover, exercise programs to reduce the physical deconditioning that can occur secondary to fatigue may be particularly important (MacAllister & Krupp, 2005).

Most relevant to neuropsychologists, however, is the treatment of cognitive impairment. As noted, cognitive dysfunction occurs rather frequently in both adults and children/adolescents with MS. Clinical attention to variables such as mood, sleep disturbance, fatigue, and pain is important in considering treatment directions for those MS with cognitive difficulties. It should also be stated that the disease-modifying therapies, which have the overall goal of reducing relapses and lesion burden on MRI, no doubt preserve cognition to some extent. However, because cognitive variables are seldom included as primary outcome variables in research validating these therapies, their overall effect on neuropsychological function remains unclear (Amato et al., 2013). Beyond this, however, some therapies directly target cognition.

Unfortunately, pharmacological interventions for MS-related cognitive dysfunction remain somewhat limited. Although there was some initial enthusiasm for the use of donepezil to treat memory impairment

in MS (Christodoulou et al., 2006), larger multicenter studies failed to find a significant effect for this medication (Krupp et al., 2011). Further, the results of studies on the use of psychostimulants or modafinil to treat attention deficits in MS are mixed, but there is some support for the use of amphetamines to improve memory, attention, and processing speed (Benedict et al., 2008; Morrow et al., 2009; Morrow & Rosehart, 2015; Sumowski et al., 2011).

Cognitive rehabilitation programs have also shown some preliminary support and are worth consideration. Although a recent Cochrane review had concluded that there was insufficient evidence to recommend cognitive rehabilitation for memory dysfunction in MS (das Nair, Ferguson, Stark, & Lincoln, 2012), there are several interventions that do boast positive effects. For example, a randomized controlled trial to improve learning via the use of imagery improved memory on both neuropsychological measures and self-reported daily activities. Further, the effects of this intervention showed increased activation on functional MRI, suggesting that the treatment is linked to the recruitment of additional brain regions, leading to greater depth of encoding of material (Chiaravalloti, DeLuca, Moore, & Ricker, 2005; Chiaravalloti, Wylie, Leavitt, & DeLuca, 2012).

Despite the growing popularity of computer-based cognitive training interventions, their effectiveness remains quite uncertain. Numerous controlled and uncontrolled trials of various platforms have yielded mixed results. Still, there may be some hope. For example, one double-blind, randomized, placebo-controlled study of a relatively large group of patients with MS undergoing an adaptive computer-based training program showed that the treatment group manifested improved cognition relative to controls (Charvet et al., 2016). In short, although certainly not proven, computer-based interventions may not be entirely without merit.

Perhaps most interesting may be the effect of exercise on cognition in MS, with aerobic exercise being best supported. A recent study demonstrated that aerobic exercise resulted in a significant increase in hippocampal volume in patients with MS, with corresponding improvements in memory. In contrast, nonaerobic exercise was not effective in increasing hippocampal volume or memory (Leavitt et al., 2014). Thus, the benefits of exercise in patients with MS may be multifold; it improves cardiovascular health, prevents the physical deconditioning associated with MS-related fatigue, may improve spasticity, and can lead to memory improvement.

In addition to medications, cognitive rehabilitative techniques, and exercise, some newer technologies are currently being assessed. For example, some research on the effectiveness of transcranial direct current stimulation to improve cognition, mood, and fatigue in MS is presently under way (Chan et al., 2017; Dobbs et al., 2017; Kasschau et al., 2015). Transcranial direct current stimulation is a noninvasive brain stimulation technique in which low-amplitude direct currents are passed through the brain to change cortical excitability. Although initial results are mixed and the utility of this technique remains speculative, this is another body of literature to follow moving forward.

Implications for Clinical Practice

Neuropsychological assessment plays a vital role in the clinical care of patients with MS because cognitive and emotional symptoms are common and can cause significant negative impact on daily activities.

MS impacts different people in many different ways, particularly at different developmental stages, and patients typically present with wide-ranging symptoms, requiring care from a team of providers that may include neurologists, neuropsychologists/clinical psychologists, rehabilitation psychologists, sleep specialists, occupational therapists, and physical therapists.

Education about cognitive and emotional symptoms that can develop in MS is critical in helping patients better manage their symptoms and plan for their future.

Assessment of cognitive and emotional symptoms is useful at all stages of the disease and is important for developing comprehensive treatment plans.

Cognitive dysfunction is the primary symptom that causes vocational difficulties and results in the need for disability support. Neuropsychologists are uniquely positioned to assess and describe the functional impact of MS with consideration of the patient's developmental and psychosocial context.

Understanding neuropsychological symptoms of an individual diagnosed with MS will allow the treatment team to design a tailored treatment plan, prioritizing the most salient issues.

Although the clinical presentations and cognitive profiles of individuals with MS differ significantly from person to person, researchers have identified several core domains of neuropsychological

functioning that are considered to be at risk in light of the underlying disease pathology. Clinicians may choose to begin by assessing these core areas to inform subsequent assessment decisions.

Research has suggested both brief and comprehensive methods for assessing neuropsychological symptoms in MS. This flexibility allows for a tailored approach to assessment, depending on the patient's course and current needs.

Because medications such as corticosteroids can affect cognition and emotional functions, clinicians should guide the timing of assessment to assure that these factors are not confounding the neuropsychological profile.

Clinicians must consider how issues such as sleep, mood, pain, and fatigue are affecting cognitive functions. By appreciating the role(s) of these factors, treatment plans can be optimally designed to improve cognitive functions, prioritizing the most salient needs.

Given that MS is a chronic condition and that cognitive function is likely to evolve over time, serial assessments are typically warranted. As with any situation of repeated cognitive testing, clinicians must also consider issues such as test-retest reliability and practice effects.

Future Directions

Considerable gains have been made in increasing knowledge regarding the pathophysiology and disease course of MS, refinement of diagnostic criteria, and expansion of treatment options. In addition to the role in clinical care, neuropsychologists also play a critical role with regard to clinical research and have contributed significantly to what is known about the neuropsychological impact of MS across the lifespan. As noted earlier in the chapter, knowledge about the neuropsychological manifestations of pediatric onset is less developed than that of adult MS and requires further attention. Related, pediatric-focused research would benefit from increased attention on the validation of cognitive screening tools. As progress continues to be made relative to characterizing cognitive deficits associated with MS, treatment studies have emerged as described throughout this chapter; however, this work is limited and there is a significant need for research on cognitive rehabilitation to address cognitive problems associated with MS. Such studies are particularly needed for pediatric patients.

Research on longitudinal outcomes is greatly needed in MS patient populations, particularly given the changing landscape of medical treatment options. For example, given that the first FDA-approved drugs for MS were not established until the 1990s, there remains limited understanding of the ways in which disease-modifying therapies may slow neuropsychological decline, and possibly change neuropsychological outcomes over time. The same questions apply to the newer continually emerging medications. This work is particularly needed in the pediatric-onset MS population.

In summary, great strides have been made in research on MS. As medical treatments continue to emerge, neuropsychologists have a role to play in examining their impact on cognitive functioning and in establishing cognitive rehabilitation techniques.

References

Alonso, A., & Hernan, M. A. (2008). Temporal trends in the incidence of multiple sclerosis: A systematic review. *Neurology*, *71*(2), 129–135.

Amato, M. P., Goretti, B., Ghezzi, A., Hakiki, B., Niccolai, C., Lori, S., … Cilia, S. (2014). Neuropsychological features in childhood and juvenile multiple sclerosis: Five-year follow-up. *Neurology*, *83*(16), 1432–1438.

Amato, M. P., Goretti, B., Ghezzi, A., Lori, S., Zipoli, V., Portaccio, E., … Patti, F. (2008). Cognitive and psychosocial features of childhood and juvenile MS. *Neurology*, *70*(20), 1891–1897.

Amato, M. P., Langdon, D., Montalban, X., Benedict, R. H., DeLuca, J., Krupp, L. B., … Comi, G. (2013). Treatment of cognitive impairment in multiple sclerosis: Position paper. *Journal of Neurology*, *260*(6), 1452–1468.

Amato, M. P., Portaccio, E., Goretti, B., Zipoli, V., Hakiki, B., Giannini, M., … Razzolini, L. (2010). Cognitive impairment in early stages of multiple sclerosis. *Neurological Sciences*, *31*(2), 211–214.

Applebee, A., Goodman, A. D., Mayadev, A. S., Bethoux, F., Goldman, M. D., Klingler, M., … Carrazana, E. J. (2015). Effects of dalfampridine extended-release tablets on 6-minute walk distance in patients with multiple sclerosis: A post hoc analysis of a double-blind, placebo-controlled trial. *Clinical Therapeutics*, *37*(12), 2780–2787.

Belman, A. L., Krupp, L. B., Olsen, C. S., Rose, J. W., Aaen, G., Benson, L., … Lotze, T. (2016). Characteristics of children and adolescents with multiple sclerosis. *Pediatrics*, *138*(1), 10.1542/peds.2016-0120.

Benedict, R. H., Cookfair, D., Gavett, R., Gunther, M., Munschauer, F., Garg, N., & Weinstock-Guttman, B. (2006). Validity of the minimal assessment of cognitive function in multiple sclerosis (MACFIMS). *Journal of the International Neuropsychological Society*, *12*(4), 549–558.

Benedict, R. H., Munschauer, F., Zarevics, P., Erlanger, D., Rowe, V., Feaster, T., & Carpenter, R. L. (2008). Effects of l-amphetamine sulfate on cognitive function in multiple sclerosis patients. *Journal of Neurology*, *255*(6), 848.

Bobholz, J. A., Rao, S. M., Lobeck, L., Elsinger, C., Gleason, A., Kanz, J., … Maas, E. (2006). fMRI study of episodic memory in relapsing-remitting MS: Correlation with T2 lesion volume. *Neurology*, *67*(9), 1640–1645.

Braley, T. J., & Chervin, R. D. (2010). Fatigue in multiple sclerosis: Mechanisms, evaluation, and treatment. *Sleep*, *33*(8), 1061–1067.

Chabas, D., Ness, J., Belman, A., Yeh, E. A., Kuntz, N., Gorman, M. P., … Rodriguez, M.(2010). Younger children with MS have a distinct CSF inflammatory profile at disease onset. *Neurology*, *74*(5), 399–405.

Chan, W., Dobbs, B., Shaw, M., Kasschau, M., Sherman, K., Krupp, L., … Rodriguez, M. (2017). Baseline affect predicts improved fatigue with telerehabilitation using remotely-supervised transcranial direct current stimulation (RS-tDCS) in adults with multiple sclerosis (MS)(P3. 343). *Neurology*, *88*(16 Supplement), P3. 343.

Charvet, L., O'donnell, E., Belman, A., Chitnis, T., Ness, J., Parrish, J., … Krupp, L. B. (2014). Longitudinal evaluation of cognitive functioning in pediatric multiple sclerosis: Report from the US pediatric multiple sclerosis network. *Multiple Sclerosis Journal*, *20*(11), 1502–1510.

Charvet, L., Yang, J., Shaw, M., Sherman, K., Xu, J., Haider, L., & Krupp, L. (2016). An adaptive computer-based cognitive training program improves cognitive functioning in adults with multiple sclerosis (MS): Results of a double-blind randomized active-placebo-controlled 12-week trial (P2. 170). *Neurology*, *86*(16 Supplement), P2. 170.

Chiaravalloti, N. D., & DeLuca, J. (2008). Cognitive impairment in multiple sclerosis. *The Lancet Neurology*, *7*(12), 1139–1151.

Chiaravalloti, N. D., DeLuca, J., Moore, N. B., & Ricker, J. H. (2005). Treating learning impairments improves memory performance in multiple sclerosis: A randomized clinical trial. *Multiple Sclerosis Journal*, *11*(1), 58–68.

Chiaravalloti, N. D., Wylie, G., Leavitt, V., & DeLuca, J. (2012). Increased cerebral activation after behavioral treatment for memory deficits in MS. *Journal of Neurology*, *259*(7), 1337–1346.

Chitnis, T., Glanz, B., Jaffin, S., & Healy, B. (2009). Demographics of pediatric-onset multiple sclerosis in an MS center population from the northeastern united states. *Multiple Sclerosis Journal*, *15*(5), 627–631.

Christodoulou, C., Melville, P., Scherl, W. F., MacAllister, W. S., Elkins, L. E., & Krupp, L. B. (2006). Effects of donepezil on memory and cognition in multiple sclerosis. *Journal of the Neurological Sciences*, *245*(1), 127–136.

Comi, G., Radaelli, M., & Sørensen, P. S. (2017). Evolving concepts in the treatment of relapsing multiple sclerosis. *The Lancet*, *389*(10076), 1347–1356.

das Nair, R., Ferguson, H., Stark, D. L., & Lincoln, N. B. (2012). Memory rehabilitation for people with multiple sclerosis. *Cochrane Database Syst Rev*, *3*.

Dobbs, B., Shaw, M., Kasschau, M., Frontario, A., Krupp, L., & Charvet, L. (2017). Telerehabilitation using remotely-supervised transcranial direct current stimulation (RS-tDCS) enhances the benefit of at-home cognitive training in multiple sclerosis (P4. 335). *Neurology*, *88*(16 Supplement), P4. 335.

Feinstein, A. (2011). Multiple sclerosis and depression. *Multiple Sclerosis (Houndmills, Basingstoke, England)*, *17* (11), 1276–1281.

Fiest, K., Walker, J., Bernstein, C., Graff, L., Zarychanski, R., Abou-Setta, A., ... Fisk, J. D. (2016). Systematic review and meta-analysis of interventions for depression and anxiety in persons with multiple sclerosis. *Multiple Sclerosis and Related Disorders*, *5*, 12–26.

Goretti, B., Ghezzi, A., Portaccio, E., Lori, S., Zipoli, V., Razzolini, L., ... Patti, F. (2010). Psychosocial issue in children and adolescents with multiple sclerosis. *Neurological Sciences : Official Journal of the Italian Neurological Society and of the Italian Society of Clinical Neurophysiology*, *31*(4), 467–470.

Gourraud, P., Harbo, H. F., Hauser, S. L., & Baranzini, S. E. (2012). The genetics of multiple sclerosis: An up-to-date review. *Immunological Reviews*, *248*(1), 87–103.

Graves, J. S., Chitnis, T., Weinstock-Guttman, B., Rubin, J., Zelikovitch, A. S., Nourbakhsh, B., ... Waubant, E. (2017). Maternal and perinatal exposures are associated with risk for pediatric-onset multiple sclerosis. *Pediatrics*, *139*(4), e20162838.

Hedström, A., Olsson, T., & Alfredsson, L. (2016). Smoking is a major preventable risk factor for multiple sclerosis. *Multiple Sclerosis Journal*, *22*(8), 1021–1026.

Hind, D., Cotter, J., Thake, A., Bradburn, M., Cooper, C., Isaac, C., & House, A. (2014). Cognitive behavioural therapy for the treatment of depression in people with multiple sclerosis: A systematic review and meta-analysis. *BMC Psychiatry*, *14*(1), 5.

Holland, A. A., Graves, D., Greenberg, B. M., & Harder, L. L. (2014). Fatigue, emotional functioning, and executive dysfunction in pediatric multiple sclerosis. *Child Neuropsychology*, *20*(1), 71–85.

Julian, L., Serafin, D., Charvet, L., Ackerson, J., Benedict, R., Braaten, E., ... Zaccariello, M. (2013). Cognitive impairment occurs in children and adolescents with multiple sclerosis: Results from a United States network. *Journal of Child Neurology*, *28*(1), 102–107.

Kasschau, M., Sherman, K., Haider, L., Frontario, A., Shaw, M., Datta, A., ... Charvet, L. (2015). A protocol for the use of remotely-supervised transcranial direct current stimulation (tDCS) in multiple sclerosis (MS). *Journal of Visualized Experiments*, (*106*):e53542. doi(106), e53542.

Kennedy, J., O'Connor, P., Sadovnick, A. D., Perara, M., Yee, I., & Banwell, B. (2006). Age at onset of multiple sclerosis may be influenced by place of residence during childhood rather than ancestry. *Neuroepidemiology*, *26*(3), 162–167.

Koch-Henriksen, N., & Sorensen, P. S. (2010). The changing demographic pattern of multiple sclerosis epidemiology. *Lancet Neurology*, *9*(5), 520–532.

Krupp, L. B., Christodoulou, C., Melville, P., Scherl, W. F., Pai, L. Y., Muenz, L. R., ... Schwid, S. R. (2011). Multicenter randomized clinical trial of donepezil for memory impairment in multiple sclerosis. *Neurology*, *76*(17), 1500–1507.

Krupp, L. B., Tardieu, M., Amato, M. P., Banwell, B., Chitnis, T., Dale, R. C., ... Rostasy, K. (2013). International pediatric multiple sclerosis study group criteria for pediatric multiple sclerosis and immune-mediated central nervous system demyelinating disorders: Revisions to the 2007 definitions. *Multiple Sclerosis Journal*, *19*(10), 1261–1267.

Langer-Gould, A., Smith, J. B., Hellwig, K., Gonzales, E., Haraszti, S., Koebnick, C., & Xiang, A. (2017). Breastfeeding, ovulatory years, and risk of multiple sclerosis. *Neurology*, *89*(6), 563–569.

Leavitt, V., Cirnigliaro, C., Cohen, A., Farag, A., Brooks, M., Wecht, J., ... Sumowski, J. F. (2014). Aerobic exercise increases hippocampal volume and improves memory in multiple sclerosis: Preliminary findings. *Neurocase*, *20*(6), 695–697.

Lublin, F. D., Reingold, S. C., Cohen, J. A., Cutter, G. R., Sorensen, P. S., Thompson, A. J., ... Bebo, B. (2014). Defining the clinical course of multiple sclerosis: The 2013 revisions. *Neurology*, *83*(3), 278–286.

MacAllister, W. S. (2010). Multiple sclerosis in children and adolescents: Neurocognitive disorders. In D. Riva and C. Njiokiktjien (Eds.), *Brain lesion localization and developmental functions*. Milan: John Libbey Eurotext.

MacAllister, W. S., Belman, A. L., Milazzo, M., Weisbrot, D. M., Christodoulou, C., Scherl, W. F., ... Krupp, L. B. (2005). Cognitive functioning in children and adolescents with multiple sclerosis. *Neurology*, *64*(8), 1422–1425.

MacAllister, W. S., Christodoulou, C., Milazzo, M., & Krupp, L. B. (2007). Longitudinal neuropsychological assessment in pediatric multiple sclerosis. *Developmental Neuropsychology*, *32*(2; 2), 625–644.

MacAllister, W. S., Christodoulou, C., Milazzo, M., Preston, T. E., Serafin, D., Krupp, L. B., & Harder, L. (2013).

Pediatric multiple sclerosis: What we know and where are we headed? *Child Neuropsychology, 19*(1), 1–22.

MacAllister, W. S., Christodoulou, C., Troxell, R., Milazzo, M., Block, P., Preston, T. E., ... & Krupp, L. (2009). Fatigue and quality of life in pediatric multiple sclerosis. *Multiple Sclerosis, 15*(12), 1502–1508.

MacAllister, W. S., & Krupp, L. B. (2005). Multiple sclerosis-related fatigue. *Physical Medicine and Rehabilitation Clinics of North America, 16*(2), 483–502.

Mikaeloff, Y., Caridade, G., Tardieu, M., Suissa, S., & KIDSEP Study Group. (2007). Parental smoking at home and the risk of childhood-onset multiple sclerosis in children. *Brain, 130*(10), 2589–2595.

Mokry, L. E., Ross, S., Ahmad, O. S., Forgetta, V., Smith, G. D., Leong, A., ... Richards, J. B. (2015). Vitamin D and risk of multiple sclerosis: A mendelian randomization study. *PLoS Medicine, 12*(8), e1001866.

Morrow, S. A., Kaushik, T., Zarevics, P., Erlanger, D., Bear, M. F., Munschauer, F. E., & Benedict, R. H. (2009). The effects of L-amphetamine sulfate on cognition in MS patients: Results of a randomized controlled trial. *Journal of Neurology, 256*(7), 1095–1102.

Morrow, S. A., & Rosehart, H. (2015). Effects of single dose mixed amphetamine salts-extended release on processing speed in multiple sclerosis: A double blind placebo controlled study. *Psychopharmacology, 232*(23), 4253–4259.

Narula, S., Hopkins, S. E., & Banwell, B. (2015). Treatment of pediatric multiple sclerosis. *Current Treatment Options in Neurology, 17*(3), 10.

Nielsen, N. M., Munger, K. L., Koch-Henriksen, N., Hougaard, D. M., Magyari, M., Jorgensen, K. T., ... Stenager, E. (2017). Neonatal vitamin D status and risk of multiple sclerosis: A population-based case-control study. *Neurology, 88*(1), 44–51.

Olek, M. J. (2005). Differential diagnosis, clinical features, and prognosis of multiple sclerosis. *In M. J. Olek (Ed), Current Clinical Neurology: Multiple Sclerosis*, 15–53, Human Press, Totowa, NJ.

Pastò, L., Portaccio, E., Goretti, B., Ghezzi, A., Lori, S., Hakiki, B., ... Moiola, L. (2016). The cognitive reserve theory in the setting of pediatric-onset multiple sclerosis. *Multiple Sclerosis Journal, 22*(13), 1741–1749.

Planche, V., Gibelin, M., Cregut, D., Pereira, B., & Clavelou, P. (2016). Cognitive impairment in a population-based study of patients with multiple sclerosis: Differences between late relapsing– remitting, secondary progressive and primary progressive multiple sclerosis. *European Journal of Neurology, 23*(2), 282–289.

Polman, C. H., Reingold, S. C., Banwell, B., Clanet, M., Cohen, J. A., Filippi, M., ... Lublin, F. D. (2011). Diagnostic criteria for multiple sclerosis: 2010 revisions to the McDonald criteria. *Annals of Neurology, 69*(2), 292–302.

Portaccio, E., Goretti, B., Lori, S., Zipoli, V., Centorrino, S., Ghezzi, A., ... Amato, M. P. (2009). The brief neuropsychological battery for children: A screening tool for cognitive impairment in childhood and juvenile multiple sclerosis. *Multiple Sclerosis Journal, 15*(5), 620–626.

Pucak, M. L., Carroll, K. A., Kerr, D. A., & Kaplin, A. I. (2007). Neuropsychiatric manifestations of depression in multiple sclerosis: Neuroinflammatory, neuroendocrine, and neurotrophic mechanisms in the pathogenesis of immune-mediated depression. *Dialogues in Clinical Neuroscience, 9*(2), 125–139.

Rao, S. M., Grafman, J., DiGiulio, D., Mittenberg, W., Bernardin, L., Leo, G. J., ... Unverzagt, F. (1993). Memory dysfunction in multiple sclerosis: Its relation to working memory, semantic encoding, and implicit learning. *Neuropsychology, 7*(3), 364.

Strober, L., Englert, J., Munschauer, F., Weinstock-Guttman, B., Rao, S., & Benedict, R. (2009). Sensitivity of conventional memory tests in multiple sclerosis: Comparing the Rao brief repeatable neuropsychological battery and the minimal assessment of cognitive function in MS. *Multiple Sclerosis Journal, 15*(9), 1077–1084.

Sumowski, J. F., Chiaravalloti, N., Erlanger, D., Kaushik, T., Benedict, R. H., & DeLuca, J. (2011). L-amphetamine improves memory in MS patients with objective memory impairment. *Multiple Sclerosis (Houndmills, Basingstoke, England), 17*(9), 1141–1145.

Suppiej, A., & Cainelli, E. (2014). Cognitive dysfunction in pediatric multiple sclerosis. *Neuropsychiatric Disease and Treatment, 10*, 1385–1392.

Tan, A., Hague, C., Greenberg, B. M., & Harder, L. (2017). Neuropsychological outcomes of pediatric demyelinating diseases: A review. *Child Neuropsychology*, 1–23.

Till, C., Ghassemi, R., Aubert-Broche, B., Kerbrat, A., Collins, D. L., Narayanan, S., ... Banwell, B. L. (2011). MRI correlates of cognitive impairment in childhood-onset multiple sclerosis. *Neuropsychology, 25*(3), 319–332.

Till, C., Ho, C., Dudani, A., Garcia-Lorenzo, D., Collins, D., & Banwell, B. (2012). Magnetic resonance imaging predictors of executive functioning in patients with pediatric-onset multiple sclerosis. *Archives of Clinical Neuropsychology, 27*(5), 495–509.

Till, C., Racine, N., Araujo, D., Narayanan, S., Collins, D. L., Aubert-Broche, B., ... Banwell, B. (2013). Changes in cognitive performance over a 1-year period in children and adolescents with multiple sclerosis. *Neuropsychology, 27*(2), 210.

Vollmer, T. (2007). The natural history of relapses in multiple sclerosis. *Journal of the Neurological Sciences, 256*, S5–S13.

Weisbrot, D. M., Ettinger, A. B., Gadow, K. D., Belman, A. L., MacAllister, W. S., Milazzo, M., ... Krupp, L. B.(2010). Psychiatric comorbidity in pediatric patients with demyelinating disorders. *Journal of Child Neurology, 25*(2), 192–202.

Yeh, E. A., Chitnis, T., Krupp, L., Ness, J., Chabas, D., Kuntz, N., & Waubant, E. (2009). Pediatric multiple sclerosis. *Nature Reviews. Neurology, 5*(11), 621–631.

Yeh, E. A., Weinstock-Guttman, B., Ramanathan, M., Ramasamy, D. P., Willis, L., Cox, J. L., & Zivadinov, R. (2009). Magnetic resonance imaging characteristics of children and adults with paediatric-onset multiple sclerosis. *Brain : A Journal of Neurology, 132*(Pt 12), 3392–3400.

Stroke

Robyn Westmacott, Angela Deotto, and David Nyenhuis

Introduction

Stroke is a major cause of acquired brain injury in both pediatric and adult populations. Although the pathophysiology of stroke is similar across the lifespan, pediatric and adult stroke differ significantly in terms of etiology and outcome. A lifespan approach to the study of neuropsychological outcome after stroke provides a unique opportunity to evaluate the impact of a focal brain injury at different stages of development. In this chapter, we review the current literature on diagnosis, etiology, treatment, and prevention of pediatric and adult stroke, as well as important factors determining poststroke neuropsychological outcome across the lifespan. We also discuss the unique role of the neuropsychologist in pediatric and adult assessment after stroke, important considerations for clinicians in working with these populations, and the current literature on rehabilitation and intervention. Finally, directions for future research are highlighted, with emphasis on increased lifespan perspective.

Epidemiology and Pathophysiology

A stroke is a clinically defined, sudden, focal loss of neurologic function that is caused by a blocked vessel (ischemic stroke) or a burst/leakage from a vessel (hemorrhagic stroke) (Ropper, Samuels & Klein, 2014). Ischemic strokes are caused by disrupted blood flow in the arterial system (arterial ischemic stroke), or the venous system (cerebral sinovenous thrombosis; CSVT), resulting from thrombotic or embolic mechanisms. In thrombosis, a blood clot locally develops on a blood vessel wall, occluding the vessel. An embolus is another ischemic mechanism, in which a mass of material (e.g., blood clot, tissue, cholesterol, or amniotic fluid) detaches from its point of origin and travels throughout the circulatory system to occlude a blood vessel downstream (Kirton & deVeber, 2009). Hemorrhagic strokes are classified as subarachnoid (bleeding on the brain surface), intraventricular (bleeding into the ventricles),

or intracerebral (bleeding into the brain tissue). Large-scale studies have suggested that rates of ischemic and hemorrhagic strokes in children are relatively equal. This is a striking discrepancy from the adult population, wherein approximately 80% of strokes are ischemic in origin (Riel-Romero, Kalra, & Gonzalez-Toledo, 2009). Several important definitions pertaining to stroke across the lifespan are presented in Table 13.1.

Perinatal stroke and childhood stroke are very different in terms of clinical presentation, risk factors, and outcome. Perinatal ischemic stroke occurs between 20 weeks' gestation and 28 days after birth, and has an incidence of approximately 1 in 2,500 live births (Cardenas, Rho, & Kirton, 2011). The term neonatal arterial ischemic stroke is used when the diagnosis of stroke is made acutely, typically due to focal seizures in the newborn period. The term presumed perinatal ischemic stroke refers to a retrospective diagnosis of suspected stroke in the perinatal period, usually due to emerging hemiparesis at 4–8 months of age (Kirton & deVeber, 2009). Childhood arterial ischemic stroke is much less common, with yearly incidence found to range from 0.6 to 13 cases per 100,000 children (Kirton, Westmacott, & deVeber, 2007). Similar to adults, stroke symptomatology in childhood commonly involves acute hemiparesis (weakness on one side of the body) and other focal motor deficits. Altered mental state, seizures, lethargy, vertigo, and dysphasia are also common. Severe headache along with nausea or vomiting tend to be hallmark signs of childhood hemorrhagic stroke, and are documented in more than 50% of cases. Overall, pediatric stroke survival rates are far greater than those seen in the adult population; however, it is estimated that pervasive neurological morbidity will occur in more than half of pediatric survivors (Cardenas et al., 2011).

Most pediatric ischemic strokes occur within the cerebral arteries, with an embolic etiology. The arterial system within the human brain consists of the anterior circulation provided by the internal carotid arteries and the posterior circulation provided by the vertebral

Table 13.1 Stroke and Cerebrovascular Disease Definitions

Term	Definition
Neonatal stroke	A cerebrovascular event occurring within the first 28 days of life.
Presumed perinatal stroke	Retrospective diagnosis of suspected stroke in the perinatal period, usually made due to emerging hemiparesis and/or seizures at 4–8 months of age. An old lesion is observed upon neuroimaging.
Childhood stroke	A cerebrovascular event occurring between 1 month and 18 years of age.
Adult stroke	A cerebrovascular event occurring after 18 years of age.
Arterial ischemic stroke	Occurs when blood flow to a cerebral artery is suddenly blocked (e.g., due to embolism or thrombosis), resulting in death of affected brain tissue.
Sinovenous thrombosis	Sudden blockage of the venous sinuses resulting in impaired blood drainage and death to affected brain tissue.
Intraventricular hemorrhage	Hemorrhagic stroke caused by bleeding into the brain's ventricular system, which consists of fluid filled spaces containing cerebrospinal fluid.
Subarachnoid hemorrhage	Hemorrhagic stroke caused by bleeding on the brain's surface, in the area between the arachnoid membrane and pia mater.
Intracerebral hemorrhage	Hemorrhagic stroke caused by bleeding within the brain tissue.
Thrombosis	Local coagulation (formation of a blood clot) inside of a blood vessel, resulting in obstruction of blood flow within the circulatory system.
Embolism	The lodging of a blockage-causing piece of material (i.e., embolus) inside a blood vessel. The embolus forms elsewhere in the body and travels throughout the circulatory system to occlude a vessel downstream. The blockage-causing material may consist of a blood clot, air bubble, tissue, plaque, bacteria, or amniotic fluid.
Cerebral small vessel disease (CSVD)	Primarily subcortical gray or white matter pathology associated with distal penetrating arterioles.
Lacunar infarction	CSVD caused by arteriolar occlusions, most commonly in basal ganglia structures, the thalamus, the internal capsule, and deep hemispheric white matter.
White matter degeneration	Likely due to diffuse, incomplete ischemia of small vessels, often seen as caps and bands around lateral ventricles on axial brain MRI slices.
Diffuse cerebral atrophy	Often inversely correlated to white matter hyperintensity volume, likely secondary to diffuse gray and white matter degeneration.
Microhemorrhage	Very small hemorrhagic events. Lobar microhemorrhages are associated with cerebral amyloid angiopathy; deep, subcortical events are associated with stroke risk factors, such as hypertension.
Microinfarct	Tiny lesions, most often seen at autopsy, that are related to cognitive impairment and dementia.

arteries (Kirton & deVeber, 2009). Specifically, the internal carotid arteries give rise to the anterior cerebral arteries and the middle cerebral arteries (MCAs), whereas the basilar artery (formed by the fusion of the two vertebral arteries) gives rise to the posterior cerebral arteries. The three main arteries produce a number of branches that travel over the surface of the brain, within the subarachnoid space, which then divide into smaller, penetrating branches that supply the cortex, underlying white matter, and deep brain structures. In both pediatric and adult populations, the MCA is the most common source of arterial ischemic stroke (Cardenas et al., 2011). The predominance of MCA infarcts has been partially attributed to the large territory covered by this cerebral artery, which includes the lateral portions of the frontal, temporal, and parietal lobes. Furthermore, emboli can easily lodge within the deep penetrating arteries of the MCA (i.e., lenticulostriate arteries), which are smaller arteries supplying regions of the basal ganglia and internal capsule. Occlusions of these vessels are referred to as lacunar strokes. Large MCA infarcts are often seen in term infants, with both cortical and subcortical brain

Table 13.2 Primary Risk Factors for Stroke across the Lifespan

Fetal Risk	Maternal Risk	Adult Risk
• Male gender • Resuscitation at birth • Low Apgar score • Cardiac anomalies • Infection • Coagulation abnormalities • Hematologic diseases (e.g., sickle cell disease and polycythemia) • Vascular abnormality (e.g., moyamoya disease)	• Emergency cesarean section • Vacuum extraction • Infection (esp. urinary tract infections) • Autoimmune disease • Advanced maternal age • Preeclampsia • Low amniotic fluid • First child • Twin gestation	• Age • Male sex • Race (increased risk in Blacks) • Cardiovascular risk factors (e.g., hypertension, diabetes mellitus, hyperlipidemia, tobacco habit, obesity, lack of physical activity, poor dietary practices) • Cardiac conditions (e.g., atrial fibrillation, peripheral arterial disease, heart failure)

regions frequently impacted. Moreover, most perinatal strokes involve the left hemisphere due to anatomical differences between the left and right common carotid arteries (Cardenas et al., 2011).

CSVT is relatively uncommon in adulthood, but represents an important source of pediatric infarction. Approximately 25% of all pediatric cases of ischemic stroke involve the venous system, with the neonatal period carrying the highest lifetime incidence of CSVT (Kirton & deVeber, 2009). Seizures characterize symptomatic neonatal CVST, but diffuse neurological signs may also be present. CSVT occurs with thrombosis of veins or major venous sinuses, which often results in subsequent hemorrhagic transformation due to the pressure produced by blocked blood drainage. The superficial venous system is commonly involved. Infarction deep within the venous system, adjacent to the ventricular system, frequently produces intraventricular hemorrhage, and epidemiological studies have noted that nearly one-third of term neonates with intraventricular hemorrhage have underlying deep CSVT. However, hemorrhage may also occur without venous system involvement, and small-scale intracerebral arterial hemorrhage is estimated to be as high as 26% in neonates (Kirton & DeVeber, 2009).

The incidence of stroke peaks twice throughout the lifetime: first in the perinatal period and then later in older adulthood (Cardenas et al., 2011). The neonate stroke prevalence rate is approximately 25 per 100,000 live births. This rate drops quickly, and the risk of stroke in children (through age 18 years) is estimated to be 11 per 100,000 per year, or about 3,000 stroke events each year in the United States (Lloyd-Jones et al., 2009). By comparison, approximately 790,000 adults experience stroke each year in the United States (373

per 100,000). Of these strokes, approximately 17% occur in persons over the age of 85 (Mozaffarian et al., 2016). In Canada, approximately 62,000 experience a stroke or transient ischemic attack each year (171 per 100,000; Hebert et al., 2016).

In adults, stroke is the fifth-highest cause of death in the United States, killing approximately 129,000 each year. It is also the leading cause of disability. The good news is that the rate of stroke has declined by 34% during the past 10 years and the rate of stroke death has decreased by 18%. This may be due to increased surveillance and treatment of stroke risk factors (Mozaffarian et al., 2016). The single most important risk factor for stroke in adults is age; the chance of having a stroke roughly doubles each decade after age 55. Stroke is more common in men but more lethal in women. Pregnancy and use of hormonal contraception increase women's risk for stroke. Blacks are at particularly high risk; their risk of first stroke is twice that of Whites in the United States, and is also more lethal. Table 13.2 summarizes the primary risk factors for stroke across the lifespan. Lifestyle (diet and exercise) and risk factor modification (high blood pressure, etc.) will be covered in the Prevention section.

Risk factors for pediatric stroke are quite different from those associated with stroke in adults, given that lifestyle factors (e.g., elevated cholesterol levels and unhealthy diet) are rarely implicated. For reasons that are not well understood, there is a preponderance of male pediatric stroke for all stroke subtypes and ages, with males comprising approximately 60% of pediatric stroke samples (Golomb, Fullerton, Nowak-Gottl, & Deveber, 2009). Perinatal stroke usually occurs during the third trimester of pregnancy, during the process of labor and delivery, or during the neonatal timeframe.

Maternal risk factors for neonatal ischemic stroke include preeclampsia, gestational diabetes, advanced maternal age, autoimmune disease, twin gestation, low amniotic fluid, and infection (especially urinary tract infection). Labor-related pediatric stroke risk is highest with emergency caesarian section, vacuum extraction, and birth trauma (Cardenas et al., 2011). Neonatal ischemic stroke has also been attributed to emboli arising from the degenerating placenta around the time of birth and traveling to the left MCA. Through use of Doppler ultrasound, Coker, Beltran, Myers, and Hmura (1988) documented that the amniotic embolus travels from the umbilical cord veins to the aortic arch, where turbulent flows from the ductus tend to direct its passage into the left common carotid artery. The embolus then travels into the left internal carotid and continues until it reaches and occludes the left MCA or its penetrating branches.

The presence of congenital or acquired heart disease is a primary risk factor for perinatal and childhood ischemic stroke, with the heart being the most common source of cerebral emboli (Roach, Heyer, & Lo, 2012). Vascular anomalies (arteriopathies) have also been implicated and account for half of all arterial ischemic strokes in children (Amlie-Lefond et al., 2009). Specifically, blood disorders such as sickle cell disease increase the risk of blood clots within the vascular system, whereas small vessel disease (e.g., moyamoya disease) increases the likelihood of thrombi or emboli occluding the narrowed vessels. Arterial dissection of the carotid arteries is another prominent arteriopathy that occurs when a small tear forms in the innermost lining of the arterial wall, increasing the risk for clotting and occlusion of the vessel. Traumatic or "spontaneous" arterial dissections account for up to 20% of childhood ischemic stroke cases. Head and neck infections (such as sinusitis, otitis, and meningitis) also commonly co-occur with childhood stroke and have been associated with emboli and infarcts via the inflammatory immune response (Cardenas et al., 2011).

With regard to hemorrhagic stroke, trauma is reported to be the most common risk factor among children in the United States. When trauma is not implicated, the remainder of hemorrhagic strokes in children is generally accounted for by arteriopathies, such as arteriovenous malformation (AVM). AVM constitutes abnormal connections between the interfacing arterial system and venous drainage system, in which the interface lacks the normal branching structures that allow for a steady drop in blood pressure. Abnormal connections

and high pressure of AVM increase the risk of spontaneous hemorrhaging. AVMs can become symptomatic within the first few days of life and account for a greater percentage of hemorrhagic strokes in children than in adults. Hemorrhaging can also result from small vessel disease, as seen in William syndrome, where blood vessel walls can become weaker and more prone to rupturing over time due to increased blood pressure within the narrowed cerebral arteries (Roach et al., 2012).

As with childhood stroke, there is a prominent role for focal events occurring in large brain vessels in adults. However, to fully understand stroke in adults, one must also pay attention to small vessel events (lacunar infarctions), chronic, diffuse white matter degeneration, and cerebral atrophy. Often, acute and chronic conditions co-occur in both large and small vessels. It is the combination of these conditions that often results in cognitive and behavioral change.

Cerebral small vessel disease (CSVD) (i.e., lacunar infarctions and white matter degeneration) may be the most common cause for vascular cognitive impairment (VCI) in adults (Pantoni, 2010). CSVD refers to the primarily subcortical gray or white matter pathology associated with distal penetrating arterioles most often branching from the middle, posterior, or basilar arteries. Arteriolar occlusion results in focal lacunar infarction, which shows up as dark spots on T1 and light dots on T2 and fluid attenuation inversion recovery magnetic resonance imaging (FLAIR MRI). The most common locations for lacunar infarctions are in basal ganglia structures, the thalamus, the internal capsule, and deep hemispheric white matter areas.

White matter degeneration is much more diffuse than lacunar infarctions. It is identified by hyperintensities on T2 and FLAIR sequences and is not as apparent on T1 images. On FLAIR MRI, the hyperintensities are often seen as caps and bands, surrounding the lateral ventricles (see Figure 13.1). The mechanisms of white matter degeneration are not fully known but are likely related to chronic, incomplete ischemia, perhaps venular in addition to arteriole occlusion (Black, Gao, & Bilbao, 2009). White matter pathology may also reflect glial swelling, demyelination, enlarged perivascular spaces, spongiosis, amyloid angiopathy, and cyst formation (Pantoni, 2010). Diffuse cerebral atrophy co-occurs with white matter degeneration, and there are often strong inverse correlations between these two vascular markers. More specific atrophy, in the area of the thalamus, has also been associated with VCI in a sample of patients with ischemic stroke (Stebbins et al., 2008).

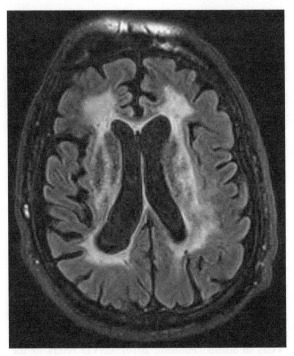

Figure 13.1. An axial FLAIR MRI image showing periventricular caps and bands for a patient with extensive white matter hyperintensities.

Two other types of CSVD have more recently been described. Microhemorrhages/microbleeds are identified via gradient-echo MRI sequences. Their etiology may depend on their location in the brain. Lobar microbleeds have been associated with cerebral amyloid angiopathy, which in turn is associated with Alzheimer disease. However, deep, subcortical microbleeds are associated with stroke risk factors, such as hypertension, and subsequent cognitive decline (Patel et al., 2013). Microinfarcts are very small lesions, difficult to identify with conventional MRI. More often, they are identified during brain autopsy. They are linked with cognitive impairment and dementia in studies such as the Honolulu Asia Aging Study (Launer, Hughes, & White, 2011).

Vascular pathology and risk factors have also been associated with Alzheimer disease, suggesting linkages between the two diseases. Midlife stroke risk factors, such as hypertension and diabetes, are associated with later-life cognitive decline and dementia, including Alzheimer disease (Gorelick et al., 2011). In addition, the most common pathology associated with dementia is not Alzheimer disease alone, but Alzheimer disease with comorbid cerebrovascular pathology. Finally, the neuropathic study of persons who completed neuropsychological assessment before death finds an additive relationship between cerebrovascular disease and the neuronal plaques and neurofibrillary tangles associated with Alzheimer disease. In these studies, such as the nun study, less Alzheimer pathology was needed to produce cognitive decline and/or dementia in persons who also showed cerebrovascular disease (Mortimer, 2012).

Prevention

Pediatric Stroke Prevention. Overall, it can be difficult to prevent a first stroke in childhood because stroke is often the initial sign of a problem in a child. Thus, guidelines for stroke management in the pediatric population often focus on prompt diagnosis and future stroke prevention. The 5-year cumulative recurrence rate of arterial ischemic stroke in children had been found to range from 5% to 18% among studies conducted in Germany, the United Kingdom, and California (United States). Although there have been no controlled trials in children, aspirin at doses of 1–5 mg/kg/day is frequently used for secondary stroke prevention when there is history of childhood arterial ischemic stroke. Current medical practice involves assessing and, if possible, addressing any treatable underlying risk factors that could contribute to stroke recurrence. For instance, pediatric stroke associated with sickle cell disease is often managed with intravenous hydration and supplementary oxygen. Although there are beneficial effects of blood transfusion in sickle cell disease, this is an expensive procedure that is associated with several potential complications. Neonates with stroke are treated for dehydration and anemia and also require replacement of deficient coagulation factors if there is a history of intracranial hemorrhage linked with coagulation factor deficiency (Roach et al., 2012). Because of the high incidence of stoke in moyamoya disease, surgical revascularization procedures are generally used as a preventive measure, especially when patients have experienced cognitive decline or progressive symptoms. Treatment for congestive heart failure is also recommended to reduce the likelihood of cardiogenic embolism. Medical guidelines also dictate that, when possible, congenital heart lesions should be repaired to improve cardiac function and to reduce subsequent stroke risk (Roach et al., 2012).

Adult Stroke Prevention. Recent studies have suggested that 85% of all strokes in adults may be preventable (O'Donnell et al., 2010), primarily through medical management and lifestyle modification.

As would be expected, stroke risk factors often mirror risk factors for cardiovascular events, such as heart attacks and heart disease.

Medical Management and Stroke Prevention. Of all of the risk factors under study, hypertension is believed to be the most important. In a recent, large (n > 26,000) case-control study conducted in 32 countries, stroke risk was approximately three times higher in persons with a history of hypertension or measured blood pressure of 140/90 mmHg or higher (O'Donnell et al., 2016). Moreover, decreased stroke risk is noted even in persons with borderline hypertension (130–140 mmHg systolic blood pressure; 80–89 mmHg diastolic blood pressure) who lower their blood pressure. Although stroke risk increases with age, even persons older than 80 years may benefit from better blood pressure management. Beckett and colleagues showed that lowering systolic blood pressure from 160 mmHg to 145 mmHg resulted in a 30% stroke reduction across 2 years in an elderly sample (Beckett et al., 2008).

The relationship between stroke and cholesterol levels is less clear than it is between stroke and hypertension. Hypercholesterolemia is clearly related to carotid atherosclerosis and is an established risk factor for myocardial infarction. Statin use has not been found to lower stroke risk in otherwise healthy adults with hypercholesterolemia without vascular disease. However, statin use has been found to lower risk in persons with other risk factors, such as coronary heart disease, diabetes mellitus, and/or carotid stenosis.

Persons with diabetes mellitus are also at higher risk for stroke and cerebrovascular disease. Diabetes is especially associated with subcortical ischemia and small, lacunar infarctions. Blood sugar control appears to have greater effect on small artery rather than large artery events. Control of other stroke risk factors, such as hypertension and hypercholesterolemia, lowers risk in persons with diabetes.

Atrial fibrillation is the leading cause of stroke in the elderly. Persons with atrial fibrillation are also at higher risk for large, fatal strokes than persons with strokes that are associated with other conditions. Prevention begins with detection; persons older than 65 years are recommended to undergo regular assessments to detect cardiac arrhythmias. Treatment with anticoagulant agents show reduced ischemic stroke risk of up to 70% in persons with atrial fibrillation (Hart, Benavente, McBride, & Pearce, 1999), but also increases risk of bleeding after a fall and hemorrhagic stroke.

The bleeding risk, however, may be small in comparison to the stroke reduction benefits of anticoagulation. Perhaps surprisingly, aspirin has not been shown to lower stroke risk in persons with atrial fibrillation.

Other medical treatments have had mixed success with stroke prevention. Sleep-disordered breathing (SDB) caused by obstructive sleep apnea and other conditions may increase stroke risk, although to date, there are stronger links between treatment of SDB and cardiovascular events than SDB and stroke events (Barbe et al., 2012). Use of antithrombotics, such as aspirin, for stroke prevention has received some weak support in stroke prevention in some studies. However, a recent meta-analysis found no association between aspirin use and primary stroke prevention, whereas increased risk of bleeding was noted in groups that took aspirin (Baigent et al., 2009). There is greater support for aspirin use to prevent recurrent stroke than first stroke.

Lifestyle Modification and Stroke Prevention. There is growing evidence that healthy lifestyle decisions have significant effects on stroke risk. Chiuve and colleagues combined data sets from the US Nurses' Health Study and the Health Professionals Follow-Up Study (combined n = 114,928). They found up to 80% lower stroke risk in adult women's stroke risk and up to 70% lower risk in men who a reported healthy lifestyle, such as avoidance of excess body weight, smoking, heavy alcohol consumption, unhealthy diet, and physical inactivity (Chiuve et al., 2008). Physical activity/exercise is a key component of a healthy lifestyle. For example, Zhang and colleagues have found that physical activity was associated with reduced stroke risk, primarily because of a reduction in ischemic strokes. There was a nonsignificant trend for lower hemorrhagic events (Zhang et al., 2013). Finally, a meta-analysis of 23 studies found that moderate to vigorous regular physical activity was associated with reduced total stroke risk as well as reduced risk for both ischemic and hemorrhagic stroke events (Lee, Folsom, & Blair, 2003). Most investigators agree that the mechanism for lower stroke risk with greater physical activity is by control of other known risk factors, such as hypertension, diabetes, and obesity.

Diet has also been linked to stroke risk. Several observational studies have linked regular fish intake to lower stroke risk (Larsson, Virtamo, & Wolk, 2011), whereas other studies have noted that frequent red meat (pork or beef) consumption may increase stroke risk (Micha, Wallace, & Mozaffarian, 2010). Other dietary elements for which there has been some support for lowering stroke risk include vegetables (O'Donnell et al., 2010), coffee (Larsson & Orsini, 2011), and chocolate (Buitrago-Lopez et al., 2011). Moderate alcohol use (up to two drinks per day for men and one drink per day for women) has also been associated with lowered stroke risk, while a higher consumption level may increase stroke risk. Of interest, to date there has not been a significant relationship found between stroke risk and fat intake, fat type (saturated vs. polyunsaturated), or fat origin (vegetable or animal). Also, although omega-3 polyunsaturated fatty acid intake has been associated with decreased cardiovascular events, there have not been consistent, similar findings associated between this marine-based fat and stroke risk. Obesity independently increases stroke risk; each increased body mass index point has been found to be associated with an increased 5% stroke risk.

Salt intake that is greater than 5–6 g/day is associated with both ischemic and hemorrhagic stroke. However, a recent Institute of Medicine review found no evidence that salt reduction diets are an effective means of lowering the risk of myocardial infarction, stroke, or death (Institute of Medicine of the National Academies, 2013). Cigarette smoking increases stroke risk, both by itself and in combination with other stroke risk factors. Smoking cessation lowers stroke risk. To a lesser extent, passive smoke intake is also associated with increased stroke risk.

The mechanisms for many of the lifestyle factors associated with stroke risk are believed to be their relationships with known risk factors, such as hypertension, hypercholesterolemia, heart health, and diabetes. This hypothesis fits with recommendations of global lifestyle modifications that include physical activity, diet, and smoking cessation. The American Heart Association's Life's Simple 7 is an example of this global approach, and studies have found associations between the degree of adherence to this global approach and lower stroke risk (Kulshreshtha et al., 2013).

Clinical Manifestation

Despite the widely held belief that increased plasticity of the young brain protects against significant neurological and neuropsychological deficits, a substantial body of evidence indicates that individuals with a history of perinatal or childhood stroke experience difficulties in motor, cognitive, academic, and psychosocial functioning that emerge over the course of development (Fuentes, Deotto, Desrocher, deVeber, & Westmacott, 2014). Consistent with research from other pediatric populations, the literature on pediatric stroke highlights the vulnerability of the developing brain, the long-term neuropsychological deficits that often result from early disruption of brain function and subsequent brain development, and the significant variability in outcomes seen across individuals. Heterogeneity in outcomes within the pediatric stroke population has been linked to a range of clinical and demographic factors, including those related to the brain (e.g., lesion location, size, and volume), the child (e.g., age at stroke, age at assessment, co-occurring neurological conditions, stroke etiology, genetic predispositions), and the environment (family stress/functioning, parent mental health, sibling interactions, educational support, rehabilitation therapy) (Fuentes et al., 2014). We are just starting to understand how these factors interact to affect neuropsychological outcome and resilience after pediatric stroke. In this section we summarize the literature on outcomes after perinatal and childhood stroke across important cognitive domains (e.g., intellectual ability, language, visual-spatial ability, attention, and executive function), and we discuss several important determinants of neuropsychological outcome (see Table 13.3).

Intellectual Ability. As a group, children with perinatal and childhood stroke consistently score broadly within the average range on tests of intellectual ability, although statistically lower than the normative mean (Hajek et al., 2013; Studer et al., 2014; Westmacott, Askalan, Macgregor, Anderson, & Deveber, 2010). However, variability in intellectual function across individuals is significant, and it has been difficult to pinpoint determinants of outcome because many studies have included a diverse group of children with pediatric stroke who differ on many other relevant factors (e.g., extent of lesion, presence of seizure disorder, age at stroke, age at test, and presence of other neurological comorbidities). Nonetheless, several important themes have emerged from recent research. First, there is considerable evidence that stroke earlier in childhood is more detrimental to overall intellectual ability than stroke in later childhood (Jacomb, Porter, Brunsdon, Mandalis, & Parry, 2016; Studer et al., 2014; Westmacott et al., 2010), highlighting the vulnerability of the immature brain. However, recent studies suggest that the relationship between age at stroke and intellectual outcome is complex and modulated by other variables such as lesion location. One large study of 145

Table 13.3 Summary of Notable Neuropsychological Outcomes and Common Difficulties After Pediatric Stroke

Domain	Notable Neuropsychological Outcomes
Intelligence	• Generally low-average to average • Poorer outcomes associated with larger lesions, younger age at stroke, older age at assessment
Language	• Delayed onset of language • Slower rate of grammar acquisition • Spared vocabulary and comprehension • Word-finding difficulties and simpler sentence structure
Visual-spatial	• Left hemisphere injury = feature processing deficits • Right hemisphere injury = pattern configuration deficits • Mild to severe impairment that is persistent
Sensory-motor	• Deficits in stereoagnosis • Hemiparesis in arm and hand contralateral to lesion • Apraxia, weakness, spasticity, impaired dexterity • Cerebral palsy in approximately 40% of perinatal cases • Motor tracts capable of reorganization to compensate for motor loss. However, little plasticity in sensory cortex leads to persistent sensory deficits
Memory	• Verbal memory deficits (subtle, nonlateralized) • Reduced encoding, less use of learning strategies to enhance recall, and reduced delayed free recall and recognition
Executive functioning and attention	• Greatest impairments noted in sustained attention, inhibitory control, working memory and mental flexibility
Academic achievement	• Low-average math, spelling, and reading • Left hemisphere injury linked to reading difficulties
Social-emotional	• Subtle deficits in facial affect recognition, especially with parietal lobe involvement • Up to 40% of patients struggle with internalizing or externalizing problems • Difficulty navigating social situations (making attributions and understanding the role of social context)

children with arterial ischemic stroke (Westmacott et al., 2010) found that subcortical lesions were most detrimental to intellectual outcome when they occurred in the perinatal period, whereas cortical strokes were most detrimental to intellectual outcome when they occurred in early childhood (1 month to 5 years). Other studies have suggested a nonlinear relationship between age at stroke and intellectual outcome – for example, Allman and Scott found that stroke in early childhood (1–5 years of age) had better intellectual outcome than those with stroke at an earlier or later age (Allman & Scott, 2013), whereas Everts and colleagues reported peak intellectual resilience for those with stroke between 5 and 10 years of age (Everts et al., 2008). These conflicting findings likely reflect the fact that factors such as lesion size, age at assessment, and extent of neurological deficit are not consistently accounted for across studies. There does appear to be a general trend toward poorer overall intellectual outcome associated with earlier age at stroke, but the relationship is complex and likely depends on many other factors. Moreover, determinants of outcome may differ depending on the specific cognitive ability in question.

Another consistent trend in the literature is that large lesions (i.e., encompassing multiple lobes), bilateral lesions, and lesions involving both cortical and subcortical structures are most likely to be associated with poor intellectual outcome at school age compared with strokes classified as small and strokes that are isolated to either subcortical or cortical structures (Ballantyne, Spilkin, Hesselink, & Trauner, 2008; Studer et al., 2014; Westmacott et al., 2010). Moreover, children with seizure disorders exhibit significantly weaker intellectual ability than those without (Studer et al., 2014), and children with more severe neurological impairment tend to do more poorly from a cognitive standpoint than those with milder neurological deficits. Gender differences have also been found – males are more likely to suffer perinatal and childhood stroke (Golomb et al., 2009) and they demonstrate poorer intellectual outcomes compared with females with similar strokes (Westmacott, Macgregor, Askalan, & Deveber, 2009). There is some evidence that gender and laterality may interact to impact intellectual outcome, with left hemisphere lesions being more detrimental for males and right hemisphere lesions being more detrimental for females. Finally, there is considerable evidence to support the notion of emerging deficits over time, such that older age at assessment is associated with poorer intellectual performance and slower than expected rates of skill development (Westmacott et al., 2009). However, other studies have suggested a significant amount of stability in intellectual ability over time (Ballantyne et al., 2008; Jacomb et al., 2016). More work is needed to explore how all of these factors interact to determine intellectual outcome after pediatric stroke.

Language. Unlike in adults, left MCA strokes in the perinatal period do not typically result in persistent aphasic disorders later in childhood. Early language milestones are often achieved somewhat more slowly for children with perinatal stroke, but equally so for those with left and right hemisphere lesions. Moreover, core language skills, including vocabulary and comprehension, tend to be age-appropriate by the time children enter school. The resilience of speech and language function in the event of early stroke has been attributed to enhanced plasticity of the young brain. However, there is growing evidence to suggest later-developing challenges with complex language skills, including verbal fluency and word retrieval, grammatical expression, discourse processing, and narrative expression, which are particularly pronounced in children with left hemisphere perinatal strokes (Reilly, Wasserman, & Appelbaum, 2013). In contrast, strokes impacting classic left hemisphere language areas later in childhood may result in acute aphasic deficits, as seen in adults. Because left hemisphere cortical lesions in later childhood are exceedingly rare, however, the nature and extent of the associated aphasic deficits are poorly understood. Although younger children do to tend to recover more quickly from acute-stage language deficits then older children or adults, many go on to develop significant problems with more sophisticated language skills as they get older, such as narrative discourse, written expression, and verbal fluency (Reilly et al., 2013). Thus, enhanced plasticity is not necessarily associated with more positive

outcome if compensatory mechanisms are ineffective or disrupt the development of higher-level skills. The functional neuroimaging literature on language reorganization after pediatric stroke is limited, but findings generally suggest increased recruitment of right hemisphere regions during language task performance as compared with similar studies in adult stroke. However, one study (Raja Beharelle et al., 2010) found a positive correlation between left frontal lateralization and language function in individuals with a history of left perinatal stroke, even though the group as a whole showed increased right hemisphere lateralization relative to controls. Thus, children with perinatal and early childhood stroke show a remarkable amount of resilience with respect to the development of core language skills, but higher-level verbal abilities are often negatively affected, and there is some evidence to suggest that persistent left hemisphere lateralization is associated with better outcome.

Visual-Spatial and Motor Ability. Most research on visual-spatial processing has been carried out in children with perinatal stroke, with some evidence to suggest that visual-spatial and visual-motor skills are more profoundly impacted than verbal abilities (Everts et al., 2010). Moreover, lateralized effects have been more consistently documented in visual-spatial ability than in verbal ability. Stiles and colleagues report evidence of a double dissociation in visual-spatial processing, such that children with right hemisphere perinatal stroke exhibit specific deficits in global processing (i.e. the overall gestalt), whereas those with left hemisphere perinatal stroke exhibit specific deficits in local processing (i.e., the specific details). These findings are very consistent with the adult stroke literature showing lateralized effects in global and local processing. Children with early right hemisphere stroke were also found to show poorer strategy use and slower improvement with practice on an "impossible house" task of visual-spatial organization as compared with children with early left hemisphere stroke. These findings have been interpreted as evidence for the limited capacity of the developing brain to reorganize visual-spatial processing after early right hemisphere injury (Stiles et al., 2008).

With regard to motor outcomes, approximately 30–60% of children with histories of stroke are reported to have motor disabilities, with severity dependent upon lesion location (e.g., region of the motor strip, basal ganglia, or internal capsule) and volume within the brain. The upper extremities (i.e., hand, arm) tend to be most frequently affected, such as through compromised finger dexterity and poor movement planning of the hand. Perinatal stroke has been noted as the most common cause of congenital hemiplegic cerebral palsy, which is often marked by weakness, impaired dexterity, spasticity, apraxia, and a circumducting gait (Stiles et al., 2008). Overall, persisting neurologic impairment in pediatric stroke is associated with poorer cognitive and behavioral outcomes across a variety of domains (Fuentes et al., 2014).

Learning, Memory, Attention, and Executive Function. Several studies indicate that verbal learning and memory challenges are common after pediatric stroke involving either hemisphere. Rote learning and retrieval from memory appear to be more significantly affected than long-term retention. Moreover, high incidences of attention and working memory difficulties have been documented after pediatric stroke (Fuentes, Westmacott, Deotto, DeVeber, & Desrocher, 2016; Jacomb et al., 2016; Max et al., 2003). In a sample of 29 children with pediatric stroke, Max and colleagues found that 46% met criteria for a diagnosis of attention-deficit/hyperactivity disorder (ADHD), with some association with lesions of the ventral putamen and the mesial prefrontal and orbitofrontal cortex (Max et al., 2003). Interestingly, ADHD diagnosis was not associated with lesion size, laterality, age at stroke, age at assessment, or family history, but it was associated with additional cognitive and academic deficits. A more recent study involving a large clinical sample ($n = 124$) of children with pediatric stroke found a much lower incidence of ADHD, but again demonstrated increased cognitive and academic deficits as compared with those with similar strokes but no ADHD. With respect to executive functioning, deficits have been found to occur frequently after pediatric stroke, on both psychometric measures and reports of everyday functioning (Roberts et al., 2016). Long and colleagues (2011) reported significant executive function deficits in a group of children with pediatric stroke, independent of intellectual ability. There was a trend toward increased deficits after lesions involving frontal and basal ganglia regions, as expected based on the broader executive function literature, but deficits were present even in those with lesions elsewhere in the brain. Earlier age at stroke was associated with increased executive dysfunction (Long et al., 2011). Finally, some recent work suggests an important role

for executive function in the academic performance of children with stroke, particularly in mathematics. Academic ability appears to be an area of particular vulnerability for children with a history of stroke (Jacomb et al., 2016).

Social-Emotional Functioning. Quality of life is poor for many children with a history of pediatric stroke, although recent studies indicate that most do well with respect to social participation, mental health, and family relationships (Greenham et al., 2015; Neuner et al., 2016). Several risk factors for poor quality of life and social participation have been identified, including significant neurological deficit, low overall intellectual ability, gender (females experience worse outcome), older age at stroke, and larger lesion size. Recent research has highlighted the critical importance of family functioning, parent mental health, and parent education in promoting social competence in children and reducing internalizing problems (Greenham et al., 2015).

A central theme of this chapter is that as one moves from neonate to child to adult to aged, some factors associated with stroke remain the same, whereas others vary widely. Age and developmental factors matter. Factors in pediatric stroke that remain salient in adults include the importance of the triad of location, volume, and number of stroke-related lesions. Where the lesion is located, how large it is, and how many lesions there are have ramifications to cognitive, functional, and behavioral outcomes. However, in the adult stroke world, one must also look at additional factors, such as the presence or absence of diffuse white matter disease, total brain volume, and the potential presence of other degenerative conditions such as Alzheimer disease, when assessing stroke's impact. As shown in Figure 13.2, there are striking similarities in the appearance of a left MCA stroke in a neonate, a child, and an adult, but the clinical manifestations of the lesion are very distinct.

Tomlinson, Blessed, and Roth (1970), in their seminal paper, found that lesion volume was important in predicting cognitive outcome; they found dementia in patients with lesions larger than 100 mL. The importance of the paper, however, was more in their attempt to show clear, measurable brain–behavior relationships rather than the correctness of their hypothesis. Indeed, subsequent studies have been mixed in finding volume-cognition relationships, with some finding that larger lesions were more likely to result in dementia/cognitive impairment whereas others have not. The number of lesions

(a)   (b)   (c)

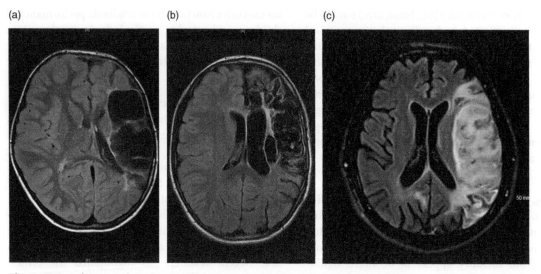

Figure 13.2. Left MCA stroke in a neonate (A), 10 year-old child (B), and 59-year-old adult (C)

may also be an important factor. Multiple strokes, both large and small, are associated with the stepwise deteriorating cognitive course that led to diagnoses of multi-infarct dementia (Hachinski, 1983), or in the case of multiple lacunar infarctions, the condition of *état criblé* (the cribriform state), which is associated with slowed processing speed and cognitive decline.

The relationships between lesion location and cognitive or behavioral change are a foundation of modern neuropsychology, and strokes have been the primary source for the lesions in this line of research. It is beyond the scope of this chapter to examine all hypothesized location–behavior relationships, and the reader interested in this topic is directed to any comprehensive neuropsychology textbook. However, some of the strongest, most enduring relationships between a single, focal lesion and cognitive skills include most aspects of language and the frontotemporoparietal region of the (usually) left hemisphere, visual agnosias and the posterior (usually) right hemisphere, hemispatial neglect and the temporoparietal region of the (usually) right hemisphere, and both primary and associative visual disturbances and the occipital lobe. Memory skills, because of their complexity, are associated with many locations. Some of the most prominent include single, well-placed lesions in the angular gyrus or thalamus of the (usually) left hemisphere, or in the basal frontal structures in the distribution of the anterior communicating artery. Behavior disturbance and pervasive personality change are also associated with focal lesions, such as relationships between depression

and (usually) left hemisphere lesions, disinhibition and orbitofrontal lesions, and apathy with mesial frontal lesions.

CSVD also contributes to cognitive and behavioral changes. The two primary components of CSVD are diffuse white matter deterioration and lacunar infarction. Of these two, lacunar infarcts likely have a stronger relationship between cognitive function than white matter lesions. The relationship of white matter lesions and cognition is still debated. It is clear that white matter lesions are ubiquitous in the elderly. In both the Rotterdam Scan Study and the Cardiovascular Health Study, more than 90% of nonpatient, community elderly subjects (age > 65 years) showed MRI evidence of white matter lesions. Some factors that are associated with the presence of greater white matter load include stroke risk factors such as hypertension and diabetes (Gorelick et al., 2011). The Cardiovascular Health Study showed that small amounts of white matter lesions had little or no effect on their cognitive outcome measure, the Modified Mini-Mental State Examination (MMSE). However, there appeared to be a threshold effect with a moderate degree of white matter lesion; as the load increased, the Modified MMSE score declined. It is not clear whether the location of the white matter lesions is an important factor. Swartz and colleagues (Swartz, Sahlas, & Black, 2003) found greater executive dysfunction when the lesions appeared to involve cholinergic tracts. However, other studies found executive dysfunction regardless of lesion location.

Cerebral atrophy in the context of stroke and cerebrovascular disease is another important factor. For example, Mungas and colleagues (Mungas et al., 2001) found atrophy to be a stronger predictor of cognitive abilities than lacunar infarct volume. There is a frequent, inverse relationship between white matter lesion volume and atrophy, leading some to hypothesize close linkages between the two factors. However, in other studies (Swartz, Stuss, Gao, & Black, 2008), both whole-brain atrophy and white matter lesion volume independently predicted cognitive function, suggesting potentially different mechanisms for the two conditions.

Because the location of large artery stroke is so varied, and presents with a wide array of cognitive impairment (e.g., primary language vs. primary visuospatial deficits), it is not surprising that there is no single stroke pattern that would be akin to the prominence of memory impairment in Alzheimer disease. However, because large artery stroke is often added to a foundation of preexisting CSVD, it is not surprising that recurrent, modal cognitive patterns have been found in samples of patients with stroke. Several studies have found a pattern of slowed information processing, executive dysfunction, immediate memory deficits and mood disturbance in patients after stroke (Nyenhuis et al., 2004). Difficulties with these studies include potential sample bias, however, because they are not able to include persons in the sample with moderate to severe expressive or receptive language deficits because these patients are not able complete formal neuropsychological assessment.

Neuropsychological Assessment

With the incredible advances in brain imaging over the past few decades, neuropsychologists are no longer called upon to determine the presence, location, or extent of a stroke. However, neuropsychological assessment continues to be the gold standard for determining the impact of stroke on an individual's cognitive, academic, vocational, social, emotional, and adaptive functioning. Information is gathered from multiple sources, including interviews and standardized questions completed by patients and families. In pediatric cases, parents and teachers may be involved, and there may be review of school documentation and child works samples. Direct behavioral observation at school may also take place. In adult evaluations, such observations at the workplace are rare. However, workplace performance evaluations may be reviewed and spouses, children or other family member may be interviewed in addition to the patient. Finally, standardized performance on validated psychometric tests is measured, with the goal of

determining the patient's strengths, areas of challenge, and needs to optimize development and/or recovery. Neuropsychologists are often asked to make predictions about long-term outcome and long-term needs, and it is critical for clinicians to have a solid grasp on the current research literature. Early assessment and long-term follow-up are of paramount importance in both pediatric and adult settings. With the pediatric stroke population, access to motor, language, cognitive, and academic intervention can alter the child's developmental trajectory and maximize adaptive ability in daily life; with adults, tracking the presence and speed of cognitive recovery may be important factors in determining the long-term cognitive impact of stroke on their lives.

As discussed in the previous section, the pediatric stroke population is extremely heterogeneous, and the neuropsychologist must take into consideration a variety of important factors when interpreting data and making predictions about later outcome. Clinicians must be well informed about the stroke mechanism, brain regions impacted, extent of lesion, age at stroke, and other neurological and medical comorbidities to interpret neuropsychological findings appropriately. Conditions such as congenital heart disease, sickle cell disease, and moyamoya disease are all associated with an increased risk of pediatric stroke, and also with their own unique patterns of neurocognitive deficit. Establishing a prestroke baseline of function is also extremely important, but this can be challenging when the stroke occurred in the perinatal period or very early childhood. Gathering information about family history of cognitive or attention difficulties, parent education and employment status, and functioning of siblings is very helpful when a clear baseline of function cannot be established for the child.

A comprehensive yet flexible test battery is optimal given the heterogeneous nature of the pediatric stroke population and the presenting neuropsychological issues. Some preliminary work from our group, involving a clinical sample of 151 children after pediatric stroke, suggests that nearly half were given at least one psychological diagnosis and 15% were given two or more diagnoses (Williams, McDonald, Roberts, Dlamini, & Westmacott, 2017). The most common diagnoses given were learning disorder/disability (25%), ADHD (14%), intellectual disability (12%), and anxiety disorder (5%). Moreover, more than 30% of children diagnosed with learning disability experienced significant deficits in two or more academic areas. The presence of seizure disorder was found to be strongly associated with the diagnosis of learning disability or ADHD, and more so than stroke characteristics (e.g., lesion location, lesion size) or family history. Moreover, children who were older at the time of assessment were more likely to receive a diagnosis of learning disability, and many of the children who did not receive any diagnosis were younger than 6 years of age at the time of assessment. These findings underscore the importance of long-term follow-up assessment.

For children with perinatal stroke, an initial assessment at between 4 and 5 years of age can be extremely helpful for determining educational needs as they transition into school. This preschool assessment should evaluate intellectual, visual-motor, language, and preacademic skill development, as well as early executive, behavioral, and social-emotional functioning. Parent and educator reports are particularly critical for evaluating daily functioning at this early age, and there is some evidence to suggest that parent reports of preschool executive functioning predict later academic ability. A follow-up assessment in the primary grades (grades 1–3) is important for early identification of learning disorders, ADHD, and intellectual disabilities, and also for elucidating the complexities of the child's individual neuropsychological profile in areas such as speed of information processing, attention regulation, inhibitory control, visual-spatial organization, higher level verbal abilities, rote learning, contextual learning, and problem-solving. Additional follow-up assessments at the time of transition to middle school, secondary school, and adult care are also helpful for developmental tracking and updating of recommendations.

After childhood stroke, a baseline neuropsychological assessment at 6–8 months poststroke is optimal, in line with recommendations for those with adult stroke. In the first days, weeks, and months poststroke, recovery is rapid and functioning fluctuates significantly on a daily basis. Inpatient screening may be appropriate in some cases to target specific cognitive abilities in question or to address pressing questions regarding rehabilitation planning or patient safety. However, neuropsychological assessment carried out in the early stages of recovery must be interpreted cautiously, because performance may have limited predictive validity. After the initial baseline assessment, additional follow-ups at transition points are also recommended. Little is known about very-long-term neuropsychological outcomes of pediatric stroke survivors into adulthood, but there is some evidence that functional outcome at 1-year poststroke

as assessed by the Pediatric Stroke Outcome Measure (Kitchen et al., 2012) remains stable into the early 20s (Elbers, deVeber, Pontigon, & Moharir, 2013). In a study of 26 young adults with a history of pediatric stroke (mean age = 21 years), Elbers and colleagues found that approximately three-quarters of the sample reported independence with driving, relationships and employment, but one-quarter also reported significant mental health issues. Long-term neuropsychological follow-up into adulthood is ideal because it can assist with postsecondary education planning, access to academic accommodations, access to disability funding and community resources, and screening for significant mental health concerns.

Comprehensive evaluation of attention, working memory, executive function, verbal learning, and memory is essential for children of school age because deficits in these skills are common in the pediatric stroke population, regardless of lesion location, size, and age at stroke. In addition, a thorough understanding of an individual's information processing strengths and challenges can inform educational strategies and interventions. Integrative skills such as visual-motor ability, problem-solving, and deductive reasoning are also often affected after pediatric stroke, perhaps because these high-level skills are mediated by complex and widespread brain networks.

Poststroke cognitive impairment and dementia are common in adult populations, with 50–90% of stroke survivors showing some cognitive impairment within 3 months of stroke and approximately one-third developing dementia by 3 years poststroke. The two most common cognitive deficits after stroke are aphasia and hemispatial neglect (Gottesman & Hillis, 2010). As in pediatric populations, the goals of neuropsychological assessment in poststroke adults are most often to assist with diagnosis, to explain functional capacity, and, in the months after stroke, to assist with rehabilitation. As in pediatric assessment, a flexible protocol that assesses all primary cognitive areas (attention, executive functions, processing speed, language skills, visuospatial skills, new learning, memory, personality/behavior) is required, with additional or substitute tests added as needed, for patients who present with variable performance on first-line assessment, and/or challenges (e.g., cortical blindness, hemiparesis, expressive aphasia) presented by specific patients. Also, as in pediatric assessments, formal cognitive assessment is but one of many tools used by the clinician; to provide context for test data, one must interview the patient and family members and review medical and (sometimes) occupational information, and one must integrate observed behavior with other information sources.

Of course, there are differences in practice patterns of pediatric and adult neuropsychological services for patients with stroke. Some assessment questions encountered almost uniquely by adult practitioners include decisional capacity evaluations during the acute or subacute recovery phase (e.g., if a stroke patient with significant cognitive impairment wishes to return home against medical advice), work capacity evaluations in patients who wish to return to work, and disability assessments of patients who do not believe themselves capable of returning to work. This may require additional test strategies (e.g., greater use of performance validity measures, the use of formal capacity measures) not often used during pediatric assessments. On the other hand, there may be less need for extensive intellectual or academic testing with many adult patients with stroke.

As in all neuropsychological assessments, it is important to sample each of the primary cognitive domains. However, two domains deserve special mention because of their prominence in VCI research. The first are executive functions, which are viewed as a core deficit in adult and elderly persons with stroke and cerebrovascular disease. Some have suggested that executive dysfunction be a required deficit when diagnosing VCI. However, although tests of executive function are sensitive to poststroke impairment (Nyenhuis et al., 2004), they are not specific, even when comparing patients with cerebrovascular disease to an Alzheimer disease sample (Reed et al., 2007), which may limit their diagnostic utility.

The second prominent cognitive domain is memory. Memory deficits are prominent in patients with VCI, but unlike in earlier diagnostic classification systems, such as the criteria developed jointly by the National Institute of Neurological Disorders and Stroke and the Association Internationale pour la Recherche et l'Enseignement en Neurosciences, more recent systems do not require memory impairment to diagnose dementia or vascular mild cognitive impairment (Gorelick et al., 2011). The pattern of memory deficit in VCI may be qualitatively different than in patients with Alzheimer disease, in that rapid forgetting of newly learned information is not seen as often in the former as in the latter patient group. Instead, patients with stroke and cerebral vascular disease

show inefficiencies in the encoding process, perhaps secondary to attention and executive dysfunction.

It stands to reason, given the modal cognitive pattern of slowed processing, impaired executive function, and inefficient learning, that neuropsychological tests that emphasize these cognitive areas will be validated when used in patient groups with stroke and cerebrovascular disease. This has been the case. The Montreal Cognitive Assessment Test (MoCA), with its greater reliance on executive function, is more sensitive to cognitive impairment than the MMSE when used with stroke patients (Rossetti, Lacritz, Munro Cullum, & Weiner, 2011). This sensitivity, however, may come at the price of lower specificity and there may be need for greater educational corrections when using the MoCA. A modification of the MoCA that allows it to be administered by telephone has also been shown to be sensitive to stroke-related cognitive impairment (Wong, Nyenhuis, et al., 2015). In 2005, the National Institute of Neurological Disorders and Stroke teamed with the Canadian Stroke Network to produce harmonization criteria for patients with stroke and cerebrovascular disease (Hachinski et al., 2006). The neuropsychological subcommittee recommended a 60-minute, 30-minute, and 5-minute cognitive protocol to be used with patients with suspected VCI. The protocols were dominated by tests of speeded executive function. Wong and colleagues (Wong et al., 2013) showed a high degree of sensitivity in a sample of patients with stroke when compared with nonpatient controls.

There is a small but growing literature that is examining the ecological validity of measured cognitive impairment in patients after stroke in adults and the elderly. Yantz and colleagues (Yantz, Johnson-Greene, Higginson, & Emmerson, 2010) demonstrated that patients with stroke with measured neuropsychological impairment showed deficits on a standardized cooking test, and Vordenberg and colleagues (Vordenberg, Barrett, Doninger, Contardo, & Ozoude, 2014) demonstrated that the Brixton Spatial Anticipation Test was independently related to discharge functional independence measure scores in a sample of patients with ischemic stroke. On a more global functional level, neuropsychological performance within 7 days of first-ever stroke predicted discharge destination (home or dependent living) in a sample of 287 patients (Van Der Zwaluw, Valentijn, Nieuwenhuis-Mark, Rasquin, & Van Heugten, 2011), and performance on the Repeatable Battery for Assessment of

Neuropsychological Symptoms during inpatient rehabilitation for stroke predicted cognitive disability 6 months later (Larson et al., 2003). It is hoped that more research will be completed that demonstrates relationships of stroke patient neuropsychological performance with everyday life and function.

Intervention

Given the disparate risk factors associated with adult and childhood stroke, it follows that acute treatment and measures for long-term prevention are often different for children than for adults. With regard to immediate management poststroke, recombinant tissue plasminogen activator (rt-PA), commonly used in adult patients with ischemic stroke to facilitate the breakdown of blood clots, has not been tested for its safety and efficacy in children. Thus, rt-PA is generally not recommended for use in the pediatric population, especially in young children and infants. However, immediate treatment with anticoagulant drugs such as aspirin, heparin, and warfarin is considered reasonable in pediatric ischemic stroke, especially when cardiac embolus or arterial dissection is present. Notably, there is considerable variability in the immediate application of pharmaceuticals due to lack of evidence and limited drug trials in children. Medical guidelines suggest that extremely high intracranial pressure produced by hematoma can be alleviated by surgical evacuation, but its impact on outcome is unclear. The benefits of surgical intervention are more defined with progressive hydrocephalus caused by intraventricular hemorrhage, in which draining and, if indicated, later shunting is often necessary (Roach et al., 2012).

Pediatric stroke remains underrecognized within the health-care system and community organizations that provide rehabilitation. Pediatric rehabilitation services are largely allocated using the model of congenital/developmental disorders (e.g., genetic conditions, cerebral palsy), which may not adequately address the needs of children with acquired, focal lesions (Ganesan, 2013). Occupational therapy, physical therapy, and speech-language therapy make up the bulk of the intervention offered to children with stroke, but services are often discontinued or significantly reduced after the age of 5 or 6 years. For children with stroke at an older age, it can be very challenging to find appropriate longer-term intervention services akin to what is offered as standard of care to adults. Access to cognitive intervention is particularly difficult, and the financial burden is significant.

Many children with stroke receive specialized supports through the education system, including the development of an individualized education plan, access to educational technology, academic accommodations, and/or assistance from an education assistant for physical needs. However, accessing these services can be challenging for children who do not have a psychological diagnosis recognized by the education system.

There is very little research on effective interventions for children with stroke. The importance of early assessment and intervention is recognized among clinicians, but there is little empirical support to distinguish between effective and ineffective therapies. Constraint-induced therapy, whereby the strong limb is constrained for a period of weeks to promote recovery of the affected limb, is largely unique to the pediatric stroke population and has been found to improve outcomes (Gordon et al., 2007). Some newer research has also documented benefits of transcranial magnetic stimulation on motor function for children with neonatal and childhood stroke (Kirton et al., 2016). Transcranial magnetic stimulation was also found to improve expressive language ability in a recent case study of childhood left MCA stroke (Carlson et al., 2016). With respect to cognitive intervention, therapies targeting attention, working memory, processing speed, and executive function are of particular interest because these are common areas of concern in this population. The Cogmed working memory training program has received promising support in studies of children with ADHD and some preliminary support in children with stroke (Westerberg et al., 2007), but a more recent study failed to find evidence supporting its effectiveness in children with arterial ischemic stroke (Eve et al., 2016). The literature on cognitive rehabilitation after traumatic brain injury in children is more extensive and highlights the importance of considering the child's age at the time of intervention and appropriate developmental expectations (Anderson & Catroppa, 2006). For example, although early intervention is critical, some later-developing skills and abilities (e.g., executive functions) may not be amenable to remediation until the child is older. Early interventions often focus on adaptive skills and reintegration into school. Evaluating the impact of cognitive remediation in children can also be challenging because it may be difficult to distinguish between recovery due to the intervention and normal developmental gains (Anderson & Catroppa, 2006).

In adult stroke, the advent of hyperacute therapies, such as rt-PA therapy, has revolutionized ischemic stroke treatment. Stroke is now called a "brain attack" and phrases like "time is brain" emphasize that, in some patients who are able to get to treatment quickly (usually within a 4-hour time window), cerebral vessels may be reopened, emboli that block vessels may be reduced, and blood flow restored. Broome and colleagues (Broome, Battle, Lawrence, Evans, & Dennis, 2016) completed a recent review of three studies that examined cognitive outcomes after thrombolytic therapy. They noted the nascent character of this literature, which detracts from extrapolation of results across studies. Overall, they found that therapeutic cognitive outcomes were modest and inconsistent, especially when studied over longer periods, such as 6 months. They emphasize the need for future large-scale studies with primary cognitive outcomes. Of note, a few other studies have examined whether persons with prestroke dementia or significant cognitive impairment should be given rt-PA treatment. A recent review (Paciaroni & Pantoni, 2016) concluded that this decision should be made on an individual basis, with consideration given to such factors as prestroke disability level, dementia severity, and possible increased risk of hemorrhage due to leukoaraiosis and cerebral amyloid angiopathy.

To date, pharmacotherapy for vascular dementia has been disappointing. No medications for stroke-related cognitive impairment or dementia have been approved by the Food and Drug Administration. Many of the agents under study – for example, cholinesterase inhibitors (e.g., donepezil) and N-methyl-D-aspartate agonists (e.g., memantine) – were originally developed to treat Alzheimer disease. In pivotal trials, these agents have at times shown modest cognitive effects, but inconsistent global or functional effects, when compared with placebo. Several methodological barriers to clinical trial success have been discussed, including the potential for having mixed dementia (Alzheimer disease + stroke/cerebrovascular disease) patients in the clinical samples, difficulties in assigning functional impairment to cognitive cause because of the high rate of physical disability (e.g., hemiparesis) and, in some trials, a dementia definition that required memory impairment (which increased risk of Alzheimer disease). In addition, many of the early trials suffered from cognitive outcome instruments (e.g., Alzheimer Disease Assessment Scale-Cognitive, MMSE) that had very limited executive function emphasis, which may have led to decreased sensitivity to VCI (Gorelick et al., 2011).

The risk factors for stroke, including hypertension, hypercholesterolemia, diabetes mellitus, cigarette smoking, obesity, and a sedentary lifestyle, are well known and several studies have linked midlife risk factors to later-life cognitive decline and dementia (Birns & Kalra, 2009). However, it is not possible to design multidecade clinical trials, with random assignment and treatment protocols, due to cost and complexity. Later-life clinical trials that examine risk factor control with cognitive outcomes have met with inconsistent success (Birns & Kalra, 2009). It may be that the physiologic and cognitive damage is done by late life. Also, there has been a dearth of cognitive primary outcomes for these trials; thus, if the primary endpoint (e.g., stroke) has been examined in a trial, it may stop before the secondary cognitive outcome has sufficient power to be tested. Finally, in some cases, a negative midlife risk factor may transform into a protective factor in the elderly. For example, hypertension at midlife may increase risk for stroke and cognitive impairment. However, hypertension in the elderly may be necessary to ensure proper perfusion; and lowering blood pressure in the elderly may result in cognitive decline (Gorelick et al., 2011).

The effectiveness of poststroke cognitive rehabilitation remains a controversial topic. It is beyond the scope of this overview chapter to cover this area in depth. Cicerone and colleagues have published three reviews of evidence-based cognitive rehabilitation that include patients with stroke (Cicerone et al., 2011). They conclude that, "there is substantial evidence to support interventions for attention, memory, social communications skills, executive functions, and for comprehensive-holistic neuropsychological rehabilitation after TBI [traumatic brain injury]. Evidence supports visuospatial rehabilitation after right hemisphere stroke, and interventions for aphasia and apraxia after left hemisphere stroke. ... There is now sufficient information to support evidence-based protocols and implement empirically-supported treatment for cognitive disability after TBI and stroke" (p. 519).

However, several Cochrane reviews are not supportive. For example, reviews of cognitive rehabilitation after stroke (Nair & Lincoln, 2007), for treatment of spatial neglect (Bowen, Hazelton, Pollock, & Lincoln, 2013), and for executive dysfunction in adults with nonprogressive acquired brain damage, including stroke (Chung, Pollock, Campbell, Durward, & Hagen, 2013), all concluded that there was insufficient evidence for effectiveness of cognitive treatment for cognitive-based disorders. Reasons cited include the lack of high-quality clinical trials that include randomized assignment, adequate control groups, and consistent, high-quality outcome measures. In another recent review, Cumming et al. (2013) noted that the lack of a consistent pattern of cognitive impairment after stroke is another complicating factor that inhibits the study of this area. They also noted that more progress is apparent in the rehabilitation of focally based cognitive deficits than in cognitive treatment of deficits that are related to more diffuse neuropathology.

Implications for Clinical Practice

Neuropsychologists working with children who have a history of stroke must keep in mind several unique considerations. First, up-to-date knowledge of the research literature on the complex interactions among brain, child, and environmental factors and their impact of long-term neuropsychological outcome is essential. Brain–behavior relationships evolve over the course of development, and assessment data must be interpreted in the context of these changing dynamics. Second, it is important for the clinician to recognize that the impact of an early focal lesion will unfold and evolve gradually over time, and to help parents make the connection between their child's current struggles and the remote brain injury. However, with this understanding should also come the recognition that parents, educators, and other professionals have the capacity to alter the child's trajectory with tailored treatments, interventions, and styles of interaction. Longitudinal follow-up assessments are also critical in pediatric stroke, given that the richness and subtlety of a child's cognitive profile may not become clear until higher-level skills have started to develop. It is important for the neuropsychologist to distinguish between the recovery and relearning of lost skills versus the acquisition of new skills, and to explain to families and educators why the latter may be particularly difficult for the child with stroke (Dennis et al., 2014). Third, many children with stroke have focal motor deficits that must be accommodated during the assessment and taken into consideration when interpreting findings. A stroke affecting the dominant hand often results in switched hand dominance, which clearly affects educational needs. Development of secondary dystonia after basal ganglia stroke in childhood is also common, and there is evidence to suggest additional intellectual, academic, and inhibitory control deficits in

this subgroup of children (Westmacott et al., 2017). Fourth, pediatric stroke remains underrecognized and poorly understood within the general population, and even within some health-care settings. The neuropsychologist must assist in educating family members and educators about the impact of stroke on the developing brain, and must advocate for access to services within the education system and the broader community. Although many children do meet criteria for well-known psychological diagnoses (e.g., learning disorder/disability, ADHD, intellectual disability), often their needs cannot be understood entirely in the context of these labels. Furthermore, many children present with clear neurocognitive deficits but do not meet criteria for any specific psychological diagnosis. Helping parents and educators appreciate how the early stroke has affected systems in the child's brain that mediate cognitive, academic, motor, attention, and/or social development is critical for tailoring recommendations and setting appropriate expectations. This task can be particularly challenging in the case of a child with stroke who has no focal motor or sensory deficits. These children appear to be typically developing and it may not be until they are asked to cope with heavy academic, social, or emotional demands that challenges with attention, working memory, problem-solving, verbal fluency, learning, or memory retrieval become apparent. Finally, the transition to adult care can be challenging and overwhelming for patients and families. In the case of those with pediatric stroke, it may be difficult to find an adult neurologist with experience working with young people affected by stroke. Pediatric stroke and adult stroke differ tremendously in terms of etiology, associated medical issues, and outcome, and the young adult with a history of pediatric stroke may feel quite out of place in an adult neurology setting. Table 13.4 outlines important considerations for clinicians working with stroke populations.

Similar comments can be made for adult evaluations. One must keep in mind that neuropsychologists are not testing a stroke, they are assessing the effects of a stroke on a person. With this in mind, the clinician first needs to establish the context of the patient by interviewing the patient and his or her family and/or friends. The more specific contextual information that is known about topics such as prestroke education, occupation, behavior/psychiatric disorders, personality features, quality of relationships, substance use/abuse, potential legal situations, potential

Table 13.4 Unique Considerations for Clinicians Working with Stroke Populations

Principles and Considerations	Explanations and Examples
Evolving brain–behavior relationships	Age at the time of injury will impact neuropsychological outcome.
Emerging deficits over time	Children may grow into deficits as they are expected to achieve new developmental milestones.
Focal motor deficits and switched handedness	Testing accommodations are frequently required and test scores must be interpreted cautiously.
Lack of public awareness and understanding of pediatric stroke	Education of patients, families, teachers, and other professionals is critical.
Traditional psychological diagnoses may not apply or fully capture a child's neurocognitive profile	For instance, multiple areas of neurocognitive impairment may lower scores on tests of intelligence without being equivalent to an intellectual disability.
Transition to adult care can be challenging	Individuals with a history of neonatal or childhood stroke have very different needs and issues than those with adult-onset stroke.
Consider nonstroke factors affecting neuropsychological outcome	Genetic influences, family history, school experiences and opportunities, cultural differences, and individual differences have a tremendous impact on outcome. The impact of the acquired brain injury depends on complex interactions with these other factors.
Two-step process for cognitive assessment	Step 1: A complete examination of focal cognitive features (e.g., language impairment after cerebrovascular accident involving the language zone.
	Step 2: An assessment of remaining cognitive domains that minimizes the impact of the focal cognitive impairment.
Assessment of functional impairment	Differentiating between cognitive and motor/sensory impact on activities of daily living.
Assessment of depression	Ascertain that depression symptoms include mood symptoms (e.g., sadness, diminished self-worth), not just vegetative symptoms (e.g., fatigue, apathy, attention difficulties), which may due to medical/neurological aspects of stroke rather than psychological symptoms.

disability applications, and social support, the more helpful and accurate the resulting report will be to the referent, the patient, and the patient's family.

Patients with stroke may bring special cognitive, functional, and psychological challenges for the clinician. A common cognitive challenge when completing neuropsychological testing with a patient who has experienced a stroke is how best to deal with focal cognitive deficits. A two-step assessment approach may be useful. The goal of the first step is to discover as much as possible about the focal deficit. For example, if the patient experienced a left MCA ischemic stroke, she may be left with significant language disturbance. For this patient, in the first step, the clinician's goal is to characterize all areas of language, such as spoken expression, auditory comprehension, reading output and comprehension, repetition skill, confrontation naming skill, and phonemic and semantic fluency.

Once the first step is complete, the goal of the second step is to evaluate the other primary cognitive areas. In this step, the clinician wishes to keep the effects of the focal deficit to a minimum, knowing that (especially in the case of language) it is not possible to do this absolutely. An example of this is to use a recognition format for assessing vocabulary (e.g., Peabody Picture Vocabulary Test) with a patient with an expressive aphasia rather than a test that requires a narrative explanation. A recognition format may also be used when assessing spatial reasoning skills (e.g., with the Wechsler Abbreviated Scale of Intelligence, 2nd ed., Matrix Reasoning), and memory skills (e.g., with the Continuous Visual Memory Test or the Neuropsychological Assessment Battery Shape Learning Test).

A functional challenge when assessing patients who have experienced a stroke is determining whether functional deficits are due to physical or cognitive difficulties. Such a determination is important when determining the presence of dementia. One technique that may be helpful is to modify the instructions of a functional instrument, such as the Activities of Daily Living Questionnaire. Request that the friend or family member label items (e.g., bathing) assigned with impairment with a "P" if the impairment is due to physical limitations, a "T" if it is due to thinking/cognitive difficulties, or a "P" and a "T" if both physical and cognitive limitations contribute to the deficit. After they complete this task, review the questionnaire with them to find out more information about the reasoning behind their choices. The Disability Assessment for Dementia (Gélinas, Gauthier, McIntyre, & Gauthier, 1999) does something similar. It is an activities of daily living scale that incorporates not only the physical act, but also scores initiation and planning, thus taking into account cognitive factors for performing physical acts.

Finally, a psychological challenge when examining patients with stroke is how best to measure depressive symptoms. Depression is the most common psychiatric disturbance after stroke in adults and the elderly, with upwards of one-third of patients with stroke experiencing depression in the months after the stroke event. Vascular contribution to late-life depression is an important topic of study, and medication such as serotonin reuptake inhibitors has been shown to be effective in treating stroke-related depression. For these reasons it is important to examine the presence and severity of depression in patients with stroke. Self-report screening instruments, such as the Beck Depression Inventory or the Geriatric Depression Scale, cannot diagnose depression, but do provide a time-efficient means of collecting important mood-related data. However, when using such a scale, one must be careful to not overdiagnose depression by including vegetative items which may be more related to the person's physical/cognitive deficits instead of their mood disturbance. Scales such as the Chicago Multiscale Depression Inventory (Nyenhuis et al., 1998), which categorize depression symptoms into mood, cognitive, and vegetative items, can be used to ensure that a mood disturbance is present when diagnosing depression in patients with stroke.

Future Directions

Neuropsychological outcome after pediatric stroke is very heterogeneous due to variability in factors related to the child, the brain, and the environment. Future research should focus on understanding the complex interactions among these factors in determining outcomes across a range of neuropsychological domains. More work examining long-term outcome (into adolescence and adulthood) and developmental trajectories over time is needed, and attention should be paid to identifying specific risk factors (e.g., seizure disorders, maladaptive patterns of reorganization) and protective factors (e.g., parent mental health, educational support, access to early intervention) that can be modified to optimize outcomes. Many studies to date have produced inconclusive or conflicting results because they are statistically underpowered. Efforts should be made to promote collaborative, multisite, international studies that can maximize sample sizes. Finally, functional neuroimaging promises to provide further insight into individual responses to early stroke, which may be adaptive or maladaptive for long-term neuropsychological outcome.

Research investigations into the etiology of post-stroke cognitive impairment in adults has been impeded by several barriers, including reliable, in vivo indicators of Alzheimer disease, which may co-occur with vascular pathology in many patients with stroke, especially in the very old; the lack of a uniform, common classification system to diagnose poststroke cognitive impairment; and a dearth of studies examining the effect of preexisting CSVD on cognitive outcomes after large vessel infarction. However, progress is being made on each of these three fronts. Liu and colleagues (Liu et al., 2015) have completed a longitudinal study of cognitive decline after stroke or transient ischemic attack. They divided their patient sample, based on the presence or absence of amyloid beta, as measured by carbon 11-labeled Pittsburgh Compound B positron emission tomography. They found that patients with stroke with amyloid beta, a marker of Alzheimer disease, declined significantly more on the MMSE than did patients without evidence of Alzheimer disease during the 3-year trial. These results showed the significance of having a "pure" vascular sample. Future clinical trials and epidemiological study of patients with stroke may be able to use this technique to increase confidence that Alzheimer disease is not lurking in the background of what purports to be a pure stroke group.

In regard to the second problem, Gorelick et al., (2011) updated criteria for vascular dementia and

Table 13.5 Classification of Vascular Cognitive Impairment in Adults

Domain	Description
Probable vascular dementia	Generalized cognitive impairment causing disruption of activities of daily living; imaging evidence of cerebrovascular disease; and either: (a) a clear temporal relationship between a vascular event and cognitive impairment; or (b) a clear relationship in the severity and pattern of cognitive impairment and diffuse, subcortical cerebrovascular disease. No history of gradually progressive cognitive deficits before or after the stroke.
Possible vascular dementia	Generalized cognitive impairment causing disruption of activities of daily living; but no clear relationship between cognitive impairment and cerebrovascular disease; or no imaging (CT or MRI) is available; or severity of aphasia precludes a proper cognitive assessment; or there is evidence of other neurodegenerative diseases or conditions.
Probable vascular MCI	As probable vascular dementia above, but no significant decline in activities of daily living, independent of motor or sensory deficits. Also, cognitive impairment may be limited to a single cognitive area (e.g., memory skills).
Possible vascular MCI	As possible vascular dementia above, but no significant decline in activities of daily living, independent of motor or sensory deficits. Cognitive impairment may be limited to a single cognitive area (e.g., memory skills).
Unstable vascular MCI	Persons who meet criteria for either probable or possible vascular MCI, but whose symptoms revert to normal.

Note. MCI = mild cognitive impairment; CT, computed tomography; MRI = magnetic resonance imaging.
Adapted from "Vascular Contributions to Cognitive Impairment and Dementia: A Statement for Healthcare Professionals from the American Heart Association/American Stroke Association," by P. B. Gorelick, A. Scuteri, S. E. Black, C. Decarli, S. M. Greenberg, C. Iadecola, … S. Seshadri, 2011, *Stroke, 42*, p. 2672.

vascular mild cognitive impairment (see Table 13.5). In addition, a group of VCI investigators are developing VCI criteria using a consensus-based approach that required a 67% threshold for criteria agreement. These new standardized terminologies will be useful in future investigations. Finally, in regard to the third problem, Wong and associates (Wong, Wang et al., 2015) recently demonstrated that white matter hyperintensity volume and atrophy significantly affected cognitive function in patients with stroke. This investigation demonstrated the need to understand both acute and chronic and both focal and diffuse neurovascular processes when attempting to understand poststroke cognitive function. Findings such as this can lay a foundation for future investigation, with the goal being a more complete understanding of patients with stroke. It is hoped that this improved understanding will lead to improved treatment and cognitive outcomes for persons with stroke.

In conclusion, the neuropsychological impact of stroke varies tremendously according to the age at which it was sustained. The increased plasticity of the young brain does not necessarily protect against negative effects of a very early stroke. Deficits in intellectual ability, academic achievement, attention, language processing, visual-spatial ability, learning, and executive function are common after perinatal and childhood stroke, with complex interactions among many factors determining outcome. Focal stroke in adults is associated with both specific cognitive deficits that correlate more predictably with the affected brain regions and the more diffuse effects of CSVD and degenerative conditions. Adopting a lifespan approach to the study of neuropsychological outcome after stroke will further inform models of neuroplasticity, neurodevelopment, and neurodegeneration.

References

Allman, C., & Scott, R. B. (2013). Neuropsychological sequelae following pediatric stroke: A nonlinear model of age at lesion effects. *Child Neuropsychology, 19*(1), 97–107.

Amlie-Lefond, C., Bernard, T. J., Sébire, G., Friedman, N. R., Heyer, G. L., Lerner, N. B., ... Fullerton, H. J. (2009). Predictors of cerebral arteriopathy in children with arterial ischemic stroke: Results of the international pediatric stroke study. *Circulation, 119*(10), 1417–1423.

Anderson, V., & Catroppa, C. (2006). Advances in postacute rehabilitation after childhood-acquired brain injury: A focus on cognitive, behavioral, and social domains. *American Journal of Physical Medicine & Rehablitationi, 85* (9), 767–778.

Baigent, C., Blackwell, L., Collins, R., Emberson, J., Godwin, J., Peto, R., ... Zanchetti, A. (2009). Aspirin in the primary and secondary prevention of vascular disease: Collaborative meta-analysis of individual participant data from randomised trials. *The Lancet, 373*(9678), 1849–60.

Ballantyne, A. O., Spilkin, A. M., Hesselink, J., & Trauner, D. A. (2008). Plasticity in the developing brain: Intellectual, language and academic functions in children with ischaemic perinatal stroke. *Brain, 131*(11), 2975–2985.

Barbe, F., Durán-Cantolla, J., Sánchez-de-la-Torre, M., Martinez-Alonso, M., Carmona, C., Barceló, A., ... Montserrat, J. M. (2012). Effect of continuous positive airway pressure on the incidence of hypertension and cardiovascular events in nonsleepy patients with obstructive sleep apnea: A randomized controlled trial. *Journal of the American Medical Association, 307*(20), 2161–2168.

Beckett, N. S., Peters, R., Fletcher, A. E., Staessen, J. A., Liu, L., Dumitrascu, D., ... HYVET Study Group. (2008). Treatment of hypertension in patients 80 years of age or older. *The New England Journal of Medicine, 358*(18), 1887–1898.

Birns, J., & Kalra, L. (2009). Cognitive function and hypertension. *Journal of Human Hypertension, 23*(2), 86–96.

Black, S., Gao, F., & Bilbao, J. (2009). Understanding white matter disease: Imaging-pathological correlations in vascular cognitive impairment. *Stroke, 40*, S48–52.

Bowen, A., Hazelton, C., Pollock, A., & Lincoln, N. B. (2013). Cognitive rehabilitation for spatial neglect following stroke. *The Cochrane Database of Systematic Reviews, 7*, CD003586.

Broome, L. J., Battle, C. E., Lawrence, M., Evans, P. A., & Dennis, M. S. (2016). Cognitive outcomes following thrombolysis in acute ischemic stroke: A systematic review. *Journal of Stroke and Cerebrovascular Diseases, 25*, 2868–2875.

Buitrago-Lopez, A., Sanderson, J., Johnson, L., Warnakula, S., Wood, A., Di Angelantonio, E., & Franco, O. H. (2011). Chocolate consumption and cardiometabolic disorders: Systematic review and meta-analysis. *BMJ (Clinical Research Ed.), 343*, d4488.

Cardenas, J.F., Rho, J.M., & Kirton, A. (2011). Pediatric stroke. *Child's Nervous System, 27*(9), 1375–1390.

Carlson, H., Jadavji, Z., Mineyko, A., Damji, O., Hodge, J., Saunders, J., ... Kirton, A. (2016). Treatment of dysphasia with rTMS and language therapy after childhood stroke: Multimodal imaging of plastic change. *Brain and Language, 159*, 23–34.

Chiuve, S. E., Rexrode, K. M., Spiegelman, D., Logroscino, G., Manson, J. E., & Rimm, E. B. (2008). Primary prevention of stroke by healthy lifestyle. *Circulation, 118*(9), 947–954.

Chung, C., Pollock, A., Campbell, T., Durward, B., & Hagen, S. (2013). Cognitive rehabilitation for executive dysfunction in adults with stroke or other adult nonprogressive acquired brain damage. *Stroke*. http://doi.org/10.1161/STROKEAHA.113.002049

Cicerone, K. D., Langenbahn, D. M., Braden, C., Malec, J. F., Kalmar, K., Fraas, M., ... Ashman, T. (2011). Evidence-based cognitive rehabilitation: Updated review of the literature from 2003 through 2008. *Archives of Physical Medicine and Rehabilitation, 5*, 519–530.

Coker, S. B., Beltran, R. S., Myers, T. F., & Hmura, L. (1988). Neonatal stroke: Description of patients and investigation into pathogenesis. *Pediatric Neurology, 4*(4), 219–223.

Cumming, T. B., Marshall R. S., & Lazar, R. M. (2013). Stroke, cognitive deficits, and rehabilitation: Still an incomplete picture. *International Journal of Stroke, 8*(1), 38–45.

Dennis, M., Spiegler, B. J., Simic, N., Sinopoli, K. J., Wilkinson, A., Yeates, K. O., ... Fletcher, J. M. (2014). Functional plasticity in childhood brain disorders: When, what, how, and whom to assess. *Neuropsychology Review, 24*, 389–408.

Elbers, J., deVeber, G., Pontigon, A.-M., & Moharir, M. (2013). Long-term outcomes of pediatric ischemic stroke in adulthood. *Journal of Child Neurology, 29*(6), 782–788.

Eve, M., O'Keeffe, F., Jhuty, S., Ganesan, V., Brown, G., & Murphy, T. (2016). Computerized working-memory training for children following arterial ischemic stroke: A pilot study with long-term follow-up. *Applied Neuropsychology. Child, 2965*(May), 1–10.

Everts, R., Lidzba, K., Wilke, M., Kiefer, C., Wingeier, K., Schroth, G., ... Steinlin, M. (2010). Lateralization of cognitive functions after stroke in childhood. *Brain Injury, 24*(6), 859–870.

Everts, R., Pavlovic, J., Kaufmann, F., Uhlenberg, B., Seidel, U., Nedeltchev, K., ... Steinlin, M. (2008). Cognitive functioning, behavior, and quality of life after stroke in childhood. *Child Neuropsychology, 14*(4), 323–338.

Fuentes, A., Deotto, A. A., Desrocher, M. M., deVeber, G., & Westmacott, R. R. (2014). Determinants of cognitive outcomes of perinatal and childhood stroke: A review. *Child Neuropsychology, 22*(November), 37–41.

Fuentes, A., Westmacott, R., Deotto, A., DeVeber, G., & Desrocher, M. (2016). Working memory outcomes following unilateral arterial ischemic stroke in childhood. *Child Neuropsychology*, *18*, 1–19.

Ganesan, V. (2013). Outcome and rehabilitation after childhood stroke. *Handbook of Clinical Neurology*, *112*, 1079–1083.

Gélinas, I., Gauthier, L., McIntyre, M., & Gauthier, S. (1999). Development of a functional measure for persons with Alzheimer's disease: The disability assessment for dementia. *American Journal of Occupational Therapy*, *53*(5), 471–481.

Golomb, M. R., Fullerton, H. J., Nowak-Gottl, U., & Deveber, G. (2009). Male predominance in childhood ischemic stroke: Findings from the international pediatric stroke study. *Stroke*, *40*(1), 52–57.

Gordon, A., Connelly, A., Neville, B., Vargha-Khadem, F., Jessop, N., Murphy, T., & Ganesan, V. (2007). Modified constraint-induced movement therapy after childhood stroke. *Developmental Medicine and Child Neurology*, *49*, 23–27.

Gorelick, P. B., Scuteri, A., Black, S. E., Decarli, C., Greenberg, S. M., Iadecola, C., … Seshadri, S. (2011). Vascular contributions to cognitive impairment and dementia: A statement for healthcare professionals from the American Heart Association/American Stroke Association. *Stroke*, *42*, 2672–2713.

Gottesman, R. F., & Hillis, A. E. (2010). Predictors and assessment of cognitive dysfunction resulting from ischaemic stroke. *The Lancet Neurology*, *9*, 895–905.

Greenham, M., Hearps, S., Gomes, A., Rinehart, N., Gonzalez, L., Gordon, A., … Anderson, V. (2015). Environmental contributions to social and mental health outcomes following pediatric stroke. *Developmental Neuropsychology*, *40*(6), 348–362.

Hachinski, V. (1983). Multi-infarct dementia. *Neurologic Clinics*, *1*(0733-8619), 27–36.

Hachinski, V., Iadecola, C., Petersen, R. C., Breteler, M. M., Nyenhuis, D. L., Black, S. E., … Leblanc, G. G. (2006). National Institute of Neurological Disorders and Stroke-Canadian Stroke Network vascular cognitive impairment harmonization standards. *Stroke*, *37*(9), 2220–2241.

Hajek, C. A., Yeates, K. O., Anderson, V., Mackay, M., Greenham, M., Gomes, A., & Lo, W. (2013). Cognitive outcomes following arterial ischemic stroke in infants and children. *Journal of Child Neurology*, *29*(7), 887–894.

Hart, R. G., Benavente, O., McBride, R., & Pearce, LA. (1999). Antithrombotic therapy to prevent stroke in patients with atrial fibrillation: A meta-analysis. *Annals of Internal Medicine*, *131*, 492–501.

Hebert, D., Lindsay, M. P., McIntyre, A., Kirton, A., Rumney, P. G., Bagg, S., … Teasell, R. (2016). Canadian stroke best practice recommendations: Stroke rehabilitation practice guidelines, update 2015. *International Journal of Stroke*, *11*(4), 459–484.

Institute of Medicine of the National Academies. (2013). Sodium Intake in Populations. *Advising the Nation Improving Health*.

Jacomb, I., Porter, M., Brunsdon, R., Mandalis, A., & Parry, L. (2016). Cognitive outcomes of pediatric stroke. *Child Neuropsychology*, *14*, 1–17.

Kirton, A., Andersen, J., Herrero, M., Nettel-Aguirre, A., Carsolio, L., Damji, O., … Hill, M. D. (2016). Brain stimulation and constraint for perinatal stroke hemiparesis. *Neurology*, *86*(18), 1659–1667.

Kirton, A., & deVeber, G. (2009). Advances in perinatal ischemic stroke. *Pediatric Neurology*, *40*(3), 205–214.

Kirton, A., Westmacott, R., & deVeber, G. (2007). Pediatric stroke: Rehabilitation of focal injury in the developing brain. *NeuroRehabilitation*, *22*(5), 371–82.

Kitchen, L., Westmacott, R., Friefeld, S., MacGregor, D., Curtis, R., Allen, A., … deVeber, G. (2012). The pediatric stroke outcome measure: A validation and reliability study. *Stroke*, *43*(6), 1602–1608.

Kulshreshtha, A., Vaccarino, V., Judd, S. E., Howard, V. J., McClellan, W. M., Muntner, P., … Cushman, M. (2013). Life's simple 7 and risk of incident stroke: The reasons for geographic and racial differences in stroke study. *Stroke*, *44*(7), 1909–1914.

Larson, E. B., Kirschner, K., Bode, R. K., Heinemann, A. W., Clorfene, J., & Goodman, R. (2003). Brief cognitive assessment and prediction of functional outcome in stroke. *Topics in Stroke Rehabilitation*, *9*(4), 10–21.

Larsson, S. C., & Orsini, N. (2011). Coffee consumption and risk of stroke: A dose-response meta-analysis of prospective studies. *American Journal of Epidemiology*, *174*, 993–1001.

Larsson, S. C., Virtamo, J., & Wolk, A. (2011). Fish consumption and risk of stroke in Swedish women. *The American Journal of Clinical Nutrition*, *93*(3), 487–493.

Launer, L. J., Hughes, T. M., & White, L. R. (2011). Microinfarcts, brain atrophy, and cognitive function: The Honolulu Asia Aging Study Autopsy Study. *Annals of Neurology*, *70*(5), 774–780.

Lee, C. D., Folsom, A. R., & Blair, S. N. (2003). Physical activity and stroke risk: A meta-analysis. *Stroke: A Journal of Cerebral Circulation*, *34*(10), 2475–2481.

Liu, W., Wong, A., Au, L., Yang, J., Wang, Z., Leung, E. Y. L., … Mok, V. C. T. (2015). Influence of amyloid-beta on cognitive decline after stroke/transient ischemic attack: Three-year longitudinal study. *Stroke*, *46*, 3074–3080.

Lloyd-Jones, D., Adams, R., Carnethon, M., De Simone, G., Ferguson, T. B., Flegal, K., … Hong, Y. (2009). Heart disease and stroke statistics 2009 update: A report from the

American Heart Association Statistics Committee and Stroke Statistics Subcommittee. *Circulation, 119*(3), 410–528.

Long, B., Spencer-Smith, M. M., Jacobs, R., Mackay, M., Leventer, R., Barnes, C., & Anderson, V. (2011). Executive function following child stroke: the impact of lesion location. *Journal of Child Neurology, 26*(3), 279–287.

Max, J. E., Mathews, K., Manes, F. F., Robertson, B. A., Fox, P. T., Lancaster, J. L., ... Collings, N. (2003). Attention deficit hyperactivity disorder and neurocognitive correlates after childhood stroke. *Journal of the International Neuropsychological Society, 9*(6), 815–29.

Micha, R., Wallace, S. K., & Mozaffarian, D. (2010). Red and processed meat consumption and risk of incident coronary heart disease, stroke, and diabetes: A systematic review and meta-analysis. *Circulation, 121*(21), 2271–2283.

Mortimer, J. A. (2012). The nun study: Risk factors for pathology and clinical-pathologic correlations. *Current Alzheimer Research, 9*(6), 621–627.

Mozaffarian, D., Benjamin, E. J., Go, A. S., Arnett, D. K., Blaha, M. J., Cushman, M., ... Turner, M. B. (2016). Heart disease and stroke statistics—2016 update. *Circulation, 133* (4), e38–e360.

Mungas, D., Jagust, W. J., Reed, B. R., Kramer, J. H., Weiner, M. W., Schuff, N., ... Chui, H. C. (2001). MRI predictors of cognition in subcortical ischemic vascular disease and Alzheimer's disease. *Neurology, 57*(12), 2229–35.

Nair, R. D., & Lincoln, N. B. (2007). Cognitive rehabilitation for memory deficits following stroke. *Cochrane Database of Systematic Reviews (Online)*, (3), CD002293.

Neuner, B., von Mackensen, S., Holzhauer, S., Funk, S., Klamroth, R., Kurnik, K., ... Nowak-Göttl, U. (2016). Health-related quality of life in children and adolescents with hereditary bleeding disorders and in children and adolescents with stroke: Cross-sectional comparison to siblings and peers. *BioMed Research International, 2016* (group 1), 1–8.

Nyenhuis, D. L., Gorelick, P. B., Geenen, E. J., Smith, C. A., Gencheva, E., Freels, S., & DeToledo-Morrell, L. (2004). The pattern of neuropsychological deficits in vascular cognitive impairment-no dementia (vascular CIND). *The Clinical Neuropsychologist, 18*(1), 41–49.

Nyenhuis, D. L., Luchetta, T., Yamamoto, C., Terrien, A., Bernardin, L., Rao, S. M., & Garron, D. C. (1998). The development, standardization, and initial validation of the Chicago Multiscale Depression Inventory. *Journal of Personality Assessment, 70*(2), 386–401.

O'Donnell, M. J., Chin, S. L., Rangarajan, S., Xavier, D., Liu, L., Zhang, H., ... Yusuf, S. (2016). Global and regional effects of potentially modifiable risk factors associated with acute stroke in 32 countries (INTERSTROKE): A case-control study. *The Lancet, 388*(10046), 761–775.

O'Donnell, M. J., Denis, X., Liu, L., Zhang, H., Chin, S. L., Rao-Melacini, P., ... Yusuf, S. (2010). Risk factors for ischaemic and intracerebral haemorrhagic stroke in 22 countries (the INTERSTROKE study): A case-control study. *The Lancet, 376*(9735), 112–123.

Paciaroni, M., & Pantoni, L. (2016). Thrombolysis in dementia patients with acute stroke: is it justified? *Neurological Sciences*, advanced e-publication, 1–5.

Pantoni, L. (2010). Cerebral small vessel disease: From pathogenesis and clinical characteristics to therapeutic challenges. *The Lancet Neurology, 9*, 689–701.

Patel, B., Lawrence, A. J., Chung, A. W., Rich, P., Mackinnon, A. D., Morris, R. G., ... Markus, H. S. (2013). Cerebral microbleeds and cognition in patients with symptomatic small vessel disease. *Stroke; a Journal of Cerebral Circulation, 44*(2), 356–361.

Raja Beharelle, A., Dick, A. S., Josse, G., Solodkin, A., Huttenlocher, P. R., Levine, S. C., & Small, S. L. (2010). Left hemisphere regions are critical for language in the face of early left focal brain injury. *Brain, 133*(6), 1707–1716.

Reed, B. R., Mungas, D. M., Kramer, J. H., Ellis, W., Vinters, H. V., Zarow, C., ... Chui, H. C. (2007). Profiles of neuropsychological impairment in autopsy-defined Alzheimer's disease and cerebrovascular disease. *Brain, 130* (3), 731–739.

Reilly, J. S., Wasserman, S., & Appelbaum, M. (2013). Later language development narratives children with perinatal stroke. *Developmental Science, 16*(1), 67–83.

Riel-Romero, R. M. S., Kalra, A. A., & Gonzalez-Toledo, E. (2009). Childhood and teenage stroke. *Neurological Research, 31*(8), 775–784.

Roach, E.S., Heyer, G.L., Lo, W. D. (2012). *Pediatric Stroke and Cerebrovascular Disorders* (3rd Edition). New York, NY: Demos Medical Publishing.

Roberts, S., Coppens, A., Westmacott, R., Crosbie, J., Elik, N., deVeber, G., & Williams., T. (2016). ADHD following pediatric stroke: Impact on childhood development. Abstract presented at the annual meeting of the American Academy of Clinical Neuropsychology.

Ropper, A. H., Samuels, M. A., & Klein, J. P. (Eds.) (2014). *Adams and Victor's Principles of neurology*. New York, NY: McGraw-Hill.

Rossetti, H. C., Lacritz, L. H., Munro Cullum, C., & Weiner, M. F. (2011). Normative data for the Montreal Cognitive Assessment (MoCA) in a population-based sample. *Neurology, 77*(13), 1272–1275.

Stebbins, G. T., Nyenhuis, D. L., Wang, C., Cox, J. L., Freels, S., Bangen, K., ... Gorelick, P. B. (2008). Gray matter atrophy in patients with ischemic stroke with cognitive impairment. *Stroke, 39*(3), 785–793.

Stiles, J., Stern, C., Appelbaum, M., Nass, R., Trauner, D., & Hesselink, J. (2008). Effects of early focal brain injury on memory for visuospatial patterns: Selective deficits of global-local processing. *Neuropsychology*, *22*(1), 61–73.

Studer, M., Boltshauser, E., Datta, A., Fluss, J., Mercati, D., Hackenberg, A., … Wehrli, E. (2014). Factors affecting cognitive outcome in early pediatric stroke. *Neurology*, *82*, 784–792.

Swartz, R. H., Sahlas, D. J., & Black, S. E. (2003). Strategic involvement of cholinergic pathways and executive dysfunction: Does location of white matter signal hyperintensities matter? *Journal of Stroke and Cerebrovascular Diseases*, *12*(1), 29–36.

Swartz, R. H., Stuss, D. T., Gao, F., & Black, S. E. (2008). Independent cognitive effects of atrophy and diffuse subcortical and thalamico-cortical cerebrovascular disease in dementia. *Stroke*, *39*(3), 822–830.

Tomlinson, B. E., Blessed, G., & Roth, M. (1970). Observations on the brains of demented old people. *Journal of the Neurological Sciences*, *11*(3), 205–242.

Van Der Zwaluw, C. S., Valentijn, S. A. M., Nieuwenhuis-Mark, R., Rasquin, S. M. C., & Van Heugten, C. M. (2011). Cognitive functioning in the acute phase poststroke: A predictor of discharge destination? *Journal of Stroke and Cerebrovascular Diseases*, *20*(6), 549–555.

Vordenberg, J. A., Barrett, J. J., Doninger, N. A., Contardo, C. P., & Ozoude, K. A. (2014). Application of the Brixton Spatial Anticipation Test in stroke: Ecological validity and performance characteristics. *The Clinical Neuropsychologist*, *4046*(January 2015), 1–17.

Westerberg, H., Jacobaeus, H., Hirvikoski, T., Clevberger, P., Ostensson, M. L., Bartfai, A., & Kingberg, T. (2007). Computerized working memory training after stroke – A pilot study. *Brain Injury*, *21*, 21–29.

Westmacott, R., Askalan, R., Macgregor, D., Anderson, P., & Deveber, G. (2010). Cognitive outcome following unilateral arterial ischaemic stroke in childhood: Effects of age at stroke and lesion location. *Developmental Medicine and Child Neurology*, *52*(4), 386–393.

Westmacott, R., Macgregor, D., Askalan, R., & Deveber, G. (2009). Late emergence of cognitive deficits after unilateral neonatal stroke. *Stroke*, *40*(6), 2012–2019.

Westmacott, R., McDonald, K., deVeber, G., MacGregor, D., Moharir, M., Dlamini, N., Askalan, R., & Williams, T. (2017). Neurocognitive outcomes in children with unilateral basal ganglia arterial ischemic stroke and secondary hemi-dystonia. *Child Neuropsychology* (Jul 12), 1–15. doi: 10.1080/09297049.2017.1353073 [Epub ahead of print].

Williams, T., McDonald, K. P., Roberts, S., Dlamini, N., & Westmacott, R. (2017). Prevalence and predictors of learning and psychological diagnoses following pediatric arterial ischemic stroke. *Developmental Neuropsychology*, (*42*), 309–322.

Wong, A., Nyenhuis, D., Black, S. E., Law, L. S. N., Lo, E. S. K., Kwan, P. W. L., … Mok, V. (2015). Montreal Cognitive Assessment 5-Minute Protocol is a brief, valid, reliable, and feasible cognitive screen for telephone administration. *Stroke*, *46*(4), 1059–1064.

Wong, A., Wang, D., Black, S. E., Nyenhuis, D. L., Shi, L., Chu, W. C. W., … Mok, V. (2015). Volumetric magnetic resonance imaging correlates of the National Institute of Neurological Disorders and Stroke–Canadian Stroke Network vascular cognitive impairment neuropsychology protocols. *Journal of Clinical and Experimental Neuropsychology*, *37*(9), 1004–1012.

Wong, A., Xiong, Y. Y., Wang, D., Lin, S., Chu, W. W. C., Kwan, P. W. K., … Mok, V. (2013). The NINDS-Canadian stroke network vascular cognitive impairment neuropsychology protocols in Chinese. *Journal of Neurology Neurosurgery and Psychiatry*, *84*(5), 499–504.

Yantz, C. L., Johnson-Greene, D., Higginson, C., & Emmerson, L. (2010). Functional cooking skills and neuropsychological functioning in patients with stroke: An ecological validity study. *Neuropsychological Rehabilitation*, *20*(5), 725–738.

Zhang, Q., Zhou, Y., Gao, X., Wang, C., Zhang, S., Wang, A., … Zhao, X. (2013). Ideal cardiovascular health metrics and the risks of ischemic and intracerebral hemorrhagic stroke. *Stroke*, *44*(9), 2451–2456.

Dementia

Laura Lacritz, Heidi Rossetti, and Christian LoBue

Introduction

Dementia is a clinical syndrome that involves a variety of signs and symptoms, including the presence of cognitive impairment, which represents a change from preexisting ability levels and is accompanied by functional impairment in social, occupation, and/or daily living skills. A variety of disorders can lead to dementia, some progressive and others more static. This chapter focuses on the most common neurodegenerative disorders that cause dementia, Alzheimer disease (AD), Lewy body disease (LBD), and behavioral variant frontotemporal dementia (bvFTD). Vascular dementia or vascular cognitive impairment has typically been thought of as the second most common form of all-cause dementia/mild cognitive impairment and may be caused by stroke or vascular brain injury from a variety of causes. With stroke, cognitive changes occur suddenly and in temporal relation to the stroke. Vascular disease in the absence of overt clinical stroke can lead to either slow or stepwise progression of cognitive decline. Either presentation can be seen in isolation or in conjunction with the aforementioned dementia syndromes and may constitute a mixed dementia, with AD and vascular cognitive impairment the most common dual pathology. Neuroimaging is critical in the dementia evaluation process to rule out vascular etiologies for cognitive decline and/or identify potential modifiable risk factors that may be contributing to the cognitive impairment. This chapter focuses on the most common nonvascular dementias, although more can be found on vascular cognitive impairment in a review conducted by Smith (2017), including causes for specific forms of vascular disease such as cerebral amyloid angiopathy and cerebral autosomal-dominant arteriopathy with subcortical ischemic leukoencephalopathy.

In AD, LBD, and bvFTD, there is a prodromal stage when cognition or behavior starts to decline, but does not yet produce functional changes to fully meet criteria for a dementia. This transitional stage between normal cognition and dementia is referred to as mild cognitive impairment (MCI) (Petersen, 2011). The type of initial symptoms and pattern of cognitive impairment present at this stage can be predictive of transition to AD or other forms of dementia. For example, those with amnestic MCI (i.e., isolated memory impairment) are at high risk of progressing to AD, with an estimated conversion rate of approximately 12% per year. However, up to 20% of individuals with MCI do not progress to develop dementia and some revert to normal cognition. Analysis of longitudinal data from the National Alzheimer's Coordinating Center showed that 14% of persons with MCI reverted to normal cognition, 51% remained with MCI, and 35% progressed to dementia over a 3-year period (Pandya, Lacritz, Weiner, Deschner, & Woon, 2017). As drug intervention trials for AD increasingly target mildly impaired or even presymptomatic at-risk individuals, greater emphasis has been placed on early diagnosis and incorporation of biomarkers in making more definitive diagnoses, although definite diagnoses of the dementias that are discussed in this chapter can only be made postmortem.

In the most recent *Diagnostic and Statistical Manual of Mental Disorders* (American Psychiatric Association, 2013) diagnosis of dementia has been replaced with major and mild neurocognitive disorders (NCDs) due to various etiological disorders that include AD, FTD, and LBD, among others in which there is a specific underlying pathology that can be determined. These neurocognitive disorders are acquired disorders in which there is evidence of significant cognitive decline from a previous level of performance in one or more cognitive domains (attention, executive function, learning and memory, language, perceptual motor, or social cognition). In major neurocognitive disorder, the impairment is determined to be substantial enough to impact independence in everyday activities. Alternatively, mild neurocognitive disorder is diagnosed when there is a modest impairment in cognitive performance that does not yet interfere with functional independence, although completion of daily living skills may require greater effort, use of compensatory strategies, or some other form of accommodation. Using this diagnostic classification, individuals are first diagnosed with either a mild or major neurocognitive disorder, after which the suspected etiology is then coded. There is also a provision to add a specifier to indicate the presence or absence of behavioral disturbance. Specific criteria for each of the dementias include genetic or biomarker criteria where appropriate. For example, a diagnosis of major neurocognitive disorder due to probable AD requires evidence of either a genetic mutation from family history or genetic testing, or progressive decline in memory, and at least one other domain, with no other alternative explanation for the decline. There has been some resistance to the nomenclature in the 5th edition of the *Diagnostic and Statistical Manual of Mental Disorders*, in part because the term dementia is no longer used.

Biomarkers are increasingly becoming part of new diagnostic criteria for AD, LBD, and bvFTD that, in combination with clinical data from history and pattern of cognitive impairment, have improved diagnostic accuracy within these populations. The National Institute on Aging-Alzheimer's Association workgroups on diagnostic guidelines have revised the original 1984 National Institute of Neurological Disorders and Stroke and Alzheimer Disease and Related Dementias Association diagnostic criteria, incorporating advances in biomarker detection through cerebrospinal fluid and imaging studies (McKhann et al., 2011). However, these criteria are primarily used for research because the availability of biomarker data is limited in many clinical settings. Diagnosis of LBD or dementia with Lewy bodies (terms often used interchangeably) requires obtaining a detailed clinical history for diagnostic features that differ from other forms of dementia, including cognitive fluctuations, visual hallucinations early in the course of the disease, and spontaneous parkinsonism (McKeith et al., 2017). Imaging with positron emission tomography (PET) or single photon emission computed tomography can further help differentiate LBD from AD. In particular, dopamine transporter protein imaging uses tracers that bind to the dopamine transporter to identify dopamine levels in the corpus striatum, which are reduced in LBD. This can help to confirm the diagnosis. In contrast to AD and LBD, in the case of bvFTD, early symptoms involve changes in personality and comportment that can sometimes be mistaken for a psychiatric disorder. New diagnostic criteria for bvFTD (Rascovsky et al., 2011) also include biomarker criteria (i.e., focal frontal and/or anterior temporal atrophy or hypoperfusion on PET imaging). In the remainder of this chapter we review the major features of each of these disorders.

Epidemiology and Pathophysiology

All-Cause Dementia

An estimated 35.6 million individuals are affected by dementia worldwide, with China having the largest numbers at 5.4 million followed by the United States (3.9 million), India (3.7 million), Japan (2.5 million), and several European countries (Prince et al., 2013). Specifically, approximately 58% of the worldwide burden of dementia is found in countries with low or middle incomes. Because these consist of all-cause dementia, including conditions that are static or reversible as well as those that are progressive, related to a variety of neurodegenerative etiologies, onset can occur at any age across the lifespan. See Table 14.1 for a summary of different causes of dementia. Recent data from the Framingham Heart Study has shown that the incidence of all forms of dementia, at least in the United States, has actually declined over three decades (Satizabal et al., 2016), seemingly related to earlier recognition and intervention of vascular risk factors that can lead to later cognitive decline. However, as populations continue to grow across the globe and the number of elderly individuals increases (estimates of nearly 65.7 million by 2030), the number of individuals with dementia will steadily rise because of (1) limited access to potential treatments and (2) onset of common neurodegenerative dementias in mid- to late life. See Table 14.2 for a summary of the epidemiology and pathologic features of common dementia types.

AD

Alzheimer disease is the most common dementia type, making up as much as 50% to 75% of cases (Alzheimer's Association, 2015). Onset typically occurs after age 65 (late onset), although there is a subset of early-onset cases (< 65 years of age) that are more likely to have a genetic susceptibility (see Risk Factors in the Clinical Manifestations section), and the condition is more prevalent in women. Prevalence in the United States for those >70 years of age is 9.7%, and the

Table 14.1 Causes of Dementia

AIDS

Alcoholic dementia

AD

Amyotrophic lateral sclerosis

Cerebral amyloid angiopathy

Cerebral autosomal-dominant arteriopathy with subcortical infarcts and leukoencephalopathy

Cerebellar degeneration

Creutzfeldt Jakob disease

Corticobasal degeneration

Frontotemporal dementia (behavioral variant, semantic dementia, primary progressive aphasia)

Huntington's disease

Hyper/hyponatremia

Hyper/hypothyroidism

Kidney diseases

LBD

Lupus erythematosus

Meningitis or encephalitis

Metals, poisons (lead, mercury, arsenic, manganese, carbon monoxide, solvents, some insecticides)

Metastatic brain tumor

Multiple system atrophy

Normal pressure hydrocephalus

Opportunistic infections

Parkinson's disease

Primary brain tumor

Progressive multifocal leukoencephalopathy

Progressive supranuclear palsy

Subdural hematoma

Traumatic brain injury

Vitamin deficiencies (B$_{12}$, folate)

Wilson disease

Note: AD = Alzheimer disease, LBD, Lewy body disease.

number of individuals with AD is projected to double every 5 years (Qiu, Kivipelto, & von Strauss, 2011). Classic AD involves neuronal loss, first observed in the temporal lobes, which later progresses to the frontal and parietal regions, followed by the occipital lobes (Braak & Braak, 1991). The pathological hallmark of AD is an accumulation of amyloid-β (Aβ) plaques outside neurons and tau neurofibrillary tangles inside

neurons. A new AD neuropathological classification system has been developed that includes staging of Aβ plaques, neurofibrillary tangles stage, and neuritic plaques (Hyman et al., 2012). Once a diagnosis is made, life expectancy is approximately 8–10 years, although individuals can live as many as 20 years postdiagnosis.

Dementia with Lewy Bodies

Dementia with Lewy bodies is the second most frequent dementia type, with estimated prevalence rates ranging from 6% to 24% of all dementia cases, constituting approximately 7% of the population over age 65. Age of onset has been found to range from 50 to 85 years, and develops more frequently in men (4:1). Its pathological features involve the accumulation of alpha-synuclein proteins in neurons diffusely throughout the brain (McKeith et al., 2017). Dementia with Lewy bodies has a fairly rapid course, with a life expectancy of 4–7 years after symptoms begin (Brodaty, Seeher, & Gibson, 2012).

FTD

Frontotemporal dementia encompasses two main related dementia types, a behavioral variant and language variant, of which there are three subtypes: nonfluent/agrammatic primary progressive aphasia, logopenic primary progressive aphasia, and semantic dementia (Gorno-Tempini et al., 2011; Rascovsky et al., 2011,). Of these types of FTD, the behavioral variant is more common, and is the third most frequent dementia type, making up approximately 3–4% of all dementia cases. Age of onset of bvFTD is usually earlier than other dementia types, often occurring between 45 and 65 years of age. In addition, women have a slightly higher predilection for developing this condition. As its name suggests, bvFTD involves neuronal atrophy of the frontal and temporal lobes. Its pathological features predominantly consist of an accumulation of tau inclusions or transactive response DNA-binding protein. The life expectancy depends on the FTD phenotype and ranges from 3 to 14 years after diagnosis (Onyike & Diehl-Schmid, 2013).

Clinical Manifestations

AD

Alzheimer disease is characterized by an insidious onset and slow progression of cognitive difficulties, usually with initial symptoms of short-term memory

Table 14.2 Epidemiology and Pathological Features of Common Dementia Types

Dementia Type	Prevalence	Ratio Females: Males	Age of Onset (years)	Pathological Markers	Life Expectancy (years)
Alzheimer disease	60–80%	3:2	≥65	Aβ, τ	8–10
Dementia with Lewy bodies	6–24%	1:4	50–85	α-synuclein	4–7
Frontotemporal dementia	3–4%	3:1	45–65	TAR DNA, τ	3–14

Note. Aβ = amyloid-β plaques, τ = tau neurofibrillary tangles, α-synuclein = alpha-synuclein proteins, TAR DNA = transactive response DNA-binding protein inclusions.

loss that is later accompanied by deficits in executive functioning, language, and visuospatial skills. Overlearned verbal abilities and simple attention remain relatively intact in the early stages of the disease. However, atypical presentations exist whereby individuals may show relatively greater impairment of frontal lobe systems (e.g., executive functioning abilities), as well as lateralized deficits, with relatively greater verbal or visuospatial difficulties. Social graces tend to be well preserved in early stages that in combination with reduced insight or awareness of cognitive changes can lead to minimization of symptoms and reluctance to use compensatory strategies or enlist the help of others. Increased incidence of depression in the prodromal (MCI) stage has been reported that may relate to greater insight of cognitive slippage at that point. Over time, apathy becomes more prevalent, and as the disease progresses, greater behavioral disturbance can be seen in the form of anxiety and agitation. Hallucinations and delusions may occur later in the course of the disease, and are sometimes related to cognitive deficits (e.g., believing that someone has stolen their possessions when they have misplaced them). See Table 14.3 for a summary of cognitive features.

Functional difficulties become increasingly common and may include losing personal belongings, trouble with finances, problems managing medications, getting lost while driving, reduced ability to perform household tasks (e.g., cook, operate appliances), and ultimately attend to their own self-care (e.g., require prompting and/or assistance with basic activities of daily living). Physically, individuals with AD may remain relatively healthy in the early to middle stages of the disease, although decreased awareness of health-related issues and poor memory can result in a delay in seeking medical attention for new symptoms and ignoring or forgetting symptoms. Dehydration and urinary tract infections are a common cause of acute deterioration in functioning later in the disease course that is reversible with proper treatment. An overview of common clinical features of the disease can be found in Table 14.4.

LBD

The dementia associated with LBD also has an insidious onset and gradual progression, although it is often accompanied by behavioral features that can help distinguish LBD from AD. In particular, the presence of parkinsonism, cognitive fluctuations, and early visual hallucinations should raise suspicion of possible LBD, as well as nighttime behaviors in the form of dream enactment behaviors (i.e., REM behavioral disorder). More specifically, parkinsonism may involve postural instability, gait difficulty, and masked faces; resting tremor is less common, but possible. The presence of fluctuating cognition may be difficult to assess, although typically involves variation between states of relative clarity and states of confusion. There are several measures designed to assess cognitive fluctuations that can help determine the presence of this symptom (see McKeith et al., 2017). Visual hallucinations early in the course of the disease, when present, may help to increase confidence of the diagnosis. As a precursor to hallucinations, individuals may experience visual misperceptions in which they misperceive stimuli in their environment as something else (e.g., water hose as a snake, shadows on the wall as spiders) or see shadows in their peripheral vision. The presence of dream enactment behaviors can be difficult to determine if an individual does not have a bed partner to provide the

Table 14.3 Early Neuropsychological and Behavioral Features Across Dementias

Domain/Disorder	AD	LBD	bvFTD
Intelligence/achievement	Largely intact; processing speed may be reduced	Nonverbal IQ subtests may show mild impairment	Largely intact
Attention/concentration	Simple attention usually intact; Complex attention may be impaired and some difficulty with working memory can be seen	Impaired early, particularly working memory and vigilance	May be impaired or negatively impacted by impulsivity or perseveration
Processing speed	Some inefficiencies can be seen on more complex tasks	Impaired early	Some inefficiencies can be seen if mental flexibility or initiation involved
Language	Confrontation naming and verbal fluency (semantic > phonemic) often impaired	Variable deficits in verbal fluency and confrontation naming early on with progression over time; hypophonia may be present	Naming usually intact early, may become impaired later; verbal fluency may be impaired (phonemic > semantic)
Visuospatial	Impairment can vary early on, but eventually declines	Early, marked impairment in visuospatial and constructional abilities common	Intact initially unless there is an organizational component
Learning and memory	Impaired early with reduced learning, rapid forgetting, poor recognition, and a tendency to make an elevated number of intrusion and false positive errors	Learning and memory reduced but not as impaired as other domains (e.g., executive functioning) early on, although memory becomes more impaired as disease progresses (similar to AD)	Initial learning of new material may be impaired; can benefit from cues, recognition, and recall aids, but have difficulty initiating/generating the strategies
Executive functions	Impaired early, although typically after memory	Impaired early	Impaired early
Sensorimotor functions	Preserved until late stage	Micrographia, parkinsonism (tremor less common than gait problems, rigidity, and bradykinesia)	Preserved until late stage
Emotional functioning	Depression can predate onset of dementia; anxiety and agitation in later stages	Well-formed visual hallucinations early that can become more disruptive as disease progresses; delusions (e.g., Capgras syndrome) can occur	Early symptoms may include apathy, impulsivity, loss of empathy, personality change, disinhibition, irritability

Note. AD = Alzheimer disease, LBD = Lewy body disease, bvFTD = behavioral variant frontotemporal dementia.

observations; they also can be confused for other movements during sleep, such as restless leg syndrome. To be certain that nighttime behaviors are occurring during REM sleep, a formal sleep study is needed. However, questioning regarding hitting, kicking, and purposeful activity during sleep will help identify individuals with this symptom. In some instances, this symptom is significant enough to drive

Table 14.4 Clinical Features of Common Dementia Types

Sign/Symptom	AD	LBD	FTD
Abrupt onset	–	–	–
Insidious onset	+	+	+
Early personality change	–	–	+
Cognitive fluctuations	–	+	–
Insight	–/+	+	–
Apathy	–/+	–	–/+
REM behavioral disorder	–	+	–
Psychosis	–/+ [a]	+	–
Motor symptoms	–	+	–/+

Note. AD = Alzheimer disease, LBD = Lewy body disease, FTD = frontotemporal dementia. + = expected, - = not expected. Any of these elements may be present in MCI depending on the underlying etiology.
[a] Can be seen later in the disease.

the bed partner from the bed. Review of medications when REM behavioral disorder is present is suggested, given that use of a selective serotonin reuptake inhibitor can cause REM behavioral disorder. Cognitively, individuals with LBD may demonstrate greater visuospatial and executive function difficulties early in the course of the disease relative to language functions, and memory may not be as impaired in comparison with those who have AD. However, as the disease progresses, global cognitive impairment develops. From a functional standpoint, declines similar to those seen in AD will develop over time. Early visuospatial and processing speed difficulties can cause problems with driving, and there is increased risk of falls due to parkinsonism. See Tables 14.3 and 14.4 for neuropsychological and clinical features of LBD.

FTD

The presence of early personality change and behavioral symptoms distinguishes bvFTD from the other dementias. Early in the course of the disease, cognitive functions may be relatively preserved on formal testing, although functionally, individuals often have significant difficulty related to executive dysfunction, inappropriate social behaviors, impulsivity, apathy, and decreased empathy. Perseveration and stereotyped or compulsive/ ritualistic behaviors can be seen (e.g., repetitive movements, compulsive behaviors, stereotypy of speech). Hyperorality (e.g., binge eating) and changes in food preferences, such as a proclivity for sweets or junk food to the exclusion of other foods, may also be present. In some cases, it may be difficult to distinguish behavioral features of FTD from certain psychiatric disorders (e.g., bipolar disorder, personality disorder), although determining the chronology of symptoms and change from long-standing abilities can help make this distinction. Because individuals with FTD often have functional as well as social difficulties, accompanied by poor awareness, they can be difficult to manage behaviorally. See Tables 14.3 and 14.4 for neuropsychological and clinical features of bvFTD.

Risk Factors

A variety of genetic, medical, psychiatric, and psychosocial factors have been found to increase overall risk of dementia. These are summarized in Table 14.5. Because the neurodegenerative process develops over decades, symptoms only manifest once a pathological threshold has been reached, making aging one of the greatest risk factors for developing dementia. Among individuals diagnosed with AD in the United States, approximately 4% are younger than age 65 and 15% between 65 and 75 years, whereas 81% are older than age 75 (Alzheimer's Association, 2018). Genetic susceptibility can also play an important role, with nearly 1% of Alzheimer cases being the result of inheriting one of three possible mutated genes, whereas 10% to 20% of bvFTD cases are the result of inheriting one of six possible genes (Piguet, Hornberger, Mioshi, & Hodges, 2011). Also, inheritance of an apolipoprotein ε4 allele, which is linked to fewer synaptic networks and disrupted neuronal repair, has been found to increase the risk for developing dementia by threefold for one allele and more than eightfold for those with two alleles. However, a family history of dementia alone only slightly increases an individual's risk. In addition to these nonmodifiable risk factors, increasing evidence suggests that central nervous system insults, including conditions associated with cardiovascular disease (obesity, diabetes, hypertension, hypercholesterolemia, and tobacco smoking), toxin exposure, alcohol/substance abuse, and moderate to severe head injury can increase the

Table 14.5 Factors Associated with Increased Risk for Developing Common Dementia Types

Factors	AD	LBD	bvFTD
Genetic			
Family history of dementia	+		+
Apolipoprotein ε4 allele	+	-/+[a]	+
Mutations			
Amyloid precursor protein	+		
Presenilin protein 1	+		
Presenilin protein 2	+		
Microtubule-associated protein Tau			+
Chromosome 9 open reading frame 72			+
Chromatin-modifying protein 2b			+
Valosin-containing protein			+
TDP 43			+
Granulin protein			+
RNA-binding protein fused in sarcoma			+
Medical			
Cardiovascular disease	+		+
Diabetes	+		
Moderate to severe head injury	+		+
Substance			
Toxin exposure	+		
Alcohol abuse	+		
Substance abuse	+		
Psychiatric			
Depression	+	+	
Anxiety		+	
Posttraumatic stress disorder	+		
Psychosocial			
Aging	+	+	+
Low education	+		

Note. AD = Alzheimer disease; LBD = Lewy body disease, bvFTD = behavioral variant frontotemporal dementia. += factor associated with increased risk for developing dementia syndrome.
[a] Inconsistency in reports that may relate to mixed AD/LBD pathology in clinical studies.

likelihood for developing certain types of dementia in some individuals and may reduce the threshold for onset of symptoms, by either contributing pathological burden or disrupting neuronal functioning. A history of depression, anxiety, and/or posttraumatic stress disorder has also been reported to increase the risk for later cognitive decline, but whether these are actual risk factors is questionable. Psychiatric symptoms are common in individuals with dementia and may represent the earliest symptoms of a dementia process, a reaction to having awareness of cognitive decline, or the result of other known risk factors. For more detailed discussions of possible mechanisms underlying the association between dementia and psychiatric symptoms, see Byers and Yaffe (2011), Boot et al. (2013), and Greenberg, Tanev, Marin, and Pitman (2014).

Prevention

Neurodegenerative dementias are insidious, appearing to develop over several decades, and aside from those with a genetic mutation, predisposing factors are less clear. Given the many failed clinical trials and long presymptomatic period before disease expression, it is believed that effective treatments, when discovered, will likely have to be administered years before symptom onset (i.e., prevention vs. treatment). Efforts to develop a vaccine for the treatment or prevention of AD have thus far focused on amyloid clearance and prevention of further deposition, but have resulted in excess immune activation, causing serious adverse effects. More recent vaccine efforts have focused on tau pathology, but these studies are only in Phase 1 and clinical benefit is not yet known. Given that, there is no treatment at present that can prevent the development of neurodegenerative dementias. However, there are a few nonpharmacological agents that have been shown to reduce the risk of developing later cognitive impairment and may slow the onset of symptoms.

Well-Supported Factors for Reducing Risk for Cognitive Impairment

Regular physical exercise has been associated with improved cognitive functioning and a reduced risk for cognitive decline (Baumgart et al., 2015). Individuals aged 60 years and older engaging in at least 150 min of weekly exercise, primarily of moderate or vigorous intensity, have been found to show increased brain volume in areas vulnerable to aging (e.g., temporal lobe) compared with those with lower levels of exercise (Dougherty et al., 2016). It would appear then that regular physical exercise at or above these levels can protect against the deleterious effects of normal aging, and subsequently may slow the onset of cognitive impairment in some individuals who later develop dementia. Similarly, participation in mentally stimulating activities in midlife or late life, such as reading, playing games, or learning, has also been found to delay the onset and reduce the likelihood for dementia (Fratiglioni & Wang, 2007). In a study of 147 monozygotic twin pairs, where one was diagnosed with dementia and the other remained nondemented for at least 3 years afterward, greater participation in cognitive activities in

Table 14.6 Evidence for Factors That Delay Onset of Dementia Syndromes

High	• Physical exercise (2–3 hours of moderate to vigorous exercise weekly) • Regular engagement in mentally stimulating activities (e.g., reading, playing games, socializing) • Mediterranean diet (high in fish, fruits, and vegetables) • Light to moderate alcohol consumption • Higher education
Limited	• Estrogen hormone therapy initiated in women within 5 years of menopause • Nonsteroidal antiinflammatory drugs • Vitamin supplements (C, E, and/or B) • Folic acid supplements • Omega-3 fatty acid supplements (fish oil) • Coconut oil • Coenzyme Q10
None	Avoidance of: • Use of aluminum (in cooking utensils, dental fillings, etc.) • Silver dental fillings • Flu vaccinations • Aspartame (artificial sweetener)

midlife, most notably social involvement, was associated with a 26% reduced risk for dementia onset, and this effect was even higher (30%) for those with an increased genetic risk (presence of an apolipoprotein ε4 allele) (Carlson et al., 2008). Other lines of evidence show that more years of formal education, regular intake of Mediterranean diet–based foods (fruits, vegetables, oats, nuts, fish, and olive oil), and light to moderate consumption of alcohol can reduce the risk for developing dementia (Baumgart et al., 2015). Although these mechanisms are not well understood, it has been posited that higher years of schooling may enable individuals to better develop compensatory strategies to help cope with neuronal damage, and a Mediterranean diet and some alcohol intake might reduce the oxidative stress and inflammation seen in those with dementia. See Table 14.6 for a summary of variables associated with delaying the onset of dementia symptoms.

Factors for Reducing Risk for Cognitive Impairment with Limited Support

Despite a few factors having received mounting support for reducing risk for developing dementia, there are others that have shown mixed results. There have been numerous investigations into whether agents with antioxidant, antiinflammatory, dietary supplement, or, in women, hormone replacement therapies delay onset of cognitive decline due to their link with neuroprotective effects in laboratory studies. Table 14.6 summarizes which agents may have potential, but currently show a lack of research support. For a detailed review of these agents, see Côté et al. (2012), Dangour et al. (2010), Shao et al. (2012), and Young, Johnson, Steffens, and Doraiswamy (2007).

Unsupported Factors for Reducing Risk for Cognitive Impairment

Avoidance of some environmental factors, such as aluminum, silver dental fillings, and flu vaccinations, was previously believed to reduce the risk of developing dementia. However, these strategies have not received any research support, and it would be a mistake to assume that they have an association with later-life cognitive decline. For a list of unsupported factors previously believed to delay the onset of dementia, see Table 14.6.

Diagnostic Evaluation

The diagnostic evaluation for identification and differential diagnosis of dementia involves a thorough clinical interview to determine the onset and progression of symptoms, functional problems, behaviors changes, and potential comorbid or contributory factors. Preferably, an informant is present to provide additional information and can be interviewed separate from the patient to obtain the most accurate information. Neurological/medical evaluation that includes blood chemistries and neuroimaging are standard practice to help rule out other potential causes for the symptoms (e.g., stroke, tumor, metabolic dysfunction), and when possible, biomarker data are obtained (e.g., cerebrospinal fluid analysis of Aβ/tau for AD). Standard imaging procedures can now be augmented by more sophisticated neuroimaging techniques specific to various forms of dementia. For example, PET amyloid imaging can now be obtained that measures the amount of amyloid deposition in the brain. However, barriers such as availability of scans, cost, and lack of coverage by insurance carriers limit the frequency with which these scans are obtained. Tau imaging is an emerging technique, but is currently only available for research purposes. See Table 14.7 for a review of various neuroimaging techniques and common findings across dementia types. Despite advances in neuroimaging, the neuropsychological evaluation continues to be the gold standard in assessing cognitive abilities and helping to determine the degree of functional decline.

Neuropsychological Assessment

Neuropsychological assessment serves an important role in the evaluation and care of patients with dementia. It can detect the presence of subtle cognitive changes, aid in early diagnosis, identify cognitive phenotypes associated with different neurodegenerative diseases, predict and monitor disease trajectory, characterize strengths and weaknesses, estimate functional status, and inform treatment planning. There is strong concordance between clinical dementia diagnoses and ultimate neuropathological diagnoses, with particularly high accuracy in multidisciplinary settings in which comprehensive neuropsychological assessment forms an integral part of the diagnostic workup. For example, estimates of clinical diagnostic accuracy of AD and FTD in memory clinics range from 88% to100% (see, for example, Grossman et al., 2007; Snowden et al., 2011). Neuropsychological differences among neurodegenerative disorders are usually most apparent in the early stages, and differential diagnosis is more difficult in later stages because nuances of cognitive features are no longer discernable as the disease process advances.

The incremental value of neuropsychological assessment is well supported with evidence that cognitive markers independently predict conversion from MCI to dementia (Ewers et al., 2012). For example, in a large, community-based study examining the cognitive predictors of all-cause dementia, select measures (Rey Auditory Verbal Learning Test short delay recall, Wechsler Adult Intelligence Scale Digit Symbol, and animal fluency) predicted onset of dementia after 5 years with a sensitivity and specificity of 75% and 74%, respectively, and after 10 years with a sensitivity of 78% and specificity of 72% (Tierney, Moineddin, & McDowell, 2010), and other studies have shown predictive accuracy as high as 86% (Tabert et al., 2006).

Table 14.7 Neuroimaging in Dementia

Technique	Description/Utility	Typical Findings		
		AD	LBD	bvFTD
CT	Rapid, widely available, useful for ruling out underlying pathology such as hemorrhage, hydrocephalus, or mass	Unremarkable	Unremarkable	Unremarkable
MRI	Better delineation of anatomy, more sensitive to vascular changes than CT	Global volume loss, medial temporal atrophy, enlarged ventricles (due to atrophy)	Global volume loss	Frontal and anterior temporal atrophy
fMRI	Generates high resolution anatomic images, detects regional changes in brain activity	Reduced medial temporal lobe activity	Increased temporal activation compared with AD	Decreased frontal and temporal activity
SPECT	More widely available than fMRI or PET, measures cerebral blood flow	Temporoparietal hypoperfusion	Low dopamine transporter uptake in the basal ganglia	Frontal hypoperfusion
PET	Characterizes resting regional brain metabolism	Bilateral parietal hypometabolism/hypoperfusion	Diffuse hypometabolism, disproportionate involvement of occipital lobes	Frontal hypometabolism
Amyloid PET	View amyloid plaque deposition using compounds that bind to amyloid (e.g., Pittsburgh compound B, florbetapir F)	Increased tracer uptake in posterior cingulate and parietal regions	Often positive; similar pattern but less burden compared with AD	Negative

Note. AD = Alzheimer disease, LBD = Lewy body disease, bvFTD = behavioral variant frontotemporal dementia, CT = computed tomography, MRI = magnetic resonance imaging, fMRI = functional MRI, SPECT = single photon emission computed tomography, PET = positron emission tomography.

Cognitive measures predicted conversion above and beyond other AD biomarkers such as regional brain volumes and cerebrospinal fluid studies (Gomar et al., 2011). Alternatively, neuropsychological evaluation can also identify protective factors that are associated with reduced risk of dementia. For example, the risk from old age and family history of dementia was mitigated by a memory score 1 *SD* above the mean (Locke et al., 2009).

Screening Assessment

Brief mental status examinations are useful for the evaluation of dementia and for tracking change over time. Screening batteries are also practical when there are time constraints or concerns for patient fatigue. Short cognitive screening can help quickly and inexpensively identify patients who warrant a referral for a more in-depth neurocognitive examination. Cut scores to define dementia are commonly used and often have good sensitivity but may lack adequate specificity. In addition, brief mental status examinations and neurocognitive screening measures often have poor sensitivity to MCI in part because they commonly have limited assessment of areas such as executive function and visuospatial ability. There are many mental status scales and inventories available (see Ruchinskas & Curyto, 2003, for a review), and we briefly highlight a few selected tools here.

The Dementia Rating Scale–2 (Jurica, Leitten, & Mattis, 2001) assesses overall level of cognitive functioning and provides information on five specific domains: attention, initiation/perseveration, construction, conceptualization, and memory. It offers a total score with a maximum of 144 points, and provides scoring ranges for dementia staging (125–134 = mild, 115–124 = mild to moderate, 105–114 = moderate, 95–104 = moderate to severe, <95 = severe). It can be completed in 20–30 min and provides norms for ages 56 to 105. Various cut scores have been proposed; for example, a cutoff of 123 differentiated patients with AD from healthy controls with 83% specificity and 100% sensitivity (van Gorp et al., 1999), whereas a higher cutoff score of 133 was more appropriate (96% sensitivity and 92% specificity) in a highly educated sample of mild AD versus normal controls (Salmon et al., 2002).

The Montreal Cognitive Assessment (Nasreddine et al., 2005) is a brief (10-min) 30-point cognitive screening measure that has become increasingly popular. A score below 26 was originally recommended as a cutoff for MCI, although subsequent studies have suggested lower cutoffs to improve specificity. For example, in a study of patients with AD or MCI matched for sex, age, and education to cognitively healthy community dwellers, a cutoff of below 22 for MCI and below 17 for AD showed significantly better sensitivity, specificity, positive predictive value, negative predictive value, and classification accuracy compared to the Mini-Mental State Examination (Freitas, Simoes, Alves, & Santana, 2013). Determining the most optimal cut score may depend on the population because studies have shown lower mean scores in population-based and minority samples (Rossetti, Lacritz, Cullum, & Weiner, 2011; Rossetti et al., 2017).

The Repeatable Battery for the Assessment of Neuropsychological Status (RBANS) is a brief battery of 10 subtests that assess five cognitive domains and provides a summary score that ranges from 40 to 160. Administration is typically about 30 min and normative data are available for ages 20–89. Analysis of the utility of the RBANS in detecting AD suggested a cutoff of 1 SD below the mean best discriminated patients with AD from comparison participants on most of the RBANS subtests and indexes, with a total score of 77 producing 98% sensitivity and 82% specificity (Duff et al., 2008).

Comprehensive Assessment

A comprehensive neuropsychological evaluation for dementia includes the integration of a clinical interview, collateral information, and an assessment of multiple cognitive domains, typically memory, language, executive functions, attention, and visuospatial and motor skills, as well as assessment of mood and emotional functioning. An estimate of premorbid abilities is an important aspect of the assessment given that the diagnosis of dementia requires evidence of a decline from prior levels of functioning. Tests that are typically resistant to dementing illness and correlate well with premorbid intelligence are useful for this purpose, and would include word recognition reading tests such as the Wechsler Test of Premorbid Function or the Wide Range Achievement Test Reading subtest. Of all cognitive domains, tests of declarative/episodic memory, language, and executive function are the most sensitive for differentiating AD from normal aging (Cullum & Lacritz, 2012). This was illustrated in a study of 98 patients with early AD (i.e., scored ≥24 on the Mini-Mental State Exam) and 98 gender-, age-, and education-matched normal control participants, in which receiver operating characteristic curve analysis showed robust sensitivity (SN) and specificity (SP) for detection of mild AD with classic measures such as the California Verbal Learning Test (SN: 95–98%, SP: 88–89%), category fluency (SN: 96%, SP: 88%), and Trail Making Test Part B (SN:85%, SP: 83%) (Salmon et al., 2002).

An older adult's ability to function independently is an important aspect of the evaluation, in part because functional impairment is a key feature of the diagnosis of dementia and for practical considerations such as safety, living arrangement, and quality of life recommendations. Functional assessment includes basic everyday skills (e.g., personal grooming) and complex abilities (e.g., managing finances, taking medications, and driving). Appropriate assessment of functional status is of particular importance in civil competency/

capacity cases (Moye, Marson, & Edelstein, 2013). An estimation of functional ability commonly relies upon the patient's self-report or the informant report gathered during clinical interview; however, individuals with dementia typically overestimate their functional abilities and caregivers are also prone to misestimation (Schulz et al., 2013). Scales commonly used to assess activities of daily living include the Functional Activities Questionnaire, the Instrumental Activity of Daily Living Scale, and the Everyday Cognition scales. Measures such as the Everyday Cognition scales help draw comparisons to prior levels of ability, which can be helpful in the assessment of individuals with limited education for whom low cognitive scores may represent long-standing abilities. Performance-based measures, such as the Texas Functional Living Scale, provide an objective, ecologically valid way to measure the ability to execute everyday tasks (Cullum et al., 2001) and can guide recommendations.

Normative Considerations

Common neuropsychological tests have age and education norms. Some argue that removing the effect of age, the main risk factor for dementia, undermines the sensitivity of cognitive measures (O'Connell & Tuokko, 2010); however, the use of demographically corrected norms improves the specificity of test results and in turn optimizes the positive predictive values of the test (Fields, Ferman, Boeve, & Smith, 2011). In addition to age, education, and sex, cultural and ethnic differences exert an effect on test performance. Most neuropsychological measures were designed and normed in majority White European ethnic groups. It is important to carefully consider whether tests are appropriate for the individual being served, and seek the best available measures and norms when assessing older adults of diverse ethnic or cultural backgrounds. Furthermore, the examiner should be aware of stereotype threat, a confirmatory bias in which an individual's performance may be influenced by his or her own expectations and society stereotypes (Nguyen & Ryan, 2008). The use of ethnicity-specific norms can improve diagnostic accuracy in minorities, and the availability of such data has improved greatly in the past decade through work such as Mayo's Older African American Studies (Lucas et al., 2005); however, many tests still lack representative normative data. Texts such as Conducting a Culturally Informed Neuropsychological Evaluation (Fujii, 2017) and Minority and Cross-Cultural Aspects of Neuropsychological Assessment – 2nd Edition

(Ferraro, 2015) can help guide assessment of individuals from diverse backgrounds.

It can be useful to supplement standard norms with so-called robust norms, which identify and exclude individuals who develop diagnosable dementia after baseline assessment (Holtzer et al., 2008). An additional normative consideration in dementia evaluations is that data for elderly samples is often limited because cell sizes tend to be much smaller, and this issue is compounded in minorities.

Serial Assessment

Dementia is a progressive condition with a dynamic time course that varies by etiology and by individual. Repeated neuropsychological evaluations can chart the rate of progression, track areas of cognitive change over time, and help plan and adapt treatment and interventions. The use of various statistical methods can aid in determining whether a clinically significant change has occurred across time, such as Reliable Change Indices and standardized regression-based formulas (see Duff, 2012, for a review).

Specific Assessment Considerations

FTD. In addition to collateral interview, informant measures such as the Neuropsychiatric Inventory and the Frontal Behavioral Inventory may also assist in assessment and diagnosis. Executive function measures such as the Executive Interview or the Frontal Assessment Battery have also been validated in this population. Efforts to characterize a neuropsychological profile specific to bvFTD have not been successful (Wittenberg et al., 2008). Instead, attention to the relative pattern of test scores can aid differential diagnosis, such as a relative sparing of declarative memory and visuospatial function. Overall performance on classic executive function tests does not consistently differ between bvFTD and AD and may not always be impaired early in the course (Johns et al., 2009); however, within-task performance differences such as rule violations on the Stroop task may improve diagnostic accuracy (Carey et al., 2008).

Lewy Body Disease. Given that visuospatial deficits are often disproportionally prominent in Lewy body disease, visuoconstructional tasks are particularly important to include when an LBD diagnosis is suspected. Simple tasks such as intersecting pentagons may be flawed (Troster, 2008), and both clock drawing to command and clock copy may be poor. It is also worth noting that visual memory may be impaired secondary to visuoperceptual impairment. Incorporating a measure of sustained attention could help uncover evidence of cognitive fluctuations, and the use of a collateral report scale may also assist in gauging this aspect of LBD. For example, the Mayo Fluctuations Composite Scale (Ferman et al., 2004) requires three or more "yes" responses from caregivers to structured questions about the presence of daytime drowsiness and lethargy, daytime sleep >2 hr, staring into space for long periods, or episodes of disorganized speech to suggest cognitive fluctuations.

Intervention

Disease-modifying interventions for dementia do not currently exist. Rather, interventions are aimed at reducing symptoms, slowing progression, and/or helping individuals and their families compensate for the cognitive decline. There are two standard forms of intervention that may be used depending on the type of dementia: (1) pharmacological and (2) nonpharmacological. It is important to note that although these interventions can improve the quality of life of those with dementia, increasing assistance and support with daily functioning will be required as the disease progresses. That is, individuals may be able to work around deficits initially to enhance autonomy, but full-time assistance and supervision from caregivers will be required at some point.

Pharmacological

Medication has proven to be a first-line intervention for those with AD because the pathology appears to result in an abnormal production of some neurotransmitters in the brain, namely decreased acetylcholine. Thus, several acetylcholinesterase inhibitors have been developed that can slightly improve cognitive difficulties seen in AD and they are typically well tolerated, but most notably have been found to slow cognitive deterioration for many AD patients in randomized controlled trials (Atri, Shaughnessy, Locascio, & Growdon, 2008). It has also been posited that increased glutamate may result from the pathogenesis of AD, and there is now one Food and Drug Administration-approved medication targeting glutamate that shows similar benefits to the acetylcholinesterase inhibitors. Overall, there have been more than 200 drug trials in the last decade to address the cognitive symptoms in AD, but only five have received approval from the Food and Drug Administration. These medications are summarized in Table 14.8. Although these medications have also shown some utility with LBD (Stinton et al., 2015), support for their use in bvFTD is lacking (Piguet et al., 2011). Unfortunately, there are no pharmacological interventions approved at present that target the cognitive and/or behavioral changes in bvFTD, although some psychotropic medications are used off-label to address the behavioral issues with varying success.

Nonpharmacological

Lifestyle changes for individuals with any type of dementia appear to be important, either alone or in combination with pharmacological intervention because they can help individuals to compensate for cognitive changes as the disease progresses. Several randomized controlled trials have shown

Table 14.8 Approved Medications to Address Cognitive Symptoms in Alzheimer Disease

Drug Name	Brand Name	Mechanism	Dementia Severity
Donepezil	Aricept	AChEI	All stages
Rivastigmine	Exelon	AChEI	All stages
Galantamine	Razadyne	AChEI	Mild to moderate
Memantine	Namenda	NMDA	Moderate to severe
Donepezil–memantine blend	Namzaric	AChEI/NMDA	Moderate to severe

Note. AChEI = acetylcholinesterase inhibitor, NMDA = N-methyl-D-aspartate receptor antagonist. Acetylcholinesterase inhibitors increase acetylcholine transmission in the brain by slowing down its breakdown, compensating for the decreased acetylcholine levels associated with AD. N-methyl-D-aspartate receptor antagonists reduce glutamate excitoxicity resulting from AD.

participation in exercises that involve regular practicing of activities of daily living (e.g., making a phone call, opening/closing a door lock), orientation to one's situation (e.g., date, location, current events), and/or engagement in recreational activities reduced cognitive difficulties and improved the quality of life for many individuals with mild to moderate AD compared with controls (Buschert, Bokde, & Hampel, 2010). Also, although progression occurred in both groups over time, those who engaged in several of the above activities evidenced a slower rate of decline than those with no participation. From a practical perspective, it would seem that establishing a daily routine in which activities are rehearsed along with regular engagement in hobbies may reinforce actions, making them overlearned behaviors and possibly more resilient to disease progression. Along these lines, the Mayo Clinic has developed a program called Healthy Action To Benefit Independence or Thinking (also known as HABIT) to help those with MCI or early AD establish a routine involving compensatory strategies such as memory aids, physical exercise, and social support to bolster independence (Mayo Clinic, 2016). Furthermore, engagement in mentally stimulating activities, as described previously (see the Prevention section), has been found to delay cognitive decline in some individuals; in light of this, immersive computerized cognitive training programs (e.g., virtual reality) are currently being developed to help individuals preserve functional abilities and enhance quality of life to some degree (Hill et al., 2016).

Implications for Clinical Practice

Despite the lack of effective treatments for the dementias discussed in this chapter, new neuroimaging techniques, identification of biomarkers, and greater understanding of disease manifestations have helped to aid earlier detection and differential diagnosis of dementia. This will be particularly important for when more effective treatments are developed because it is likely that they will have to be administered in the early or even preclinical stages of the disease evolution. As dementia awareness has increased in our society, suspected cases are presenting for evaluation earlier in the disease course, which can make differential diagnosis more challenging. Neuropsychology has the potential to play an integral role in the early detection and behavioral management of these patients through education, diagnostic clarification, and prospective follow-up to help address functional implications of the cognitive disorder and to respond to the needs of family members in managing the daily needs of

Table 14.9 Clinical Overview of Dementia Diagnosis and Management

Delay Symptom Onset	Diagnosis	Behavioral Management
• Control metabolic risk factors in midlife (diabetes, hypertension) • Vigorous exercise 2–3 hr per week • Engage in mentally stimulating activities • Mediterranean diet • Light to moderate use of alcohol	• Detailed clinical interview (with collateral source) • Medical/neurological workup (including imaging) to rule out potential contributing factors and identify any focal neurological deficits • Utility of DaT scan, PET, or SPECT imaging when diagnosis unclear • Use of available biomarkers to confirm/support diagnosis • Neuropsychological evaluation to characterize pattern of deficits and help with differential diagnosis and behavioral management	• Review need for driving restrictions • Increase support for financial and medication management • Establish routines to make schedule predictable • Encourage socialization and cognitive stimulation, but be alert for overstimulation or frustration • Put compensation strategies in place (e.g., posting daily events, alarms for medications, regular notetaking to augment memory) • Redirect from topics or situations that increase agitation (e.g., driving) • Restrict access to finances or mail to avoid negative monetary implications • Find meaningful activities that enhance quality of life (e.g., time with family) • Support for family to help with management when patient is not safe to be alone

patients. Table 14.9 provides an overview of evidence-based factors that may delay onset of dementia symptoms, core components of the diagnostic process, and some behavioral management strategies to address common issues that occur as cognition declines. Quality of life after dementia diagnosis can be enhanced by early interventions to slow progression of the disease, minimize responsibilities, provide proper support (to ensure safety, medication compliance, and financial well-being), and structure daily life to include enjoyable and appropriate activities.

Future Directions

Test Design and Normative Development

As with neuropsychology as a whole, dementia assessment will continue to require innovative development of tests that are valid, reliable, ecologically valid, and culturally sensitive. Test norms require regular updating to reflect generational and cultural shifts. Similarly, there is a need to ensure we are measuring cognitive constructs that relate to modern society, in which adaptive functioning is increasingly based on digital and technological activities. Ecologically valid measures will allow more precise and practical prescriptive recommendations for functional activities such as management of medication and finances as well as driving (Spooner & Pachana, 2006).

Refining Neuropsychological Biomarkers

There are several innovative drug therapies under investigation and large trials aimed at disease prevention. However, despite the huge financial burden dementia poses to society, it remains an underfunded area of research with significant discrepancies in funding compared with cancer and heart disease (Luengo-Fernandez, Leal, & Gray, 2015). The reasons for this are multifactorial, and include issues such as the failure of animal drug studies to translate to human clinical trials (Hall & Roberson, 2012), the necessarily long timeframe for human clinical drug trials, the challenge of recruiting symptom-free but at-risk volunteers (Watson, Ryan, Silverberg, Cahan, & Bernard, 2014), and societal stigma. It is likely that the various neurodegenerative disorders will respond differently to the potential treatments for dementia that are in development. Therefore, accurate early classification and neuropsychological characterization of at-risk patients is a particularly important goal. To ensure accurate participant selection, group assignment, and appropriate selection of cognitive outcome measures, we must further refine our understanding of the differences in cognitive profiles associated with very mild AD and other dementias.

Clinical Utility

Clinical neuropsychological assessment has an established role in the detection and diagnosis of dementias. However, there is a need to go beyond diagnosis and expand our role in treatment planning to meet the needs of patients and referral sources. Future work should help determine how best to leverage neurocognitive data to make accurate and relevant predictions for clinical care. Higher predictive validity would be extremely useful for establishing early prognosis and helping patients and caregivers estimate important transition points, such as expected length of time to nursing home placement (Tun, Murman, Long, Colenda, & von Eye, 2007).

References

Alzheimer's Association. (2018). 2018 Alzheimer's disease facts and figures. *Alzheimer's & Dementia*, *14*, 367–429.

American Psychiatric Association. (2013). *Diagnostic and statistical manual of mental disorders* (5th ed.). Arlington, VA: American Psychiatric Publishing.

Atri, A., Shaughnessy, L. W., Locascio, J. J., & Growdon, J. H. (2008). Long-term course and effectiveness of combination therapy in Alzheimer's disease. *Alzheimer Disease and Associated Disorders*, *22*(3), 209–221.

Baumgart, M. Snyder, H. M., Carrillo, M. C., Fazio, S., Kim, H., & Johns, H. (2015). Summary of the evidence on modifiable risk factors for cognitive decline and dementia: A population-based perspective. *Alzheimer's & Dementia*, *11*(6), 718–726.

Boot, B. P., Orr, C. F., Ahlskog, J. E., Ferman, T. J., Roberts, R., Pankratz, V. S., … Knopman, D. S. (2013). Risk factors for dementia with Lewy bodies: A case-control study. *Neurology*, *81*(9), 833–840.

Braak, H., & Braak, E. (1991). Neuropathological staging of Alzheimer-related changes. *Acta Neuropathologica*, *82*(4), 239–259.

Brodaty, H., Seeher, K., & Gibson, L. (2012). Dementia time to death: A systematic literature review on survival time and years of life lost in people with dementia. *International Psychogeriatrics*, *24*(7), 1034–1045.

Buschert, V., Bokde, A. L., & Hampel, H. (2010). Cognitive intervention in Alzheimer disease. *Nature Reviews Neurology*, *6*(9), 508–517.

Byers, A. L., & Yaffe, K. (2011). Depression and risk of developing dementia. *Nature Reviews Neurology, 7*(6), 323–331.

Carey, C. L., Woods, S. P., Damon, J., Halabi, C., Dean, D., Delis, D. C., … Kramer, J. H. (2008). Discriminant validity and neuroanatomical correlates of rule monitoring in frontotemporal dementia and Alzheimer's disease. *Neuropsychologia, 46*(4), 1081–1087.

Carlson, M. C., Helms, M. J., Steffens, D. C., Burke, J. R., Potter, G. G., & Plassman, B. L. (2008). Midlife activity predicts risk of dementia in older male twin pairs. *Alzheimer's & Dementia, 4*(5), 324–331.

Côté, S., Carmichael, P. H., Verreault, R., Lindsay, J., Lefebvre, J., & Laurin, D. (2012). Nonsteroidal anti-inflammatory drug use and the risk of cognitive impairment and Alzheimer's disease. *Alzheimer's & Dementia, 8*(3), 219–226.

Cullum, C., & Lacritz, L. (2012). Neuropsychological assessment. In M. W. A. Lipton (Ed.), *Clinical manual of Alzheimer's disease and other dementias* (pp. 66–88). Arlington, VA: American Psychiatric Publishing.

Cullum, C. M., Saine, K., Chan, L. D., Martin-Cook, K., Gray, K. F., & Weiner, M. F. (2001). Performance-based instrument to assess functional capacity in dementia: The Texas Functional Living Scale. *Cognitive and Behavioral Neurology, 14*(2), 103–108.

Dangour, A. D., Whitehouse, P. J., Rafferty, K., Mitchell, S. A., Smith, L., Hawkesworth, S., & Vellas, B. (2010). B-vitamins and fatty acids in the prevention and treatment of Alzheimer's disease and dementia: A systematic review. *Journal of Alzheimer's Disease, 22*(1), 205–224.

Dougherty, R. J., Ellingson, L. D., Schultz, S. A., Boots, E. A., Meyer, J. D., Lindheimer, J. B., … Koscik, R. L. (2016). Meeting physical activity recommendations may be protective against temporal lobe atrophy in older adults at risk for Alzheimer's disease. *Alzheimer's & Dementia: Diagnosis, Assessment & Disease Monitoring, 4*, 14–17.

Duff, K., Humphreys Clark, J. D., O'Bryant, S. E., Mold, J. W., Schiffer, R. B., & Sutker, P. B. (2008). Utility of the RBANS in detecting cognitive impairment associated with Alzheimer's disease: Sensitivity, specificity, and positive and negative predictive powers. *Archives of Clinical Neuropsychology, 23*(5), 603–612.

Duff, K. (2012). Evidence-based indicators of neuropsychological change in the individual patient: Relevant concepts and methods. *Archives of Clinical Neuropsychology, 27*(3), 248–261.

Ewers, M., Walsh, C., Trojanowski, J. Q., Shaw, L. M., Petersen, R. C., Jack, C. R., … Vellas, B. (2012). Prediction of conversion from mild cognitive impairment to Alzheimer's disease dementia based upon biomarkers and neuropsychological test performance. *Neurobiology of Aging, 33*(7), 1203–1214.

Ferraro, F. R. (Ed.). (2015). *Minority and cross-cultural aspects of neuropsychological assessment: Enduring and emerging trends* (2nd ed.). Hove, UK: Psychology Press.

Ferman, T. J., Smith, G. E., Boeve, B. F., Ivnik, R. J., Petersen, R. C., Knopman, D., … Dickson, D. W. (2004). DLB fluctuations: Specific features that reliably differentiate DLB from AD and normal aging. *Neurology, 62*(2), 181–187.

Fields, J. A., Ferman, T. J., Boeve, B. F., & Smith, G. E. (2011). Neuropsychological assessment of patients with dementing illness. *Nature Reviews Neurology, 7*(12), 677–687.

Fratiglioni, L., & Wang, H. X. (2007). Brain reserve hypothesis in dementia. *Journal of Alzheimer's Disease, 12* (1), 11–22.

Freitas, S., Simoes, M. R., Alves, L., & Santana, I. (2013). Montreal cognitive assessment: Validation study for mild cognitive impairment and Alzheimer disease. *Alzheimer Disease and Associated Disorders, 27*(1), 37–43.

Fujii, D. (2017). *Conducting a culturally informed neuropsychological evaluation.* American Psychological Association.

Gomar, J. J., Bobes-Bascaran, M. T., Conejero-Goldberg, C., Davies, P., Goldberg, T. E., & Alzheimer's Disease Neuroimaging Initiative. (2011). Utility of combinations of biomarkers, cognitive markers, and risk factors to predict conversion from mild cognitive impairment to Alzheimer disease in patients in the Alzheimer's disease neuroimaging initiative. *Archives of General Psychiatry, 68*, 961–969.

Gorno-Tempini, M.L., Hillis, A.E., Weintraub, S., Kertesz, A., Mendez, M., Cappa, S.F., … Grossman, M. (2011). Classification of primary progressive aphasia and its variants. *Neurology, 76*, 1006–1014.

Greenberg, M. S., Tanev, K., Marin, M. F., & Pitman, R. K. (2014). Stress, PTSD, and dementia. *Alzheimer's & Dementia, 10*(3), S155–S165.

Grossman, M., Libon, D. J., Forman, M. S., Massimo, L., Wood, E., Moore, P., … Trojanowski, J. Q. (2007). Distinct antemortem profiles in patients with pathologically defined frontotemporal dementia. *Archives of Neurology, 64*(11), 1601–1609.

Hall, A. M., & Roberson, E. D. (2012). Mouse models of Alzheimer's disease. *Brain Research Bulletin, 88*(1), 3–12.

Hill, N. T., Mowszowski, L., Naismith, S. L., Chadwick, V. L., Valenzuela, M., & Lampit, A. (2016). Computerized cognitive training in older adults with mild cognitive impairment or dementia: A systematic review and meta-analysis. *American Journal of Psychiatry,* 1–12. doi: 10.1176/appi.ajp.2016.16030360

Holtzer, R., Goldin, Y., Zimmerman, M., Katz, M., Buschke, H., & Lipton, R. B. (2008). Robust norms for selected neuropsychological tests in older adults. *Archives of Clinical Neuropsychology, 23*(5), 531–541.

Hyman, B. T., Phelps, C. H., Beach, T. G., Bigio, E. H., Cairns, N. J., Carrillo, M. C., … Mirra, S. S. (2012). National Institute on Aging–Alzheimer's Association guidelines for the neuropathologic assessment of Alzheimer's disease. *Alzheimer's & Dementia, 8*(1), 1–13.

Johns, E. K., Phillips, N. A., Belleville, S., Goupil, D., Babins, L., Kelner, N., … Chertkow, H. (2009). Executive functions in frontotemporal dementia and Lewy body dementia. *Neuropsychology, 23*(6), 765–777.

Jurica, P. J., Leitten, C. L., & Mattis, S. (2001). *DRS-2 : Dementia rating scale-2 : professional manual.* Lutz, FL: Psychological Assessment Resources.

Locke, D. E. C., Ivnik, R. J., Cha, R. H., Knopman, D. S., Tangalos, E. G., Boeve, B. F., … Smith, G. E. (2009). Age, family history, and memory and future risk for cognitive impairment. *Journal of Clinical and Experimental Neuropsychology, 31*(1), 111–116.

Lucas, J. A., Ivnik, R. J., Willis, F. B., Ferman, T. J., Smith, G. E., Parfitt, F. C., … Graff-Radford, N. R. (2005). Mayo's older African Americans normative studies: Normative data for commonly used clinical neuropsychological measures. *The Clinical Neuropsychologist, 19*(2), 162–183.

Luengo-Fernandez, R., Leal, J., & Gray, A. (2015). UK research spend in 2008 and 2012: Comparing stroke, cancer, coronary heart disease and dementia. *BMJ Open, 5*(4), e006648. doi:10.1136/bmjopen-2014–006648

Mayo Clinic. (2016). HABIT Health Action to Benefit Independence & Thinking. Retrieved from: http://www.mayo.edu/pmts/mc2800-mc2899/mc2815-10.pdf.

McKeith, I. G., Boeve, B. F., Dickson, D. W., Halliday, G., Taylor, J. P., Weintraub, D., … Kosaka, K. (2017). Diagnosis and management of dementia with Lewy bodies fourth consensus report of the DLB consortium. *Neurology, 89*, 1–13.

McKhann, G. M., Knopman, D. S., Chertkow, H., Hyman, B. T., Jack, C. R., Kawas, C. H., … Mohs, R. C. (2011). The diagnosis of dementia due to Alzheimer's disease: Recommendations from the National Institute on Aging-Alzheimer's Association workgroups on diagnostic guidelines for Alzheimer's disease. *Alzheimer's & Dementia, 7*(3), 263–269.

Moye, J., Marson, D. C., & Edelstein, B. (2013). Assessment of capacity in an aging society. *American Psychologist, 68*(3), 158–171.

Nasreddine, Z. S., Phillips, N. A., Bedirian, V., Charbonneau, S., Whitehead, V., Collin, I., … Chertkow, H. (2005). The Montreal Cognitive Assessment, MoCA: A brief screening tool for mild cognitive impairment. *Journal of the American Geriatrics Society, 53*(4), 695–699.

Nguyen, H. H., & Ryan, A. M. (2008). Does stereotype threat affect test performance of minorities and women? A meta-analysis of experimental evidence. *Journal of Applied Psychology, 93*(6), 1314–1334.

O'Connell, M. E., & Tuokko, H. (2010). Age corrections and dementia classification accuracy. *Archives of Clinical Neuropsychology, 25*(2), 126–138.

Onyike, C. U. & Diehl-Schmid, J. (2013). The epidemiology of frontotemporal dementia. *International Review of Psychiatry, 25*(2), 130–137.

Petersen, R. C. (2011). Mild cognitive impairment. *The New England Journal of Medicine, 364*, 2227–2234.

Pandya, S. Y., Lacritz, L. H., Weiner, M. F., Deschner, M., & Woon, F. L. (2017). Predictors of reversion from mild cognitive impairment to normal cognition. *Dementia and Geriatric Cognitive Disorders, 43*(3–4), 204–214.

Piguet, O., Hornberger, M., Mioshi, E., & Hodges, J. R. (2011). Behavioural-variant frontotemporal dementia: Diagnosis, clinical staging, and management. *The Lancet Neurology, 10*(2), 162–172.

Prince, M., Bryce, R., Albanese, E., Wimo, A., Ribeiro, W., & Ferri, C. P. (2013). The global prevalence of dementia: A systematic review and metaanalysis. *Alzheimer's & Dementia, 9*(1), 63–75.

Qiu, C., Kivipelto, M., & von Strauss, E. (2009). Epidemiology of Alzheimer's disease: Occurrence, determinants, and strategies toward intervention. *Dialogues in Clinical Neuroscience, 11*(2), 111–128.

Rascovsky, K., Hodges, J. R., Knopman, D., Mendez, M. F., Kramer, J. H., Neuhaus, J., … Hillis, A. E. (2011). Sensitivity of revised diagnostic criteria for the behavioural variant of frontotemporal dementia. *Brain, 134*(9), 2456–2477.

Rossetti, H. C., Lacritz, L. H., Cullum, C. M., & Weiner, M. F. (2011). Normative data for the Montreal Cognitive Assessment (MoCA) in a population-based sample. *Neurology, 77*, 1272–1275.

Rossetti, H., Lacritz, L., Hynan, L., Cullum, C. M., Van Wright, A., & Weiner, M. (2017). Montreal Cognitive Assessment performance among African Americans. *Archives of Clinical Neuropsychology, 32*(2), 238–244.

Ruchinskas, R. A., & Curyto, K. J. (2003). Cognitive screening in geriatric rehabilitation. *Rehabilitation Psychology, 48*(1), 14–22.

Salmon, D. P., Thomas, R. G., Pay, M. M., Booth, A., Hofstetter, C. R., Thal, L. J., & Katzman, R. (2002). Alzheimer's disease can be accurately diagnosed in very mildly impaired individuals. *Neurology, 59*(7), 1022–1028.

Satizabal, C. L., Beiser, A. S., Chouraki, V., Chêne, G., Dufouil, C., & Seshadri, S. (2016). Incidence of dementia over three decades in the Framingham Heart Study. *New England Journal of Medicine, 374*(6), 523–532.

Schulz, R., Cook, T. B., Beach, S. R., Lingler, J. H., Martire, L. M., Monin, J. K., & Czaja, S. J. (2013). Magnitude and causes of bias among family caregivers rating Alzheimer disease patients. *American Journal of Geriatric Psychiatry, 21*(1), 14–25.

Shao, H., Breitner, J. C., Whitmer, R. A., Wang, J., Hayden, K., Wengreen, H., … Welsh-Bohmer, K. (2012). Hormone therapy and Alzheimer disease dementia: New findings from the Cache County Study. *Neurology*, *79*(18), 1846–1852.

Smith, E.E. (2017). Clinical presentations and epidemiology of vascular dementia. *Clinical Science*, *131*(11), 1059–1068.

Snowden, J. S., Thompson, J. C., Stopford, C. L., Richardson, A. M., Gerhard, A., Neary, D., & Mann, D. M. (2011). The clinical diagnosis of early-onset dementias: Diagnostic accuracy and clinicopathological relationships. *Brain*, *134*Pt (9), 2478–2492.

Spooner, D. M., & Pachana, N. A. (2006). Ecological validity in neuropsychological assessment: A case for greater consideration in research with neurologically intact populations. *Archives of Clinical Neuropsychology*, *21*(4), 327–337.

Stinton, C., McKeith, I., Taylor, J. P., Lafortune, L., Mioshi, E., Mak, E., … O'Brien, J. T. (2015). Pharmacological management of Lewy body dementia: A systematic review and meta-analysis. *American Journal of Psychiatry*, *172*(8), 731–742.

Tabert, M. H., Manly, J. J., Liu, X., Pelton, G. H., Rosenblum, S., Jacobs, M., … Devanand, D. P. (2006). Neuropsychological prediction of conversion to Alzheimer disease in patients with mild cognitive impairment. *Archives of General Psychiatry*, *63*, 916–924.

Tierney, M. C., Moineddin, R., & McDowell, I. (2010). Prediction of all-cause dementia using neuropsychological tests within 10 and 5 years of diagnosis in a community-based sample. *Journal of Alzheimer's Disease*, *22* (4), 1231–1240.

Troster, A. I. (2008). Neuropsychological characteristics of dementia with Lewy bodies and Parkinson's disease with dementia: Differentiation, early detection, and implications for "mild cognitive impairment" and biomarkers. *Neuropsychology Review*, *18*(1), 103–119.

Tun, S. M., Murman, D. L., Long, H. L., Colenda, C. C., & von Eye, A. (2007). Predictive validity of neuropsychiatric subgroups on nursing home placement and survival in patients with Alzheimer disease. *American Journal of Geriatric Psychiatry*, *15*(4), 314–327.

van Gorp, W. G., Marcotte, T. D., Sultzer, D., Hinkin, C., Mahler, M., & Cummings, J. L. (1999). Screening for dementia: Comparison of three commonly used instruments. *Journal of Clinical and Experimental Neuropsychology*, *21*(1), 29–38.

Watson, J. L., Ryan, L., Silverberg, N., Cahan, V., & Bernard, M. A. (2014). Obstacles and opportunities in Alzheimer's clinical trial recruitment. *Health Affairs*, *33*(4), 574–579.

Wittenberg, D., Possin, K. L., Rascovsky, K., Rankin, K. P., Miller, B. L., & Kramer, J. H. (2008). The early neuropsychological and behavioral characteristics of frontotemporal dementia. *Neuropsychology Review*, *18*(1), 91–102.

Young, A. J., Johnson, S., Steffens, D. C., & Doraiswamy, P. M. (2007). Coenzyme Q10: A review of its promise as a neuroprotectant. *CNS Spectrums*, *12*(1), 62–68.

Index

AAIDD. *See* American Association of
    Intellectual and Developmental
    Disabilities
ABA. *See* applied behavioral analysis
ACA. *See* anterior cerebral arteries
academic outcomes
    with epilepsy, 193
    with FASD, 86
    with LBW/preterm birth, 7–10
        prevention strategies for, 8–9
        special education services, 8
    with LD
        for basic academic skills, 118
        for complex academic skills, 118
    with pediatric cancer, 171
    with PHIV, 214–215
    with SBM, 28
        clinical treatment practices for, 37
        IEPs and, 33–34, 35
        intervention strategies for, 35
        neuropsychological evaluations
            of, 32–33
acquired immune deficiency syndrome
    (AIDS), 210
activities of daily living (ADL), with
    HIV, 213
acute lymphocytic leukemia (ALL),
    162
    intellectual functioning with, 170
acute myeloid leukemia (AML), 162
AD. *See* Alzheimer's disease
ADA. *See* Americans with Disabilities
    Act
ADA Amendments Act (ADAAA)
    (2008), 54, 117
adaptive functioning
    with FASD, 86–87
    with PHIV, 215
ADDM Network. *See* Autism and
    Developmental Disabilities
    Monitoring Network
ADHD. *See* attention deficit
    hyperactivity disorder
ADL. *See* activities of daily living
adolescence. *See also* pediatric cancer;
    pediatric HIV; pediatric
    ischemic stroke
    ADHD during, 94
    HIV and, 215–216

behavioral and emotional
    functioning, 216
cognitive functioning, 215–216
HAND, 217–219
intellectual disability syndromes
    during, 73
MS in, 234–235
SBM during, 30
TBI and, behavioral and emotional
    outcomes with, 145
ADT. *See* androgen deprivation
    therapy
adult care, transition to
    with ASD, 54–55
        for college and university
            attendance, 54
        for employment, 54–55
        for independent living skills, 55
    in epilepsy treatment, 203
    with intellectual disability
        syndromes, 73–74
    with LD, 130
    RD, 123
    after pediatric TBI, 145–146
    with SBM, 38
adult patients with cancer. *See* cancers
AEDs. *See* antiepileptic drugs
African Americans, SBM among, 24
age
    intellectual disability syndromes by,
        73–74
    maternal, DS and, 65
    MS and, age of onset for, 228
aging. *See also* adult care
    HIV and, 212, 217
AIDS. *See* acquired immune deficiency
    syndrome
AIM program. *See* Attention
    Intervention and Management
    program
alcohol-related birth defects (ARBD),
    79
alcohol-related neurodevelopmental
    disorder (ARND), 79
alemtuzumab, 237
ALL. *See* acute lymphocytic leukemia
all-cause dementia, 269
Alzheimer's disease (AD), 268,
    269–271

behavioral features, 272
clinical features, 273
neuropsychological features,
    272
American Association of Intellectual
    and Developmental Disabilities
    (AAIDD), 61
Americans with Disabilities Act (ADA)
    (1990), 54, 117
AML. *See* acute myeloid leukemia
androgen deprivation therapy (ADT),
    165–167
anticipatory guidance, 37
antiepileptic drugs (AEDs), 186,
    201–202, 204
antiretroviral (ARV) treatments, 210,
    220. *See also* combination
    antiretroviral therapy
anxiety, cancer and, 175
anxiety disorder, 45, 235
aphasia, 256
applied behavioral analysis (ABA), 51–52
aptitude-achievement discrepancy
    model, 127
ARBD. *See* alcohol-related birth
    defects
ARND. *See* alcohol-related
    neurodevelopmental disorder
arteriovenous malformation (AVM),
    247
ARV treatments. *See* antiretroviral
    treatments
ASD. *See* autism spectrum disorders
Asian populations, SBM among, 24
ATN. *See* Autism Treatment
    Network
atomoxetine, 101
atrial fibrillation, 249
attention deficit hyperactivity disorder
    (ADHD)
    assessment of
        CPTs, 99–100
        EF, 100
        multi-informant, 99–100
        through rating scales, 99–100
    CBT for, 105–106
        group metacognitive therapy,
            105–106
        individual, 105

comorbid psychiatric disorders, 95
  CD, 9, 95
  MDD, 95
  ODD, 9, 95
DSM-5 diagnostic criteria, 93
employment outcomes with, 94
epidemiology, 93–94
  gender distribution, 94
  by race, 94
epilepsy and, 192–193, 195
etiology, 107
functioning domains with, 94–95
  during adolescence, 94
  during childhood, 94
intervention strategies, 101–107
  academic, 103
  BPT, 103–104
  classroom-based, 102–103
  cognitive training, 106–107
  organizational skills, 104–105
  pharmacological, 101–102
  physical activity, 107
  school-based, 102–103
  self-regulatory, 103
  skill-based, 104
LBW/preterm birth and, 9
PAE and, 86–87
pathophysiology, 95–97
  brain development, 96–97
  through fMRI imaging, 96–97
  heritability factors, 95–96
  phenotype, 97
pediatric ischemic stroke and, 253
SBM and, 26
subtypes, 93
attention deficits
  with ASD, 50
  with DS, 65–66
  with epilepsy, 192–193
  with FASD, 84–85
  iFC and, 5
  LBW/preterm birth and, 5–7
  with MS, 234
  with pediatric, 170
  with SBM, 25–26
    intervention strategies, 33–34
    neuropsychological evaluations of, 31
  with stroke, pediatric ischemic stroke, 253
  top-down abilities, 26
Attention Intervention and Management (AIM) program, 152–153
Autism and Developmental Disabilities Monitoring (ADDM) Network, 46
autism spectrum disorders (ASD)
  ADHD and, 45

adult care practices, transition to, 54–55
  for college and university attendance, 54
  for employment, 54–55
  for independent living skills, 55
  under Americans with Disabilities Act, 54
anxiety disorder and, 45
clinical features, 45–46
clinical practices, 56
  future research on, 57
  pharmacological interventions, 55–57
clinical presentation, 47–51
  attentional deficits, 50
  brain development, 48
  cognitive function, 49
  EF deficits, 50
  language skills development, 49–50
  megencephaly, 48
  memory impairment, 50–51
  motor function impairments, 51
  social interaction issues, 9–10, 47
diagnostic criteria, 45, 48–49
  by CDC, 47
  in DSM-5, 45, 46
  with fMRI, 48
  testing instruments in, 48–49
epidemiology, 46–47
  ADDM Network, 46
  prevalence rates, 46
intervention approaches, for children, 51–54
  ABA, 51–52
  Early Social Interaction Project, 53
  ESDM, 52–53
  NDBI, 52
  PRT, 52
LBW/preterm birth and, 9–10
mood disorder and, 45
pathophysiology, 46–47
  genetic factors, 46
pharmacological interventions, 55–57
Autism Treatment Network (ATN), 56
AVM. See arteriovenous malformation

Bayley Scales of Infant Development, 219–220
Behavior Rating Inventory of Executive Function (BRIEF) scores, 7
behavioral parent training (BPT), 103–104
behavioral variant Frontotemporal Dementia (bvFTD), 268, 273
behavioral features, 272

clinical features, 273
neuropsychological features, 272
specific assessment considerations, 279
biomarkers, in dementia, 269, 282
birth defects. See also spina bifida myelomeningocele
  prevalence rates for, 24
  by race, 24
BPT. See behavioral parent training
brain attack, 259. See also stroke
brain development
  with ADHD, 96–97
  with ASD, 48
  with HIV, 212
  LBW/preterm birth and, 4
  LD and, 120
  with SBM, 31
  white matter development, with megencephaly, 48
Brief Repeatable Battery of Neuropsychological Tests (BRB), 236
BRIEF scores. See Behavior Rating Inventory of Executive Function scores
bvFTD. See behavioral variant Frontotemporal Dementia

cancer-related cognitive impairment (CRCI), 163–164
cancers. See also pediatric cancer
  ALL, 162
    intellectual functioning with, 170
  AML, 162
  anxiety and, 175
  assessment recommendations, 177
  clinical manifestations, 166–167
  clinical practice implications, 168
  CLL, 162
  CML, 162
  CNS tumors, 162
    surgical interventions for, 163–164
  depression and, 175
  diagnosis rates, 162
  interventions for, 175–177
    CBT, 175
    future research on, 177–179
    neuropsychological, 176–177
    pharmacological, 175–176
  liquid tumors, 162
  neuroanatomical correlates, 166–167
  neuropsychological functioning, 172–173
    assessment tests, 172
    genotype associations, 173
  prevalence rates, 162

cancer (cont.)
  prevention strategies, 170
  solid tumors, 162
  treatment factors, functioning
      influenced by, 163–170
    chemotherapy, 164
    CRCI, 163–164
    CRT, 163–164
    endocrine therapy, 165–168
    hormonal therapy, 165–168
    HSCT, 164–165
    radiation therapy, 165
    SES as factor in, 169
cART therapy. *See* combination
    antiretroviral therapy
CAS. *See* Cognitive Assessment System
CBT. *See* cognitive behavioral therapy
CD. *See* conduct disorder
Centers for Disease Control (CDC)
  ASD diagnostic criteria, 47
  FASD estimates, 80
  intellectual disability rates, 61–62
central nervous system (CNS) tumors,
    162
  surgical interventions, 163
cerebral atrophy, 254
cerebral palsy (CP), 3
cerebral sinovenous thrombosis
    (CSVT), 244
  ischemic stroke, 244
cerebral small vessel disease (CSVD),
    247, 248, 254
cerebral vascular accident, epilepsy
    and, 188
chemoprotectants, 169
chemotherapy, 164
Chiari-II malformation, 25
Chicago Multiscale Depression
    Inventory, 262
children. *See* infants and children
cholesterol level management, 249
chronic lymphocytic leukemia (CLL),
    162
chronic myeloid leukemia (CML), 162
chronic traumatic encephalopathy
    (CTE), 146–147
CIFASD. *See* Collaborative Initiative
    on Fetal Alcohol Spectrum
    Disorders
CIS. *See* clinically isolated syndrome
clinically isolated syndrome (CIS), 233
CLL. *See* chronic lymphocytic
    leukemia
CML. *See* chronic myeloid leukemia
CNS tumors, 162
"cocktail party syndrome," 32
Cognitive Assessment System (CAS),
    31
cognitive behavioral therapy (CBT)
  for ADHD, 105–106

group metacognitive therapy,
    105–106
  individual, 105
in cancer interventions, 175
for epilepsy, 202–203
cognitive function
  with ASD, 49
  with FASD, 81–87
    academic outcomes, 86
    EF, 84–85
    language skills development,
        85
    learning impairments, 85–86
    memory impairments, 85–86
  with HIV, 212–213
    in adolescence, 215–216
  LBW/preterm birth, 5
  metacognition, 26
  with MS, 234–235
    in adults, 234
    attention deficits, 234
    in children and adolescents,
        234–235
    EF, 235
    language skills development,
        234–235
    memory deficits, 234
  with PHIV, 213–215
  with stroke, 263–263
    pediatric ischemic, 257–258
  with TBI, 141, 142–144
cognitive rehabilitation
  for HAND, 221
  for MS, 238–239
cognitive reserve, 212
Cogstate program, for pediatric cancer
    assessment, 178–179
Collaborative Initiative on Fetal
    Alcohol Spectrum Disorders
    (CIFASD), 84
combination antiretroviral (cART)
    therapy, 212, 217, 220
  for HAND, 220–221
Comprehensive Assessment of Spoken
    Language, 32
conduct disorder (CD), 9, 95
continuous performance tests (CPTs),
    99–100
corticosteroids, 237
CP. *See* cerebral palsy
CPTs. *See* continuous performance
    tests
cranial radiation therapy (CRT),
    163–164
  for pediatric cancer, use limitations
    in, 169
CRCI. *See* cancer-related cognitive
    impairment
CRT. *See* cranial radiation therapy
CSVD. *See* cerebral small vessel disease

CSVT. *See* cerebral sinovenous
    thrombosis
CTE. *See* chronic traumatic
    encephalopathy
culture, epilepsy considerations
    influenced by, 197
  neuropsychological assessment of,
    200

daclizumab, 237
DAI. *See* diffuse axonal injury
DART. *See* Dual Attention to Response
    Task
delayed onset dementia, 275
dementia
  AD, 268, 269–271
    behavioral features, 272
    clinical features, 273
    neuropsychological features, 272
  all-cause, 269
  assessment strategies
    comprehensive, 278–279
    neuropsychological, 276–277
    normative considerations in, 279
    screening tests, 277–278
    serial, 279
    specific considerations in,
        279–280
    test design for, 282
    utility of, 282
  bvFTD, 268, 273
    behavioral features, 272
    clinical features, 273
    neuropsychological features, 272
    specific assessment
        considerations, 279
  causes of, 270
  common causes of, 268
  comprehensive assessment of,
    278–279
  definitions, 268
  diagnostic criteria, 268–269
    biomarkers in, 269, 282
    clinical overview, 281
    NCDs, 268–269
  epidemiology of, 271
  with epilepsy, 194–195
  frontotemporal, 270
  interventions for, 280–282
    clinical overview, 281
    non-pharmacological, 280–281
    pharmacological, 280
  LBD, 268, 270, 271–273
    behavioral features, 272
    clinical features, 273
    neuropsychological features, 272
    specific assessment
        considerations, 279–280
  neuroimaging in, 277
  prevention strategies, 275

risk factors, 273–274
support factors for, 275–276
  for delayed onset, 275
  limited, 276
  from TBI, 146–147
    CTE, 146–147
  unsupported factors for, 276
Dementia with Lewy Bodies. *See* Lewy
    Body Disease
depression
  cancer and, 175
  Chicago Multiscale Depression
    Inventory, 262
  with MS, 235
  stroke and, 262
developmental MD, 121
diabetes, management of, 249
*Diagnostic and Statistical Manual of
    Mental Disorders, 5th Edition*
    (DSM-5)
  ADHD diagnostic criteria, 93
  ASD, 45, 46
  intellectual disability, 61, 63
  LD diagnostic criteria, 117–119
    for basic academic skills, 118
    for complex academic skills,
      118
    IQ levels in, 118–119, 127
diet and nutrition
  ketogenic, 202
  stroke prevention and, 249
diffuse axonal injury (DAI), 140
diffuse TBI, 140
dimethyl fumarate, 237
Donepezil, 173–174
Down syndrome (DS), 64–66
  attention deficits with, 65–66
  epidemiology, 64–65
  etiology, 64–65
    chromosome 21 overexpression,
      64–65
    maternal age, 65
    race and ethnicity factors, 65
  language development and,
    65–66
  medical comorbidities, 65
  motor function and, 65–66
  neurobehavioral profile, 65–66
  neurological basis, 66
  phenotype, 65
  prevalence rates, 64–65
  survival prognosis, 66
DS. *See* Down syndrome
DSM-5. *See Diagnostic and Statistical
    Manual of Mental Disorders,
    5th Edition*
Dual Attention to Response Task
    (DART), 31
dyslexia. *See also* reading disorder
  heritability of, 120

Early Social Interaction Project, 53
Early Start Denver Model (ESDM),
    52–53
Education for All Handicapped
    Children Act (1975), 116
education services. *See* special
    education services
EF. *See* executive functioning
ELBW. *See* extremely low birth weight
employment outcomes
  with ADHD, 94
  with ASD, 54–55
endocrine therapy, 165–168
endoscopic third ventriculostomy with
    choroid plexus cauterization
    (ETV/CPC), 38–39
EP birth. *See* extremely preterm birth
epilepsy
  ADHD and, 192–193, 195
  in adults
    cognitive manifestations, 193–195
    psychoclinical features, 193–195
  assessment techniques, 188
  behavioral manifestations of, 192
  cerebral vascular accident and, 188
  in children
    cognitive manifestations, 188–193
    psychosocial features, 195
  clinical practice implications,
    205–206
  cognitive manifestations of, 188–195
    academic outcomes, 193
    attention deficits, 192–193
    EF deficits, 193
    memory deficits, 193
  cultural considerations across
    lifespan, 197
  neuropsychological assessment of,
    200
  defined, 186
  dementia with, 194–195
  EF and, 193
    neuropsychological assessment of,
      201
  ischemic stroke and, 188
  longer-term outcomes with, 197
  longitudinal development studies,
    197
  medically refractory, 192
  memory functions and, 193
    neuropsychological assessment of,
      200–201
  mental health disorders with,
    202–203
  neuropsychological aspects of,
    189–191
  neuropsychological assessment of,
    199–201
    cultural considerations, 200
    for EF, 201

ILAE Neuropsychology Task
    Force, 199–200, 204, 205–206
  for intellectual functioning, 200
  language skills, 200
  for memory, 200–201
new-onset, 194
prevalence rates, 186–187
prevention strategies, 187
  early, 187
  against infection, 187
PTE, 187–188
seizures, 186
  PNES, 197–199
after TBI, 187–188
treatment strategies, 201–202
  with AEDs, 186, 201–202, 204
  with CBT, 202–203
  through ketogenic diet, 202
  transition to adult care, 203
  VNS, 202
ESDM. *See* Early Start Denver Model
ETV/CPC. *See* endoscopic third
    ventriculostomy with choroid
    plexus cauterization
executive functioning (EF)
  with ADHD, 100
  with ASD, 50
  BRIEF scores, 7
  epilepsy and, 193
    neuropsychological assessment of,
      201
  with FASD, 84–85
  with HIV, 212–213
  LBW/preterm birth and, 5–7
  with MS, 235
  neuroanatomical correlates of, 7
  with pediatric cancer, 170
  with SBM, 26–27
    clinical treatment practices for, 37
    intervention strategies for, 34
    neuropsychological evaluations
      of, 31
  with stroke, 257–257
    pediatric ischemic stroke, 253
Expanded Disability Status Scale,
    233–234
extremely low birth weight (ELBW), 2
extremely preterm (EP) birth, 2

facilitative intervention training (FIT),
    106–107
families, functioning skills for, with
    SBM, 29–30
  clinical manifestations, 29–30
  interprofessional team partnering
    with, 36–37
  intervention strategies for, 35–36
  neuropsychological evaluations of,
    33
  SES factors, 29–30

families, TBI and, psychosocial
	outcomes for, 145
FAS. *See* fetal alcohol syndrome
FASD. *See* fetal alcohol spectrum
	disorders
fatigue, with MS, 235
females. *See* women
fertility treatments, preterm birth rates
	and, 2
fetal alcohol spectrum disorders
	(FASD)
	ARBD, 79
	ARND, 79
	behavioral functioning, 87
		neuroanatomical correlates,
		82–83
	CDC estimates, 80
	during childhood, 82–83
	clinical care practices, 89–90
	cognitive impairments, 81–87
		academic outcomes, 86
		EF, 84–85
		language skills development, 85
		learning impairments, 85–86
		memory impairments, 85–86
	defined, 79
	diagnostic criteria, 79
	epidemiology, 80
	FAS, 79
		pFAS, 79
	interventions, 88–89
		future directions for, 90
		non-pharmacological, 88–89
		pharmacological, 88
	neuropsychological impairments,
		81–87
		adaptive functioning, 86–87
		assessments of, 87
		attentional difficulties, 84–85
		CIFASD program, 84
		intellectual disability, 82–84
		motor function, 86
		visual-spatial processing, 85
	NIAAA guidelines, 79
	PAE, 79, 81
		ADHD and, 86–87
		ND-PAE, 79–80
	pathophysiology, 80
	prevention strategies, 80–81
		UPPSs, 81
	psychopathology with, 87
	psychosocial functioning, 87
fetal alcohol syndrome (FAS), 79
	pFAS, 79
fingolimod, 237
FIT. *See* facilitative intervention
	training
Flair MRI, 247–248
fMRI. *See* functional magnetic
	resonance imaging

focal TBI, 140
Fragile X syndrome (FXS), 66–67
	ADHD and, 66
	ASD and, 66
	comorbidities, 66
	epidemiology, 66
	etiology, 66
	gender factors, 67
	long-term prognosis, 67
	neurobehavioral profile, 67
	neurological basis, 67
	phenotype, 66
	prevalence, 66
frontotemporal dementia, 270
Full Scale IQ (FSIQ), 68
functional adaptation, with SBM, 30
	intervention strategies for, 36
	neuropsychological evaluations of,
		33
functional magnetic resonance
		imaging (fMRI)
	for ADHD, 96–97
	for ASD diagnosis, 48
FXS. *See* Fragile X syndrome

gender. *See also* males; women
	ADHD and, 94
	FXS and, 67
		long-term prognosis by, 67
	MS and, 228
glatiramer acetate, 237
glucocorticoids, 168–169
goal-setting. *See* metacognition
Gordon Diagnostic System, 31
group metacognitive therapy, 105–106

HAND. *See* HIV-associated
		neurocognitive disorders
health-related quality of life (HRQoL)
	with HIV, 213, 217
	with SBM, 29
hematopoietic stem cell transplant
		(HSCT), 164–165
hemispatial neglect, 256
hemorrhagic stroke, 244, 247
Hispanic populations, SBM among,
		24
HIV. *See* human immunodeficiency
		virus
HIV-associated neurocognitive
		disorders (HAND), 211, 212
	in adolescents, 217–219
	in adults, 217
	cART and, 220–221
	in children, 217–219
	cognitive rehabilitation, 221
	development of, 216–217
hormonal therapy, 165–168
HRQoL. *See* health-related quality of
		life

HSCT. *See* hematopoietic stem cell
		transplant
human immunodeficiency virus
		(HIV). *See also* HIV-associated
		neurocognitive disorders;
		pediatric HIV
	in adolescence, 215–216
		behavioral and emotional
			functioning, 216
		cognitive functioning, 215–216
		HAND, 217–219
	adults with
		evidence-based guidelines, 221
		HAND, 217
	aging and, 212, 217
	AIDS and, 210
	clinical manifestation, 212–216, 222
		ADLs, 213
		behavioral function, 213
		cognitive function, 212–213
		EF, 212–213
		emotional functioning, 213
		motor function, 213
	cognitive functioning with, 212–213
		in adolescence, 215–216
		in infants and children, 213–215
	cognitive reserve, 212
	development history for, 210
	epidemiology, 211–212
		UNAIDS projections, 211
	HRQoL with, 213, 217
	interventions for, 210–211
	longitudinal development, 216–223
	mood disorders with, 213
	neuropsychological development,
		216–223. *See also* HIV-
		associated neurocognitive
		disorders
		assessment methods, 219–220
	pathophysiology, 211–212
		brain development, 212
		CNS damage, 211. *See also* HIV-
			associated neurocognitive
			disorders
		in perinatal acquisition, 211–212
	prevalence rates, 211
	prevention, 212
	research on, 210–211
	treatment strategies
		ARV, 210, 220
		cART, 212, 217, 220–221
		evidence-based guidelines,
			223
hybrid models, for LD testing, 128
hydrocephalus, 25
hypercholesterolemia, 249
hyperfractionation, 169

ICD-10. *See* International
		Classification of Diseases

IEP. *See* individualized education program
iFC. *See* intrinsic functional connectivity
ILAE Neuropsychology Task Force, 199–200, 204, 205–206
individualized education program (IEP), 33–34, 35
  development strategies for, 116
Individuals with Disabilities Education Act (1990), 116
infants and children. *See also* pediatric cancer; pediatric HIV; pediatric ischemic stroke
  ADHD in, 94
  ASD and, intervention approaches for, 51–54
    ABA, 51–52
    Early Social Interaction Project, 53
    ESDM, 52–53
    NDBI, 52
    PRT, 52
  epilepsy in
    cognitive manifestations, 188–193
    psychosocial features, 195
  FASD during, 82–83
  intellectual disability syndromes
    from environmental exposure, 63–64
    from infants to preschool age, 73
    during school age, 73
  MS in, 230
  WISC-V, 31
intellectual disability syndromes. *See also* Down syndrome; Fragile X syndrome; Williams Syndrome
  during adolescence, 73
  adult care with, transition to, 73–74
  assessment considerations, 73
    by age, 73–74
    behavior observation, 73
    sensory and motor conditions, 73
  in childhood
    from environmental exposure, 63–64
    from infants to preschool age, 73
    school age, 73
  clinical manifestations, 69
  defined, 61
  diagnostic criteria
    AAIDD, 61
    classification systems, 62–63
    DSM-5, 61, 63
    dual, 73
    ICD-10, 61, 63
  epidemiology, 61–62
  etiology, 62–64

environmental exposure, during childhood, 63–64
  genetic disorders, 63
  LBW/preterm birth, 63
  prenatal risk factors, 63
  from TBI, 63, 64
  with FASD, 82–84
  interventions for, 71–73
    resources for, 74
  neuropsychological assessment, 68–71
  PKU, 64
  prevalence for, 61–62
    CDC estimates, 61–62
  prevention strategies, 64
  treatment strategies, 71–72
intellectual functioning
  with ALL, 170
  with epilepsy, 200
  with pediatric cancer, 170
  with pediatric ischemic stroke, 250–252
intelligence quotient (IQ)
  FSIQ, 68
  LBW/preterm birth and, 5
  with LD, 118–119, 127
International Classification of Diseases, 10th Edition (ICD-10), intellectual disability diagnosis, 61, 63
intra-individual differences model, 126–127
intrauterine growth restriction (IUGR), LBW/preterm birth and, 2
intrinsic functional connectivity (iFC), 5
IQ. *See* intelligence quotient
ischemic stroke, 188
  CSVT, 244
IUGR. *See* intrauterine growth restriction

Joint United Nations Programme on HIV/AIDS (UNAIDS), 211

Kanner, Leo, 48
Kaufman Test of Educational Achievement-Third Edition, 32
ketogenic diet, 202

language skills
  with ASD, 49–50
  "cocktail party syndrome," 32
  Comprehensive Assessment of Spoken Language, 32
  with DS, 65–66
  with epilepsy, 200
  with FASD, 85
  with MS, 234–235

with pediatric ischemic stroke, 252
with PHIV, 214–215
with SBM, 27
  intervention strategies for, 34
  neuropsychological evaluations of, 31–32
late preterm (LP) birth, 2
LBD. *See* Lewy Body Disease
LBW. *See* low birth weight
learning disabilities (LD). *See also* academic outcomes
  definitions, 116–117
    under ADA/ADAAA, 117
    IEP development strategies influenced by, 116
    NJCLD guidelines, 116
    under RSA, 116
    unexpected underachievement as core aspect in, 130–131
  DSM-5 diagnostic criteria, 117–119
    for basic academic skills, 118
    for complex academic skills, 118
    IQ levels in, 118–119, 127
  under Education for All Handicapped Children Act, 116
  epidemiology, 119–122
  etiology, 119–122
  under Individuals with Disabilities Education Act, 116
  intervention/prevention strategies, 122–125, 129–130
    for adults, 130
    for MD, 129
    for RD, 122–124, 129
  LBW/preterm birth and, 7–10
    ADHD, 9
    diagnostic evaluations of, 14–15
    prevention strategies, 8–9
    special education services, 8
  MD, 120–121
    comorbidity with, 121
    developmental, 121
    genetic risk factors, 121
    intervention strategies, 129
    prevalence rates, 120–121
  pathophysiology, 119–122
  RD, 119–120
    brain development and, 120
    comorbidities with, 119–120
    intervention/prevention strategies, 122–124, 129
    meta-analysis of adults with, 123
    prevalence rates, 119
    risk factors for, 120
  testing for, limitations in, 125–130
    aptitude-achievement discrepancy model, 127
    discrepancy approaches, 129
    future strategies for, 130–133
    hybrid models, 128

learning disabilities (LD). (cont.)
  intra-individual differences
      model, 126–127
  low achievement model, 126
  regression to the mean model,
      127–128
  RTI model, 128
learning skills. *See also* academic
      outcomes
  with FASD, 85–86
    non-verbal, 86
    verbal, 85
  with pediatric ischemic stroke, 253
lesions
  with MS, 229
  with stroke, 254
leukemias. *See specific leukemias*
Lewy Body Disease (LBD), 268, 270,
      271–273
  behavioral features, 272
  clinical features, 273
  neuropsychological features, 272
  specific assessment considerations,
      279–280
liquid tumors, 162
low achievement model, 126
low birth weight (LBW)
  academic outcome issues with, 7–10
    prevention strategies for, 8–9
    special education services, 8
  ASD and, social issues as result of,
      9–10
  classifications, 2
  decline of, 2–3
  defined, 2
  developmental disorders
    ADHD, 9
    ASD and, 9–10
    diagnosis of, 11
    interventions for, 11–13
    personality issues, 10–13
  ELBW, 2
  emotional issues and, 10
  epidemiology, 2–16
  intellectual disability and, 63
  LBW, 2
  learning disabilities and, 7–10
    ADHD, 9
    diagnostic evaluations of, 14–15
    prevention strategies, 8–9
    special education services, 8
  mortality rates, 3
  neurodevelopmental complications,
      3, 4, 14–16
    attention issues, 5–7
    brain development, 4
    cognitive ability, 5
    CP, 3
    diagnostic evaluations of, 14–15
    EF deficits, 5–7

IQ, 5
  long-term, 4–16
  PVL, 3
  visuomotor skills, 7
pathophysiology, 2–16
personality issues, 10–13
  corrected age evaluations, 10–11
  prevalence rates for, 2
  prevention strategies, 3
  risk factors for, 2
  WHO demographics for, 2
LP birth. *See* late preterm birth

MACFIMS. *See* Minimal Assessment
      of Cognitive Function in MS
magnetic resonance imaging (MRI)
  Flair, 247–248
  fMRI
      for ADHD, 96–97
      for ASD diagnosis, 48
Major and Mild Neurocognitive
      Disorders (NCDs), 268–269
major depressive disorder (MDD), 95
males
  ADHD in, 94
  with FXS, 67
math disorder (MD), 120–121
  comorbidity with, 121
  developmental, 121
  genetic risk factors, 121
  intervention strategies, 129
  prevalence rates, 120–121
MCA. *See* middle cerebral arteries
MD. *See* math disorder
MDD. *See* major depressive disorder
medically refractory epilepsy, 192
megencephaly, 48
memory
  with ASD, 50–51
    recall ability, 51
  epilepsy and, 193
      neuropsychological assessment of,
        200–201
  with FASD, 85–86
    non-verbal learning, 86
    verbal learning, 85
  with MS, 234
  with pediatric cancer, 170, 171
  with PHIV, 214
  prospective, 27
  retrospective, 27
  with SBM, 27
    intervention strategies for, 34–35
    neuropsychological evaluations
        of, 32
  with stroke, 257
    pediatric ischemic stroke, 253
  working, 27
mental retardation, 61. *See also*
      intellectual disability

metacognition, 26
methylphenidate, 173
middle cerebral arteries (MCA), 254
mild TBI, 139, 140
  assessment following, 147
  clinical characteristics, 142
  clinical implications, 153–154
  intervention strategies, 150–151
Minimal Assessment of Cognitive
      Function in MS (MACFIMS),
      236
mitoxantrone, 237–238
MITP. *See* Mother-Infant Transaction
      Program
moderately preterm (MP) birth, 2
moderate-severe TBI, 142
  AIM program, 152–153
  assessment following, 147–148
  clinical implications, 154
  intervention strategies, 151–153
  pharmacological interventions for,
      153
mood disorders, 45. *See also* anxiety
      disorder; depression
  with HIV, 213
  with MS, 235
mortality rates
  LBW/preterm birth, 3
  SBM, 25
mosaic trisomy, 64–65
Mother-Infant Transaction Program
      (MITP), 12
motor function
  with ASD, 51
  with DS, 65–66
  with FASD, 86
  with HIV, 213
  with intellectual disability
      syndromes, 73
  LBW/preterm birth and, 7
  with pediatric cancer, 170
  with pediatric ischemic stroke,
      252–253
  with SBM, 28
    intervention strategies for, 35
    neuropsychological evaluations
        of, 32
MP birth. *See* moderately preterm
      birth
MRI. *See* magnetic resonance imaging
multiple sclerosis (MS)
  clinical manifestations, 230–235
    in children, 230
      CIS, 233
  clinical practice implications,
      239
  cognitive functioning, 234–235
    in adults, 234
      attention deficits, 234

in children and adolescents, 234–235
EF, 235
language skills development, 234–235
memory deficits, 234
disease course, 233–234
epidemiology, 228–229
age of onset, 228
by gender, 228
by race, 228
etiology, 229
future research on, 239–240
interventions, 237–239
cognitive rehabilitation, 238–239
with corticosteroids, 237
pharmacological, 238
neuropsychological assessment, 235–236
BNBC, 236
BRB, 236
MACFIMS, 236
MS Society Neuropsychological Core Battery, 237
pathophysiology, 228–229
lesions, 229
pediatric, 229
prevention strategies, 229–230
psychosocial impact, 235
anxiety disorders, 235
depression, 235
fatigue, 235
mood disorders, 235

natalizumab, 237
National Comprehensive Cancer Network (NCCN), 177
National Institute on Alcohol Abuse and Alcoholism (NIAAA), 79
National Joint Committee on Learning Disabilities (NJCLD), 116
Naturalistic, Developmental Behavioral Interventions (NBDI), 52
NCCN. See National Comprehensive Cancer Network
NCDs. See Major and Mild Neurocognitive Disorders
ND-PAE. See neurobehavioral disorder associated with prenatal alcohol exposure
neonates. See infants and children; low birth weight; preterm birth
neurobehavioral disorder associated with prenatal alcohol exposure (ND-PAE), 79–80
neuroimaging. See also functional magnetic resonance imaging
for dementia, 277

neuropsychological functioning, learning skills, 253. See also perinatal stroke
new-onset epilepsy, 194
NIAAA. See National Institute on Alcohol Abuse and Alcoholism
NJCLD. See National Joint Committee on Learning Disabilities
non-verbal learning, with FASD, 86
nutrition. See diet and nutrition

obstructive sleep apnea (OSA), 249
oppositional defiant disorder (ODD), 9, 95
OSA. See obstructive sleep apnea

PAE. See prenatal alcohol exposure
partial fetal alcohol syndrome (pFAS), 79
PBRT. See photon beam radiation therapy
PCA. See posterior cerebral arteries
pediatric cancer. See also specific cancers
assessment strategies, 173
Cogstate program, 178–179
behavioral functioning, 171–172
clinical manifestations, 166–167
clinical practice implications, 168
emotional functioning, 171–172
longitudinal outcomes, 171–172
interventions for, 173–175
cognitive, 174
educational, 174
future research on, 178, 179
online, 174–175
pharmacological, 173
socioemotional, 175
long-term effects into adulthood, 163
neuropsychological resources, 176
neuroanatomical correlates, 166–167
neuropsychological functioning with, 170–171
academic outcomes, 171
attention deficits, 170
EF, 170
genetic moderators of, 172
intellectual functioning, 170
memory functions, 170, 171
speed and motor functions, 170
pharmacological preventions, 169–170
psychosocial functioning, 171–172
longitudinal outcomes, 171–172
treatment strategies
chemoprotectants, 169
CRT, use limitations of, 169
hyperfractionation, 169

PBRT, 169
pediatric HIV (PHIV), 213–216
academic outcomes, 214–215
acquisition pre-birth, 211–212
adaptive functioning, 215
behavioral and emotional functioning, 215
cognitive functioning, 213–215
evidence-based guidelines, 221–223
language acquisition skills, 214–215
memory deficits, 214
pediatric ischemic stroke, 244
ADHD and, 253
aphasia, 256
clinical practices, 257, 260–261
hemispatial neglect, 256
heterogeneous population for, 255–256
intervention strategies, 258–260
rt-PA therapy, 258
neuropsychological functioning, 250–258
attention deficits, 253
cognitive functions, 257–258
EF, 253
intellectual ability, 250–252
language skills development, 252
learning skills, 253
memory deficits, 253
motor function, 252–253
post-stroke, 262–263
visual-spatial ability, 252–253
prevention strategies, 248–248, 258–260
risk factors, 246–247
social emotional functioning, 253–258
pediatric MS, 229
pediatric TBI. See also mild TBI; moderate-severe TBI
adult outcomes from, 145–146
behavioral and emotional outcomes, 144–145
clinical implications, 153–154
psychosocial outcomes, 145
return-to-school guidelines with, 150–151
perinatal stroke, 244
ADHD and, 253
assessment for, 256
MCA and, 254
neuropsychological functioning, 250–258
attention deficits, 253
EF, 253
intellectual ability, 250–252
language skills development, 252
learning skills, 253
memory deficits, 253

perinatal stroke (cont.)
   motor function, 252–253
   visual-spatial ability, 252–253
  risk factors, 246–247
periventricular leukomalacia (PVL), 3
personality deficits, LBW/preterm
   birth and, 10–13
  corrected age evaluations, 10–11
pFAS. *See* partial fetal alcohol
   syndrome
phenobarbital, 168–169
phenylketonuria (PKU), 64
PHIV. *See* pediatric HIV
photon beam radiation therapy
   (PBRT), 169
Pivotal Response Therapy (PRT), 52
PKU. *See* phenylketonuria
PNES. *See* psychogenic non-epileptic
   seizures
posttraumatic amnesia (PTA), 139,
   142–143, 147
posttraumatic epilepsy (PTE), 187–188
posttraumatic stress disorder (PTSD),
   144–145
prenatal alcohol exposure (PAE), 79,
   81
  ADHD and, 86–87
  ND-PAE, 79–80
preterm birth
  academic outcome issues with, 7–10
   prevention strategies for, 8–9
   special education services, 8
  ASD and, social issues as result of,
   9–10
  classifications, 2
  decline of, 2–3
  defined, 2
  developmental disorders
   ADHD, 9
   ASD and, 9–10
   diagnosis of, 11
   interventions for, 11–13
   personality issues, 10–13
  emotional issues and, 10
  EP, 2
  epidemiology, 2–16
  fertility treatments and, 2
  intellectual disability and, 63
  IUGR and, 2
  learning disabilities and, 7–10
   ADHD, 9
   diagnostic evaluations of, 14–15
   prevention strategies, 8–9
   special education services, 8
  LP, 2
  medical complications, 3, 4
  mortality rates, 3
  MP, 2
  neurodevelopmental complications,
   3, 4, 14–16

  attention issues, 5–7
  brain development, 4
  cognitive ability, 5
  CP, 3
  diagnostic evaluations of, 14–15
  EF deficits, 5–7
  IQ, 5
  long-term, 4–16
  PVL, 3
  visuomotor skills, 7
  pathophysiology, 2–16
  personality issues, 10–13
   corrected age evaluations, 10–11
  prevalence rates for, 2
  prevention strategies, 3
  risk factors for, 2
  SGA birth and, 2
  VP, 2
  WHO demographics for, 2
prospective memory, 27
PRT. *See* Pivotal Response Therapy
psychogenic non-epileptic seizures
   (PNES), 197–199
PTA. *See* posttraumatic amnesia
PTE. *See* posttraumatic epilepsy
PTSD. *See* posttraumatic stress
   disorder
PVL. *See* periventricular leukomalacia

race. *See also* African Americans; Asian
   populations; Hispanic
   populations
  ADHD and, 94
  birth defects and, 24
  DS and, 65
  MS and, 228
radiation therapy, 165
  CRT, 163–164
   for pediatric cancer, use
    limitations in, 169
  PBRT, 169
RBANS. *See* Repeatable Battery for the
   Assessment of
   Neuropsychological Status
reading disorder (RD), 119–120
  brain development and, 120
  comorbidities with, 119–120
  intervention/prevention strategies,
   122–124, 129
  meta-analysis of adults with,
   123
  prevalence rates, 119
  risk factors for, 120
recall ability, 51
recombinant tissue plasminogen
   activator (rt-PA) therapy,
   258
regression to the mean model, 127–128
Rehabilitation Services Administration
   (RSA), 116

Repeatable Battery for the Assessment
   of Neuropsychological Status
   (RBANS), 278
response to intervention (RTI) model,
   128
retrospective memory, 27
return-to-school guidelines, after TBI,
   150–151
rituximab, 237
RSA. *See* Rehabilitation Services
   Administration
RTI model. *See* response to
   intervention model
rt-PA therapy. *See* recombinant tissue
   plasminogen activator therapy

SBM. *See* spina bifida
   myelomeningocele
SDB. *See* sleep disordered breathing
seizures, epileptic, 186
  PNES, 197–199
SES. *See* socioeconomic status
severe TBI. *See* moderate-severe TBI
SGA birth. *See* small for gestational age
   birth
sleep disordered breathing (SDB), 249
small for gestational age (SGA) birth
  classifications, 2
  preterm birth and, 2
social functioning
  with ASD, 9–10, 47
  with SBM, 29
   intervention strategies for, 35–36
   neuropsychological evaluations
    of, 33
socioeconomic status (SES)
  cancer treatment and, 169
  SBM and, 29–30
solid tumors, 162
special education services, 8
  IEP and, 33–34
spina bifida myelomeningocele (SBM)
  during adolescence, 30
  clinical manifestation, 25–31
   academic outcomes, 28
   ADHD, 26
   attentional deficits, 25–26
   EF deficits, 26–27
   family functioning issues, 29–30
   functional adaptation issues, 30
   language deficits, 27
   memory dysfunction, 27
   metacognition deficits, 26
   motor function deficits, 28
   psychological dysfunction, 28–29
   social functioning deficits, 29
   visual-spatial abilities, 27–28
  clinical treatment practices, 36–39
   for academic outcome success, 37
   anticipatory guidance, 37

for developmental issues, 37
for EF, 37
through interprofessional team
partnering, with families, 36–37
through medical care, 37
for psychological functioning,
37–38
transition to adult care, 38
defined, 24
epidemiology of, 24–25
ETV/CPC and, 38–39
features, 24
HRQOL with, 29
intervention strategies, 33–37
for academic outcome success, 35
for attention deficits, 33–34
for EF, 34
for family functioning, 35–36
for functional adaptation, 36
for language skills development,
34
for memory deficits, 34–35
for motor functioning issues, 35
for psychological functioning,
35–36
for social functioning, 35–36
for visual-spatial difficulties, 35
vocational training, 37
mortality rates with, 25
neuropsychological evaluations
with, 30–33
for academic outcomes, 32–33
for attention deficits, 31
brain development, 31
for EF, 31
for family functioning, 33
for functional adaptation, 33
for language skills, 31–32
for memory, 32
for motor functioning, 32
for psychological functioning, 33
for social functioning, 33
for visual-spatial abilities, 32
pathophysiology, 24–25
Chiari-II malformation in, 25
hydrocephalus in, 25
non-genetic factors, 25
prevalence rates, by race, 24
prevention strategies, 25
tectal beaking and, 26
stroke. See also pediatric ischemic
stroke
cerebral atrophy, 254
clinical practices, 260–261
CSVD, 247, 248, 254
definitions, 244, 245
depression and, 262
diet and, 249
Flair MRI, 247–248
hemorrhagic, 244

AVM and, 247
risk factors, 247
incidence rates, 244
intervention strategies, 258–260
rt-PA therapy, 258
ischemic, 188
CSVT, 244
MCA and, 254
neuropsychological functioning,
250–258
cognitive functions, 257–258,
263–263
EF, 257–257
lesion location and, 254
memory deficits, 257
post-stroke, 262–263
OSA and, 249
prevention strategies, 248–250,
258–260
cholesterol level management, 249
diabetes management, 249
through lifestyle modification,
249–250
through medical management,
249
risk factors, 244, 259–259
atrial fibrillation, 249
SBD and, 249
types, 245
VCI and, 263–263
Sunitinib, 173–174

tamoxifen, 167–168
TBI. See traumatic brain injury
tectal beaking, 26
teriflunomide, 237
Theory of Visual Attention (TVA), 31
top-down attentional abilities, 26
topiramate, 168–169
training. See behavioral parent
training; facilitative
intervention training;
vocational training
translocation trisomy, 64–65
traumatic brain injury (TBI)
behavioral and emotional outcomes
with, 144–145
in adolescents, 145
in children, 144–145
blast injuries and, 140–141
clinical manifestations of, 141–142
cognitive characteristics, 141
magnitude of impairment,
141–142
mild TBI, 142
moderate-severe TBI, 142
neuroanatomical correlates, 141
neurobehavioral characteristics,
141
over time, 143

cognitive outcomes with, 141,
142–144
DAI, 140
definitions, 139
severity in, 139
dementia risks, 146–147
CTE, 146–147
diffuse, 140
epidemiology, 139
epilepsy after, 187–188
focal, 140
functional outcomes, 145
future research on, 154–155
intellectual disability from,
63, 64
intervention strategies, 149–154
for mild TBI, 150–151
moderate-severe TBI, 151–153
return-to-school guidelines, for
children, 150–151
mild, 139, 140
assessment following, 147
clinical characteristics, 142
clinical implications, 153–154
intervention strategies,
150–151
moderate-severe, 142
AIM program, 152–153
assessment following, 147–148
clinical implications, 154
intervention strategies, 151–153
pharmacological interventions
for, 153
pathophysiology, 140–141
pediatric. See also mild TBI;
moderate-severe TBI
adult outcomes from, 145–146
behavioral and emotional
outcomes, 144–145
clinical implications, 153–154
psychosocial outcomes, 145
return-to-school guidelines with,
150–151
prevention strategies, 148–149
psychosocial outcomes, 145
for children, 145
for families, 145
PTA and, 139, 142–143, 147
PTSD and, 144–145
treatment strategies, 149–150
trisomy 21, 64–65
TVA. See Theory of Visual Attention

UNAIDS. See Joint United Nations
Programme on HIV/AIDS
unexpected underachievement,
learning disabilities and,
130–131
universal prevention programs
(UPPSs), 81

vagal nerve stimulator (VNS), 202
vascular cognitive impairment (VCI),
    263–263
verbal learning, with FASD,
    85
very low birth weight
    (VLBW), 2
very preterm (VP) birth, 2
visual-spatial abilities
    with FASD, 85
    LBW/preterm birth and, 7
    with pediatric ischemic stroke,
        252–253
    with SBM, 27–28
        intervention strategies for, 35
        neuropsychological evaluations
            of, 32
VLBW. See very low birth weight
VNS. See vagal nerve stimulator

vocational training, as SBM
    intervention strategy, 37
VP birth. See very preterm birth

Wechsler Intelligence Scale for
    Children (WISC-V), 31
Wechsler Preschool and Primary Scale
    of Intelligence, Revised
    (WPPSI-R), 12
white matter development, with
    megencephaly, 48
WHO. See World Health Organization
Williams syndrome (WS),
    67–68
    comorbidities, 67
    epidemiology, 67
    etiology, 67
    life expectancy, 68
    neurobehavioral profile,
        68

neurological basis, 68
phenotype, 67
prevalence, 67
WISC-V. See Wechsler Intelligence
    Scale for Children
women. See also low birth weight;
    preterm birth; small for
    gestational age birth
    ADHD and, 94
    FXS and, 67
    MS and, 228
Woodcock-Johnson IV Tests of
    Achievement, 32
working memory, 27
World Health Organization
    (WHO), 2
WPPSI-R. See Wechsler Preschool and
    Primary Scale of Intelligence,
    Revised
WS. See Williams syndrome